CROSSING'S GUIDE
TO DARTMOOR

CROSSING'S GUIDE TO DARTMOOR

The 1912 Edition
reprinted with new introduction

by
BRIAN Le MESSURIER

DAVID & CHARLES: NEWTON ABBOT

7153 4034 4

First reprint of this edition 1965
Reprinted 1966, 1968, 1970, 1972

Reprinted 1976

Printed in Great Britain by
Redwood Burn Ltd Trowbridge and Esher
for David & Charles (Publishers) Ltd
Brunel House, Forde Road
Newton Abbot, Devon

PUBLISHER'S NOTE

THERE has been a growing demand for the republication of this classic of Dartmoor literature. The work was first published by *The Western Morning News* at Plymouth and later by Wheaton & Company of Exeter. Some difficulty arose because the records of both these earlier publishers were destroyed in air raids while the author had no known descendants. Although neither *The Western Morning News* nor Wheaton & Company were in a position formally to authorise this edition, the present publishers are nonetheless grateful for their co-operation. To Plymouth City Library and its librarian, Mr W. Best Harris, who made available the copy used as the basis of this edition, the publishers' thanks are also due.

In lieu of the royalties they might have had to pay for this edition, the publishers will make a grant for a new work on Dartmoor, which they will publish at a later date. The grant will be paid to the chosen author in addition to the usual commercial royalties, and will permit of a more detailed study than might otherwise have been possible. The book might be of topographical or historical nature. The lack of a full history of the moor has always been one of the biggest gaps in West Country literature. William Crossing devoted much of his life to collecting historical data but this was unfortunately destroyed before it could be put in circulation, and much spade work has to be tackled again.

After this note there follows the new introduction. Thereafter the entire text minus advertisements of the 1912 edition is followed, from the first sketch map and the title page to the index and lists of road and rail distances and maps. No changes whatever have been made to the text except that a black line has been added in the margin against those passages which have become particularly out of date and are especially referred to in the new introduction.

Although most of the work is as valuable today as when first published, the passing of time has of course brought some changes to the moor, and the publishers cannot accept any liability for any of the information given.

INTRODUCTION TO THE 1965 REPRINT

WILLIAM CROSSING:
THE MAN AND THE MASTERPIECE

THE MAN

The story of William Crossing's life is a strange one, and is little known. It is a story of success, with none of the monetary reward that this brings, and of failure too, with not a little pain and heartache.

Although Crossing was recognised as the leading Dartmoor authority during his lifetime, his voluminous writings barely provided a living for himself and his wife, and in the closing years it was only the magnanimity of an old friend that kept him out of the workhouse. Perhaps it is only now that his work is truly appreciated; it stands head and shoulders above the rest of Dartmoor topographical literature.

Crossing was a pioneer. He discovered stone crosses whose whereabouts had long been forgotten, and recorded their position in his books on the subject. He was the accurate chronicler of customs now gone from the country calendar, and his collection of folklore tales was made before the memory of them was lost forever.

Who was he, and what were the events that led to the writing of his *Guide to Dartmoor?*

William Crossing was born in Plymouth on 14 November 1847 and spent most of his boyhood in that city. As a child he was encouraged by his mother to interest himself in the antiquities and traditions of the countryside, and since the family spent holidays in a cottage on Roborough Down he was introduced to Dartmoor at an early age.

When he left school he was apprenticed to a sail-cloth manufacturer, but, disliking the trade, ran away to sea and sailed to Canada. By the time he was twenty he had returned to Plymouth and was working for his father. In his spare time he wrote poetry and plays, and also took every opportunity to visit the moor, which remained his chief interest.

Mr Crossing senior, no doubt feeling that a position of responsibility would benefit his son, sent William to supervise the family mill at South Brent. But away from parental control William indulged in his twin delights of drama and Dartmoor more freely than ever; he ran a local theatre, which after an initial success failed financially, and the moor was at his doorstep.

Theatricals continued to attract, and so William formed his own professional drama group with which he went on tour. When this venture failed too he returned to the South Brent mill, which his long-suffering father had kept going, and resumed his Dartmoor explorations. Perhaps because of his lack of interest it was not long before the mill closed down and he was left struggling for his livelihood. He had married in 1872 and shortly afterwards began to keep careful records of his Dartmoor excursions and studies. With no desire to return to business he determined to earn his daily bread by writing, but he and his wife Emma stayed on at South Brent until the 1890s, when they moved to Brent Tor, and then to Mary Tavy.

Until the end of the century, when his health began to deteriorate, Crossing constantly walked or rode the moor. Wherever he went he made friends with the moormen, and he was a popular figure in the group round the peat fire in the evenings, when he would play tunes on his tin whistle, or recite an improvised rhyme describing his wanderings of the day.

By 1893 one senses he was finding it difficult to make ends meet. He became editor of *The Westcountry Annual* and two years later brought out a small book called *Cricket Averages*. At the turn of the century his output was truly astonishing. One series of articles after another appeared in the *Mid-Devon & Newton Times*, *The Western Morning News*, the *Devon Evening Express* and the *Western Weekly News*. Two of these series, *A Hundred Years on Dartmoor* and *Gems in a Granite Setting*, which first appeared in *The Western Morning News*, were published later in book form.

Crossing never shirked a soaking on the moor, but later paid the penalty: he was so stricken by rheumatism that he was unable to write, and his livelihood was in jeopardy. A public testimonial was organised in 1904, the signatures including such well-known names as Lord Clifford, Robert Burnard, the Rev S. Baring-Gould, Eden Phillpotts and A. T. Quiller Couch. Two years later his fortunes changed for the better. He became tutor to the three sons of Mr W. P. Collins, and teaching was carried on alongside work on his magnum opus, the *Guide to Dartmoor*.

There came the time when Crossing needed an illustrator for his book, and on one of his visits to the Duchy Hotel at Princetown he asked the landlord, Aaron Rowe, if he knew an artist who could help him. As it happened Rowe knew just the man, for his youngest daughter was being courted by a clerk at the prison who, besides being knowledgeable about Dartmoor, had artistic gifts.

Thus it was that William Crossing was introduced to Philip Guy Stevens. At frequent intervals thereafter Crossing sent postcards to Stevens bearing such terse requests as 'Please get me a view over Post Bridge from Lakehead Hill.' For the young man this entailed getting up at 5 a.m., walking five miles each way, and being back at the prison by 9 a.m. The remark by Crossing in the preface, where he thanks Stevens for the sketches 'he has been at such pains to furnish', has a special meaning to anyone acquainted with the rigours of Dartmoor weather.[1]

At last the book was ready, and it was published by *The Western Morning News* on Monday, 24 May 1909 at 3s. The newspaper gave it a banner announcement in letters an inch high. Three years later a second edition, slightly corrected and printed on better paper, was published,[2] to be followed in 1914 by the third (revised) edition in five separate parts at 6d each. Publication then passed to A. Wheaton & Company Limited, of Exeter, who bound the five parts in two volumes, one containing three parts and the other two parts. The last time the *Guide* appeared on sale as a new book was in the early days of the second world war, when Wheatons sold large numbers of three of the parts in a fawn paper cover at 1s each. Since that time the value of 'Crossing' has soared, and copies have been much sought-after in the second-hand market. The success of his masterpiece cheered Crossing greatly.

Another event that gladdened his heart during these years was the knowledge that at last his abilities as a playwright had been recognised. He collaborated with Florence Eaton to write *The Triumph*, and this was given a matinée performance at the Royal Court Theatre on 27 November 1912 before an audience that included King George V and Queen Mary.

Crossing's last years are touched with sadness. Mr Collins arranged a public subscription for him on his 70th birthday, but shortly afterwards the old couple had to move to Ivybridge, where relations lived, for Mrs Crossing was ailing. When constant nursing became necessary she was admitted to Tavistock Institution and she died on 6 June 1921.

Mr Collins found accommodation for his old friend at Mary Tavy, and Crossing lived there for a while. In 1924, while he was away from home, the woman who looked after his rooms found a mass of papers and, because mice had damaged them, burnt the lot. Since Crossing had been preparing a history of Dartmoor, and the notes represented a lifetime's work, the loss was irreplaceable. For twelve weeks from 9 July 1925 he was a patient at Tavistock Institution, but in October he was taken to Cross Park Nursing Home, in Plymouth, where he spent his last three

---

[1] Philip Stevens rose to be Governor of Shrewsbury and Norwich Prisons, and retired to Somerset, where he died in 1944, aged 61.

[2] This is the edition reproduced here.

years. During this time Mr Collins paid the bills, which amounted to several hundred pounds. While at Cross Park he published his last book, a volume of poems called *Cranmere*, after the principal work it contained. His first book, *Leaves from Sherwood* (1868), was also poetry.

William Crossing died on 3 September 1928, and is buried with his wife in Mary Tavy Churchyard. The grave is north-east of the church, and standing by it one can see the western slopes of Dartmoor swelling up less than a mile away.

Since his death two memorials to him have been raised on Dartmoor. In 1938 Dr J. W. Malim and a band of walkers called Dobson's Moormen fixed a plaque to a boulder at Ducks' Pool (page 374).[1] Its inscription reads, 'In memory of William Crossing, author of many inspiring books on Dartmoor, whose Guide is a source of invaluable information to all lovers of the moor. Died 3rd Sep. 1928, aged 80.'

Mr Hamlyn Parsons, who died in 1961, and on whose notes about Crossing I have leaned heavily for this account, initiated a plan for a second memorial — a tablet affixed to the house at Mary Tavy where Crossing lived.[2] It was unveiled in 1952 by the chairman of the Dartmoor Preservation Association, Mrs (now Lady) Sylvia Sayer. The tablet is of plain slate, and the inscription reads, 'In this house William Crossing (1847–1928) lived for many years and wrote his "Guide to Dartmoor" and other works. The Dartmoor Preservation Association, 1952.'

THE MASTERPIECE

Although the *Guide* was written sixty years ago (we may be sure it took several years to complete) it remains the best topographical book about Dartmoor that has ever been published. This is because no other writer has explored the moor so extensively in all seasons and in all weathers. It was Crossing's complete familiarity with his subject that gives the *Guide* such accuracy and atmosphere. He gained the confidence and respect of Dartmoor people and from them learned the customs and obscure place-names that enables the *Guide* to speak with rural authority.

The *Guide* is encyclopaedic in content but, it must be realised, does not mention every antiquity. Space simply did not permit this ideal for one thing, and even Crossing did not know every hut circle and stone row. (But it should not be assumed that because Crossing omits an antiquity it is unimportant.) Then, too, there have been discoveries since 1909, particularly with the development of air photography. This has, for example, shown

---

[1] There is also a 'Cranmere'-type letter-box and visitors' book here.
[2] The house is the first on the left as one approaches Mary Tavy from the Okehampton direction.

the existence of numerous medieval village sites on the Dartmoor borders, of which Crossing knew nothing.

Crossing was a well-read man, and the historical asides show that he was a scholar of some ability. His humorous remarks enliven what could easily have become a dull book. In addition to giving posterity 'A Topographical Description of the Forest and Commons' (as the subtitle reads), Crossing has provided a valuable glossary of Dartmoor terms (page 9 *et seq.*), and the comprehensive index, in two parts, enables the reader to find his way about the book without difficulty.

Every Dartmoor lover is eternally grateful to Crossing for the *Guide*. It may be relied upon to present the authentic Dartmoor, unadorned by flights of fancy, and it has stood the test of time. Reference to it often strengthens the hand of present-day defenders of Dartmoor by its evidence of the existence and value of particular features of national, historical or traditional interest in some threatened area. Although he died many years ago, William Crossing is still, in a very real sense, helping to defend the moor he loved.

SIXTY YEARS OF CHANGE

This is not a full revision. Such a task would take years to complete, and the result would not be Crossing's *Guide*, but someone else's product, itself becoming out of date with the passing of the years. Neither is it a partial revision. It claims only to point out the chief changes that have taken place on Dartmoor since the *Guide* was first published.[1]

The list of items selected for mention is bound, in the end, to be a personal one, but considerations of space have eliminated many points worthy of note, so that or · the large issues are left: the reservoirs, the plantations, the Services, and so on. The subjects mentioned fall naturally under two headings, 'General' and 'Specific'.

The visitor is urged to read the *Guide* in conjunction with the latest 1-inch Ordnance Survey maps, or better still the 2½-inch maps. These will show him the extent of the areas planted with trees, or used as reservoirs. They do not mark the limits of the live-firing danger areas (see the paragraph 'The Services').

Under the list of 'Specific' changes only the chief page references to each place are given.

GENERAL

Access and the National Park

In 1951 Dartmoor was designated as one of Britain's National Parks under the National Parks and Access to the Countryside

---

[1] Because this remains Crossing's book, his spelling of Dartmoor place-names is retained in this introduction, except for the list of danger-flag sites under 'The Services'.

Act 1949. No physical changes resulted — the land remained in private ownership — but as well as setting out to preserve and enhance the natural beauty of the landscape, the Act acknowledged that there must be facilities for public access and enjoyment so far as possible.

On the open moor and in moorland newtakes, there is a *de facto* right of access for walking and riding (but see the paragraph 'The Services'). Because the Devon definitive rights-of-way map is not yet complete, and because a full revision is not being undertaken here, it is more difficult to pronounce upon the rights of the visitor in enclosed land, even when Crossing states that a track or path exists. If in doubt the visitor is advised to enquire locally. Unfortunately, access to some of the moorland newtakes is now made more difficult by barbed-wire fencing, unknown in Crossing's day; and there has been some recent ploughing of moorland which has obliterated ancient monuments — a development with serious implications if allowed to continue uncontrolled.

Motorists are reminded of the clause in the Road Traffic Act 1960, that forbids the driving of motor vehicles more than fifteen yards from a public road.

It will be clear by reference to some of the specific changes listed below that Dartmoor's designation as a National Park has not always afforded the hoped-for degree of protection. But a deep and widespread knowledge of the area, which Crossing's *Guide* provides, must inevitably help towards a greater understanding of the need for such protection in this present age.

Public Transport

Since the *Guide* was first published there has been a revolution in public transport. At the beginning of the description of each district there are details of distances from the various stations, but many of these are now closed. The following are the only stations that may be said to serve Dartmoor directly at the time of writing: Okehampton, Bridestowe, Lydford, Brent Tor and Tavistock. The following stations in large centres with bus connections give an indirect link with Dartmoor: Exeter, Newton Abbot, Totnes and Plymouth.

Bus services run through the larger moorland villages.

The Services

When Crossing walked the moor the area used by the Services was confined to ranges near Okehampton and Willsworthy and firing took place only from May to September. Largely as a result of the retention of land used by the Services during the 1939–45 war, the area over which live firing is now carried out is about 30,000 acres, and firing takes place all the year round.

The warning notice on page 191 is completely out of date and of historic interest only, except where it warns of the danger of handling shells. As regards live firing, the following table shows the present location of the poles from which red flags are flown when firing is in progress.

OKEHAMPTON FIELD FIRING AREA	St Michael's Bungalow Halstock Watchet Hill Steeperton Tor Hangingstone Hill Blackdown (Okehampton)	Quintin's Man Amicombe Knoll Rattlebrook Hill Kitty Tor Yes Tor
	Cranmere Pool and Fur Tor are in this danger area.	
WILLSWORTHY FIELD FIRING AREA	Hare Tor Ger Tor Lanehead	Blackdown (Mary Tavy) Whitehill
	Tavy Cleave is in this danger area.	
MERRIVALE FIELD FIRING AREA	Lynch Tor Great Mis Tor Roos Tor Beardown Tor	Walkham Spur Holming Beam Rough Tor
	Great Mis Tor is in this danger area.	
RIPPON TOR RIFLE RANGE	Hemsworthy Gate Saddle Tor 600 yard firing point	Old Summer House Cold East Cross

The flag-poles do not denote the limit of the range boundary; this is marked by notice boards and white posts with two red bands. When red flags are flying the range boundary must not be crossed. If red flags are not flying, any explosions or firing will only be blank cartridges or fireworks. When there is firing at night, red lights are hoisted on the flag-poles.

The firing notices and maps of the ranges may be seen by the visitor at post offices, police stations and most hotels and inns in the vicinity of Dartmoor. The firing notices are published every Friday and give details of firing for the following week. They appear in *The Western Morning News*, the *Western Times & Gazette* and the *Express & Echo*. It cannot be too strongly emphasised that anyone intending to visit a part of the moor where live firing is carried out should first ascertain the dates and times of such activities.

Large tracts of south-west Dartmoor at Ringmoor Down, Shaugh Moor, Wigford Down and Roborough Down are used by the Services for other forms of training which do not affect public access. A hutted camp was established at Plaster Down, near Tavistock, during the second world war, and a vast Royal

Marines' Barracks has recently been built at Bickleigh to replace a wartime camp on the same site.

The Services' use of Dartmoor has meant damage to antiquities and natural features, the construction of miles of new roads where none existed and the proliferation of various concrete, wood and tin buildings and "works". One cannot think that Crossing would have approved of this state of affairs.

Tree-felling

Many of the oak woods in Dartmoor's border valleys are now being felled and replanted with conifers — a drastic change of the landscape since Crossing's time.

SPECIFIC

The Avon reservoir Page 367

The dam across the Avon valley two miles up river from Shipley Bridge was constructed for the South Devon Water Board between 1954 and 1957. The water area is 50 acres, and 150 acres of moorland are enclosed within steel fencing to prevent pollution. The fenced area extends upstream to Huntingdon Cross.

Bear Down Page 121

Crossing's 'great bare hill' of Bear Down is now partly clothed with conifers. These were planted by the Duchy of Cornwall in 1919–20, and taken over by the Forestry Commission some years later. The planted area was enlarged in 1949.

Bellaford — Lough Tor (Bellever — Laughter) Pages 469 and 470

The large Forestry Commission plantations extending north, west and south of the ancient tenement of Bellaford have come into being since 1931–2.

There are still numerous Bronze Age remains in the area, especially on Lakehead Hill, but some destruction has occurred. Several antiquities may be seen in the unplanted tongue of land that extends north of Bellaford Tor to Kraps Ring, but the ungrazed, rank vegetation hinders their discovery. Others, in the planted area, are difficult to find in their isolated clearings.

Brimpts Page 457

The plantations at Brimpts, above Dartmeet, have been extended since the *Guide* was written. At the end of the first world war much of the old wood was cut, and removed by an overhead cableway constructed between Brimpts and Princetown railway station, over five miles away. The supporting standards, and the rest of the cableway apparatus, were afterwards dismantled.

Burrator Page 450

In 1928 the Burrator dam was heightened to increase the capacity of the reservoir. The water surface area was thus enlarged from 116 to 150 acres. The plantations around the reservoir are owned by Plymouth Corporation, who started planting in 1921.

Fernworthy   (a) The plantations.   Pages 243, 244 and 246.

The first conifers were planted by the Duchy in 1919, and at the same time Fernworthy farm was abandoned. The Forestry Commission took over the area in 1931, and planting has continued spasmodically up to the present time.

The antiquities, planted around with trees, can still be found, but their environment has completely altered. The stone row and circle on Froggymead Hill (page 244) are adjacent to the Fernworthy — Teignhead track. The Assacombe antiquities (page 246) are more difficult to find, but are near forest roads. The Lowton remains (page 246), being not far from the main entrance of Fernworthy forest, can be found without difficulty.

(b) The reservoir. Page 243. Torquay Corporation began to extract water from the South Teign at Fernworthy in 1928, when an intake works was constructed just below the farm. As the demand of the growing seaside town rapidly increased, powers were sought for the erection of an impounding dam, and work began on this in 1936. It was not completed until 1942. A new road was built around the head of the reservoir, but Fernworthy Bridge and the nearby clapper may be seen only when conditions of extreme drought lower the water level. The water reaches Torquay via the lower of the Trenchford reservoirs (near Hennock) to which it is piped.

Dendles Waste and Hawns   Page 414

Much of this area, a spur made a peninsula on the west by Broadall Lake, and on the east by the river Yealm, has been planted with conifers since March 1960.

Lee Moor — Cholwich Town — Wigford Down area

The china clay industry was already well established in south-west Dartmoor in Crossing's day. On page 427 he writes (of the upper Torry valley): 'It is now the centre of a great clay industry, of which we see abundant evidence on every hand.' More than half a century has since elapsed, and many of the clay workings have grown considerably. The spoil heap of the Cholwich Town works recently obliterated the stone row mentioned on page 410.

North Hisworthy (Hessary) Tor   Page 85 *et seq.*

The British Broadcasting Corporation's 750-foot steel mast and associated buildings were erected in 1954-5.

The Princetown railway   Page 82 *et seq.*

The last public train used the Princetown branch line on 3 March 1956, and all the paraphernalia of a railway line has now been removed. A walk along the track is an enjoyable experience.

The railway track from Bridestowe to the disused peat works at Rattle Brook head was removed in the 1930s. Crossing mentions that attempts to re-start operations in that lonely spot had been made during his lifetime, without success. Further schemes have been put into effect in the intervening years, one as recently as 1951, and all have ended in failure.

The pyramidical china-clay spoil-heap on the Avon — Erme watershed at Red Lake is a prominent landmark on this part of the moor, and the disused railway track that reaches out to it from the extreme southern tip of Dartmoor provides an easy approach to the Ducks' Pool — Aune Head area for the walker approaching from the Ivybridge direction.

The clay was pumped in solution to a pipe-line whence it travelled by gravity to the drying works beside the main railway line at Bittaford. Communication between the drying works and the southern terminus further up the hill was by cable incline.

The permanent way to Red Lake was completed in 1911, and was used chiefly for the conveyance of coal, men and their supplies to and from the workings. The men stayed on the moor for weeks at a time in the summer, and during the winter as weather permitted. Burys (see page 13), for the propagation of rabbits, were thrown up at several places near the line to provide food and sport for the workers.

In 1922 the Left Lake china-clay works were re-opened (Crossing speaks of them as 'long-deserted'). Ten years later the whole undertaking failed, and the rolling stock and equipment were sold by auction.

The present R.A.F. mast dates from 1957. It replaced a wooden mast put up during the second world war.

Soussons Common was planted with conifers by the Forestry Commission in 1946. Crossing used the common for several of his routes. By following the forest tracks one may still pass through the area. This, in fact, applies to all Forestry Commission plantations.

The small reservoir in the Swincombe valley dates from 1926, and augments Paignton's supply from the Wennaford (Venford) reservoir on Holne Moor, to which the water is piped.

Taw Marsh Pages 211, 212
The visitor will notice a number of concrete and steel protuberances sticking out of the floor of this vast natural amphitheatre; these are the pumping and aeration installations of the North Devon Water Board. Trial boring to discover if water existed in any quantity beneath Taw Marsh began in 1957, and a road from Belstone was made to enable the heavy drilling equipment to be brought into the valley.

Yelverton Page 444
The runways of the second-world-war aerodrome, generally known as Harrowbeer, are now being torn up, and the site is being restored to natural moorland. Bunkers and emplacements associated with the wartime use of the area remain.

The changes listed above are those that have significantly affected the descriptive accuracy of the *Guide*, or have made a substantial impact on the moorland landscape during the last half century.

But, for all these changes, and allowing for the many other facts that the reader will find are not in accord with Crossing's description, the Dartmoor of 1965 is essentially the moor he knew. The wind whispering through the heather and bending the bog cotton; the tors standing stark on the skyline like so many ruined castles; the peat-stained rivers hurrying to the sea — these are the things that are timeless. May they last for ever.

ACKNOWLEDGMENTS
I wish to thank the following for help in the preparation of this introduction: Surg. Capt. R. G. Anthony, Col D. C. Campbell-Miles, Mr E. J. Coombe, Lt-Col C. A. McLaren, Mr M. J. Passmore, Lady Sayer, Mr J. V. Somers Cocks, Mr A. Stevens, Mr H. L. Watkins.

Brian Le Messurier
March 1965

SKETCH MAP

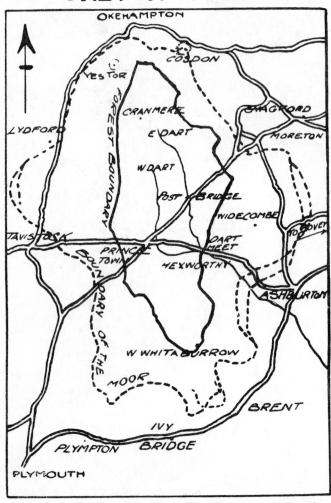

OKEHAMPTON

COSDON

YES TOR

FOREST BOUNDARY

CRANMERE

E DART

W DART

CHAGFORD

MORETON

LYDFORD

POST BRIDGE

WIDECOMBE

TO BOVEY

TAVISTOCK

PRINCE TOWN

DART MEET

HEXWORTHY

BOUNDARY OF THE

ASHBURTON

W WHITA BURROW

MOOR

BRENT

IVY

BRIDGE

PLYMPTON

PLYMOUTH

BOUNDARIES OF DARTMOOR
FOREST & COMMONS.

GUIDE TO DARTMOOR:

A TOPOGRAPHICAL DESCRIPTION OF THE
FOREST AND COMMONS

BY

WILLIAM CROSSING.

———

WITH MAPS AND SKETCHES.

SECOND EDITION.

———

"If you want sternness and loneliness you may pass into Dartmoor. There are wastes and wilds, crags and granite, views into far-off districts, and the sound of waters hurrying away over their rocky beds, enough to satisfy the largest hungering and thirsting after poetical delight."

WILLIAM HOWITT: *Rural Life of England.*

Plymouth :
"The Western Morning News" Co., Ltd., Printers and Lithographers,
31, George Street and Notte Street.

OUT OF THE LAND OF GORSE AND HEATHER

TO

THE RIGHT WORSHIPFUL THE MAYOR,

AND MAYORESS,

OF PLYMOUTH,

A. EDMUND SPENDER, B.A.,

AND

HELEN FRANCES SPENDER,

GREETING.

PREFACE TO THE SECOND EDITION.

———◆◆◆———

THIS Guide to Dartmoor was written with the purpose of furnishing the visitor with such directions as would enable him to find his way to any part of it from whatever starting-point on its borders he might choose; and to give him a description of the scenery, antiquities, and other objects of interest. The demand which the book has met with, and the very gratifying testimony of many who have used it on their rambles, is, I venture to think, sufficent proof that this end has been attained, and that the needs of the Dartmoor explorer have been supplied. The first edition being exhausted the publishers have promptly responded to the call for a second issue, encouraged by the belief that the book has been of service not only to the tourist but to all who desire to learn something of a district that possesses so many charms.

For the reception the book has been accorded I offer my best thanks, and would take this opportunity of acknowledging the pleasure it has given me to learn that by its means I have been able to be of some assistance to those who find enjoyment in a ramble over the wild Highlands of the West.

BLACK DOWN, DARTMOOR,

MAY, 1912.

PREFACE.

———

DURING recent years the claims of Dartmoor as a holiday and health resort have become widely recognized. Those to whom an old world region is an attraction will find in it a field of surpassing interest, No district in England of similar extent is so rich in pre-historic remains, and in none does Nature wear a wilder aspect.

To this elevated tract of land no guide book, in the true sense of the term, has hitherto appeared. It has, of course, been noticed in county guides, and there are also topographical works and hand-books descriptive of it, but in the former the accounts are necessarily superficial, while in the latter the visitor is not given any directions for finding his way over those parts of the waste remote from roads. To enable him to learn what Dartmoor really is he needs something beyond notices of the more celebrated, because more readily accessible, places and objects of interest. He should be led from the beaten track, and wander among the hills where signs of man's occupancy are not, where silence broods over the sea of fen, and the pasture grounds of the cattle that range at will are as they were when the Norman herdsman drove his beasts there ; or he should stray into solitary combes encumbered with the ruined huts and fallen rock-pillars of the people who once made this wild land their home. As my acquaintance with Dartmoor is a life-long one, and as it has been with me a subject of study and of systematic investigation during many years, it is with some degree of confidence that I take upon myself the task of conducting the visitor over it, and leading him into its remoter parts.

This book is the first to give a complete topographical description of Dartmoor, and the reader may depend upon its being correct. Its aim is to furnish the visitor with an account of all that is to be found on the moor worthy of note, and to acquaint him with the best means of reaching the various objects from any point. the districts into which the moor has been divided are described in the excursions, and at the end of these are given routes to each of the other districts. By this arrangement the moor is crossed in every conceivable direction, so that it is not possible to find any part of it that is not noticed somewhere in the book. For the sake of convenience the terms used in connection with the forest and commons are given, with their meanings, in glossarial form, some archæological terms being also included.

I desire to express my thanks to Mr. PHILIP GUY STEVENS, of Princetown, for the series of pen-and-ink sketches he has been at such pains to furnish, and which were executed on the spot. It is hoped they will be found useful as a means of helping the visitor to identify the principal tors and hills.

If I gain the confidence of the rambler who uses this book my satisfaction will be complete. There is some reason for me to hope that I shall do so, as I venture to believe that he will discover ere we have gone far on our wanderings together that I am really and truly a Dartmoor man.

CONTENTS.

CONTENTS.

CONTENTS.

Where reference is made to other of the Author's books the
titles are thus abbreviated.

GUIDE TO DARTMOOR.

SITUATION AND EXTENT OF DARTMOOR.

DARTMOOR is situated in South Devonshire, and towards the Western part of the county. At its nearest approach to the Tamar at Plaster Down, it is about five or six miles from that river, but it is not so many years since that commons stretched from it almost to the Morwell Rocks, and even now the breaks of cultivated land between the two are not extensive. Wigford Down is part of Dartmoor, and this is separated from Roborough Down only by the farms in the narrow valley of the Mew, while adjoining the last-named common is Buckland Down, which extends to the Tavy where it flows under Blackmoorham Wood. From that point to the Tamar at New-quay the distance, measured in a straight line, is not much over a mile, or to the Morwell Rocks about two miles, and far into the nineteenth century much of this intervening tract, now cultivated and planted, was open common. The eastern verge of Dartmoor is about sixteen miles from Exeter, but there are outlying commons, once no doubt forming part of it, that approach much nearer to that city. The district in which these are situated, and the moor itself, constitute the granite area of Devon. The part of the moor nearest to Plymouth is Crownhill Down, in the parish of Plympton St. Mary, the gate of which, near Bottle Hill Mine, is only seven miles from it.

On the northern verge of Dartmoor is situated the town of Oke-hampton, the suburbs and the railway station being quite close to the commons. On the south is the large village of Ivybridge, which is rather over half-a-mile from the edge of the down below the Western Beacon. The distance between these two places, as shown on the recent Ordnance Map, is rather over twenty-three miles, the extreme length of the moor being a little less than this Its breadth varies. At its widest part it is seventeen miles across ; this is from the edge of Black Down, near Brent Tor, to the border of Ilsington Common under Hey Tor, but its average breadth is about ten or twelve miles. It covers an area of about two hundred square miles, but this does not include the borderland, which is usually regarded as Dartmoor country, and in which are a number of outlying commons. Its highest hill attains an elevation of 2,039 feet, but its mean altitude is about 1,400 feet. [100 *Years*, Intro. ; *Crosses*, Chap. I.]

The principal market towns and holiday centres surrounding the moor are Okehampton, Belstone, Sticklepath, on the north ; Chagford, Moretonhampstead, Lustleigh, and Bovey Tracey, on the east ; Ash-burton, Buckfastleigh, Brent, Ivybridge, and Plympton, on the south ; and Yelverton, Horrabridge, Tavistock, Mary Tavy, Brent Tor, Lydford, and Bridestowe, on the west.

Although the whole of the moorland region was in all probability once known as Dartmoor, or perhaps as the Dartmoors, the name has for several centuries been supposed to belong only to the ancient forest, which forms the central part of the great waste, and which is at some considerable distance from the towns and villages of the borderland.   But for many years what seems to have been the earlier order of things has been reverted to, and the forest and the broad belt of commons surrounding this old-time royal hunting-ground, have together borne the name of Dartmoor, though many of the dwellers in the district do not recognize this general term. [100 *Years*, Chap. VII.]

Each of these border commons belongs to a different parish, the name of which it usually bears.   They are of the same general character as the forest, except that some parts of the latter are much more desolate, the depth of the peat greater, and the surface more uneven. The boundary between the forest and these purlieus is marked, with a few exceptions, by natural objects, and there is nothing to show the stranger when he passes from one to the other.   The bounds of the commons are viewed at certain times, and copies of perambulations and surveys exist showing the bounds of the forest, which lies wholly within the parish of Lydford.

Dartmoor thus consists of an ancient forest and its purlieus, but it is also naturally divided into five districts.

I.   The great central depression extending from near Prince-town to the West Webburn, below Hameldon, and comprising the lands of the early forest settlers lying near the East Dart, the West Dart, and the Walla Brook.

This is noticed in the Excursions from Princetown, Post Bridge, and Hexworthy.

II.   That part of the moor to the north of this depression, and extending to Okehampton, but not including the Tavy Valley below the Cleave.

Noticed in the Excursions from Princetown, Tavistock, Lydford, Okehampton, Belstone, and Chagford, and in the routes to Cranmere.

III. That part of the moor to the south of the depression, and extending to Ivybridge.

Noticed in the Excursions from Princetown, Hexworthy, Brent, Ivybridge, Plympton, and Yelverton,

IV.   The Tavy Valley below the Cleave.

Described in the Excursions from Tavistock and Lydford.

V.   Hameldon, the Widecombe Valley, and the commons to the east of it.

This district, which extends from Manaton and Lustleigh to Ashburton, is described in the Excursions from Moreton, Bovey Tracey, and Ashburton.

All these districts are also crossed by the different routes.

HINTS TO THE DARTMOOR RAMBLER.

THE explorer of the moor who is a stranger to the locality, will naturally desire to know something of the nature of the ground he will have to traverse in his rambles, and it may, therefore, be well to offer a few remarks on this and one or two other kindred subjects. He will probably have read of the dangers of Dartmoor, and may have formed the idea that it is a land of mists and bog. It certainly cannot be denied that the moor is often enveloped in a mist in the winter, but such will not be found to be frequently the case during the season usually chosen by the visitor to make acquaintance with it. And it must also be confessed that bogs are by no means rare. But to be overtaken by the former, though sometimes proving rather awkward, is never dangerous, while the latter are only so to the rider to hounds who may be a stranger to the district. The cautious pedestrian will come to no harm, unless he should be benighted, and in the darkness walk into a swamp, or plunge into what is known as a "feather bed." But even at such a time these may generally be avoided, while by day there is, of course, no difficulty whatever in doing so.

My own experience is that the worst obstacles on Dartmoor are not such as Nature has placed there, but those that owe their existence to man. It is usually much easier to pass over the worst parts of the fen than to make headway across a tract covered with old turf-ties. Such a hillside, for instance, as that down which Outer Redlake runs to fall into the Tavy, where peat has been cut for generations, presents greater difficulties to the pedestrian than the boggy ground near by, which the peat-cutters have left untouched. The bogs are not a source of danger to the rambler who will exercise judgment and proceed with care.

The fen, or "vain," as the moormen calls it, and which covers so much of the more remote parts of the forest, consists entirely of peat, on which bog-grasses grow, in certain spots to a great height. There is no top-soil, and consequently no herbage suitable for cattle. Often this ground will be found seamed in every direction, the rains having worn channels in the peaty surface, and these gradually widening and deepening, the whole tract is broken up into innumerable hummocks. The fissures are frequently so wide that it is impossible to leap across them, and progress can then only be made by descending into them and wading to the next hummock. In a dry season one may indeed pass through the fissures, for although the peat is soft he will not sink very far into it. I have many a time walked for a considerable distance through these channels, my head being occasionally two or three feet below the surface of the ground. When they are found of such a depth the gravel is often exposed, the whole of the peat having been washed away. Northward of Cut Hill there is an extensive tract of ground of this character.

Sometimes a considerable area will be met with where the hummocks are very few, and dotted about the bare peat like small islands in a sea of mud. In these cases they are invariably low.

When the season is wet the peat is very soft and yielding, and it would then be exceedingly unwise to attempt to cross the worst parts of the fen, for though the adventurous explorer would hardly be in danger of sinking so far into it as the man who, according to the story, was discovered by his hat, which, while on his head, yet appeared to rest upon the surface, he would certainly be what is locally termed " stugged."

Very little ground of this nature is to be found on the commons surrounding the forest, for there the peat is usually not deep, and is covered with turf. It is only when the central and higher parts of the moor are reached that the true fen, or bog, is seen. Of this two tracts exist ; one, which is very extensive, in the north quarter of the forest, and the other in the south quarter. In the latter there are, however, no deep channels in the peat similar to those just described. The surface of the other parts of the forest resembles that of its purlieus.

A mire is of a totally different character from the fen ; it is really a swamp, and is usually found at the heads of streams. Should the rambler inadvertently walk into one, he must at once retrace his steps, and on no account seek to go forward. Tussocks of rushes often grow on the edges of the mires, and these will afford a secure foothold. Where such are plentiful a mire may even be crossed by means of them, though it is not advisable for those unaccustomed to the moor to attempt it. To these mires the name of Dartmoor Stables has been given, but it is not often heard now. This was in playful allusion to the belief that ponies often found a " resting place " in them, one, however, we can well believe, they would not have been loth to quit could they have done so. I have certainly known instances of these animals, and of cattle and sheep, being lost in the mires, but speaking generally such accidents are by no means of frequent occurrence. In the northern part of the moor, among other places, there are mires at Dart Head, at Broad Marsh, on the Walla Brook, and at Rayburrow Pool ; and in the southern at Aune Head, and in the valley below Fox Tor.

The weary wanderer on Dartmoor is probably not sorry when he is able to seek his couch, but however tired he may be he would hardly care to avail himself of the kind of " feather-bed " he will sometimes meet with there, notwithstanding its inviting look. What is known as such is a deep hole, usually not more than ten or twelve feet in diameter, filled with ooze, hidden beneath a covering of moss of a beautiful bright green colour. Should this matted surface, or *raim* (that is, ream) as the moorman calls it, be broken by anyone unwittingly crossing it, there would be nothing to prevent him from plunging into the slush. No one would set foot on such spots intentionally, for in spite of their attractive appearance their real nature betrays itself on a very slight examination, and it is therefore only by night that the " feather-bed " is likely to have an occupant. I have walked across them in the darkness, but never came to any harm. Animals, with an apparent perception of the fitness of things, shun the " feather-bed."

Quaker is another not inappropriate name for these. It is derived from their tremulous motion when trodden upon.

Mists sometimes suddenly envelop the moor in an impenetrable shroud. I have known my surroundings to be entirely obscured, and objects twenty or thirty yards distant rendered invisible, where ten minutes before there was not a sign of what was coming, and the mist has continued for several days. If a stranger be overtaken by one, he should, when not certain of his bearings, endeavour to find a stream, and having done so, follow it till he reaches the borders of the moor, or some road. Attempts to strike a straight course over the moor will assuredly fail ; he will only wander in a circle. It is obvious that the stream may lead him away from the point he is desirous of reaching, but it will, nevertheless, act as a guide to the enclosed country, which to those unacquainted with the locality is in such circumstances " a consummation devoutedly to be wished." When the mist comes on the rambler should take particular care to keep descending ; immediately he finds an ascent before him he must turn, and unless he should be unfortunate enough to be pixy-led, it cannot be long before running water will be reached. Should it be suspected that the little elves of the moor are playing pranks, let him take off his outer garment, turn it inside out, and put it on again. The pixies will then have no further power over him. This is a potent charm that has never yet been known to fail. [*Pixies*, Chap. I.]

But this plan of following a stream, though effective enough in enabling the rambler to reach the borders of the moor, leaves much to be desired. It is far better to be able to go in the direction he wishes, and this he may, of course, do if be has taken the precaution to provide himself with a pocket compass. I would strongly advise all who are unacquainted with the moor to carry one when they penetrate into those parts of it that are far removed from the beaten tracks. In describing the various routes in the pages that follow I have presumed that the rambler is so provided. With this, and the maps and directions here furnished, he may mark out his course, and the mist will prove but little hindrance to his progress. At the same time, if his knowledge of Dartmoor is slight, it will not be unwise for him to make his way to a stream, provided there is one near him running *towards* his destination. But in all such cases his judgment must be his guide.

It is also possible to steer by the wind. I have done this on many occasions, and do not remember that I have ever gone wrong, though such a plan is not altogether satisfactory, for there is always the contingency of the wind changing. But many years of Dartmoor rambling have made me so familiar with every part of the district, that I never think about steering for any particular point ; even in the most dense mist the nature of the ground passed over is usually sufficient to assure me of my situation. Nevertheless, I have invariably carried a compass. Then when the moor has hidden itself, and my way has lain, as it were, through cloudland, I have been able, by consulting it occasionally, to satisfy myself that I was not straying from the course. It must not be forgotten that objects appear so distorted in a Dartmoor mist that the most familiar scenes when come upon suddenly are hardly recognizable. [*Dev. Alps.*, Chap. VIII.]

To cross the moor on a dark night is a much more difficult matter than to make one's way over it through the mist. The latter, it is true, is sometimes confusing, and one is apt to be led astray by the strange appearance worn by those objects, which from their nearness, happen to be visible, but it is at all events possible to see the ground around one. In the darkness, however, every inequality—and these are not usually slight on Dartmoor—becomes a stumbling block. When you have mist and darkness combined, and it is raining in addition, you may justly consider that you are being treated to about the worst that Dartmoor has to offer. But this is an experience that the ordinary rambler on the moor is not likely to meet with, since he will probably prefer to visit it in the summer and confine his wanderings to the day-time.

There is one matter to which attention has been called by the late Rev. E. Spencer, of Tavistock, that it may be well to mention, though as it is so seldom known to occur, it can scarcely be regarded as a danger. Should by any chance the peat become ignited by the heather being set on fire, it might possibly continue to smoulder for some time, that is, if the weather be very dry. As it gives out carbonic acid it would, of course, be dangerous for anyone to pass near such a spot, unless he kept to the windward side of it. This, however, could never arise from any action of a Dartmoor man, for swaling, as the practice of burning the heather and furze is termed, is confined to the spring, at which season the peat is never sufficiently dry to ignite. Only after a period of exceptionally dry and hot summer weather could such a thing be possible.

During recent years Scotch cattle have been introduced on Dartmoor, and their wild, and sometimes rather fierce appearance, has caused some to dread encountering them. I do not think there is any real ground for alarm. The general opinion among the moor folk seems to be that these animals are no more dangerous than our own Devon cattle ; that if they are not worried they will take no notice of the passer-by. The rambler becomes the centre of attraction to all cattle that he approaches on the moor, which is not to be wondered at when it is remembered that they see so few people. They will generally stop grazing, and watch him till he has gone by, and then quietly go on feeding as before. If he has a dog with him he should keep it under control, and not allow it to disturb the animals. Speaking generally, it is just as well to avoid passing too near to cattle on the moor, particularly during hot weather, when they are teased by the flies.

Among my Dartmoor experiences I can number most of the things that may happen to a man there, and I can recollect one or two adventures with Scotch cattle. About twenty-five years ago, when crossing a part of Ugborough Moor in company with my wife, a whole herd came down upon us. The first intimation we had of it was the thundering of hoofs upon the turf, and then we were suddenly aware that a large number of black Scotch bullocks were rushing down the slope in pursuit of my dog, which was coming straight towards us. Fortunately, we were at no great distance from the wall of Glascombe Newtake, and seizing my wife's hand, I ran towards it with all speed. When we got to it I almost threw her on the top of the wall, which I knew was banked with turf on the inner side, and then pitching my dog after her, clambered over myself, just as the cattle came up. But they were not so infuriated as I had imagined ; in fact, no longer seeing the dog, they looked at us with an indifferent air. This I was able to return, though had they been so near to us two minutes previously my face would probably have worn another expression.

A few years ago I was going over the moor from Okehampton to Chagford, and when descending from Little Hound Tor towards Ruelake Pit, I saw some way in advance a herd of Scotch cattle crossing my path. They were going at a rapid pace, being evidently much tormented by flies. I halted for a few minutes to allow them to go on their way, and leave mine clear for me. When the main herd had passed I resumed my walk, not caring to wait until the stragglers, of which there were several, had gone by. I had just crossed their track when one of the latter, detaching himself from two or three companions, came in a very threatening manner towards me. I did not wait for him, but continued on my way at a quicker pace than before. I deemed it possible that he might attribute to my influence some of the pain the flies were inflicting upon him, and had no wish to meet him. But casting a look backwards I saw that he also had increased his pace, and was whisking his tail in a very excited manner. Not far off was a mire from which a little feeder of the Walla Brook drains, and this I lost no time in gaining, for I saw it would prove a haven of safety. Planting my feet upon the tussocks of rushes I made my way out upon it, knowing that the animal could not follow me. And he knew it, too, for he did not attempt to do so. But he was nevertheless quite aware that a means existed of crossing the mire, for he set off, without even so much as bestowing a look upon me, for a ford lower down. At first I thought that he intended to come up on the other side ; but he did not, choosing instead to mount the hill towards Wild Tor. My last view of him showed me only the part corresponding to that which Washington Irving's Traveller concealed beneath a broad disc of corduroy.

Readers of Eden Phillpotts' story *The River* will remember that it was a Scotch beast that attacked Nicholas Edgecombe in the lonely region round Devil's Tor, but though there is nothing improbable in the incident, they need be under little apprehension of meeting with a similar experience to the warrener. The animal in question was a bull, and had he been of Devonshire breed instead of Scotch, would have rushed upon Edgecombe all the same, as I can testify, having once had to run at topmost speed across Brown Heath, near the Erme, to escape from one of them. But the rambler's chief safeguard against such an occurrence lies in the fact that bulls are not now allowed to be placed on the moor.

To these few inconveniences—I will not call them dangers—I will add that of losing one's way in a solitary part of the moor. It is fortunately one that can easily be avoided. If the reader will allow me to become his guide I promise him that he shall not stray from his path. If he follows my instructions he will learn enough about the district to enable him to reach all the important objects in it with ease and safety.

All that the visitor needs to take with him on his rambles over the moor is a stout stick, a sandwich case, and—as before named—a pocket compass. If when he reaches his destination at night his boots are wet, let him fill them with oats. These, which are usually procurable at the farm-houses, answer the purpose of boot-trees. The grain absorbs the moisture and swells, and when shaken out in the morning the boots will be found to have preserved their shape. Let him, however, be sure that he shakes out every grain. Should he neglect to do so it will probably not be long before he finds himself able to form a very correct idea of the feelings of the man who omitted to take the precaution to boil his peas. But having exercised proper care he may set out over the moor again ; and if he is fond of a long tramp, he may go from one end of it to the other. I have left Okehampton in

the morning, passed over Yes Tor and Willes, also Cranmere, and
lunched at East Dart Head ; made my way to Fox Tor, thence by
Black Lane and Green Hill to Western Whitaburrow, and so down to
Shipley, reaching Brent in the evening.

When we consider how much Dartmoor has to offer, what scenes
of wild grandeur meet the eye of those who penetrate into it, and what
interest attaches to its memorials of other days, the few inconveniences
inseparable from a long ramble in a hilly region that gives birth to
many rivers are as nothing.   They have been magnified into dangers
by those whose knowledge of the moor is slight ; when one becomes
familiar with it they take their proper place, and are unheeded.

I would particularly request the visitor's attention to one point.
Never omit to fasten a gate after passing through it.   Much trouole
is often caused to the farmers when these are left open.   Cattle may
stray from the field or newtake, or other cattle turned loose on the
forest may enter, and much inconvenience ensue.   The Dartmoor
farmer will always willingly allow strangers to pass through his ground,
and it is surely a small thing to ask in return that they should not
forget to shut his gates.

The latest Ordnance Survey maps, and maps that have been
made from them, are the only ones that are reliable.   Those published
previous to about 1884 are of very little use, being full of inaccuracies.

At the time Dartmoor was being surveyed a list of the place-
names from the old map was sent to me for revision ; I also added
fresh ones, and supplied other information.   As I have already mentioned, there are a large number of objects on the moor the names of
which, often purely local, are not generally known, and these are, of
course, not given on the Ordnance map ; but all the more important
ones are there shown.

In calculating distances on Dartmoor I have found it a safe plan
to add one fourth to those shown on the map.   What the moorman
calls the " ups and downs, and ins and outs " may not make a journey
across the moor quite so much as a fourth longer than the crow's would
be, supposing that bird to be in the habit of indulging in straight and
extended flights ; but the rambler will nevertheless not be far wrong
if he regards a tramp of eight miles as measured on the map as being
nearer one of ten.

The excursions in this Guide have been so planned as to embrace
everything worthy of notice on the moor within about three or four
miles of the centre of each district into which it has been divided ;
objects outside that radius are described in the routes.   These are
given from each district to all the others, with the exception of
Yelverton, Hexworthy, and Post Bridge.   In these cases they were
not required, those from Princetown or Shaugh, serving for the first-
named, while the latter two are crossed by routes between other places.
The visitor can begin his moorland rambles at any point.   He should
first read the paragraphs giving the important landmarks around the
district from which he starts, as by so doing he will learn what there
is in his locality that he should see.   It is also advisable before setting
out across the moor to read the route and its reverse, as the objects
met with on it will be found to be noticed in the latter should that
have been first described.   This is also necessary as in many cases an
alternative route is given.   All places and objects of importance

mentioned in the routes, but not described, will be found more fully noticed in one or other of the excursions, these being always indicated. The compass bearings are sufficiently accurate for the purpose for which they are intended ; they have, of course, not been reduced to points.

At the head of each district a table of road distances is given. If the name of a required place should not be found in a particular table, it must be looked for in the district in which the place is situated, and the distance can then be calculated Thus, if it should be desired to find the distance between Lydford and Sticklepath, the Okehampton district, which is between the two, should be consulted. This will give the distance to both places.

By studying the routes, with the aid of the map, the visitor will find that he can connect one with another, and plan rambles for himself. Thus, the route from Princetown to Lydford is given direct. But should he desire, for instance, to visit Great Kneeset (which is altogether out of his way) *en route*, he may readily do so by following the Princetown and Okehampton route as far as that hill, and return to Lydford by the route to that place from Chagford, or from Cranmere. He can, in fact, by means of this Guide, reach any part of the moor from whatever point upon it he may happen to be.

TERMS USED IN CONNECTION WITH THE

FOREST AND COMMONS.

IN order to avoid stopping to explain the meaning of certain Dartmoor terms in those places where they will be met with, I have here brought them together, and arranged them alphabetically, for facility of reference. Whilst it was primarily terms connected with the forest, and forest law, that seemed to call for some explanation, it also appeared not undesirable to include others relating to archæology and mining, as well as some of a general character. Although the meanings of many will be well known, it was nevertheless thought that they should be given a place in the list, since they often have besides their general signification a peculiar application to the moor. It must not be supposed that the following list is an exhaustive one. Such, indeed, is very far from being the case ; but it is believed that every term necessary to a proper understanding of the usages of Dartmoor will here be found. It was imperative that the remarks on each subject should be as brief as possible.

[a, Antiquarian ; f, Forest ; g, General ; m, Mining.]

Afforestation, f. The turning of a large tract of land into a forest, which can only be done by the Sovereign. It was marked with certain boundaries. Under the Norman kings immense tracts were afforested in every English county. [See *Forest*.]

Agistment, f. The pasturage of cattle in the forest. The conditions under which this is now exercised on Dartmoor are in some respects similar to those formerly existing, but not entirely so. The commoners had the right of agistment, but this was limited. The feeding of the game was first considered ; the surplusage of the pasture alone belonged to the commoner On a tract so extensive as

Dartmoor there must always have been a very large surplusage, and consequently the commoner has enjoyed his grazing rights without hindrance. *Wrongful Agistment* was putting beasts out to pasture without licence.   [See *Commoners, Forest, Moorman.*]

Ammil, The. g. A phenomenon said to be sometimes witnessed in the north of England, but otherwise peculiar to Dartmoor. It consists of a thin coating of ice, which envelopes every projecting object down to the smallest, the effect produced being most remarkable, and when the sun shines upon the ice-cased blades of grass and sprigs of heather, one singularly beautiful. Mr. John Shelly, of Plymouth, points out that the name by which this unusual natural appearance is known is the old English word *ammel*, equivalent to *enamel*.

Ancient Tenements, f. Certain farms of great antiquity, lying within the bounds of the forest. They were probably in existence before the latter were set out, and not encroachments upon the royal demesne. With the exception of some that have been purchased during recent years they are not the property of the Duchy. They are held by copy of Court Roll, and certain privileges are attached to their possession. The holders, or tenants, as they are called, have a right of turbary and pasturage, and until 1796 had also a right of enclosing eight acres of land if the father and grandfather of the tenant had held the farm successively. This enclosure was termed a newtake, q-v. These forest tenants are bound to do suit and service at the Duchy Courts, and to assist at the drifts. The ancient tenements are 35 in number : Babeny, immediately above the confluence of the East Dart and Walla Brook, 3 ; Bellaford, higher up the East Dart, and not far below Post Bridge, 2 ; Brimpts, on the East Dart above Dartmeet, 3 ; Broom Park, on the West Dart, just above the bend under Dunnabridge Pound, but on the right bank of the river, 1 ; Brown Berry, on the road between Two Bridges and Dartmeet, and immediately opposite to Dunnabridge Pound, 1 ; Dunnabridge, adjoining Brown Berry, 4 ; Dury, near Bellaford, 1 ; Hartland, on the left bank of the East Dart, a short distance above Post Bridge, 1 ; Hexworthy, on the West Dart, below Sherberton, 3 ; Huccaby, separated from Hexworthy by the Dart, 5 ; Lower Meripit, near Post Bridge, 1 ; Pizwell, on the Walla Brook, in the vicinity of Post Bridge 3 ; Prince Hall, on the West Dart, below Two Bridges, 1 ; Riddon, on the Walla Brook, not far above Babeny, 1 ; Runnage, on the Walla Brook, above Pizwell, 2 ; and Sherberton, on the West Dart near its confluence with the Swincombe River, 3. Of these old tenements the Duchy have purchased Babeny, Brimpts, Dunnabridge, Huccaby, Prince Hall, Riddon, and Sherberton. It will be seen that two or more tenements are now grouped together under one name ; it would appear, however, that formerly each had its distinctive appellation.

Avenue, a. [See *Stone Row.*]

Ball, g. Hills of a rounded form are often distinguished as such, as Coryndon Ball, Cuckoo Ball, Pinchaford Ball, Red Brook Ball, etc.

Barrow, a. Granite being so abundant on Dartmoor, cairns, or heaps of stone, much more frequently mark the resting-places of the dead than barrows, or mounds of earth. Many examples of the latter nevertheless occur. It was in a barrow on Hameldon that Mr. Spence Bate found the pommel of the dagger now in the museum of the

Plymouth Institution. It is rather strange that the fine hill in the south part of the moor should be known as Three Barrows, when it is really crowned with three immense cairns. But the Celtic term—*Carn*, a heap—though still seen in some place-names on the moor, is much less often met with than barrow, or borough (burghe). In a document of sixteenth century date the hill referred to appears as " Tryberie Boroughs," alias Tre Boroughs," and the great cairn marking the ancient boundary line between the forest and Brent Moor is called by the Perambulators of Henry III's time Whyteburghe.

Beacon, g. There are several hills on the moor to the names of which this word is attached, but whether they were all eminences on which beacon fires were lighted is doubtful. On the southern verge of the moor we have Ugborough Beacon, but I have heard aged people speak of it as Picken Hill, and it appears to me that there is good reason for supposing its name to have once been Peak Down Hill. At its foot is a moor gate, which was known in the sixteenth century as Picke Gate, and still bears that name in the modernized form of Peek, as also does a farm close by. On a map of Dartmoor of the same century the hill is shown as Pigedon. We have also Cosdon Beacon, Hameldon Beacon, Pen Beacon, and others. Two fires would have been sufficient to signal across the longest part of the moor, for from Western Whita-burrow, where the in-country south of Dartmoor is in full view, the hill of Cosdon can be seen, and the latter overlooks the whole of the north of Devon. The watching of beacons was a duty at one time imposed upon the inhabitants of certain places. Reference is made to this in a document relating to Sheepstor, of the date 1626, from which it appears that the "antient privileges and ffreedom of the mannor of Sheepstor were ever heretofore used and accustomed, and then were, that all such persons as did or should thereafter inhabit and dwell within the said hamlett, were ffree from payment of all ffifeteens, which are commonly called ffifth dole, and from payment of Sheriff silver, and from any appearance at the Court called the Sheriffs' Turn, and from the office of tything man, and all manner of limbs belonging to the same, and from watching and warding of all beacons, or any other where, save only within the same hamlett." On Brent Hill there are the remains of a small building, sometimes called the Chapel, which may have been used as a place of shelter for the watchers of the beacon, for we may well suppose a signal fire was lighted on this prominent height. In 1887 I discovered the foundations of another building close to the former.

Beam, m. This word has a mining signification, and where it is found on the moor a deep, open working will usually be seen. Gibby's Beam is a trench running from the Wellabrook across the shoulder of the hill of Snowdon ; Piper's Beam is a gully near the Avon at Hunt-ingdon ; in the vicinity of Princetown is Omen Beam, or as it appears to have been formerly called, Holming Beam ; and near Aune Head is Caters Beam. In the two latter cases the name has attached itself to the hill near the workings. Caters Beam is wrongly marked on the Ordnance map, being there placed more than a mile too far to the west.

Beck, g. This, the northern term for a small stream, is not found as a common name on Dartmoor. But we probably see it in Becky Fall, near Manaton, and in Beckamoor Combe, under Cock's Tor Hill.

Beehive Hut, a and m. [See *Cache, Hut Circle*.]

Blackwood, g.   Peat ; used occasionally by the moor people instead of the more usual word *turf*.   The former is with them *black'ood*, and the latter *turve*.

Blowing House, m.   Small buildings in which tin was smelted on the moor, and worthy of examination as throwing much light on the manner of working adopted by the mediæval tinners.   They are oblong in form, and the door is invariably near one corner and in one of the longest sides.   The remains of a furnace can occasionally be seen, and perhaps a recess in the wall.   Some examples have mould-stones and pounding troughs (q. v.) in or near them.   Sometimes a wheel-pit adjoins, and leading towards this a partly choked water course may often be traced.   These houses are always in a very ruinous condition, and it is possible that they may sometimes have been in-tentionally destroyed.   At all events, Carew, the historian of Cornwall, says that in that county it was customary to burn them down, as by so doing the tinners found sufficient tin in the ashes of the thatched roof to pay for the erection of new buildings and to give them " a gainful overplus."   The size of these blowing houses varies ; some are small, and others as much as 26 or 27 feet long, and about half that in width, The more important examples are noticed in the Excursions.

Bog, g.   This does not mean quite the same as a mire on Dartmoor, although the term is often used to signify any miry ground.   [See *Fen, Mire*.]

Bond-mark, g.   The forest bond-marks have already been noticed. [See *Bond Stones, Perambulation*.]   According to forest law objects forming its boundary are regarded as being wholly within it.   At Mis Tor, the line is drawn *through* the tor, and this appears at first sight to conflict with this view.   But it is not the tor itself that forms the bond-mark, but the rock called Mis Tor Pan, and it is therefore only this that we may expect to find within the forest.

Bond Stones, g.   Very few of these mark the limits of the forest, natural objects such as a hill, tor, or stream, having mostly been fixed upon for that purpose.   But the boundary line between one common and another is usually defined by means of upright granite posts, and these often bear names.   Thus we have Old Jack, and Old William, Aaron's Knock, Petre on the Mount, and the U Stone, and many more.   In addition to the boundary stones of commons there are others marking the limits of manors and of ground over which mineral rights extend.

Bottom, g.   Most of the valleys on the moor are referred to by this name by the inhabitants, and to some it is attached as a proper name.

Boundary, g.   [See *Bond-mark, Bond-Stones, Bound Beating, Perambulation*.]

Bound Beating, g.   At certain times the bounds of a common are viewed by the inhabitants of the parish in which it lies, mostly at the instance of the Lord of the Manor, but sometimes at that of the com-moners.   For the most part the custom is a septennial one.   The day is generally observed as a holiday, though it must be confessed it does not always pass off without an element of discord.   Commoners of the adjoining pieces of waste make a point of being present, and it would be wonderful indeed if the bondmarks were in every instance in the places where each party considered they should be.   There are consequently frequent discussions, and these have been known to grow so heated that blows have resulted. It is all forgotten by the next day, however ; but the bond-viewers would not be Dartmoor men if they did not stand up for their rights. Lads are encouraged to accompany the party making the circuit of the common. This is done in order that there may always be some parishioners having a personal knowledge of the bond-marks.

British Village, a. [See *Hut Settlement.*]

Brook, g. Many tributary streams on the moor are distinguished as brooks. Among others may be named Walla Brook—the brook of the Wealas, *i.e.*, " foreigners," or " strangers " to the Saxons— ; Red Brook, Black Brook (always called Blackabrook) ; Bala Brook, and Rattle Brook.

Burn, g. Like *Beck*, this northern term for a stream is not found as a common name on the moor, though it occurs as a proper one. The stream under Brent Tor is called the Burn, and we have also the Harbourn, the Dean Burn stream, and others.

Burrow, g. A term applied by the moormen to any heap, whether cairns, barrows, or rubble heaps. At the same time they always refer to the mounds in warrens that have been thrown up for the rabbits to burrow in as *burys*. In old documents relating to the forest the word sometimes appears as a form of barrow.

Cache, m. The name recently given to the tiny erections found near stream works, it being supposed that they were intended as places of concealment by the tinners. They are arched with stone in the manner in which it is thought some of the dwellings were roofed, and which from their domed form have been called bee-hive huts. Caches were covered with soil, and when the grass and heather grew on this, and the low entrance was closed (probably with stones and turf) presented, as they do now, the appearance of a natural mound. In this tools, or perhaps ingots of tin, could be left with safety. There is a good example close to a tributary of the Erme on Stall Moor, in the south of Dartmoor, but they are met with in a more or less ruined condition in many parts of the moor. The country people regard them as being places in which contraband spirits were concealed, and that some were used for such a purpose there are many stories to show. The cache referred to is sometimes spoken of as the Smugglers' Hole.

Cairn, a. These ancient places of burial are noticed in our remarks on the barrow. In the south part of the moor there are some remarkably fine examples crowning the hills. It is to their situation that many of the Dartmoor cairns owe their present existence ; those that happened to be near the enclosed lands were despoiled long ago, but the more remote have escaped the hands of the vandal. Vestiges of these ancient stone heaps are to be seen in many places on the verge of the moor. But I have known stone to be taken even from cairns situated at some distance from the in-country. I was once acquainted with a man who about sixty years ago obtained stone for building from Three Barrows. It is, however, near the farms, or roads, where the spoliation has for the most part taken place. During a part of 1878 I was in the habit of riding over Holne Moor almost daily, and I remember seeing a fine cairn by the roadside near Combstone Tor gradually disappear under the hammer of the stone-breaker. Stone of another kind was abundant near by, but it would probably have cost the contractor for the repair of the roads more money to break up, so the cairn had to go. On Black Down, in the parish of Mary Tavy, the vestiges of a number of cairns may be seen. The stones of which they were composed were in all likelihood carted away by the miners for building cottages, in the days when Wheal Friendship and Wheal Betsy were flourishing. On the summit of Corn Down, not far from Yar Tor, above Dartmeet, are some very fine cairns, and to them the hill probably owes its name. In the locality it is, indeed, usually called Carndon, or Carnon ; it is, of course, not to be expected that the Dartmoor native would trouble himself to sound the " d." His pronounciation of the name is rather strange, and this led to the hill being marked on the map made from a survey early in the nineteenth century, as Quarnian Tor. Cairns were sometimes surrounded by a circle of slabs, set on their edges in the ground. The body to be interred was sometimes laid on the surface and the cairn built over it ; sometimes it was placed in a kistvaen which was then covered by the stones. When the body was first cremated the ashes were either placed in a cinerary urn, or gathered into a little heap on the ground. It is noticeable that on Dartmoor cairns frequently occur in groups of three.

Camp, a.　[See *Hill Fort*.]

Cave, g.　Any small hollow, whether natural or artificial, is called a cave.

Censarii, f.　[See *Liberties of the Forest, Priour*.]

Charter of the Forest, f.　This was granted by King John in 1215, and although it contained a promise to disafforest all English forests that had been recently created, little effect was given to it. In 1224 another Charter of the Forest was granted by Henry III., and this provided that all lands which had been turned into forests by Henry II., Richard I., and John should be disafforested. General perambulations of forests throughout England, under royal commissions or writs, followed. The first recorded perambulation of Dartmoor was made in 1240. [See *Perambulation*.]

Chase, f.　A tract of unenclosed land set apart for hunting in the same manner as a forest, but unlike the latter it could be owned by a subject, and did not possess the special privileges belonging to the hunting-ground of the king. When Dartmoor was bestowed by Henry III. upon Richard, Earl of Cornwall, it became in law a Chase, but as it reverts to the crown in certain circumstances it is still termed a forest. According to Maine the beasts of the Chase were the buck, the doe, fox, marten, and roe.　[See *Forest*.]

Circle, a.　There are several kinds of stone circles on the moor : small ones surrounding kistvaens ; larger ones in which no remains of kists are now to be seen ; and hut circles.　[See *Hut Circle, Kistvaen, Stone Circle*.]

Clam, g.　A wooden footbridge ; seldom seen on Dartmoor.

Clapper, g.　A bridge composed of immense slabs of unwrought granite laid upon buttresses and piers of the same. Their rude and massive appearance renders the larger ones very striking, and this is perhaps in some degree responsible for their age having been overestimated. They are mostly on the line of pack-horse tracks, and were probably built by the farm settlers in the forest. The finest example is on the East Dart at Post Bridge.

Clatter, g. There is sometimes a softening of the first vowel, the word being then pronounced clitter. The name given to the collections of boulders frequently seen covering a considerable area on the side of a hill. These rock-fields are really the ruins of tors.

Cleave, g. This word is pronounced *claive* by the native, and often *clay*, the v requiring too much effort to be sounded. It is the name by which certain valleys, mostly on the borders of the moor, are known. But in all that are so called there are crags, and it is questionable whether the term is not derived from these ; *i.e.*, it may possibly be a corruption of cliff, and not of cleft. There is strong evidence pointing in this direction. [*Gems*, Chaps. IX., XXIV.]

Coal, f. Peat is referred to by this name in some of the documents relating to the forest—*carbo*. In the 51st of Edward III., Walter Smith, of Sampford, was fined for carrying away coals from a coal place in the forest without licence ; and in the 2nd of Henry VI. Walter Bird was accused of digging " turves whereof he made coals."

Colt, g. The name by which all ponies running on the moor are called by the moormen.

Combe, g. A small valley, usually closed at its upper end. From the Celtic *cwm*.

Commoner's Rights, g. These are enjoyed by three classes of persons : the holders of the ancient tenements, with which are now included the tenants in that part of Lydford parish not within the forest ; the Venville tenants ; the holders or occupiers of land in Devon outside Venville, excepting the inhabitants of Barnstaple and Totnes. The latter class of commoners have only rights upon the commons of Devon, and these are limited to pasturage ; the two former possess rights of pasture, turbary, and the taking of stone, rushes, etc. They are entitled to take from the forest " all that maye doo thym good excepte grene ocke and venyson." [100 *Years*, Chap. VII.] [See *Venville*.]

Commons of Devon, The. g. The moors surrounding the forest, and lying between it and the in-country, were formerly so called. The term is, however, not now usually applied to these purlieus.

Corn Ditches, g. By this name the hedges, or walls, of the enclosed lands where they abutted upon the moor, were formerly known.

Cooking Stones, a. Sometimes called pot-boilers. Large round pebbles, showing the action of fire, and discovered occasionally in the hut circles. After being heated they were placed with the flesh that was required to be cooked in holes in the ground, or plunged into water contained in a skin when such was to be made hot.

Court, g. Small enclosures, or sometimes nothing more than a space formed by an intentional inward sweep of a wall, into which ponies are driven by the moormen for the purpose of securing them. There is one where the road over Coryndon Ball enters upon Brent Moor, formed by two gates placed across the track, the wall on each side of it between the gates being carried higher than usual. Some of these courts were probably first used for the purpose of capturing deer. [See *Leapyeat*.]

Creep, g. A shallow gulley is often referred to as a creep, and the term sometimes appears in proper names.

Cromlech, a. [See *Dolmen*.]

Crooks, g. A wooden appliance by means of which loads were carried on the backs of horses. Ponies with crooks were at one time always employed for conveying peat from the ties, and a considerable load could be piled on their backs.

Crosses, a. There are a number of stone crosses on Dartmoor, the majority of which were undoubtedly set up for the purpose of marking certain ancient tracks that ran between the abbeys situated on its southern and western borders. [See the section dealing with the Ancient Tracks 1, 2, 69.] Until the publication of my book on the subject [*Crosses*] the first edition of which appeared in 1884, many of the crosses now to be seen on the moor were unknown. For some years previous to that date I had been giving much attention to these venerable memorials, and having formed the opinion from the situations of the few then standing that they were originally intended to mark paths over the moor, I followed the matter up, and by dint of much searching discovered others (often broken and partially buried in the soil) on the line which I supposed the paths to have taken. The latter, it will be understood, could in many places not be seen at all, but I found traces of them here and there, especially near the fording-places on the streams. Since the date mentioned I have given further attention to the subject, and in the later editions of my book (1887 and 1902) I have added to the number of those I originally described. The result of my investigations in this direction I am pleased to say has been the setting up of a number of crosses on the moor, and in the parishes surrounding it, that were before in a neglected state. The Dartmoor cross is usually a simple Latin cross, and altogether unlike some of the elaborate examples found in Cornwall. Most of them are briefly noticed in the excursions.

Cry, g. The sound of hurrying waters borne upon the breeze, and usually heard as evening approaches, is termed the cry of the river.

Danmonii, g. The name given to the ancient inhabitants of the western parts of Britain. Danmonia, the name of their kingdom, it has been supposed, is the same with the Cymric *Dvfnaint*, which, it is thought, is seen in the present *Devon*. Its import—deep or dark hollows—is descriptive of the country. Danmonia has also been derived from the Celtic *Moina*, signifying *Mines*, and *dun, a hill*—thus it would mean the hilly, mining country, or country of the hill mines. Richard of Cirencester, after referring to the early inhabitants of Cornubia (Cornwall) speaks of the Damnonii. He says, "Near the above-mentioned people on the sea-coast towards the south, and bordering on the Belgæ Allobroges, lived the Damnonii,* the most powerful people of those parts ; on which account Ptolemy assigns to them all the country extending into the sea like an arm.† Their cities were Uxella (probably near Bridgwater), Tamara (on the Tamar), Voluba (on the Fowey), Cenia (on the Fal), and Isca (Exeter), the mother of all, situated upon the Isca. Their chief rivers were the Isca (Exe), Durius (Dart), Tamarus (Tamar), and Cenius (Fal). . . .

---

* The transposition of the letters nm is of little consequence. The form *Damnonii* also occurs in Ptolemy.

† Cornwall, Devon, Dorset, and part of Somerset.

This region was much frequented by the Phœnician, Grecian, and Gallic merchants, for the metals with which it abounded, particularly for its tin."*

Deer, g. Deer do not now inhabit Dartmoor, though stragglers from Exmoor are sometimes seen there. In the eighteenth century they were almost exterminated by the hounds of the Duke of Bedford, which were sent down from Woburn for the purpose. This was at the request of the farmers in the neighbourhood of Tavistock, the deer causing great injury to the crops. In 1627 a deponent in a law suit, Thomas Taverner, of Chagford, stated that there were deer on the moor, but he thought only a few. That they continued fairly plentiful on its borders, however, there is good evidence to show. As far as recorded, it was in 1780 that the last deer was killed by hounds on Dartmoor. This stag was roused in Brook Wood, near Buckfastleigh. [100 *Years*, Chap. IX.]

Deer Leaps, f. In the charter by which King John purported to disafforest Devon, in 1204, the terms *saltatoria* and *haias* occur, and these are translated deer leaps and hedges. Permission was therein given to the men of Devon to make deer leaps except within the bounds of Dartmoor and Exmoor. It has been thought that *leap* in this case is derived from the high German *lippe*, an enclosure. A deer leap would therefore be, if this is so, the same as what is now often known as a *court*, q. v. [See *Leap Yeat.*]

Disafforestation, f. The reduction of forests to common ground. This was done in the case of the tracts of land afforested by the Norman kings by means of a solemn perambulation of the bounds of the forest, and the return of this into Chancery was the record of disafforestation.

Dolmen, a. From the Celtic *daul*, a table, and *maen*, a stone. Dolmen is therefore literally a stone table, and this term conveys an idea of its usual appearance. The word has taken the place, among antiquaries, of *Cromlech*, as being more suitable to the object it represents. The dolmen marked a place of sepulture. It consists of a huge flattish stone, supported by others at an elevation of several feet above the ground, thus forming a rude canopy. The supporters are generally three in number, but there are instances in which these are more. Trevethy Stone, at St. Cleer, in Cornwall, has seven. Dolmens are found in many parts of the world. They were sometimes buried beneath a tumulus, but this was certainly not always the case. The finest example in the Dartmoor country (and outside that district there are none in Devon) is the Spinsters' Rock, near Drewsteignton. One or two others on the moor are noticed in their places.

Drift, f. At certain times the moor is searched for the purpose of ascertaining that no cattle or ponies are pastured on it except those whose owners are entitled to place them there, and this is called the drift. The time when this is to be done is fixed by the Duchy authorities, and notice is then given to the moormen. All estrays are driven to Dunnabridge Pound, and fees, and a charge for watering, must be paid by their owners before they can be removed. [See *Moorman, Venville Tenant.*]

Druids, g. Antiquaries of a former day, and those who followed

---

* Richard of Cirencester on the *Ancient State of Britain.*

them, ascribed the erection of the stone monuments of Dartmoor to the Druids. Not only is there no proof that Druids ever were on Dartmoor, but some evidence that they were unknown in Devon.

Duchy of Cornwall, The. g. Henry III. granted the manor of Lydford, with the forest of Dartmoor, to his brother Richard, Earl of Cornwall, and these then became a part of the Earldom. This was raised into a Duchy by Edward III., his son, the Black Prince, being the first duke. The Commons of Devon (q. v.) are not within the Duchy, but belong to various manors lying round the moor. The Duchy Courts, which took the place of the ancient forest courts, formerly held at Lydford, are now held at Princetown.

The amount received by the Duke of Cornwall from the Duchy during 1905 was £77,490.

Duke of Cornwall, The. g. The duke is the eldest son of the reigning king. Should there be no heir apparent, the dukedom reverts to the crown until there is one.

Early Inhabitants, g. The evidence afforded by the names of the hills and streams of Dartmoor shows us that this upland tract was inhabited in some far away time by a race of Celts. (See *Danmonii*). Scattered over it are the remains of their dwellings and the shattered monuments of their dead. The discovery in and near the ruins of their huts of arrow heads and other articles of flint, while indicating that iron was probably not employed by them, does not, to my mind, preclude the supposition that they sought the inhospitable hills of the moor for tin. There are instances of tribes being in what is termed the stone age even in very recent times ; they have continued to use stone implements while around them were those who employed iron. It is well known that the Greeks, and perhaps the Phœnicians, came to the southern part of Britain for tin, and a native tribe may very well have furnished the strangers with the ore they required, in exchange for certain articles, without understanding the process of smelting it, or working the metal. However this may have been, that the remains of primitive dwellings in this part of Britain are mostly found near ancient stream-works is a fact that cannot be disputed.

Enclosures, g. These are now numerous on Dartmoor. Some land was filched by those who had the right to a newtake. [100 *Years*, Chap. I.] It was by the Duchy that the tracts of land round Two Bridges and Post Bridge were enclosed.

Farlieu, g. Under this head certain sums were payable by farms to the lord of the manor in some places.

Farm of Forest, f. From time to time the forest has been let out on lease, the system being introduced in 1425, when it was let to Sir Philip Courtney and Sir Walter Hungerford for seven years. For some time past, however, the Duchy have retained it in their own hands, but let out the right to take cattle to pasture to moormen, q. v.

Feather Bed, g. These are sometimes called Quakers, and are noticed in our " Hints to the Dartmoor Rambler." When a depression in the granite occurs the water collects in it, and, vegetation forming, the result is a deep hole filled with slush, the surface being always covered with bright green moss.

Fen, g. This is also alluded to in our " Hints to the Rambler."

Those parts of the forest are so called where the soil consists of nothing but peat, and on which the only growth is bog-grass. There are two principal tracts of it ; one in the north part of the moor, extending from Ockment Hill to the sources of the West Dart, and the Cowsic, and in which the East Dart, the Taw, the West Ockment, and the Tavy take their rise ; and the other in the south part, and lying round the head waters of the Avon, Erme, and Plym. This word is always pronounced *vain* by the moor people.

Fines Villarum, f. The rents of the vills, or those lands on the borders of the moor having rights on the forest. They probably grew out of older customary payments. [See *Venville*].

Flint Weapons, etc., a. Flint arrow heads and scrapers have been found in considerable numbers in many parts of the moor. At Walkham Head the late Mr. Francis Brent, of Plymouth, found two polished celts in the peat. In 1887 the late Mr. F. N. Budd, of Batworthy, on the borders of the moor near Chagford, discovered flint flakes in his fields, and subsequent examination revealed the fact that they were exceedingly numerous. Within two or three years several thousands were found there. The presence of these flakes in such large numbers has led to the supposition that somewhere within the area over which they were scattered there must have been a place where it was customary to chip flints and fashion weapons and implements—a kind of manufactory of arrow heads and spears, so to speak. The flint must have been brought from a distance, as there is none obtainable in the neighbourhood. On the slope of White Tor, on Cudlipp Town Down, flakes are also found in considerable numbers. A few bronze weapons and fishing spears have also been discovered on and near the moor. Mr. Robert Burnard, of Huccaby, has a very fine collection of flints, as also has Mr. J. D. Prickman, of Okehampton.

Flood, g. The rivers of the moor are subject to sudden risings, particularly in the summer, when the ground being dry the rain runs off the slopes, filling every little channel leading to them. In an incredibly short space of time a clear stream will be turned into a rushing torrent, and yet there may be no indications of rain. That has fallen a few miles away and perhaps only over a limited area. During these floods the water is of a dull reddish brown colour, and though when they begin to subside the rivers grow clearer it is a few days before they resume their ordinary appearance. [100 *Years*, Introd.]

Fold, f. These are mentioned in the returns of profits of the moor. In 1300 there is an entry of £20 1s. 3d. for cattle " returning to divers folds there " ; and another of 13s. 10d., " fines of 83 folds this year at 2d. per fold."

Foldepeny, f. A customary payment due at Michaelmas. In 1502 the sum of 2s. is returned under this head in the reeve's account of Lydford borough.

Folk-lore, a. Notwithstanding its wild character legendary stories are not numerous on Dartmoor. The Wish Huntsman and his hounds are said to be heard when the wind is howling over the moor, and there is a black dog which haunts the waste, while one or two stories are related of Binjie, the dwarf of Cranmere. There is also the traditionary story of Childe of Plymstock, and stories of a Lord of the Forest which probably points to Gaveston, and also the wild tales related of Lady Howard, besides several of a similar character. But we do not find such a number of these stories as we might expect in a region that breathes so much 'of the romantic ; where rocky ravines and lonely glens seem to form a fitting home for the wonder story. But while this is so folk-tales of another kind are exceedingly numerous. I have collected hundreds of these, chiefly relating to the doings of the pixies (q. v.), and to encounters with the Evil One. Some of them are related in these pages.

Foot, g.   The name given to that part of a stream where it falls into another, as Rattle Brook Foot, etc.   It is sometimes applied to the foot of a hill, as Kneeset Foot.

Foreigners, g.   Ever since the time when the Saxon settlers on Dartmoor gave to the Celts whom they found there the name of foreigners, or in their own tongue *Wealas*, the term has been in use in the district to signify those who do not belong to it.   It is found in documents relating to the tin mining as well as in the forest records, and is heard to-day.   The inhabitants of Devon, outside Venville, are referred to in documents of the seventeenth and eighteenth centuries as foreigners, wraytors, countrymen and strangers, or strange men.

Forest, f.   Wistman's Wood, near Two Bridges, is often spoken of as a relic of the ancient forest of Dartmoor, as though the district was at one time clothed with trees.   It is altogether a mistake to suppose anything of the sort.   That in many of its more sheltered valleys groves similar to Wistman's Wood were once to be seen there is no doubt ; in fact, there are still such on the West Ockment and on the Erme, but nothing can be more certain than that Dartmoor was never a wooded district.   The word forest is generally understood to mean an extensive wood, but that was not its true signification.   A forest was really a tract of land set apart as a hunting-ground for the king, and governed by certain laws having for their object the preservation of deer and other wild animals of the chase.*   A forest can only be created and possessed by the sovereign ; should he bestow one upon a subject it is no longer a forest, but a chase, unless there be a special grant.   When Dartmoor Forest was given by Henry III. to his brother Richard there was no such special grant.   It therefore became a chase, but it is nevertheless always called a forest, the fact of its having been at times in the possession of the crown (when there has been no Duke of Cornwall, q. v.), possibly accounting in some measure for this.   But there was a great change in its legal status when it passed from Henry to his brother.   It was no longer under forest law, and the Courts thereafter held at Lydford, though sometimes on the Rolls called Courts of the Forest, were not the same as the ancient Forest Courts.   The beasts of the forest were the hart (which was called a royal hart when six years old if it had been chased by the king and had escaped), the hind, hare, boar, and wolf, and the laws which governed the preservation of these were very strict.   A man possessing land in a forest, as in the case of the holders of the ancient tenements on the moor, had to exercise his rights with particular care, so that he might not injure the *vert* and *venison*, that is the cover and game.   Should he do so his offence was termed a Nuisance of the Forest, and he was liable to punishment.   The Forest Courts were the Court of Attachment,

---

* The word has been derived from *foris*, *outside*, *without* ; *i.e.*, a place outside the bounds of cultivated land.

the Court of Swainmote, and the Court of Justice Seat. The officers of the forest were the Lord Chief Justices of Forests (one of whom sat in the Court of Justice Seat, held once in three years), verderers, a chief warden, rangers, an agister, a regarder, foresters, a beadle, and others of a less important character. There was also a Steward of the Court of Swainmote. [For the bounds of the forest see *Perambulation ;* and for Forest Law see *Lydford Law.*]

Gates, g. These were formerly placed on every drift road, or other approach to the moor. There are numerous entries on the Court Rolls of Lydford of persons being presented at the Court for permitting the gates to be in a dilapidated condition. At present the greater number of the approaches to the moor have gates, in order that the cattle and ponies may not stray from the commons, but there are none to some of the high roads that run across it, which is justly a subject of complaint with the commoners.

Gert, m. A deep, open working of the miners ; larger than a gulley.

Goyle, m. Has the same meaning as *gert,* but is heard chiefly on the north-western side of the moor.

Granite, g. A chain of granite masses extends through Devon and Cornwall, Dartmoor being the most easterly and the largest. Its granite is of a brownish grey colour, coarse-grained, and composed of large prisms of orthoclase felspar, quartz, and black or white mica. [100 *Years.* Introd.]

Green, g. Certain spots are known as such on the moor ; they are sometimes smooth and grassy, but not always so.

Gurgey, g. On the moor this word is applied to a steep gully through which water is sometimes carried from mine workings, but it is only occasionally heard. There is a deep gurgey running from the slope of Gibbet Hill, on Black Down, to the Cholwell Brook. It is usually dry, but when the rain is very heavy, and pours into it from the side of the hill, the water rushes through it in a foaming torrent.

Head, g. The source of every river and brook on the moor is referred to by this name.

Heath, g. Certain spots on the moor bear this name, as Brown Heath, on the Erme, and Bala Brook Heath, near Zeal Hill.

Hills, g. Many of the hills of Dartmoor are crowned with a tor, and then they are often found to possess no name of their own, but are indicated by that of the tor. This, however, is not always the case. The hill on which Cock's Tor is situated is, for example, known as Cock's Tor Hill, and the pile called Lowery Tor is on Peak Hill. When there is no tor the hill invariably bears a name, no matter how small it may be.

Hill Forts, a. There are no hill forts or camps actually on the moor (unless we suppose the enclosure on White Tor to have been one), with the exception of the camp near Ashbury Tor, above the Moor Brook and East Ockment. But there are several on its borders, the chief being on the Teign below Chagford. These are Cranbrook, Prestonbury, and Wooston. There is also the remains of one near the road between Plympton and Shaugh. Brent Tor Down and Brent Hill were both fortified.

Hole, g. Equivalent to hallow. The name is sometimes applied to the head of a combe, but oftener to the narrow part of a river valley.

Holt, g. A subterranean hollow, or small cave ; a rabbit burrow or fox earth.

Houses, g. Clusters of hut circles. The name is seldom heard, and is only used by moormen.

Hut Circle, a. The name given to the remains of the circular dwellings of the primitive inhabitants of the moor. These consist of low walls, usually about 3 or 4 feet in height, and generally formed of granite slabs set on their edges. In some examples, however, the stones are laid in courses, and in others the wall is formed of stone and turf. The mode of construction was evidently dictated by the nature of the materials near at hand. In a few instances that will be noticed the walls are of immense thickness. The roof was formed of poles laid on the wall and converging to a point, and was probably not very high. Rushes, and perhaps heather, served as a covering. A few of the smaller ones seem to have been built entirely of stone, and in a domed form, as already has been mentioned [see *Beehive Hut*], but this was very exceptional. The entrance, which faced the south, can nearly always be distinguished ; in a great number of examples, indeed, the door jambs, often formed of slabs set at right angles to those in the wall, yet remain. Excavations in the interior of the hut circles have shown that in many of them a section of the floor was slightly raised, and this, it is conjectured, was the bed-place. Flat stones have also been found in them, which may have been used for splitting bones upon, as well as cooking holes, and pot boilers. [See *Cooking Stone*.] A curtain of skins was probably hung across the entrance, which in some instances is protected by a dwarf wall. The average diameter of a hut circle is about 17 or 18 feet ; some, however, are much smaller, while others are as much as 28 or 30 feet.

Hut Settlement, a. A group of hut circles, sometimes called a village. These are found both unenclosed, and surrounded by a wall, always in a ruined condition. Enclosures of this kind are known on the moor as *Pounds*, q. v.

In-country, g. The name by which the Dartmoor man refers to the cultivated land off the moor. Formerly the same was known as the *In-ground*.

Inscribed Stones, a. There are not many stones bearing inscriptions in the Dartmoor country. Those which are to be found are noticed in the Excursions.

Island, g. On most of the principal rivers it will be found that the stream has in places formed a second channel for itself, thus leaving a small island. Sometimes it is covered with grass, or ferns. These generally bear distinctive names.

Journey, g. Evidently from the French *journee* ; a term that has probably been in use on Dartmoor since Norman times. It signifies a certain quantity of peat ; *i.e.*, as much as can be cut throughout a length of forty yards and a width of twice that of the cutting-iron. Two journeys are considered a good day's work for an experienced cutter.

Jurats, m. The stannators at the Tinners' Parliament from the Stannary districts were so-called. [See *Stannaries*.]

Kistvaen, a. A stone coffin, from the Celtic *cist*, a chest, and *maen*, stone, v being used as a mutation of m. These are very numerous on Dartmoor, and some are still in a good state of preservation, notwithstanding that they have all been rifled. They take the form of small oblong pits, about three feet long, and two feet wide. Some examples are larger. Each side and end is usually composed of a single slab, and another was laid on these as a covering. The cover stones are missing in some examples ; where they remain they will be seen lying by the side of the kist. These rude coffins were buried beneath a mound of earth, round which was set a small circle of stones. When a body was placed in the kist it was laid in a contracted position, but it was often cremated, and the ashes sometimes deposited in a cinerary urn. Several stories are related on the moor of treasure seekers despoiling kistvaens.

Lair, g. Certain spots where the pasturage is good, and to which the moormen are in the habit of driving their cattle when they turn them on the forest in the spring. Places of this kind were formerly termed Predas. [100 *Years*, Chap. VII.]

Lake, g. Many of the tributary streams on Dartmoor are called lakes, as Dark Lake, Red Lake, Hook Lake.

Lane, g. Paths and natural passes through bogs, are often so called, as Black Lane, Cut Lane.

Leat, g. There are a number of water-courses on the moor, some formed for the purpose of supplying power to mines, and others for conveying water for drinking, as the Devonport Leat, and the Prison Leat.

Leapyeat, f. Leap gate ; an old term for the moor gates. *Lippe*, an enclosure. [See *Deer Leap*.]

Levancy and *Couchancy*. [See *Venville*.]

Liberties of the Forest, f. Certain liberties enjoyed by right, or under grant. In 1199 John, Earl of Mortein (afterwards King John), confirmed by charter to the earls, barons, knights, free tenants, clerics and laymen, in Devonshire, their rights of the forest which they had in the time of Henry I. ; a writ of the date 1221 directs that Roger de Toeny shall have the same liberties in Dartmoor which his father had ; the Abbot of Buckfast released by charter to Richard, Earl of Cornwall, his liberty and right of having a stud farm in the forest ; and in 1296, in an account of the ministers of Richard, there is a sum of 2s. 2d. returned from the " censarii," afterwards called moormen, for having a liberty, the same being the right of dwelling in the forest while not holding any tenement there.

Loaf, g. This corruption of the Celtic *llof* is only found in the names of objects on Dartmoor in two or three instances. Its meaning is an excrescence, and it well describes the appearance of those rocks to which it is attached. These are noticed in the Excursions.

Logan, g. Formerly all rocks so nicely poised as to move with very slight pressure were thought to have been in some way connected with Druidical rites. [See *Druids*.] There are a number of such rocks on the moor.

Longstone, g. The name by which the menhir is always known on Dartmoor. [See *Menhir*.]

Lords of the Forest, f. Dartmoor is first mentioned by name in 1204, in the Charter of John, but it is referred to in another Charter granted by John before he became king. He then held it presumably under grant, and that it had been similarly held by others previously there is some evidence to show. He possessed the forest during his reign, and at his death it came into the hands of his son, Henry III., who held it until 1239, when he bestowed it upon Richard, Earl of Cornwall, who was also king of the Romans. Dartmoor then became in law a chase, and at Richard's death passed to his son Edmund. In 1300 Edmund died, and the forest reverted to the crown, and remained in its possession during the reigns of Edward I. and Edward II., and part of that of Edward III. Edward I. put the forest into the custody of John de Tresympel, and Edward II., in 1307, granted it to Piers Gaveston. After the execution of the favourite, Thomas le Ercedekne became the custodian of Dartmoor, and it was subsequently granted to Hugh de Audley and Margaret his wife, the king's niece, to hold for the life of the said Margaret, licence being given them in 1319 to demise it to the Abbot of Tavistock for five years. In 1337 Edward III. bestowed the forest upon his son Edward, the Black Prince, whom he created Duke of Cornwall. Since that time it has frequently reverted to the crown, and there have been several violations of the charter to the Black Prince. The revenues of the Duchy have not only been diminished by the sale of properties, which is altogether contrary to one of its provisions, but although the charter appoints the dukedom to the eldest son of the reigning king and heir apparent to the crown, and enjoins it to remain in suspense should there be none until such time as there is, this course has not always been followed. The present Lord of the Forest of Dartmoor is Edward Albert, Prince of Wales, who succeeded to the Dukedom of Cornwall on his father, His present Majesty, ascending the throne.

Lydford Law, f. This, which is described as "hanging first and trying afterwards," is commemorated by Browne in his humorous lines, written about 1644, entitled *The Lydford Journey.* In Lydford Castle those who offended against the harsh forest laws were confined, and it was also the Stannary prison. The treatment meted out to the unhappy captives appears to have been most rigorous, and the place early obtained an evil repute in consequence. But it was the justice dispensed in the forest courts that were held there, and not its connection with the Stannaries that probably gave rise to the saying concerning Lydford law, the severity of which was proverbial, nearly 250 years before Browne wrote. He says:—

> " I oft have heard of Lydford law,
> How in the morn they hang and draw,
> And sit in judgment after "——

and this has been supposed to be merely a playful allusion to the tyranny exercised in the castle in early days. But, strange as it may seem, it is probable that what Browne had so often heard was not far from the truth. The lowest Forest Court was the Court of Attachments, held every forty days by the verderers, and part of their business was to make presentments to the Court of Swainmote, which was held three times a year. A presentment concerning any offender against the forest laws would there be delivered to a jury composed of forest freeholders, and if they found it true the indictment was sealed. Sentence, however, could only be passed by the Court of Justice Seat, held once in three years. But as there was very little doubt about what this would be, it was frequently anticipated, and the offender straightway hanged. Later on, when the Court of Justice Seat met, his case would come before it, and sentence be passed. The tyrannical Stannary laws fully kept alive the bad repute into which those pertaining to the forest had first brought the castle of Lydford. In a Parliament Roll of the 50th of Edward III., in which the commonalty of the County of Devon petitioned the king to remedy certain evils which they suffered at the hands of the tinners, it is stated that there was no gaol delivery at Lydford oftener than once in ten years. In an Act of the 8th of Henry VIII. the prison in Lydford Castle is described as " one of the most annoious, contagious and detestable places within this realme." When we further learn that Sir Richard Grenville, who is chiefly notorious for his ruffianly acts, was governor of the castle for the king during the Civil Wars, and that the cruel Jeffreys is also said to have presided in its Courts, we shall hardly wonder that Lydford Law was once regarded as being anything but justice. But this Devonshire parish was not the only one in the country with a reputation for dealing harshly with prisoners. In Yorkshire, there was formerly a custom known as Halifax Law. The inhabitants had a right to try any felon found within a certain district with stolen goods in his possession, and to hang him forthwith. The last execution took place in 1650. Lydford is sometimes spoken of as a Stannary town. This is erroneous. There was no Stannary of Lydford.

Lynch, g. A rough road, or track. The word usually indicates a track that is lower than the ground on each side of it—a cutting. It is possible that Lynch Tor, Walkham, and Lynch Down, Meavy, may both have been named after old tracks. Near the former runs the Lich Path, and through a cutting ; carried up the steep side of the latter is the Abbots' Way, and the monk's path from Tavistock and Sampford Spiney to Plympton. The last named is also cut below the level of the common.

Marsh, g. This word is not used so much on Dartmoor as a common name as part of a proper one. Among other places in which it appears are Broad Marsh, Lade Hill Marsh, Deeper Marsh, the Marsh, at Huccaby, and Langa Marsh. The word is pronounced *maish* by the moor people.

Meads and *Meadows,* g. Certain spots on the moor are so called, as Prayley Mead, Bush Meads, and the Meadows, on the Erme.

Menhir, a. A rude commemorative pillar, usually found on Dartmoor with other remains, often of a sepulchral character. They are always known as Longstones, which name is indeed precisely the same as menhir, the latter being merely the two Celtic words *maen*, stone, and *hir*, long.

Meet, g. The confluences of some of the streams are so called, but it is not found attached to all. Dartmeet, Swincombe Meet, Lizwell Meet, and Glaze Meet, may be named as examples.

Mining, m. Many of the stream works on Dartmoor are probably of great antiquity, but it is also quite certain that we do not now see them as they were left by the early searchers for ore, the mediæval tinner having worked in all of them. And he has left us much that is interesting, especially when it is read in the light thrown upon his rubble heaps, and his ruined blowing-houses, by old writers, and certain records of the Tinners' Parliament. Down to the reign of

Elizabeth there were probably a good many stream works on the moor, but after that period the industry seems to have considerably declined. Towards the close of the eighteenth century it commenced to revive, but before the nineteenth century was many years old most of the mines had ceased working. Vitifer, on the commons belonging to North Bovey, has perhaps been one of the most prosperous of the Dartmoor mines. Others are the Golden Dagger, near it ; White Works, near Fox Tor Mire ; and the Hexworthy Mine on Skir Hill. [100 *Years*, Chap. III.]

Among those who have been connected with modern mining enterprise on Dartmoor, Mr. Moses Bawden, of Tavistock, stands pre-eminent. From 1879 onwards Golden Dagger was worked by him. At times he had from 30 to 40 miners employed there, and paid close upon £20,000 for labour. [See *Stannaries, Stream Works.*]

Mire, g. Applied to a swamp, or marsh, and not to the bog, or fen. This is noticed in our *Hints to the Rambler.*

Mists, g. A few remarks on Dartmoor mists are offered in our *Hints to the Rambler.*

Moor, g. This name is attached to many of the parish commons surrounding the forest and forming its purlieus. It is, however, found more particularly in the southern part of the moor. It is also attached to certain parts of a common, and occurs in the forest as well.

Moormen, g. Men whose business it is to take in cattle to pasture are called moormen. They rent the quarters of the forest, either direct from the Duchy, or as sub-renters from others. [100 *Years*, Chap. VII.] The modern moorman is the successor of the ancient priour or herdsman, and seems to have originated in the first half of the eighteenth century, when Frederick, eldest son of George II., having demised the forest to Abram Elton and Mrs. Mary Heywood for a long term of years, the lessees licenced certain persons as herdsmen in the four quarters to take in cattle to pasture, and receive the usual fees. This practice still continues, so that instead of the charges payable for pasturage being collected by the Duchy, they belong to the moormen, the former receiving a fixed rent in lieu of them. [See *Priour.*]

Mort gabel, f. In the earlier records this appears among the profits of Dartmoor as "mortuo gabulo," and probably represented payment received for dead wood.

Mouldstones and *Mortars*, m. Granite blocks having moulds cut in them for the smelted tin are found near some of the blowing-houses, as also are others with small circular hollows which probably served as pounding mortars. Troughs are also occasionally found. The moulds are usually about a foot in length and three or four inches in width, and have sloping sides in order that the ingot of tin might be readily removed. Some, however, are larger than this. Their depth is about three inches.

Newtake, f. The right of enclosing newtakes has been referred to under *Ancient Tenements*. These were supposed to be eight acres in extent, exclusive of rock and bog. Much more was often enclosed under the plea that the additional acreage consisted of the latter. Grants of newtakes of one acre are often met with in the Lydford Court Rolls. No newtakes under the old conditions have been allowed for more than a century. The enclosing of large newtakes such as those

formed towards the end of the eighteenth and beginning of the nine
teenth centuries, was altogether contrary to the custom of the forest.

Night-rest, f. [See *Venville*.]

Old men, m. The name by which the earlier tinners, are always
referred to by the people of the moor. They do not usually call those
who set up the stone monuments old men, but apply the term almost
exclusively to the tin streamers. The sites of their labours are always
spoken of as Old Men's Workings.

Oxen, g. As in the in-country, oxen were formerly employed on
the moor. I have known many old men who have worked with them
there, and have collected several stories in which their employment
is spoken of. In some of the border farms oxen were put to work on
the roads, and then they were usually shod, the shoe being called a
" Q " in consequence of its being shaped something like that letter.

Pack-saddle, g. These were formerly in use for carrying burdens
on the backs of ponies. For certain loads, such as ferns and peat,
the crooks, already noticed, were attached to them.

Park, g. A name used to describe a small area on the moor, as
Sand Parks, under Fox Tor, and Horsey Park, at Walkham Head.
It is not found in many parts of the moor.

Peat, g. [See Turf-tie.]

Perambulation, f. In the Charter of King John already mentioned [see *Charter of the Forest*], and which is dated the 18th May,
1204, all Devon is purported to be disafforested " up to the metes of
the ancient regards of Dartmoor and Exmoor, as those regards were
in the time of King Henry I." Thirty-six years later there was a
Perambulation of the bounds of the Forest of Dartmoor, made by order
of Henry III., shortly after it was bestowed upon his brother Richard.
There are several copies of the return to the writ ordering this perambulation, and though they do not agree exactly it is possible to
identify most of the objects named as bond marks with those recorded
at a later date, and which are regarded as the bounds at present. The
perambulation was made by twelve knights, summoned by the Sheriff
of Devon in the 23rd of Henry III. (1240). The bounds set forth are
as follows :—Hogam de Cossdonne—Parva Hundetorre—Thurlestone—
Wotesbrokelakesfote — Heighestone — Langestone — Turbariam de
Alberysheved — Wallebroke — Furnum Regis — Wallebrokeshede—
Wallebroke usque cadit in Dertam—per Dertam usque ad aliam
Dertam—per aliam Dertam ascendendo usque Okebrokysfote—
—ascendendo Okebroke usque ad la Dryeworks—Dryfeld Ford—
Battyshull—Caput de Wester Wellabroke—Wester Wellabroke usque
cadit in Avenam—Ester Whyteburghe—Redelake—Grymsgrove—
Elysburghe—Crucem Sywardi—Ysfother—aliam Ysfother—Mystor—
Mewyburghe — Lullingesfote — Rakernesbrokysfote — la Westsolle—
Ernestorre—vadum proximum in orientali parte capelle Sancti Mich-
aelis de Halgestoke—Hogam de Cossdonne. In the 6th of James I.
(1609), a survey of the bounds of the forest of Dartmoor was made by
twenty-five jurors, and presented at a Survey Court held at Okehampton, on the 16th August. The bounds were returned as follows :—
Casdon—Little Houndetorr—Thurleston, or Waterdontorr—Wotes-
brooklakefoote (at that time called Whoodelake)—Hingeston, or
Highstone—Yeston, or Geston (at that time called Hethstone)—
Turfehill — Kinge's Oven — Wallebrookeheade — by Wallebrooke to

Easter Dart—thence to Wester Dart—thence to Wobroovefoote—
Drylake — Crefeildfford, or Dryefeild ford — Knattleburroughe —
Wester Wellebrooke headd—thence by Wester Wellebrooke to Owne,
or Aven—Easter Whitaburrowe—Redlake foote whir it falleth into
Erme—Arme headd—Plimheadd—Elisboroughe—Seaward's Crosse—
Little Hisworthie—another Hisworthie—Mistorrpan—Dedlakeheadd
—Luntesborowe—Wester Redlake—Rattlebrooke foote—thence to
the headd of the same Rattlebrooke—Steinegtorr—Langaford, or
Sandyford—thence to the ford wch lyeth in the east syde of the chapple
of Halstocke—Cosdon. [100 *Years*, Appendix.] The bounds that
the Duchy recognize to-day do not always agree with those of the
commoners whose wastes they touch, though except in the north and
north-east part of the moor, and in the extreme south, where the
latter have greatly encroached, the difference is not considerable.
From the point of view of the commoner the bounds would be as
follows. It must be explained that, as a rule, the commoner only
knows the forest boundary where it abuts on his own common, or on
those adjacent). From the foot of Cosdon, where Small Brook falls
into the Taw, the line runs over Metheral Hill to White Moor Stone,
and thence to Little Hound Tor—Wild Tor Well—Thurlestone, or
Watern Tor—Hew Thorn Clitter—Manga Rock—across the North
Teign—Stonetor Hill—Longstone — Woodlake Head — across the
South Teign—along Hurston Ridge to King's Oven—Walla Brook
Head (near the Warren House Inn)—down the Walla Brook to the
East Dart—down the Dart to Dartmeet—up the West Dart to Wo
Brook Foot—up the Wo Brook to Dry Lakes—up Dry Lakes and
across the hill to Corfield Ford—Knattleborough on Ryder's Hill—
West Walla Brook Head—down the West Wella Brook to the Avon—
a short distance up the Avon, thence up the hill to Western Whita-
burrow—thence to Red Lake Mires and down Red Lake to the Erme—
up the Erme to Erme Head—Boundary Stone—Broad Rock—Plym
Head—a short distance down the Plym, and thence to the carn on
Eylesbarrow—Siward's, or Nuns' Cross—South Hisworthy Tor—North
Hisworthy Tor—Rundle Stone—Great Mis Tor—across the Walkham
under Greena Ball—Dead Lake Head—White Barrow—Higher Pile of
Lynch Tor—Homer, or Wester Red Lake, a short distance below its
source—down Red Lake to the Tavy—down the Tavy to Rattle
Brook Foot—up the Rattle Brook to its source—Stinka Tor—Sandy
Ford—across Dinger Plain to Curtory Clitters—across the Blackaven
under Row Tor—then down by the right bank of that stream to Crovenor Steps—up the hill to the summit of the Belstone ridge, to a point
just north of Winter Tor—down the further side, and across Taw Plain
to the starting point at the confluence of the Taw and Small Brook.
That the bounds recognized by the Duchy are the true ones, or at all
events are much nearer to the true ones, than those that the commoners
contend are correct, there cannot be a doubt. The perambulation of
1240, and the surveys of the forest made since that date, show this to
be the case. Nothing can be clearer, for instance, that the line drawn
from Eastern Whitaburrow to the Erme by the jurors of 1609. They
name the boundary as running from the Avon to Eastern Whitaburrow
" and from thence liniallie to Redlake foote whir it falleth into Erme."
Now the boundary line, as contended for by the commoners, leaves
Eastern Whitaburrow outside the forest altogether, and running to

Western Whitaburrow goes thence to Red Lake—not, however, to its foot as the jurors say, but nearly to its head. By this very convenient arrangement a considerable portion of the forest has been claimed by the commoners as belonging to Brent, Ugborough and Harford Moors. The fact that they do so does not, however, make this tract less a part of the forest, and the Duchy maintain their rights over it, and over all other disputed tracts, by annually driving them for estrays.

Pillion, g. A saddle on which a woman rode behind a man on horseback. They were formerly much in use in the West of England, and also in other parts of the country. One was exhibited in the Northampton Museum some years ago that was said to have been used in 1830. It was on a pillion that the Devonshire parson suggested that the man should have brought his wife to the supper to which he had been invited, instead of making the frivolous excuse that in consequence of his being married he was unable to be present. For the purpose of assisting women to mount, what were called uppingstocks were provided. These consisted of a small mass of masonry about 3 or 4 feet in height, one of its sides forming steps. They are yet to be seen in nearly all the villages and hamlets round the moor.

Pixies, g. The former belief in these little elves was one of the most interesting of the Devonshire superstitions. But their existence is now regarded by the peasantry with something more than doubt. They were said to be the souls of unbaptized children, and though they sometimes appeared as a small bundle of rags, were more often seen in the form of tiny beings dressed in fantastic garments, mostly of a green colour. The pixy is the brownie of the north. Many stories are related on the moor of their doings. While sometimes found to be mischevious, they more often evince a desire to aid the industrious housewife or husbandman. Their favourite haunts on Dartmoor were the Pixie's Cave on Sheeps Tor, the Piskie's Holt, in Huccaby Cleave, and New Bridge on the Dart, below Holne. [*Pixies*, Chaps. I., II.] [See *Folk Lore*.]

Place-names, g. These are very numerous on Dartmoor, almost every combe and hillock bearing some appellation. The greater number are of comparatively modern date, having been bestowed upon the various objects by the moormen as a means of indicating localities. But many of the names of the chief streams and hills and tors are of Celtic derivation, and it is to the Gaelic branch of that tongue we must mainly look to read their meanings.

Plain, g. This word is found attached to certain localities on the moor, as Zeal Plains, Erme Plains, and Dinger Plain ; but it does not mean a stretch of level ground. It could, indeed, hardly be used in such a sense on the moor, for the reason that it would be difficult to find a piece of level ground there of any extent. Its true signification is a tract of plain moorland ; that is, ground comparatively free from rocks and inequalities.

Ponies, g. These have roamed for centuries over Dartmoor, and are referred to in some of the earlier records as horses. They are very hardy, and being foaled on the open moor, and seeing little of man, grow up in a semi-wild state. Except during very severe winter weather, when their owners may drive them to the enclosed country, they remain on the hills throughout the year. Wet and cold they can endure, but snow is their deadly enemy, for it robs them of their food, and should it happen that their owners are unable to gather them in they are sometimes starved to death. After a heavy fall of snow, when the moor has been thickly covered for some time, I have seen numbers of them dead. I remember once seeing one at the foot of Stony Bottom, near the Erme, and the marks on the ground, which it had evidently made by pawing in its efforts to reach the buried herbage, were plainly visible. Unless the fall of snow is of such a character as to quickly render progress over the moor impossible, these animals usually make their way to the borders on its approach, and in such cases those to whom they belong, or in whose charge they may be, are able to watch over them. During late years much attention has been paid to the breeding of the Dartmoor pony, and the animals are now becoming of greater value than formerly.

Pool, g. With the exceptions of the Burrator Lake, in the valley of the Mew, formed as a storage reservoir for the town of Plymouth, and another in the Wennaford valley on Holne Moor for the supply of Paignton, there is no large sheet of water on Dartmoor. But there are a number of pools, and so-called pools, on the moor, not one of them, however, being of the slightest importance as such. Certain associations lend some interest to one or two of them, but for the most part they possess little to attract the visitor. The much-talked of Cranmere Pool has contained no water for a century, and is now nothing more than a hollow in the fen. But it deserves to be visited nevertheless ; for though disappointing to those who expect to see a lonely tarn and find only a boggy depression in the peat, the journey to it will lead the rambler, from whichever point he may start, through desolate parts of the moor, and enable him to see it in its wildest aspect. Crazy Well 'Pool, on Walkhampton Common, though filled with water, is simply an excavation of the miners ; and Raybarrow Pool, on South Tawton Common, is a mire. On the tract of fen in the south part of the moor is the little known Ducks' Pool, which, however, has been drained by the tinners. When filled with water it was a much finer sheet than ever Cranmere could have been. Between the Western Beacon and Butterdon Hill is Black Pool ; but this, even in a rainy season, is very shallow. The pool that is perhaps more deserving of notice as such than any on the moor is one that has never yet received mention. This is Knattleborough Pool, on Brent Moor, which though in great measure artificial has little of it in its appearance. Crazy Well is of regular form ; Knattleborough Pool presents a more natural outline. These are all noticed in the Excursions. The pools on the streams of Dartmoor for the most part bear names, as Timber Pool, on the Dart : Shiny Pool, on the Avon ; and Long Pool, on the Tavy.

Pound, g. It has been stated in the remarks on the *Hut Settlements* that many of the groups of ruined dwellings on the moor are surrounded by a wall. These enclosures are always spoken of by the moor people as pounds, and that they were places of shelter for cattle by night, as well as for their owners, there is, I think, little doubt. The walls of some are composed of very large stones, and in others they are found to be comparatively small. These enclosures, which usually approach a circular form, may in some cases have been intended to protect the dwellers in the huts against the assaults of an enemy, but such could not have been their primary purpose. The best known of these enclosed hut settlements is Grim's Pound, situated on the common belonging to the parish of Manaton, and between Hameldon Tor and Hookney Tor. It covers an area of about four acres. [*Gems,* Chap. VIII.] Pounds are numerous on the moor, and many fine examples exist in the south part of it. The walls having fallen in every case, and the turf that probably formed part of them having been washed away, these are now nothing more than an agger of granite blocks, though in some examples there are parts that show that the stones were originally laid in courses. *Drift pounds* are altogether of a different character, and, as the name indicates, were enclosures to which estrays were driven at the time of the drifts. Two of these, Dunnabridge Pound and Erme Pound, though of considerable antiquity, are formed on the site of still older enclosures, the remains of the vallum that once encircled a hut settlement being plainly visible at the foot of the wall of each. Erme Pound has not been used for many years, but to Dunnabridge estrays are still driven. There are other pounds at Halstock and Creaber. On the verge of the moor will also be found a number of small manor pounds ; some of them are evidently of great antiquity.

Preda, f. Pasturage grounds, both within the forest and on the commons. In an account of the constable of Lydford Castle of the fourteenth century several predas in different parts of the moor are mentioned. [See *Lair.*]

Priour, f. Herdsmen in whose charge were placed the cattle agisted in the forest. Their duties were very probably similar to those of the moorman of the present time, but they differed from him in that they were hired for the work at a certain wage. These are referred to in early documents as censarii. [See *Liberties of the Forest* and *Moorman.*]

Quakers, g. [See *Featherbed.*]

Quarters of the Forest, f. The forest is divided into four quarters, north, east, south, and west, and these are leased out by the Duchy separately. Previous to 1404 there were only three quarters, but in that year a readjustment of the divisions took place, and the south quarter was then formed. The boundary line of the forest has already been given [see *Perambulation*] ; the bounds of the quarters are as follows :—North : From the confluence of Wester Red Lake and the Tavy to the head of Spriddle Combe, and thence to Horse Hole on the West Dart ; thence to a pile of rocks, formerly bearing the name of Kit Tor, on the East Dart ; thence to Teign Head, and down the Teign to the boundary of the forest.—East : Conterminous with the north from the forest line on the Teign back to Horse Hole ; thence down to Dart Hole and by the West Dart past Two Bridges, Prince Hall and Hexworthy, to Wo Brook Foot.—South : Conterminous with the east from Wo Brook Foot as far back as Cholake Foot, about a mile below Two Bridges ; thence to Cholake Head and across part of Tor Royal Newtake to Strane Head ; thence down to Strane Foot, near the White Works and on to Plym Head.—West : From the confluence of Wester Red Lake and the Tavy the line is conterminous with that of the north as far as Horse Hole ; from that point it is conterminous with the boundary of the east to Cholake Foot ; and from Cholake Foot is conterminous with the south quarter boundary to Plym Head.

As these boundaries now run through newtakes, or other enclosures, the whole area of each quarter is not, of course, let to the moormen, but only so much of it as is open forest. It will be seen that the east and west quarters touch each other, and that each also touches the north and south ; but the two latter do not touch. The north is by far the largest.

Reave, g. Banks of earth and stone, sometimes running for a considerable distance, are known by this name on the moor, and are found in all parts of it. That they were boundaries, and that many were thrown up by the tinners, there can be no doubt. When met with near groups of hut circles they are usually small, and are probably of some antiquity. Trackline is a name that has been given to them, but not very happily, as it suggests that they were formed to serve the purpose of marking a track, which they certainly were not. There are, however, those who consider that the larger examples were roads, and have given to them the name of trackways. I confess that I have never been able to regard them as such, and until it is explained how those who used them contrived to ride through rocks, or immense cairns, I am afraid I shall be unable to accept the view that they were designed for purposes of traffic. A large reave runs from the East Glaze (a stream which after joining the West Glaze falls into the Avon not far below Brent Bridge) to the summit of Three Barrows, and down the further side towards the Erme, and this is one that has been looked upon as a road. It is, however, difficult to see on what grounds. It starts abruptly at the stream, and ends as abruptly on the slope of the hill above the Erme. For centuries it has served to mark the boundary between Brent Moor and Ugborough Moor, and the Glaze is a continuation of that boundary. It is named in a survey of Brent Moor as presented by jurors at Brent on the 25th August, 1557. This reave is certainly much larger than those usually seen, but that is no reason for supposing it to have served a different purpose. The three cairns which give name to the hill over which it runs stand directly in the line of it, and this being the case it is impossible to see how it could ever have been a road. We must believe one of three things : that the reave and the cairns were thrown up at the same time ; that the reave was made first ; or that the cairns were built first, and in either case the conclusion arrived at must be that the bank was not a road. If we suppose the first to have been the case this is plain, for nobody would take the trouble to make a road, and then render it impassable by building cairns upon it ; if we consider the reave to be older than the cairns we have to believe that those who threw up the latter deliberately blocked the road, which is absurd ; and if we suppose the cairns to have been placed on the hill before the bank was formed (and they most certainly were) we must imagine the road makers to have been stupid enough to carry their track towards an obstacle instead of trying to avoid it. No men with a grain of sense would have made a road in the line of this reave. It climbs a lofty hill for no apparent purpose but that of descending its further side. Another large reave is to be seen near Archeton, on Chittaford Down, and this also is regarded by some as a road, and has been termed the Great Central Trackway. It runs directly into Lower White Tor after climbing the precipitous side of a hollow, and there terminates. There is not a trace of it on the other side of the tor, nor on the commons.

near by. Four and a half miles to the west, and nearly two miles to the south, is another reave, and with this it has been sought to connect it, though when it stops at the tor its direction is due west. No explanation has been offered why this so-called trackway should be carried straight into a tor, and none, in fact, could be given unless the tor were its terminal point. I am sorry I cannot agree with those who think otherwise, but whatever purposes the reave on Chittaford Down may have served, I am certainly not inclined to consider that a road was one of them.

Reeve, f. The forest reeve is elected at the Duchy Court, held annually at Princetown, by the Duchy officers and the holders of the ancient tenements. He has certain duties to perform in connection with the drifts, and with rights of common, but they are not so important as formerly. There is also a deputy-reeve.

Ridge, g. This word appears in place-names in all parts of the moor, as Hickley Ridge, on Brent Moor ; Down Ridge, in the south quarter of the forest ; Riddon Ridge, in the east quarter ; and Row Tor Ridge, on Okehampton Common.

Rings, g. The name by which pounds and hut circles are sometimes known, as Erme Pound Rings, and The Rings, on Ryder's Plain.

Ripping, g. Rinding, or stripping trees of their bark. Dartmoor labourers sometimes obtain work of this kind in the oak coppices on the borders of the moor. Any clothes are supposed to be good enough to go ripping in. The moorland saying with regard to this is : "If you go in dressed, you come out ragged ; and if you go in ragged, you come out naked."

Rocks, g. The moor folk often add this word to the name of a tor, as Hey Tor Rocks, and Hound Tor Rocks. It also sometimes appears properly as part of a name, as Tristis Rock, Hangershell Rock, and Tor Rocks. The moor people have also a habit of duplicating the word tor. Thus they will speak of Henter Tar, instead of Hen Tor, or of Ingater Tar, instead of Inga Tor.

Rock Basin, g. Hollows found on the summits of some of the tors. Ascribed to the Druids until the geologist refused to allow them to have a hand in the matter. Produced by the action of rain, frost, and wind.

Rock Idol, a. Not to be found on Dartmoor, though it was once believed to the contrary. The rocks that were formerly thought to be idols still remain, but the Druids having been banished they are no longer regarded as such.

Rye, g. This was formerly grown on some of the Dartmoor farms. Rye straw has been found in the thatch of old buildings there.

Sacred Circle, a. A term once in favour with the Druid school of antiquaries who looked upon all columnar circles of stone as temples. [See *Stone Circle.*]

Side, g. A indefinite term, usually employed in conjunction with the words *higher* and *lower*. Thus a Dartmoor man will speak of that part of a hill near its summit as the " higher side," and of its foot as the " lower side."

Sledge, or *Slide*, g. Still used occasionally on the moor—principally for drawing heavy stones—but not nearly so much as formerly.

Spading, g. Paring and burning the surface of the moorland ; the first step towards bringing it into a state of cultivation. Now seldom practised, but afforded the labourer much work in the times when attempts were being made to reclaim certain parts of the moor.

Spalliard m.   The name by which the labourer in the tin works was formerly known.   Westcote in his *View of Devonshire in* 1630, in speaking of the Spalliard, or spador, as he calls him, says, " no labourer whatsoever undergoes greater hazard of peril or danger, nor in hard or course fare and diet doth equal him ; bread, the brownest ; cheese, the hardest ; drink, the thinnest ; yea, commonly the dew of heaven ; which he taketh, either from his shovel or spade, or in the hollow of his hand, as Diogenes, the cynic, was taught by a boy."

Squatting, g.   This practice was once not unknown on Dartmoor. It was a sort of recognized custom that if a house could be built and land enclosed between sunrise and sunset, the builder could claim it. The last instance of such a proceeding occurred about 1835, the house that was erected being Jolly Lane Cot, near Hexworthy.   [100 *Years*, Chap. I.]

Stables, g.   Mires are sometimes known as Dartmoor Stables. This is mentioned in our *Hints to the Rambler*.

Stannaburrow, m.   Small heaps of soil thrown up by the miners to mark the bounds of their sett, or grant, are so called.

Stannaries, m.   The mining districts of Devon and Cornwall. In a Charter of the 9th of Richard I. (1198), which is referred to by Sir George Harrison in his *Report on the Laws and Jurisdiction of the Stannaries in Cornwall* as " the earliest authoritative document upon the subject of the Stannaries," are certain expressions that prove that the mining of Devon and Cornwall was under the jurisdiction of the crown at a very early period, and that at the date of the charter the tinners had long been possessed of rights and privileges in connection with the same.   The dues were a source of considerable profit, and at an early date pertained to the earldom of Cornwall.   The laws regulating the Stannaries were of a very stringent character, and the tinners possessed great power.   The origin of these laws is entirely unknown. They were passed and amended at assemblies called Stannary Parliaments, which were held on Hingston Down, in Cornwall.   But prior to 1305 the tinners of Devon and Cornwall had separated and become distinct bodies.   This is evident from a charter of that date, in which among other matters the towns of Tavistock, Ashburton and Chagford are appointed as the places at which all tin, wherever found and wrought in the County of Devon, should be weighed and stamped.   In 1328 Plympton was created a Stannary town in the place of Tavistock, as being much nearer the sea, and therefore more likely to be visited by merchants.   How long such an arrangement continued is not certain, but in the following century, at all events, Tavistock was once more one of the weighing and stamping places.   As Plympton retained its status there were then four Stannary towns, and no further changes were made.   The tinners of Devon on separating from the tinners of Cornwall held their own Parliaments, and having regard to the situation of the Stannary towns, there is hardly a doubt that it was at that time they fixed upon Crockern Tor, on Dartmoor, as the place of their deliberations.   The first Parliament on the tor of which we have an account was held on the 14th September, 1494.   It has been considered that the ancient tinners' courts formed the model for the higher legislative assembly of our land.   In a report to the prince's council in 1785, the vice-warden of the Stannaries remarked that the Tinners' Parliament was similar in constitution to the British; the lord warden representing the king; the stannators, the lords; and the assistants, chosen by the stannators, the commons. Each of the Stannary towns sent 24 stannators, or jurats, to the court. An early writer has stated that any tinner convicted of mixing impurities with his metal was to have three spoonfuls of it poured down his throat in a molten state. While this is probably nothing more than a tradition, it is still certain that the laws by which the tinners were guided were very stringent. The Stannary Prison was at Lydford, and the " depe pitte vnder the grounde " in the castle there, in which Richard Strode was confined in the reign of Henry VIII., is still to be seen. Strode was member of' Parliament for Plympton, and having brought a Bill to prevent the tinners choking up the harbours by sending down sand in the streams, incurred their displeasure, and was cited to appear before them at Crockern Tor. This he refused to do, and he was heavily fined in his absence, afterwards being seized and sent to Lydford. He had to give a bond for £100 to Thomas Denys, deputy-warden of the Stannaries, to obtain his release, and an Act was then passed making his condemnation by the tinners utterly void. The supremacy of the Imperial Parliament was thus asserted, and from that time the power of the tinners gradually declined. A Parliament is said to have been held on Crockern Tor as late as 1749 ; indeed, it has been stated that even this was not the last. The later practice, however, was to open the Court on the tor, and then adjourn it to Tavistock. A large slab of granite, forming a stone table, and seats of granite for the stannators, were once to be seen on the tor, but had disappeared before the close of the eighteenth century. The spoliation is noticed in the excursions from Princetown and Two Bridges. [*Stannaries.*]

Stent, g. A space somewhat similar to a stroll, but not so confined, and usually on sloping ground.

Steps, g. Stepping stones are often found on the streams near the enclosed parts of the moor, and these always bear names, as Swincombe Steps, Stannon Steps, and Crovenor Steps. The ford on the Plym where it is crossed by the Abbots' Way is known as Plym Steps, but there are no stepping-stones there, nor does it seem very probable that there ever were any, for although the miners have been at work near by it is hardly reasonable to suppose that they would have removed them.

Stone Circle, a. Circles of upright stones often defined the bases of grave mounds, but there are no remains of a tumulus to be seen in any of the larger examples on Dartmoor. Though formerly looked upon as temples, they are now known to be sepulchral in their origin. The small circle so often seen enclosing a kistvaen served exactly the same purpose ; that is, it was a monument marking the resting-place of the dead. They are altogether unlike the hut circle in appearance. The latter are either built like a wall, or the slabs composing them are set quite close together ; the stones composing the sepulchral circle stand at some distance from each other, and in the finer examples are several feet in height. The largest sepulchral circle on Dartmoor is that at Scorhill, on Gidleigh Common, but the one that has come down to us in the most complete state·is the circle known as The

Dancers, on Stall Moor, in Cornwood Parish. There is also a fine circle on Langstone Moor, in Peter Tavy parish, but this is a restoration.

Stone Remains, a. The pre-historic monuments of Dartmoor consist of barrows and cairns, dolmens, or cromlechs, menhirs, stone rows, kistvaens and stone circles ; other remains of the same period being pounds, hut circles, and reaves. To the early historical period belong the hill forts on its eastern borderland, and to mediæval times the stone crosses and some of the clappers. The tinners' remains are blowing houses, moulds and mortars.

Stone Row, a. Rows of stones placed a few feet apart, and often extending for a considerable distance, are seen in many parts of the moor, and no other monument has perhaps occasioned so much speculation as to its purpose. Had they been more carefully studied it is probable we should not have seen this. Suggestions have been made that the rows were intended for gymnastic performances, that they were used for solemn Arkite ceremonials, that they are parts of serpent temples, that they formed the processional roads of the Druids, that they were race-courses, that they were once roofed in and formed shelters, that they represented armies drawn up in battle array, that they were intended to guide people over the moor in misty weather, that they have an astronomical signification, and that they are a representation of the passages that led to the chamber in a tumulus. From these hypotheses it certainly should be possible for the visitor to select one to his mind, though I confess that the latter alone commends itself to me. An examination of the rows must, I think, convince anyone that they are sepulchral. It will be found that they are generally associated with remains we know to be so. These rows are sometimes single, sometimes double, and there are instances where several parallel lines are found.

Streams, g. Risdon, writing early in the seventeenth century, speaks of Dartmoor as the mother of many rivers. The chief of these is the one that gives name to the district, and of this there are two branches, the East Dart and the West Dart. These unite on the eastern border of the forest, and the stream then runs between Holne Moor and the commons in the parish of Widecombe. With the exception of the two Ockments and the Taw, with their tributaries, all the Dartmoor streams empty themselves into the English Channel. The former find their way into the Bristol Channel at Bideford Bay.[*]

Stream Works, m. The workings of the tinners are found on every stream on the moor, and consist for the most part of heaps of stones thrown up on the banks. These heaps are in no sense disfiguring, as time has weathered the stones and coated them with moss and lichen. Streaming is the washing of the ore from the surface gravel. This was placed on an inclined plane, which was agitated while water from the river flowed rapidly over it. The grit, and other refuse, were carried away, and the ore was left behind. " Tinners," says an old writer, " covet to have always a River as nigh their Work as they can." There are many references to stream works during the 16th, 17th, and 18th centuries, but that some are of much earlier date

[*] A list of the streams of the moor, and also of the hills and tors, is given in *A Hundred Years on Dartmoor.*

there can be no doubt. They were probably often formed on the sites of the very early workings. [*Stannaries.*]

Stroll, f. A space between two enclosures. These are useful as affording shelter to cattle during stormy weather, and are also of service to the moormen for driving cattle into occasionally for certain purposes. When newtakes have been formed on the banks of a stream a stroll becomes necessary in order to permit of the cattle or ponies reaching the water. There are instances of land grabbers having turned strolls into enclosures. As it required the building of only one, or at most two walls, to effect this the process was easy.

Sull, g. An old name for a plough, still heard on the moor. It is the Saxon *suhl*.

Swaling, g. The burning of the furze and heather, which is done in order that the grass may spring up and afford pasturage for the cattle. Only those in charge of beasts have any right to swale, and its practice is confined to the months of March and April. On the commons that border the forest swaling is often regulated by Parish Councils.

Tin Bounds, m. A few stones set up in the form of a brandis, that is a tri-angular stand on which kettles are set on a hearth, often mark the bounds of a tin sett. Tin bounds had always to be entered on the books of the nearest Stannary town. [See also *Reave* and *Stannaburrow*.]

Tinners' Parliament, m. [See *Stannaries*.]

Tolmen, a. A holed stone; from the Gaelic *tol*, a hole, and *maen*, stone. Said to have been used for mysterious purposes—by the Druids, of course, one of whose great objects in life seems to have been the puzzling of posterity. In some ancient monuments there are certainly artificial holes, but nothing of the kind is seen on Dartmoor. The only stones having holes that are the work of man are such as were used by the miner, and those to which gates were formerly hung, or in which they swung. Nature made the tolmens on Dartmoor, and she has a number in process of fashioning there now. By far the most striking is the holed stone in the Teign, immediately below the stone circle at Scorhill.

Tor, g. These granite masses, of which there are about 170 on Dartmoor, form one of its most striking features. The word is really the Celtic *twr*, tower, and it not inaptly describes their appearance, for many of them rise to a considerable height above the ground. Usually they are seen crowning a hill, but this is not always the case. The finest tors are situated on the western side of the moor, between Mis Tor and Yes Tor, and on the eastern side above the Widecombe Valley. There are, however, very striking ones in other parts of the moor; indeed, there is hardly one without some feature of interest. One of the grandest is Fur Tor, situated on the edge of the great tract of fen, in a remote part of the north quarter of the forest. [100 *Years*, Intro., Appendix. *Gems*, Chap. II. *Dev. Alps.*, Appendix.]

Town, g. The Saxon *ton*, a settlement; often applied only to one farmhouse, as Davy Town, in the Walkham Valley, and Tor Town, near Cocks' Tor. Cudlipp Town, in Peter Tavy parish, is a collection of several farms.

Track, g. Old tracks are numerous on the moor. [See the section in which the chief of these are described.]

Trackway, g.   [See *Reave.*]

Trial, or Tin, Pits, m.   Small pits a few feet in depth are met with in certain parts of the moor.   These show where a trial has been made to discover tin.

Trough, g.   In places a river is seen pent up between walls of rock, that form a miniature cañon, as it were.   These are called troughs, or as the Dartmoor native has it, traws.   Thus we have Long-a-traw, Henchertraw, and others.   In the former case the name has also attached itself to the valley in which the cañon is situated.

Turbary, g.   The commoners' and the forest tenants' right of turbary has existed from the earliest times.   One of the places where peat was cut is mentioned in the Perambulation of 1240, as the "turbariam de Alberysheved," or Aberesheved, but which the Jury of Survey in 1609 called Turf Hill.

Turf-tie, g.   The pits where peat is cut.   Each farmer has his own tie, and it is a recognized rule that no one else must cut any peat in it. Another rule compels the owner of the tie to replace the surface turf, so that a green side shall be preserved.   Peat is still used in considerable quantities in the forest, and in some of the border farms, but very little is consumed in the villages surrounding the moor.   Since these have been brought within easy reach of railways, coal has taken its place.

Upping Stock, g.   [See *Pillion.*]

Vags, g.   Slabs of turf cut for fuel on those parts of the commons encircling the forest where there is no peat.   Speaking generally it is only within the forest, that is to say, in the more central and elevated parts of Dartmoor, that peat is found in abundance.   There are a few exceptions, notably on Outer Stall Moor, where there are a large number of old ties, but as a rule those who dwell on the borders of the moor find a journey of a few miles necessary before they can obtain peat. They therefore make use of surface turf from the commons near their homes.   When cut the slabs are turned face downward, and are allowed to remain where they are for a short time to dry, when they are brought in to the farms and stacked for the winter in the same manner as peat.   The jurors of 1609 present that the Venville tenants have a right to take from the moor "turves, vagges, heath, stone, cole and other thinges according to their custombes."

Valley, g.   The valleys of Dartmoor run in all directions, but for the most part preserve a north and south line.   The finest on the moor are Tavy Cleave, the valley of the West Ockment from Meldon to Lints Tor, the gorge of the Dart below Dartmeet, and the Erme valley above Harford.   Nearer the borders, where on the sides of the valleys is often a happy mingling of crag and coppice wood, are the valley of the Plym above Shaugh Bridge, the Walkham Valley below Merivale, Belstone West Cleave, valley of the Teign at Gidleigh, the Dart Valley at Holne Chase, and Stowford Cleave, where the Erme comes down from the moor to Ivybridge.   The gorge of the Teign below Drewsteignton is some distance from the borders of the moor, on the verge of the granite area.

Venison, f.   The forest and Venville tenants were prohibited from taking two things in the forest—green oak and red venison. [See *Vert.*]

Venville, f.   A term derived from fines villarum, the rents of the vills. These are certain " towns " (q. v.) that is, farms, situated on the borders of the moor, to which belong rights on the forest of Dartmoor and commons of Devon. It is not known how these rights originated, but it is probable that they were exercised before Dartmoor was afforested, or that they grew out of trespasses upon it after such was effected. The rights were chiefly those of pasturage and turbary, and were subject to a small fee, this being the fin ville. No one was allowed in a royal forest after nightfall ; all beasts put there to pasturage had to go in " by sonne and goo home by sonne." When it became the custom to permit them to remain there by night as well as by day, the possessors of the rights of pasturage were called upon to pay 4d. yearly for what was termed " night-rest." Sometimes the Venville rights extend over a whole border parish, and the rent is then paid collectively. In an account rendered by the foresters of the four quarters of the forest in 1502, venville rent is accounted for from the following places. In the north quarter : the vills of Throulegh, Collerowe, Sele, Hallestoke, and Willesworth, and the parishes of South Tawton, Belston, Sourton, and Briddestowe. In the east quarter : the vills of Chagford, Hereston, Litterford, Shirwyll, Higher Catrowe, Grendon, Fenne, Jurston, Willuhede, Edworthie, Higher Jurston, and Chalnecombe, and the hamlets of Tenkenhamhorne, Hokyn, Kyndon, North Werthiehed, North Catrowe, and a hamlet in the parish of Widecombe not named. In the south quarter : the vills of Helle, Skyridon, and Ugbirough, and the hamlet of Stouton. In the west quarter : the vills of Shawe, Brighteworth, Godemewe, Mewey, Dennecumbe, Chodlype, Twyste, Raddyche, Pytcheclyff, and Margaret Land, the hamlet of Lonnington, and the parishes of Shidford, Sampford Spanley, Whitechurch, and Petarstavie. The owners, or occupiers, of venville lands are regarded as the king's special tenants, and were once called upon to perform certain duties, and to appear at the Duchy Courts. [100 *Years*, Chap. VII.] One of the duties was that of assisting at the drifts, but since the farming out of the forest this service has rarely been demanded of them. According to a deposition taken in a suit in 1702, the forest tenants, who had also to assist in driving the moor, could demand a halfpenny cake for their trouble at the close of the day on which the drift took place. The rights of the venville men are fully set out in a document of the time of Henry VIII., entitled, " Instructions for my Lord Prince to the King's most honourable Council concerning my Lord Prince's Forest of Dartmoor," and in this it is distinctly stated that they shall have all that may do them good except green oak and venison. The limitation of levancy and couchancy attached to these rights. No man might pasture more cattle upon the forest than he could winter on his farm. If he did so the document in question states that he must then pay " as a strange man." This condition is still in force.

Verderer, f. Forest officers holding their appointment by writ of the king. They enrolled the attachments of all trespasses. [See *Forest*.] In the Close Rolls is a writ dated 28th June, 1219, commanding the Sheriff of Devon to convoke his county, and elect two knights of the neighbourhood of Dartmoor as verderers. When the forest became in a law a chase verderers were no longer elected.

Vert, f. Whatever grows and bears a green leaf in a forest. The jurors of 1609, in referring to the venville tenants, say that they may take " in and uppon the forrest of Dartmoore all thinges that maye doe them good, savinge vert (which they take to be green oke) and venison." In the document " Instructions for my Lord Prince," it is plainly stated that it was " grene ocke and venyson " the venville men were prohibited from taking. [See *Venville.*]

Vills, f. [See *Venville.*]

Vooga, m. The name given on the western side of the moor to small earth caves, and miners' caches.

Warren, g. Like a forest and a chase, a warren was land set apart for the preservation of game, and the beasts and birds of the warren were the hare and the coney, the pheasant and the partridge. As breeding-places for rabbits alone there are several warrens on Dartmoor, and some of them have probably been in existence for a long period. Trowlesworthy Warren, on the Plym, dates back to the thirteenth century.

Waste, g. This term, attached to the name of small downs, or commons, is only found in the southern part of the moor. In the parish of Cornwood there are several in which it appears as part of the name, as Highhouse Waste, Dendles Waste, Watercombe Waste, and Yadsworthy Waste.

Water, g. Used very often instead of *brook*, or *stream*, but only in the case of tributaries, as Cut Combe Water, in the north quarter ; Evil Combe Water, a small tributary of the Upper Plym ; and Ruddy-cleave Water, a stream falling into the Dart in Buckland Woods.

Wells, g. Certain springs are so called, but the only true well on the open moor is Fitz's Well, on the Blackabrook. As instances may be named—Broady Well, on the Avon ; Dead Lake Well, on the Walkham ; Dick's Well, at the head of Doe Tor Brook ; Wild Tor Well, near Wild Tor, on the verge of the north quarter ; and Wapsworthy Wells, above the hamlet of that name.

White Works, m. Although this name occurs as a proper one on Dartmoor, the mine (now disused) on the edge of Fox Tor Mire being so called, it also appears in places as a common one. Some mining remains on a tributary of the Walla Brook (the stream that falls into the North Teign) are generally spoken of in the neighbourhood as White Works, and so also are other disused mines.

Whortleberry, g. This berry, the vaccinium myrtillus, grows in great abundance on Dartmoor. Large quantities are annually gathered during the months of July and August, chiefly by women and children from the border villages. They are sold in the market towns, and there are those who make a substantial addition to their income by gathering them. In most of the moorland villages the day on the moor " pickin' hurts," as the berries are always called by the native, is regarded as a holiday, and looked forward to with pleasurable anticipations.

Worthy, g. This word—the Saxon *worthig*, a settlement—is frequently found as a terminal in the place-names of Dartmoor.

IMPORTANT POINTS AND LANDMARKS, CHIEF PLACES
AND OBJECTS OF INTEREST, AND PRINCIPAL
GROUPS OF ANTIQUITIES ON THE MOOR.

B Y means of this list the visitor may ascertain at a glance what
there is of note in that part of the moor in which he happens to
be staying. The places or objects classed as Important Points
are in most cases of equal interest with those given under the second
head, but are kept separate as forming landmarks which the visitor
who wishes to gain a good knowledge of Dartmoor, will do well to
acquaint himself with. It is, indeed, in this sense that they are named
as being important. Everything mentioned is described in the excursions or routes, and when a place is not noticed in the District in
which it here appears (consequent upon being outside the three or four
miles radius of the excursions) it must be sought for in an adjoining
one. The index will show which this is, and to this also the reader is
referred for the names of such places and objects as he may not find
here, since only the more important of these are included in this list.
When objects are common to two Districts they are named under each.

1.—PRINCETOWN AND TWO BRIDGES DISTRICT. *Important
Points.* Bear Down Man — Bellaford Tor—Dartmeet—Merivale
Bridge—Mis Tor—North Hisworthy Tor—Nosworthy Bridge—Plym
Steps—Rundle Stone—Siward's, or Nun's Cross. *Other Places of
Interest.* Childe's Tomb—Cowsic Valley, under Bear Down—Crazy
Well Pool—Crockern Tor—Dean Combe—Dunnabridge Pound—
Fitz's Well—Prince Hall—Tor Royal—Valley of the Walkham—
Wistman's Wood. *Prehistoric Antiquities.* Conies' Down : hut
circles and stone row—Crock of Gold, and other kistvaens in Tor Royal
Newtake—Down Tor : row, menhir, and circle, on Hingston Hill—
East Tor Bottom : hut circles—Hart Tor : hut circles and stone row,
and remains on Raddick Hill—Roundy Farm : hut circles—Lower
Watern Newtake : kists and cairns—Merivale : rows, huts, and menhir
on Long Ash Hill—Thrushelcombe (on the Plym) : rows, cairns, and
menhirs. *Mining Remains.* Hart Tor : blowing houses and stream
works—Dean Combe Head : tinners' excavations — Newleycombe
Lake : extensive stream workings—Plym : workings near Eylesbarrow—Riddipit : mould stones—Walkham : blowing houses above
Merivale Bridge.

2.—TAVISTOCK DISTRICT. *Important Points.* Hill Bridge—
Merivale Bridge—Mis Tor—Sandy Ford (Walkham)—Warren's Cross.
Places of Interest. Brent Tor—Black Down—Cocks' Tor, Staple Tors
and Roose Tor—Lydford (Lydford District)—Peter Tavy Combe—
Pu Tor—Sampford Spiney—The Tavy below Horndon—Valley of the
Walkham—Vixen Tor—Whitchurch Down—White Tor. *Prehistoric
Antiquities.* Langstone Moor : stone circle and menhir, and hut
circles at White Tor, or Whittor, and Wedlake—Merivale : rows, huts,
and menhir. *Mining Remains.* Walkham : blowing houses near
Merivale Bridge, and streaming remains above Mis Tor.

3.—LYDFORD DISTRICT. *Important Points.* Forstall Cross—
Great Links Tor—Hill Bridge—Noddon Gate. *Places of Interest.*
Black Down (Tavistock District)—Bra Tor—Branscombe's Loaf—
Brent Tor (Tavistock District)—Lydford Gorge and Waterfall—The

Lyd below Doe Tor—Skit Steps—Tavy Cleave. *Prehistoric Antiquities.*
Arms Tor : hut circles—The Rings, Watern Oke : hut circles—Noddon
Rings, on the Lyd : hut circles—Rattle Brook : hut circles—Standon
Houses, on the Tavy : hut circles.

4.—OKEHAMPTON DISTRICT. *Important Points.* Cosdon—High
Willes—Moor Gate—Sandy Ford (Ockment)—White Moor Stone.
Places of Interest. Belstone Cleave, and the West Cleave—Black Tor
Copse—Branscombe's Loaf (Lydford District)—East Hill Camp—
Fitz's Well—Halstock Woods—Island of Rocks—Okehampton Castle
—Raybarrow Pool—Taw Marsh—Yes Tor. *Prehistoric Antiquities.*
The Cemetery : kists and stone rows on South Tawton Common—
Clannaborough Down : hut circles and reaves—Cosdon : cairns and
other remains—Hound Tor : stone circle—The Nine Stones : circle
near Belstone — Small Brook : pounds and hut circles. *Mining
Remains.* Brim Brook : tinners' huts—New Bridge : stream works—
Skit Bottom : stream works, and on the Taw above Steeperton Hole
and at Taw Marsh.

5.—CHAGFORD AND MORETON DISTRICT. *Important Points.*
Beetor Cross—Kes Tor—Metheral—Moor Gate (Princetown Road)—
Newhouse, or Warren House Inn, on the Princetown Road—Teign
Head Farm—Watern Tor—White Moor Stone. *Places of Interest.*
Becky Falls—Bowerman's Nose—Bradford Pool—Cranbrook Castle—
Fernworthy—Fingle Bridge and Gorge—Gidleigh Castle and Chase—
Hameldon—Holy Street—Lustleigh Cleave—Prestonbury Camp—
Raybarrow Pool—The Tolmen—Week Down—Whiddon Park—
Wooston Castle. *Prehistoric Antiquities.* Assacombe : row, menhir,
and circle—Challacombe : stone row—Clannaborough Down : huts
and reaves—Froggymead stone circle—Grim's Pound : large hut
enclosure—Little Hound Tor : stone circle—Metheral : huts—Scorhill
Down : stone circle — Shapley Common : hut circles — Shovel
Down : rows and sepulchral remains—Spinsters' Rock : dolmen, near
Drewsteignton—Water Down : stone row. *Mining Remains.* North
and South Teign, and Walla Brook : stream works—South Teign below
Metheral : blowing houses.

6.—BOVEY TRACEY DISTRICT. *Important Points.* Hemsworthy
Gate—Hey Tor—Rippon Tor—Swine Down Gate, or Swallerton Gate
—Widecombe. *Places of Interest.* Becky Falls—Bottor—Bowerman's
Nose—Hound Tor—Lustleigh Cleave—Manaton. *Prehistoric Antiqui-
ties.* Black Hill : tumuli—Holwell Tor : hut circles—Torhill : hut
circles and reaves—Tunhill : kistvaen.

7.—ASHBURTON DISTRICT. *Important Points.* Cold East Cross
—Hemsworthy Gate—Holne—New Bridge—Pound's Gate—Welstor
Cross—Widecombe. *Places of Interest.* The Coffin Stone—Buck-
land Beacon—Buckland Woods—Dartmeet—Gorge of the Dart—
Hembury Castle — Holne Chase — Leusdon — Liswell Meet — The
Nutcracker (logan on Rippon Tor). *Prehistoric Antiquities.* Money
Pit : kistvaen near Yar Tor—Saddle Bridge : old enclosures—Sharp
Tor Circles—Torhill : huts and reaves—Tunhill : kistvaen—Yar Tor
Hill : huts.

8.—BRENT AND IVYBRIDGE DISTRICT. *Important Points.* Broad
Rock—Brent Hill—Coryndon Ball Gate—Harford Bridge—Hunting-
don Cross—Owley Gate—Pen Beacon—Petre's Bound Stone—Petre's
Cross, and the Cross Ways—Pupers—Shipley Gate—Three Barrows—

Ugborough Beacon—Watercombe Waste Gate—Western Beacon. *Places of Interest.* The Abbots' Way—Black Pool—Cornwood— Erme Pound—Harford—Hawns and Dendles—Knattleburrow Pool —Piles Wood—Red Brook Bottom—Shipley—Stowford Cleave— Valley of the Avon—Valley of Dean Burn—Zeal Falls. *Prehistoric Antiquities.* Addicombe, and Butterdon and Weatherdon Hills, and Tor Rocks : hut circles, cairns, and stone row—Biller's Pound— Burford Down : stone row—Broadall : hut circles—Cholwich Town : stone row—Erme Plains : hut circles—Erme Pound Rings : enclosed hut settlements—Glascombe Ring : enclosed hut settlement—The Glazes : stone row—Gripper's Pound : hut settlement—Hickaton Hill : hut enclosures—Red Brook Bottom : huts and enclosures— The Rings : hut enclosure—Stall Moor : stone circle, rows, cairns, kist, and hut enclosures—Three Barrows : cairns and reave—Ug- borough Moor : stone rows—Yealm Head Ring : hut enclosure. *Mining Remains.* Brock Hill : stream works and miners' huts— Erme Head : stream works and deep excavations—The Erme, at Hook Lake and below : blowing houses and streaming remains— Huntingdon : blowing house and streaming remains—Stall Moor : stream works and miners' huts—Yealm : blowing houses.

9.—PLYMPTON AND SHAUGH DISTRICT. *Important Points.* Cada- ford Bridge—Pen Beacon—Tolch Moor Gate. *Places of Interest.* Cornwood—The Dewer Stone—Hawk Tor—Hawns and Dendles— Shaugh Bridge—Trowlesworthy. *Prehistoric Antiquities.* Cholwich Town : stone row—Ringmoor Down : stone circle—Shaugh Moor : hut circles—Trowlesworthy : hut circles and stone row.

10.—YELVERTON DISTRICT. *Important Points.* Cadaford Bridge —Marchants Cross—Nosworthy Bridge—Plym Steps—Sheeps Tor. *Places of Interest.* The Abbots' Way—Burrator Lake—Crazy Well Pool—Dean Combe—The Dewer Stone—Down Tor—Lether Tor— Pixies' Cave—Valley of the Walkham. *Prehistoric Antiquities.* Down Tor : row, menhir, and circle on Hingston Hill—Kingset : hut circles—Plym Valley : hut circles and other remains—Peak Hill : stone row—Thrushelcombe (on the Plym) : rows, cairns and menhirs— Wigford Down : hut circles and kists. *Mining Remains.* Dean Combe Head : tinners' excavations—Plym Valley : stream works— Shady Combe : deep cuttings on Greenwell Down.

11.—HEXWORTHY DISTRICT.—*Important Points.* Aune Head— Bellaford Tor—Black Lane—Dartmeet—Fox Tor—Hapstead Ford— Horn's Cross—Petre's Bound Stone—Prince Hall Bridge—Pupers. *Places of Interest.* Cater's Beam—Childe's Tomb—The Coffin Stone— Combestone Tor—Dunnabridge Pound—Gorge of the Dart—Huccaby Cleave—Piskies' Holt—Prince Hall—Sherburton Firs—Wo Brook Foot—Yar Tor. *Prehistoric Antiquities.* Corndon Tor : cairns—Holne Lee : tumuli—Mardle Ring : hut enclosure on the Mardle—Money Pit : kistvaen near Yar Tor—Saddle Bridge : enclosures—Sharp Tor Circle—Snowdon : cairns and enclosures—Swincombe Valley : hut circles—Yar Tor Hill : huts. *Mining Remains.* Aune Head : stream works and tinners' huts—Black Lane : stream works and tinners' huts—Deep Swincombe : blowing house and other remains—Dry Lakes : old workings—Gobbet : old workings—Hangman's Pit : workings—The Mardle : workings—Swincombe Valley : workings— Week Ford : blowing house.

12.—POST BRIDGE DISTRICT. *Important Points.* Babeny Bridge —Bellaford Tor—Cator Gate—'Grendon Cot—Newhouse, or Warren House Inn—Row Tor Gate—Sandy Hole—Siddaford Tor—Teign Head Farm—White Ridge. *Places of Interest.* Bellaford Clapper— Broad Down Falls—Dart Valley—Dunnabridge Pound—Laugh Tor Hole—Meripit Hill—The Sheepfold—Walla Brook Valley. *Prehistoric Antiquities.* Assacombe Hill : hut circles and stone row—Bovey Combe Head : huts—Broad Down : hut enclosures—Challacombe Down : stone row—The Grey Wethers : stone circles—Grim's Pound : hut enclosure—Lakehead Hill : enclosures and kistvaens—Roundy Park : kistvaen—Water Down : stone row. *Mining Remains.* The Barracks : Mould Stone—Broad Marsh : extensive workings and tinners' huts on the East Dart—Dart Valley : workings—King's Oven : ancient smelting place—Vitifer Mine : old workings.

Other important points in the more remote parts of the moor (a few of which are, however, named in the foregoing Districts) are as follows. They are passed on the routes.

IN THE NORTHERN PART OF THE MOOR : Bear Down Man ; menhir close to Devil's Tor, a short distance from the head of the Cowsic, and to the eastward of that stream.—Broad Marsh ; on the East Dart, below the point where the river bends to the south-east two miles from its source.—Cranmere ; a hollow on the fen near the sources of the East Dart, West Ockment, and Taw, formerly a pool. [See Cranmere Routes.]—East Dart Head ; the source of the East Dart, about two miles N.N.E. of the summit of Cut Hill.—Fur Tor ; a fine tor overlooking the valley of the Upper Tavy and the Amicombe, four miles N.N.E. of Great Mis Tor, and four miles S. by E. of High Willes. —The Guide Stones, Cut Hill ; two slabs marking the path known as Cut Lane, q. v. ; they are not far from the summit of the hill, and on its northern slope.—Great Kneeset ; a conspicuous hill above the West Ockment, 2½ miles E. by S. of Great Links Tor ; the latter is situated on the commons belonging to Bridestowe and Sourton.—Kitty Tor ; a pile at the northern end of Amicombe Hill ; tracks lead to it from Prewley Moor, Sourton, and Southerly.—Newtake ; a hill eastward of Cranmere Pool ; on some maps it is erroneously shown as Newlake.— Red Lake Hill Foot ; the confluence of the Tavy and the Amicombe.— Sandy Ford ; a ford on the West Ockment, on the forest boundary line.—Tavy Hole ; the hollow down which the Tavy runs just above where it receives Outer Red Lake.—Travellers' Ford ; crossing-place of the Lich Path, q.v., on the Cowsic, rather over a mile from its source. —Walkham Head ; the source of the Walkham, but the name is often applied to that part of the moor lying round it, the highest point of which, on the E., attains an elevation of 1,800 feet.—West Dart Head ; the source of the West Dart, ¾ mile S.S.E. of the summit of Cut Hill ; ½ mile E.S.E. of Tavy Head ; and 1 mile W.S.W. of Broad Marsh, on the East Dart.—White Horse Gate ; a gate in the wall of a newtake belonging to Teign Head, opening on to White Horse Hill, in the neighbourhood of East Dart Head.

IN THE SOUTHERN PART OF THE MOOR : Aune Head ; the source of the Avon, on high ground, two miles southward of Hexworthy ; a track leads to it from that place.—Black Lane : a path, q. v., running from Fox Tor to Erme Head.—Broad Rock ; a natural boundary mark, on the Abbots' Way, q. v., near Erme Head.—The Crossways ;

the point where the Abbots' Way is crossed by the disused Zeal Tor tramroad ; less than ½ mile north westward of Western Whitaburrow, a cairn on the forest boundary line.—Erme Pits ; very deep tinners' excavations, close to the head of the Erme.—Green Hill ; a favourite pasturage ground above the Erme, between the Black Lane Brook and Red Lake.—Heng Lake Gully ; a stream work on the Avon, above Higher Bottom.—Huntingdon Hill ; the highest part of Huntingdon Warren, on the Avon.—Petre's Cross, on Western Whitaburrow : See The Crossways.—Plym Head ; the source of the Plym ; 1 mile S. by W. of Fox Tor, and 1½ miles S.E. of Nuns' Cross.—Plym Steps ; the point where the Abbots' Way, q. v., crosses the Plym, about 2 miles from its source.—Red Lake Ford ; the point where the Abbots' Way crosses Red Lake, about 1 mile N.W. of Western Whitaburrow. —Ryder's Hill ; a lofty height, rather over ½ mile E.S.E. of Aune Head.

PACKHORSE TRACKS AND OTHER OLD PATHS.

MOST of the roads on the moor are formed on the line, or nearly so, of old packhorse tracks. Several of the latter yet remain in those parts where no roads have been made, though not quite in the state they once were, vegetation having so encroached upon them that in places they are entirely obliterated. [100 *Years*, Chap. II.] Others have been formed by the peat cutter, but are now little used by him, the quantity of peat brought in from the forest at the present time being comparatively small. But the moormen and the hunter find them of service, and so will the rambler, for in places where they are well defined they are not only excellent guides, but will often enable him to pass with ease over rough or miry ground. The principal ones are here enumerated, and are numbered for convenience of reference. When the reader becomes acquainted with them he will see that Dartmoor is not quite the trackless waste that it has sometimes been represented. The paths are named in the order in which they would be met with in going round the moor, starting on its west side and proceeding northward. They commence with the Abbots' Way as being a track of considerable interest. This, and others of more than ordinary importance, are marked with an asterisk.

In the north part of the moor there are only three tracks of historical interest—the Lich Path, Cut Lane, and the King Way. But in the south part the case is different. On its borders were four important religious houses, and we consequently find several tracks leading from one to the other of these, all of them being marked by stone crosses, which, it is pleasing to add, have, after lying on the ground neglected for a long period, been re-erected during recent years.

The visitor will do well to make himself acquainted with the tracks in his locality, as some are referred to in the routes ; additional particulars are given when he is conducted over them. It must not be imagined that they can always be easily followed. Those who formerly used them did not concern themselves about keeping to any particular line on ground that was easily passed over, and consequently traces of a path are sometimes lost for a considerable distance. But if their general direction is known they can usually be picked up again at a ford, or on boggy ground.

With the exception of those noticed by me elsewhere [*Crosses* ; 100 *Years*] the following tracks are described for the first time.

1.—* *The Abbots' Way.*   This path formed a means of communication between Buckfast Abbey, on the south-eastern side of the moor, and Buckland Abbey, on its western side ; a branch of it also led to Tavistock Abbey.   It enters the moor at a spot known as Cross Furzes, which is about three miles from Buckfast, and at the head of the valley of Dean Burn.   Whether the track running up over Lambs Down is a part of it cannot be determined, but less than half-a-mile beyond the boundary wall of that down it is plainly discoverable. This is at a ford where it crosses the Brock Hill stream, a feeder of the Avon.   On the further side of it the path passes through an ancient hut enclosure, the wall of which has been broken down in two places to admit of this.   It then runs down the side of Hickaton Hill to the Avon, being here a good track, except for a few boggy places where the drainage of the hill has been caught.   It reaches the Avon at its confluence with the Wellabrook, both of which streams it crosses.   It is next seen a short distance up the valley, where is a ford over a little affluent of the Avon, and from this point becomes a plainly marked path for a considerable distance.   In the name of this crossing-place —Buckland Ford—there is no doubt we see an allusion to the monastic house to which the track leads.   From the ford the path climbs the hill by the side of a gully known as Pipers' Beam, soon after being crossed by the old Zeal Tor tramroad at the Crossways.   It then passes down between Brown Heath and Red Lake Mires to a ford over the Red Lake, and here it is lost.   But it is seen again at Hux Lake, close to the Erme, and a little further on it crosses the Black Lane Brook.   It then passes through a part of the mire at Erme Head, and ascends the hill to Broad Rock, where the branch to Tavistock diverges.   From Broad Rock the Buckland path descends to the Plym, between which two points it is still well defined.   Crossing the stream at Plym Steps it goes on towards the northern end of Ringmoor Down, but this portion of it now partakes of the character of a moor road, having been used in comparatively recent times in connection with Eylesbarrow Mine. From the down it descends to Marchants Cross, where it leaves the moor.   The Tavistock branch of the Abbots' Way was probably little used by travellers proceeding direct from Buckfast to that town, as it would have been more to their advantage to follow the Buckland track from Broad Rock to Ringmoor Down, and cross the Mew either at the ford near Marchants Cross, or at some other point higher up the stream.   It is more likely that the branch was used as a link between the path at Broad Rock and the Ashburton track and another near the Rundle Stone.   It cannot be traced with certainty, but apparently crossed the Plym near its source and passed over the hill to Siward's Cross, whence it ran to Merivale, either by way of the Rundle Stone, or by Black Tor Ford and the present Foggintor Quarries.   There is evidence tending to show that the former was the route.   At Merivale it crossed the Walkham a short distance below the present bridge, at a ford, the approaches to which can still be seen.   Passing to the north of Vixen Tor it crossed the little stream flowing through Beccamoor Combe, and over the hill on which the Windy Post now stands, and so to Moortown and the present Quarry Lane.   From the Western end of this the way lay over Whitchurch Down, which it left by the steep bridle path leading down towards the Tavy, where it now enters Tavistock at Vigo Bridge. Between Merivale and Tavistock the track is well defined, but this is owing in great measure to this part of it having been used long after the monks had ceased to pass over it. For several miles it served as the old road from Tavistock to Ashburton, and the guide-stones showing its direction, and bearing the letters T and A, are still to be seen on Long Ash Hill, which rises from the eastern bank of the Walkham at Merivale. Although the Abbots' Way passes through a lonely part of Dartmoor it does not enter far within the forest. It touches the boundary line at the Wellabrook, and runs very close to it as far as Broad Rock, while the Tavistock branch almost follows the line to the Rundle Stone. There are several ancient crosses on this interesting track, and these I have elsewhere described. [*Crosses*, Chap. IX. ; this chapter deals entirely with the Abbots' Way.] On the moor this old way is usually called Jobbers' Path, or, as the moormen have it, Joblers' Path. This name is in all probability derived from being used in former days by the yarn jobber. Both Buckfast and Buckland were Cistercian houses, an order that traded extensively, and we may therefore well suppose that considerable quantities of wool were once carried over this ancient pack-horse road of the monks. Buckland Abbey was founded in 1280 ; Buckfast and Tavistock, q. v., were in existence much earlier.

On the Ordnance map a road leading from Plym Ford to Nuns' Cross is marked as the Abbots' Way, but I am not of opinion that the old track followed that course. The map also shows the track running from Ball Gate to Bala Brook (T. 61) as Jobbers' Path, which is wrong ; it merely leads towards that path.

2.—*Track from Buckland to the Eastern side of the Moor.* This track enters the moor at Lowery, about a mile and a half from Dousland, and, like the Abbots' Way, was a monks' path. This is shown both by its direction and by the number of old crosses that mark it. Indeed, it was the discovery of some of the latter that revealed its existence to me. [*Crosses*, Chap. X.] But besides being used by the monks, that part of it extending eastward from Lowery afterwards served the farm settlers in the valleys of the Upper Mew and its tributaries, who had found their way there at least as early as the sixteenth century. Reference is made by the jury who surveyed the bounds of the forest in 1609 to " certayne howses " that the " auncestors " of Gamaliel Slanning had caused to be erected on Walkhampton Common, and that they used the path as a means of communication between their holdings and the in-country is certain. In recent times the tinners at the White Works used not only that part of it, but much more, so that at the present day it is seen as an ordinary moor road running from Lowery to Older Bridge, where the miners left it and followed their own track. From Lowery the road skirts the present Burrator Lake, afterwards crossing the Mew at Lether Tor Bridge. Thence it runs below Roundy Hill, and along the slope of Newleycombe Bottom to Older Bridge, where it crosses the Devonport leat. The old path went to Siward's Cross, where it entered the forest, and ran down the Swincombe valley to the foot of the hill on which Fox Tor is situated. Crossing the Fox Tor stream, near which is a track known as Sandy Way, noticed further on (T. 56) it passed up the slope, somewhere near the present boundary of Fox Tor Farm, to Ter Hill, where two crosses,

long fallen, but now once more erect, mark its course. From the hill
it went to the higher bend of the Wo Brook, and over Down Ridge,
where it is also marked by two crosses (re-erected, like the others,
during recent years) to Horse Ford. On the further side of this it
branched, one path running to Holne, but the main one turning down
the valley. The former is marked on the hill above the stream by the
remains of a cross, known as Horn's Cross, from which point it went
direct to Workman's Ford, on the Wennaford Brook, and thence to
the Moor Gate. For some distance all traces of the path down the
valley are lost, but it reappears immediately below Saddle Bridge,
on the right bank of the Wo Brook, and crosses the West Dart at
Week Ford. It can then be seen running between the enclosures
towards the modern chapel of St. Raphael at Huccaby, whence it
passed over the side of the hill to Dartmeet, where a clapper, the
remains of which are still to be seen, spanned the river. From that
point the present road has probably been formed upon it. [*Crosses*
Chap. X.]

3.+—*Track from Kingsett to Princetown.* Close to the path just
noticed (T. 2), and half a mile eastward of Lether Tor Bridge, is Kingsett Farm, from which a cart track leads to Princetown. It is probably
not older than that place. It passes over the Devonport leat at Crazy
Well Bridge, not far from the pool of that name. It then runs near
Cramber Tor to the Hart Tor Brook, where there is a ford, and leaving
the tor on the left, passes up the slope to Princetown. The traffic over
the path being practically nil, it is only defined in a few places.

4.—*Farm Tracks on Walkhampton Common.* There are several
paths on that part of Walkhampton Common lying to the west of the
Dousland and Princetown road, but none of any importance. One
path comes up from Walkhampton to the present highway, its junction
with it being marked by a stone known as Goad's Stone ; this is not
far from the highest point on the road where it climbs the shoulder of
Peak Hill. Near Walkhampton Vicarage this is a paved track, and is
there known as the Packhorse Road. Other tracks lead from the
moor gate near Eggworthy to Crip Tor and Routrendle Farms, and
to the same places from the Princetown road. There is also a track
from the Foggin Tor Quarries to Yes Tor Green. A road leads to
these quarries, passing the Red Cottages and Yellowmead. It
branches from the Princetown and Tavistock road half-a-mile W. of
Rundle Stone.

5.—*Frenchmen's Road.* This path leads from the Plymouth
highway, just where it enters Princetown, to the foot of the hill crowned
with North Hisworthy Tor. It is interesting as having been made by
the prisoners of war confined there in the early part of the nineteenth
century. A green path branching from it leads towards the quarries.

6. — * *Ivybridge Lane, and Track to Siward's Cross.* A track, very
nearly straight, leads from Princetown to Siward's Cross. It is really
a portion of the Tavistock branch of the Abbots' Way, supposing that
old path went by way of the Rundle Stone, of which, as already has
been mentioned, there is some evidence. [*Crosses*, Chap. II.] It
leaves Princetown by the side of the Railway Inn, and runs for a short
distance between enclosures. This part of it now bears the name of
Ivybridge Lane, in consequence of its having been customary in the
early days of the convict prison, when there was only one railway in

this part of the country, to take discharged prisoners along this route, on foot, and entrain them at Ivybridge. On entering upon the common the track runs for a considerable distance by the wall of an enclosure on the left, past South Hisworthy, or, as it is called in the locality, Lookout Tor. The stones seen on the right mark the boundary line of the forest from South to North Hisworthy. On leaving the tor the ancient way runs on this line to Siward's Cross. Some way beyond the tor the wall is carried in another direction, and no longer acts as guide, but the path being well defined, and perfectly straight, cannot be missed. A little further on the forest boundary is marked by a reave, or bank of turf, and at Siward's Cross this will also be seen running up the hill to Eylesbarrow. It was probably thrown up as a tin bound. Half a mile before the cross is reached the path is crossed by the road running from Older Bridge (T. 2) to Peat Cot and the White Works. Two tracks pass over the hill southward of Siward's Cross. One, which runs parallel to the reave—a little to the left of it —goes to Eylesbarrow mine, whence it is continued to the Abbots' Way where it comes up from Plym Steps (T. 1); and the other, a peat track, runs left from the cross, but turns abruptly to the right on the top of the hill and descends to the Plym, whence it also goes to Eylesbarrow mine.

7.—*Castle Road.* This leads from Princetown to Peat Cot and the White Works, and is now a parish road. The approach to Tor Royal leaves the highway not far from the Duchy Hotel. Near Tor Gate it bends L., and descends the hill to the lodge. Here the Peat Cot road turns R., and passing the house, continues southward.

8.—*Princetown to Hexworthy.* The way passes the entrance to Tor Royal (T. 7), shortly afterwards reaching a small farm called Bull Park, where it enters Tor Royal Newtake, the highest part of which now bears the name of Royal Hill. The path runs nearly due east from Bull Park, and at the distance of a little more than half a mile passes close to a kistvaen called The Crock of Gold. The track is here a well-defined green path, and may be followed without any difficulty. Rather over a quarter of a mile from the kist it passes the springs of the Cholake, a little feeder of the West Dart, and about half a mile further on reaches a gate in a newtake wall. The path does not enter this, but runs on with the enclosures L., and passes in front of Swincombe Farmhouse to the stream of that name. (If the gate is entered a course roughly parallel to the wall on the R. must be followed to another gate near the house (T. 10), whence a narrow lane leads to the river). Here there is a ford and stepping-stones, and also a modern footbridge erected some years ago for the convenience of men working at Hexworthy mine. From the stream the road, which is well defined, runs upwards to Gobbet Plain, below which the little settlement of Hexworthy is situated.

9.—*From Princetown to Moorlands.* This path leaves the Two Bridges road just before it passes New London, and runs first to Bachelor's Hall, and by this way also the track to Hexworthy just described (T. 8), may be reached. From Bachelor's Hall the path runs due east with the Blackabrook to the left. Crossing Lanson Brook, and passing the small pile of rocks which seems to have formerly borne the name of Colden Tor, it reaches the Cholake, from which Moorlands is less than half a mile distant.

10.—*From Prince Hall Lodge to Swincombe and Hexworthy.* About a mile from Two Bridges, on the Ashburton road, is the approach 'to Prince Hall. This road is continued beyond the house to a bridge over the West Dart, placed amidst most charming surroundings. It then climbs the hill to Moorlands, which lies a little to the right, but the track to Swincombe goes straight on and speedily enters on the common. From this point to the gate at Swincombe, previously mentioned (T. 8), the distance is exactly a mile, and the direction of the track about S.E. It is very rough, but though not at all suitable for wheels, I have driven over it often. The route from Swincombe to Hexworthy has already been noticed (T. 8). There is a footpath to Prince Hall from Roundhill Farm, which is not far from the Ockery, below Princetown. The West Dart is crossed by stepping-stones just above its confluence with the Blackabrook.

Opposite to Prince Hall Lodge is Muddy Lakes Newtake. A short distance W. of the lodge a track runs across this enclosure to the Moreton road N. of Two Bridges.

11.—*From Two Bridges up the West Dart Valley.* An old track runs northward from the road behind the hotel, but during recent years it has been contended that it is merely an approach to Crockern Tor Farm. Wistman's Wood is reached by way of it. [See Ex. 5.]

12.—*Path by the Blackabrook to Cudlipp Town.* This track seems to have been used principally for the conveyance of peat to Princetown on the one hand, and to Cudlipp Town and Wapsworthy on the other. It leaves the Two Bridges road about 300 yards E. of Rundle Stone Corner, and runs northward through the prison ground for one mile. It then enters on the open' moor, but crosses the Blackabrook just before doing so. [If the rambler desires to follow this path and cannot pass through the prison enclosures, he may reach it by making his way to Mount View, less than ½ mile N.W. of Rundle Stone, and ascending the hill towards Mis Tor, with the wall on his R. (Exs. 5, 6). At the corner he will turn eastward and crossing the prison leat and the Blackabrook, will find the path on the left bank of the latter]. The track then runs northward for ¾ mile to the source of the stream, which is L. in ascending. It then turns to the N.W., and passing the leat at a ford, runs down to the Walkham to Shallow Ford, just below. (Ex. 6). Thence it runs to Dead Lake Head, and across the northern part of Langstone Moor towards White Tor. (R. 2A). The branch to Cudlipp Town passes to the S. of the tor, crossing the track from Peter Tavy to Walkham Head, but is not here plainly defined. But due W. of the tor it is to be seen passing between the walls of two newtakes, just beyond which it turns into a stroll to a moor gate, from which a road runs direct to the hamlet. The Wapsworthy branch, which is also ill-defined, crosses the Peter Tavy track like the former, but runs N.W., leaving the tor L., and having the walls of some enclosures R. Keeping near to the latter it descends to a moor gate from which Wapsworthy is about ¼ mile distant.

13.—*From Sampford Spiney to Merivale.* From the village this path runs to the bottom of the enclosure belonging to Pu Tor Cottage, and is carried along the hill above the beautiful valley of the Walkham, and close to the enclosures. After passing Heckwood Tor, a small pile which it touches, there is a steep descent, and the lower end of Beckamoor Coombe is crossed. It climbs the further side, and

passing the well-known Vixen Tor, joins the highway near the settlement to which it leads, close to the fourth milestone from Tavistock.

14.—*Merivale to Peter Tavy.* That there has always been a path
over the moor between these two points is certain, but its present
well-defined state is owing to its having been used during recent years
by the workmen at the granite quarries at Merivale and Walkhampton
Common. The track leaves the highway just above Tor Quarry, and
passes over the hill between Great and Mid Staple Tors, but nearer to
the former than the latter. On the further side it descends into the
hollow formed by the ridge on which the Staple Tors are situated and
Cocks Tor Hill, and this part of it is roughly paved. This was done by
workmen, who added a stone each time they passed that way, to ensure
their being able to follow it through the darkness. In the hollow
there is but little scattered granite, so the work could not there be
continued. But another plan for marking the path was devised. The
men made a practice of carrying with them pieces of broken crockery,
and strewing them by the side of the way. These can be readily seen
even in the darkest night, as I can testify from experience, and there is
consequently no fear of the wayfarer straying from the path. The
fragments of ware mark it from the hollow to the enclosures north of
Cocks Tor Hill. There it crosses to Great Combe Tor and descends
the southern side of Peter Tavy Comoe, to the little stream flowing
through it, over which there is a wooden footbridge, whence a good
path leads to the village. On the common above Great Combe Tor
this track crosses another leading to Godsworthy. (T. 15). For an
alternate route see T. 15.

15.—*Moortown to the high road by Dennithorne ; thence to Higher
Godsworthy and Wedlake.* This track branches from the Abbots' Way
between Moortown and the Windy Post, and runs northward, with the
enclosures on the L. to the Princetown road. This it crosses, and
still runs northward, with the farm lands L. and Cocks' Tor Hill R.
About ¾ mile from the road a branch runs L. to a moor gate, above
Harragrove farmhouse, whence a lane leads to Peter Tavy village.
Half a mile further on there is another branch L. ; this leads to Higher
Godsworthy, a farm on the Peter Tavy Brook. At this point the
track bears E., afterwards turning N.E., and runs up close by the
Wedlake enclosures, which are L., towards Langstone Moor. Between
the high road and Godsworthy this track is a well-kept road.

The lane to Harragrove forms an alternative route to R. 14. On
leaving Merivale the Tavistock road is followed for one mile, when a
little rivulet a short distance W. of Beckamoor Combe will be reached.
Here a track runs off R. to the Godsworthy road.

16.—**Peat Track from Peter Tavy to Walkham Head.* Very near
to the church at Peter Tavy is a short piece of road leading to a moor
gate, which opens on to Smeardon Down. The road goes on past
Godsworthy to the common, but about half a mile from the gate
a rough track branches from it and ascends the hill on the left. This
runs out to the source of the Walkham, a distance of about five miles,
and although not used as a peat track nearly so much as formerly,
is yet of considerable service. It communicates with the old Lich
Path (T. 18), and by means of it those parts of the forest round the
head waters of the Cowsic and West Dart are easily reached. Shortly
after branching from the Godsworthy road the track passes near

Boulters Tor, the easternmost of several piles that crest the ridge. Not far from this the track leaves the down, and passes between the walls of some enclosures to the open common. This part of it is called Twyste Lane, after the farm of that name on the left, and which is one of the ancient vills. About half a mile further on, and close to the track on the right, is a low mound, marking the burial place of a suicide, and known as Stephens' Grave. The path then runs about E.N.E. with White Tor, or Whittor, as it is always called, rising on the left, and at the distance of another mile is marked by a tall menhir. This, which was re-erected a few years ago, seems to have given name to the common to the eastward, and which is probably Langstone, and not Lanson, Moor, as it is always called in the neighbourhood. Soon after leaving the stone the track runs by the side of the enclosures extending up the hill from Wapsworthy, and near the corner of Longbetor Newtake bends a little to the right towards the forest boundary at White Barrow. Here it is no longer a grassy track, but a rather deep cutting, and this portion of it is certainly one with the Lich Path. Passing into the forest it descends towards the Walkham between Stooky Moor on the north and Cocks Hill on the south. The Lich Path goes straight on, and crosses the river at a ford, but the peat track runs a short distance up the valley to the left, and crosses the stream at a bridge. This is one of a kind not often seen on Dartmoor, being of wood, and is always referred to in the locality as Timber Bridge. From this point the track runs along the slope to the east of the Walkham for about a mile, terminating very near to its head in the midst of the peat beds.

Close to Timber Bridge the track forks, the R. branch passing up into Spriddle Combe. It crosses the Spriddle, and runs for a short distance up the side of Maiden Hill, E. This name is probably a corruption of the Gælic *meaton*, a path ; Latin *meatus*.

17.—*Paths from Cudlipp Town.* From the foot of Broad Moor two paths lead upward, the one on the right going to Twyste and the end of Smeardon Down ; that on the left leading up through the enclosures to a moor gate opening on to Cudlipp Town Down, under White Tor (T. 12). One branch of the latter then turns right between the enclosures and an outlying newtake, and joins the Walkham Head track between Twyste Lane and Stephens' Grave ; the other branch runs over the down to the west of White Tor, then bends round to the north of it, and reaches the same track not far from the menhir. Near this menhir the track runs E. to the Walkham, Blackabrook Head, and Rundle Stone. (T. 12, R. 20).

18.—*The Lich Path.* This ancient track, which has been already mentioned, is of more than ordinary interest. It led from the early farm settlements on the east side of the forest to the village of Lydford, and although portions of it are now obliterated, it can still be traced for a considerable distance, and is of much service as affording a means of passing easily from the upper West Dart valley to the valleys of the Cowsic and Walkham. Over this path the dead were formerly carried from the settled parts of the forest to Lydford for burial. The name of the Lich Path, indeed, indicates its use ; it was really a church way. There is another path from the forest farms to Lydford, known in one part of its course as Cut Lane (T. 79), and which would have served more particularly the settlements in the neighbourhood of the present Post Bridge, on the East Dart, while the holders of the ancient tenements lying in the valley of the West Dart would use the Lich Path. [100 *Years*, Chap. II.] These paths are referred to, though not by name, in a document of thirteenth century date, included in the Exeter Episcopal Registers. By this instrument Bishop Walter Bronescombe, in 1260, granted permission to the inhabitants of the villages of Balbeny and Pushyll to attend Widecombe Church instead of their parish church of Lydford, for the reason that they were so far distant from the latter. The " villages " in question were the ancient tenements on the Walla Brook, now known as Babeny and Pizwell, and are situated just within the forest boundary. In the document Lydford Church is stated to be eight miles further from the places named than Widecombe Church ; that is, if the weather was fair ; when it was stormy the journey made a difference of fifteen miles. " *Et quod loca predicta a matrice ecclesia de Lideford sereno tempore per octo, et tempestatibus exortis in circuitu per quindecim, distant miliaria.*" When the moor was in a suitable condition, and the streams not in flood, the forest settlers journeyed to Lydford over the green paths that led them there direct ; when the state of the weather rendered these routes difficult to follow a more circuitous one was chosen. The Lich Path cannot be identified with absolute certainty in the neighbourhood of the forest farms, though there is little doubt that the track that now leads from Higher Cherry Brook Bridge, near the powder mills, to the clapper at Bellaford, is a part of it. Even if the path went to the clapper at Post Bridge, it must have gone to the one at Bellaford also, for the latter was very much nearer than the former, not only to Babeny, but also to the forest farms of Riddon and Dury, and a little nearer to Pizwell as well. That a branch of the Lich Path did, however, go to Post Bridge we may be sure. We cannot, of course, suppose any other than that a track led there from the crossing-place over the Cherry Brook, but this was not the branch to which I allude. There is a track running from the East Dart to a part of the moor known as Rowtor, and which is very plainly defined near the source of the Cherry Brook. This I have heard called the Lich Path by some on the moor, and though it is rather further north than we should suppose that old way to have gone, there is yet good reason for believing that it really is such. It will be noticed when I have sketched the probable route of the branch from Bellaford to the point on the Cowsic where it is yet a clearly defined track. From the modern bridge over the East Dart, close to the Bellaford clapper, (Post Bridge District) the road ascends between enclosures to the farm of the same name, and shortly afterwards enters on the common called Lakehead Hill. Here it becomes a narrow track, and runs down the hill by the side of the wall of Bellaford Newtake to the Princetown highway, where the latter crosses the Cherry Brook. From this point for a distance of about two miles and a half it cannot be traced, but a crossing-place on the West Dart in the line it would take in running to the ford on the Cowsic, and some evidence afforded by the names of the tors in the locality, enable us to be pretty sure of its course. These tors are the Littaford Tors, on the ridge eastward of the West Dart ; Longaford Tor, on the same ridge, but further to the north ; and Lydford Tor, on the ridge between the West Dart and the Cowsic. The final syllable of these names is probably the Celtic *ffordd*, a way, a passage, or highway ; it cannot be the English *ford*, a crossing-place over a stream, since the tors are all on elevated land, and at some distance from a river.   The line we should suppose the Lich Path to have taken passes between the first two and close to the third, and we shall prob- ably not be far wrong in believing such to be the correct route, par- ticularly as the crossing-place on the West Dart adds a link to the chain. Less than half a mile from Lydford Tor* the Lich Path is seen running down to a ford on the Cowsic, sometimes called Travellers' Ford, and from this point westward for about two miles is a clearly defined track. West of the stream is Conies Down, over which the Lich Path takes a W.N.W. course, and it was somewhere about here that the track I have referred to as passing over Rowtor joined it.

[This is a continuation of another, known as Drift Lane, and which is noticed further on (T. 78).   It leaves the Dart less than half a mile above Post Bridge, and runs up the hill to Rowtor Gate, its direction being about W.N.W.   Passing over Rowtor, as the piece of moor south of Broad Down is usually called by the moormen, it runs near the head of Cherry Brook, as already named, and for a short distance is really a good hard road.   It then descends to the West Dart, which it crosses at a point a mile or more above that at which we may suppose the track just traced to have passed over it.   Running over the ridge to the Cowsic it reached Conies Down, and may possibly have passed to the north of the tor of that name.   The supposition is not only warranted by its direction as it approaches the Dart, but the situation of Bear Down Man also appears to favour it.   The name of this rude obelisk, which is undoubtedly a corruption of the Celtic *maen*, *stone*, points to its being a genuine menhir of antiquity, but while such may be the case there is no reason why it should not have been chosen for a guide to a path.   The Longstone, near White Tor, and the menhir at Merivale, were so adapted, as we have seen, and there are other instances of a similar kind on the moor.   The route appears to be rather far to the north having regard to the point at which the path crosses the Walkham, but it must not be forgotten that such a line would touch the rivers near their sources where they are so small as not to be rendered impassable by floods, and this was a matter that had to be studied.   When the Dart could not be forded under Longa- ford Tor, it could be crossed a short distance below its springs, so that an alternative route actually became necessary.]

From Conies Down the Lich Path runs to the Walkham ; a great sea of fen to the north of it, and a lesser tract to the south.   It is carried over the prison leat immediately before reaching the river, which it crosses at Sandy Ford.   (T. 16).   Passing up the side of the ridge towards White Barrow it is joined, as already mentioned (T. 16) by the track from Walkham Head to Peter Tavy.   The latter we have traced

---

* It may be that Lydford Tor is called after the parish in which the forest is situated, and if such is the case the evidence referred to could not perhaps be adduced from the second syllable of the name. But other evidence would be afforded that the old track passed very near to it, for if it were named after the parish, one of the best reasons we can imagine for this particular tor being selected is that it was on the road to Lydford church.   But I am not of opinion that the name borne by the tor has any reference to the parish or the church.

but the course of the Lich Path from near White Barrow is not clearly defined. That it went towards Bagga Tor is certain, but there is no track between those two points that we can safely identify with the old way, though it is possible that we may see it in the path running by the wall of Longbetor Newtake. The reason is not far to seek. The Peter Tavy track was until comparatively recent years, and, indeed, is to some extent to-day, used for the conveyance of peat (T. 16), while over this part of the Lich Path the traffic would be very trifling. But there can be no doubt, I think, that we see it again in the old piece of road, now nothing more than a gully, running from the moor gate at Bagga Tor to Brouzen Tor Farm, whence it may be followed to the Bagga Tor Brook, which is here crossed by a clapper, probably built as a means of communication between the farms in the locality. The track then went to the Tavy, where there is a ford, with approaches, below Willsworthy Farm. At such times as the river was flooded those who journeyed over this old churchway no doubt went direct from White Barrow to Hill Bridge, where was formerly a clapper. From Willsworthy the Lich Path cannot be traced, though it is met with again at Forstall Cross (T. 21, 25), a mile to the N.W. Midway between Willsworthy and the point just named is Yellowmead Farm, and tradition comes forward with some evidence to show that the ancient path passed by it. It is related in the locality that an avenue of trees once extended from Yellowmead to Watervale, on the Lydford side of Black Down, and as throughout half this distance the Lich Path is still traceable, there is little doubt that the avenue has reference to it. [100 *Years*, Chap. II.] It may, therefore, be safely assumed that the track went from the ford below Willsworthy to the present Yellowmead Farm, and thence to Forstall Cross. There is a footpath from Willsworthy Pound (Ex. 10) to this point, and it very probably runs on the line of the old track. From the cross (Lydford District) this interesting path may be followed towards the enclosures extending eastward from Watervale. It leaves the common at a gate opening on Down Lane, which is undoubtedly a part of it, and reaches the high road near Beardon Farm, within a short distance of Lydford village.

19.—* *Black Lane, N.* The letter N is placed after the name of this track in order to distinguish it from another of the same name in the south quarter of the forest. Over this old road very large quantities of peat were formerly annually conveyed on the backs of packhorses, as I have learnt from old men who at one time worked at the turf-ties to which it leads. These are situated at a spot called Brook's Head, the stream to which the name has reference being the Outer, or Easter, Red Lake, a tributary of the Tavy. The ties cover a considerable area, and the peat is of great depth, but very little has been cut there during recent years. The track enters the moor at Bagga Tor Gate, above Wapsworthy, and for a short distance ran on the line of the old Lich Path. Passing through the stroll outside the gate it is carried along by the wall of the enclosures of Bagga Tor Farm, at the end of which it bends to the left, or northward, having on one side, across the narrow valley, the great rounded hill of Standon, and on the other the ridge from which Lynch Tor rises. Soon after passing the latter a branch runs up over the ridge, R., and descends to the deserted Walkham Head peat works, and to some ties further to the N.

It also sweeps round to the S. of Lynch Tor. But this branch was made long before those works were started. It was used in the days of the Wheal Betsy mine, situated on Black Down, at which much peat was consumed, and this was cut at Walkham Head. Up to about this point Black Lane is still a good track, but where it runs up the hill beyond it is now impassable. The rains have worn it into a deep gully and during a wet season it more resembles a water-course than a track. On its edge, however, there is a narrow path, formed by the moormen, so that it is of just as much practical use as ever. When it reaches the level ground at the top of the hill and turns to the right, it becomes a good hard road, and may be ridden over nearly to its termination, which is about three quarters of a mile further on. This part of it was known to the peat-cutters by the name of Belson, in reference to the village of Belstone on the other side of the moor, which they playfully said they must reach if they carried their track much further.

The rambler who wishes to reach Fur Tor or Cranmere from the Mary Tavy side of the moor, will find Black Lane of great service. It will bring him within one mile of the tor, and the intervening ground is such as can always be traversed with ease. This route is noticed in the Tavistock District, and also in the section on Cranmere.

20.—*Track from Lane End.* About three miles and a half from Tavistock, on the Okehampton highway, is the hamlet of Lane Head, consisting of a roadside hotel and a few cottages. Here a road leads down to the village of Mary Tavy, and passing through a part of it, turns off near the schoolhouse and runs by way of Horndon, Zoar Down, and Willsworthy, to the moor gate at Lane End. The distance from Lane Head to this point is rather over three miles and a half. As the parish road terminates at the moor gate, the name borne by the spot, and by the farm close by, is not inappropriate, but there is nevertheless a continuation of the way, though it now becomes merely a grassy track. A short one leads east to Nat Tor Farm, but that we are about to notice runs up the hill towards Ger Tor, crossing the Wheal Friendship leat about midway up the ascent. The track leaves Ger Tor to the right, and runs over a plain piece of common towards Hare Tor, having the enclosures of Redford Farm on the west and Tavy Cleave on the east. Near Hare Tor the track is particularly well defined. Passing below that pile it descends the hill and crosses Dead Lake at Dead Lake Ford, shortly afterwards reaching the Rattle Brook where it enters the forest. A large mound marks the spot where it climbs the bank on the E. side of that stream. This track soon grows very faint, but it is possible to trace it half way across Watern Oke.

21.—* *The Dartmoor Path.* Although there are several tracks on Black Down, and all of them still of service, only two or three are of real importance. Chief among these is the Dartmoor Path, so called because it runs out to the forest. It leads from Brent Tor to the Rattle Brook, its length being about six miles, and for the greater part of that distance is well defined. It enters the commons at the moor gate close to Brent Tor railway station, and runs up by the side of the school house. At the corner of the enclosure just beyond, another track runs by the side of the edge in the direction of Lydford, but the Dartmoor Path crosses this, and also another a short distance further up, and climbs the hill towards Gibbet. About a quarter of a mile from the summit of this eminence the path turns abruptly to the left and thence runs over fairly level ground to the Tavistock and Okehampton high road. Just before it reaches this it is joined by the Burn Lane Path, which comes up from Ironcage Gate, and also by the Henscott Path from the moor gate near Lydford railway station. A track also branches from it in the opposite direction and runs to Horndon Down Bridge, where it joins another which we shall shortly notice. Crossing the high road between the fifth and sixth milestone from Tavistock (nearer the latter than the former) the Dartmoor Path, still pointing about N.E. by E. goes on to Black Hill, over which it passes quite near to the despoiled cairn crowning its highest point. This is known as the Ring o' Bells, but nothing now remains of it beyond a low bank enclosing a circular space about 19 yards in diameter. The path now descends the north-eastern slope of Black Down to Forstall Cross (T. 18, 25) from which point it runs for some distance by the enclosures of Redford Farm, with White Hill rising on the left. This part of the moor has lately been acquired by the War Office for rifle practice. Leaving the wall where it sweeps round towards the east, the path runs up the hill towards Hare Tor, but is not here very clearly defined, and passing over the ridge to the north of that pile, descends to the Rattle Brook, which stream throughout its course acts as part of the forest boundary. On its bank is the deserted Rattle Brook Mine, and it was by the workmen who were there employed that this track was chiefly used. Now it is of service in other ways, particularly that part of it extending from Brent Tor to Redford. The Rattle Brook is only about two miles from Great Kneeset, and the ground between the two is good. Kneeset is less than a mile from Cranmere, so that this path forms an excellent route to the pool from the neighbourhood of Lydford railway station and Brent Tor. From the N. side of Hare Tor to the Rattle Brook, which it reaches near where the Green Tor Water falls into that stream, and just beyond which it terminates, it is a plainly marked track. [See Tavistock and Lydford Districts, and the Cranmere section.]

From the Redford enclosures there was a branch of this path that ran to the S. of Hare Tor, where parts of it are now to be seen, and joined T. 20, which crosses the Rattle Brook half a mile below T. 21.

22.—*Paths on Black Down.* Among other paths on Black Down may be named the Brent Tor track, which runs from Iron Gate to the moor gate near Brent Tor station ; another from Iron Gate to Iron Cage Gate, leading to Burn Lane ; the Higher Spring Path, leading into the two former from near the Ashburys (the name of some fields by the road just above the village of Black Down), and passing Higher Spring ; another from Moorside to Burn Lane passing over the southern shoulder of Gibbet ; a track running from the Ashburys to the summit of Gibbet, and communicating with the Dartmoor Path (T. 21) ; the Lydford Path, which next to the Dartmoor Path is the most important on this part of Black Down, and is therefore noticed separately ; the Burn Lane Path and the Henscott Path, already mentioned as joining the Dartmoor Path (T. 21) ; Warren's Path, and a track running along the edge of the down from Brent Tor station to Lydford station.

On that part of Black Down eastward of the high road there are other tracks. One has already been referred to as branching from the

Dartmoor Path, where it approaches the road, to another at Horndon
Down Bridge (T. 21). This crosses the road to the northward of
Barrett's Bridge, and pursuing a course a little south of east, passes at
the head of a gully known as Goosey Creep, and joins the other track
alluded to a short distance before the latter reaches Horndon Down
Bridge. This other track runs from Zoar to Watervale, and is noticed
further on. A path runs from near the Ashburys by way of Wheal
Betsy Bridge to Kingsett Down, and by Allaclauns Corner to Zoar
Down, and another from Kingsett Gate communicates with it. Besides these there is a track from Will at Down Lane, the greater part
of which is on the line of the old Lich Path (T. 18); and is described
hereafter (T. 25); and one from the gate at Down Lane, eastward by
the long plantation above Bear Walls, to the northern end of the
Redford enclosures, and from which other short tracks branch.

23.—*The Lydford Path.* This path leads from the settlement of
Black Down to Lydford railway station. It leaves the highway soon
after the latter enters on the common, the point being marked by four
granite posts. These are placed on the right of the way as a protection to a culvert, and about a hundred yards further on, but on the
opposite side, the track commences. It runs up the slope, leaving
Gibbet on the left, and when the highest part of the down over which
it passes is reached, the Lydford stations and the Manor Hotel are in
full view in the valley below. From this point the track, hitherto
rather rough, assumes the character of a green path. A little further
on it is crossed by the Dartmoor Path (18), and lower down by its
branch that comes up from Ironcage Gate. At the bottom of the
ascent it is joined by the Henscott branch of the Dartmoor Path, and
is identical with it to its termination at the moor gate. This opens on
the road close to the dwellings of the South Western Railway Company's
employees.

24.—*Zoar to Watervale.* From the hamlet of Zoar a rough track
runs over the rock-strewn Zoar Down, and passing between enclosures
emerges on Horndon Down. It pursues a northerly course for about
half a mile to Horndon Down Bridge, which is a clapper thrown over
the Wheal Friendship Mine leat. A little beyond this it is joined by
the track already referred to as branching from the Dartmoor Path
(T. 21), and crossing the highway at Barrett's Bridge. Further on it
passes near the Ring o' Bells, and descending the north western slope
of Black Hill reaches the high road a short distance from the point
where the latters enters the enclosed country at Watervale.

25.—*Will to Down Lane.* We have already referred to the road
crossing the Tavy at Hill Bridge as being probably used by those
journeying over the Lich Path (T. 18) when the river could not be
forded, and it now becomes necessary to notice the track from the
bridge to Forstall Cross, as it is still in use. As the country near the
bridge is now enclosed we cannot be certain what line it followed, but
it could not have been very far from that taken by the existing lane,
even if that be not formed upon it. This passes Hill Town Farm, and
shortly after turning to the left, runs up by Will Farm to Yard Gate,
being crossed between these two latter points by the road from Lane
Head to Lane End (T. 20). At Yard Gate the path is seen as a genuine
moor track. It first runs through an enclosure, and is then carried
along the side of Snap and Yellowmead Hill, south-eastward of Black

Hill. Below is Yellowmead Farm, and soon after passing this it crosses the Wheal Friendship Mine leat, and reaches Forstall Cross. From this point onward to Down Lane it has already been noticed (T. 18).

26.—*The King Way.* The old road from Tavistock to Okehampton, which was in use previous to 1817, did not run like the present one through the vale of Parkwood, but was carried over the high ground to the west of it, and left the town by the steep hill now bearing the name of Exeter Street. It crossed the Walla Brook a short distance below Indiscombe, thence running on by Wilminstone, to which place it may still be followed. Beyond this it crossed the Burn near Wringworthy Farmhouse, and ascended the hill on the opposite side, and from this point onward to the Lyd followed practically the same line as that taken by the existing highway. But a track belonging to a time much earlier than that of this old road also ran this way, and that the latter was formed upon it, at least as far as the Lyd, or a little beyond, is more than probable. Further, however, the old road did not follow it, but was carried along the verge of the moor instead of across a part of it as the track was. This is known in the locality, that is to say, from Mary Tavy to Sourton, as the King Way, and though much of it is now obliterated, I have been able by careful examination to trace it from the village of Black Down to Higher Bowden, near Meldon, a distance of between eight and nine miles. There are now no remains of it in the village named, nor, with the exception of a few faint traces at its northern end, can it be seen on Black Down itself, but the line it took can nevertheless be determined. Former inhabitants used to speak of it as running quite near to the site of the present Black Down Wesleyan Chapel, while on the down it has often been come upon by those engaged in repairing the road when they have had occasion to remove surface turf near by. It ran parallel to it, and not many yards from its western side. But the King Way is to be plainly seen in a field near Watervale, running down towards the Sounscombe Brook. It is much overgrown, and several feet below the level of the field. (100 *Years*, Chap. II.) At the seventh milestone from Tavistock, near Beardon, it is again to be seen, as also is the old bridge where it crossed the Lyd, and which is a little further down stream than the present Skit Bridge. Passing up the hill and turning right, it either took the same line as the present highway as far as Downtown,' or, which is more probable, it passed through the short lane leading to the moor gate opening on High Down. But however this may have been, it is seen again at Noddon Gate in the north east corner of Vale Down, and from this point forward, although it is obliterated in places, there is no difficulty in tracing it to the enclosed country at Higher Bowden. Just inside Noddon Gate it crosses the Rattle Brook Head peat railway by a bridge, and running parallel to another rough track for about a mile, converges with it soon after passing the smooth, round hill of Noddon. It then runs close to the peat railway, which at one place cuts into and follows its line for a short distance. On leaving the railway it passes through the dip formed by the Sourton Tors on one side and Corn Ridge on the other, and reaching Iron Gates, which is a bond mark between the Sourton and Okehampton Commons, runs down the hill to the lane leading to Higher Bowden and Meldon. This track is crossed by others from Southerly and Sourton, hereafter noticed.

27.—*Tracks over High Down.* Two short tracks run over High Down, as well as another that extends to the forest (T. 28), and they are of use to the rambler as they will lead him to places where he can cross the Lyd. One enters the down at the gate at the end of the lane which crosses the high road N. of Skit Bridge, and runs E. to Doe Tor Gate Ford, close to the confluence of the Lyd and the Walla Brook. From the stream it passes up over a part of Doe Tor Common to Doe Tor Farm. The other track crosses the down from the gate near the Dartmoor Inn, running nearly E. to Mary Emma Ford and some stepping-stones. This ford is about ⅓ mile above the one just mentioned, and between them there is a clam so that the river can be crossed here when it is flooded.

28.—*From High Down to Amicombe.* This is a peat track, and also runs from the gate near the Dartmoor Inn. Immediately on entering upon the down it bears L., or N.E., to High Down Ford on the Lyd, at which point a branch goes southward to Doe Tor Farm. From the ford it runs up the hill between Arms Tor, L., and Bra Tor, R., to Dick's Well at the head of the Doe Tor Brook, where is a boundary stone marking the limits between the common lands of Bridestowe and Sourton on the N., and those of Lydford on the S. Just beyond Dick's Well there is a branch, R., to the disused Rattle Brook mine. The track then runs along the slope under the Dunnagoat Tors to the Rattle Brook, its course here being N., and crossing that stream at a ford, reaches Amicombe Hill within the forest.

29.—*From Vale Down to Arms Tor Down.* This short track leaves Vale Down at Noddon Gate, and running R. down the hill, reaches Noddon Ford on the Lyd, where also are some stepping-stones. It is then carried up the hillside N. of Arms Tor.

30.—* *Track from Southerly to Kitty Tor.* From the hamlet of Southerly, on the Okehampton road, a track runs in an easterly direction, and crossing the railway emerges on the common, where it is joined by a short path coming up from Combe Farm. It passes up over Southerly Down, and crosses the King Way near the point where that old road is cut into by the peat railway. The latter is carried over it, and the track then runs to the head of the Lyd valley, again crossing the peat railway, and also the stream, by a rude bridge a short distance from its source. It then runs by Gren Tor and ascending Woodcock Hill passes also by Hunt Tor, and reaches Rattle Brook Head. It then bends a little to the N., afterwards turning southward to Kitty Tor, just beyond which it terminates, having attained an elevation of about 1,920 feet. A track from the hamlet of Lake runs into this one on Southerly Down, and tracks also join it before it reaches Lyd Head from Sourton and Frewley Moor. (T. 31, 32). This track, which is really a peat track, will be found of considerable use to the rambler who wishes to reach the Cranmere district from the neighbourhood of Sourton. The route from its termination to Great Kneeset and the pool is described in the Cranmere section.

31.—*Track from Lake.* On the Okehampton road, 1½ miles from the Fox and Hounds, is the hamlet of Lake. Here a green path leads from under the viaduct up the hill with Withycombe Bottom, L. The traces of it are faint near the top, but it leads to the King Way (T. 26), which is one mile from the viaduct.

32.—* *Tracks from Sourton and Prewley Moor to Kitty Tor.*

Between Lake and Sourton a road branches R. from the road at Higher Collaven, and passing over the railway (L.S.W.) runs between enclosures to the common. Here it bends N., but a little in advance, due E., will be found again, and runs on to the King Way (T. 26) half mile distant, which it reaches in the dip between the Sourton Tors and Corn Ridge. Another track leaves the road a little nearer to Sourton, and passing under the railway, joins the former on the verge of the down. A third track leaves Sourton near the church, and taking a course to the northward of the Sourton Tors, also reaches the King Way. A fourth leaves the high road on Prewley Moor, and passing under the railway, runs up the hill to Iron Gates, where it, too, meets the King Way. From about the centre of the dip referred to a track leaves this ancient path, and passing up over the southern shoulder of Corn Ridge reaches the head of the Lyd (T. 30) and goes on to the peat beds.

From the track running up from the road at Collaven another is carried along the side of the hill under the Sourton Tors, and between them and the village. This, which runs to a quarry, close to the enclosures at Vellake, crosses the tracks from Sourton Church and from Prewley Moor.

33.—*Tracks by the West Ockment in Meldon Gorge.* These paths may be useful to the rambler. Just above the hamlet of Meldon, a lane runs from that leading up to Higher Bowden in a south-easterly direction to the down, where a path descends its steep side to the Ockment. Along the left bank of the stream a track leads down to the old quarry near the Meldon viaduct, and from here returns to the hamlet. At the spot where the river is first reached there are stepping-stones, known as Higher Bowden Steps, so that it may here be crossed. If it is desired to pass up the valley the descent to the stream should not be made. Along the side of the down is an old disused watercourse, and this forms a capital path to Vellake Corner, where the Ockment makes a bend. When the little Vellake is nearly reached a narrow zigzag path will be seen leading down to it.

On the right bank of the Ockment is also a track. This may be followed from Okehampton along the hill forming the northern side of the park, to the Meldon viaduct. Passing under this it crosses the Redaven, and about half-a-mile further up makes an abrupt turn to the left and climbs Longstone Hill. (Higher Bowden Steps are R.) When on high ground it turns to the right, and runs to the head of the combe in which the Fishcombe Water rises. Another track, part of which is now a camp road, leads upwards from near the Meldon viaduct, but in a different direction. It passes through the enclosures eastward, and then turning S. crosses Black Down to a ford on the Redaven, a little over half-a-mile below Yes Tor. A branch from a track now to be described also reaches this ford.

34.—* *From Okehampton to Dinger Plain.* (Ex. 15). This is a very important track, and in the early days of the forest farm settlers was probably used, in conjunction with two others, Cut Lane (T. 79) and Drift Lane (T. 78), as the chief means of communication between that part of the moor in which their homesteads were situated, and the town of Okehampton. It is very plainly marked, having been in constant use as a peat track. The three tracks still form the only

direct route for horses between the locality named and the town, and
are used by the moorman and the hunter. The Dinger Path is again
noticed in our account of Cut Lane (T. 79). From the corner of the
enclosures near Fitz's Well on the brow of the hill above Okehampton
Station, the track runs southward across the park to Moor Gate, where
it enters on the common.* Here the little Moor Brook comes down
from the dip between Row Tor and West Mil Tor, and the track is
carried very near to its L. bank to its source. About half a mile from
the gate another path branches from it R. ; this is the one already
alluded to (T. 33) as running to the ford on the Redaven below Yes
Tor. A camp road also crosses this part of it. Passing up between
Row Tor and West Mil Tor, where on the level is a branch over the
moor brook, L., it continues due S. to near Dinger Tor. This part of
the track can be plainly seen in certain states of the weather from
Cranmere, which is only two miles distant. Beyond Dinger Tor it
cannot be traced with certainty, but it probably went to Sandy Ford,
on the West Ockment, ¾ mile off, in a direction W. by S. A more
direct way from this point for the pedestrian would be to go by Lints
Tor, leaving it a little to the R., to Kneeset Foot, about one mile S.S.W.
[See remarks on continuation of Cut Lane, T. 79.]

35.—* *Okehampton to Ockment Hill.* This track branches from
the former (T. 34) at Moor Gate. It runs S. by the enclosures of
Pudhanger, and for the first half mile is now a well kept road, being
used by the artillery. Near Row Tor, which is R., the track proper
leaves the road, which bends L. The old path runs S., with Row Tor
Combe, through which the Blackaven flows, L., and reaches that
stream below East Mil Tor. It here crosses it by a clapper, known as
New Bridge, on the other side of which a short track turns L. The
path still runs southward, with the Blackaven R., and climbs the
southern shoulder of East Mil Tor. One mile from the bridge it reaches
a ruined wall, running E. and W. (Ex. 16), beyond which it continues
for ¾ mile further to the highest point of Ockment Hill. On the Mil
Tor side of the wall the track is well worn, but outside this it becomes
a green path. It terminates about 1¼ miles northward of Cranmere,
and is noticed in the routes to the pool.

Branches from this track formerly led over the side of Halstock
Down to Crovenor Steps, on the East Ockment, and to Stone Ford,
on the Blackaven. These are now camp roads.

36.—*Path from Okehampton Park to Halstock and Belstone.* On
the verge of the park above the station, just before Fitz's Well is
reached, a path turns to the left through a gate. This leads down to
the Moor Brook, which it crosses a little above where that stream enters
Halstock Cleave, and runs on to Halstock Farm. Beyond this it is
continued to the common, but a path branches from it to the left and
passes over a field known as Chapel Lands, in which are one or two
mounds marking the site of the ancient St. Michael's Chapel. On the
further side of the field the path enters Halstock Wood, and descends
through it to the East Ockment, which it crosses at a ford where also
are stepping-stones. Here it ascends the hill to the left, and at some

---

* Many of the tracks in this locality have been put in order by
the War Office, and are used as roads in connection with the artillery
practice on Okehampton Common.

distance up strikes another path running from the moor gate near Cleave Tor to the track leading from Belstone to Crovenor Steps (T. 37). From the moor gate referred to a lane leads by the entrance to the old vicarage to the village of Belstone.

There seems to have been a path running from Okehampton Park to Halstock Down ; between Halstock Farm and Pudhanger is a gully, known as Symons' Ditch, which certainly has the appearance of an old road.

37.—*From Belstone to Crovenor Steps.* This track passes over the side of Watchet Hill, which is quite near to the village, and then runs down in a south-westerly direction to the East Ockment, leaving Skir Tor on the right as it approaches the stream. Soon after passing Watchet Hill it is joined by the path coming along the side of the hill from the moor gate near Cleave Tor (T. 36). From Crovenor Steps another road runs up the hill towards the south-east, and joins the Knock Mine track described below. (T. 38).

38.—*From Belstone to Knock Mine.* There is no historical interest attaching to this track, nor does it serve the purpose like some others of conducting the rambler over a part of the moor otherwise not easily traversed, since the ridge along which it runs is of solid ground covered for the most part with short turf, but it is nevertheless of considerable use to the stranger as a guide to the Upper Taw. For about half a mile it is one with the last-named track, but leaves it just before reaching a small circle called the Nine Stones, and keeping higher up, on the side of the ridge crowned with the Belstone Tors, runs to the top of it at Winter Tor. Passing close to Ock Tor a mile further south, it is carried above the narrow defile through which the Taw comes down at the foot of the western flank of Steeperton. At the head of this, where the valley opens, it descends to the stream, L., here crossed by a clapper, now partly ruined. The remains of mining operations are abundant. The head waters of the East Ockment are only half a mile to the west, and one would be inclined to imagine, from the proximity of that stream, and of Ock Tor, that Ock rather than Knock was the true name of this mine on the Taw. But Knock it is with the natives, or sometimes Knack, and Ock appears to have nothing to do with it. Whether this was derived from *Cnoc*, a Celtic term for a hill (for around the more recent workings there are those of an earlier time), or whether the name has reference to a former disused mine on the spot, I am not able to say. When a mine is abandoned the miners describe it as being " knacked," and we can very well suppose that at some period prior to the last time it was worked, it would be referred to as the knacked mine.

39.—*Birchy Lake to Taw Plain.* A rough track runs from Birchy Lake, which is close to Belstone, by the side of the Taw, and at the eastern foot of the Belstone Tor range. It goes out to a ford on the river, and though on the further side of this it is not so plainly defined, it may be followed across the plain to Small Brook, where it meets another (T. 40) coming out from Ford on the high road south-east of Sticklepath.

40.—*Ford to Small Brook.* About midway between the village of Sticklepath and Ramsleigh Mine, and a little removed from the road, is Ford Farm, R., situated on a tributary of the Taw, known as the Ford Brook, and sometimes as the Cosdon Brook. The lane by which the farm is approached, after passing the house, runs up by the bank of the stream, which here comes down through a steep and narrow gully.. A short distance up the path turns L., and a little way on, in the midst of some small enclosures, is joined by another coming up the hill L. from Ramsleigh Mine. This one goes southward, and is the track to Steeperton, next described (T. 41). The Small Brook path turns R., and runs up the hill to meet the Ford Brook again. Here a path branches S., towards the summit of Cosdon. The track is carried by the side of the brook to the W. shoulder of the hill, and nearly ¾ mile from the branch crosses it, and also the Ivy Tor Water. Thence it runs S. along the W. side of White Hill to Small Brook, where there is a ford, but beyond this it cannot be traced far.

A narrow footpath from the ridge S. of Winter Tor crosses Taw Plain and runs up to this track. The two form a direct route from East Ockment Farm to Ramsleigh and South Zeal.

41.—*South Zeal to Hangingstone Hill.* This track is useful to the visitor as affording an easy means of reaching the upper Taw and Cranmere from South Zeal and Ramsleigh Mine, and also from Throwleigh. (From the latter place the track next mentioned (T. 42) would be followed as far as the southern end of Raybarrow Pool, where it would be left for the one now under notice, as hereafter described). From South Zeal a lane leads to the Okehampton highway at Providence Place, and immediately opposite to the point where it reaches it is a gate. It is at this gate that the track commences, and it runs up the side of the hill for a considerable distance between the numerous enclosures that have here been formed. Before it enters on the common it is joined by another track on the right, which comes in from Ford, the starting-place of the Codson Hill (T. 40) path to Small Brook. Here it turns L., and one mile further on passes the triple stone row known as The Cemetery, and then, still pursuing a course a little westward of south, runs along the slope of Codson, with Cheriton Combe on the left. Here for a short distance it passes between banks, being about four or five feet below the surface of the common, and it also assumes the character of a road, which it maintains until reaching the forest, when it becomes more rugged. Not far beyond Cheriton Combe is the mire known as Raybarrow Pool, and this it skirts throughout its whole length. A little further on it passes the restored circle near White Moor Stone, and then runs across the ridge that forms the watershed between the Teign and the Taw. Its course is then below Little Hound Tor, about ¾ mile beyond which it approaches the Steeperton Brook, and here a branch crosses that stream to Chimney Bow, where it forks, but is not continued very far. The main track runs up through Bow Combe, with the Wild Tor ridge L., or E., and the brook close by on the R. This it crosses about ¾ mile above the other fording-place and reaches Ockside Hill, thence running southward to the foot of Hangingstone Hill.

42.—*Clannaborough Down to Gallaven.* A part of Throwleigh Common near Payne's Bridge is known as Clannaborough Down, and from here a path runs out to another part of the same common bearing the name of Gallaven. This is quite close to the forest boundary, and in its midst rises a little stream, which joins the Rue Lake, a feeder of the Walla Brook, itself a tributary of the North Teign. Just below where the brook first referred to (and which is sometimes called the

Gallaven Water) has its source is a crossing-place named Gallaven Ford. One branch of the track leading out to that spot leaves the road close to the house by Payne's Bridge, and another a little further up the hill. They unite about three parts of a mile to the west, and the path then follows the Blackaton Brook, which it crosses in two places, to its source at Raybarrow Pool. It skirts the eastern side of the mire, running between it and Kennon Hill, and then descends the slope to Gallaven. To reach the South Zeal track (T. 41), the Gallaven path must be left when the mire is passed, and a direction due west pursued. This will lead to White Moor Stone, which is in view from the path, and the Zeal and Steeperton track (T. 41) is only a short distance beyond it.

43.—*Tracks from Ensworthy.* A track leaves the road that runs along the edge of the moor at Ensworthy, and at a short distance from the latter branches into two. The lower one passes between the enclosures of Higher Ensworthy, and runs for about half mile S. to the slope below the rocks that crown Buttern Hill, and which are some-times referred to as Buttern Tor. The other branch runs up the hill for a short distance, and then also turns S., its course being almost parallel to the former, but on the other side of Buttern Hill. It runs up the bottom for about ¾ mile with White Moor Marsh R., and passing Buttern Circle (Ex. 19) runs S.W. to Rue Lake, a little below the weir W. of Rival Tor.

44.—*South Zeal to Widecombe : Part of an Ancient Way from Bideford to Dartmouth, with Notice of the Plymouth and Tavistock Track.* Only in places can this old path now be traced. Though I have heard it spoken of as being merely a way from Zeal to Widecombe Church, there is good reason for believing that it extended right across the county. It is said that it was once used by sailors passing from one of the above-named ports to the other, and that at intervals of about 8 or 10 miles there were rest-houses for their accommodation. It seems to have approached the moor from the north by way of Week and Throwleigh or Clannaborough, thence running through Deave Lane to Forder, where it is seen crossing a field. From there it probably went on by Chapple to Gidleigh village and Gidleigh North Park, below which it crossed the Teign at Glassy Steps. It then climbed the hill to Teigncombe, and crossed Yeo Farm, within half mile of Kes Tor, and here it still exists as a footpath. Thence it crossed the farms of Frenchbere, Yardworthy, Shapley, Hurston, Venn, Jurston, Littaford, Liapa, or Leeper as it is usually called, and went on to Combe, where it runs through the passage of a dwelling-house. From this curious circumstance it has been supposed that one of the rest-houses formerly stood on the site of the present building. From Combe it went to Hookney, and thence to Widecombe.

The high roads that now cross Dartmoor, the Act for making the first of which was obtained in 1772, are all formed on the line of old tracks (100 *Years*, Chap. II.) The most important of these ancient ways was one running from Chagford to the West Dart Valley below Bear Down, where Two Bridges now stands, and here it forked, one branch going to Tavistock and the other to Plymouth. We have stated that the path just described ran between Yardworthy and Shapley, and it therefore crossed the Two Bridges track near the first-named farm, for in Owen's *Britannia Depicta*, published in 1720, the road from Exeter to Tavistock is shown as passing over the moor from that farm, or rather from Yadrey, the plan following the local pro-nounciation. It ran by the enclosures of Willandhead, as a wall is mentioned as existing on the L. of the way, and a stone that stands not far from Metheral Farm gate probably marked its course towards Hurston Ridge, over which it passed to a point not far from the present Stats Brook Bridge. It is shown on Ebden's Map of Devonshire, published in 1811, and may still be traced in many places. This part of it is often regarded on the moor as a branch of the old Bideford track, but of course incorrectly so, and it is related that old-fashioned tobacco pipes with small bowls have been picked up upon it. Midway between Metheral and Stats Brook, a distance of rather over two miles, an object marking this path is figured and named on Owen's plan. This is Heath Stone, and it is mentioned in 1702 by William French, of Widecombe, a deponent in a law case, and is also probably identical with the Heathstone named in the Survey of the forest made in 1609. It stood at a point where another track crossed the main one, and exactly 19 miles from Exeter, and it is curious to note that on Moll's Map of Devon, published in 1713, it is the only object shown on the whole of Dartmoor.* That this stone was originally a menhir, afterwards becoming a forest bondmark, as in the case of the Longstone near Kes Tor, and subsequently an adapted guide-stone, I think there can be little doubt. Its name, and that of the ridge on which it stood, are plainly indicative of its origin, while its situation on the forest boundary line renders clear the purpose it served later. The Saxon *hare-stane*, or *hoar stone*, is a cognate term with the Celtic *men-hir*, *high*, or *long*, *stone*, and that these ancient monoliths were often fixed upon as boundaries there is ample proof; indeed, there is evidence that the Saxon name in question also denoted that purpose. That Hurston Ridge derived its name in Saxon times from the hare-stane that stood upon it we may regard as certain (the farm of Hurston, which is named after the ridge, actually appears as Hareston in a forester's account of the time of Henry VII.), and it is not difficult to see how the stone itself would in time come to be called Hethstone, and later, Heath Stone. This track across the forest, although marked with guide-stones and carried over the wider streams by clappers, was probably not much used in Owen's time except by the dwellers on the moor. When the present road across Dartmoor was made, although it mainly followed the line of the ancient track, it was not carried from Stats Brook over Hurston Ridge to Chagford, but was formed on another old path that ran across Bush Down to Beetor Cross, and thence to Moretonhampstead.

Another path crosses the Teign above Glassy Steps. It leaves the stroll running from the common to Berry Down, and forms an entrance to Scorhill House. From this it descends to the islands in the Teign, where are two foot bridges, and climbs the hill to Batworthy. It is a church path from the latter place to Gidleigh.

45.—*Metheral to Teign Head Farm.* The road from Chagford to the moor past Waye is probably on the line of the old track leading to

---

* The map is on a very small scale. On the latest edition of the Ordnance Map the stone not far from Metheral is marked Heath Stone, which is incorrect.

Tavistock and Plymouth already referred to (T. 44). It enters the moor at the gate near Yardworthy, whence a road now runs by Metheral Farm to Fernworthy, another farm lying just within the border of the forest. From this a lane goes through the enclosures to the common, and at the top of it the track to Teign Head Farm commences. It is by no means plainly marked, but may be seen here and there pursuing a course across Froggymead Hill in a direction little north of west. About a mile from the head of the lane, close to which is the Froggymead circle, a gate in a newtake wall is reached, and here the track is well defined as it runs down to the Teign, which is crossed by means of a clapper of three openings. It then passes up to the lonely farm which is in full view on the hillside. This road is very useful to the rambler who desires to reach Carnmere from Moorgate on the Moretonhampstead highway, or any place in its immediate neighbourhood. Teign Head Farmhouse is not very much more than two miles from the pool, while the outer wall of its enclosures on the western side is only about 1½ miles from it. [See Cranmere Routes.]

46.—*Paths on Bush Down.* A footpath runs over Bush Down which the rambler may find of service to him. It leaves the Moreton road about half mile N.E. of the Warren House Inn, very near to Bennet's Cross, and strikes down L. to the enclosures of Lakeland Farm. It passes through these, and is continued down Broad Moor Bottom to the moor gate near Jurston, where two rocks take the place of gateposts. Another footpath leaves the Chagford road, which branches from the Moreton one about one mile N.E. of Bennet's Cross. This path leads to the same moor gate.

A path runs eastward from Bennet's Cross over Headland Warren, and below Shapley Tor, to Westcombe. (See T. 47).

47.—*Tracks near Challacombe.* A road, cut in 1874, branches from the Moretonhampstead highway on North Bovey Common, and runs down to Grendon Cot, where it joins another. It was formed to connect the main road with Grendon, Blackaton, and Cator. About a mile from the point where it commences a path branches from this road to the right, and runs down to Headland Warren house in the valley below, and thence to West Webburn. This it crosses and goes on to Challacombe. Just before this path diverges from the road the latter is crossed by a track leading from Westcombe, on the eastern verge of North Bovey Common to Bennet's Cross on the Moreton road. In this locality are several other paths, mostly formed by the miners, but none likely to prove of much service to the rambler. A path also led from the enclosed lands in Manaton parish to Headland and Vitifer, It ran through Grim's Pound, the wall of which was broken down in two places. Another path runs off S.E. from the Blackaton road S. of Challacombe, along the verge of Blackaton Down (See Ex. 85), and joins the Church Way (T. 76) at the top of Gore Hill.

48.—*Paths at Lustleigh Cleave.* Several foot-paths cross the side of the valley. There is one from near Hammerslake to Foxworthy Bridge, whence it is continued up through the wood to Manaton ; several branches from this to the Bovey below Water Cleave and Wanford Wood ; and there is also another branch leading to Higher and Lower Hisley. These are noticed in the description of the cleave. [Bovey Tracey District.]

49.—*Paths on Ilsington Common.* There are a couple of tracks on Ilsington Common, which, though short and unimportant, deserve notice as having probably formed an early means of access to the moor from the neighbourhood of Sigford. They both came up from near Bag Tor, one of them reaching the road to Hensworthy Gate just under Hey Tor, and the other, which branches from the former a short distance below Bag Tor, following the little Sig to its source and joining the road much nearer to the gate. On the same common is a green path running over the shoulder of the hill by Saddle Tor, by means of which the pedestrian, or horseman, may shorten the distance between that part of the road under Hey Tor and the gate named. There is also a track running from the road that comes up from Bovey Tracey just where it enters on the common, to the Higher Terrace Drive above Yarner Wood. This track passes very near to a boundary mark known as Owlacombe Burrow.

50.—*Path on Hound Tor Down.* Where the narrow lane from Great Hound Tor Farm enters upon the down below Swine Down Gate,* a path runs southward to Holwell Farm. It is carried along the side of the hill between Hound Tor and Grea Tor, the former being above it, and the latter between it and the valley.

51.—*The Tunhill Road.* About midway between Newhouse under Rippon Tor, and Cold East Cross a track leaves the road and runs down in a northwesterly direction to the Ruddycleave Water, which it crosses[not far below its source. Here is a gateway, formed by the old walls of the Newhouse enclosures on the right and those of the Blackslade enclosures on the left. Passing through this the track ascends the hill, and runs down on the further side to Tunhill Farm, leaving the gate leading to Blackslade on the left. Just where it commences to descend the hill is a fine kistvaen.

52.—*Track over Dunstone Down, and from Rowden Down to Shallowford.* About a quarter of a mile from Widecombe, on the Ponsworthy road, a lane turns up on the right to Westcombe Farm, just beyond which it enters on Dunstone Down. Over this a track runs to the road coming down the valley from Blackaton. A short distance to the right of the point at which it touches it, another track runs down a narrow piece of common between two enclosures to Rowden Down. Passing over this the path enters the enclosures and descends to the West Webburn, where is a clapper of three openings. West Shallowford Farm is just beyond, and here the track, which now assumes the character of a moor road, enters on Corndon Down, and joins the road coming down from Cator, and the ancient tenements in the Walla Brook valley. By passing over Corn Down from Shallowford, in a S.W. direction, Sherwell would be reached in about one mile. The line of route here sketched forms the direct way between Widecombe and that place.

53.—*Path from Dartmeet.* On the L. bank of the Dart above the bridge at Dartmeet, a road runs N. to Dartmeet Cottage. From this point a footpath, also running N., climbs the hill between Yar Tor and the river. It goes on to the enclosures N. of the tor, and passes across them to Sherwell, which is about 1¼ miles from the bridge.

---

* Usually known as Swallerton Gate, which name, however, appears to be a corruption of Swine Down.

From this place another path runs northward, along the N.W. edge of Corn Down, to Riddon, about one mile from Sherwell.

54.—*Hexworthy to Aune Head.* The Avon, which stream is always called the Aune on the moor, has its source a short distance westward of Ryder's Hill, the summit of which lofty height forms a boundary mark of the forest. A track runs from the hamlet of Hexworthy to the edge of the mire in which this river rises, where it meets another shortly to be noticed (T. 56). This track leaves the Gobbet and Sherberton road above, and at the back of, the Forest Inn. It passes up through a newtake, crossing the Wheal Emma leat, and climbs the side of Down Ridge, and goes on to Skir Ford on the Wo Brook. Near this point it is crossed by the track already described as running from Buckland across the forest (T. 2), which, however, is here undefined. A little further up is Sandy Ford, and thence the track runs parallel to the Wo Brook to its source. Not far beyond this it reaches Sandy Way (T. 56), which is here very plainly defined. There are traces of a continuation of this Hexworthy path ; or, at all events, of one running from Aune Head across the side of Ryder's Hill to Wella Brook Gert, but the ground is usually there very boggy, and such a course could not always be followed. (T. 58).

*55.—*Combestone Tor to Dockwell Gate.* This path forms the most direct route between Hexworthy and Brent. It leaves the Holne road exactly opposite to Combestone Tor, and runs up over Holne Moor in a direction due south to the head of Ringleshutts Gert, crossing the track from Horse Ford to Holne (T. 2) not very far from the tor. Beyond the gert it also crosses Sandy Way (T. 56) and descends to the Mardle, which here runs through a hollow having very steep sides. From Hapstead Ford on this stream it pursues a southerly course along the side of Snowdon to Snowdon Hole, a rocky hollow forming the eastern end of a gert known as Gibby's Beam. Here the path is very narrow, there being only sufficient room for a horse to pass, as the rocks encumber the ground above it, and there is a mire below. Beyond this point traces of the path are lost for some distance (indeed it is indistinct from Hapstead Ford to the hollow) but the next point is the tor, or group of tors, called Pupers, a corruption of Pipers. Some who use this track pass below and to the east of the principal pile, while others prefer to ascend the hill immediately on leaving Snowdon Hole, and do not turn towards the tor until they are some distance up. By following this course a piece of common encumbered with rocks is avoided. From the eastern tor a reave running S.S.E. for more than a mile is followed, and when a little water-course is reached the track becomes once more a clearly defined grassy path, and was here crossed by the Abbots' Way (T. 1). A branch runs by the wall enclosing Lambs Down from the open common to the gate giving access to Skerraton Down, which it crosses and reaches a point whence a lane leads to Brent. The main track runs between Small Brook Plains and Parnell's Hill, and passing the head of Dockwell Hole, goes onward to Dockwell Gate. Here the path runs up to the left to another gate opening on the same lane that is reached by the track crossing Skerraton Down. From this point Brent is rather more than two miles distant.

*56.—*Sandy Way.* This path runs from Holne and Scoriton to the lower end of Fox Tor Mire and the White Works. A steep lane leads to the moor from Mitchellcombe, a hamlet in the valley of the

Holy Brook, and usually called by the natives Mutchecum, and the track is a continuation of this. It enters on the moor at Lane Head, near Whithedges, and takes a direction west by north to Holne Ridge, running roughly parallel to the Mardle, which stream is about half a mile south of it. When the source of this, which is just under Ryder's Hill, is passed, the track enters the forest, and goes due west to Aune Head. Here, where it skirts the mire, it is very clearly defined, appearing for a short distance like an ordinary road. Passing between Cater's Beam and Ter Hill it runs down the side of the hollow through which courses the Fox Tor stream, one of the branches of the Swincombe river, though it is not here plainly marked, to a ford not far below the White Works. Sandy Way may be reached from Holne Moor Gate by the Ringleshutts Mine road, which branches from the highway near the gate.

From Scoriton another track runs out to Holne Ridge and joins Sandy Way. It passes up over Scoriton Down, and crosses the Mardle at Chalk Ford, and runs up by it to Hapstead Ford, a quarter of a mile beyond which it reaches the main track.

In the days of the war prison at Princetown, when there was frequent communication between that place and the villages surrounding the moor, there is little doubt that Sandy Way was much traversed. It would form with a connecting path from Princetown to the upper Swincombe (and more than one now exist) a direct way to Holne, if instead of being followed down the Mardle valley it was left on Holne Ridge, and a straight course pursued towards the village. Thus it would be an alternative route to the Ter Hill and Down Ridge path (T. 2), and in early times may have been used by travellers from Tavistock to Ashburton. (T. 1).

57.—*Chalk Ford and Lid Gate to Huntingdon.* Close to Chalk Ford a track leaves the branch just noticed (T. 56), and passing up the slope bends round the shoulder of Pupers, and runs to Huntingdon Warren, crossing the Wella Brook near the house. It is by no means a clearly defined track, as it is simply an approach to the warren and to Huntingdon Mine, now disused. Here and there it is marked by an upright granite stone. About midway in its course it is joined by a track coming from Lid Gate, which is situated at the end of a lane leading from Cross Furzes to the moor, and which passes near Hayford.

58.—*Track to Wella Brook Gert.* Faint vestiges of a track are seen in places on the side of the hill under Pupers, in a line between Water Oke Corner and Wella Brook Gert. The corner is close to the fording-place on the water-course named in the notice of the Combestone and Dockwell track (T. 55), and the gert is a short distance above Huntingdon Warren house. Here two tracks are to be seen amid the workings with the fords where they crossed the Wella Brook. The higher one points in the direction of Ryder's Hill, across the side of which are the traces of a path as already named (T. 54). The lower one is a branch of this and runs to a side working known as T Gert.

*59.—*Buckfast to Plympton.* As I have pointed out in another place [*Crosses,* Chap. XVI.] it is evident that a path once ran from Buckfast and Ashburton by way of Dockwell, Harford, and Cornwood, to Plympton and Plymouth. Though now unknown as a continuous track, there are portions of it still used, and as these are of service to the rambler on the moor it was thought desirable to notice it here‧ We first meet with it near the southern gate of Skerraton Down (T. 55), where two roads cross. Here is an old guide stone on each of the four faces of which is an incised letter. These indicate the places to which the roads lead, namely, Ashburton, Plympton, Totnes and Tavistock. Crossing Gigley Bridge, which is just below, the Plympton track probably ran through the Dockwell enclosures. Its course cannot here be traced with any certainty, but the path running from near Dockwell Gate to Yolland Farm seems to be a part of it. From the farm it went to the Avon, and in the present Diamond Lane, a rugged bridle path branching from the road between Shipley Bridge and Didworthy Bridge, it is undoubtedly seen. On the common at the head of the lane are some newtakes, but a space has been left between two of them for the old road. Near Coryndon Ball it is again seen, and there is a ford on the East Glaze, and another on the West Glaze, directly in the line of it. From the latter it ascended the side of Ugborough Moor to Spurrell's Cross, whence it went to Harford. At the cross it is joined by another path, coming from Owley (T. 62), and is also intersected by a peat track (T. 63), both of which are noticed further on.

60.—Shipley to Red Lake Mire. This track is really an old tram road, over which peat was once conveyed to some naphtha works at Shipley, on the verge of Brent Moor. It has been disused for a very long time, but I can remember when the rails, which were of wood, bolted to blocks of granite, were to be seen in places. [100 *Years,* Chap. III.] The buildings at Shipley still remain, having been put in a good state of repair by a china clay company, about the year 1872, but operations in connection with this venture did not long continue. To the rambler this track is valuable, as enabling him to readily reach the forest and the Abbots' Way from the neighbourhood of Brent. By passing up by the wall on the left, immediately on entering the moor at Shipley Gate, the track will soon be reached where it comes up from the rear of the factory buildings. It sweeps round Zeal Hill, and leaving Bala Brook Heath to the left, runs towards Broad Rushes. Here it turns again and shortly after passes the old workings at the head of Bala Brook, and, a little further on, the old clay pits. This part of it has long been filled with bog, and rendered impassable, but the ground on the north side of it is good, so that it can readily be followed. Further on it becomes a hard track again, running between high banks, but it is here so rough that the ground by the side of it is preferable, both for the pedestrian and the rider. When it reaches the cairn known as Western Whitaburrow, close to which it passes, and where was a siding, it begins to descend, and runs down a steep incline to its termination among the old turf pits at Red Lake Mire. Rather over a quarter of a mile from the cairn it crosses the Abbots' Way, which is here a well-defined path. The distance from Shipley to the Crossways, where the monks' path is reached, is about three miles and a half. The railway was formerly known as the Zeal Tor tram-road.

61.—*Ball Gate to Bala Brook Head.* A road runs up the hill from the hamlet of Aish, near Brent, to Aish Ridge and Cornydon Ball, terminating at Ball Gate, which opens on Brent Moor. From this point there is a track to the head of the Bala Brook, over which clay

was at one time brought in from the pits there. It is, however, not
very well defined in places. It passes up the hill to the E. of Three
Barrows, and, crossing the head of Red Brook at Higher Ford, runs
on by Knattle Barrow to the pits. There are other fords on Red Brook
lower down, but these are merely crossing-places made by the moormen. As this track leads to the Zeal Tor tram-road, which crosses
the Abbots' Way (T. 1, 60), it is sometimes spoken of as Jobbers'
Path.

62.—*Owley to Harford.* From the moor gate at Owley, which is
about a mile and a half from Wrangaton, a green path runs over the
moor to the gate at Harford. It climbs the hill to the north of
Ugborough Beacon, and on reaching the piece of level ground at the top
is crossed by the Blackwood Path, presently noticed (T. 63). This
point was formerly marked by Spurrell's Cross, of which nothing now
remains but the fractured head. It was here that the Buckfast and
Plympton track (T. 59) crossed Ugborough Moor as it ran towards
Harford. From Spurrell's Cross onward the green path is marked
by little heaps of stones, its direction being south of west. It passes
very near to the head of Butter Brook, which is at no great distance
to the north of Hangershell Rock, and then descends the slope to
Harford Gate.

*63.—*Blackwood Path.* As its name indicates, this has been used
as a peat track, but it was also an approach to Erme Pound, and may
have joined the Abbots' Way, the latter not being far from the pound.
It enters the moor near Wrangaton, and, passing up the hill, leaves the
Eastern Beacon on the right. A little further on it is joined by another
track that comes up from the verge of the common under the Western
Beacon. Passing Spurrell's Cross (T. 62), it goes on over the level,
and then ascends the hill towards Sharp Tor. It runs through the dip
between that pile and Three Barrows, and parallel to some upright
stones that mark the boundary between Ugborough and Harford Moors.
A little further on it crosses this line close to one of the stones, and runs
over Erme Plains to Stony Bottom. This part of it, however, is now
very ill-defined. In places it is altogether lost, and where discoverable
is little more than a narrow footpath. In Stony Bottom it is seen
crossing Hook Lake at a ford. Beyond this is Brown Heath, at the
foot of which, and close to the river, is Erme Pound.

On Piles Hill, just before this track reaches Sharp Tor, it is joined
by another that comes up from Harford Gate.

64.—*Paths near Addicombe.* From the moor gate above Stowford,
near Ivybridge, a track runs by the enclosures of Lukesland to
Addicombe. Green paths branch from it to Weatherdon Hill and
Butterdon Hill, but do not extend far.

65.—*Track by the Erme under Stalldon Barrow.* A track enters
the commons at the gate close to Harford Bridge, and runs up the right
bank of the Erme. About a mile and a half from the gate it is carried
along the foot of the steep hill crowned with the cairn known as Stalldon
Barrow, and which name is often given to the hill itself. On the further
side of the Erme at this point is the interesting old oakwood of Piles.
Some distance further up the track is lost.

*66.—*Track over Stall Moor.* From Watercombe Waste Gate,
in the parish of Cornwood, and about a mile and a half from the village,
a track runs in a northerly direction over Stall Moor. Like the Black-

wood Path (T. 63), this track was formerly much used as a peat road, but like that path also it was an approach to Erme Pound. In the days when this served as a drift pound, there must at times have been a good deal of traffic over these tracks. In an Agistment Roll attached to an account of John D'Abernon, Constable of Lydford, in the reign of Edward III., mention is made of the "Preda de Irm," so that we know that one of the recognized pasturage grounds at that time was in the Erme Valley. This was not improbably Green Hill, a little northward of the pound, and within the forest. It still affords the best pasturage in the south quarter. On leaving Watercombe Waste Gate the track ascends the side of the hill crowned with Stalldon Barrow, which is about ¾ mile E. About one mile N. of the gate a path comes up from the corner between Dendles Wood and Harrowthorn Plantation, and crosses it. It is this path that leads to the pound ; the other, from Watercombe Gate, goes on towards Yealm Rocks. At the crossing-place, therefore, the way lies R. Passing Downing's Brook the track runs northward to a little tributary of the Erme, which it crosses, the direction here being east of north. A short distance further on the stone circle known as The Dancers is passed, and half mile beyond this the track reaches Green Lake Bottom. It crosses this hollow (there are two fords here), and then bends R. to a ford on the Erme, just below the pound. The track ends here, but from this point onward a moorman's path, only distinguishable in places, connects it with the track running out from Hexworthy to Aune Head (T. 54). Usually the Erme is not crossed at the ford, but half mile higher up, below Stinger's Hill. From that point the way lies up the side of Green Hill, with Red Lake R., to a spot where the fen stretching northward from Red Lake Mire can be crossed. The path through this boggy ground is narrow and winding, but it is the only means by which horsemen can pass from Green Hill to the Avon without making a considerable detour. It runs into Heng Lake Gully, which extends to the river. Above this a narrow strip of solid ground between the fen and the right bank of the stream forms a natural path to Fish Lake, beyond which the way lies over the shoulder of Cater's Beam. It then crosses Nakers Hill, leaving the mire known as Little Aune to the right, a short distance from which it reaches the Hexworthy track at Aune Head. These paths, therefore, form a continuous way from the in-country at Cornwood to Hexworthy, and the settled parts of the forest beyond, and are of great service to those engaged in looking after cattle pastured in the south quarter. I know one moorman who was in the habit of passing over it constantly during nearly fifty years.

67.—*Path to Broadall.* A lane leads from Heathfield Down, close to Cornwood village, to the common under Rook Tor, where it finds a continuation in a track running up the hill to the head of the little stream bounding High-house Waste on the west. It then bends to the right, and crossing the waste reaches Broadall Lake, where it terminates. This stream is a tributary of the Yealm, and falls into it in Dendles Wood.

68.—*Tracks on Heddon Down and Crownhill Down.* On Heddon Down, in the parish of Cornwood, and on the adjoining Crownhill Down, in Plympton St. Mary parish, are a few paths, but they do not call for any particular notice. From the hamlet of Lutton, on the road between Cornwood and Sparkwell, a track runs northward over Heddon Down, and crossing the little stream that flows under Quicks Bridge to join the Piall Brook, reaches the Lee Moor road near the gate opening on the lane leading to Cholwich Town. On Crownhill Down there are paths forming a continuation of the lanes above Goodamoor and Bottle Hill Mine, and one also branches from the road leading down to Coleland Bridge just inside the moor gate. These run by the clay pits to Broomage, from which place another goes down the side of Ridding Down to Cholwich Town Gate. For the most part the paths on these downs have been made, and are used, by the labourers at the clayworks in the vicinity.

69.—*From Plympton to Sampford Spiney and Tavistock.* A good road now connects these places, but as it is certain that it is formed on the line of an ancient one, it seems fitting to mention it here. Like the Abbots' Way (T. 1), and other old tracks that have been noticed (T. 2, 59), this was formerly a monks' path, or at all events, was much used by them. Sampford Spiney belonged to Plympton Priory, and it was along this road that the monks journeyed when they desired to visit their church at the former place. The line is a direct one, and it was marked at certain points by stone crosses. The road passes through Colebrook and runs up past Boringdon to Browney Cross, a short distance beyond which it enters the commons at Niel Gate. Skirting Shaugh Moor it descends to Cadaford Bridge, where it crosses the Plym. It then climbs the hill to Lynch Down, along the edge of which it runs to its north-western corner, leaving it by the steep Lynch Hill, at the foot of which stands Marchants Cross (T. 1), and reaches the Mew. Then leaving the village of Meavy a short distance to the left it runs up to Yennadon Down, and along the verge of it to Dousland. Thence its descends to Walkhampton, and a little further on reaches the Walkham river at Huckworthy Bridge. On Huck-worthy Common just above is an old cross, placed where the Sampford Spiney road diverges from the one leading to Tavistock. The former skirts the common to the right, afterward branching left to the village, which is rather more than a mile distant. The latter goes on to the corner of Plaster Down, and thence to Warren's Cross, where it enters upon Whitchurch Down. Near this point the ancient track joined the Abbots' Way, as already described (T. 1). Tavistock is about two and a half miles from this, the eastern, end of Whitchurch Down.

70.—*Paths on Shaugh Moor.* There are a number of paths on Shaugh Moor, many of them having been made by the workmen engaged at the clayworks in the neighbourhood in passing to and from their labour. There are none of any particular importance, the chief perhaps being one that runs from the road near Beatland Corner to Emmet's Post. Another leads from Brag Lane End to the road under Stewart's Hill ; and a third from near Shaden Plantation to the clay pits at Wotter.

71.—*Paths to Ditsworthy Warren House.* In the valley of the Plym, above Cadaford Bridge, is Trowlesworthy Warren, which is approached by a narrow road branching from the Lee Moor road about half a mile from the bridge. Still further up the valley is Dits-worthy Warren, and to the house connected with this, which is situated very near to Eastern Tor, several paths lead. A track runs to it from

Brisworthy, a group of farmhouses seen on the right in ascending from Cadaford Bridge towards Lynch Down (T. 69), and there is also an approach to it by a footpath which starts near the bridge and follows the course of the Plym upward. The track enters on Ringmoor Down just above the farms, and crossing Legis Lake at the lower end of Legis Mire runs north of Legis Tor to an enclosure, by the wall of which it descends towards the river, and then goes direct to the house. The footpath leaves the road a short distance from the northern end of the bridge, and runs eastward by the wall of the Brisworthy enclosures to the Plym, on the bank of which it is carried to its termination, just below the house. Another track, and the one by which the house is usually approached, runs straight across Ringmoor Down from Ringmoor Cot, on the road leading from Meavy to Sheeps Tor, and at the upper, and north-eastern corner, of Lynch Down. Close to the Cot a moor road branches to the right from the one running to Sheeps Tor. This road is the old Abbots' Way, the course of which has already been sketched (T. 1). A very short distance from the point where it leaves the Sheeps Tor road the Ditsworthy track springs from it, R. At first this is clearly defined, but further out on the down it would only be possible to trace it by the marks of wheels here and there were it not that its course is indicated by stones placed some distance apart. These are not posts, and being low and few and far between, are not quite such excellent guides as might be wished. They were once coated with whitewash, and then answered their purpose admirably. The distance from Ringmoor Cot to the warren house is under two miles. A branch of this track runs into the Sheeps Tor road southward of the Cot, and from this point paths lead towards Brisworthy Plantation and the farms. About half a mile on the Eylesbarrow road—or Abbots' Way (T. 1)—a footpath runs from it, R., up over the common to Gutter Tor, and descends to Ditsworthy ; and at the distance of another half mile, a track, known as Edward's Path, also leaves the road, R., and runs to the warren house. These two last-named paths form the means of communication between the warren and Sheeps Tor. Around Ditsworthy there are also other footpaths used by the warreners.

72.—Paths on Lynch Down, Meavy. The road to Sheeps Tor from Meavy branches L. at the top of Lynch Hill, and runs across Lynch Down to Ringmoor Cot. Above this road a couple of paths lead from the gate near the cot to the Cadaford Bridge road ; and a track also runs from the gate down the hill, with the enclosures on the R., to the road at Marchants Cross. This latter track is on the line of the old Abbots' Way (T. 1).

73.—Path at Sheeps Tor. A footpath runs over the common at the foot of Sheeps Tor, on the E. side of the Burrator Lake, to Narrator, whence a short track leads to Nosworthy Bridge.

74.—Paths on Yennadon. Several green paths run over Yennadon, the principal one being a track that leaves the Meavy road near where the lane comes up from Lake ; this path goes northward to Lowery Cross.

75.—*Black Lane, S. One of the most important paths in the southern part of Dartmoor, from the moorman's point of view, is Black Lane, a natural pass extending from a large stream work on a tributary of the Erme to Fox Tor, and forming with the hollow down which that tributary flows below the stream work, a track from Erme Head to the tor named. It runs through the tract of fen bounded on one side by the springs of the Plym, and on the other by the upper waters of the Avon. By means of it the herdsmen are able to drive cattle direct from the pasturage grounds at Green Hill to the slopes in the neighbourhood of the Fox Tor stream. The tributary referred to is usually called Dark Lane, and sometimes the Black Lane Brook, but the true name of it is the Wollake. It falls into the Erme immediately below the source of that river, thus giving the latter a considerable volume ere it has run far on its course. Close to the confluence there is a ford on the Wollake, where it is crossed by the Abbots' Way (T. 1). At the northern end of Black Lane near Fox Tor is the old path from Buckland across the forest (T. 2), so that this pass connects these two tracks of the monks. From the ford the ground on the eastern side of the Wollake is good up to Stony Hole, the tin working already referred to. But above this is the fen, and it is here that Black Lane commences. On the left in ascending, and at the top of this working, is Ducks' Pool, from which one branch of the Wollake issues. The pool is now a boggy hollow, but must once have been a tarn of some considerable size. Black Lane passes the narrow entrance to this hollow, and runs northward. Half a mile further up another gully runs off to the right, and by means of this it is possible for a rider to cross the fen and reach the head of Fish Lake, under Cater's Beam. The Wollake, which is here merely a tiny rivulet, rises not far above where this gully branches off, and beyond its source the pass becomes a shallow trench. At its head the path turns right for a very short distance, then left, and runs into Fox Tôr Gert, beyond which the tor may be seen.

76.—*The Church Way.* From Meripit Hill, and three-quarters of a mile from the Dart at Post Bridge, a road turns from the Moreton highway, and, quitting the forest at Runnage Bridge, goes on to Widecombe. This, there is no doubt, is formed on the ancient track by which the occupants of the forest tenements made their way to the church at that place. In a forester's account of the year 1491 there is a reference to this track. It is there called the Church Way, and is described as leading from a certain tenement on the Walla Brook to the church at Widecombe. Part of this old track still remains. The road runs from Runnage Bridge to Grendon Bridge on the West Webburn, and then ascending to Hill Head, passes Blackaton, turning at the foot of the steep and going down to Bittleford Down, around which it sweeps, and reaches the Ponsworthy and Widecombe lane. But the old track took a more direct course from Blackaton Bridge to the village of Widecombe, and this part is still in use, though not fitted for wheels. It runs between the walls of the enclosures straight up the ascent known in the vicinity as Gore Hill. At the top it enters on the common forming the southern part of the great ridge of Hameldon, where it is joined by a path coming L. from Challacombe (T. 47). Here it strikes off obliquely to the R., and, crossing the down to Church Lane Head, descends into the Widecombe valley, this part of it being very steep. It emerges on the road a short distance from the green north of the church.

77.—*Paths in the neighbourhood of Meripit Hill. To the Grey Wethers and Teign Head. To Fernworthy.* Between Post Bridge and the Warren House Inn several paths branch from the Moreton highway.

A moor road leads from the Stannon Lodges at Post Bridge to Stannon House, and a green track, marked in places by stones, runs by Stannon Tor and over the western shoulder of White Ridge to the Grey Wethers. The ground is good, and it is possible to drive this way. Near these circles there is a gate in the wall of the newtake belonging to Teign Head Farm, and from this a track leads down to the clapper under that solitary dwelling. Inside the gate a branch of the track runs L.; this must be followed by visitors driving towards Cranmere. The newtake is left further on at another gate. From Stannon a footpath runs across Meripit Hill eastward to Stats Bridge. A path leads from Meripit Hill to Fernworthy. It runs N. from the road, close to the enclosures of Higher Meripit, and Stannon Little Newtake, which are L., to Assacombe. Thence down by Assacombe House with the enclosures L., and then on about midway between the Assacombe Brook L., and the Lowton Brook R., to a track which runs down E. of Silkhouse, to a ford on the Teign, near Fernworthy farmhouse. When the river cannot be crossed at the ford the way will be by the bridge just below (Ex. 20). A road, which there is no doubt is formed on an ancient track, runs from the Methodist Chapel at Post Bridge to the way leading to Runnage Bridge. It passes through Lower Meripit, close to which there is a footbridge over the Lury Brook. From the road near Runnage an old path runs through the enclosures to the Warren House Inn. From the inn a path leads to the deserted Wheal Caroline, and another to the Golden Dagger Mine. (See also Ex. 44, 45. T. 44, 46).

*78.—*Drift Lane.* This path runs up by the right bank of the Dart at Post Bridge, and is important as an approach to others, viz., the northern branch of the Lich Path (T. 18) and Cut Lane (T. 79), which latter forms a part of the path, as already mentioned, from Post Bridge to Okehampton (T. 34). Drift Lane leads from the enclosed parts of the moor lying around Post Bridge to the open forest, and forms, as its name denotes, a way by which cattle are driven there from that district. It runs perfectly straight for nearly half a mile, having the river on one side and the Archeton enclosures on the other side. At the north-eastern corner of these it turns a little to the left, and passes up the hill to Broad Down.

*79.—*Cut Lane.* No path in the northern part of Dartmoor is of greater service to the moorman and the hunter than this. Like Black Lane, in the south quarter (T. 75), it forms a pass through the fen, and though this is not entirely, as in the case of the other, a natural one, it is so in great measure. The main track of fen in northern Dartmoor extends from Ockment Hill to the head waters of the West Dart and Cowsic, a distance of five miles, and this can only be crossed on horseback in one place. Two miles below East Dart Head a strip of hard, grassy ground stretches from the river to the summit of the ridge running parallel to it on the west ; and on the further side of this ridge is a larger tract of similar ground extending to the foot of the hill. To the north and to the south of this hard ground is deep fen, and it is evident also that the whole of the flat summit of the ridge was once covered with it. Between these two solid tracts the fen was removed at some early time from the top of the ridge, a wide path, long since covered with grass like the hard ground it unites, thus being formed. This pass is not on the lowest, or flat, part of the ridge, but runs over it where it begins to rise towards the south to form the bold eminence of Cut Hill, the name of which there can be on doubt is derived from this ancient way cut through the fen. Elsewhere [*Gems*, Chap. II.] I have brought forward some evidence to show that Fur Tor, below which the track passes on the western side of the ridge, may also owe its name to it. The part of this path thus artificially formed is marked by two square slabs of granite, one on each side of the way. These are set on little mounds, and are placed a short distance from the edges of the track, which here pursues a north-westerly direction. Fur Tor is seen beyond the combe nearly due west. From the point where the cut terminates in that direction to the foot of the hill near Cut Combe Water, stone posts are placed on tiny cairns at intervals, so that a traveller approaching the pass from the west is able to find his way from the stream named direct to it. This stream runs into the Amicombe, a branch of the Tavy, so that Cut Lane forms a means of communication between the Tavy valley and the valley of the East Dart. It has already been mentioned (T. 34, 78) that this path forms part of a track from Post Bridge to Okehampton ; it also formed part of another from the same place to Lydford, thus affording an alternative way to the Lich Path (T. 18). On reaching Broad Down by Drift Lane, a direction N.W. by N. is followed to the East Dart, which is struck just below a place called Sandy Hole. (There is some reason for supposing that Broad Down was also reached by way of the L. bank of the Dart, that stream being crossed under Hartland Tor). Above Sandy Hole there is a path of sufficient width only for the stream, which here runs between walls formed of boulders, and a path on its right bank. [*Dev. Alps.*, Chap. VII., Ex. 45.] At the head of this pass is Broad Marsh, where is a large stream work, extending up to a point where the Dart turns abruptly to the right, and is joined by a tributary. The approach to Cut Lane is indicated by the latter ; to the left of it in ascending is the strip of hard ground leading to the artificial cut on the ridge. Westward of this ridge is Cut Combe, down the side of which the path runs, as already stated. The entrance to this combe is between the hill from which Fur Tor rises and Little Kneeset, and just without this the Cut Combe Water falls into the Amicombe. Here, on the western, or right bank, of the last-named stream the path to Lydford diverged. It ran across Watern Oke to the Rattle Brook, the direction being almost due west. The stream is crossed at Dead Lake Foot, and that little tributary is followed to its source. The path then runs by a cairn between Hare Tor and Sharp Tor, and descends to the Lyd, either by way of the Doe Tor Brook to the right or by the Walla Brook to the left. In the first case when the Lyd is crossed the path on High Down leading directly to the Dartmoor Inn is reached, and in the second the path running to the moor gate at the end of the short lane near Skit Bridge (T. 27). From the confluence of the Cut Combe Water and the Amicombe the track to Okehampton takes a line due north, following one of the branches of the last-named stream to its source. This is in a hollow between Great Kneeset and that part of Amicombe Hill usually known as Broad Amicombe, and rather more than a mile from the confluence. This hollow, which goes by the name of Broad Amicombe Hole, forms a pass into the valley of the West Ockment. At its northern end, and only about a quarter of a mile from the head of the branch of the Amicombe, another little stream rises, but flows in an opposite direction. It is a tributary of the Ockment, and the way lies by its bank to the point where it joins that river at Kneeset Foot. The old track is all probability then ran down the valley for nearly a mile to Sandy Ford, where it crossed the Ockment, and passing up the hollow down which runs the Lints Tor stream, reached Dinger Plain. By crossing the Ockment at Kneeset Foot, and passing to the S. of Lints Tor, a more direct route might have been followed, but a precipitous hill would then have had to be climbed. Besides, the passage of the river had to be considered, and that the usual way was by the ford there is not much doubt (cf. T. 34). In the survey of the forest bounds of 1609 this is referred to as " Langaford, al's Sandyford." On Dinger Plain is the track running out from Okehampton between Row Tor and West Mil Tor, over which peat is conveyed from the ties, and which in all probability is the ancient way we have been tracing (cf. T. 34).

80.—*Post Bridge to Dunnabridge Pound.* A path runs across the newtakes from Post Bridge to the road at Dunnabridge Pound, and is of much service as forming a direct means of communication between the farms around the former place and those in the valley of the West Dart. It enters the newtakes through a gateway opposite to the end of Drift Lane (T. 78), and passes over Lakehead Hill. At the next gate, which is in the wall between Lakehead Hill and Bellaford Tor Newtake, it crosses the path which we have referred to as forming part of the old Lich Path (T. 18), where it runs between the bridge over the Cherry Brook on the Princetown and Moreton road and Bellaford Bridge. From here the way lies by the side of Bellaford Tor to another gate in the corner of the newtake at the foot of the slope beyond it. It then runs by the walls of other enclosures R. to the pound, where is a gate opening on the highway. The direction of this path is N. and S., and its length about two and a half miles.*

81.—*Post Bridge to Dartmeet, Huccaby, and Hexworthy.* This old track runs down the R. bank of the Dart from the clapper, passing close to the ruined tinners' building known as The Barracks. It then runs by Lakehead and below Bellaford Farm, and still keeping near the river goes on to Lough Tor Hole Farm, where it passes through the yard in front of the house. Then it turns upward towards Huccaby Tor, and leaving that small pile R., descends to the Dartmeet road, which it enters upon close to Huccaby Cottage, which stands near the edge of Snider Park Plantation, L. Formerly it appears to have gone straight down the hill to Huccaby, but that place, as well as Hexworthy and Dartmeet, is now approached by the modern road.

Much more could have been said about these old paths, but sufficient is here given to enable the visitor to utilise them as aids to his rambles over the moor. Many of them have never before received a mention, and there are yet others that could have been named, but it seemed hardly necessary for the present purpose to do so. There are paths, for instance, on the downs of Heytree, Cripdon, Hangher, Greenwell, Wigford, Roborough, and Fernworthy, and in other parts, but they are of little service to the rambler, and in only two or three instances have they any historic interest. The visitor must not forget

---

* This path has lately been closed to the public.

that many of the paths that we have here traced are ill-defined, and cannot always be followed with certainty. Where further directions regarding them appeared necessary they are given in the Excursions or Routes.

PRINCETOWN AND TWO BRIDGES DISTRICT.

DISTANCES. By Road. *ASHBURTON, via* Dartmeet, P.T. 14½ m., T.B. 13; *via* Hexworthy, P.T. 16, T.B. 14½. *BOVEY TRACEY, via* Dartmeet, Widecombe, and Hemsworthy Gate, P.T. 19, T.B. 17½. *BUCKFASTLEIGH, via* Hexworthy, P.T. 15½, T.B. 14. *CHAGFORD*, P.T. 12, T.B. 10½. *CORNWOOD, via* Dousland and Cadaford Bridge, P.T. 12¾, T.B. 14¼. *DARTMEET*, P.T. 6½, T.B. 5. *DOUSLAND*, P.T. 4½, T.B. 6. *EXETER, via* Moreton, P.T. 25½, T.B. 24. *HEXWORTHY*, P.T. 6¾, T.B. 5¼. *HOLNE, via* Hexworthy P.T. 11½, T.B. 10. *IVYBRIDGE, via* Dousland, Cadaford Bridge and Cornwood, P.T. 15¾, T.B. 17¼. *LYDFORD, via* Moor Shop, Harford Bridge, and Skit, P.T. 13½, T.B. 14. *MERIVALE*, P.T. 3¼, T.B. 3¾. *MORETON*, P.T. 13½, T.B. 12. *OKEHAMPTON, via* Moor Shop and Harford Bridge, P.T. 21½, T.B. 22. *PLYMOUTH, via* Roborough, P.T. 14¾, T.B. 16¼. *PLYMPTON, via* Dousland, Cadaford Bridge, and Niel Gate, P.T. 14, T.B. 15½. *POST BRIDGE*, P.T. 5, T.B. 3½. *POUND'S GATE, via* Dartmeet, P.T. 9¾, T.B. 8¼. *RUNDLE STONE*, P.T. 1½, T.B. 2. *SHAUGH, via* Dousland and Cadaford Bridge, P.T. 9½, T.B. 11. *SHEEPSTOR, via* Lowery Cross and Burrator Dam, P.T. 5¾, T.B. 7¼. *SOUTH BRENT, via* Hexworthy and Buckfastleigh, P.T. 20½, T.B. 19; *via* Dousland, Cadaford Bridge, Cornwood and Ivybridge, P.T. 21, T.B. 22½. *TAVISTOCK*, P.T. 7½, T.B. 8. *WARREN HOUSE INN*, P.T. 7¼, T.B. 5¾. *WIDECOMBE, via* Dartmeet and Ponsworthy, P.T. 11½, T.B. 10; *via* Post Bridge and Grendon Cot, P.T. 13, T.B. 11½. *YELVERTON STATION*, P.T. 6, T.B. 7½.

By Rail (from Princetown). *EXETER, via* Plymouth (G.W.) 74 m.; *via* Tavistock (G.W. to Tavistock, thence by L.S.W.) 58. *PLYMOUTH* (G.W.) 21½. *TAVISTOCK* (G.W.) 16. *YELVERTON* (G.W.) 10½.

BY ROAD AND RAIL TO THE CAPITAL OF THE MOOR.

Within the confines of Dartmoor there are several small settlements, two of which, Post Bridge and Hexworthy, have grown up around some of the ancient tenements. Foggin Tor owes its origin, and Merivale its expansion, to the granite quarrying industry, while White Works was called into being by mining enterprise, which has also helped to promote the growth of the two first-named. There are a few others consisting of groups of farmhouses, and there is also the old village of Widecombe. Cultivation has so spread itself throughout the valley in which this settlement is placed, that pastures and woodlands now link it with the in-country, and it appears less deserving of its adjunct than in the days when it was known as Widecombe-in-the-Moor. Still, although it is possible to approach it without actually entering on the commons, it belongs as much to Dartmoor as ever it did. The parish is conterminous with the forest for a distance of nearly four miles, and there has always been a connection between them. A larger settlement than any of those named is that of Lee Moor, in the parish of Shaugh, the seat of an extensive china clay industry, and a larger and more important still is Princetown, which is justly regarded as the capital of the moor. Time was when Lydford held that distinction. There the mother church was situated, and there was the castle in which the forest courts were held, and in later days the Duchy courts. But when Princetown sprang into being these were removed to it, and a church being built, journeys to Lydford or to Widecombe became less frequent. Interest centred round the new town, which speedily became the largest settlement on the moor.

In the section dealing with the tracks we have stated that the roads on the moor were formed on the lines of ancient ways (T. 44). One ran from Tavistock to Moreton and Chagford, and from this there were branches to Ashburton and Widecombe, and it was also joined by one from Plymouth. The latter is now the present Plymouth and Princetown road. It enters on Roborough Down at the sixth milestone from the first-named town, and leaves it just beyond the ninth. All the way across this fine open common there is a good view of the western frontier of Dartmoor, the grouping of the tors above the Walkham Valley, and Sheeps Tor, above the valley of the Mew, being particularly noticeable. Yelverton is delightfully placed between the eighth and ninth milestone, the residences being situated on the verge of the down. One mile beyond it is Dousland, where the road is crossed by another running from Plympton and Ivybridge to Tavistock. About a mile from Dousland the road passes under the Princetown Railway, and shortly after enters Dartmoor. It climbs the shoulder of Peak Hill, a grand prospect opening towards the west as the higher ground is reached. For the next 3½ miles it runs over Walkhampton Common, passing near to Leedon Tor, which rises on the L., and Black Tor, which is seen on the R., with Hart Tor just across the shallow valley below it. Crossing Devil's Bridge the road climbs the steep ascent from the hollow, and soon after reaches the limits of the common in this direction and enters the forest. A granite post on the right of the way serves as a bondmark of the latter. Princetown is only a little way beyond, being situated just within the forest bounds.

The Tavistock road leaves the town by way of Vigo Bridge, or by the Abbey Bridge and Dolvin road, and passing the entrance to Mount Tavy, runs on to Moor Shop, where it is crossed by a road from Horrabridge to Harford Bridge and Peter Tavy. Here the ascent of Pork Hill commences, the commons being entered before the top of it is reached, and at about 2¾ miles from Tavistock. The road now runs across the common belonging to the parish of Whitchurch, with Cocks Tor and the Staple Tors to the L., and Vixen Tor R. The Walkham is crossed at Merivale Bridge, 4¼ miles, and Walkhampton Common is entered. Here a long ascent to the Rundle Stone commences, the dominant object in the view being Great Mis Tor, which rises grandly above the river valley on the L. At Rundle Stone, 6 miles, the road enters the forest, and turning R. runs past the prison to Princetown. The church is 7 miles from Tavistock.

The Moretonhampstead road crosses the Bovey river a little over

two miles from the town, and then ascends Worm Hill, after passing
over which it reaches Beetor Cross, 3 miles. Here it is crossed by the
Ashburton and Chagford road. Exactly a mile further on is Moor
Gate, where the commons are entered. Its former presence is indicated
by the name only, for no gate is now to be seen there. A little further
on a branch of the Bovey is crossed, and at the top of the hill beyond
it the road is joined by one coming from Chagford, and which enters
the moor about three quarters of a mile from the junction. For the
next mile or more the road runs over a fairly level piece of common,
and enters the forest shortly before the Warren House Inn is reached.
Further on it crosses Stats Brook, passes over Meripit Hill, and descends
to Post Bridge, where the East Dart is crossed, $8\frac{1}{2}$ miles from Moreton.
From the river the road runs up between Archeton R., and Lakehead
Hill L., and after crossing the Cherry Brook, passes in succession the
Powder Mills Cottages, Cherry Brook Farm, and Crockern Tor, and
descends to Two Bridges. Here the Princetown road branches L.,
the one to the R. leading to Tavistock.

The road from Ashburton to Two Bridges runs by way of North
Street to Holne Bridge, which is two miles from the town. It then
ascends Holne Chase Hill, having the chase and the Buckland Woods
to the right. At the top of the hill a road branches left, being joined
a little further on by one from Buckfastleigh. This runs through the
village of Holne to the moor gate, about a mile distant, and crosses
Holne Moor to the forest, which it enters at Saddle Bridge, on the
Wo Brook. The view is particularly fine, the tors above the gorge of
the Dart here showing to great advantage. Not far from the gate is
the Paignton storage reservoir, the formation of which has turned the
Wennaford Valley into a Lake. Further on the hollow known as
Hangman's Pit is passed, and afterwards Combestone Tor, to the R.,
a very steep hill following. At its foot flows the Wo Brook, and about
a mile further on is Hexworthy, where, at the Forest Inn, the road
turns down the hill to the R., being here known as Jolly Lane. Crossing the West Dart at Hexworthy Bridge it runs by the little chapel of
St. Raphael's at Huccaby, and ascending the hill joins the road from
Ashburton to Two Bridges more usually followed.

The last-named road having climbed Holne Chase Hill, two miles
from Ashburton, descends to the Dart, which it crosses at New Bridge,
and enters the commons. Here there is a steep ascent to the hamlet
of Pound's Gate, where the enclosed country is reached, to be left again,
however, about a mile further on, when the road skirts Sherberton
Common. Turning L. at Ouldsbroom Cross it passes between Yar
Tor Down and Dartmeet Hill, and descends to Dartmeet Bridge, on
crossing which it enters the forest. Climbing the hill with the estate
of Brimpts on the R., it reaches the gate where the road previously
mentioned comes up from Huccaby, and then runs above the valley
of the West Dart to Dunnabridge. A mile further on it crosses Cherry
Brook, and in another mile and a half reaches Two Bridges, being
joined by the Moreton road on the brow of the hill above that place.

The objects passed on these roads, and on others in different parts
of the moor, are noticed more fully in the Excursions.

The Princetown Railway branches from Yelverton, on the Plymouth and Launceston line. It was opened in 1882, and from a point
about midway between Yelverton and Dousland Stations follows very

nearly the route taken by a tramroad constructed in the earlier part of the nineteenth century.

On leaving Dousland the railway is carried over Yennadon Down, which it nearly encircles in order to reach a point on the hill leading to Walkhampton Common by an easy gradient. Soon after the train enters on the down a good view of the valley of the Mew is presented, one object in it that will not fail to catch the eye being the tower of the little church of Meavy. On the further side of the valley is Calisham Down, with Wigford Down, the common above the Dewer Stone, beyond it. To the L. of the first-named is Lynch Down, backed by Shaugh Moor, and then the bold sweep of Ringmoor Down comes into view. To the L. is the giant mass of Sheeps Tor, with the village nestling at its foot, and at the further end of the opening between the down and the tor, is seen Gutter Tor, with a green path running up the common towards it. Below is the narrow Burrator Gorge, with the dam thrown across it for the purpose of storing the waters of the Mew, which, filling the valley between Peak Hill and Sheeps Tor, present the appearance of a true lake. This fine sheet of water, the storage reservoir for the town of Plymouth, is noticed in our Excursions from Yelverton. At its head is seen Down Tor, and the more distant Cramber Tor, while, rising above it to the L., are Lether Tor* and Sharp Tor, the first-mentioned being particularly striking. After passing a small plantation the upper valley of the Mew, and the Newleycombe Valley to the R. of it, are seen, with another fine tor near Down Tor. This is Combe Tor, and behind it rises the lofty height of Eylesbarrow. On Lowery Siding being passed the view is lost, but another speedily discloses itself. After crossing the Plymouth and Princetown road a wide stretch of hill and dale, farm lands and woods, with distant heights, is seen to the L. of the railway as the train advances. A conspicuous object in the near view is Walkhampton Church, situated on a hill near the village. This is seen from many points on the railway as the train proceeds, and from both sides of it, consequent upon the windings of the line. Just here, although the train has to attain an elevation of about 1,400 feet, there is a down gradient. This was planned with a view to the more easily bringing up the train when running from Princetown to Dousland, or stopping a carriage, or truck, should such happen to become detached from a train proceeding to the first-named place. At this point the line draws nearer to Walkhampton Church, then all at once turns away from it, and the train passes out on to the open moor.

The beautiful valley of the Walkham now partially reveals itself, the glimpses obtained from certain points to which the winding of the line bring the visitor speaking eloquently of its hidden beauties. Far down below is a wealth of trees, and where these cease to climb from the wooded depths, the granite-strewn commons are seen. On the down above its further side is Pu Tor, here a very prominent object, and far away beyond it the church-crowned summit of Brent Tor. Further up, and overhanging a small lateral valley not far from

---

* The *th* has the heavy sound, the name being pronounced like the word *leather*. Indeed, in its earlier form it appears as *Ledder*, the true sound of which would be the same as *leather*, *dd* being actually the heavy *th*.

Merivale, is the curiously-shaped mass of Vixen Tor, with Cocks' Tor and the Staple Tors behind it, 'and to the R. the lofty Mis Tor, the monarch of this part of the moor, while much nearer to us is King Tor. Passing Routrendle the line sweeps out around Inga Tor, below which the ground is rather marshy, and then making a great bend to the right runs up to Yes Tor Green. Here, at the turn, the old tramroad, which made a rather longer sweep, will be noticed, with the little bridge that carried it over the brook. This is just below the pile known as Fur Tor. On the slope above, to the N.E., and exactly a quarter of a mile distant, the visitor may see the railway on which he is travelling. But that portion of it is more than 200 feet above him, and it is necessary for the train to make a journey of two and a half miles to attain that elevation. The line runs out under the granite quarries of the Messrs. Pethick Bros., and from here Inga Tor is again seen, also Walkhampton Church, and there is a fine view of the Cornish hills. Near King Tor, around which the railway runs, doubling back upon itself, the tram road is seen in several places where the line has left it a few yards on one side. Here the valley near Merivale and Mis Tor Moor is in full view, and the menhir on Long Ash Hill, near the double stone rows, can be plainly discerned.

The Red Cottages—a misnomer since their colour has been changed to black—the cottages at Rundle Stone, with Hollow Tor on the hill to the right, are also in sight. Passing the Royal Oak siding and the Foggin Tor Quarries, the line is carried by White Rock along the slope seen from below, and now the visitor looks down upon it as it winds round Yes Tor Green. Inga Tor is also seen once more, and to the L. of it the upper part of the tower of Walkhampton Church.

And now quite another part of the moor is opened up, although many tors seen during the first stage of the journey again become visible. But they are looked at from a different side, and in many instances their outlines are not the same. Sheeps Tor and Down Tor, Lether, Sharp, and Cramber are all in sight, as well as Gutter Tor. Further away is Trowlesworthy Tor, on Lee Moor. In the direction of Walkhampton Leedon Tor is seen, and not very far from the railway is Black Tor, with Hart Tor just beyond it. Soon the Plymouth road is noticed where it crosses the hollow at Devil's Bridge, and a short distance further on the station, close to which is one of the stones marking the forest boundary, is reached.

Princetown was called into existence by the building of a war prison below North Hisworthy, the foundation stone being laid on the 20th March, 1806, by Sir Thomas Tyrwhitt, who had suggested its location here. Sir Thomas built Tor Royal, and had great hopes of reclaiming Dartmoor. After 1816 the prison was untenanted for some time, but was subsequently used as a naphtha factory, for the production of which large quantities of peat were cut on Holming Beam. In the meanwhile the little town fell into decay, and it was only when the prison was turned into a depot for convicts that its fortunes began to revive. This was in 1850. Since that date it has gradually improved, and now fully justifies its title of the capital of the moor. The church was built and fitted up by the French and American prisoners.

The hamlet of Two Bridges is pleasantly situated in the valley of the West Dart, a mile and a half from Princetown. The trees under Bear Down near by were planted by Mr. Edmund Bray, a solicitor, of

Tavistock, who began operations here about 1780. Bear Down is probably *bear dun*, the promontory hill. The semi-circular belt at the foot of the hill is known as the Cowsic Horse Shoe. The inn, the forerunner of the present hotel, was built by Judge Buller, of Prince Hall.]

[The Princetown and Two Bridges, Hexworthy and Post Bridge Districts, embrace the whole of the central part of the moor.]

EXCURSIONS FROM PRINCETOWN AND TWO BRIDGES.

Tracks in the vicinity, Nos. 1 to 15, 18, 56, 75, 80. [The visitor is advised to read up these, as having been already described, they hereafter only receive mention. The numbers are appended thus : (T. 1) ; Excursions are numbered (Ex. 2 or S. Ex. 3) ; Routes (R. 4) ; and Cranmere Routes (C.R. 5). It will also be well to consult the section in which the Important Points and Objects of Interest in each District are given. The Excursions are mostly within a radius of three miles of Princetown. The commons westward of the Walkham are noticed in the Tavistock District, and the neighbourhood of Sheeps Tor and Walkhampton in the Yelverton District.]

North Hisworthy Tor. Before setting out on our Excursions from Princetown and Two Bridges we shall ascend the hill rising above the first-named place to the tor locally known as North Hessary, as an excellent view of the district over which our rambles are to extend is to be obtained from that breezy height. We therefore leave the main street by the turning opposite to the school, and passing through a gate, make our way up the hill, keeping close to the wall of the enclosures on the right. This will lead us directly to the tor, just before reaching which we find ourselves walking over the ground traversed by the perambulators who viewed the bounds of the forest in 1240. The boundary line is drawn from South Hisworthy to North Hisworthy, and here is marked by some granite posts of comparatively recent erection, which may be seen from the point we have now attained. The tor is by no means striking in appearance, but as a forest bond-mark mentioned in the return to the perambulation made in the thirteenth century, it is not altogether devoid of interest. The visitor will, however, find his chief reward in the wonderful view commanded from its summit. No less than about sixty tors are to be seen, besides a number of important hills. As Simon Renard read from the battlements of the White Tower the history of England, so one may look down from the crest of Hisworthy and read the history of modern Dartmoor. Northward and southward are the untamed hills, rising grim and bare ; vast solitudes where nothing of man's work is seen. Between these wild tracts is the more sheltered part, where the settler has formed his enclosures, and planted his few trees and made his roads. Immediately below, the prison and the town that grew up around it, and on the other side the iron way that has penetrated to the verge of the forest. Man has done something here, but when the beholder again looks upon the dusky sweeps that roll away into the blue distance, he realises how little it is.

In order to enumerate the tors seen from this hill, and at the same time to indicate their situations, it will be most convenient to

commence with those on the common north of the road leading to
Tavistock. If, therefore, we look in a W.N.W. direction we shall see
this road winding up the side of the Walkham Valley. Immediately
to the R. of it is Little Staple Tor, a small group of rocks, and R. of
that again Mid Staple Tor, with Cocks' Tor rising behind it, the latter
being situated at the southern extremity of a long hill with a rounded
outline.* In a line with these tors, on the slope of Hisworthy and
not far from us, is Hollow Tor. The fine tor to the R. of Mid Staple
Tor is Great Staple Tor, and R. of this is Roose Tor. Between these
two is seen the distant Brent Tor, with the little church on its summit.
Beyond the dip R. of Roose Tor is Black Down, a fine common mostly
in the parish of Mary Tavy, and R. of that is White Tor, or Whittor,
as it is always called. The line of junction between the granite and
the altered rocks runs through the shallow valley beyond the ridge
on which rise the Staple Tors and Roose Tor. Cocks' Tor and White
Tor are therefore not within the granite area ; they are composed of
trap rock, and the difference in form between them and the granite
hills is very striking, particularly when they are seen from Black
Down. Right of Roose Tor, and on the nearer side of the Walkham
Valley, is Great Mis Tor, one of the finest of the rock-piles on Dartmoor.
Just below is Little Mis Tor, a square mass of granite, and quite near
to us, at the foot of Hisworthy, is Rundle Stone Tor.

To the R. of Mis Tor, and in a direction a little W. of N. we look
away to the ridge above the Rattle Brook, from which Hare Tor,
Sharp Tor, and Great Links Tor rise in succession. The first-named is
of a pyramidal form, and will be easily recognised, as also will Links
Tor, the rocks of which rise to a considerable height above the turf.
The rounded hill below it, and three miles nearer to us, is Standon,
or Stannon, as it is usually called ; on its summit is a cairn presenting
from this distance the appearance of a small mound. A little to the
R. of Links Tor, the Dunnagoat Tors are seen, and R. of these is
Amicombe Hill. From Links Tor the ground dips towards the north,
where there is a great opening in the hills. This marks the deep gorge
of the West Ockment, and above it to the R. is High Willes, the most
elevated of the Dartmoor eminences. This height is exactly nine miles
from the point on which we stand as measured on the map.

In a line with Amicombe Hill, but much nearer to us, being in fact
only four miles distant, is Walkham Head, and if we look beyond
this, and to the R. of it, we shall see the rocks of Fur Tor, with Cut
Hill rising still further R. Peeping over its shoulder, far away in a
direction N.N.E., is Newtake, the hill near Cranmere and East Dart
Head. Less than two miles south of the summit of Cut Hill, and in a
line with it and our standpoint, is Cowsic Head. On one side of this,
the L., we may see Conies Down Tor, and on the other side Devil's Tor.
Quite close to the latter is Bear Down Man, but this can only be made
out with the aid of a glass.

Rising against the sky to the R. of Devil's Tor is Row Tor, and
under it, but more than a mile nearer to us, is Lydford Tor, at the
northern end of Bear Down. To the R., but further away, is Crow
Tor, and then the Bear Down Tors, with White or Whitten Tor, seen
between. It should be noticed that in Row Tor and Crow Tor the

---

*This is known as Cocks' Tor Hill.

" ow " has the same sound as in crowd. One form of spelling the latter is Crough. To the R. of the Bear Down Tors, and on the ridge above the West Dart, we see Longaford and Littaford Tors, the former rising like a pyramid from the down.

Beyond these tors, and some four miles further away, is White Ridge, with Waters Down to the right of it. Near the latter the Moreton road is seen climbing the shoulder of Meripit Hill. Below us, and only two and a half miles distant, is Crockern Tor, close to which the Moreton road is also seen, as well as the Ashburton road between Two Bridges and Prince Hall. Further distant, E. by N., is Bellaford Tor, and bounding the view in this direction is the huge ridge of Hameldon.

Three quarters of a mile from Bellaford Tor is Lough Tor—Lafter Tor, as it is generally called—and this is in full view to the R. of the former. Far away beyond these is seen Chinkwell Tor and Hey Tor, with the steep road leading up from the village of Widecombe. To the R. of Hey Tor is Saddle Tor, and R. of that Rippon Tor.

Much nearer than Rippon Tor, but seen a little to the R. of it, is Corn Down, with Yar Tor, the fine height that rises above Dartmeet ; and in the distance above the hanging woods that line the valley of the Dart, the granite boss of Buckland Beacon, and amid the trees below, the crag called Auswell Rock.* The road winding up the hill from Dartmeet is plainly visible, and above it Sharp Tor, and the crest of its neighbour, Mil Tor.

And now we look upon a part of the moor westward of the Dart. Four and a half miles away in a direction E. by S. the road running from Sherberton Bridge to Gobbet Plain is seen, and in a line with it and nearly three miles further distant, Bench Tor, on Holne Moor. Right of this we see the Holne road, where it climbs the steep hill above the eastern bank of the Wo Brook. The hill to the right of this is Down Ridge, above Hexworthy, and the next the swelling eminence of Cater's Beam, rising from the fen beyond Fox Tor, the piles of which are placed about midway up the hill-side. The direction of the tor is about S.E.

Peeping over the hill that bounds the view to the R. of Fox Tor are some distant heights. The first of these is Eastern Whitaburrow, and the next Western Whitaburrow, the highland between them being the summit of Bush Meads, at the foot of which the Avon runs. A little further to the R. is the prominent hill known as Three Barrows, eight and a half miles distant.

Less than two miles from our standpoint is South Hisworthy Tor. Its direction is S.E., and it is in a line with Eastern Whitaburrow.

Looking in a direction S.S.E. we notice a combe on the hillside beyond the first ridge. This is Langcombe Bottom, through which runs a tributary of the Plym ; it falls into that stream at Plym Steps. The high land on this side of the combe is Eylesbarrow, and the distant point to the right of it is Shell Top, a fine height overlooking the in-country in the neighbourhood of Cornwood. On the side of the hill under Shell Top, and a mile nearer to us, is Hen Tor. This rises above the Plym, and gives name to one of the warrens in the valley through which that stream runs. Rather over two miles nearer, and in a line

---

* This is sometimes known as Hazel Tor.

with it, is Combeshead Tor, so named from its situation at the head of the Dean Combe valley.

To the right of Combeshead Tor is Down Tor, and in a line with it, a mile and a half beyond, is Gutter Tor, a pile at the eastern end of Ringmoor Down, and overlooking Ditsworthy Warren. The same distance beyond Gutter Tor, and in a line with it, are Great and Little Trowlesworthy Tors, which are situated on the common lands belonging to the parish of Shaugh. The name of these tors is pronounced as though it were spelt without the first " w," and with the " o " long. The high land to the R. of these tors is that part of Shaugh Moor known as Saddlesborough.

But the most striking tor in this direction is Sheeps Tor, whose giant mass is only three and a half miles distant. Its direction is S. by W. Below it, to the R., is the Meavy Valley, above the western side of which we see Lether Tor, and close to it one of the numerous Sharp Tors on the moor.

Now we must let our eyes wander a little to the L., and on the common below us we shall observe three tors. The first, which lies S. by E., is Cramber Tor; the next, and nearer to us, is Hart Tor, always called Harter Tor, which, however, is probably only a duplication of the final syllable; and the other is Black Tor, which is quite near to the Plymouth road. The latter is in a direct line with Sheeps Tor.

Once more we look towards Sharp Tor, and on the common to the R. of this shall notice another pile. This is Leedon Tor, and below it to the R. is Inga Tor, close to which is the Princetown Railway. Nearer to us, to the R., is Swell Tor, and further in that direction, and less than a mile and a half from where we stand, the fine pile of King Tor.

Below King Tor is the beautiful valley of the Walkham, and beyond this, and nearly in a line with the pile named, we see Pu Tor, conspicuously placed on the common near Sampford Spiney. Right of this is Feather Tor, and then the curiously-shaped mass of Vixen Tor, and near it the Tavistock road, where we began our survey.

Although many of the Dartmoor hills attain an elevation of 1,700 or 1,800 feet, and some an even greater height, there is not one from which an uninterrupted view of half-a-dozen miles in every direction can be obtained. There is always another hill rising within that distance to obstruct the range of vision. Even High Willes and Cut Hill are not exceptions.

The view from North Hisworthy—or Ysfother, as the perambulators of 1240 have it*—cannot fail to impress, on account of its extent. But while it reveals so much of the moor it fails to convey that idea of it which is obtained from High Willes, or Great Links Tor, and a few other prominent hills. The wilder parts of the moor are hidden from the beholder on Hisworthy, or when glimpses of such are afforded it is of spots too far off for the nature of them to be properly estimated. He cannot look down as from the heights mentioned, or as he may from Three Barrows and from Ryders' Hill, upon a scene of wildness

---

* By the jury who surveyed the bounds of the forest in 1609 the tor is mentioned as Hisworthie. In 1786 another jury refer to it by the same name, but with the modern terminal " y."

and desolation ; the eye has to range over the enclosed parts of the moor before it can rest upon the heathery slopes that cultivation has not disturbed. He sees, indeed, scarcely anything of the remote parts of the south quarter of the forest, and not much of the recesses of the north.

Westward of Hisworthy, beyond the commons, is a wonderful view of the south-western part of Devon, with the Channel off Plymouth, and of East Cornwall. Pasture lands and woods, towns and villages, make up the picture over which the eye wanders till it lights upon the Cornish hills that rise up against the western sky.

On the slope of Hisworthy, and not far from the tor, is a rainguage, placed on the line bounding the water-collecting area of the Burrator Lake. This suggests the question of rainfall, one into which it will perhaps be wise not to enter. A town cannot very well occupy so elevated a site as Princetown, which is placed about 1,400 feet above sea level, without receiving its full share of moisture, but it may perhaps be some consolation to the visitor if we assure him that by far the greater proportion of the rain is reserved for the inhabitants : during the holiday season blue skies are usually above it.

And now, having looked upon so many of the Dartmoor tors, we will bid adieu to Hisworthy, with its overhanging rock, and set out on our way to make closer acquaintance with them, or at least with such of them as present features more than ordinarily interesting, as well as to examine others not seen from its crest. But, though we bid the tor good-bye, we shall not readily forget it, for much that we see will recall our visit to it. Often, too, our eyes will rest upon it when we are in distant parts of the moor, so that it will be neither out of sight nor out of mind.

(It was thought that to burden this description with references would be inconvenient to the reader ; the Index will show where a notice of each tor named is to be found).

[From Two Bridges the visitor will take the left hand road to Princetown, passing the Ockery on his way, but he will find it a good plan to return by the Tavistock road. To do this he will descend the northern slope of Hisworthy, keeping near to the wall, to Rundle Stone (Ex. 1), whence the highway from Tavistock runs due E. to Two Bridges (2 m.) Just before reaching the road Rundle Stone Tor is passed ; the tor seen to the left, and not far off, in descending the side of Hisworthy, is Hollow Tor.]

Ex. 1. *The Soldiers' Pond—Devil's Bridge—Stone Rows near Sharp Tor—Routrendle—Yes Tor Bottom—Ward Bridge—Okel Tor—Merivale Bridge—Mining Houses on the Walkham—Merivale Antiquities—Rundle Stone. About 12 miles from Princetown.* Add $3\frac{1}{2}$ m. if from Two Bridges.

Among the interesting objects in the vicinity of Princetown not a few are to be found on Walkhampton Common, and to a brief examination of some of the more striking of these we shall first devote our attention. For the present our ramble will extend only over that part of the common lying between the Plymouth road, the Tavistock road, and the Walkham river. Other divisions of it will be noticed in furture excursions. We leave Princetown by the first-named highway, and shortly after passing the corner of the enclosures R., where the old path known as the Frenchmen's Road branches (T. 5), shall reach one of the row of stones marking the forest boundary where it runs from South Hisworthy to North Hisworthy Tor. Here we leave the ancient royal hunting-ground and enter upon Walkhampton Common. About 200 yards further on, and L. of the road, is an object associated with one of Dartmoor's sad memories. It is a small hollow filled with water, and surrounded by a bank rising above the level of the common, which goes by the name of the Soldier's Pond, and marks the spot where a corporal of the 7th Royal Fusiliers perished in the snow, in February, 1853. The bodies of two privates who were accompanying him were found at a spot known as Double Waters, where a little stream runs under the road. The event is recorded on a tablet in Princetown Church.

The road now descends into a hollow where it crosses the springs of the Mew at Devil's Bridge. The name suggests a legend, but in reality became attached to the spot in a very prosaic manner. The bridge, which is merely a culvert, was built by a labourer who rejoiced, or otherwise, in the sobriquet of Devil. That is all; "story, I have none to tell." His Santanic Majesty has left his name in other places on Dartmoor, but not at this particular spot.

On the slope above Devil's Bridge, that is to the N.W. and W. of it, are a number of hut circles. One group is close to the railway. In connection with the other there is a pound, overlooking Yes Tor Bottom. In this combe fragments of a vessel of highly glazed ware were discovered a few years ago under some slag, and also the bottom of a cooking-pot, as well as sherds and charcoal.

Black   Lether   Sharp
Tor.   Tor.   Tor.

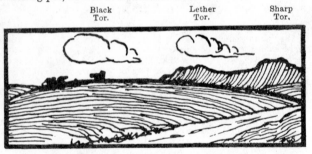

FROM DOUBLE WATERS, LOOKING S.W.

Proceeding on our way we soon reach Double Waters, which is about half a mile from the hollow. Here we notice Black Tor, a short distance across the common to the L. Near it are some prehistoric antiquities, and also an extensive stream work with two mining houses, which are noticed in our next excursion. West of Double Waters, and about a quarter of a mile from it, are several hut circles; in fact, these ancient ruined dwellings are exceedingly numerous in that part of the common now under notice.

As we pass on, we shall be struck with the bold appearance of two tors immediately in front of us. The one L. is the principal pile of

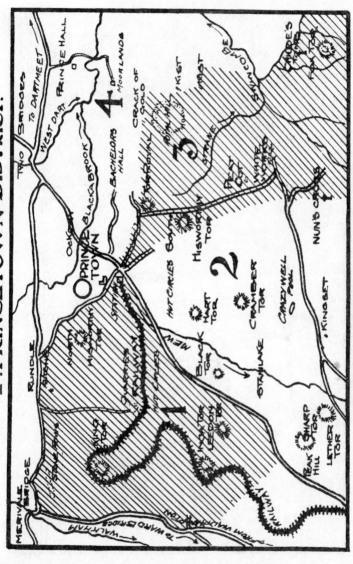

EXCURSIONS 1, 2, 3, 4.

1. PRINCETOWN DISTRICT.

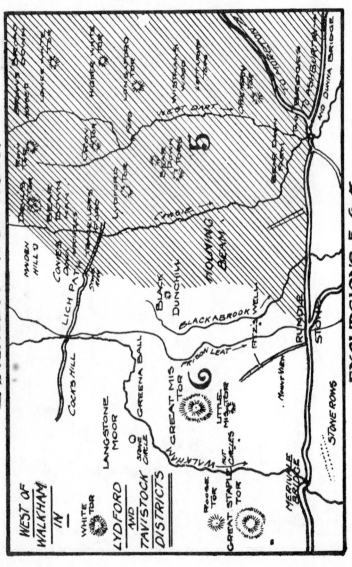

Lether Tor ; the other is Sharp Tor, which has a rather greater elevation. R., and much nearer to us, is Leedon Tor, consisting of several
fine groups of rocks in which the granite is fantastically piled. Looking
back in a northerly direction we see the pound just mentioned. It is
situated on the slope below the railway, where the latter begins to hide
itself behind the hill on the nearer side of which are the granite quarries.
Below us, L., are the enclosures of Stanlake Farm, the house itself
also being visible. On the hill beyond it is Cramber Tor (Ex. 2), and
across the valley to the R. of the farm, is Down Tor (Ex. 2, 38), with
the fine mass of Sheeps Tor (Ex. 38) still further R.

At a point about 2¼ miles from Princetown our road begins to
ascend the flank of Peak Hill. Here it is crossed by a track (T. 4)
coming up in front of us from the direction of Walkhampton, and
running down the hill L. to Stanlake. Half mile further on we reach
the twelfth milestone from Plymouth. This is known as Goad's Stone,
and on the upper half of the face are some markings, but they are not
readily distinguishable. Passing up the hill we soon reach a pond on
the L. of the road, on the brink of which is a double stone row. It is
in a very ruined condition, but may be traced for some distance. It
appears to terminate at a boulder, but is really continued, as a careful
examination will show, to the remains of a kistvaen at its northern
end. Near it is also a single row. From the pond, which, by the way,
has never been known to be dry, we may ascend Sharp Tor and the
summit of Peak Hill, the view from which points is exceedingly fine,
and is noticed in our Excursions from Yelverton. (Ex. 39).

In his progress towards Sharp Tor from Double Waters the rambler
will probably have noticed a reave running from the pile down the hill
towards the road. From our station near the pond we shall, on looking north-eastward, perceive another of these objects on the left. It
runs across the track we saw at the foot of the ascent, and like the
former, climbs the hill capped by Leedon Tor. These reaves have
been said to extend for a very considerable distance ; one of them,
indeed, as far as Chagford. If the visitor considers that a hiatus of a
few miles here and there does not render this doubtful, and is quite
ready to believe, if he picks up a line anywhere to the north or south
of the point at which all traces were lost, that he is still following the
same reave, he may, if he cares for a long tramp, satisfy himself that it
really does go to Chagford. It may, therefore, be as well to inform
him that it is the Sharp Tor reave that was once said to lead to that
moorland town, although it is highly probable that if he chooses the
other the result of his endeavours will be precisely the same.

Hut circles occur between the track before-named and the summit
of Leedon Hill. To the fine rocks crowning that eminence we shall
now make our way, and strike thence towards Inga Tor, which bears
N.W., and is close to the Princetown Railway. When about 300 yards
from the last-named tor, and in a direct line between the two, we shall
come upon a kistvaen surrounded by a circle of stones about 20 feet
in diameter. Both are unfortunately in a dilapidated condition.
The cover of the kist is four feet in length, and nearly three feet in
width. Turning southward towards the railway we shall direct our
steps to a crossing-place to which two white gates give access, and
which forms an approach to Routrendle, a moor farm in full view
from the road at Goad's Stone. On reaching the further side of the

railway we shall follow a road that will lead us to the farmhouse. This we leave on the L., and shall shortly regain the open common, not far from Inga Tor, which we see rising immediately above the line. On passing this pile, the rocks of which are poised in a similar manner to those of Leedon Tor, the line makes a bend towards the east, and crossing the lower end of Yes Tor Bottom,* turns again to the west, and runs out to King Tor.

[This spot may be reached from Princetown direct by following the road to Devil's Bridge, and then striking up over the common westward, with the railway on the R., or by crossing the bridge near the station from the Frenchmen's road (T. 5) and then turning L. If the latter route is followed the visitor will pass under the line at the first cattle creep he comes to, where is a little stream. From this point he will see the railway far down below, as it sweeps round towards Inga Tor. He must then make for it, keeping well to the R. Should the way by Devil's Bridge be chosen, the railway will be similarly seen below.

From Yes Tor Bottom the rambler may make his way around King Tor, noticing Little King Tor on the L., to the Royal Oak level, by taking the railway for his guide. He will keep it on his R., crossing it on reaching the tor if he wishes to ascend the pile. If he desires first to see the quarries he will ascend the hill above the line, whence he may look down upon them. Granite quarrying on this part of Dartmoor commenced on the opening of the Plymouth and Dartmoor Railway in 1823. [100 *Years*, Chap. III.] From the Royal Oak level the visitor may return to Princetown either by way of the Red Cottages and Rundle Stone, or by following the line to the station. If the former route be chosen he will make his way to the cottages, which are seen near by, and passing them will gain the high road from Tavistock, just above the Mission Room. Directions for reaching Princetown from this point are given at the end of the present excursion.]

Making our way over the common from Routrendle, with the wall of the enclosures on our L., we shortly reach a moor gate opening upon a lane. This we descend, and shall soon find that it is crossed by another, which comes up from Walkhampton and runs on to Merivale. Here we turn R., the latter now becoming our road, unless it be desired to visit Ward Bridge before proceeding up the valley, in which case we continue to descend the hill. The bridge, which is not far distant, is situated in one of the most charming parts of the valley of the Walkham, and is noticed in our excursions from Tavistock (Ex. 7).

At a distance of less than ½ m. from the point where the lanes intersect each other we shall reach Whithill Farm, where the road crosses the Yes Tor Brook by a clapper of two openings. It is of comparatively modern date, and presents nothing remarkable. Beyond this we pass Davy Town Farm (see *Town* in the list of terms),

---

* Apparently a corruption of East Tor. Yes Tor Green, below the bottom, is shown on a map of Sir Thomas Tyrwhitt's projected railway as Easter Green. The date of this is 1818. Here is Crip Tor Farm, and adjoining it are the ruins of another Dartmoor homestead.

when our road becomes exceedingly rough. But we shall regard the inconvenience of traversing it as a very light matter when we arrive at Okel Tor Gate,* for we shall then have reached one of the most beautiful of the rock piles of Dartmoor. [*Gems*, Chap. XXI.] The gate, which is at the top of a slight ascent, is hung to the rocks of the tor, and, having passed through it, we find ourselves in their midst. The piles do not rise high above the ground, and there is nothing of the grandeur that belongs to such granite crowns as Mis Tor, or Staple Tor, or Hound Tor ; but the masses are so delightfully shrouded in dwarf oaks and mountain ash, tufts of heather, and patches of the bright green whortleberry plants, that they present an appearance that cannot fail to enchant the beholder. In place of sternness we have beauty ; the rugged is lost in the softening effect of the foliage that so happily mingles with the weather-stained rocks. A number of tors are in view, and away to the south, beyond the farm lands, rise the heights that look down upon Plymouth Sound. Beneath us is the charming Walkham Valley, but the length of our present excursion will prevent us from visiting it now. To do so it will be better to proceed by the road from Princetown to Merivale (R. 1), and on reaching that place to follow the directions given in Excursion 7.

Leaving Okel Tor, with its drapery of living green, we continue on our way, and soon the sound of falling water strikes upon the ear. Coming down from the moor in the neighbourhood of Rundle Stone, the Long Ash Brook here crosses our track on its way to join the Walkham. The road is carried over it by a clapper, which, though not of great size, is yet an excellent example of these rude bridges. The banks of the stream being so thickly covered with bushes little of the structure can be seen in crossing, but a good view of it is to be obtained from a point a few yards below it on the southern side. The clapper has two openings, and the centre pier and buttresses are formed of massive stones. Just beyond we reach Long Ash Farm, and shortly afterwards find ourselves on the Princetown and Tavistock road, near Merivale Bridge. Our walk from the cross lanes has been a rough one, but it has brought us through some of the finest Dartmoor border scenery. [If the visitor does not desire to go to Merivale he may strike up across the enclosures from Long Ash Farm to the common on which the stone rows shortly to be noticed are situated. The distance is very short.]

Merivale Bridge spans the Walkham, which stream here forms the boundary between Walkhampton Common and the common lands belonging to the parish of Whitchurch. The hamlet of Merivale is situated in the latter parish, and consists of a roadside house of entertainment called the Dartmoor Inn, a few cottages, a modern Wesleyan Chapel, and a row of dwellings erected during recent years for the men working in the adjoining Tor Granite Quarries of Messrs. Duke and Company. The stone is conveyed by road to the railway at Tavistock, which town is 4½ miles from the bridge.

On the common between the road leading from the bridge towards Princetown and Great Mis Tor, which rises high above the left bank of the Walkham, are some deep cuttings of the tinners, and close to the stream the remains of two small buildings in which they smelted

---

* Often called Hucken Tor.

their ore are to be seen. The rambler will find these on the left bank, the first being about a furlong above the bridge. A door jamb marks the entrance, and near to this is a mould stone. The mould is a large one, being about 18 inches in length, and as usual has bevelled sides. In one end of it is a notch, no doubt intended for the more easy withdrawal of the block of metal. In the stone there is also a tiny mould, four inches long. Similar small cavities are to be seen in other mould stones on the moor, and it is thought they were intended for sample ingots. Above the house traces of a leat are observable, by which water was probably conducted to a wheel. Under the house is a small culvert leading from that part of the building in which the wheel appears to have stood. Another stone will be noticed in this blowing-house which has been hollowed out in the manner of a shallow trough. This it is not unlikely formed the bottom of the furnace, in the midst of the remains of which it lies. The second building will be found about half-a-mile further up stream. Here also is a stone with a large and small mould, as well as the remains of a leat.

Near the head waters of the Walkham are other mining remains ; these are briefly noticed in the excursions from Lydford. (Ex. 10).

In making his way back to the road the rambler may forsake the guidance of the river, and keeping a little up the hillside pass Over Tor, where Mrs. Bray alighted upon a rock basin filled with water, and having washed her hands in it her husband bestowed upon it the name of "Mrs. Bray's Wash-hand Basin."

On Long Ash Hill, above Merivale Bridge, are the well-known stone rows.* To reach these from the bridge the rambler will pass up the Princetown road for a short distance, and will then strike up across the common to the R., when the tall menhir near the Long Ash enclosures will come in sight and serve as a guide to the other objects of which he is in search. There are two rows, both being double, and some faint indications of a third nearer to the menhir. The direction of the two former is nearly due east and west, and they are roughly parallel to each other. The length of these rows of stones has been variously given, showing discrepancies of about 200 feet in the northern row and about 300 feet in the southern. This reminds us of what used to be said of the Giant's Grave, near Kenford. It was formerly marked by two stones, and the country people declared that no matter how often the distance between them was measured the result was never the same. But some who have used the tape at Merivale have proved a little more fortunate, for the measurements of the rows given by Sir Gardner Wilkinson have been verified by more than one.† The length of the southern row is 850 feet, and that of the northern 590. About the middle of the former is a stone

---

* This group of remains was formerly known in the neighbourhood as the Potato Market, and also as the Plague Market, and a tradition stated that provisions were brought here by the country people and deposited as supplies for Tavistock, at a time when the plague ravaged that town. See *Tamar and Tavy.* Letter IX.

† The Merivale remains are drawn to scale and figured in Sir Gardiner Wilkinson's paper, entitled, *The Rock Basins of Dartmoor, and some British Remains in England*, Journal of the British Archæological Assoc., 1860.

circle, and at the eastern end of the latter a large stone. This is placed between the lines, and closes the end of the row, as it were. Near the north-western end of the southern row is a small cairn, much dilapidated, and about 600 feet south-east of this, and also near the same row, is a ruined kistvaen. This was formerly regarded as a dolmen, or cromlech, and is marked as such on a plate illustrating a paper by the Rev. Samuel Rowe, in the first volume of the *Transaction of the Plymouth Institution* (1830) ; and it is also so marked on a plate accompanying the paper in which these remains are mentioned by Sir Gardner Wilkinson. Unfortunately the cover stone is broken, and one of the side stones also. This damage was done about the year 1860 ; gate posts being cut from the former, and part of the latter being removed. A few years ago an examination was made of the kist, and a flint scraper and flake and polishing stone were found. About 300 feet southward of the small dilapidated cairn previously mentioned, and not far from the menhir, are the remains of a stone circle. The menhir, which stands on the line of the old Tavistock and Ashburton track (T. 1, 7, 56), and which was in this part of its course identical with a branch of the Abbots' Way (T. 1), is a good example. Its height is ten and a half feet.

Near by is a corner formed by the walls of the Long Ash enclosures, and here there is a gateway, whence a path leads towards the farm house. Built into this wall is the half of a large circular stone, about ten feet in diameter.

North-eastward of the rows, and not very far from the road, is a small enclosure formed of upright blocks set on their edges in the ground. Hut circles occur within and without it, and in some of these charcoal has been found. A large number of these ruined dwellings are also to be seen northward of the road, on the slope above the Walkham. (Ex. 6). Near the enclosure is a round stone resting on some supporters. Visitors are cautioned not to allow their antiquarian zeal to carry them so far as to suppose this to be a dolmen. It is true that a well-known archæologist once made this mistake, but with the history of the stone before us there can be no danger of our doing so. He afterwards discovered that what he had regarded as an ancient monument had been fashioned by a man then living in the vicinity. The piece of granite had been intended for a millstone, but was found to be unfitted for the purpose.

The stones in the Long Ash rows and circles are small, and the general effect cannot be said to be particularly striking. Finer examples of the stone row exist on Dartmoor, as we shall see, but at the same time it must be confessed that the megalithic monuments on the moor are not imposing. Of pounds and remains of ancient habitations fine examples exist there, but the same cannot be said of the sepulchral circles, while the stones in many of the rows rise only a foot or so above the turf. This is the more surprising seeing that in so many parts of the moor stones of large size and of suitable shape are scattered abundantly over the surface of the ground. One has only to look upon the clatter on the slope of Mis Tor to see what a striking effect might have been produced had choice been made of the kind of stones found there instead of such comparatively small ones as compose the rows. It is the vast number of its stone remains that renders Dartmoor remarkable from an archæological point of view, and not the size or importance of individual groups of antiquities.

But though the visitor to Merivale may be somewhat disappointed when he views the long lines of stones, and remembers what he has read of Carnac, he will certainly not fail to be pleased with his surroundings. And after all, it is the scenery of Dartmoor and not its antiquities that constitutes its chief charm. In its wildness, its old associations, and its stories of other days, the visitor will probably find an attraction far greater than in the mouldering monuments of its early people, important as these may seem to the antiquary. As the late Mr. W. F. Collier has well observed, " in comparison to the work of nature all interest in them vanishes."

From the plateau near the menhir we look across the Walkham valley, and in a direction about W.S.W. see the piles of Pu Tor ; to the right of these, and much nearer to us, is the granite mass of Vixen Tor, and still further to the right, and immediately below us, the hamlet of Merivale. On the ridge above it are placed Mid Staple Tor and Great Staple Tor, and further north, Roose Tor. To the N.N.E. Great Mis Tor, the giant of the moor, uplifts his rocky crest. Turning to the south we see King Tor, with the Princetown Railway winding round its base.

The guide stones marking the old Tavistock and Ashburton track (T. 1, 7, 56) and bearing the letters T and A [*Ancient Crosses*, Chap. XIV.] may be seen on this part of the common, leading from the menhir eastward.

These guide stones run towards Yellowmead Farm, which will be noticed on the hillside, E. A short distance from the lower corner of the enclosures is a pound having hut circles within it.

Leaving the rows we make our way to the road, and passing up the hill shall shortly reach the Mission Room. Just beyond this we cross the Long Ash Brook near its source, and here a road turns R. to the Foggin Tor granite quarries, passing the Red Cottages. About a quarter of a mile further on we reach the first of the dwellings at Rundle Stone. Opposite to a row of granite posts on the right of the way is the wall of an enclosure. It was close to this wall that a schoolmaster belonging to the prison at·Princetown lost his life in the snow many years ago. When on his way home from Tavistock snow commenced to fall, and though urged to remain for the night in a cottage at which he called, near Moor Shop (R. 1), he determined to continue his journey. I have been told by one who was present that he appeared very anxious to get to his home, saying that he feared his wife would be alarmed if he did not return that night. After his departure the storm increased in fury, and the next day his body was found at the spot indicated. It was said that he possessed some artistic skill, and that the very last picture he produced represented a man meeting his death in the snow. [100 *Years*, Chap. X.]

It is not so very long since that the dwellings at Rundle Stone were merely miserable huts, as the ruins of some still attest. Passing on, with Mount View, a modern house, on the L., we soon reach the site of the object that gave name to this spot. This was a granite pillar known as the Rundle Stone, which stood on the forest boundary line. It is not named as a bondmark in any of the surveys, but was, however, recognized as such in 1702. It was formerly to be seen on the S. of the way, immediately opposite to the modern boundary stone, which we shall observe on the L. This bears the names of the parishes that here meet each other—Lydford and Walkhampton—and on passing it we again enter the forest. The Rundle Stone was broken up several years ago, when a wall was being built near by. It is much to be regretted that an ancient landmark should have been wantonly destroyed ; unfortunately the spoliator has been busy on Dartmoor, and has swept away many interesting objects. About the year 1881 I took measurements of the Rundle Stone. It stood 7 feet above the stones in which it was set, and was four feet in girth. Near the top was the letter R, cut in relief. It is marked on a map dated 1720 as a " Great stone call'd Roundle." Rundle Stone Tor is a short distance up the hill to the south.

A few yards further on, and exactly six miles from Tavistock, is Rundle Stone Corner, where a road branches R. to Princetown ; the Duchy Hotel is 1½ miles distant. This we shall follow, and shortly after passing the prison shall enter the town. If our destination be Two Bridges, 2 m., we keep straight on from Rundle Stone, crossing the Blackabrook on our way.

[A direct route from Princetown to Yes Tor Bottom has been given. Direct route to Ward Bridge : First to Yes Tor Bottom— thence down the common W. by S. to the moor gate near Withill Farm. Those who prefer to do so may make their way from Prince- town to the Long Ash Rows by North Hisworthy Tor, instead of taking the road to Rundle Stone as described in S. Ex. 3. From the tor the way lies N.W. to Hollow Tor, which is near by and in sight, and then down by the Red Cottages. Thence down the hill W., crossing the Long Ash Brook, to the rows. The road to Merivale Bridge is described in Route 1.]

Ex. 2.—*Hart Tor—Cramber Tor—Crazy Well Pool—Roundy Farm —Lether Tor Bridge—Riddy Pit—Mining Houses on the Mew—Raddick Hill—Stone Rows near Black Tor. About 7 miles from and to Prince- town.* EXTENSION *to Hingston Hill Stone Rows* add 2 *miles.* ALTERNATIVE RETURN ROUTE *from Crazy Well by Older Bridge and South Hisworthy.* DIRECT ROUTE *to Siward's Cross,* 2½ m. from Princetown.

One of the curiosities of Walkhampton Common is Crazy Well Pool, which, unlike the more famous Cranmere Pool in the northern part of the moor, is really deserving of its title. Between the pool and Princetown, from which it is distant about 2½ miles, are several objects of antiquarian interest, and the border scenery being of a fine character, the rambler should not neglect to visit it.

We leave Princetown by the Plymouth road as in Ex. 1, but when reaching a gate on the R. near the top of Devil's Bridge Hill, shall forsake it and strike across the common L., our course now being almost due S. Ahead of us are seen two tors, the left hand one being Sheeps Tor and the other Lether Tor. We make for a point about midway between these two, and very soon Hart Tor, which is quite near to us, comes into view, in a direct line with Sheeps Tor, but much under it. Other rock piles seen to the R. of Lether Tor are Sharp Tor and Leedon Tor, with Inga Tor far down below the latter. Beyond Hart Tor, and on the further side of the Mew, is Black Tor. A straight line to Crazy Well Pool would leave Hart Tor a little to the right, but the rambler will perhaps hardly pass it by without a visit. As we progress other tors come into view. Pu Tor and Heckwood Tor (Ex. 7), on the down beyond the Walkham Valley, will be observed on the R., as also will Swell Tor, the latter marking the sight of the granite quarries, which are comparatively near to us, while behind us the summit of North Hisworthy is seen. On the slope down which we pass before commencing the ascent of the tor is a cluster of hut circles.

In itself Hart Tor presents nothing remarkable, though it is rather striking when seen from some points, particularly from Black Tor, but the view from it is good. In addition to the tors already named a dozen others are in sight, including the range beyond Merivale, with Mis Tor, and Higher and Lower White Tor. Brent Tor, with its little church, rises N.W. by W., and far away to the N. is the summit of the lonely Cut Hill.

On the slope south-westward of the tor are a pair of stone rows. These are noticed further on.

Our next point is Cramber Tor, which is about half a mile distant, in a direction S. by E. We therefore descend to the Hart Tor Brook, which we shall cross at a ford, and find ourselves on the Princetown and Kingsett track (T. 3). This will, however, afford us little guidance here, as it is by no means clearly defined ; but we shall hardly need any, for ere we have proceeded very far up the hill in front of us we come in sight of the tor. On reaching it we shall find that our view southward is greatly extended.

Hen Tor and Gutter Tor, in the Plym Valley, are seen, with Shell Top, the height overlooking Cornwood, beyond. Across the valley below us is Down Tor, with Combeshead Tor to the L. of it. Between these two tors and Sheeps Tor, whose giant bulk here looms largely, is the beautiful Dean Combe (Ex. 38). To the L. of Sheeps Tor we look far away to the Staddon Heights, on the eastern side of Plymouth Sound. A striking feature in the scene is the Burrator Lake (Ex. 39),

BURRATOR LAKE FROM CRAMBER TOR.

with Lether Tor, the fine proportions of which are strikingly presented from this point, rising above its northern shore. We get a glimpse of Yennadon, and a view of the distant Kit Hill, on the Cornish side of the Tamar, an eminence conspicuous in all this part of the moor. It is marked by a lofty mine chimney on its crest.

Leaving this spot, the view from which is rendered so impressive by the fine grouping of the nearer tors, we shall make our way to Crazy

Well Bridge, where the cart track to Kingsett crosses the Devonport Leat. This is about three furlongs distant, and if we pursue a course due S. we shall not fail to strike it. The pool is situated just below, but is not visible until we reach the edge of the deep hollow in which the waters are gathered. That this hollow is artificial is evident at a glance. It is an excavation of the tinners, who were once very busy on this part of the common, as even a cursory examination will show. It is said to cover about an acre of ground. Its depth is about 15 feet, though it used to be related on the moor how the bellropes belonging to Walkhampton Church were once tied together and let down into it, and yet no bottom was found. It was also said to rise and fall with the tide ; but that was " yeers agone." That the water does, however, sometimes rise very rapidly, we shall probably not care to dispute if we have ever experienced a true Dartmoor downpour.

In my *Ancient Stone Crosses of Dartmoor* there is a brief notice of Crazy Well Pool (Chap. X.), and in connection with it mention is made of a poem by the Rev. John Johns, entitled, *Gaveston on Dartmoor.* There was formerly a tradition in the forest that the favourite of Edward II. sought concealment there during one of his banishments from Court. Mr. Johns, with a poet's license, discovers Gaveston at early morn beside the waters of Crazy Well, where he meets the Witch of Sheeps Tor, and his fate is revealed to him, though he does not read the prophecy aright. But no tradition regarding Gaveston is found in the neighbourhood of Crazy Well ; the choice of the spot for the scene of the poem was merely fanciful on the part of its author. Whether another story of a knight who came secretly to Dartmoor, and which is related further on (Ex. 20), has any reference to the favourite I cannot say, but it belongs to the eastern side of the forest and not to Walkhampton Common. Gaveston held the forest under grant from Edward II. At his death it reverted to the Crown.

A short distance southward of the pool is the track leading from Lowery to White Works, which is formed on the line of an ancient one running across the forest to Dartmeet and Holne. This is the track which, as already mentioned (T. 2), the discovery of certain stone crosses revealed to me. A portion of one of the objects that evidently marked its course, consisting only of the head and arms, is to be seen near the N.E. corner of the pool. Its original site was probably a little nearer to the old path. [*Crosses*, Chap. X.]

Not far from Crazy Well Pool are the ruins of Roundy farmhouse, and thither we shall now direct our steps. A gully will be seen extending from the S. side of the pool, and this we must leave on the L. as we descend the slope. We soon come in sight of some enclosures, R., within which, and a short distance above the track just referred to, the remains of the ancient homestead are situated. The building below us, and on the further side of the track, is Kingsett farm house, and a little over a quarter of a mile to the E., or L., of this, though not in sight, are the ruins of another, which bears the same name as the pool. In the valley is the Newleycombe Lake, a stream that joins the Mew immediately below Nosworthy Bridge, and very near to the upper end of the Burrator Lake (Ex. 39).

Roundy Farm is interesting as an example of an old Dartmoor dwelling, though there are several on the moor that boast a far greater antiquity. A stone over the doorway bears the letters R.C., and the date 1668, cut in relief, and about six inches in height. The initials have been thought to be those of Richard Crymes, whose family were long seated at Crapstone, in Buckland Monachorum parish, and to which the manor was granted at the Dissolution. Crapstone was built by them, and afterwards became the property of the Elfords by purchase. (Yelverton District). If the date on the stone is that of the erection of the house, and not of a restoration, it is not improbable that the latter was built on the site of a still older dwelling. There were farm enclosures on this common at the beginning of the seventeenth century, and it is more than likely that Roundy was one of these. The jury which made a presentment respecting the forest, in 1609, refer to this part of the moor, and speak of " certayne howses " that had been erected there, and of land that had been enclosed. In going through the ruins the large fireplace will be noticed, also a recess in the wall, and in the garden what was evidently a cooling-place for butter.

Northward of the farmhouse, and inside the enclosures, are a number of hut circles, some of them being good examples. There is one small circular enclosure of a kind not usually met with. This will be found a short distance above the ruin.

Before setting out on his return to Princetown the visitor who is interested in mining remains will do well to visit Riddy Pit, where are some stones with hollows in them. To do this he will make his way down the track below Roundy, and turning right will follow it to Lether Tor Bridge, a clapper of two openings, but evidently not of very ancient construction. Just above the bridge he will notice a track running up on the left bank of the Mew. This will lead him to Riddy Pit, which is indeed quite near, and where are the ruins of two houses. A little beyond these he will find the stones with the cavities. They now form part of the paving of the rough track. Close by is an old wall, and near to this, and built into the hedge, is a stone in which there is a circular cavity on each side. Another curious stone having a rounded top, and with a small piece of iron leaded into it, will also be seen. This was probably the upper stone of a crushing mill. On his way back the rambler may strike L. at about a quarter of a mile from the bridge, into Raddick Lane, and so gain the common northward of Roundy Farm.

Below Lether Tor Bridge the Mew flows between farm enclosures, and by the edge of the common, to Nosworthy Bridge. The latter we have named as an important point in the Princetown District, as it marks the confluence, as already stated, of the Mew and Newleycombe Lake. A track opposite to Raddick Lane leads down to it (R. 8), but the approach most frequently used branches from the Lowery road at Cross Gate. The bridge is noticed in the excursions from Yelverton. (Ex. 39),

[*Extension from Crazy Well Pool to Hingston Hill.* On that part of the common bearing the name of Hingston Hill, and situated to the south of Newleycombe Lake, is an interesting group of pre-historic remains, and these the visitor may very well include in the present ramble. Having examined Roundy Farm he will make his way to the track before referred to (T. 2), and leaving Kingsett on the R. will pass down by the ruins of Crazy Well Farm, to which a path branches, and descend to Newleycombe Lake. There is a fording place where he will strike the stream, but usually it can be crossed at any point without much difficulty. If preferred the rambler may turn R. on reaching the track, and then L. to Kingsett. If he does this he will find just across the stream, and opposite to the farm house, a ruined building, very much overgrown. It is so decayed that it is not possible to determine its character, but it may have been connected with mining operations. A stone with a cavity will be observed in the doorway, and this certainly seems to indicate that such was the case. The hollow has all the appearance of an unfinished tin mould. But whether the stream be crossed below Crazy Well or Kingsett, the visitor will have no difficulty in discovering the object that has brought him to this part of Walkhampton Common. He will mount the hill, keeping a course about S.E., with Down Tor on his R., and the remains, which are less than half a mile from the stream, will soon come in sight. These consist of a single row of stones running nearly east and west, with a menhir at each end. Very near to the western menhir, which is much the higher of the two, is a stone circle about 36 feet in diameter, enclosing a barrow. About 300 yards from the eastern menhir is a cairn 500 feet or more in diameter, and not far distant is a pound. Some of the stones in the row are of large size, and the monument is more than usually striking. The menhirs, which had fallen, were set up in the summer of 1894. The length of the row is about 340 yards. South of the row is Combeshead Tor, and below this is the charming Dean Combe, both of which are noticed in the Yelverton Excursions. (Ex. 39). Returning to the stream we may cross at Kingsett Steps, below the farm, and, mounting the hill, shall once more find ourselves on the common near Roundy.]

Passing onward from Roundy with the enclosures L., our course at first being northerly and then N.W., we soon come in sight of Stanlake Farm (Ex. 1), on the opposite side of the valley. Shortly after we reach the Devonport leat, where it runs down the side of a steep hill, the water forming one long rapid, to an aqueduct known locally as Iron Bridge, which carries it over the river. We follow it to that point, where it is easily crossed, and shall then make our way up the L. bank of the Mew to its confluence with the Hart Tor Brook, in the midst of an extensive stream work. We cross the brook, and then the Mew itself, and shortly afterwards reach one of the beauty spots of Dartmoor This is Black Tor Fall, where the stream comes swiftly round a heathery bank to glide over moss-covered stones ; where dripping ferns margin the waters, and the mountain ash waves her branches gracefully above them.

In this charming little dell are two mining houses, one on each side of the stream, and both are worthy of examination. The one on the eastern bank has the doorway in a particularly perfect state. It is about 5 feet high, and rather over 3 feet wide. There is a groove in the jamb and the lintel for the door On one side of it is a wheel pit, the wall of which is built of very large stones. The building measures 22 feet by 16. The ruin on the western bank is not so large, measuring only 16 feet by 12. In this one the chimney to the height of several feet was until recently intact. In August, 1907, a colt belonging to Mrs. Gill, of Stanlake, fell into it, and was imprisoned in the wide hearth for three days, when it was rescued by Mr. Pearse, of Kingsett, who noticed its dam grazing near by. This, however, could only be accomplished by destroying the chimney. Two stones having circular cavities in them are to be seen here ; these were probably mortars in which the tin ore was pounded. 'To reach this spot direct from Prince-town the rambler will proceed as in Ex. 1, and soon after passing Double Waters will leave the road and make his way to Black Tor, which he will see on the common left. The Mew is just below the tor, and by following it downward for a short distance he will be led to the dell.

[On the further side of the stream work, in a S.E. direction, is a pound of an irregular shape on the slope of Raddick Hill. It contains several hut circles, and in one of these a fine vessel of rude hand-made pottery was found intact by Mr. Robert Burnard, when exploring the remains in 1895. It measured 10½ inches in height, and was 10 inches in diameter at the top. Unfortunately, the bottom of the vessel went to pieces when it was taken out of the cooking hole in which it was discovered. In the other huts cooking stones, flint, and sherds were found. On Raddick Hill there are also several barrows. Should the rambler desire to visit Raddick Hill on his way from Roundy Farm, the best plan will be for him to cross the Devonport leat at Crazy Well Bridge, and then proceed north-westward with the leat on his L. To reach the hill direct from Princetown he can go either by way of Black Tor, or Hart Tor. From the former the pound bears about S.E., and from the latter about S.W., and is plainly visible from both points. It is on the hillside just above the Hart Tor Brook.]

Passing upward from the little dell we speedily reach Black Tor Ford, where we shall cross the stream. On the slope between the ford and Hart Tor, but much nearer the former, are two stone rows, one double and the other single. They each start from a cairn, the one at the commencement of the double row being placed within a stone circle. They are here about 36 feet apart, but they do not run parallel, and that distance is doubled at their termination. The length of the double row is about 460 feet, and of the single one 260 feet. A tinners' working crosses these remains. The visitor will have no difficulty in finding them whether they be approached from the ford or from Hart Tor, if he follows a straight course from one object to the other.

Passing Hart Tor we regain the high road at the top of Devil's Bridge Hill, where we left it on setting out on our excursion ; or, if the rambler prefers it, he may make his way to the road by tracing the stream upward.

[ALTERNATIVE ROUTE *from Crazy Well Pool to Princetown.   Older Bridge—Siward's Cross—South Hisworthy Tor.* Add 2 m.
If the remains in the valley of the Mew have already been visited, or if it is intended to visit them direct from Princetown, the rambler may prefer to return from Crazy Well Pool by another route than the one already sketched, as offering a change of scenery. Supposing this to be decided upon, we shall follow the track (T. 2) below the pool up the valley, our direction being easterly. When we have advanced about half a mile we shall pass a broken cross lying on the ground a short distance to the R. of the way. Only the head and arms, and the socket stone in which the shaft was fixed, now remain. [*Crosses,* Chap. X.] The view from this point, looking down the valley, is good. Among the tors Sheeps Tor and Down Tor are conspicuous, while

Lether Tor, and its companion Sharp Tor, present a particularly fine appearance.

As we proceed along the track we shall not fail to be struck with the great amount of work the " old men " performed here. On every hand are evidences of their labours in search of tin, and that they were rewarded with success can hardly be doubted. That the valley was rich in the metal is shown by the fact that where they delved the more modern mining adventurer has also conducted operations. Less than half a mile from the broken cross we reach a ravine, called in the neighbourhood Drivage Bottom, near the head of which our track crosses the Devonport leat at Older Bridge. We are, however, not now on the line of the ancient track. That kept a little lower down the hill, and passed direct from the cross just noticed to Siward's, or Nun's, Cross, the interesting object already mentioned as a forest bondmark. (T. 1, 2). It may be reached from Older Bridge by following the Devonport leat upward, and will be found very near where this enters an adit, or tunnel, 1,400 yards in length.

Before describing this cross it will perhaps be well to sketch the route to it from Princetown direct. Should the rambler not include it in the present excursion, he will pass up to the head of the ravine above Older Bridge, and pursuing a northerly course will soon come in sight of an enclosure. The wall of this he will keep on his R., and, passing South Hisworthy Tor (rather over 1 m. from the bridge), will reach the gate opening upon Ivybridge Lane. (T. 6). For the pathway inside the wall see *post.*]

[*From Princetown to Siward's Cross.* Leaving the town by way of Ivybridge Lane (T. 6), we soon gain the common, and ere we have proceeded very far shall notice a stile in the wall on the L. Here a path leads to South Hisworthy Tor and Peat Cot (Ex. 3), and we may avail ourselves of it if we will. It is carried along a bank raised to the level of the top of the wall, and will bring us direct to the tor named. As we proceed we notice the bond stones that mark the limits of the forest between this pile of rocks and North Hisworthy Tor, and which we were able to see when on our way to the latter. On the top of South Hisworthy, which is usually known in the vicinity as Look Out Tor, is an iron spike. From the tor the path to Peat Cot (Ex. 3)

| Ter Hill. | Stream Hill. | Hand Hill. |

PEAT COT FROM SOUTH HISWORTHY TOR.

runs down across the newtake L., but we continue on our way by the wall, and on reaching the corner of the enclosure, climb over it and regain the common. Those who do not care for the work of scaling had perhaps better make their way along the common outside the wall. At the corner referred to this wall must be left, and a course the same as that previously followed from the tor, that is to say about S.S.E., must be kept. Very soon we shall strike a reave which here marks the forest boundary, and by following this we shall be led directly to the cross, which is under 2½ miles from the Duchy Hotel. The track passed about ½ mile S. of the newtake corner leads to Peat Cot, and a branch passed further on to the White Works (Ex. 3). It comes up from Older Bridge, to which point we followed it in the previous excursion.]

More than one of the Dartmoor crosses is referred to in documents relating to the forest and commons, but none receives so early a mention as Siward's Cross. It is named as a forest bondmark by the perambulators of 1240, who draw the line from " Elysburghe " (now Eylesbarrow) " et sic linealiter usque at crucem Sywardi," but that it was in existence long before that time there is good reason for believing. Standing on the line of a branch of the Abbots' Way (T. 1), it may possibly have been set up by the monks of Tavistock as a mark to that path, and their house was founded before the close of the tenth century ; but it is quite likely that it is of rather later erection, and that its name is indicative of the period. There could never have been much traffic over this branch of the Abbots' Way, and during the earlier years of Tavistock Abbey it is questionable whether there was any. We may with more probability look upon the cross as having been erected in the time of the Confessor, when Siward, Earl of Northumberland, held the manors of Tavei and Wifleurde. The former was probably the manor of Mary Tavy, in the parish of that name, and the latter has been thought to be Warne, a former manor in the same parish, but I am now inclined to regard it as being the manor of Willsworthy, in the parish of Peter Tavy. *Worthy*, a farm place, appears in the Devonshire Domesday as *orda*, *orde*, and *urde*, and while Wifleurde might become Willsworthy, it is difficult to see how the name could have changed its form to Warne. The manor of Willsworthy includes a considerable portion of the moor (see Lydford District), and abuts on the forest, which latter was also probably held by the earl. There are several instances of the royal hunting ground having been granted temporarily to a subject. It will be noticed that the earl's name is graven on that side of the cross which looks towards the forest. The letters are not particularly clear, but there is still no uncertainty about them, except that the second may be either an " i " or a " y."

The inscription on the western side of the cross is one that puzzled antiquaries for a long time, and it was not until my book on the crosses of the moor appeared (1st Ed., 1884) that this was understood. It had been variously read as *Roolande*, *Bod Bond*, and *Booford*, but after much careful examination of the letters, coupled with various references, I was able to decipher them. The inscription is BOC LOND, the ancient form of *Buckland*,* and the name was in all probability cut on the cross by the monks of Buckland Abbey to mark the limits of

---

* *Boc Lond, i.e., Book Land,* or land held by charter.

their lands, which included the manor of Walkhampton, which extends as we have seen, to the boundary line of the forest. These lands were given by Amicia, Countess of Devon, to endow the abbey, and the gift was confirmed by her daughter, Isabella de Fortibus. Immediately above the name a small incised cross will be observed.

This interesting relic is seven feet four inches in height, and measures two feet eight inches across the arms. It will be noticed that the shaft is broken, and is now held together by an iron clamp on each side. This damage resulted from the cross being intentionally thrown down by two lads when searching for cattle in this part of the moor. This was in 1846, but it was soon after repaired by a stone mason, named John Newcombe.

I have ventured to suggest elsewhere that the second name of the cross may be derived from the Cornu-Celtic word *nans*, a valley, dale, or ravine, standing, as it does at the head of the Swincombe valley. But it is quite possible that Nuns is a comparatively modern name, or corruption of one. The earliest record of it is in 1699, when it appears as Nannecross. A full account of this interesting object is given in the book to which reference has just been made. [*Crosses*, Chap. IX.]

Quite near to the cross is Nun's Cross Farm, enclosed about 1870 by John Hooper. A few years ago a modern dwelling-house took the place of the quaint little thatched cottage that he erected. Near by are the remains of Nun's Cross Mine.

(For route from Siward's Cross to Childe's Tomb, see Ex. 3).

To return to Princetown we follow the reave northward, with the farm enclosures on the R. When these latter are passed we continue on the same course, and at the distance of nearly a mile from the cross shall reach the corner of the newtake already noticed. The wall will then become our guide to South Hisworthy Tor, and to the moor gate at the end of Ivybridge Lane. (T. 6).

(This excursion may be extended to Childe's Tomb. See Ex. 3).

Ex. 3. *Peat Cot—White Works—Fox Tor Mire—Childe's Tomb—Fox Tor—Mining Remains—Kists in Tor Royal Newtake.* 7 m. from and to Princetown. *With route from Siward's Cross to Childe's Tomb,* 1½ m. ; *from Peat Cot to Princetown by the leat,* 2 m. ; *and direct route to the kists in Tor Royal Newtake.*

Leaving Princetown by the road leading to Tor Royal we shall make our way to Peat Cot, as in T. 7. for the purpose of visiting the Swincombe valley, in which are several objects of interest. (On reaching the entrance to South Hisworthy House, R., which is just beyond Tor Gate, L., we shall notice a gate L. of it, and into this it will be worth while to turn for a few minutes. In the second field is a circle resembling the fringe of a turfy mound, 36 yards in diameter, and within this is another, across which is a short piece of wall cutting off a segment of it). Shortly before the road reaches Peat Cot we leave it and enter a field L., where a footpath runs to the hamlet.

Peat Cot may also be reached by way of Ivybridge Lane (T. 6, Ex. 2). At South Hisworthy Tor strike into the green path L., and descend to Castle Road. Vide *supra*.

From Two Bridges Peat Cot may best be reached by way of Round Hill Farm. The visitor will cross the Blackabrook at the steps

S. of the farmhouse, and then strike S.W. over Tor Royal Newtake, leaving Tor Royal House R., to the corner of the enclosures in front of the latter. Thence as in R. 34. To go direct to Childe's Tomb from the steps a course S. by E. must be followed across the newtake, keeping Royal Hill R. This will bring the rambler to the hunting-gate mentioned *post*. From Prince Hall Lodge to the tomb, see R. 27.

Peat Cot, though not dating back to early times like Babeny, or Pizwell, or Hexworthy, is yet not devoid of interest. It shows what the nineteenth century settler has been able to accomplish on Dartmoor, and is a realization of a small part of Sir Thomas Tyrwhitt's dream. The mother of Peat Cot, Charlotte Worth, died in March, 1906, aged ninety four, and in possession of all her faculties. She came of a long-lived stock ; not, however, natives of Dartmoor, but of Wembury, on the coast near the mouth of the Yealm. Mrs. Worth's father, Richard Edwards, died at White Works, aged ninety-nine ; his mother lived till she was over a hundred, as also did his brother. Peat Cot, which is fairly sheltered from the westerly winds that are so detrimental to the agriculturists on the moor, consists of a few small farms. The Devonport leat runs quite close to it, and is carried round the hill on the side of which the settlement is situated.

Leaving this little group of Dartmoor dwellings we pass over the hill to the S.E., and make our way to White Works, which place is less than half a mile distant. Just before reaching the first of the cottages we again meet the Devonport leat as it comes round the hill from the E., and this we cross by a granite footbridge. White Works owes its existence and its name to a mine. This has been closed for some years, but the evidences of it are abundant around the few dwellings that now constitute the place. We remember when two large waterwheels were to be seen revolving here, and when the blacksmith's hammer was constantly heard ringing on the anvil. For some time the mine was worked by Mr. Moses Bawden, of Tavistock, a gentleman who has been connected with other similar operations on the moor of an extensive character. Those who now live at White Works look not to the bowels of the earth for their support, but to its surface. By breeding ponies and rearing other stock, and doing such labour as their hands may find for them to do, they contrive to get a living, and if the prize of wealth is not to be obtained, they have what is far more than its equivalent—health.

The cottages first reached are of recent erection, and take the place of older ones that had gone to decay. Those seen lower down are part of the original settlement, and with their thatched roofs present a picturesque appearance. Around them are the grey walls of a number of small enclosures.

The wide flat in front of White Works is Fox Tor Mire, and looking across this in a S.E. direction, a tor will be observed, the only one that is here in sight. This is Fox Tor, and below it, and a little to the L., a plain piece of ground will be seen, which is known as Sand Parks. Here, if the visitor looks carefully, he will notice a dark object. Its form cannot be distinguished at this distance, but it is the tomb to examine which is one of the objects of our present excursion.

[Before leaving White Works it will be well to mention two objects described *post* (in the route from Siward's Cross to Childe's Tomb), as the rambler may wish to take them on his way to Sand Parks, instead of proceeding by the more direct way hereafter sketched. The first of these is a cross on the further side of the mire, and the other a stone pillar near Wheal Anne Bottom. To reach the cross, which is about half a mile S.E. by S. of White Works, the visitor will pass over the upper end of the mire. This he may readily do, as the few swampy places in this part of it are easily avoided. He should not, however, attempt to cross it lower down. Though not so dangerous as formerly, there are yet many parts of it where the ground is treacherous, and it is as well to give it a wide berth. A branch of the Swincombe river, here only a small brook, runs through the middle of it. On the further side, *i.e.*, the south, the ground rises, and some short distance up the slope is a new newtake wall. The cross is about midway between the edge of the mire and this wall. It is set up on a rock, and around it is much scattered granite. Wheal Anne Bottom is westward of the cross, and in full view ; a little stream crosses through it, and joins the Swincombe river. By following this up for a short distance, and then striking R., the stone pillar will be seen.]

Making our way down by the lower cottages at White Works, and crossing the Strane, a small tributary of the Swincombe, we pass onward with the wall of Tor Royal Newtake L. Ere long we reach Stream Hill Ford, close to the Wheal Emma weir, where we shall cross the Swincombe, and by directing our steps a little to the L. of Fox Tor shall reach Sands Parks. We shall find the object of which we are in quest about ¼ m. northward of the tor. To be exact, it is ½ m. from the confluence of the two streams near the weir, S.S.E. by E. But unfortunately what the rambler will see is not the ancient monument spoken of by Risdon in the early part of the seventeenth century as one of Dartmoor's " three remarkable things," but a late nineteenth century erection that bears little resemblance to it. I have elsewhere given a full account of Childe's Tomb, and the legend of the luckless hunter, and have also related how I found the kist, and the stones that once surmounted it,* but it is perhaps necessary that my notices of this object should be briefly recapitulated here. Before doing so, however, we will sketch the route to the tomb from Siward's Cross.

[*Siward's Cross to Childe's Tomb*, 1½ miles. Passing down with Nun's Cross Farm on our L., we cross the little brook of the same name. and then the Plym road S. of Nun's Cross Ford. We pursue an easterly direction up the slope, keeping rather higher than a direct route would necessitate, in order to examine the stone pillar already referred to. Presently we shall reach a reave running along the side of the hill, and following this toward the E., shall soon arrive at the stone. This we shall find to be an ordinary shaft, about 5½ feet in height. The head, which was discovered near by a few years ago, has part of a cross cut in relief upon it. Eastward is the little stream running down Wheal Anne Bottom, and when we reach this we must make for the newtake wall below. (The latter has only recently been erected ; it runs on the line of an old reave). Reaching the newtake we strike about E., gradually leaving the wall on the R., and when nearly opposite White Works, shall come upon the cross already mentioned as being set up

---

* *Ancient Stone Crosses of Dartmoor.* Chap. X. *Folk Rhymes of Devon.* Chap. X.

on a rock. There is much scattered granite near by, but if the directions here given be followed, the object will not be missed. It was discovered by Lieut. M. Lennon Goldsmith, in 1903, after the latest edition of my book on the Dartmoor crosses had appeared. He found it lying on the ground near the rock in which the socket was cut, and afterwards had it re-erected, and secured in its place with cement. A portion of the shaft appears to be missing, but otherwise this ancient relic is in an excellent state of preservation. It faces E. and W. It is 41 inches high; the bottom of the shaft is 43 inches in girth; the arms measure 22 inches across; and the head rises 7 inches above the shaft. Near the cross is a kistvaen within a circle of stones.

The discovery of this cross adds another to the line of those objects extending from Buckland Abbey across the forest (T. 2), and, as Lieut. Goldsmith observed when acquainting me with his find, tends to confirm my contention that they marked an old track. [*Crosses*, Chap. X.] Since this cross was discovered another on the same line has come to light; it is described further on (Ex. 39).

Continuing on our way eastward to Sand Parks, with the newtake wall R., we soon reach the tomb, which is distant only a little over ½ m. from the cross.]

The story of Childe, the hunter, which I have frequently heard in the forest, was first related by Risdon nearly three hundred years ago. It is to the effect that one Childe, of Plymstock, " a man of fair possessions," being overtaken by a snowstorm when hunting on Dartmoor, slew his horse and disembowelled him, hoping to preserve himself by seeking shelter in the carcase. But he was there frozen to death, and having, as our old topographer states, "ordained, by his will, that wheresoever he should happen to be buried, to that church his lands should belong," he was carried by Tavistock men to the Abbey Church for interment. They were, however, able to accomplish this only by a stratagem. The people of Plymstock having learnt what was taking place, assembled at the bridge over the Tavy, with the intention of preventing the Tavistock men taking the body to the Abbey. But the latter, hearing of this, threw a slight bridge across the river, and carrying over their prize in triumph, became the possessors of Childe's lands. The people of Plymstock "were deceived," says Risdon, "by a guile"; "in memory whereof the bridge beareth the name of *Guilebridge* to this day." Our author also tells us that Childe's Tomb was to be seen on the moor in his time, though he does not say in what part of it, and that it once bore the following lines:

" They fyrste that fyndes and brings mee to my grave,
The priorie of Plimstoke they shall have."*

This story is probably a version of some early legend. Childe does not seem to have been a proper name, though some writers not only apparently think it was, but have gone so far as to furnish the supposed hunter with another—indeed, he has had no less than three Christian names given to him, Amyas, John, and Oswald. In all probability it was the Saxon Cild, a common appellation. Further, nothing is known of any Priory of Plymstock, and this perhaps accounts for the word " lands " being substituted for " priorie " in later versions

---

* Risdon's *Survey of Devon*, p. 223. Edit. 1811.

of the couplet. Tavistock Abbey possessed the manor of Plymstock, but it belonged to it at the time of the Domesday Survey. That Guile Bridge was simply the Guild Bridge, or bridge that led to the Guildhall of Tavistock, is much more likely to be the case than that it obtained its name in the manner the tradition states. It is difficult also to understand how we find the hunter's grave in the forest, when the story says he was buried at Tavistock. It is true that the body of a stranger found on the moor might have been interred on the spot, and afterwards exhumed on his identity being discovered, but that could hardly have happened at so late a period as the end of the tenth century, when Tavistock Abbey was founded. The grave, consisting of a kist within a stone circle, is precisely similar in plan to those which we know to belong to pagan times, and there can be little doubt is very much older than that religious house, though there are indications that the kist itself is not of such great antiquity as those generally seen on the moor. That a Christian monument should have been erected upon it is not inexplicable, since we know that the cross was frequently planted in similar situations in early times. Menhirs have been fashioned into the symbol of that faith, or have had it graven upon them, as we shall see in places on the borders of the moor. The story of Childe the Hunter must be regarded as a myth, but at the same time there is no doubt that, like most legends, there is an element of truth underlying it.

Although Risdon does not state in what part of the moor Childe was said to have been buried, forest tradition has always pointed to the tomb under Fox Tor as that of the unfortunate lord of Plymstock. This tomb remained intact until about 1812, when it was destroyed by a Mr. Windeatt, who enclosed Fox Tor Farm, and built the house, the ruins of which will be seen on the slope eastward. It consisted of a calvary of three stages, surmounted by a large worked stone in which a cross was fixed. In the first edition of Carrington's poem of *Dartmoor* (1826), the tomb is figured, but as this was probably drawn from memory, it is not a true representation of it in every particular, though no doubt correct in its main features. A note to the poem states that Mr. Windeatt removed some of the stones from the tomb, and used them for building purposes and for door steps. More than half a century after this was written I discovered the whole of the stones with the exception of three, but not in the place the note would seem to indicate.

When I was engaged in my investigations of the Dartmoor crosses in the seventies, Childe's Tomb naturally attracted my attention. But its exact site appeared to be then unknown, and it was not without some trouble that I discovered it. I was, however, aided in my search by some information obtained from Richard Eden, a moorman with whom I was well acquainted, and who was born at Fox Tor Farm. All that was then to be seen was a small mound, and some half buried stones. An account of my exploration is given in my book on the crosses, and it is therefore only necessary to state that I discovered the greater part of the missing stones. Some of these yet form a bridge over the brook below the ruined farmhouse. With the "restoration" I had nothing to do, beyond raising my voice against the manner in which it was carried out. The present cross and stone in which it is fixed were cut at Holne, in 1885.

Mining operations near Fox Tor were evidently of an extensive character. Fox Tor Gert, as the deep gully running up to the tor is named, has been worked for tin, as also has the branch of the Swincombe that runs down in front of the farmhouse, and which rises not far from Little Aune. (Ex. 43). The visitor to Childe's Tomb will probably wish to ascend Fox Tor, and here he will see the gert on the eastern slope of the hill, and also behind, or to the S. of the tor.

He will likewise be able to examine an old mining house, which is not wanting in interest. It will be found at the end of Black Lane (T. 61), where that old path runs into the gert, and S. of the tor. It stands on the W. side of the way, which here passes through a gully, and consists of the walls of a building, $23\frac{1}{2}$ feet by 14 feet on the outside. The doorway, as is usual in these houses, is near one corner, and the fireplace appears to have been at the opposite end.

Adjoining the southern wall of the farm enclosures, and near the bank of the Swincombe branch that flows in front of it, are the remains of another mining house, about the same width but a little longer than the one just noticed. It is built against a bank, a plan often followed by the constructors of these huts on the moor. Most of the wall that formed the western end has disappeared.

The path known as Sandy Way (T. 56), runs from Sand Parks up the hollow to the E.S.E., down which the stream comes. This it leaves on the right in ascending and goes on to Aune Head, where it becomes a plainly-marked track.

Fox Tor farmhouse presents nothing that will detain the visitor, unless it be that he desires to look more closely upon the building with which so many of the incidents of Eden Phillpotts' novel, *The American Prisoner*, are associated. If such be the case he may amuse himself for half-an-hour in searching for Maurice Malherbe's wine cellar, but we fear the result will be disappointing.

Passing down to the ford on the Swincombe we again cross that stream, but instead of returning to White Works we shall make for a hunting gate in the wall of Tor Royal Newtake, which we see near by. Our first point will then be a tumulus about $\frac{1}{2}$ m. N.N.W., and which will come in sight as we mount the slope. On our R. are some other enclosures near the river, one of which is known by the name of Joan Ford's Newtake, in which are three small upright stones standing in a row.

A few hundred yards in a north-easterly direction from the tumulus we shall come upon a ruined kistvaen, close to the source of a rivulet ; and a little further on, but in a more northerly direction, are two others, also dilapidated. Here we are near the summit of Royal Hill, the highest point in the newtake, and if we leave this a little to the L., and proceed in a north-westerly direction for about $\frac{1}{3}$ m. beyond it we shall reach the kistvaen known as the Crock of Gold. It is situated close beside the track leading from Princetown to Hexworthy (T. 8), and is a well preserved kist, with some of the stones that once encircled it yet remaining. The track we shall now follow W. to Bull Park, where, passing through a gate, we soon reach the entrance to Tor Royal, the residence of Mr A. E. Barrington, the High Bailiff of Dartmoor. Passing upward we bend R., and speedily find ourselves at Princetown.

[A pleasant way of returning from Peat Cot is by the Devonport leat. The best plan is to cross it at the bridge at the little settlement, and passing for a short distance over the newtake, strike it again above the bend. There is a path on the bank which the rambler may follow. Just before reaching Tor Royal the woods are passed, and when the trees are in leaf the contrast between the slope on which they grow and the bare moor around it is very striking. A short distance beyond Tor Royal the road from Bull Park (*supra*) is reached.]

[The kistvaens in Tor Royal Newtake may be visited from Princetown direct by following the Hexworthy track (T. 8) to the Crock of Gold, and then crossing over Royal Hill to the others. This will be the reverse of the latter part of the homeward route from Childe's Tomb just sketched. The walk may be extended to White Works, and the return made by way of Peat Cot and the lea t

Ex. 4.—*The Ockery—Antiquities on Round Hill Farm—Prince Hall—Swincombe—Crock of Gold—Bull Park.* About 9 m. from and to Princetown. WITH ALTERNATIVE RETURN ROUTES *from Swincombe, via White Works or Tor Royal Newtake,* and *from Prince Hall, via Moorlands and Bachelor's Hall.*

From Princetown our way takes us along the Two Bridges road past New London. This is the name given to the four blocks of dwellings on the R., and considered to be appropriate since they were erected under the superintendence of a London man; much of the material of which they are constructed was brought from there, and being several storeys in height they much more resemble town houses in plan than they do those usually seen on Dartmoor. Beyond them

| Holming Beam. | Devil's Tor. | Lydford Tor. | Row Tor. | Beardown Tors. |

FROM MAIN ROAD NEAR NEW LONDON.

we descend the hill to the Ockery, having Arrow Head Field on our L., so called in consequence of the finding there of some flint implements. We cross the Blackabrook by a modern bridge, formerly known as Trena Bridge, and turn R. On the R. bank of the stream is the Ockery, the approach to it being by means of a clapper. Though not of great size this is a good example of these structures, and consists of buttresses with centre pier, but the addition of parapets to some extent destroys its primitive appearance. The Ockery was formerly a very picturesque building, having an exterior gallery; renovation has altered it, but has not altogether destroyed its old-time air.

Entering Lower Watern Newtake by a gate near the bridge, we

pass down by the Blackabrook, and noticing some low tumuli near the
bank as we proceed, shall shortly reach the wall of one of the enclosures
belonging to Round Hill Farm. On the further side of this, and quite
near to the stream, is a group of kistvaens, and less than 200 yards
from these in a N.E. direction are the remains of two others, placed
side by side. Further on in the same direction, and on the slope of
Round Hill where it declines towards the Dart and the lower part of
the Blackabrook, are other examples of kists, as well as tumuli and hut
circles. Having examined these we shall turn westward, and leaving
Round Hill Farm to the L., shall reach the track by which it is
approached from the Two Bridges road. This we follow N. to Round
Hill Cottage, once the home of Jonas Coaker, locally renowned as the
Dartmoor poet, where we regain the road we left at the Ockery, within
a short distance of Two Bridges.

In Lower Watern Newtake the Princetown and Hexworthy Races
have been held. These consist of races for ponies, galloways, and
horses.

[As the Round Hill antiquities are situated in enclosed land, it
will be well for the visitor to obtain permission at the farm to examine
them. From Two Bridges they are, of course, reached by way of
Round Hill Cottage.]

On leaving Two Bridges we pass up the hill behind the hotel.
On the brow the road forks, the L. branch running to Moreton and
the R. to Ashburton. We follow the latter, with Muddy Lakes Newtake on our L., and during our progress towards Prince Hall Lodge
shall look upon several fine tors. Across the newtake, and at no
great distance from us, is Crockern Tor (See *post.*) To the R. of
this, and standing up boldly on a lofty ridge, is " Longaford's strange
mitre of earth and stone,"* and beyond it Higher and Lower White
Tors. In front is Bellaford Tor, a prominent object in every view
in this part of the moor. Away to the R. we see the high land of
the south quarter of the forest rising like a huge barrier from the
Swincombe valley, and extending from Cater's Beam, L., to Hand
Hill and Eylesbarrow, R. If we look carefully at it we may discern
a pile of rocks, not defined against the sky, but rising from its dusky
side. This is Fox Tor, already noticed [Ex. 3], which, like Crockern
Tor, is chiefly interesting on account of its associations, in this instance
only legendary.

At the distance of about 1 m. from the fork of the roads we arrive
at Prince Hall Lodge, R., and passing through the gate make our way
along the road that leads to the house (T. 10). This is bordered with
trees, but they have bowed before the prevailing westerly winds.
Stunted in growth they tell but too plainly that it is only in the
sheltered spots on the moor that planting can be undertaken with any
success.

Prince Hall was one of the ancient tenements of the forest [see
Ancient Tenement in the *Terms* section], and was known by the name
it at present bears several centuries ago, being mentioned at Prynshall
in a forester's account of the time of Henry VIII., while in a document
of a later date it appears as Prynce Hall. In 1702 it was in the
possession of William Gidley, and in the last quarter of the eighteenth

---

* *The Rive:*. Book I., Chap. XIII.

century was held by a Mr. Gullet, one of those who about that time entertained hopes that the forest might be profitably cultivated. From him it passed to Judge Buller, and was afterwards held by Mr. G. W. Fowler, whose operations on the farm were on a very large scale. [*Dev. Alps*, Chap. 3.] But they proved unsuccessful, except in one respect ; he certainly showed that such a style of farming as he adopted was not suited to Dartmoor. Some of the older people still speak of him, and will tell you that there was one thing Mr. Fowler deserved special praise for : he grew the largest turnips ever seen on the moor. "Proper gert benders, zure 'nuff—but most o' mun was holla."

The road will conduct us by the side of the house, which is large, and, for the moor, of imposing appearance, and down the lawn in front of it to Prince Hall Bridge, which spans the West Dart. Here the scene is of a very attractive character, particularly in the summer, when the trees are in leaf, and the hedgerow that borders the little lane that leads up from the bridge on the southern bank of the river is bright with young ferns and wild flowers. Near the top of the ascent the lane turns R. to Moorlands, a farm close by, but our way will be as in T. 10. Crossing the little Rue Lake, which falls into the Dart below Cherry Brook Foot, we enter Swincombe Newtake, and soon reach the gate at Swincombe Farmhouse. This building formed one of Sir Thomas Tyrwhitt's lodges, and appears to have been erected on land long enclosed. In a list of the newtakes in the forest made over two hundred years ago there are three enclosures named respectively Swancombe Head, Swancombe, and Swancombe Ford.

A short lane leads to Swincombe Ford, over the stream of that name, the farmhouse being on the R. as we proceed, and a cottage on the L. The latter was the abode for many years of John Bishop, a true specimen of the old style of Dartmoor man. He retained his primitive manners to the last, insisting on using a flint and steel in place of matches, among other things, and "couldn' abide any new fashioned notions." The footbridge at the ford is usually known as the Fairy Bridge.

We shall return to Princetown by the track running between that place and Hexworthy (T. 8), and for this purpose shall either retrace our steps to the gate of the newtake, and then turn L. behind Swincombe farmhouse, or pass in front of it. Though we now pass over the track the reverse way of that in which it has been described, it will be followed without difficulty, and we shall soon be led to the gate opening upon Tor Royal Newtake, across which the green path is well defined. About midway we shall pass the kistvaen called the Crock of Gold, noticed in Ex. 3, from which point we make our way to Bull Park, and thence by the road to Princetown.

[To return by way of the Swincombe Valley, noticed in the Hexworthy District, will be found very interesting. The visitor will cross the stream by the footbridge, and follow it up to the point where it receives the tributary that comes down from under Fox Tor farmhouse, whence he may make his way to Princetown either by the White Works or by Tor' Royal Newtake (Ex. 3). The walk may be shortened by returning direct to Princetown from Prince Hall Bridge. The visitor will follow the postman's path from Moorlands (T. 9), which will lead him across the northern side of Tor Royal Newtake, where he

will pass over the Cholake and the Lanson Brook, the former a tributary of the West Dart and the latter falling into the Blackabrook.
The path will bring him to Bachelor's Hall, whence the road will lead
him past New London, R., to the highway on the outskirts of Princetown.   The view from Bachelor's Hill Newtake, above New London,
is very fine.   It embraces Mis Tor, Maiden Hill, Cowsic Head, Bear
Down, Row Tor, Meripit Hill, Hameldon, the valley of the Dart, Holne
Moor, and many other prominent objects.]

   Ex. 5.   *Wistman's Wood—Foxholes—Crow Tor—Row Tor—Bear
Down Man—Antiquities on Conies Down—The Cowsic Valley.*   8¼ m.
from and to Two Bridges.   FROM THE COWSIC TO PRINCETOWN : *Black
Dunghill—The Blackabrook—Rundle Stone.*   IF TO BEAR DOWN MAN
BY WAY OF *Crockern Tor—Littaford Tors—Longaford Tor—The White
Tors—Brown's House,* 9 m.   IF BY WAY OF *Bear Down Clapper—Bear
Down Tors—Lydford Tor,* 7½ m.   IF FROM AND TO PRINCETOWN (returning by Black Dunghill) add 1½ m.
   For *Cut Hill* see Ex. 11.
   From the southern edge of the great fen which we have described
as covering so much of the N. quarter of the forest, two lofty ridges,
each about 1 m. in width, extend for about 3 m. in a southerly direction,
and terminate at Two Bridges.   These ridges, which are crowned with
tors, forming prominent objects when viewed from the road at Princetown, are separated by the valley of the West Dart.   Along the foot
of the Western ridge runs the Cowsic, the other being bounded on the
east for some distance by the Cherry Brook.   The three streams here
flow southward, their courses being roughly parallel.   The greater
part of the western ridge and the whole of the eastern, are now enclosed
within newtake walls.   Those who, some century ago, took in these
large tracks of land—" improvers " they delighted to call themselves—
under grant from the Duchy, were careful to select the best parts of
the forest, and pushed their walls out to the verge of the fen, thus
leaving those who possessed an undoubted right to the pasturage of
the moor, here only the boggy parts of it.   In this excursion the
rambler will see much enclosed moorland, and will be able to form
some idea of what Dartmoor would have been reduced to had those,
of whom Sir Thomas Tyrwhitt was the chief pioneer, been permitted
to realize their idle dreams.
   In the valley of the West Dart, about 1½ m. above Two Bridges,
is situated one of the curiosities of Dartmoor.   This is Wistman's
Wood, and consists of three small groves of dwarf oaks growing from
the midst of a clatter, and extending for about ½ m. along the L. bank of
the river.   Several suggestions as to the derivation of the name have
been made, one being that it is a corruption of the Celtic words *uisg
maen coed,* signifying the stony wood by the water, but there is also
reason for believing the word to be derived from *wealas,* meaning
foreigners, a term applied by the Saxons to all not of their race.   At all
events, the older people living on the moor used to speak of this oak
grove as Welshman's Wood, and it seems not at all improbable that
Wistman is merely a corruption of this.   *Wealasman's Wood* would
thus be the wood of the Celts, regarded as foreigners by the Saxon
settlers.   [*Gems,* Chap. I.]
   The path from Two Bridges to the wood lies through the enclosures

of Crockern Farm, at one time known as Board'n House, and these are entered at a gate on the L. in ascending the hill immediately behind the hotel (T. 11.)* No directions are needed, as the path is followed through the enclosures beyond which the wood is seen. The oaks grow quite near to the Dart amongst the rocks forming the clatter, and are so dwarfed that their boughs will often be seen resting upon the blocks of granite. The site of the wood, a stone-covered slope, seems altogether unsuited to the growth of trees, but in reality it is to the presence of the boulders that the oaks owe their preservation. These have not only sheltered them, but probably prevented their being cut down for fuel by the tinners. Trunks and boughs are thickly coated with moss, and consequently appear much larger than they really are. In 1886 the central grove took fire, by what means was never satisfactorily explained, and much damage was done. Time has, however, healed the wound the flames inflicted.

When the belief was held that the Druids once turned Dartmoor into one wide temple, Wistman's Wood was regarded as being a spot they particularly patronised ; indeed, it was said to have obtained its name from them, this meaning neither more nor less than the wood of the wise men. The Druids, by the way, showed their wisdom by cutting mistletoe (though where they found it on Dartmoor it is rather difficult to say) and by making stones rock, and other similarly useful acts. The valley, with its ruined hut dwellings, its oak groves, and the Dart perhaps as its oracle, was presumably regarded as another Dodona. But the Druids have gone now, and left only snakes and foxes to occupy the wood. As a holt for the latter it probably serves a much more popular purpose than when it was given over to the white-bearded priests. Many a fox has been bolted there, and one game little terrier, who often showed his prowess among the moss-covered rocks, now lies beneath one of its aged trees. This is Jumbo, which belonged to Mr. Sam Adams, Master of the Lamerton Hounds. One day in April, 1904, after being as active as ever in the field, the game little animal died suddenly, and was buried in the wood.

To reach the higher end of the wood it will be better that we keep on its upper side, that is to say, along its eastern verge. About 50 paces above the central grove is a large triangular-shaped stone in the midst of the clatter, on which is an inscription setting forth that a tree was cut down on this spot in 1866 by Mr. Wentworth Buller. A section of the trunk is now in the Albert Memorial Museum at Exeter.

About a third of a mile above the higher oak grove, which is due W. of Longaford Tor, is Wistman's Wood Ford on the Dart, and to this we shall now direct our steps.† On our way we pass a small deserted dwelling, constructed of wood, once the abode of a warrener, and in which readers of the *River* will recognise the home of Nicholas Edgecombe. In full view as we descend towards the stream is Crow

---

* The public right of way, as already stated (T. 11), is now disputed. This is one of the results of the work of the forest "improvers." *Board'n* is equivalent to *wooden*.

† Here the rambler passes over what was formerly Wistman's Warren. If he cannot cross the river at the ford he will perhaps be able to do so at the weir where the Devonport leat is taken from it.

Tor, placed on the southern extremity of the hill peninsulated by its two branches. (*Crow* rhymes with *now*. See View from North Hisworthy). The ford is situated about 200 yards below the confluence, and it was here that the Lich Path (T. 18) crossed the Dart.

The side of the valley in which Wistman's Wood is situated is included within Longaford Newtake, the wall of which is carried along the L. bank of the Dart. The other side of the valley is in Bear Down Newtake, and in this we shall find ourselves after having crossed the river at, or near, the ford, which, unless it be in flood, is not difficult. Passing up the R. bank we soon reach the smaller branch of the Dart

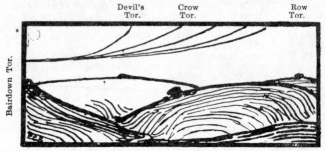

FROM ABOVE WISTMAN'S WOOD.

already referred to, and which is immediately without the northern wall of the last-named enclosure. This stream flows down from a hollow called Dart Hole, and is sometimes known as the Foxholes Water, and also as Methern Brook. It forms the boundary between the east and west quarters of the forest, the line running from Horse Hole southward to Dart Hole, and thence down to the West Dart. (See *Quarters* in the *Terms* section). Just above the confluence the northern wall of Longaford Newtake runs off in a direction E. by N., crossing the Dart and passing up the hill to Higher White Tor. At the point where this wall leaves the little stream another will be seen running up the hill in a direction N. by E. through a clatter, known as Foxholes. This we follow up the slope to Crow Tor, about ¼ m. distant, not far beyond which it terminates. Many years ago I learnt from one whose memory carried him far back into the nineteenth century, that it was intended to take in more land here from the forest, the example of those who had enclosed Longaford and Bear Down, and the other large tracts in the vicinity, presumably inciting others to follow in their steps. Much of the wall was built, but fortunately it was never completed. The fragment at Crow Tor forms a part of it, and another, and larger part, is to be seen near Row Tor, whence it runs down to the Dart, and up the hill in a N. easterly direction, for about ¾ m., to a point not far from Cherry Brook Head, and then turns southward, and is carried for some little distance down by the side of that stream. This part of the enclosure is known as Wild Banks Newtake.

Crow Tor we shall find to consist of several lumps of rock, one of which, placed exactly on the brow of the hill where the latter drops rather suddenly to the streams, is a conspicuous object from some parts of the lower valley.

Less than ¾ m. almost due N. from Crow Tor is Row Tor, to which, as it affords a good view of the moor, the rambler up this valley will no doubt desire to make his way. The ground is good, and the rise gradual, the tor being only about 150 feet higher than Crow Tor. It is, however, of considerable elevation, being no less than 1,793 feet, and is seen standing up boldly from the surrounding moor from the street at Princetown. The tor gives name to that part of the forest extending a little to the N. of it, and a considerable distance to the E. This is known as Rowter, and it abuts on Broad Down, about 1½ m. in the latter direction. At that end of it is Rowter Gate, already mentioned (T. 18, 78), and to a miry spot near this, and a small stream issuing from it, have been given the name of Rowter Marsh, and Rowter Brook, though I have not heard them so spoken of by the moormen. The latter is sometimes called Middle Brook.

The name of the tor became attached to this area in consequence of the latter forming what was probably to have been called Rowtor Farm, and of which Wild Banks Hill would have constituted a part. Rowtor Gate was the approach to it from the Post Bridge district. A ruined dwelling (see *post*) stands within this uncompleted enclosure, and is now known as Brown's House.

Before proceeding to Bear Down Man from Row Tor we shall sketch the route to the latter by way of the ridge between the West Dart and the Cherry Brook. This will lead us first to Crockern Tor, which is reached from the hotel at Two Bridges by following the Moreton road for about ½ m. to Parson's Cottage, close to which a gate gives access to the newtake in which the tor is situated. The cottage, which is now in ruins, was built in the early part of the nineteenth century by the Rev. J. H. Mason, Vicar of Widecombe, who held land here under a grant from the Duchy. It is also known as Billy Clack's Cottage, having once been in the occupation of the Rev. William Clack, a sporting parson, of Moretonhampstead.

Crockern Tor will be seen on the brow of the hill behind the cottage, from which it is distant only about 300 yards. In itself it presents nothing remarkable, consisting only of a small group of rocks, and attaining an elevation of no more than 1,295 feet. But it is one of those objects to which interest is lent by its historic associations. Without these it would fail to appeal to the beholder, but viewed in its connection with the Stannaries it at once claims attention. We shall, however, defer our notice of it until we have finished our excursions in this district, as it will be more convenient to deal with it separately.

Passing Crockern Tor and proceeding along the ridge in a direction a little W. of N., with the wall on our R., we shall, at the distance of about ½ m., reach Longaford Newtake, just within which are the three groups of rocks known as the Littaford Tors, of which mention has already been made. (T. 18). On a map drawn from a survey made at the beginning of the last century, and which was spoken of soon after its publication as being defective in names, these groups of rocks are marked as Little Bee Tor, although the name as we have it to-day was that by which they were then called on the moor. In a book published in 1832 this name occurs, only it is there rendered Littleford.

From this it seems probable that the error on the map occurred in the transcription of the name, and other mistakes on it may perhaps be explained in the same way ; or they may in some instances be due to a wrong reading of his copy by the engraver. This was very likely the case with regard to Beetor Cross (R. 4), which is shown on the map in question as Bector Cross. But though these errors are to be deplored, they have nevertheless served one useful purpose. They have been re-produced in more than one book dealing with the moor, and thus have shown the Dartmoor student that their writers have not gathered their information on the spot, but have adopted the much easier plan so delightfully described by Captain Marryat in his article on writing a book of travels.

Passing the northernmost of the Littaford Tors, we make our way to Longaford Tor, less than ½ m. distant, with the Dart valley on our L., and the great dun slope that stretches away to the Cherry Brook on our R. The rambler will do well to ascend Longaford, which attains an elevation of 1,595 feet, for the view from it is exceedingly fine. The pile is rather different in character from most of the tors on the moor, consisting not of rocks alone, but of rocks and turf, and is thus very easy of ascent. It is somewhat of a conical form, and a conspicuous object in all those parts of the moor centering round what we have called the Great Central Depression. (See Situation and Extent, etc.) From Cut Hill it at once arrests the attention of the beholder who looks down upon the valley of the West Dart by its striking form, though it is 400 feet lower than that eminence. Cut Hill is seen rising against the sky in a direction about N.N.W. (Ex. 11).

The next pile on this ridge is Higher White Tor, or Whitten Tor, as it is usually called, and which, like Longaford, is also a conspicuous object. It is of greater elevation than that tor, being placed on the highest part of the ridge, which is here 1,712 feet high. Its distance from Longaford is about the same as the distance of that tor from the nearest of the Littaford group. To this pile we make our way, and thence to a gate in the northern wall of the newtake, a short distance due N. of which is Lower White Tor.

The masses of rock so named are placed upon the brow of a steep declivity forming the western side of Hollowcombe Bottom. The tor is interesting as being the point where a reave of stone and turf, which may be traced for some distance eastward, has its termination. This is noticed in the Excursions in the Post Bridge District. (Ex. 46).

Leaving Lower White Tor we turn our steps in a north-westerly direction, or, to be more precise, N.W. by N., and crossing a slight depression in the side of the hill shall reach Brown's House, which is about ½ m. distant. The situation of this ruined dwelling is such as would certainly satisfy the greatest lover of solitude. From what I have been able to gather it never became what its builder intended it to be. As we have already seen, the work of enclosing the land around it was never completed, and consequently, instead of becoming the home of a settler, it was suffered to fall to decay.

Across the valley of the Dart, and in full view, is Row Tor, and to this we now make our way direct. Should the river prevent the visitor striking a beeline it must be followed upward for a short distance, when a means of crossing it by the natural stepping-stones will no doubt present itself. The distance from Brown's House to the tor is rather over ½ m.

We have already stated that Row Tor is a prominent object in the view from several points in this part of the moor. It does not greatly exceed in elevation the stretches of heath surrounding it, except on one side where the ground drops some 200 feet to the Dart, but the form of the hill renders it conspicuous. The rocks of the tor are disposed in a form approaching that of an oval, and enclose a small area. Almost due W. of the tor, and less than ½ m. from it, are the springs of Summer Brook, a feeder of the Dart, which pursues a course directly opposite to that of the river into which it falls. Just below its source, and near its L. bank, is the bottom known as Horse Hole, where is the junction of the north, west, and east quarters of the forest, as already mentioned. (See *Quarters* in *Terms* section). This is about ½ m. N. W. of Row Tor. A short distance to the N. of it is Summer Hill, on which are some rocks known as Flat Tor, but they present nothing remarkable. Still further N. is West Dart Head, distant, if the line *via* Crow Tor be followed, about 2 m. from the ford above Wistman's Wood, or 4 m. from Two Bridges.

Bear Down Man is a little over ½ m. from Row Tor in a south-westerly direction. Our way thither will lead us across a part of Methern Hill with Dart Hole on our left. The menhir is quite close to Devil's Tor, which does not consist of piles of granite, but merely of flat rocks scattered about the hill. Although it bears a name suggestive of some tradition I have never been able to gather any in connection with it. It was the opinion of one moorman whom I consulted that the pillar represented the Devil, and that the tor, which can hardly be truly regarded as such, "was plenty good enough vur he."

Man is, of course, the Celtic *maen*, *stone*, and the word is found so corrupted in all parts of the country. The pillar is nearly 11 feet high, and about 8 feet in girth.

Horse Hole is about ½ m. N.N.E. of Bear Down Man, and Cowsic Head ½ m. N.N.W. The course of the Cowsic is at first almost due S., and the Walkham, a little over 1 m. to the W., runs parallel to it. Between the springs of the Cowsic and Spriddle Lake, W., is Maiden Hill, 1,774 feet, and southward of this is Conies Down, which is probably the Condyshull of a fourteenth century document. The Lich Path (T. 18) runs along the southern verge of this. Rather over ½ m. due N. of Cowsic Head are the upper waters of the Tavy, and between the two the ground is very heavy, this being the southern edge of the great fen that extends northward to Ockment Hill.

The rain gauges seen in this part of the moor are in connection with the Devonport Water Supply.

[Should the visitor desire to make his way direct to Bear Down Man from the ford on the Dart above Wistman's Wood, he will follow the Methern Brook for about ½ m., keeping it on his R. Then, leaving it, he will pursue the same course, *i.e.*, N.W., up the hill, and will soon reach his objective.]

On leaving Bear Down Man we shall strike S.W. to the Cowsic, which we cross, and make our way down the stream with Conies Down Tor (T. 18) on our R. Just below this is a group of hut circles, and ⅓ of a mile to the W. a double stone row, but the stones of the latter are not very large. It is close to the Lich Path, and extends for a distance of about 350 feet, running nearly N. and S. Not far from the southern end of it are what appear to be the remains of a small cairn, probably despoiled by the builders of the Bear Down enclosures, which are not far off. A little way below the hut circles is Travellers' Ford, where the Lich Path (T. 18) crosses the Cowsic, and if, on reaching this old track, we follow it for a short distance towards the W., we shall observe the row on the R., or northern, side of it.

Continuing on our way down the stream we soon arrive at Cowsic Fork, which is just below the ford. The branch which comes from the N.W. rises close to the Lich Path, and is sometimes known as the Conies' Down Water. The Cowsic here runs through a deep hollow, called Broad Hole, where, some seventy-seven years ago, the remains of an oak were discovered in the bank. When dug out the tree was found to consist of the trunk, with a part of the root and a branch, and was thought to be larger than any of those in Wistman's Wood. In Broad Hole is Bear Down Newtake Corner, where the northern wall joins the western one. The former runs up the hill eastward, and passing close to Lydford Tor is carried to the West Dart, which it reaches near the confluence under Crow Tor, as we have already seen. A few hundred yards below the corner the western wall leaves the eastern for the western bank of the stream, so as to include this part of the Cowsic within the Bear Down enclosures. Passing down through Broad Hole we soon after cross a small tributary rivulet, and find ourselves on the eastern edge of Holming Beam, or, as the name is now often rendered, Omen Beam. This comprehends that part of the moor lying between the Cowsic and the upper waters of the Blackabrook. A considerable portion of it is now included in that part of the prison enclosures to which the name of the New Forest has been given. Holming Beam is noted for the abundance of its whortleberry plants. and has long been a favourite place with the gatherers of that fruit. Old mine workings exist here, as the name would indicate, and much peat was formerly cut near the Blackabrook. About 1 m. below the Bear Down Newtake Corner the wall is carried to the eastern bank of the Cowsic, and very near to this point the Devonport leat crosses that stream. Making our way southward with the leat and the river on our L., and the prison enclosures on our R., we reach the Tavistock road at a point ½ m. W. of Two Bridges, and exactly 2 m. from Travellers' Ford.

This excursion will be found particularly interesting, and will enable the visitor to gain a good idea of the upper valley of the West Dart as well as of the Cowsic valley. To reach Bear Down Man by way of the]latter it will, of course, only be necessary to follow the stream upward, and cross it at, or above, Travellers' Ford.

[If our destination be Princetown we leave the Cowsic just where the Bear Down wall is brought across it, near the lower end of Broad Hole, and climbing the steep on the R., make our way to Black Dunghill, the summit of which (1,615 feet) is a little over ¾ m. distant, in a direction S.W. by W. A quarter mile beyond this we reach a track (T. 12), and this we follow southward with the Blackabrook on our R. Soon we arrive at the wall of the New Forest Prison enclosures, and entering them shall cross the stream. Still following the track we shall pass Fitz's Well (Ex. 6), and speedily reach the high road a short distance from Rundle Stone (Ex. 1, 6). When the convicts are at work in the enclosures here it is very likely that the visitor will not be allowed to pass this way. In that case he will turn R. on reaching the wall, and follow it up the hill to the corner, near Little Mis Tor (Ex. 6). Here he will turn L., and still keeping close to the wall will, at the distance of 1 m., reach Rundle Stone. (Ex. 1, 6)]

Another route to Bear Down Man from Two Bridges is by way of Bear Down Hill. The distance from the hotel is 3½ m. On leaving the latter the visitor follows the Tavistock road, and just after passing the entrance to Bear Down Lodge will reach a gate on the R., where a road leads direct to Bear Down Farm. The bridge over the Cowsic takes the place of one erected by Mr. Edward Bray, the encloser of the farm, and who died in 1816. This was swept away in the great flood of July, 1890. Some of the rocks in the bed of the stream near here, and on its bank, bear inscriptions. These are the work of Mr. Bray's son, afterwards Vicar of Tavistock, who, presumably lamenting the absence of the Druids, and the stir and bustle consequent upon their frantic endeavours to discover mistletoe on Dartmoor, conceived the idea of consecrating the rocks in this part of the valley to Theocritus and Virgil, and to British bards, and suitably inscribing them, and thus, as he says, " give more animation to the scene." His method of proceeding was to trace the letters on the stone with a paint brush, and then get them cut by a labourer with a pick. It is fortunate that he recorded what he had done, for had this been omitted he would have caused no end of trouble. The speculations of the antiquaries upon the work of Mr. William Stumps would have been as nothing compared to the theories that would have been advanced by the modern Dryasdusts. In sparing us these Mr. Bray has proved more fortunate than in his endeavours to impart " animation " to the district.

A very short distance above the bridge, and in the beautiful dell that renders this part of the Cowsic so charming, is an interesting clapper. It was swept away in 1873, but the stones were afterwards replaced, and some of them secured with iron clamps. In 1890 it was again partly destroyed by the flood that did so much damage in this part of the moor, and was then rebuilt by the Dartmoor Preservation Association. Its length is about 37 feet, and its breadth rather less than 4 feet, while its height above the stream is 3½ feet. There are five openings.

Ascending the hill we soon reach the farmhouse, where we shall be readily accorded permission to pass up through the enclosures. Above the house is the Devonport leat, here crossed by foot bridges, and just beyond that is the great bare hill. Our first point is the chief of the Bear Down Tors, which is exactly 1 m. distant from the spot at which we cross the leat, and in a direction almost due N. On a small map in Bellamy's *Natural History of South Devon* (published in 1839), illustrative of the zoology of Dartmoor, Bear Down is shown as the principal station of the stone-chat. Whether this bird is now to be observed in greater numbers here than in any other part of the moor I cannot say, but so far as I have been able to discover they are as plentiful on Lakehead Hill, between the Cherry Brook and Post Bridge, as anywhere. Two-thirds of a mile from the leat we reach the outer, or northern, Bear Down Newtake, within which the tors are situated. They consist of a group of four, the southernmost being the smallest. Very near to it is the principal pile, which rises to a height of 1,681 feet, and forms a conspicuous object from many of the hills in the surrounding parts of the forest. Viewed from a distance from any point from N.E. to S.E., it presents the appearance of a huge cairn, with a small conical pile in the centre of it. This is especially noticeable from the slope of the hill above Broad Marsh (Ex. 46) on the East Dart, and from the high ground round Aune Head (Ex. 43). Another of the tors is placed on the brow of the hill nearer the West Dart, and the fourth is a short distance northward of this. Lydford Tor, which is the last we shall pass, is about ¼ m. N.W. of the latter, or less than ½ m. N. by W. of the chief of the group. As already stated, the northern wall of the Bear Down enclosures passes close to Lydford Tor as it runs across the hill from the Cowsic to the West Dart.

In the Rev. E. A. Bray's journal mention is several times made of Hannaford, who was his tenant at Bear Down. From his two grandsons I have been able to learn something respecting him. His Christian name was John, and he was the father of James Hannaford, who lived for so many years at Headland Warren (Ex. 22). John Hannaford, it appears, built a great part of the newtake wall at Bear Down, but for some reason that I could never discover, was unable to obtain payment for his work. Having spent a considerable sum upon it the loss so crippled him that he was compelled to relinquish the farm. He was buried at Mary Tavy.

Bear Down Man is rather under a mile from Lydford Tor, and lies a little W. of N. Our way thither will take us over gently rising ground, with Dart Hole to the E. and the Cowsic to the W. The return to Two Bridges may be made by way of the Cowsic Valley, as already described, or by the valley of the West Dart. As the latter route has been given *from* Two Bridges *to* the menhir, the objects named in it must, of course, be looked for conversely as the rambler makes his way *to* the former. In a similar manner he will be able to vary any of the excursions here described.

Several objects, indicative of a prehistoric and medieval population, have been discovered in the vicinity of Two Bridges. Flint flakes and chips have been found near the bridge, as well as in Lower Watern Newtake (Ex. 4), at Crockern Farm, and in the track leading to it. John Hannaford, the occupant of Bear Down, told Mr. Bray in 1827 that his uncle had found silver coins about the size of a sixpence in some of the cairns on the moor, and that he himself had found human hair in a kistvaen that he had destroyed. Hannaford, by the way, was, on his own confession, guilty of many acts of vandalism, a statement that will perhaps incline some to think that since he was so prone to interfere with the erections of others he was justly rewarded by the failure of his own building operations. Some human bones are also said to have been found near the road under Bear Down Farm. In a kist not far from the same place, which Mr. Bray opened in 1832, a small fragment of pottery of coarse texture was found. Some oak bowls were dug up many years ago in that part of the moor lying between the Moreton and Ashburton roads, and which is now enclosed and known as Muddy Lakes Newtake. In Gawler Bottom, much nearer Post Bridge (Ex. 46), an oak bowl was also found about seventeen years ago. These were probably used for measuring tin. In February, 1905, Mr. F. Rounsfell, when raising stone for road mending a little to the E. of Parson's Cottage in the newtake below

Crockern Tor, found a stone axe-hammer head. While engaged in his work he came upon a flat stone about 18 inches square, just below the surface, and on breaking this up discovered the implement beneath it. In the centre of it was a neat perforation for the reception of a wooden handle. It had been ground and polished, and one end was fashioned as a celt, with a cutting edge, and the other as a hammer. Its weight was 1 pound 9 ounces.

[For the route to Cut Hill from Princetown or Two Bridges see Ex. 11.]

Ex. 6.—*Rundle Stone—Great Mis Tor—Greena Ball—The Walk-ham—The Blackabrook—Holming Beam—Fitz's Well. About 7¾ m., Princetown. Two Bridges add about* 1 m. EXTENSION TO *Sandy Ford, the Lich Path, and the Cowsic.*

To *Fitz's Well* direct (return) 4½ m.

If our starting-point is Princetown we take the road running past

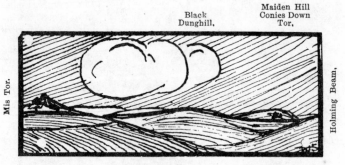

Black   Maiden Hill
Dunghill,   Conies Down
                            Tor,

Mis Tor.   Holming Beam,

FROM ROAD ABOUT 100 YARDS S. OF RUNDLESTONE.

the church and the prison to Rundle Stone, and if we set out from Two Bridges we follow the Tavistock road to the same spot. As we have already spoken of the Rundle Stone (Ex. 1), there will be little to detain us now. The destruction of the monolith is greatly to be deplored, for, though we hear nothing of it until 1702, it is exceedingly probable that it was standing long prior to that time. It was one of the few objects set up on the forest boundary line, most of those by which it is marked being natural ones. The house near by, on the R. as we reach Rundle Stone Corner from Princetown, was formerly an inn, and near here at one time there was a gate across the road. Several years ago the house was greatly damaged by lightning.

Proceeding a short distance on the Tavistock road we take the first turning on the R. and make our way towards Mount View, a house which stands not far from the highway. After passing some enclosures beyond this we emerge upon the common with the wall of the New Forest Prison ground (Ex. 5) on our R. This wall is built just within the forest bounds, and our way lies along by it. On our L. is that part of Walkhampton Common which, together with a tract on our R., formerly bore the name of Mis Tor Moor. It is spoken of as such by the jurors who surveyed the bounds of the forest in 1609, but is seldom so referred to now. Ancient workings extend from near Rundle Stone to the Walkham, and in close proximity to these are a number of hut circles and some small pounds. The latter are on the side of the hill below Wain Tor, or Little Mis Tor, and almost due W. of it. This Tor will be seen a little to the L. just before we reach the corner of the prison enclosure (Ex. 5). Though not of great size, Wain Tor is a conspicuous object from many points, owing to its situation, and square, compact form.

Passing upward, and still pursuing the same course we have been following from Rundle Stone, we speedily reach Great Mis Tor, one of the grandest of the rocky crowns of the moor. From whichever side it is seen it presents an imposing appearance, but the best view of it is probably that obtained from near Merivale Bridge. It is also seen to great advantage from Langstone Moor (Ex. 8), while from Roborough Down the grouping of this fine pile, with Roose Tor and Staple Tor and Cocks' Tor Hill, presents all the appearance of a mountain chain. The view from the tor is extensive and varied. On one side is seen the whole of West and North-West Devon, and much of the eastern part of Cornwall. Away to the south is Mount Edgcumbe, and the Tamar at Saltash, with the masterpiece of Brunel which spans it. Thence ranging northward the eye lights upon the hills of " rocky Cornewaile," and the tors that rise from the midst of King Arthur's

Gt. Links Tor.		Waternoke Lynch Tor.	High Willes.

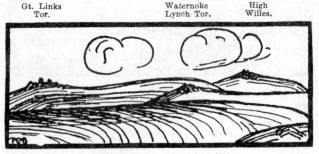

LOOKING N.N.E. FROM MIS TOR.

Land. On the other hand, we look into the great moor we are perambulating, and see much of the old-time hunting-ground, and if we have learnt to recognise the forms of the chief of its tors from the lofty summit of North Hisworthy, we shall here see many that are known to us. Westward of the Walkham are several fine piles, which are noticed in the excursions from Tavistock. The one nearest to us, in a direction W. by S., is Roose Tor; southward of that is Great Staple Tor, and beyond them the rounded Cocks' Tor Hill (Ex. 8). To the N.W., and on the further side of Langstone Moor, is another pile. This is White Tor (Ex. 8), or Whittor, as it is more often called, and beyond it is the valley of the Tavy. The stone circle on Langstone Moor, noticed in Ex. 8, is not very far from Mis Tor, and when the river can be crossed may readily be reached from it. It is about ¼ m. from the Walkham, and N.N.W. of the tor. Should the visitor decide to include this object in the present ramble he may, after having examined it, make his way to the point we shall presently reach, by following the Walkham and crossing it at Shallow Ford. Or he may return to the Rundle Stone by way of Merivale, first visiting Roose Tor and Staple Tor (Ex. 8), and then descending to the hamlet.

The meaning of the name of this tor is not apparent. The suggestion concerning it offered in the days when the Druidic theory was

Gt. Kneeset.	Walkham Hd.		Fur Tor.		Cut Hill.

Slope of High Willes.

LOOKING N.E. FROM MIS TOR.

rife, is not worth consideration. The tor was known as Mystor, or Mistorr, in the thirteenth century, and is mentioned during succeeding centuries in documents relating to the forest.

As already stated (see *Bondmark* in the *Terms* section) the boundary line between the forest and its purlieus seems to have been drawn through the tor, so that part of the pile was within the royal hunting-ground and part without. In the survey of 1609 the bondmark is specified as " a rocke called Mistorrpan," and this name also occurs more than 300 years earlier in the deed of Isabella referred to below. Mis Tor Pan is undoubtedly the large rock-basin on the mass of granite forming the southern part of the pile, and yet by some strange mistake the name has been affixed in the Ordnance Maps to Mis Tor Marsh, some third of a mile to the N.E. of the tor. That this should be corrected is important, as the forest boundary is expressly stated in the deed above referred to to be drawn from Mistorpanna, and if this be identified with the marsh the forest line is thrown considerably back. But the rock is evidently meant, and as we have seen, was specially mentioned as Mistorrpan in 1609. By this name also was the rock known to the peasantry early in the nineteenth century, and has continued to be so called. The basin is a very fine example. It is about 3 feet in diameter, and 8 inches in depth ; the bottom is flat, and there is a small channel leading from it to the edge of the rock.

But the basin also bears another name. It is sometimes referred to as the Devil's Frying-pan, and several stories are related in connection with it in which the Evil One figures.

As we have already seen, the forest boundary is drawn from North Hisworthy Tor to Mis Tor. Looking southward towards the former we have the forest on the L. of an imaginary line running from one to the other, and Walkhampton Common, as previously mentioned, on the R. The latter formed part of the lands given by Amicia of Clare, Countess of Devon, in 1280, to found the Abbey of the Blessed Mary and Benedict of Buckland. The gift was afterwards confirmed (in 1291) by her daughter, Isabella de Fortibus, Countess of Albemarle and Devon, and Lady of the Isle of Wight. Isabella was left a widow at the age of 23, and two years after succeeded to the possessions of her father, Baldwin de Redvers, her brother dying without heir male, and thus became the richest heiress of her time. Among these possions was included the Isle of Wight, the lordship of which had been bestowed upon Richard de Redvers by Henry I. She died in 1303, and on her deathbed sold the island to Edward I. for 6,000 marks. With her the line of De Redvers became extinct, and many of the estates passed to the Courtenays.

Another considerable tract of land on Dartmoor, forming part of the Chase of Okehampton, was also held by the De Redvers. (Okehampton District). It is not a little curious that in the names of these commons the termination *hampton* appears, and yet is found nowhere else on the moor, or in the border parishes. Many of the names of the latter exhibit the oft-found Saxon termination *ton*, though in more than one instance the word is apparently traceable to the Celtic *dun*, a hill, the heavy sound of the initial letter having given place to a lighter one. But *hampton* is found only in Walkhampton and Okehampton—locally pronounced Wackinton and Ockinton—though in neither does the word seem to possess its usual signification. It would, however, be unsafe to conclude that it does not. *Ham* and *ton* may, together, be taken to mean a farm, or enclosed land, with its dwelling-house and outbuildings, the *house town*, as it were, and the term came to signify an inhabited settlement. In Walkhampton the second syllable does not appear to have any connection with the third, but only with the first, the name being derived, we may reasonably suppose, from the river Walkham. Risdon, writing early in the seventeenth century, calls this river the Store [*Gems*, Chap. XXI.], but even if it were then so known, it is certain that at a much earlier time it bore a name closely resembling the one by which it is called to-day, being referred to as the Walkamp in the deed of Isabella de Fortibus. Thus, Walkhampton would mean the town, or settlement, on the Walkham, if we could be sure that the deed gave us the earliest form of the name of the river. But this is doubtful. There are many Dartmoor streams bearing the name of Walla, or Wella, and one that of Wollake, and I should be inclined to place Walkham in the same category, and to regard its early name to have been either Walla or Wollake. In Saxon times the settlement on the stream would be called Walla-hampton, or Wollakhampton, and by an easy transition Walkhampton. But it is also very probable that we do not see the word *ham* in this name at all ; that the early name of the river was the Walla, and that Walkhampton is *Walla cwm ton*, the town in the combe, or valley, of the Walla. (*Gems*, Chap. XXI.) The derivation of Okehampton is referred to in our notice of that district.

Leaving Mis Tor and its interesting traditionary and historic associations we shall make our way down the hill to the Walkham, our course being a little E. of N., thus following in the footsteps of the old perambulators. On our R. is Mis Tor Marsh, already mentioned, where the ground drops towards the Prison Leat. About ½ m. from the tor we reach Greena Ball, where are three cairns, situated a short distance to the R. of the line we are pursuing; then descending the steep slope we reach the Walkham at what is known as the Hanging Rock, immediately opposite to a combe down which flows a little stream called Dead Lake. To the Hanging Rock, which marks the extreme northern part of Walkhampton Common, the river forming its western boundary, the oft-repeated story of the sheep-stealer attaches. In the attempt to climb over it with the sheep on his shoulders he slipped, and the animal's legs being clasped round his neck, he was strangled. From the Rundle Stone to this point we have been traversing the boundary line of the forest, which here crosses the Walkham and runs up Dead Lake, but now we leave it. The suggestion that has been made that the line was once drawn from Mis Tor to White Tor rests on nothing but supposition, and is directly contrary to such evidence as we possess concerning it.

We turn eastward and trace the Walkham upwards. Soon we shall find it makes a great bend, the stream flowing from the N. Just above this bend the track leading from the Blackabrook to Cudlipp Town Down and Wapsworthy (T. 12) crosses the river at Shallow Ford. But we do not go quite so far as that, for on reaching a rivulet that comes down into the Walkham from Black Hole, R., we turn up by it, and following it for about 100 yards, shall find ourselves on the track. Following this up the hill we shall cross the Prison Leat at a fording-place, and about ¼ m. further on shall reach the springs of the Blackabrook. From this point the route to Princetown and Two Bridges has been given in Excursion 5, in which it was also stated that the path through the Prison ground lies by Fitz's Well (T. 12).

This object we shall find about ½ m. S. of the point at which our track by the Blackabrook enters the New Forest enclosure (Ex. 5). Since the formation of the latter a wall has been built round the well, otherwise it is the same as ever it was, except that it is less striking now than when it stood, as I remember it, on the open moor. Fice's Well, as it is locally called, used to be spoken of as being warm in winter and cold in summer, and according to Bellamy is a spring of the kind that are in evident connection with rivers, and which, he says, "to have attained their elevated temperature, must have descended through some passages of the river-bed to a great depth of the earth before reappearing at the surface."*

A little structure formed of slabs of granite, about 3 feet high, is raised over the well, the cover stone being oblong, and measuring nearly 4 feet in length, by rather over 3 feet in width. In the front part of this cover is a sunken panel, in which are carved in relief the letters I. F., and the date 1568. John Wilson, the Christopher North of *Blackwood*, noticed this well when on a visit to Dartmoor, and mis-read the date as 1168, "which," he says, "must be a lie." But had he been more careful in his examination he would have found that the inscription does not lie. The second figure is rather curiously formed, it is true, but this is only characteristic of the manner of writing it in

---

* *Natural History of South Devon*, p. 146.

the sixteenth century, ánd it would be recognised by anyone to-day as 5.* The letters are supposed to represent the initials of John Fitz, and there is good reason for believing this to be the case. [*Crosses*, Chap. XI.] Early in the last century there was a moorland tradition to the effect that John, or James, Fice, a traveller, experienced some great relief from the spring, and in gratitude raised the little edifice over it, while another story, related in Tavistock, told how this was set up by John Fitz, of Fitzford. He and his lady being "pixy-led" when riding over the moor, found, on drinking the water of a certain spring, that the spell of the mischievous elves was broken, and that they could no longer lead them from their way. Grateful for this deliverance he placed the granite covering over the water that possessed such miraculous power (Ex. 15). Two or three other stories are related of this well.

Quite near to it a clapper spans the Blackabrook. It was swept away in 1873 by the same flood that so greatly damaged the one under Bear Down (Ex. 5), and remained in a dismantled state for some years, but has fortunately been restored. The path that evidently passed this way seems to have been the precursor of the one on which the present high road is formed, for in the eighteenth century we find that the track which then ran across the forest passed the Rundle Stone. Continuing on our way we shall soon reach the road, which is exactly ½ m. from the well.

[Should the visitor desire to extend this walk he may, instead of returning from the Walkham by the Blackabrook Head path (T. 12), make his way up that river to the Lich Path (T. 18), where it crosses it at Sandy Ford.

This is rather less than ¾ m. above Shallow Ford. Following the Lich Path eastward he will cross the Prison Leat at a bridge, and make his way along the edge of Conies' Down to Travellers' Ford on the Cowsic, which is about 1 m. from the Walkham. Instructions for reaching the head waters of the Blackabrook from this point are given in Ex. 5. This will add about 3 m. to the ramble.]

To reach Fitz's Well from Princetown direct the first point will be the Rundle Stone ; then turn R. into the Two Bridges road, and take the first turning on the L. Here the Prison ground is entered, the path running through it as described above. From Two Bridges the way will lead the visitor along the Tavistock road to within a few hundred yards of Rundle Stone Corner, when he will enter the Prison ground on the R. Although the path to the well existed long before there were any prison enclosures on the moor, and the public have an unquestionable right of way there, visitors are, as previously observed, generally warned off when the prisoners are at work near where they may happen to be passing. It would be well therefore that the

---

* "During the whole of the sixteenth century, in inscriptions, the 5 took different forms, resembling more or less the same figure as commonly written in France at the present day, and in many instances it is easily mistaken for a 1, particularly in inscriptions of the middle and latter half of the century." Thomas Wright's *Essay on the Antiquity of Dates expressed in Arabic Numerals.* But Christopher North ought to have known that the figure could not be 1.

rambler should so time his visit to those parts of the Prison enclosures to which he has access as to be sure that no convicts will be there. They are not abroad after 5 p.m.

ALTERNATIVE ROUTE *from Mis Tor to Rundle Stone. Hut Circles —Blowing Houses on the Walkham—Merivale.*

If the rambler has not already visited the old tinners' houses on the L. bank of the Walkham, described in Ex. 1, and also desires to see the hut circles on the rock-strewn slope to the south-west of Mis Tor, he may perhaps prefer to return to Rundle Stone Corner by a route that will embrace these. From the tor he will pass down the hill to the newtake wall, his course being S.W. Entering the newtake, and still following the same course, he will come upon the hut circles when about half way between the wall and the river. These ruined dwellings are scattered on the side of the hill, and a few of them are enclosed within small pounds. One of these is situated not very far from the Walkham. By following the river downward he will soon come upon the second of the blowing-houses described in Ex. 1, and still further down, at the lower end of some mining gerts, will reach the other. On this common near Over Tor (Ex. 1), a mass of granite called the Church Rock used to be pointed out as one of the abodes of the pixies, and it was said that by placing the ear against it the sound of church bells could be heard. A similar story is told in connection with an outlying pile of White Tor, on Cudlipp Town Down (Ex. 8). Passing down the stream to Merivale Bridge we gain the Princetown road, following which we climb the hill L. to Rundle Stone.

Merivale is much in favour with the angler, but not every one of them perhaps meets with a similar experience to that of Mr. A. B. Collier, the well-known Dartmoor artist, when he was once fishing in the neighbourhood. The body of an elderly man, which had been found in the river, was brought into the Dartmoor Inn while he was there. An inquest was held, and on the foreman of the jury being asked for the verdict, he announced as their finding, " Died by the visitation of the Almighty, brought on by crossing the river when it was vlidded."

CROCKERN TOR.

Directions having been given for reaching this, the first of Risdon's " three remarkable things " in the forest (Ex. 5), and the subject of the Stannaries having received notice in the *Terms* section, we may now confine our remarks to the tor itself as a meeting-place of the tinners of Devon.

Unfortunately Crockern Tor has not escaped the hand of the vandal, and objects that formerly existed on the hill, and which would have rendered it doubly interesting to-day, are no longer to be seen there. These, we learn from Risdon, consisted of " a table and seats of moorstone hewn out of the rocks," and were presumably used by the stannators at their gatherings. A hundred and sixty-five years after that writer's book was completed, namely, in 1795, Mr. John Laskey, during an excursion on Dartmoor, visited Crockern Tor, but found that the table and seats had disappeared. Making enquiries in the locality, he discovered that the relics had been removed to Prince Hall, during the time that estate was in the occupation of Mr. Gullet. who commenced his operations there in 1780. Thirty years after

Mr. Laskey's visit the spoliation of Crockern Tor was ascribed either to Sir Francis Buller, who succeeded Mr. Gullet at Prince Hall (Ex. 4), or to Mr. Thomas Leaman. But there is good reason for believing that the information obtained by Mr. Laskey was correct, and that it was Mr. Gullet, who is known to have erected many new farm buildings at Prince Hall, and not Sir Francis, who resorted to the tor as a convenient quarry. That Mr. Leaman, however, also had a part in the despoiling of the rude court of the tinners, there is little doubt. He, I find, was the owner in the latter part of the eighteenth century of Dunnabridge Farm, at that time one of the ancient forest tenements, but now belonging to the Duchy, and to this farm it was reported the stone forming the stannators' table had been removed. In the Rev. E. A. Bray's journal of 1831, he states that the tenant of Bear Down then told him that the stone was drawn to Dunnabridge Farm by twelve yoke of oxen, and many years ago I heard the same story on the moor.

Immediately within the gate of Dunnabridge Pound (Ex. 42), is an interesting object sometimes referred to as the Judge's Chair, and which it has been said was brought from Crockern Tor. But this story has evidently arisen through confusing the pound with the farm, and was certainly never heard on the moor in the first half of the nineteenth century. In the year above named Mr. Bray visited Dunnabridge Farm for the purpose of seeing the stone his tenant had told him of, and nothing can be more certain than that such a report had not arisen at that time. After seeing the stone at the farm, which is still there (Ex. 42), he went on to the pound and examined the Judge's Chair, which, however, was not then known by that name, and which he suggested might have been the seat of an Arch-druid. He says not a word about this having been brought from Crockern Tor ; on the contrary, he expresses his satisfaction that the person who was said to have carried away the table from the tor did not have recourse to the pound for the stone he required. It is quite plain that the story originated after Mr. Bray's time. It became known, probably through the medium of Mrs. Bray's book, that something was to be seen at Dunnabridge (meaning Dunnabridge Farm) that had been taken from Crockern Tor, and it is easy to see how the relic in Dunnabridge Pound should come to be regarded as that object, and also how it should be called the Judge's Chair. I was rather amused once when, after explaining this to a driver who was in the habit of taking visitors to the pound, he said to me, "Well, I shan't have it that way. I've always told everybody it was the Judge's Chair, and that 'twas brought from Crockern Tor, and I'm not going to alter my story now."

By the side of the Moreton road, and not very far from the ruined cottage below Crockern Tor, is another stone which used to be associated with the hill of the tinners, but on what grounds I could never discover. It was brought to my notice many years ago, but all I could learn was that it was called the Judge's Corner. It is not far from Spader's Cottage, but on the R. of the way in going towards Post Bridge, and at a corner of Muddy Lake Newtake. Its situation probably accounts for its name.

[Dunnabridge Pound is reached from Two Bridges, from which it is distant 2½m., by the Ashburton road, which passes Prince Hall Lodge (1 m.) and crosses the Cherry Brook by the bridge of the same name just beyond. The pound and the farm are described in the **Hexworthy District**, Ex. 42.]

FROM ASHBURTON ROAD BEYOND TWO BRIDGES.
NEAR PRINCEHALL LODGE.

FROM ASHBURTON ROAD BEYOND TWO BRIDGES.
NEAR PRINCEHALL LODGE.

SHORTER EXCURSIONS.

By means of these the foregoing rambles may be varied. The places where descriptions of the different objects, and the directions for reaching them may be found, are indicated in brackets. As in the case of the other Excursions, the distances given include the return.

S. Ex. 1.—*Hut Circles at Head of Yes Tor Bottom*, 3½ m. T. B., 6½ m. Devil's Bridge, in Devil's Gully (Ex. 1). Strike up over common R., making towards the railway. Leave it a little on R. Hut circles will soon be seen on the common. Make towards the railway L., where it is seen at the bottom of the hill, and a hut enclosure (Ex. 1) will be observed. Return to railway (on the hill) and follow it to the siding at the quarry. Then cross, and return to Princetown by the path running near to it (Ex. 1).

[This excursion may be extended by passing down the hill from the pound to the railway, and crossing it. This can then be followed round King Tor to the siding named.]

S. Ex. 2.—*Hisworthy Tor, Hollow Tor, and Red Cottages*, 4 m., T.B., 7 m. North Hisworthy. Bear a little L. down hill to Hollow Tor. Continue down hill to road leading to Red Cottages (Ex. 1). Go on to the quarry and the railway. Turn L. and follow the latter to Princetown, as in the previous Ex.

S. Ex. 3.—*Merivale Antiquities*, 6 m. T.B., 7 m. Rundle Stone (Exs. 1, 6); before reaching this Herne Hole, where is the prison quarry, is passed L. Mission Room (R. 1 a). Down the road for ¼ m. Strike L. to the rows (Ex. 1).

S. Ex. 4.—*Ward Bridge and Vixen Tor*, 12 m. T.B., 13 m. Rundle Stone (Ex. 1, 6). Mission Room (R. 1 a.) Down the hill to gate on L. Enter (Ex. 1) and follow track to Long Ash Farm (Ex. 1). Cross Long Ash Brook by clapper, then on, still following the track, to Hucken or Okel, Tor (Ex. 1). On past Davy Town Farm and cross brook by Withil Farm (Ex. 1). Turn down the hill R. to Ward Bridge (Ex. 7). Up the hill (Ex. 7) to Sampford Spiney. Pass church on L. and on to common. (Ex. 7, T. 13). Follow track below Pu Tor Cottage and continue on with wall on R. Pass Heckwood Tor on L. of track (T. 13). Descend to Beckamoor Brook, with Vixen Tor on hill on further side (T. 13), or go by way of Vixen Tor Farm. Onward to road and turn R. to Merivale Bridge (Ex. 1). Cross bridge to gate of lane leading to Long Ash (*ante*) and return to Princetown by road, as in Ex. 1.

S. Ex. 5.—*Blowing Houses on the Walkham*, 7 m., T.B., 8 m. Rundle Stone (Ex. 1, 6). Mission Room (R. 1 a). Strike in over common R. Descend to river. Lower House about a furlong above Merivale Bridge (Ex. 1, 6). Higher House about ½ m. further up. (Ex. 1, 6). On R. bank of river is the farm of Shillapark.

S. Ex. 6.—*Mis Tor*. Rundle Stone, 6½ m., T.B., 7½ m. (Ex. 1, 6). Then as in Ex. 6.

S. Ex. 7.—*Fitz's Well*, 4½ m. See Ex. 6. Rundle Stone (Ex. 1, 6). Turn in from Two Bridges road (Ex. 6), Follow road ½ m. to Well.

S. Ex. 8.—*Blackabrook and Holming Beam*, 8½ m., T.B., 6½ m. Rundle Stone (Ex. 1, 6). Up by wall towards Mis Tor (Ex. 6). Turn R. at corner. Follow wall down to Blackabrook (Ex. 5, 6, and T. 12). Cross stream and follow wall to next corner. Turn R., keeping wall on that side, to road near Two Bridges. Turn L. for that place, and R. if for Rundle Stone. (P.T. 1½m. less if return is made by way of T.B.)

S. Ex. 9.—*Peat Cot and Nun's Cross*, 5½ m., T.B., 8¼ m. Castle Road (Ex. 3). Leave Peat Cot on L. Strike Track (T. 1, as sketched in Ex. 2), and follow it to Nun's Cross. Return to Princetown by T. 1. The distance from T.B. will be less if the visitor goes by way of Round Hill, as in Ex. 3.

S. Ex. 10.—*White Works and Swincombe*, 8½ m., T.B., 11½ m. Castle Road (Ex. 3) on to White Works (Ex. 3). Thence to the ford below Fox Tor (Ex. 3), and follow the river down to Swincombe Ford (Ex. 4). Cross by the Fairy Bridge (Ex. 4, 43). Thence home by the track through Tor Royal Newtake (T. 8, Ex. 4), or, if the destination be two Bridges, across Swincombe Newtake (T. 10), to Prince Hall

Bridge. Return, reverse of Ex. 4. If the return to T.B. is made by way of Prince Hall the distance will be 9½ m.

S. Ex. 11.—*Nun's Cross and the Rows near Down Tor*, 7 m., T.B., 10 m. Nun's Cross (T. 1, Ex. 2). Thence up the hill in front, bearing a little to the R. with the head of the Newleycombe Lake (Ex. 2), which flows W., on the R. Keep on W. to the rows which will be seen on the common (Ex. 2). Then turn N.W., and descend the hill to the Newleycombe Lake; cross, which it is usually easy to do, and up to Kingsett. Thence back as in Ex. 2.

S. Ex. 12.—*Lether Tor Bridge, Nosworthy Bridge, Combeshead, and Thrushel Combe*, 12 m., T.B., 15 m. Lether Tor Bridge, as in Ex. 2. Thence on to Nosworthy Bridge (Ex. 39), and up through Dean Combe (Ex. 39), to Combeshead Farm. Thence to Thrushel Combe. The Mining Remains at Dean Combe Head, and the Antiquities at Thrushel Combe, are described in Yelverton District.

S. Ex. 13.—*Hart Tor Hut Circles and Rows*, 3¼ m., T.B., 6¼ m. Hart Tor (Ex. 2). Circles on slope on nearing it. Rows on slope on further side (Ex. 2). Down the hill to Black Tor Ford, and return as in Ex. 2.

S. Ex. 14.—*Black Tor, Blowing Houses on the Mew, and Peak Hill*, 6 m., T.B., 9 m. Devil's Bridge (Ex. 1). Double Waters (Ex. 1). Strike L. over common to Black Tor. Descend to the ford (Ex. 2), and follow down stream for a short distance to the Blowing Houses. Mount R. bank, and make for wall of Stanlake Farm (Ex. 2). Keep wall on L., and pass over common S.W. Hut circles may be seen here. Ascend Peak Hill. Turn R. to Princetown road.

———

ROUTES FROM PRINCETOWN AND TWO BRIDGES.

The Route distances given do not include the return.

R. 1. To Tavistock. W. (A) *Rundle Stone, Merivale, Moortown*, about 7½ m. (B) *Rundle Stone, Merivale, Moor Shop*, about 7½ m.* T.B., ½ m. further. Reverse, R. 15.

[The objects passed on this route are described as follows:— Those between P.T. and T.B. and Merivale are noticed in Exs. 1, 6; those beyond Merivale in Exs. 7, 8. As already observed, it would be well that these should be consulted before starting.]

(A) Rundle Stone (Ex. 6), thence westerly by the road, passing the granite posts by the roadside (Ex. 1), and shortly afterwards cross the head waters of the Long Ash Brook (Ex. 1), near the Mission Room. A fine view of Mis Tor on the R., and in front a very extensive one of the country beyond the Tamar, with the Cornish hills in the distance. The antiquities noticed in Ex. 1 are on the plain piece of ground seen L. soon after passing the Mission Room, a short distance across the common. Here are hut circles on either hand; soon after passing them Merivale Bridge is reached. ¼ m beyond the bridge is the fourth

———

* Princetown Church is about 7 m. from Tavistock. The distances here given are from the cross roads near the Duchy Hotel.

milestone from Tavistock, near which we may leave the road, and follow a green track (L). This is part of the branch of the Abbots' Way (T. 1), and will lead us to a ford over the Beckamoor Combe Water (Ex. 7), and thence to the Windy Post (Ex. 7). The track then descends to Quarry Lane (T. 1, Ex. 7), entering it near the gate of Moortown. At the western end of Quarry Lane the path over Whitchurch Down is followed (T. 1). This leads by another cross (Ex. 7), and by the golf links, when the Tavistock road will be struck. Cross this and bear L. to the Square Seat (Ex. 7), and pass down the edge of the common with the wall of the enclosures close on the R. From the first gate reached (in the corner) a good path leads direct to the G.W.R. Station. (B) The road from the fourth milestone crosses Beckamoor Combe (Exs. 8) under Cocks' Tor (Ex. 8), and a short distance beyond the third milestone leaves the common. Descending Pork Hill it reaches Moor Shop (Ex. 8 ; cross roads, R. to Peter Tavy, L. to Horrabridge), and 1½ m. further on passes the entrance to Mount Tavy (R. Ex. 8), from which Vigo Bridge, at the N.E. end of the town, is ½ m. distant.

R. 2. To Lydford. N.W. by N., from Rundle Stone ; N.W. from T.B. (A) *Mis Tor, White Tor, Hill Bridge, Yard Gate, Forstall Cross*, about 11 m., T.B., ½ m. further. (B) *Cowsic, Black Dunghill, Walkham, White Tor*, T.B., 11 m. Reverse, R. 22.

[Objects passed E. of the Walkham are described in Exs. 1, 6 ; objects W. of that stream in Exs. 8, 9, 10.]

(A) Rundle Stone (Ex. 6) thence to Great Mis Tor as in Ex. 6, and down the steep side of the hill N.W. by N. to the Walkham, which should be struck at the weir of the Grimstone Leat. Cross the stream, and climb the bank to the group of hut circles immediately above, close to which is the stone circle noticed in Ex. 8. White Tor stands about 1 m. N.W. on the further side of Langstone Moor, but in making for this object it will be well to keep a little to the R., in order to avoid the marshy ground around the springs of the Peter Tavy Brook. By the side of the path under White Tor (T. 16) is the menhir mentioned in Ex. 8]

[Should the state of the weather render the crossing of the Walkham doubtful, it will be better for the excursionist to make his way from Rundle Stone to Merivale Bridge, and when near the fourth milestone from Tavistock turn R. to Great Staple Tor (Ex. 8). Just before reaching it the narrow path to Peter Tavy (T. 14) will be struck, and may be followed for a short distance down the hill, or the rambler may make his way N. to Roose Tor, and then descend the hill L. The point to be gained is the wall of the Wedlake enclosures, northward of Roose Tor, which is kept close on the L. to the corner of it, when the rambler makes direct for White Tor, crossing the Peter Tavy Brook, and shortly afterwards striking the green path (T. 16). The menhir is here on the R.] .

From White Tor (Ex. 8) the way lies N.W. to the foot of Cudlipp Town Down, about 1 m. distant. Here, very near to the wall of the enclosures, is a rubble heap thrown up by the miners, and close to this is a stile, whence a path leads straight down across one field to the Wapsworthy road. On reaching this the rambler will turn R., the road here running about N.E. This he will follow for about ⅓ m., when he will turn L. into Church Lane, and descend to Hill Bridge (Exs. 8, 10).

[Another route from White Tor to the bridge is by way of Wapsworthy (Ex. 10). From the tor a direction a little W. of N. is followed to a rough track that comes up through the newtakes from the settlement named. On reaching the latter turn L., and follow the Peter Tavy road for about ¼ m., and then turn R. into the lane leading to the bridge.]

From Hill Bridge pass up the road by Hill Town (Ex. 10), and where it forks choose the L. branch, but avoid taking the next turning L. Very shortly Yard Gate (Ex. 10) will be reached, on passing through which strike R., close to the wall of an enclosure to the common. Here the rambler is on an old track to Lydford (T. 18), and will follow it, with Yellowmead Farm (Ex. 10) below him on the R., to Forstall Cross (Ex. 10). Two or three paths cross here (T. 18, 21, 25), but the one that must be followed runs about N.W. by N. It passes over the ridge and in ½ m. or so reaches the gate at Down Lane (Ex. 10), which runs almost in the same direction. At the bottom of the lane is the Okehampton highway, which the excursionist, turning R., follows to the seventh milestone from Tavistock, passing Higher and Lower Beardon on his L. He enters the gate close to it, and passes down through the brake with Skit Steps on the R. to the foot-bridge near the old mill. Crossing this he follows the lane, and bearing L. will speedily enter the village.

(B) This is the better route from Two Bridges. The commons are entered just after crossing the Devonport Leat on the road to Rundle Stone. Pass up N., with the Cowsic R., and the wall of the Prison enclosures L. (Ex. 5). On reaching the corner of the wall strike N.W. by W. across Holming Beam to Black Dunghill nearly ¾ m., just beyond which the track (T. 12) passing Blackabrook is reached. Follow this, the direction still about the same, to Shallow Ford (Ex. 6) on the Walkham, ¾ m. further. Follow the track for ½ m. to Deadlake Head (Ex. 8), and then strike due W. across Langstone Moor (Ex. 8) to White Tor, From this point the directions will be found under A.

R. 3.—To Okehampton, with branches to Belstone. N.

Walkham Head, Tavy Hole, Broad Amicombe Hole, Dinger Plain, West Mil Tor, P.T. about 15½ m., T.B., 14 m. If by way of Maiden Hill (Ex. 5) from T.B. the distance from that place will be 13½ m. Belstone 1 m. less from either place. Reverse, R. 29.

[For description of objects S. of Walkham Head see Exs. 5, 6, 10 ; those between that place and Broad Amicombe are noticed in the Lydford District, Ex. 11 ; those beyond Broad Amicombe are in the Okehampton District, and are described in Ex. 15. See also C.R. 2, 10, 17.]

Rundle Stone (Ex. 6) ; thence to New Forest Corner, near Little Mis Tor (Ex. 5, 6), and down N.N.E. to the Prison leat, which is followed nearly to the point where the water is taken in from Spriddle Lake. Just before this is reached the Lich Path (T. 18) is carried over the leat, and here the rambler crosses, and turns R. Soon after this Timber Bridge is crossed, and beyond it the track forks. But the way lies straight on, with the Walkham, here a tiny stream, in sight on the L. About 1 m. above Timber Bridge is the end of the track, and the springs of the Walkham are seen a little to the R., the stream making a bend just below.

[Walkham Head may be reached direct from Two Bridges by way of the Cowsic, proceeding first as directed in R. 2 (B). When the corner of the enclosure is passed the rambler continues a northerly course, having the Cowsic on the R., but gradually leaving it, so as to strike the Lich Path (T. 18) about ½ m. to the W. of it. Crossing this track he pursues a course N.W. by N., passing over Conies' Down (Ex. 5) to Spriddle Combe (T. 16). This he also crosses, and, taking care not to keep too much to the R. will soon strike the Walkham Head track near its end.]

At Walkham Head the stream (two tiny rivulets here) must be crossed, the actual source being left on the R., and in making his way up the further bank the rambler must bear a little to the L., in order to avoid the fen on the top of the ridge. Progress will not be very rapid, the slope, which is known to the moormen as Horsey Park, being covered with old turf ties, overgrown with whortleberry plants. On reaching the summit of the ridge a part of the moor not hitherto seen comes into view. On the high ground on the L., across the valley of the Rattle Brook (Ex. 11), are several tors, chief among which is the fine pile of Great Links Tor (Ex. 12). To the R. of this, and in front of the rambler, is Amicombe Hill (Ex. 12), and to the R. of that again Great Kneeset (Ex. 14). The dip to the L. of this hill, which is of a pyramidal form is Broad Amicombe Hole, the point for which we are making. R. of Kneeset is Black Ridge, with Little Kneeset under it, and R. of that Fur Tor, the nearest pile of rocks, and Cut Hill. If the visitor has reached the top of the ridge at the proper point, Fur Tor should bear N.E. by N. The course is now about N.N.E., a little to the R. of the objective, but on reaching the Tavy, above Tavy Hole, a line due N. should be followed. The Amicombe should be struck at Fur Tor Foot, W.N.W. of the summit of the tor, and followed to its source due W. of Great Kneeset. The rambler can make no mistake if he avoids following any stream branching from it R. At its source, in Broad Amicombe Hole, he is on the track running from Okehampton to Post Bridge *via* Cut Lane, but it is not defined here. T. 79 and 34 should now be consulted. The first object to reach is Dinger Tor, a very short distance beyond which the rambler will strike the peat track, T. 34. For this purpose he will pass through the hollow, and, soon striking the head of another little stream, flowing due N., will follow it to Kneeset Foot, the point at which it meets the West Ockment. Here that river is crossed, and the hill beyond it ascended, the direction of Dinger Tor from Kneeset Foot being N.E. by N., and the distance exactly 1 m. Lints Tor, which is worth visiting, lies about midway between these two points, a little to the L. Viewed from a distance its rocks bear a striking resemblance to a tower (Ex. 14). (If the Ockment cannot be crossed at Kneeset Foot the rambler must make his way up the bank to Kneeset Nose. See *Branch to Belstone*, *Post*, and R. 29). On reaching the peat track beyond Dinger Tor, which consists of a single mass of rock, the rambler will have a well defined path to the road at Moor Gate (Exs. 14, 15. T. 34). He will leave High Willes, Yes Tor and West Mil Tor on the L., and Row Tor on the R. Between the two latter he will find himself close to the

Moor Brook, and near this his path is carried to the gate. Here the road across Okehampton Park (Ex. 14) to the town is followed.

[*From T.B. via Maiden Hill.* The Cowsic is followed upwards (Ex. 5) to Conies' Down Tor, and a course about N. by W. is then followed to the Tavy, which is about 1½ m. distant. This will lead the visitor over Maiden Hill, on the N. side of, which he will pass between the sources of the Cowsic and Spriddle Lake. Here he crosses the fen, and unless the weather be dry it is not advisable to adopt this route. On reaching the Tavy it is crossed, and a direction W.N.W. is followed down the hill, with Fur Tor on the R., to the Amicombe, when the directions given *ante* must be followed.

Branch to Belstone. On leaving Amicombe Hole a course N.E. by N. is taken, which will lead the rambler to the West Ockment at a point where it makes a sharp bend ¼ m. above Kneeset Foot. He follows it upwards for ½ m., and crosses it at Kneeset Nose, where it receives Brim Brook (Ex. 14, 16), which flows from the N.N.E. This tributary then becomes his guide, and must be followed to its source. Less than ½ m. beyond this, N.N.E., the head of the Blackaven will be struck, and this is followed to the clapper below East Mil Tor, known as New Bridge (Ex. 16, T. 35). The rambler may now either trace the stream to Crovenor Steps (Ex. 16), where it falls into the East Ockment, or he may strike N.E. across the common, and reach that river above the enclosures belonging to East Ockment Farm (Ex. 16), and follow it down to the steps, which are at the N.E. corner of the farm enclosures. From this crossing place a road runs about N.E. to Belstone village.

To Belstone from Two Bridges. N. C.R. 2 to East Dart Head. Thence due N. across the fen to Taw Head, not quite ½ m. Newtake is R. (Ex. 19, Extension), and Cranmere L. From Taw Head the way is given in C.R. 10.

[If the rambler desires to go by way of Cut Hill he will follow the directions given in Ex. 11, Extension. From the summit of the hill he will make for East Dart Head, either by proceeding N. for a few hundred yards, and then steering about E.N.E. to the Dart, which he will follow to its source ; or he may strike N. by E. over Flatters for 1¼ m., and then N.E. by N., with the summit of Black Hill L., for ½ m., which will bring him to the head of the river.]

R. 4.—To Chagford, N.E., 12 m. Moreton, 13½ m. T.B., 1½ m. less. Reverse, R. 35.

[The objects met with on these routes are described in Exs. 4, 5, 21, 46 ; see also roads.]

(Few directions are necessary, the high road being followed in each case, but should the rambler desire to make his way over the moor to Chagford he will find instructions for doing so in the Excursions in the Post Bridge District, at which place he will leave the road. Or he may pass up the West Dart by Wistman's Wood (Ex. 5), and ascend the hill to the wall beyond Brown's House (Ex. 5), when he will find himself on the line of route from Tavistock to Chagford (R. 10, B) q.v. The line comes from Row Tor, W., and crosses Broad Down to the East Dart).

The first point is Two Bridges. Thence bear L. on the brow of the hill behind the hotel, to Post Bridge, passing Crockern Tor (Ex. 5) and the Powder Mills (L) on the way. Bellaford Tor (Ex. 44) is R., a little beyond the latter. Cross the East Dart and ascend Meripit Hill (Ex. 45) to Newhouse, or as it is now called, the Warren House Inn. 1¼ m. beyond this the Chagford road branches L.

[*To Chagford.* For the first ¾ m. the road runs over the common, and then descends to Jurston, just beyond which the Bovey is crossed at Jurston Bridge. It then ascends to Meldon Hill, over the side of which the rambler makes his way, with the common L. Beyond this is Nat Tor Down, which he leaves R., and then descends into Chagford, with Padley Common L. See Chagford District.]

From the junction the Moreton road runs on to Moor Gate (Ex. 21), 4 m. from the town, where it leaves the moor. 1 m. further on is Beetor Cross (Ex. 22), where the visitor bears L., but not into the narrow road leading to Beetor Farm. Pass over Worm Hill, at the bottom of which the Bovey is crossed. 1 m. beyond this is Bughead Cross, from which Moreton is distant another mile.

R. 5.—To Bovey Tracey. E. by N. (A) *Dartmeet, Ponsworthy, Cockingford Mill, Pudsham Down, Newhouse, Hemsworthy Gate,* P.T. 16½ m. T.B., *via* Prince Hall, 17½ m. (B) *Two Bridges, Higher Cherry Brook Bridge, Bellaford Bridge, West Shallowford, Rowden Down, Dunstone Down, Blackslade, Hemsworthy Gate,* P.T. 1, m. T.B. 15½ m. (C) *Post Bridge, Runnage, Grendon Bridge, Gore Hill, Widecombe,, Hemsworthy Gate,* P.T. 18. T.B. 16½ m. Reverse, R. 42.

Route A is the most convenient.

[Objects between the starting points and Dartmeet and Post Bridge are described in Exs. 4, 42; objects beyond Grendon Cot and Dartmeet, in Exs. 28, 41; and those near and beyond Hemsworthy Gate, in Exs. 25, 26.]

(A) From P.T. by Tor Royal Lodge (T. 8) to Bull Park; across Tor Royal Newtake, passing the Crock of Gold (Ex. 4) to Swincombe Newtake and Swincombe Ford. Thence to Hexworthy, as in T. 8, and down to Hexworthy Bridge. Pass up between Huccaby and the chapel and through the gate at the top of the hill, then turn R. to Dartmeet. (*Hexworthy District*). From T.B. by the Ashburton road past the entrance to Prince Hall (Ex. 4) and on to Lower Cherry Brook Bridge and Dunnabridge Pound. Thence on by the enclosures of Brimpts, noticing Huccaby in the valley, R., and down to Dartmeet. (Or the track from Prince Hall Lodge to Hexworthy and Huccaby may be followed up, T. 10). Up Dartmeet Hill, passing the Coffin Stone (Ex. 41), and on to Ouldsbroom Cross, where the Ashburton road turns R. Straight on (the next road L. goes to Sherwell and Babeny) across Sherberton Common, and leaving this at Lock's Gate Cross, descend to Ponsworthy, on the road to Widecombe. Through the hamlet and up the hill, and 1¼ m. on take the turning R. This lane runs by Cockingford Mill (Ex. 26), and up the hill by Stone Cross, which is about ½ m. from the mill. Then keep L., passing over Pudsham Down to Ruddycleave Bridge; cross this and strike N.E. up over the common to Newhouse (Ex. 26, R. 42). Thence onward with the ruins L. and Rippon Tor high on the R., to Hemsworthy Gate, first turning R. (Exs. 26, 25).

(B) *To Hemsworthy Gate, via Bellaford.* Two Bridges, as in R. 4; thence to Higher Cherry Brook Bridge, 2 m. on the Post Bridge road.

Cross this and enter gate R., following the track by the wall over Lakehead Hill to Bellaford Bridge (T. 18). The next point is the Walla Brook, beyond Riddon Ridge, 1½ m., which stream should be struck between Riddon and Babeny, the course being S.E. (See remarks on crossing this in R. 42). Thence over the hill a trifle S. of E. to the road close to West Shallowford. Cross the West Webburn below the farm (T. 52), and pass up the side of Jordan Ball to Rowden Down (S. Ex. 86). Keeping R. the rambler will pass through the stroll on the E. side of the down to the road, which he will follow for a short distance S.E., and then strike across Dunstone Down, E., to Higher Dunstone, passing close to Wind Tor on the way. Thence we follow the Widecombe road for about 100 yards, and turning R. to Lower Dunstone, cross the East Webburn below it. A little beyond Chittleford we enter a field, L. (S. Ex. 87), and passing in front of Blackslade, gain the stroll above Tunhill (Ex. 26). Thence strike E.N.E. to Pil Tor , ¼ m., and E. by N. to Hemsworthy Gate, ½ m.

(C) *To Hemsworthy Gate via Runnage Bridge.* From Two Bridges through Post Bridge, as in R. 4, turning R. from the main road just before it enters on the common (Ex. 44). Follow the lane to Runnage Bridge, and thence across Soussons Common to Ephraim's Pinch, passing through the gate to Grendon Bridge. This road is the old Church Way (T. 76). Cross the Webburn and up to Hill Head. Descend by Blackaton Farm, and crossing the Blackaton Brook, leave the road and ascend the narrow way up Gore Hill (Ex. 28) to Blackaton Down. There is a green path over this, running S.E., by which the head of Church Lane is reached. Descend this, and at the bottom turn R. to Widecombe, which is close by. Leaving the Church R. ascend Widecombe Hill, with Bonehill Rocks L., Top Tor R., and follow road to Hemsworthy Gate. If driving it will be necessary to keep to the road at Blackaton, which is carried round Bittleford Down.

From Hemsworthy Gate the road runs E., with Rippon Tor high on the R. Skirting the head of Hound Tor Combe, it goes under Saddle Tor, L., and then bends N.E. A green path here runs over the down by which the pedestrian may shorten the distance a little. The road descends, with Punchaford Ball R., and Hey Tor L., to the Moorland Hotel (Ex. 25). 1 m. further on it leaves the commons, and leads directly to Bovey Tracey Station, which is 3 m. distant.

R. 6.—To Ashburton and Buckfastleigh. E. by S. (A) *Dartmeet, Ouldsbroom Cross, Pound's Gate, New Bridge, Holne Bridge,* P.T. 13½ m., or *via* Two Bridges, 14½ m., T.E. 13 m., to Ashburton.

(B) *Hexworthy, Saddle Bridge, Holne, Holne Bridge,* P.T., *via* Swincombe, 12½ m., T.B. 13½ m., to Ashburton.

(C) *White Works, Sandy Way, Aune Head, Ringleshutts, Holne, Holne Bridge,* P.T. 13½ m., T.B. 14 m., to Ashburton.

Reverse, R. 49.

[Objects are described (A) in Exs. 4, 27, 28, 41, 42 ; (B) in Exs. 4, 43, Holne Moor Section, and St. Ex. 96 ; (C) io Exs. 3, 43, and as in B.]

(A) To Ouldsbroom Cross *via* Dartmeet, as in R. 5 (A). Turn R. and follow road past Ouldsbroom Farm to Uppacott (Ex. 28), and thence on to Pound's Gate (Ex. 27, 28). Down the hill, with Leigh Tor on the L., turning R. at the foot, and skirting Deeper Marsh, to New Bridge. Up the hill, with Holne Chase on the L., then down Holne Chase Hill to Holne Bridge, whence road leads direct to Ashburton, distant 2 m.

(B) To Hexworthy from P.T. and T.B. as in R. 5 (A) Take the Holne road, running S.E. from the hamlet to Saddle Bridge (Hexworthy District), distant ¾ m. Cross the Wo Brook, and ascend Combestone Tor Hill. Pass tor on L. and on by Hangman's Pit to the Paignton Reservoir. Thence follow the road to Holne Moor Gate. Descend the hill, and take first turning to the L. Holne village lies R. a little further on. Pass this, and reach top of Holne Chase Hill. Descend to Holne Bridge.

(C) Leave P.T. by Castle Road (T. 7, Ex. 3) for White Works. Thence as in Ex. 3 to the confluence near Fox Tor Farm enclosures. (This point may be reached from T.B. by way of Prince Hall and Moorlands (Ex. 4). From the latter the rambler should cross the E. side of Tor Royal Newtake, in a direction due S., keeping the wall some distance on the L. The Swincombe river is 1½ m. from Moorlands). Cross stream, and follow up that branch of the Swincombe flowing down from the S.E., keeping it on the R. Soon the old track known as Sandy Way (T. 56) will be struck, and will lead the rambler by Aune Head Mire (Ex. 43) to the deserted Ringleshutts Mine, on Holne Moor. Thence a road leads to the highway very near to Holne Moor Gate. (See B. *ante*).

[If the rambler is bound for Buckfastleigh he does not turn L. below the Holne Moor Gate, as in B., but keeps straight down the steep Langaford Hill. The lane runs by Hawson, which lies L., and shortly afterwards forks. Either way leads to Buckfastleigh, but the R. branch is the shorter way, though not so well adapted for driving.]

R. 7.—To Brent, S.E., Ivybridge, S. by E., and Cornwood, S. *Siward's Cross, The Plym, Ducks' Pool, Red Lake Ford, Western Whitaburrow, Shipley,* 12 m. T.B. add 1½ m.

Branch to Ivybridge from the Plym: *Erme Head, Green Lake Bottom, Valley of Erme to Harford Bridge,* 12½ m. T.B. add 1½ m.

Branch to Cornwood from Siward's Cross: *Hart Tors, Shavercombe, Shell Top, Pen Beacon,* 9½ m. T.B. add 1½ m.

From T.B. the most direct route to Siward's Cross is by way of Round Hill Farm and Peat Cot as in Ex. 3. Reverse, Rs. 58, 59.

[The district through which these two routes run is described as follows :—Between P.T. and the Plym in Exs. 3, 37 ; between the Plym and the Erme in Exs. 33, 35 ; from the Erme to Shipley in Exs. 30, 32 ; and from the Erme to Harford Bridge in Exs. 32, 33. See also T. 1.]

To the common *via* Ivybridge Lane, and on by South Hisworthy Tor to Siward's Cross as in Ex. 2. (Here the Cornwood route branches. See *post*). The next point is Plym Ford, which lies beyond the ridge in front of the rambler in a direction S.S.E., and one mile distant. A reave will be seen running up the hill to the cairn on Eylesbarrow (Ex. 37), but this must be left well to the R., and the distance between it and the rambler gradually increased as he ascends. If he chooses he may follow the track leading from near Nun's Cross Farm (see T. 1), to Plym Ford, but the distance will then be rather greater. (At the ford the track to Ivybridge diverges from the Brent route : we will here describe the latter). The first point is a large stream work on the Black Lane Brook, nearly 1½ m. distant, its direction being E.S.E. by E. This course the rambler accordingly follows up the hill, leaving some rocks known as Great Gnats' Head (Ex. 37) a little to the R. When on the summit of the hill, and 1 m. from the ford, the line of route passes near Ducks' Pool, which will be seen L. Care must be taken in ascending this hill not to bear too much to the L., or the rambler will get on to the fen surrounding the source of the Plym ; it is better that he should err by keeping a little too much to the R. When Ducks' Pool is passed the stream work will soon be sighted. The rambler has now to make for Red Lake Ford (T. 1, Ex. 30), and crossing the stream work will strike S.E. over Green Hill, with the Erme in the valley R. (the river is not yet seen), and Stall Moor rising beyond it.

[Green Hill may also be reached from Princetown by way of White Works and Fox Tor. To the first-named T. 7 is followed ; thence the way lies to the ford, as in Ex. 3 ; up Fox Tor Gert, S. of the tor, to Fox Tor Head, where Black Lane is struck (T. 75) ; down this path to the stream work with Green Hill L. This is the best route for riders.]

Middle Mires, which is really a shallow gully, will be crossed ½ m. from the stream work, and ½ m. further on Red Lake, where also is a large working of the old miners, will be reached. The ford is nearly at the head of these remains, and as the track leading to it is plainly to be seen, the rambler will not very well miss it. On crossing the ford he will find himself on the Abbots' Way (T. 1), with a good path all the way to the moor gate at Shipley. Follow the Abbots' Way for ½ m. to the Crossways, where the ruined Zeal Tor tramroad (T. 60) intersects it at right angles. Here leave the Abbots' Way, and turn R. into the tram-road, and follow it till you lose it on the brow of the hill above Shipley. For a notice of this tram-road see Ex. 30. The road from Shipley to Brent runs down the valley with the river on the L. ½ m. outside the moor gate Didworthy Bridge is seen L. Here the rambler has a choice of paths to the village. He may either go straight on, and, passing through the hamlet of Aish, descend to Lydia Bridge (Brent District), or he may cross Didworthy Bridge, and, passing through the yard at the back of the Sanatorium (Ex. 29), reach a path that will lead him by the hedge across two fields to a narrow bridle path, which will bring him to Wash Gate. Here a road runs up to Lutton, where he will turn R., and descending Splatton Hill will soon be led to the village.

[*To Ivybridge.* The route from Flym Ford is at first along the branch of the Abbots' Way (T. 1), which, however, is not here very well defined. It runs up the hill from the river in a direction S. by E. to Broad Rock (Ex. 34), which is about 1 m. distant, S.E. Great Gnats' Head is seen L. in ascending. From Broad Rock the course is S.E. for 2 m., when the Erme will be struck near Green Lake Bottom, on its R. bank, opposite to Stony Bottom (Ex. 33). Erme Head, marked by a wilderness of stones, will be seen on leaving Broad Rock, and must be kept L., the way lying across the side of the hill that rises from the R. bank of the river. Horton's Combe, 1 m., where a little stream runs down L., is crossed near its head ; beyond this is Stinger's Hill (Ex. 33), to the S. of which Green Lake Bottom is situated. If preferred the Erme may be followed from its source to this point instead of the route over the hill. No further directions are necessary, as the Erme will lead the rambler to Harford Bridge (Ex. 32) about 4 m. below. There is good walking near the river on the R. bank. When in sight of Piles Wood (Ex. 32), which is on the L. bank under Three Barrows and Sharp Tor, a track (T. 65) running under Staldon Barrow, will be struck. In Green Lake Bottom a stone row may be seen running across the tin work. This can be followed to the fine stone circle on Stall Moor (Ex. 33), and will not take the rambler out of his way, as it runs parallel to the Erme. On emerging from the moor gate at Harford Bridge turn R. to the church, and follow the road L. past Broomhill, Lukesland, Erme Wood, and Stowford (Exs. 32, 33). (If it should be desired to visit Erme Pound and the antiquities near it, the Erme must be followed from its source, the rambler keeping on the L. bank. Soon after crossing Red Lake, where it falls into the Erme, the Pound will be reached. For a description of the remains near it see Ex. 32. After examining these the river can be crossed, and the route just sketched followed to Harford Bridge, or the rambler may make his way to Harford Church, by Quickbeam Hill and Sharp Tor (Exs. 32, 33). To do this he will cross Stony Bottom (Ex. 32), the depression down which Hook Lake runs into the Erme, at a point about ¼ m. above that river, and follow a southerly course. By doing this he should be able to see the line of granite posts defining the boundary between Harford Moor and Ugborough Moor (Ex. 32), and by following these will be led to the dip between Three Barrows and Sharp Tor. He will then see Harford Church in the valley, about 1½ m. distant, and in making towards it must be sure to keep above the enclosures on the R. When he comes abreast of the Church he will see a moor gate, where a lane runs down R. directly to it.]

[*To Cornwood.* From Siward's Cross follow the reave (see *ante*) up to Eylesbarrow (Ex. 37), and then descend the hill in a southerly direction to the Plym, passing Higher and Lower Hart Tors. The stream should be struck at Plym Steps (Ex. 37), where the Langcombe Brook falls into it. Then up the hill S. by W. to Shavercombe Brook (Ex. 37), 1 m. distant. Cross this, and continue on the same course, passing above Hen Tor (Ex. 37). On the further side of the Plym, opposite to this tor, is Ditsworthy Warren House, which is in full view. One mile S. of Hen Tor is Shell Top (Ex. 34), the loftiest eminence in this neighbourhood. This is the next point, and on reaching it Pen Beacon (Ex. 34) will be seen below, ½ m. distant and in a direction S. by E. The two are connected by a reave. This may be followed, and on passing the Beacon, a course S.S.E. must be followed for 1 m. to Broker's Plantation, where West Rrook Gate opens upon a path leading by Rook Farms to Heathfield Down, which is close to the village. (Ex. 34.)

R. 8.—To Shaugh and Plympton. S.S.W. *Nosworthy Bridge, Sheepstor Village, Cadaford Bridge*, P.T. about 8½ m. to Shaugh ; 12 m. to Plympton. T.B. add 1½ m. Branch to Cornwood and Ivybridge. Reverse, R. 67.

[Objects between P.T. and Nosworthy Bridge described in Exs. 2, 39 ; between Nosworthy Bridge and Cadaford Bridge in Ex. 38 ; between Cadaford Bridge and Plympton in Ex. 36.]

To Crazy Well Bridge, *via* Cramber Tor, as in Ex. 2. Thence descend the hill southward to the White Works track (T. 2) and turn R. About ½ m. on, near where Raddick Lane comes down R., a lane branches L. Strike into this, and in another ½ m. or so the ruined Nosworthy Farm will be reached. Cross the clapper over Newleycombe Lake L., and then almost immediately turn R. to the Narrator Brook flowing from Dean Combe (Ex. 39). Cross this and follow the path with the Burrator Lake R. (Ex. 39, T. 73) to Sheepstor village, which is 1 m. distant. Pass down near the church, leaving it L., and cross the Sheepstor Brook just below. Pass up Portland Lane, running S., to Ringmoor Cot, which is situated L. of the road. Here leave the road, which turns a little to the R., and follow the footpath over the top of Lynch Down (T. 72), which runs S., to Brisworthy Plantation, ½ m. distant, Ringmoor Down (Ex. 38) being on the L. Just beyond this, at the corner of the enclosures, the Tavistock and Cornwood road is reached (T. 69), and here the rambler turns L. for a few yards, then, leaving the lane to Brisworthy L., turns sharp to the R., just afterwards again bending L., the road running nearly S. Down the hill, with the Wigford Down Clay Works R., to Cadaford Bridge (Exs. 36, 38). At the S. end of it the road branches L. to Cornwood, R. to Shaugh and Plympton.

[The Cornwood road runs up to the grounds of Lee Moor House (Ex. 36), passing Blackaton Cross on the top of the hill. It then goes down to the Torry Brook (Ex. 36), which it crosses, and ascends the hill to Tolchmoor Gate (Ex. 36). Soon after it again descends, and nearly 1 m. from the gate Quick's Bridge is crossed. Further on the road is carried over the Piall Brook (Ex. 34), beyond which it skirts Heathfield Down and enters Cornwood village. The road to the station runs R.; that to Ivybridge, 3 m. distant, L.]

For Plympton the rambler ascends the hill R. from Cadaford Bridge, and on the top passes Shaden Plantation R., shortly afterwards reaching Brag Lane End. Here he turns R. for Shaugh (Shaugh District), which is near by. If his destination be Plympton he keeps straight on to Niel Gate, 1 m. distant, where he leaves the common. ¾ m. further on Browney Cross is passed (Ex. 36), and ½ m. beyond this the road crosses the Lee Moor Railway. Plympton Station is 3 m. distant.

[The road from P.T. to Yelverton has been described, as far as Goad's Stone, in Ex. 1. Beyond that waymark it climbs over the shoulder of Peak Hill (Ex. 39), and shortly after the descent on the further side is commenced it enters upon the enclosed land. 1 m. beyond this it passes through Dousland, and in another mile Yelverton is reached.]

TAVISTOCK DISTRICT.

DISTANCES. BY ROAD: *ASHBURTON*, *via* Two Bridges, 21 m. *BOVEY TRACEY*, *via* T.B., 25½ m. *BRENT TOR*, 3¾ m. *DO. VILLAGE*, 4¼ m. *BUCKFASTLEIGH*, *via* T.B., 22 m. *CHAGFORD*, *via* T.B., 18½ m. Cornwood, *via* Whitchurch and Grenofen Cross, Horrabridge, Walkhampton, Dousland and Cadaford Bridge (9), 13¾ m. *DARTMEET*, *via* T.B., 13 m. *DARTMOOR INN, LYDFORD*, *via* Heathfield, 8½ m., *via* Black Down, 7¾ m. *DOUSLAND*, 5½ m. *EXETER*, *via* Okehampton, 38 m. *HEXWORTHY*, *via* T.B., 13¼ m. *HILL BRIDGE*, *via* Peter Tavy, 5¾ m.; *via* Mary Tavy and Zoar Down, 7¼ m. *HOLNE*, *via* T.B., 18 m. *HORRABRIDGE*, *via* Whitchurch, 3½ m. *DO. STATION*, *via* Magpie, 4 m. *IVYBRIDGE*, see Cornwood, add 3 m. *LANE END*, for Tavy Cleave, 6¾ m. *LYDFORD*, *via* Heathfield and Manor Hotel, 7¼ m.; *via* Black Down and Skit, 8 m.; *via* Black Down and Dartmoor Inn, 8½ m. *MARY TAVY*, 3½ m. *MERIVALE BRIDGE*, 4¼ m. *MORETON*, *via* T.B., 20 m. *OKEHAMPTON*, 16 m. *PETER TAVY*, 3 m. *PLYMOUTH*, 14 m. *PLYMPTON*, *via* Roborough, George Hotel, and Plym Bridge, 14 m. *POST BRIDGE*, *via* T.B., 11½ m. *POUND'S GATE*, *via* T.B., 16¼ m. *PRINCETOWN*, 7½ m. *RUNDLE STONE*, 6 m. *SAMPFORD SPINEY*, 3½ m. *SHAUGH*, *via* Dousland and Cadaford Bridge, 10½ m. *SHEEPSTOR VILLAGE*, 2¾ m. from Dousland round Yennadon. *SOURTON*, 11 m. *SOUTH BRENT*, *via* Ivybridge, 21¾ m. *TAVY CLEAVE* (see Lane End). *TWO BRIDGES*, 8 m. *WALREDDON* (West Down Gate, for Double Waters), 2¼ m. *WAPSWORTHY*, *via* Peter Tavy, 5¼ m. *WARREN HOUSE INN*, *via* T.B., 13¾ m. *WIDECOMBE*, *via* T.B., 18 m. *YELVERTON*, 5 m.

By Rail: *EXETER* (L.S.W.), 42 m. *LYDFORD* (L.S.W., 6½ m., G.W., 7 m.) *OKEHAMPTON* (L.S.W.), 16½ m. *PLYMOUTH* (L.S.W.), 20½ m. (G.W.), 16¾ m. [Fares the same.] *PRINCETOWN* (G.W.), 16 m. *YELVERTON*, (G.W.), 5½ m.

Tavistock is about two miles from Dartmoor, but is very near to Whitchurch Down, which at one time formed a spur of the moor. As one of the stannary towns it was connected with it during several centuries, and there is early mention of lands in the parish possessing venville rights. One of the town's benefactors, John D'Abernon, held high offices in connection with Dartmoor in the fourteenth century. The Fitz family, of Fitzford, were early possessors of land on Dartmoor, and of these one of the members was the notorious Lady Howard. The Abbey was founded in 961, by Ordgar, Earl of Devon, and in it was afterwards preserved the important charter by which King John disafforested the County of Devon, with the exception of Dartmoor and Exmoor.

Three inscribed stones of early date are to be seen in the vicarage garden. One was discovered in the town, and the others in the neighbourhood of it.

EXCURSIONS FROM TAVISTOCK.

Tracks in the vicinity, Nos. 1, 12, 13, 14, 15, 16, 17, 21, 22, 23. [The area over which these excursions extend is bounded on the E. by the Walkham, and on the N. by an imaginary line drawn from 1 m. below the head of that stream to Hill Bridge, and thence to Lydford Station. The Merivale Antiquities and Mis Tor are noticed in the Princetown District, and Tavy Cleave in the Lydford District, but directions for reaching them are given here. Ex. 7, 9.]

Ex. 7.—*Whitchurch Down, Pu Tor, Sampford Spiney, Ward Bridge, Valley of the Walkham, Vixen Tor, The Windy Post*, 12 m.

We leave the town by a path opposite to the entrance to the

G.W.R. Station, which will lead us to Whitchurch Down. When we enter upon the down we pass upward with the enclosures L., and at a distance of about 150 yards from the higher corner of these shall reach what is known as the Square Seat. Here is a good view of the town we have just left, and also an exceedingly fine one of the moor, extending from the range on which Great Links Tor is situated to the Dewer Stone, and including among other prominent heights Hare Tor, above Tavy Cleave, White Tor, Cocks' Tor Hill, the Staple Tors, and North Hisworthy. (For the latter see *Princetown District*). We can also look away to the S.W. corner of the moor, where Pen Beacon, overlooked by Shell Top, rises above Cornwood (Ex. 36, R. 7). Northward is Brent Tor (Ex. 9), and to the R. of it the wide sweep of Black Down.

[From the E. end of the town a road leads to Whitchurch Down from Vigo Bridge. In ascending the hill a steep, narrow pack-horse track branching R. may be followed, or the more circuitous way of the road be chosen. In the latter case the visitor turns R. opposite to the entrance to Mount Tavy, the point gained being the same. Just where the road enters on the down there is a granite slab on the bank L. This is an old milestone. On its face, cut in deep letters, is the inscription, " 14 miles to Plymouth," and on the edge of it, " T. 1." About a couple of hundred yards further on is the head of a cross, set in its socket stone, also on the L. of the road. [*Crosses*, Chap. IX.] A little beyond this is a small parish boundary stone, bearing the letter W (Whitchurch) on one face, and the letter T (Tavistock) on the other. The road runs on to Warren's Cross (see *post*) with a branch by way of Middle Moor to the village of Whitchurch.]

Passing onward from the Square Seat we shortly cross the road just noticed, and make our way over the middle of the down by the golf links. On our R. is Middle Moor, and just beyond this we notice the entrance to Holwell, the ancient seat of the Glanvilles. A little further on we shall reach the cross mentioned in R. 1, and which stands on the line of the old Abbots' Way (T. 1). [*Crosses*, Chap. IX.] It is placed within a small circular enclosure, the low bank of which is much overgrown. From its appearance it is probable that this cross is of earlier date than the Abbots' Way. On the edge of the down to the R. are some ruined walls, which bear the name of Monkeys' Castle, but which it is not unlikely is a corruption of Monks' Castle.

Just beyond this cross, that is, a short distance E. of it, the Monks' path forked, one branch, the Abbots' Way, going straight on, and the other, the path through Sampford to Meavy and Plympton, diverging R. As we advance towards the E. end of the down we have on the R. Warren's Cross, close to a plantation, where the Tavistock and Sampford road crosses one coming up from Horrabridge. The latter runs L. to the small hamlet of Penny-come-Quick (*Pen-y-cwm-cuic*, the head of the narrow combe, or valley), and on through Moor Shop (R. 1) to Peter Tavy (Ex. 8). This we cross a little S. of the thirteenth milestone from Plymouth, and descend to Quarry Lane, which runs between the fields to the common at Moortown, ¾ m. distant.

Just before reaching the down a curious object may be observed in the wall on the L. It is a Blowing Stone, one of the kind formerly used at the time of summoning the venville tenants, and others, whose duty it was to assist in driving the moor. (See *Drift*, in *Terms* section).

On one side it is concave, and the horn being blown against this was supposed to give forth a louder 'sound. The stone has, of course, been brought to its present situation from some lofty point.

Near by is Iddymead Cottage, formerly known as Rogues' Roost, which title, if report be correct, was not inappropriate. It is said to have been the haunt of a band of sheep-stealers, whose depredations caused the farmers in the neighbourhood much uneasiness. No traces of the animals stolen from the commons were ever discovered, but it was whispered that they were driven to the Roost, and there slaughtered and cut up, the skins being concealed in a cave. The owner of the property told me some years ago that out of curiosity he had opened the so-called cave, which he found to be merely a hollow formed by some huge stones, but there were no signs of anything having been buried there.

On the R. at the end of the lane is Langstone, but the name does not owe its origin to the former presence of a menhir, as some visitors in their antiquarian zeal might perhaps be apt to imagine. The property was formerly called Lang's Stone, and being occupied by a Mr. Lang, was referred to as Lang's Stone. Instances of a similar nature are found in many places round the moor. Moortown stands on the verge of the common on the L. In Risdon's time it belonged to the Moringes, " a family which anciently wrote themselves De la More." There is a monument to this family in the church at Whitchurch. Early in the nineteenth century it was in the possession of John Ridout, whose name appears on an inscription on a paten which he presented to Sampford Spiney Church in 1811. In 1846 Moortown was the property of Jonas Ridout.

Passing up the hill in a south-easterly direction we reach Pu Tor, which, though not of great elevation, is yet a conspicuous object in this locality. The rock piles do not rise to a great height above the turf, but are nevertheless imposing. There are four principal groups, each placed towards one of the cardinal points. On the N. pile are several rock basins, the most perfect measuring 2ft. 10ins. by 2ft. 2ins. ; it is 10ins. deep. This one is furnished with a lip. Of the others two are in a fairly perfect state, but the remainder are much worn. On the W. pile there is another basin. The view from Pu Tor is exceedingly fine, much of the moor being revealed on one side, and a vast extent of cultivated country on the other. Between the S. and W. piles the distant Channel, with Mount Edgcumbe, are seen, and also the confluence of the Tamar and the Tavy, with the Cornish hills beyond. [*Gems*, Chap. XXI.]

Near the S. pile is a stone bearing the letters S.S.P. It is one of several on this common similarly inscribed, and marking the bounds of Sampford Spiney parish. The moorland part of this parish, which is defined by these stones, runs up into the common land belonging to Whitchurch, and for some little distance is but a mere strip. The boundary lines then diverge, one running towards Vixen Tor (see *post*) and the other nearly to the Windy Post (do.) They then converge, and meeting form a figure resembling a lozenge in heraldry, or, as one may be told in the neighbourhood, like the Ace of Diamonds, by which name this part of the parish is sometimes referred to.

Leaving Pu Tor we descend the hill with Pu Tor Cottage on the R., our course being S.E. At the lower corner of the enclosure we strike a moorland road, and turning R., then crossing another road, and soon after, again turning R., shall reach the small settlement of Sampford Spiney.

[The rambler may strike S. by W. from the tor to Sampford Tor, a small pile rapidly disappearing under the hand of the quarryman. Then continue the same course to the road from Tavistock, and turn L. to the village.]

Sampford Spiney hardly deserves the name of a village, consisting, as it does, only of a church, a school, an ancient manor house, now a farm, and a few dwellings. These are grouped round a green, on which is a fine old tree and an ancient cross [*Crosses*, Chap. VIII.] It is a restful place, and although some recent erections have somewhat marred its primitive aspect, it has by no means entirely lost its old-world appearance. The Church formerly belonged to Plympton Priory (T. 69, Plympton District), the arms of which religious house may be seen on the S. face of the tower. They are carved on a stone at the side of the large window, two keys, crossed. Crocketted pinnacles rise from the angles of the tower, which is perpendicular, as also is the nave. The chancel has been re-built, but retains its original decorated style. In the time of Henry II. the manor was held by Robert de Spinet, and continued in that family during several descents. It was afterwards in the possession of the Drakes, Bidgoods, and Halls. At present it belongs to Captain Hall-Parlby, of Manadon, near Plymouth.

[After noticing Ward Bridge we shall return to Sampford Spiney, and sketch the walk to Vixen Tor and Merivale.]

Leaving this secluded little place by the road running S.E. from the green, we make our way to Ward Bridge (Ex. 1), ¾ m. distant. To do this it is only necessary that we keep to the L. The bridge is delightfully placed in the depths of the Walkham Valley which is here thickly wooded. It is modern but replaces an old structure that was swept away by a flood in July 1890. Below the bridge on the R. bank of the river is Woodtown the delightful residence of Mrs. W. F. Collier. On the L. is Eggworthy where is a shooting-box belonging to Sir Henry Lopes.

Passing up the lane on the further side of the Walkham (the E.) we shall soon reach the cross ways near Withill Farm mentioned in Ex. 1 and the directions there given will enable the rambler to make his way up the valley to Merivale Bridge and to visit the antiquities near it (Ex. 1). The return to Tavistock from Merivale has already been given in R. 1.]

From the green at Sampford Spiney we shall proceed to the common leaving the church R. and make our way across its edge, with the Walkham Valley on the R. by the track already described (T. 13) to Vixen Tor ; or we may proceed to that pile by way of the path leading to Vixen Tor Farm. If we decide upon the latter we shall enter the gate at Hecklake which we see R. just after passing the track branching off for Pu Tor Cottage. Close to the gate is one of the parish boundary stones already referred to. Our road now lies along the side of the hill running parallel to the track (T. 13) but at some distance below it. Ere we have proceeded far we shall reach a small pile of rocks, L. of the way, the scene of an adventure of one Roody of Heckwood and a short distance further on we shall pass a large worked granite stone, by the roadside, R., originally intended for the Plymouth Breakwater, but rejected on account of a flaw, and soon after shall come in sight of Vixen Tor Farm, on the side of the hill on which rises the tor that gives name to it.   As it is situated within the farm enclosures, it will be better that we pass up by the house and obtain permission to visit it.

The scenery in this valley is described in *Gems*, Chap. XXI.

Vixen Tor rises to a considerable height above the turf, and is a conspicuous object from many parts of the commons surrounding it. On the summit are three rock basins, one being 14ins. deep, another

Cocks   Staple
Tor.   Tors.

FROM WINDY POST, LOOKING N.E.

9ins., and the third 8ins.   The resemblance to the Egyptian Sphinx borne by this tor has often been noticed.   This is particularly observable from the Merivale and Tavistock road.   This road runs about ½ m. N. of the tor, the point where the rambler will strike it in going direct to it being less than ⅓ m. from Merivale Bridge.   Directions for reaching the antiquities from the gate of Long Ash Farm, which is on the side of the hill above the E. end of the bridge, are given iu Ex. 1.

[Mis Tor is 1½ m. N.E. by N. of Merivale Bridge, and can readily be reached.   It is in full view.   The tor is noticed in Ex. 6.]

For the routes from Merivale to Tavistock see R. 1.   If the path

Cocks   Staple
Tor.   Tors.

FROM BARN HILL, ¼ M. NORTH OF WINDY POST.

by Moortown and Whitchurch Down be chosen the rambler will pass the Windy Post soon after crossing the Beckamoor Combe Water. This cross, which is about 7 feet in height, stands on a plain piece of ground extending from Barn Hill to Feather Tor, and is close to the latter, which is a pile of small size. Its type proclaims it to be of the sixteenth century, and as it stands beside a path which existed long before that time (T. 1), it is probable that it replaced an older cross. [*Crosses*, Chap. IX.]

[¼ m. S. of Warren's Cross is Plaster Down, over which the Horra-bridge road runs for about 1¼ m. The down adjoins the common on which Sampford Tor and Pu Tor are situated. (See Yelverton District).]

Ex. 8.—*Pork Hill, Cocks' Tor, The Staple Tors, Roose Tor, Lang-stone Moor Antiquities, White Tor, Smearn Down, Peter Tavy Combe,* 13½ m. WITH EXTENSIONS TO *Walkham Head, Cudlipp Town, and Wapsworthy,* and RETURN ROUTES BY *Hill Bridge, Horndon, and Mary Tavy.*

For the first three miles our way will take us over the Princetown road. We leave the town by way of Vigo Bridge, and ascending the hill with the grounds of Mount Tavy L., and avoiding all turnings, shall, at the distance of nearly two miles from Tavistock, reach Moor Shop (R. 1). Here we cross the Horrabridge and Harford Bridge road, and passing up Pork Hill, shall soon find ourselves on the common. We strike L. over the turf to Cocks' Tor Hill, which rises close at hand, crossing on the way the track described in the section dealing with the old moor paths (T. 15). At the southern end of this hill, which runs about N. and S. for the distance of ½ m., are a number of rock piles, among which may be seen a small shelter of the kind formerly erected by herdsmen and shepherds on the tors. Below these piles a reave runs E. and W. to the head of Beckamoor Combe (Ex. 7), and may also be seen again on the side of the hill near Roose Tor. Between it and the rock piles is a single hut circle, and other examples of these occur further W. near the track. Ascending the hill at this point we proceed northward to Cocks' Tor, of which the rocks just noticed may be regarded as an outlying portion. We shall find it to be of rather large size, though the blocks composing it are not particularly so. The higher pile is surrounded by a low vallum of stones, but for what purpose it was designed is not very clear, unless it may have been intended to build a cairn round the rocks, as in the case of Shell Top (Ex. 34) and Linch Tor (Ex. 10). On the N.E. side is another small shelter.

The view from this commanding border height, which attains an elevation of 1,452 feet, is very fine. Northward, beyond White Tor, is seen the ridge above the Rattle Brook, from which rise the rocks of Hare Tor and Great Links Tor ; across the Beckamoor Dip eastward are the Staple Tors and Roose Tor, and further away the great crown of Mis Tor. To the south is the common above Sampford Spiney, with Vixen Tor and Pu Tor. From this the cultivated land stretches away to the groves of Mount Edgcumbe, and thence, ranging westward, the eye looks upon a diversified tract of country, backed by the Cornish hills. In the valley at our feet, as it were, is the town of Tavistock.

Cocks' Tor Hill is composed of trap rock, the junction of this with

the granite being in the valley on the E. Its summit is fairly level,
and free from heather, and except near the tor the surface is covered
with smooth turf. At its northern end are two cairns, and the remains
of a stone row, and having examined these we shall turn E. by S. and
cross the shallow valley to Great Staple Tor, which is rather less than
1 m. distant. (See *post*). On our L. as we proceed is a group of hut
circles, close to which runs the path from Merivale to Peter Tavy
(T. 14), and which we shall strike at its paved part as we near the tor.
Here, too, we cross the boundary line separating the common lands of
Peter Tavy from those of Whitchurch, which line runs up from head of
Beckamoor Combe towards Roose Tor. This was once the scene of a
quarrel which terminated in the manner usually associated in our
minds with the slight misunderstandings that occasionally arise at
Donnybrook Fair. The men of one of the parishes named were view-
ing their bounds, the operation being watched by the men of the other,
when a dispute arose about a bondmark. Heated arguments followed,
but failed to be convincing, and finally recourse was had to another
means of settling the matter. But that also failed to do so, though it
cannot be said that it was barren of results. Those who returned home
with broken heads were certainly not inclined to think so.

Great Staple Tor is one of four tors that crown the ridge running
parallel to the Walkham, and high above its western bank. Southward of it are Mid Staple Tor and Little Staple Tor ; northward is
Roose Tor. The rocks of Great Staple Tor assume very fantastic
shapes, and in some instances are poised in such a manner as to induce
the beholder to believe that a very slight effort would suffice to overthrow them. It is a striking tor from whichever side it is beheld, but
becomes really impressive when closely approached. It consists of
several piles of rocks, with a large area clothed with short turf in the
centre, and an immense number of scattered rocks, that speak only
too plainly of the havoc the forces of Nature have wrought on this
stupendous granite citadel. There are rock basins on the tor, and also
an interesting object which has been regarded as a tolmen. It will be
found on the westernmost pile, and consists of an overhanging rock, at
some distance above the ground, the end of which is supported on a
lump of granite of a roughly globular form, which rests upon the
extreme edge of another rock, and is kept in position by the first.
The object is not, however, a true tolmen, such being, as the name
implies, a holed stone, but we shall, nevertheless, be quite willing to
believe that it was employed in the mysterious Druidical rites—when
it is shown to our satisfaction that such rites were ever practiced there.
In the meantime all we can say about it is that the stones are certainly
very curiously poised, and that it is Nature's handiwork alone. It is
rather unfair on the part of a certain writer to make Mrs. Bray attempt
to scale the chief pile of Great Staple Tor, and confess that she was
compelled to stop at the third block from the top, when, as a matter
of fact, she has nowhere said that she had even visited the tor.

About ¼ m. due N. of Staple Tor is Roose Tor, the dip between
them being very slight. As we make our way thither over plain,
turfy ground, we have a fine view of the surrounding moor, in which
Mis Tor, across the valley of the Walkham, is a conspicuous feature,
In Roose Tor we have another very striking group of rocks. On its

northern side the granite forms a solid buttress of considerable height ; its other parts are formed of huge blocks. There are a number of basins on the tor, and in one example, which was furnished with a lip, the portion of the rock in which the latter was formed is broken off, and lies in a crevice below it. Around the tor, at some little distance from it, are a number of upright stones, enclosing it in a circle, as it were. These stones are about 4 feet in height, and are squarely cut, and inscribed with the letter B, as also are several similar stones which the rambler may have observed near the road as he entered on the common. They mark the boundary of lands belonging to the Duke of Bedford. Close to one of these bondstones on the northern side of the tor is a rock having a flat surface level with the ground, on which is engraved a small circle bisected by a straight line. Roose Tor is not wanting in historical interest. The common immediately around it probably formed one of the old predas to which its name was attached. I cannot find it mentioned at a very early date, but it is referred to in 1665 as the pasture of Rulestorre.* Probably this form of the name is correct, though it is usually pronounced as I have given it. On the recent Ordnance Map it appears as Rolls Tor.

Northward of Roose Tor is Langstone Moor, and over this we shall now make our way to the stone circle before referred to (Princetown District). This object we may see from the tor in a N.E. direction. The stones composing it lay prone upon the turf until the year 1894, when they were set up. Being a restoration this monument loses something of its interest, but it is at the same time a matter for congratulation that it was not allowed to remain in a ruined condition. There are 16 stones in the circle, the diameter of which is about 56 feet. Three other stones, now also set up, are supposed to have belonged to another circle standing outside the existing one, so that the monument consisted of two concentric circles, if such was really the case. Of this, however, I am by no means convinced. Between this circle and the river are a number of ruined huts, some of them being within a pound of the ordinary character. Charcoal and flint have been found in these.

[From this point we may extend our ramble to the Lich Path (T. 18), where it crosses the Walkham at Sandy Ford (Ex. 6). Proceeding N.E. for nearly ¾ m. we shall reach the head of Deadlake Well, where the track from Princetown *via* Blackabrook Head (T. 12) passes. The combe down which the little Deadlake runs is a favourite spot with the whortleberry gatherer. The water of the tiny stream is said to possess magic properties. Whichever member of a party approaching it drinks of it first will find a lover before the year closes. From this point we follow the forest boundary line, which runs N.N.E. over Cocks' Hill to White Barrow, a distance of about ½ m. The Lich Path (T. 18) is quite close to this barrow, and leads R., to Sandy Ford, on the Walkham. Before it reaches that stream the road forks, the R. branch being the ancient way and the L. one the turf track (T. 16) to Walkham Head. In the fork the remains of some mine buildings will be noticed. From White Barrow the Lich Path ran

---

* In connection with it the pastures of Crowtorre and Claytorre are also named. The latter is a small tract near the Walkham below Sandy Ford, but no tor exists there.

towards Bagga Tor, the direction being about N.W., but for some distance between these two points it is not clearly defined, as already observed (see T. 18). But if the rambler follows the course indicated, making his way towards the moor gate, with the enclosure of Longbetor L., and those of Bagga Tor Farm R., he will see the old path again near the tor. From this moor gate the road will lead him to Wapsworthy and Hill Bridge (Ex. 10).

But at White Barrow the rambler is also on the Walkham Head track from Peter Tavy (T. 16), and by this, the general direction being W.S.W., he may make his way back to the menhir on the western side of Langstone Moor, the distance being 1½ m.]

From Langstone Moor Circle our way will lead us to the menhir, under White Tor (R. 2), to which, however, we must not proceed direct, the ground about the springs of the Peter Tavy Brook, W.N.W., being rather boggy, as already mentioned (R. 2). Our course will be N.W. until, having passed the source of the stream, we can bear L. to the menhir which we shall plainly see. This fine monolith was re-erected at the same time as the circle. It stands beside the Walkham Head peat track (T. 16), and, it may be noticed, is in a direct line between Great Links Tor (Ex. 12) and Peak Hill, on Walkhampton Common (Ex. 39). From this menhir a single stone row runs to a small pond about 130 yards distant, and a little westward is another row, also single, and not quite so long. The latter has much the appearance of an old reave. There are some other remains near, but they are not in a particularly good state of preservation.

As we mount the slope towards White Tor (1,529 feet), which is quite near to these remains, we shall notice the vallum surrounding the pile, and which renders is one of the most curious tors on the moor. Several of the rock masses are incorporated in this rude wall, which, on the E. side, is in a better state of preservation than elsewhere. Remains of hut foundations occur within it, and a number of flint chips have been found among these, and around the tor. This circumvallation differs from the ordinary hut pounds, and seems to have been constructed for defensive purposes.

Descending the side of White Tor, in a direction S. by W., we cross the grassy path leading to Walkham Head, at the distance of ¾ m. from the tor, and near to the Peter Tavy Brook, and the enclosures of Wedlake Farm, shall come upon a group of hut circles. These lie along the banks of a tiny rivulet running into the brook named, and the remains of walls seem to show that they were once in enclosures ; indeed, there is one of these in a fairly perfect state, containing two huts. This settlement was explored in 1904, and charcoal, pottery, flint flakes, and cooking-stones were found. Eastward is a reave running up to White Tor.

[South-west of Wedlake Farm, and close to the wall, is a large hut settlement, but this is best visited from Cocks' Tor Hill or Roose Tor (see *ante*). The Peter Tavy Brook is sometimes known as Wed Lake.]

Retracing our steps northward to the peat track (T. 16), we turn L., shortly afterwards reaching a mound close beside it. This is known as Stephens' Grave, and marks the site where a suicide was buried with the barbarous rites once customary. George Stephens was a youth of Peter Tavy, and was driven to take his life by the unfaithfulness of the girl to whom he was betrothed. It is said that at the moment he was laid here some linen that was hanging out to bleach at Higher Godsworthy was caught up into the air and never more seen. As we proceed we shall notice two rocks on the common L.; these are known at Setters, and are composed of trap of a brownish colour. It is in layers, and there are many loose pieces lying on and around the masses. Less than ½ m. from Stephens' Grave we enter Twyste Lane (T. 16), and passing through it shall find ourselves close to Boulter's Tor on Smearn Down.

From this point we may make our way to Peter Tavy direct, either by proceeding over the down westward, or descending to Peter Tavy Combe, and turning down the valley, R ; or we may lengthen our walk by going round by Cudlipp Town. If we choose the former we shall pass along the rocky summit of the ridge, an extensive panorama of field and woodland, moor and distant hill, being spread before us. Close to the highest crag is a small poundlike enclosure, and some faint vestiges of reaves. At the W. of the ridge, on the N. side of which is the enclosure known as Black Shells, we descend to a gate close to an old sandpit, from which a short lane leads to the road near the church. On reaching this we turn L. to the village.

Peter Tavy Combe is situated to the S. of Smearn Down. We cross the road below Boulter's Tor, and in a corner of the common come upon a footpath running through some enclosures. Turning R. we follow it for a short distance, when we shall find ourselves on the N. side of the combe, just above Little Combe Tor. Great Combe Tor rises on the other side of this little valley, and beyond it is Cocks' Tor Hill. The tor seen between the two is locally known as Sharp Tor. Peter Tavy Combe is a charming spot, to which clings more than one story of the pixies. The Peter Tavy Brook runs through it, and is crossed near the lower end of the combe by a clam. Here the path between the village and Merivale (T. 14) crosses the stream, and is seen ascending the hill towards Great Combe Tor. It there passes through some enclosures and reaches the common just above. Near the clam a path runs up by South Ditch to Smearn Down, but we follow one that takes us down the valley along the bank of a mill stream, which will lead us past Peter Tavy Mill, a very picturesque building, to the village. [*Gems*, Chap. XXII.]

Should we decide to go round by Cudlipp Town from Boulter's Tor, we turn N.W., and in the corner of the common shall find a narrow path, which will lead us to Broad Moor, with Twyste, one of the ancient vills, on our R. We descend the common, with the enclosures on our L., and the farm of Broadmoor a short distance R. (T. 17). At the point where we enter the lane is a small clapper. As we proceed we shall notice the old manor pound on the R., shortly after passing which we reach the road from Wapsworthy (R.) to Peter Tavy village (L.) The manor of Cudlipp Town, which is also an ancient vill, was, previous to the Reform Bill of 1832, in the parish of Tavistock, but was then transferred to Peter Tavy. Owing to this arrangement the new franchise was not extended to the tenants of the manor, and even the owner, notwithstanding that the matter formed the subject of Parliamentary debate, knew nothing of what was going on. In Domesday Cudlipp Town appears as Culitone, and in a forester's account rendered in 1502 as Chodlype, the fine, or rent, of the vill being set down as 5d. Cudlipp occurs as a family name in the neighbourhood. The manor house, now rebuilt, is situated on the W. side of the road. The distance from Cudlipp Town to Peter Tavy village is 1 m. The latter is a quiet little place, with a church embosomed in trees, a chapel, a school, and a small inn. A cross formerly stood near the churchyard gate, but has now disappeared. [*Crosses*, Chap. XI.] The Peter Tavy Brook runs through the village and falls into the Tavy just below.

For Walkham Head direct see Track 16.

Tavistock is about 3 m. from Peter Tavy. The way lies along the road S., and then R. to Harford Bridge, where the Tavy is crossed. Soon after this the highway is reached exactly 2 m. from Tavistock, for which turn L.

[EXTENSION FROM *Peter Tavy to Wapsworthy, Hill Bridge, and Horndon.*

Passing up the road N., with the church on the L., we make our way through Cudlipp Town (1 m.) A short distance beyond this is a turning L. This leads down to Horndon Bridge, the hamlet from which the structure takes its name being high above the W. bank of the Tavy (see *post*). Rather over ½ m. further on is another turning L. This is Church Lane (R. 2), and is the approach to Hill Bridge. Wapsworthy, which is noticed in Ex. 10, is reached by continuing straight on, and is about ¼ m. distant. Should the visitor extend his walk to that place he may reach Hill Bridge by a path across some fields, instead of retracing his steps to the point he has now reached. To do this he will cross Wapsworthy Bridge and enter at the first gate on the L., and descend to the Tavy with the Wapsworthy Brook also on that hand. Hill Bridge, which is situated in the midst of picturesque surroundings, though of comparatively modern erection, yet exhibits a primitive appearance. There are three openings, the centre one only being arched; the others are formed of slabs of granite laid from buttress to pier. The parapets are very low. When Miss Rachel Evans wrote, in 1846, there was no arch, and the bridge consisted of four openings. But even that she supposes to have taken the place of an older one.* (Ex. 10). Crossing the bridge we shall pass up the lane for a short distance and enter a gate, inside which is a schoolhouse, L., just where the road bends R. Making our way upward through a field, with Chilly Wood across the brook L., we reach Lower Town, and passing through the farm yard, enter upon a very narrow lane, and keeping L. shall soon find ourselves on Zoar Down. This piece of common is plentifully strewn with rocks, said to have been placed there by the pixies. Bearing L. near Higher and Lower Creason Farms, we speedily arrive at the hamlet of Zoar, consisting of a few cottages by the side of the road running from Mary Tavy to Lane End (Ex. 9). Here we see the higher part of the down, and may observe a large mass of rock near the wall of an enclosure. This is known as the Master Rock, and here Billy Bray, the celebrated Cornish preacher, was wont to hold open air services during his visit to this neighbourhood. Turning L. by the hamlet we follow the road across Black Lion Down, where is a small chapel, to Horndon. Here a road runs down L. to Horndon Bridge, before alluded to, skirting a small down known as Common Wood. But our way lies straight on past the New Inn, 1 m. beyond which we

---

*Home Scenes ; or, Tavistock and its Vicinity. By Rachel Evans.

shall reach the village of Mary Tavy. Turning L. we pass the school, and presently arrive at the church. Immediately within the gate of the churchyard is an ancient cross. Continuing our way, and keeping L., we arrive at Mary Tavy Clam, in the midst of what was once very fine scenery, but which of late years has been sadly marred by the starting of a mine. Between this clam and Horndon Bridge are some fine crags. One of these we may see as we look up the stream. This is High Tor, the others being Fox Tor and Brimhill Tor. Further up, above the bridge named, is another range of crags, the principal pile being known as Kenter Tor. Crossing the Tavy we follow the bridle path, with the beautiful Longtimber Tor on the R. This stands near the brink of the river, and consists of a square mass of rock rising to a considerable height. It is draped with creeping plants, and bears no slight resemblance to the keep of a ruined castle. Here we pass through a gate into a narrow lane, which will lead us to Peter Tavy village.]

Ex. 9.—*Black Down, Snap, Black Hill, Gibbet Hill, Iron Gate,* 13½ m. WITH BRANCH TO *Lane End,* AND EXTENSION TO *Brent Tor.*
[Black Down may be reached by G.W.R. to Mary Tavy, and by S.W.R. to Brent Tor. In the former case the rambler will pass up the road to the post office (see *post*), and in the latter he will find himself on the down when he gets outside the station. To reach the Ashburys (see *post*) he will then pass up the hill for a short distance and take the green track L. Keep straight on when it is crossed by another, and passing the enclosures of Higher Spring R. follow the path where it bends L., and which leads direct to the road that comes up from Black Down village.]

Rather over 4 m. from Tavistock the Okehampton and Exeter highway enters upon a part of Dartmoor known as Black Down, and to this we shall now make our way. Shortly after leaving the town we pass the Kelly College, L. of the road, and ¼ m. beyond it cross the Walla Brook, a tributary of the Tavy. This comes down through the valley near the head of which Kilworthy is situated, passing, not long before we meet it, Indiscombe, the Ina's Combe of William Browne. This pastoral poet, who has been not inaptly called the bard of the Tavy, was born in Tavistock about the year 1590. Many of his descriptions of places are remarkable for their fidelity and beauty. Below Indiscombe is Two Bridges.

Opposite to the second milestone at the foot of Wringworthy Hill, a road turns R. to Peter Tavy (Ex. 8), crossing the Tavy close by at Harford Bridge. But our way lies up the long ascent, and across Burn Plain to Lane Head (3¼ m. from Tavistock), where a road turns R. down the hill to Mary Tavy village.

[This road also runs on through Horndon to Lane End, and is the direct way to Tavy Cleave. The visitor to the latter will turn L. at the bottom of the hill, and immediately after passing the school, will turn into the Horndon road R. That hamlet will be reached in about 1 m. The rambler will leave it R. and pass on over Black Lion Down to Zoar. (Thus far the route has been given the reverse way in Ex. 8). A road runs straight over Zoar Down (Ex. 8), and this he will follow. That part of it leading from the down is known as Buddla Lane, and at the end of this another lane runs at right angles to it ; L. to Yard Gate (see *post,* and T. 18) ; R. to Hill Bridge (Ex. 8) in one direction, and to Lane End in the other. The rambler turns R. but bears L. at the first fork, which is just below. This will lead him by a farm called Will, shortly after which he will reach Willsworthy Bridge, a clapper, but furnished with parapets (Ex. 10). Close to the bridge is an interesting old manor pound, long disused. A little beyond this an ancient chapel formerly stood, R. of the road (100 *Years*, Chap. IV.), and further on again a road turns R. to Willsworthy Farm, and the ford on the Tavy (Ex. 10). About ½ m. beyond this the rambler will reach the moor gate at Lane End, directions for reaching Tavy Cleave from which point are given in Ex. 11.]

Passing onward we soon reach the post-office, where a road turns L. to Brent Tor. On the R. is Wheal Friendship, once one of the most important copper mines in England (100 *Years*, Chap. III.) Before us is the village of Black Down, and through this we make our way up the hill to the common from which it takes its name. On reaching this we pass the Ashburys, as the enclosures on the R. are called, and which belong to the farm of Holditch. This is now the property of Okehampton feoffees, and probably gave name to a family once resident in that town, one of which, Walter Holditch, is mentioned as a burgess in the fourth of Henry VIII. A similar name occurs in the parish of Thorncombe, its early form, according to Risdon, being Oldich, and which he supposes to have been derived from an ancient enclosure.

[At the point where we enter on the common a moorland road branches off R., and descending to the Cholwell Brook, crosses it in the midst of the deserted workings of Wheal Betsy, at one time, like Wheal Friendship, a mine of much importance. Near the bridge over the little stream is a gate, where a path runs up through Maunder's Brake to Kingsett Down, which is seen just across the valley. A plantation, known as Allaclauns, abuts on the down, and to the L. of this a path, skirting the latter, leads to Zoar (Ex. 8), and to the R. of it another, entered at a gate, runs across fields to Horndon (Ex. 8). By this road and path the rambler may reach Horndon Down Bridge, hereafter noticed. On reaching Kingsett Down he will strike L., following a narrow footpath to the corner of Allaclauns Plantation, where are some disused workings of a mine called Wheal Jewel. From this corner he will strike over the common N. by E., and at the distance of a little over ¼ m. will reach the bridge.]

Our way lies along the high road, with Gibbet Hill, noticed further on, on the L., and the Wheal Betsy workings in the valley R. Soon four posts will be seen by the roadside, and a few score yards beyond these a path runs up over the shoulder of the hill L. This is the Lydford Path (T. 23), described in the section dealing with the old tracks, and forms the most direct way from this part of the down to Lydford Station. A short distance beyond this there is a long row of stone posts by the roadside, known locally at Annie Pinkham's Men, and here on the bank L., and opposite to the mine house, is the fifth milestone from Tavistock. It also shows Okehampton to be 10 miles distant, and Truro, in the other direction, 56 m. ¼ m. further on an old mine leat runs under the road at Barrett's Bridge. This we do not cross, but turn R. and follow the path that runs on the edge of the dry water course, with Cholwell Farm in the valley R. ⅓ m. on we cross a shallow gully known in the locality as Goosey Creep, beyond which a path branches R. from the watercourse. This we follow, and shall be led to a green track that comes in L. from the high road, and runs on to Zoar Down (T. 24), over a piece of ground usually referred to as Breast-the-Water. At the junction a number of distant tors, among them the piles above Tavy Cleave, are in sight. Close at hand is the clapper known as Horndon Down Bridge. This spans a leat by which water is brought in from the river at Tavy Cleave to the mines. It is placed at the head of a gully which extends downward to the valley in which the Cholwell Brook rises. It consists of three stones laid side by side, the road being sufficiently wide for a cart. The bottom of the leat under the bridge is paved. N.E. by E. is Tavy Cleave, at the head of which a small part of Watern Oke is revealed. This, and Limsboro, and Great Mis Tor, are the only portions of the forest that can be seen, although so much of the moor is visible.

Following the wide leat in an easterly direction we shall presently reach the wall of an enclosure R., and shall notice a bondstone on the slope L. This is one of a row marking the boundary line between the common lands of Mary Tavy and Peter Tavy. A few score yards further on we cross the leat at One Stone Bridge, and make our way a short distance down the hill known as Snap (Ex. 10), where we have as fine a picture as can be found in any part of the moorland borders. To the L. is White Hill (Ex. 11), over the crest of which is seen Bra Tor (Ex. 11) with its cross. Great Links Tor (Ex. 12) stands up boldly against the sky, with the farm of Redford (Ex. 11)—locally Ruddiver—under it R., but much nearer to us. Then on the skyline is seen Sharp Tor (Ex. 11) with the conical Hare Tor (Ex. 11) to the R. of it. To the R. of that Ger Tor and the Tavy Cleave Tors (Ex. 11). The fine hill to the R. of the cleave is Standon ; at its foot is the farm of the same name. R. of this farm is Bagga Tor, where also is a farm called after the eminence, and beyond it the range on which is Linch Tor (Ex. 10) near the head waters of the Walkham, which rises E.N.E. of it. Here we look down upon the farms formed by the ancient settlers who forced their way into this valley, and among others that may be seen are Nat Tor, Lane End, Willsworthy, Brouzen Tor, Longbetor, Will, Hill Town, and the farms at Wapsworthy. If we proceed a few yards further in a northerly direction we look down upon Yellowmead Farm.

In the corner of the down just below us R. is a gateway, where a track passes across an enclosure to Yard Gate. This is the track already described as running from Hill Bridge to Lydford (Ts. 18, 25). One of the granite posts of Yard Gate bears some ancient markings, and from a supposed resemblance of the figures to stars, it is sometimes called by the country people Seven Star Gate (Ex. 10).

Retracing our steps we cross the leat and make our way up the slope to the bondstone, and follow the line on which it is placed, our direction being N.N.W. Shortly we shall reach Down Pool and Tin Pits, and passing these shall be led to the Dartmoor Path (T. 21), where it runs over Black Hill. On the further side of this is the object known as the Ring o' Bells. It has the appearance of a small pound, the encircling bank being formed of turf and stone. It may perhaps mark the site of a cairn from which the stones have been removed. There are a number of such on this down. Regaining the track we turn towards the W.S.W., and follow it to the highway, where we shall leave it, and proceeding a short distance along the road L., shall in turn leave that and strike across the common to Gibbet Hill, which is in full view before us.

Sourton. Tors.	Corn Ridge.	Great Links Tor.	Dunnagoat Tors.	Sharp Tor.

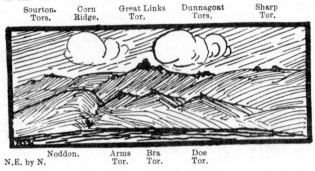

	Noddon.		Arms Tor.	Bra Tor.	Doe Tor.
N.E. by N.					

FROM GIBBET HILL.

From this fine eminence we see nearly the whole of Black Down This down is mostly in Mary Tavy, a parish which does not lie in venville, but a part of it is in Peter Tavy. Its extreme length from the Burn stream in Smallacombe Bottom, on the S., to the enclosures of Bear Walls, under White Hill, on the N., is about 3½ m., and its width about 1¼ m., though in one part it is ½ m. more than that. Gibbet

Hare Tor.	Black Ridge.	Fur Tor.

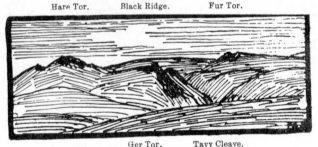

Ger Tor.	Tavy Cleave.

FROM GIBBET HILL.

attains an elevation of 1159 feet, and on its summit is a quarry in which is a pool of water. The hill obtains its name from the hideous object said once to have been erected here. The road over the down, which was the direct route from New Bridge on the Tamar to Exeter, had the evil reputation of being infested with highwaymen, and this hill being in view from it, and, indeed, from the surrounding country, was deemed a fitting place on which to expose the bodies of malefactors who had suffered at the hands of the law. There are many traditions and stories concerning the spot [100 *Years*, Chap. II.], and there are those now living in the parish whose fathers remembered when a tall post was fixed on the summit of the hill.

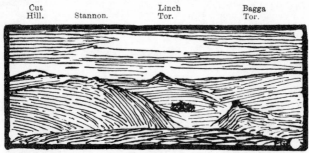

Cut Hill. Stannon. Linch Tor. Bagga Tor.

FROM GIBBET HILL.

Remains of mining operations occur on the side of the hill. It was to these workings that the water was brought in the leat we have noticed at Barrett's Bridge. After being used it was suffered to run into a deep channel known as the Gurgy (*gurges*, a whirlpool), and was by means of this carried to the Cholwell Brook, and so returned to the Tavy. The old track over the down, the forerunner of the present road, seems to have been utilized by the miners, since part of the Gurgy is formed upon it. This track we have already noticed (T. 26).

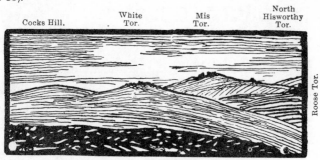

Cocks Hill. White Tor. Mis Tor. North Hisworthy Tor. Roose Tor.

FROM GIBBET HILL.

The chief interest of Gibbet Hill is the wonderful picture seen from its summit. Eastward is a wide view of the moor from the Sourton Tors N. to the Dewer Stone S., one part of which, that extending from Sourton to Hare Tor, is the finest range in the Dartmoor country. Some of the grandest tors of the moor are here visible, including Fur Tor, Great Mis Tor, White Tor, and the Staple Tors. Roborough Down, and beyond it Mount Edgcumbe, with the Channel, are in view. Across the valley W. by S. is Brent Tor, with its little church, and further away the Cornish eminences of Kit Hill, Brown Willy, and Row Tor, besides many other prominent heights. A wide expanse of diversified country is seen, embracing a great part of West and North-West Devon, and much of the country beyond the Tamar.

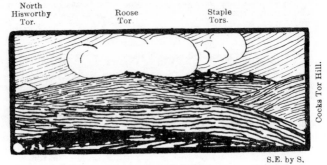

FROM GIBBET HILL.

Leaving Gibbet Hill we descend to the road near Higher Spring, by which name some enclosures and cottages on the down are known, our direction being S.W. On reaching the road, with Higher Spring on our L., we have Smallacombe Bottom below us, and on the further side of the valley the hill that extends to Heathfield, on the Tavistock and Brent Tor road. Now we turn L., and passing through Iron Gate (but a wooden one, nevertheless), shall soon reach the Mary Tavy Post Office and the high road to Tavistock.

[EXTENSION TO BRENT TOR. About ¼ m. eastward of the summit of Gibbet Hill is the Dartmoor Path (T. 21), and to this we make our way. On reaching it we turn L., and a short distance on turn abruptly R. and follow it down the hill past the school to the road near the railway station, 1 m., where we shall cross the Burn and proceed to the village of Brent Tor. The people living in this neighbourhood were formerly known as Lamerton Outer Downs. Until the year 1882 much land now included in the parish of Brent Tor belonged to the parish of Lamerton, and the name was used to distinguish those parishioners who lived so far from their village and on the edge of Black Down. At the present time the dwellers in the Burn Valley, although in Mary Tavy parish, are ecclesiastically in that of Brent Tor, and are still sometimes referred to by the Mary Tavy villagers as Outer Downs. But the valley dwellers retaliate by speaking of the Mary Tavy men as Over Downs. The village, and that part of the parish around it, is usually known as North Brent Tor, the original parish, of which the church on the hill is the centre, now being called South Brent Tor. The church, formerly a chapel-of-ease to Lamerton, was built in 1857. Passing through the village, and bearing L., we soon reach the Tavistock and Lydford road at Batten's Corner. Here we turn L. to the tor, passing the Herring Arms on our way. ¼ m. beyond this a gate gives access to the down, but if we wish to see the interior of the church, it will be necessary to apply to the caretaker at Stag's Head Farm, just opposite to the gate.

Brent Tor is of a conical shape, and forms a conspicuous landmark for many miles around. The hill has been fortified, the vallum of turf being still in a very good state of preservation. It is considered to be volcanic in its origin, and a suggestion has been made that to this circumstance it owes its name. *Brent* Tor is supposed to mean the *burnt* Tor, the word being the past participle of the Saxon verb *brennan,* to burn. But it is obvious that this cannot be its true source, for all signs such as the Saxons would be likely to recognize of the hill having been *burnt* must have disappeared long before their arrival, or before that of earlier settlers who may be supposed to have given to the hill a name equivalent to that under consideration. Another suggestion is that its name has reference to the beacon fires which it is thought were once lighted on this prominent height. This derivation seems the more probable one, but if it be correct we are forced to the conclusion that this merely superseded an older name, since it is impossible to believe that such a striking object as the tor did not possess one in the earliest times. I am inclined to think that the name is derived from the Celtic *bryn,* which means a hill, or mount. In the Cymric-Celtic *twr* (pronounced *toor,* the *w* being equivalent to *oo*), signifies a heap, or pile, so that the rocks on the crest of the height would be well described as *bryn twr,* or *hill crag,* and this name probably became attached to the settlement, on or below the tor. That there was a settlement of some kind is evident from the circumstance of the hill having been fortified. It is very likely that the name is also seen in Brinsabach, a farm on the further side of a combe to the S. of the tor. *Bach,* is a Celtic word signifying *little,* and *bryn bach* would therefore mean the *little hill.* The natives usually speak of the hill and the parish as " Brin Tar."

Several traditions of the kind usually found in connection with buildings placed in curious situations attach to the church on this hill. One says it was intended to build it at the foot of the tor, but the Evil One came continually by night and carried the stones that the builders had placed during the day up the steep sides of the hill to its crest. At length it was deemed expedient to let Satan have his way, and the church was erected on the site he had chosen for it—with the intention, perhaps, of rendering it not easily accessible. It is also related that the church was built in fulfilment of a vow, made by a merchant at sea, and that it really is a votive church is not unlikely. The fact that it seems to have been built by the monks of Tavistock Abbey does not preclude this view. Mr. James Hine, the well-known ecclesiastical architectural authority, states that the greater part of the building is of contemporary date with the earliest remains of Tavistock Abbey that at present exist, namely, the portion of the cloister arcading in the churchyard. Brent Tor Church was dedicated to St. Michael by Bishop Stapeldon on the 4th December, 1319, the name of the parish appearing on the deed as Brente Torre. But that a church existed there before that date is clear from a mention of it in a deed of Bishop Bronescombe, of the year 1269. The walls are very low, are furnished with a battlemented parapet, and are about three feet thick. The tower is forty feet high, and now contains three bells, but formerly there was only one. This bore the inscription

Gallus vocor ego, solus per omne sono. There is an east window, and
also two narrow early English windows. The nave is only 37 feet
6 inches in length.

Leaving this little church we descend the hill towards the S.E.,
where a gate opens upon a lane. We turn L. and follow this through
the few farms forming the hamlet of South Brent Tor to Wortha Mill,
on the hill beyond which we enter on Black Down. Brinsabach, to
which we have alluded, is in the combe on the further side of the Burn,
which is crossed at the bend by means of stones known as Batten's
Steps. We follow the road eastward to Iron Gate, whence we speedily
reach the Tavistock road. See *ante.*]

Should the rambler wish to return to Tavistock by the high road
direct from Brent Tor Church, he will leave the down at the gate
opposite to Stag's Head Farm, and turn L., and will also keep L.
where the road forks. Passing a part of Heathfield, most of which is
now enclosed, he will reach Pitland Corner in 1¼ m. Tavistock is
2 m. distant.

SHORTER EXCURSIONS.

FOR DESCRIPTION OF OBJECTS REFER AS INDICATED.

S. Ex. 15.—*Whitchurch Down, Plaster Down, and Pu Tor,* 7 m.
Whitchurch Down (Ex. 7). Follow road past Middle Moor, and Monkeys' Castle to Warren's Cross (Ex. 7). Turn neither R. nor L., but
follow road S.E. to northern verge of Plaster Down. Then bear L.
to the down below Pu Tor. Pass up over the common to the tor.
Descend N.W. to Moortown, and return to Whitchurch Down by
Quarry Lane (T. 1., R. 1).

S. Ex. 16.—*The Windy Post, Beckamoor Combe, and Vixen Tor,*
8 m. Over Whitchurch Down and through Quarry Lane, as in Ex. 7.
Then bear a little to the L. in passing up over the common, following
the cart tracks that will be seen on the turf, to the Windy Post near
Feather Tor. Barn Hill is L. Vixen Tor is now in view, straight
ahead. Descend into Beckamoor Combe, cross the stream at the ford,
and pass upward to the tor. Thence N. to the Tavistock road, and
turn L. ½ m. on the road passes across Beckamoor Combe, where is
a large streamwork. The ruin seen a short distance down, above the
R. bank of the stream, is an old smithy. From this point make across
to the Windy Post, and return by Quarry Lane, or follow the road
direct to Tavistock *via* Moor Shop and Mount Tavy (R. 1., Ex. 7).

S. Ex. 17.—*The Staple Tors and Merivale,* 9½ m. By road as in
Ex. 8. On reaching the moor continue on the road past Beckamoor
Combe (S. Ex. 16), then strike up over the common L. to the Little
Staple Tor, which overlooks the road. Continue northward to Mid
Staple Tor, and on to Great Staple Tor (Ex. 8). Just before reaching
the latter the path from Merivale to Peter Tavy (T. 14) is crossed. On
reaching this on returning from Great Staple Tor, turn into it L. to
Merivale, which lies S.E. From Merivale return to Tavistock as in
R. 1.

The Merivale Antiquities and Great Mis Tor. Instructions for
reaching these from Merivale are given in Ex. 1. The former **are**

3. TAVISTOCK DISTRICT.

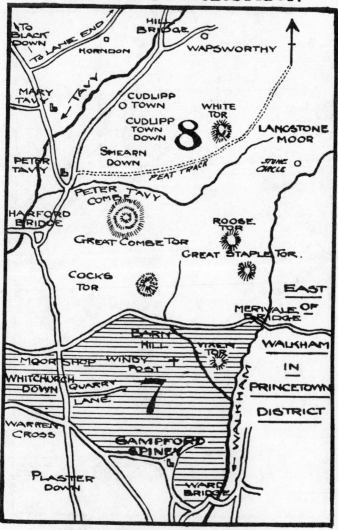

TO BLACK DOWN · TO LANE END · HORNDON · HILL BRIDGE · WAPSWORTHY

MARY TAVY · TAVY · CUDLIPP O TOWN · WHITE TOR · LANGSTONE MOOR

CUDLIPP TOWN DOWN · **8** · STONE CIRCLE O

SMEARN DOWN · PEAT TRACK

PETER TAVY · PETER TAVY COMBE

HARFORD BRIDGE · GREAT COMBE TOR · ROOSE TOR

GREAT STAPLE TOR.

COCKS TOR

EAST OF

MERIVALE BRIDGE

BARN HILL · VIXEN TOR · WALKHAM

MOOR SHOP · WINDY POST · IN

WHITCHURCH DOWN · QUARRY LANE · **7** · PRINCETOWN

WARREN CROSS · DISTRICT

SAMPFORD SPINEY · WALKHAM

PLASTER DOWN · WARD BRIDGE

EXCURSIONS 7, 8.

4. TAVISTOCK DISTRICT

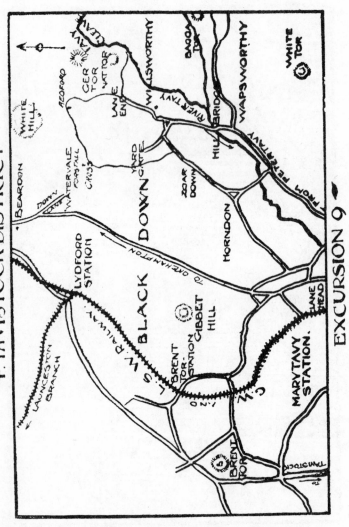

EXCURSION 9

described in Ex. 1, and the latter in Ex. 6. The blowing houses on the Walkham are also noticed in those excursions. See S. Ex. 5.

S. Ex. 18.—*Peter Tavy Combe and Cocks' Tor Hill*, 8½ m. Okehampton road for 2 m. (Ex. 9). Turn R. and cross Harford Bridge. Bend L. for Peter Tavy village. On reaching it turn up by the school ; then turn L. to the mill, and follow the path upward to the combe. Cross the clam and climb the narrow path to Great Combe Tor. Follow path through the enclosures to the commons. Climb the northern end of Cocks' Tor Hill, cross it, and descend S. to the Tavistock road. Return *via* Moor Shop (R. 1).

S. Ex. 19.—*Antiquities on Langstone Moor and Walkham Head*, 12½ m. To Peter Tavy as in S. Ex. 18. Pass the church and turn in lane R. Thence as described in the *Paths'* section, T. 16, passing in succession Boulter's Tor, Twyste Lane, and Stephens' Grave (Ex. 8). ¾ m. beyond this is the Longstone. The huts noticed in Ex. 8 are reached by striking R. over the common after passing Stephens' Grave. White Tor is visited from the Longstone (Ex. 8). The stone circle on the other side of the down (Ex. 8) lies about ½ m. E.S.E. of the menhir, but the rambler must keep to the L. of a direct line to it, the ground about the springs of the Peter Tavy Brook being rather boggy. The way to Walkham Head from the circle lies along the ridge to White Barrow (Ex. 8). From White Barrow the rambler makes his way over the Lich Path (T. 18) eastward, to the point where the peat track branches from it L., just below. Thence to Walkham Head as in T. 16. The return will be by way of this track to Peter Tavy. If the visitor extends his ramble to Walkham Head the distance will be 17 m.

S. Ex. 20.—*Wapsworthy and Hill Bridge*, 11 m. To Peter Tavy as in S. Ex. 18. Continue on road to Cudlipp Town as in Ex. 8, and then on to Wapsworthy (Ex. 10), passing Church Lane L. Cross the bridge at Wapsworthy, enter gate on L., and take the path (as in Ex. 8) across the fields to Hill Bridge. Return as in Ex. 8.

S. Ex. 21.—*Mary Tavy Clam via Peter Tavy*, 7½ m. To Peter Tavy as in S. Ex. 18. Turn L. before reaching the church. Pass Peter Tavy Inn, and take the first gate R. Follow the bridle path, and at the end of it pass through gate with Longtimber Tor L. (Ex. 8). The clam is just above this (Ex. 8). Cross the clam and on to Mary Tavy Church. After passing it take first turning L. Up the hill to Lane Head. Turn L. for Tavistock.

S. Ex. 22.—*Tavy Cleave*, 11 m. Okehampton road to Lane Head, and thence to Lane End, as in Ex. 9, passing through Horndon, Zoar, and over Willsworthy Bridge (Ex. 10). From Lane End to the cleave as in Ex. 11. *Via Brent Tor Station, G.W.R.*, 4¾ m. From the station follow the Dartmoor Path (T. 21). On reaching the higher end of the Redford enclosures keep on E. by S., with Hare Tor high on the L. Straight on till the Tavy Cleave Tors come in sight. The route from *Lydford Station, S.W.R.*, is given in the Lydford District.

S. Ex. 23.—*Black Down and Gibbet Hill*, 11 m. By road to the Ashburys, as in Ex. 9. Gibbet Hill is less than ½ m. L. on entering on the down. The return may be made by way of Brent Tor (Ex. 9).

S. Ex. 24.—*Brent Tor, by road*, 4 m. Leave Tavistock by Higher

Market Street. Notice the equestrian ridge tiles on the house L., above the market place. Pass the Union House and up the hill. ¾m. beyond this Hurdwick, formerly one of the possessions of Tavistock Abbey, lies L. 2 m. from Tavistock is Pitland Corner, where a road branches L. to Chillaton and Marystowe. Keep straight on, and the tor will soon be seen. The gate named in Ex. 9 will be found R. when the rambler is abreast of the tor. The return may be made by train from Brent Tor Station. From the tor to the station, 1½ m.

ROUTES FROM TAVISTOCK.

R. 9.—To Lydford and Okehampton, N.E. by N. (A) By Road : *Black Down, Skit Bridge, Fox Cross, Sourton.* Lydford, *via* Skit, 8 m. Reverse, Rs. 21, 23. Okehampton, 16 m. Reverse, R. 30. (B) By the Moor to Okehampton only : *Peter Tavy, Walkham Head, Broad Amicombe Hole, Dinger Plain,* 18 m. Reverse, R. 30, B.

[The road route for the most part only skirts the moor. The tors seen R. are noticed in Exs. 8 to 15. The objects passed in going to Okehampton by way of the moor are described in Exs. 8, 11, 14, 15.]

(A) The road is followed throughout. After passing over Black Down (Ex. 9) it descends by Watervale, R. and L., to Beardon, L. (Take-off Stone by the wayside, see Ex. 10), and crosses the Lyd at Skit Bridge. The path to Lydford village branches off L. at the seventh milestone, before the bridge is reached, but this can only be used by the pedestrian. Beyond the bridge the road to Lydford, which is not far off, turns L. The Okehampton road runs on past the Dartmoor Inn to Vale Down (Ex. 13), just beyond which is Fox Cross, where a road turns L. to Bridestowe Station, S.W.R., less than ½ m. At the cross is a comfortable hostelry called the Fox and Hounds. The road runs on through Southerly and Lake to Sourton (Ex. 13), the tors of which name are R. Beyond Sourton Prewly Moor is reached, where the road runs close to the railway. At the northern end of this is Jockey Down's House, two or three dwellings by the roadside to which the name of an old cottage is still attached. Pass the stone cross R. (S. Ex. 34), near where a road comes in from Bridestowe, and another runs off L. to Hatherleigh, and on to the railway bridge, from which point Okehampton is 3 m. distant.

(Lydford may also be reached by the road running past Pitland Corner (S. Ex. 24) and Brent Tor village. The latter lies R. after passing the tor. The road then runs to the Manor Hotel, and thence to Lydford by way of Lydford Bridge.)

(B) The road over Black Down is the most direct way to Oke-hampton, but in case the visitor should prefer making a detour and crossing the moor, the route is here indicated. To Peter Tavy, as in S. Exs. 18, 19. Pass the church and turn in lane R. to Smearn Down. Thence by the peat track to Walkham Head (T. 16), from which point the route from Princetown to Okehampton is followed (R. 3) q.v. (This route also shows the branch to Belstone.)

R. 10.—To Chagford and Moreton, E.N.E. (A) By Road : *Merivale, Rundle Stone, Two Bridges, Post Bridge, Warren House Inn* (1 m. branch L. to Chagford), *Moor Gate, Worm Hill.* Chagford, 18½ m.

Moreton, 20 m. Reverse, R. 36. (B) BY THE MOOR to Chagford :
*White Barrow, Maiden Hill, Devil's Tor, Row Tor, Broad Down, East
Dart, White Ridge, Fernworthy*, 19 m. Reverse, R. 36, B.

[The objects passed on the road route are noticed in Exs. 1, 5, 6,
7, 8, 44, 46, 45, 21, 22. Those on the moor route in Exs. 8, 5, 46, 21.]

(A) Merivale, either by way of Mount Tavy and Moor Shop, as in
Ex. 8, or by Whitchurch Down, Quarry Lane, and the Windy Post
(Ex. 7, S. Ex. 16). Merivale (Dartmoor Inn) (Ex. 1) is reached soon
after passing the fourth milestone from Tavistock. Cross the bridge,
and ascend the hill to Rundle Stone (Exs. 1, 6) as in Ex. 1. Keep
straight on due E. to Two Bridges, from which place the routes have
already been described. (See R. 4).

(B) Should the visitor feel inclined to walk across the moor to
Chagford he will first make his way to Peter Tavy and Smearn Down,
as in R. 9, B., and S. Ex. 18. The peat track (T. 16) must then be
followed to White Barrow (Ex. 8), where he will find himself on the
Lich Path (T. 18). This old path will bring him to the Walkham, E.
(he must be careful not to turn L. where it forks). He will cross the
Walkham at Sandy Ford, and immediately afterwards the Prison Leat.
Here he leaves the Lich Path, and makes his way across Conies' Down
(Ex. 5) in a direction E. by N., having as he proceeds Maiden Hill
(T. 16, Ex. 5) on his L. and Conies' Down Tor on his R. At the
distance of rather over 1 m. he will reach the Cowsic, just below its
source, not far to the E. of which is Devil's Tor and Bear Down Man
(Ex. 5). From the menhir he will proceed to Row Tor (Ex. 5), over
½ m. distant, the direction still being E. by N. From Row Tor he will
follow the wall N.E. of it (Ex. 5) down to the West Dart, and up the
hill to its N.E. corner, its length throughout being ¾ m. Brown's
House is R. as he ascends the hill (Ex. 5). From the corner of the wall
the way lies across Broad Down to Sandy Hole on the East Dart, the
direction being N.N.E., and the distance ½ m. (See *post*). He will
then follow the sheep path on the R. bank of the river up through the
pass above the hollow (which derives its name from the accumulation
of sand there), and having arrived at its head will be able to cross to
the L. bank. The course is then E.N.E. for 1 m., care being taken
not to bear too much to the L., and so get upon the fen, when the
Vitifer Mine leat will be reached. This he will cross, and steer E. by
N., having the crest of White Ridge R., and the Leat L. In a little
over 1 m. he will arrive at the enclosures belonging to Fernworthy.

[If the Dart can be crossed at Sandy Hole the course thence to
the leat will be N.E. The direct course to the latter from the Wild
Banks Corner is E.N.E. by N., but as it might not be possible to cross
the Dart it is better to go by way of Sandy Hole. The course, however, is here given. The Dart would be reached in ¾ m., and should
be crossed near where it begins to bend towards the E. On the side
of the hill above this point is the Vitifer Mine leat (Ex. 46), which is
taken from the river about ¼ m. higher up. It here bends N., and from
this bend the course is N.E. For ½ m. the river will be on the rambler's
R. and the leat on his L. Then they will both be lost, as the former,
after flowing a short distance N., makes an abrupt turn and runs due
S., while the leat is carried from Lade Hill to the N. and E. sides of
White Ridge (Ex. 45). Soon after these are lost a little stream flowing

southward down Lade Hill Bottom into the Dart is crossed. From this feeder (the second passed since leaving the river) the way lies over White Ridge, the course now being N.E. by E., and in 1¼ m. the leat is again met by the Fernworthy enclosures.]

The rambler now descends the hill to the Assacombe Brook (Ex. 21), and crossing this will, in about ½ m., reach the Lowton Brook, which he will also cross. ¼ m. beyond this the Fernworthy and Chagford road is reached. To this point the line is still N.E. by E., but it may have to be deviated from a little as the Lowton Rocks lie just in the way. The road is followed N.E., passing Metheral, and leaving the moor about ¾ m. beyond it. At the first fork the rambler may either bear L. by Collihole, or R. by Meldon Hill. If the former he will reach Thorn, where he turns R. to Waye Barton; if the latter he will bear L. all the way, leaving the down on the R., and will also reach Waye Barton. From this Chagford is about ¾ m. distant.

R. 11.—To Bovey Tracey, E. by N. R. 10 A. to Two Bridges (branch off R. at Rundle Stone if for Princetown). Thence see R. 5, A. B, and C, 25 m. Reverse, R. 43.

R. 12.—To Ashburton and Buckfastleigh, E. by S. To Princetown or Two Bridges see R. 11. Thence see R. 6, A, B, and C. *Via* Princetown and Holne, 20 m.; *via* Two Bridges, 21 m. Reverse, R. 50.

R. 13.—To Brent, Ivybridge, and Cornwood, S.E. round to S. To Princetown see R. 11. Thence see R. 7. Brent, 19½ m.; Ivybridge, 20 m.; Cornwood, 17 m. Reverse, R. 60, 61.

[*To Cornwood and Ivybridge by road.* Whitchurch Down to Warren's Cross, and straight on as in S. Ex. 15, but on emerging on Plaster Down bear R. at the fork. About 1½ m. from this the old stone cross on Huckworthy Common is reached (Ex. 40). A short distance beyond it turn L., and descend the hill to Huckworthy Bridge (Ex. 40); thence through the lane to Walkhampton village. Up the road S.S.E. for ½ m. to Dousland (Ex. 39). Cross the Yelverton and Princetown road, and skirting Yennadon descend to Marchants Bridge (Ex. 38) over the Mew, the village of Meavy (Ex. 38) being R. just before reaching it. Cross the bridge and pass up Lynch Hill R. At the end of the down, where a very narrow lane leads into Brisworthy (R. 8), turn sharp R., and then bend L., descending the hill to Cadaford Bridge. Thence see R. 8.]

R. 14.—To Plympton and Shaugh, S.S.E. To Cadaford Bridge, as in route 13. Thence as in route 8. To Plympton, 15 m.; to Shaugh, 10½ m. Reverse, R. 68.

R. 15.—To Princetown and Two Bridges, E. (A) *Whitchurch Down, Moortown.* (B) *Moor Shop.* This route has been described in Ex. 7, S. Ex. 16, Ex. 8, 1, and R. 10 A. P.T., 7½ m.; T.B., 8 m. Reverse, R. 1.

LYDFORD DISTRICT.

DISTANCES. BY ROAD: These may be ascertained by consulting the tables given under *TAVISTOCK* and *OKEHAMPTON* remembering that Lydford (reckoning the *DARTMOOR INN* as the starting-point) lies about midway between the two, *i.e.*, 8 m. from either, and adding or deducting that number of miles as the case may be.

By Rail : G.W. and L.S.W., the same as from *TAVISTOCK*, adding 6 m. if for *Down* trains, *i.e.*, towards *PLYMOUTH*. Deduct 6 m. for *Up* trains, *i.e.*, towards *EXETER*, L.S.W. only. *BRIDES-TOWE* Station (L.S.W. only) is 9 m. nearer *OKEHAMPTON*, and serves Lydford just as well as its own station. It is a little over ¼ m. from the Fox and Hounds, which hostelry is 1 m. from the Dartmoor Inn, on the Okehampton road.

Formerly a place of importance Lydford is now only a small village. The Castle has already been referred to in the *Terms* section, under *Lydford Law* and *Stannaries*. Early in the nineteenth century the Duchy Courts, which had long been held in it, were removed to Princetown, and it then fell into decay. A site near the river is known as the South Gate, and below the church are the remains of an entrenchment. A mound in a field W. of the cross roads in the village bears the name of Gallow's Hill.

EXCURSIONS FROM LYDFORD.

Tracks in the vicinity, Nos. 18 to 30. [These excursions extend over an area comprehended within an imaginary line drawn from Lydford Station, by Hill Bridge and Wapsworthy, to White Barrow and Sandy Ford on the Walkham ; thence to the head of that river and onward to Tavy Hole and the Amicombe ; thence N.W. across Watern Oke to the Rattle Brook, and to the head of that stream ; and thence by Stinka Tor and Branscombe's Loaf to the Sourton Tors. Within this is included the Hamlet of Willsworthy, the name of an extensive manor in Peter Tavy parish (Ex. 2), the boundaries of which are as follows : From Buddla Corner on Black Down, by the bondstones running by Down Pool, Tin Pits, and the Ring o' Bells to Prescombe Corner ; thence to Sounscombe Head and Sounscombe Foot and Beardon Gate ; thence to Lissicombe Head and down the hill to Lissicombe Foot ; thence to Greenwell, and across the marsh to the Walla Brook, and up that stream to a bond-mark in Doe Tor Bottom ; from Walla Brook Head to a cairn between Hare Tor and Sharp Tor ; thence to Dead Lake Head and so down to the Rattle Brook ; thence to the Tavy, and up the Tavy to Red Lake Foot ; up Red Lake nearly to the head, and thence to a pile of stones ; thence to the head of the Bagga Tor Brook, and down the brook by Bagga Tor Farm and the Hare's Double to the Tavy ; thence down the Tavy to Hill Bridge, and up by the stream on the edge of Chilly Wood to the enclosures, and thence to Buddla Corner—most of these points are noticed in the excursions. The hamlet includes Tavy Cleave within its boundaries, and the beautiful Hare Tor. It is a matter for regret that such a charming part of Dartmoor should be robbed of its quietude and solitariness, but much of it has lately been acquired by the War Office for rifle practice, as also has a small part of Black Down belonging to Mary Tavy. The Extension in Ex. 11 includes Fur Tor and Cut Hill.]

Ex. 10.—*Forstall Cross, Snap, Hill Bridge, Wapsworthy, Linch*

Tor, Brook's Head, Standon, Willsworthy Ford, Willsworthy Brook,
Yellowmead, 14½ m.

From Lydford village we shall first make our way by Lake to
Skit Steps, and thence by the path to the highway. Here we turn
S. at the seventh milestone, which we shall notice is rudely shaped
like a cross [*Crosses*, Chap. II.] Just beyond it, on the same side of
the road, we pass Take-off Stone [100. *Years*, Chap. II.], beyond which
in former days a third horse attached to a waggon when two only had
been charged for at the turnpike last passed, could not proceed.   Passing in succession Lower and Higher Beardon we turn L. into Down
Lane, where we are on the line of the old Lich Path (T. 18).   [A little
further up the main road the Sounscombe Brook comes down from the
common, and here on the R. there is a gate.   Just within it is a portion
of the King Way (T. 26) coming down from Black Down.   Higher up
the road, and not far from the verge of the down is Watervale, where
was formerly an inn, which may possibly have suggested to Kingsley
the one he has placed on the common.   The two stones—one near the
brook, and the other on the edge of the down above Watervale—mark
what was formerly the boundary line of Lamerton parish.]   Entering
upon Black Down at the top of Down Lane, we follow the green path
S.E. over the ridge, turning neither to the L. nor R., to Forstall Cross
(T. 18).*   L. as we descend the slope is White Hill, on which are some
tumuli, and R. is Black Hill, surmounted with the Ring o' Bells (Ex. 9).
Quite near to the cross paths the mine leat (Ex. 9) makes a bend, and
below this we follow it for a short distance southward, when we cross
it, and still follow the track as it runs nearly parallel to it, with Yellowmead Farm below us on the L.   We also see Redford, which lies about
¾ m. beyond that farm in a N.E. direction.   Our way lies across the
side of Yellowmead Hill and Snap to the corner of the down mentioned
in Ex. 9, where the view is described.

[If the start is made from the Manor Hotel the route to this point
will take the visitor to the moor gate, close to the cottages of the
L.S.W.R. Co.   Here he enters on the down, and follows the green path
that runs up by Henscott Plantations, taking care not to branch R.
towards Gibbet Hill.   When a little way from the gate he will notice
Hall Farm on the L., locally Yal, immediately below which is a small
clapper.   In rather less than a mile from the gate he will cross the high
road, and still following the track for about the same distance, will
reach Horndon Down Bridge (Ex. 9), where, turning eastward with the
mine leat on his R., he will be led to the footbridge mentioned in that
Excursion, below which is the corner of the down where the Lich Path
(T. 18) enters the enclosures.]

We follow the track across the side of the enclosure to Yard Gate
(Ex. 9), and passing through it shall make our way down the lane,
noticing Buddla Lane, which branches R., about 200 yards from it
(Ex. 9).   At the fork just below (Ex. 9) we bear R., and shortly after
passing Hilltown Farm, shall reach Hill Bridge (Ex. 8).   Instead of
passing up Church Lane (Ex. 8) we mount the steps L., of the road
immediately after crossing the bridge, and follow the path through the

---

* Roads are now being made over this part of the down by the
War Office.

fields described in Ex. 8. This path will lead us to Wapsworthy Bridge, which is about ½ m. distant.

Wapsworthy, which now merely consists of three farms, probably represents an early settlement. It is rather amusing to find the name given in one place as Waspsworthy, and to be told that Wapsworthy is merely the Devon vernacular, an idea presumably founded on the fact that in the peasant speech *wasp* is frequently *waps*. Many strange things have taken place on Dartmoor, but it is altogether beyond us to conceive of wasps ever having formed a *worthig*, or settlement, there. The name as it is pronounced to-day is met with on the Court Rolls several centuries ago. Like other dwellers in the skirts of the forest the people of this place sometimes neglected to keep up their fences. In 1609 the inhabitants were presented at the Court at Lydford for allowing the fence called Wapsworthie Hedge, hard by the forest of Dartmoor, to be in a ruinous condition.

A footpath runs from Wapsworthy to Longbetor, beyond which is the common under Lich Tor, but we shall make our way thither by the road. Longbetor was formerly the abode of a certain " old squire " who kept a pack of hounds here, and of whom more than one story is related. The present house, as appears from a tablet in the wall, was built in 1849, and is a little further removed from the Wapsworthy Brook than the original dwelling, the remains of which may yet be seen, including a part of the " old squire's oven." Above Longbetor is a miry spot known as Wapsworthy Wells, and the scene of one of the squire's adventures. Leaving the bridge we pass up the road as shown in the Paths' section (T. 19), bending gradually E., for about ¼ m., when we reach a gate on the L., where a track leads through some enclosures to Standon Farm. An immense wall, formed of the stones gathered when the enclosures were cleared, will be seen L., and immediately within the gate the turf-covered foundations of what apparently was once a building. To this we shall presently refer. The track through the fields crosses the Bagga Tor Brook at a ford, close below which is a very interesting clapper, consisting of two openings, the roadway being formed by two stones laid over each of these (T. 18). Standon Farm was formerly haunted, but the ghost does not appear to have done much harm beyond occasionally turning everything in the house topsy-turvy. We pass up the road, and presently notice another gate L., where a road runs in to Brousen Tor Farm, and is continued to the ford mentioned above. Just beyond this gate the road bends a little L., and here on the R. of the way, is a green mound. It is known as the Frenchmen's Grave, and according to the story three brothers lie buried here. These Frenchmen are said to have lived in the house, the foundations of which we were able to trace on the turf near the gate. First one died and then another, both being laid to rest at this spot. By-and-bye the surviving brother died, and was also buried here, together with everything that their house had contained. A farmer living near once thought of digging into the mound in the hope of finding something valuable. But when he heard that certain antiquaries in their searches on the moor never found anything but " a passel o' flint an' shards," he abandoned the idea, remarking that he had no time to " draw away 'pon sich foolish 'ole games."

A little further on we enter a newtake, with Bagga Tor (1,219 feet)

close by on the L., the farm of that name lying in the valley beyond it,
to which a road is seen leading.   Here we are on the line of the Lich
Path, which may be seen coming down the hill from the E., and which
ran from this point to the ford on the Tavy below Willsworthy (T. 18).
We follow this and shall soon be led to the moor gate, on passing
through which we find ourselves in a large stroll, formed by the walls
of the Bagga Tor enclosures on the L., and those of Longbetor on the R.
At the outer end of the stroll a large bush will be observed in the
corner of the Bagga Tor newtake, and which, it may be seen, is protected by a wall built across the corner.   Another will be observed in
the corner towards the N., and this is similarly fenced against the
cattle.   These shrubs were brought from abroad, and were planted
here more than fifty years ago.   A note of the circumstance was made
at the time by my old Dartmoor friend, James Stephens, who passed
the whole of his life in this neighbourhood.

From this point the Lich Path runs about S.E. to White Barrow,
having Cocks' Hill (Ex. 8) S. of it, and Green Hill on the N., the slight
depression between the two being visible from where we stand.   Green
Hill extends northward for rather over $\frac{1}{2}$ m., where is another very
slight depression, eastward of the corner bush at which we have arrived.
Northward of Green Hill is Linch Down, on which is situated Linch
Tor, in full view from the bush, and $\frac{1}{2}$ m. from it, and to this we now
make our way.   The track which runs L. goes out to Brook's Head,
with branches to Walkham Head (T. 19).

Linch Tor is not of great size, and the principal pile is on the slope
below the crest of the hill.   The southernmost pile is on the crest, and
around it stones are heaped in the form of a cairn.   This is known as
Limesboro, and forms one of the forest bondmarks, the boundary line
being drawn from it northward to the pile of stones, mentioned as
forming one of the bounds of the hamlet of Willsworthy, and thence
to Wester, or Homer, Red Lake.   Close to the cairn a small herdsman's
shelter will be noticed.   The surface level is 1,697 feet.   The western
side of this ridge, southward of the cairn, which descends to the Walkham, is known as Stookey Moor.

Proceeding northward along the ridge, with the head waters of
the Walkham in full view on the R., we shall shortly cross the old
peat track that runs out to the ties (T. 19), one branch of which went
to the Walkham Head Peat Works, now disused.   At that point there
is a ford over the shallow stream, and a track runs up the further side,
joining the path from Peter Tavy to the head of the river (T. 16).   A
little above the works is a small feeder of the Walkham, called Ninny
Lake, and here many years ago stood a building known as the Turf
House.   In this the peat cut for use at Wheal Betsy used to be stored.
The granite pillars that supported the roof are still to be seen.   This
is not far below us on the R. as we proceed.   On crossing the track we
bear a little to the E. of N., and at the distance of less than $\frac{1}{2}$ m. shall
come upon Black Lane (T. 19), which we may follow past Brook's
Head to its termination a short distance beyond.   Brook's Head,
which is really the source of Easter, or Outer, Red Lake, is on the L.
Immense quantities of peat have been cut here, but the ties are now
covered with herbage, while heather and whortleberry plants grow on
their edges.   Just below is Tavy Hole (R. 3), beyond which Fur Tor
(Ex. 11) is seen rising grandly.

Here we retrace out steps, and follow the track W. and S. until it loses the character of such, and becomes a mere washed out gully. Then we leave it and strike R. across the dip by the head of the Bagga Tor Brook, and make our way up the E. side of Standon Hill to the tumulus on its summit (which we were able to see from North Hisworthy, Princetown district), our course being about W. The view from this point is good. On leaving it we strike N.W. by N. across Standon Down, and descend towards the Tavy. Here in the wide hollow opposite to the Tavy Cleave Tors (Ex. 11) is a group of hut circles, sometimes known as Standon Houses. In the time often referred to as " back along " these, it appears, were inhabited, but the owners were driven away by the Evil One, whose bellowing at night was of so ear-splitting a character that they were unable to sleep. The remains are situated on the slope, not far from the L. bank of the Tavy, S.E. by S. or Ger Tor (Ex. 11).

From this group of antiquities we shall make our way down the valley S.W. by S. to Willsworthy Ford, or Standon Steps, as the crossing-place is more often called, keeping the Tavy near to us on the R. the whole of the way. Crossing Putty Moor we enter a stroll at the end of which is a path that will lead us directly to the ford.

[Immediately outside the wall of an enclosure S.E. of Standon farmhouse, is a kistvaen, not, however, in a very good state of preservation ; but this lies rather out of our way.]

Crossing the Tavy at Standon Steps we ascend the narrow way to Willsworthy, and on passing the farmhouse shall find ourselves in the road ½ m. from Lane End (Exs. 9, 11), which is R. We turn L. to Willsworthy Bridge (Ex. 9), and here a path will take the rambler who is on his way to Lydford village to Forstall Cross. It runs up the valley, with the Willsworthy Brook on the R., and passing very near to Yellowmead Farm, soon after crosses the mine leat at a footbridge, close to the cross. (This path passes over the ground recently acquired by the War Office). Here the rambler is on the Lich Path (T. 18), which he will follow to the village. If the visitor is returning to Lydford Station he will, on crossing Willsworthy Bridge, follow the road and take the first turning R. by Will Farm (Ex. 9), and keeping straight on up the lane will soon reach Yard Gate (Ex. 9). He will now take the path L. to some steps in the wall, and will pass up the common, with the latter on his R. Not far beyond the corner of the enclosure is Horndon Down Bridge, which he will cross (Ex. 9). Here he takes the green track running N.W., branching L. at the fork, and will follow it to the road that runs over Black Down. This he crosses, and still keeping to the green path will be led to the gate by which he entered on the down near the station.

[Should the state of the river render it impossible to cross at Standon Steps, it will be necessary to descend to Hill Bridge. To do this the rambler will make his way from Putty Moor to Standon farmhouse, near by, and follow the road thence to the clapper before referred to, and so on to the Wapsworthy road, where he turns R. He will not, however, go as far as Wapsworthy Bridge, but will enter the gate R., mentioned in Ex. 8, and follow the path through the fields to Hill Bridge, there described. (At the confluence of the Tavy and the Bagga Tor Brook, about midway between Hill Bridge and Standon Steps, there are also stepping-stones and a ford. This crossing-place over the Tavy is known as Cataloo Steps, but is not approached on the W. bank of that river by any public path.)

From Hill Bridge the Lich Path (T. 18) must be followed by the rambler returning to Lydford village, the road taking him by Hill Town, Will, and Yard Gate (*ante*). For Lydford Station he will make his way from the bridge to Zoar Down, as described in Ex. 8. Here, instead of bearing L. as in that excursion, he will make a path for himself straight up over the down, crossing the road about midway, and at its head will find an opening between the newtakes, and passing through this will reach Horndon Down. Striking N.N.W. he will, at the distance of ¼ m., reach Horndon Down Bridge, from which point the route to the station has just been given.]

Ex. 11.—*Tavy Cleave* (3¼ m. distant), *Watern Oke, Rattle Brook Hill, High Down*, 9 m. (including *Ger Tor*, 10 m.) WITH EXTENSION TO *Fur Tor* and *Cut Hill*, add 5½ m.

Our first point will be the N. end of the Redford enclosures. If we start from Lydford village we make our way by Skit Steps to Down Lane, as in Ex. 10. On reaching the common we desert the Lich Path (T. 18), and strike almost due 'E. to the corner of the plantation above Bear Walls, and under White Hill (Ex. 10), following a green track (T. 22) that runs out to the point for which we are making. We may continue along this, with the plantation L., or may still keep an easterly line, and passing over the summit of White Hill, examine the cairns there, and thence make our way to the enclosure, which is just below.

[If our starting-place is the station, we pass up the side of Black Down, with Henscott Plantations on our L., as in Ex. 10, and when near the head of the latter, shall leave the track, which bears R., and keep straight on to the high road. This we cross, going due E., and shall very soon strike the Dartmoor Path (T. 21), into which we turn L., and passing the Ring o' Bells (Ex. 9) and Forstall Cross (T. 18), shall follow the grassy track with the Redford enclosures R. to the point above named. (The stones noticed near the wall, with the letter H. cut upon them, are bondmarks formerly belonging to the Hamlyn property.]

From the N. end of the Redford enclosures we proceed in a direction S.E., with Hare Tor on the L. This beautiful Tor, which attains an elevation of 1,744 feet, is of a conical form, and a striking object from whichever side it is viewed. There is a small grassy hollow on its summit, an unusual feature in a Dartmoor tor, though something akin to it is met with on Longaford Tor (Ex. 5) and on Down Tor (Ex. 2). The view is very fine, embracing as it does so much of the forest, and such a wide extent of woodland and field. This tor, so we are told, bears a strong resemblance to a hare, which, it is said, probably accounts for its name. It requires a very strong imagination to perceive this likeness, one that would see a mouse, or an ox, or any other animal, in it had it borne a suitable appellation. Many of the Dartmoor tors bear Saxon names, their more ancient Celtic ones, if such they possessed, having been lost. Whether the name of the tor in question was given to it in Saxon times, or whether in a more recent day, it is, of course, impossible to say, but it is at least certain that it has nothing whatever to do with a hare. This is proved by an old map of Willsworthy Manor, on which the smaller pile to the N. of the main one is named Little Hay Tor, and the other Great Hay Tor. It is not difficult to see how the latter, rising as it does above the Little Hay, or High, Tor, would become the Hayer, or Higher, Tor. An analogous case occurs above Wapsworthy Wells, where a small pile on the slope above an equally small clatter, is always spoken of as Hare Tor, or, as it is sounded, Hayer Tor, the appropriateness of the name to its situation being understood.

A little N. of Hare Tor, and not far W. of the head of Dead Lake, is a small tumulus known as the Hay Tor Bound of Willsworthy Manor, and N. of this is Sharp Tor, called sometimes by the moormen Lydford Sharp, to distinguish it from the chief pile of the Tavy Cleave group of tors, which also bears that name. Some ninety odd years ago it was remarked by an antiquary that this tor well deserved its name, some of its points being as sharp as a spear, but he did not say that it was derived from this. There are eight or ten Sharp Tors in the Dartmoor country, and they have probably been given their names by moormen in comparatively recent times, their old ones being lost. The idea with them is not that the rocks are sharp, but that the pile, whatever its form, is, in a manner, a point standing sharply up from the common.

Having passed Hare Tor, our course being S.E., we shall soon reach the fine group of tors overlooking the deep Tavy Cleave. These tors are five in number, and the hill on the brow of which they are placed is so steep as to form what is practically a cliff. (See remarks on the word *Cleave* in the *Terms* section). To the N.E. of this group a clatter covers the side of the hill descending to the river, and extends up the Tavy nearly to Rattle Brook Foot. On the further side of the stream the hill is also plentifully strewn with rocks. The view from these tors, or from Ger Tor, the fine pile that rises high above the Tavy further down the valley, is not surpassed in the Dartmoor country. In none of the river valleys is there such a picture of wild grandeur as is here presented. [*Gems*, Chap. XXIV.]

[If the rambler should decide to visit Ger Tor before making his way to the Tavy Cleave group, he will, instead of striking across the common S.E. from the Redford enclosures, keep the wall of them almost close to him R., and when around the bend will proceed S.S.E. As Ger Tor is in full view, although presenting no imposing appearance from this side, there will be no difficulty in reaching it. The rambler will probably strike the green path that comes up from Lane End (T. 20) on his way. The road to Lane End from Tavistock has already been described (Ex. 9), and it now remains to sketch the route from that point to Tavy Cleave. If the rambler decides to make his way up through the cleave, which is really the best way of seeing it, he will turn R. and follow the track running close to the hedge past Nat Tor Farm. He will then turn up the slope L., and crossing the mine leat at Nat Tor Bridge, find himself close to the rocks of Nat Tor. Here a tiny enclosure of the kind formerly built by the herdsmen near the tors, will be noticed, the entrance jambs yet standing. The leat will now become the rambler's guide, and he will follow it to the weir, obtaining a grand view of Ger Tor as he passes across the foot of the clatter that descends from it to the Tavy. From the weir, or Devil's Point, as it was formerly called, the river is traced upward to the

Rattle Brook. The Tavy Cleave Tors are seen to great advantage from the river bank ; nothing like them is to be met with on any other part of Dartmoor. The strip of ground at the foot of the clatter gradually narrows as the rambler approaches the head of the defile until it disappears altogether, when he has to make the best of his way over the boulders that completely cover the side of the steep hill and stream down into the river. The return from Rattle Brook Foot to Lane End is sketched in S. Ex. 27.

Ger Tor is easily reached from Lane End, from which point it is in sight, and only ¾ m. distant. Part way up the hill the mine leat is crossed at a bridge, the situation of which can be discerned from the gate. The view of the cleave from this tor is very striking, and the pile itself, though not rising to a great height above the turf, is never-theless a fine cluster of rocks. That its true name is Great Tor, as some has supposed, Ger, or rather Gert, being simply the moorman's way of pronouncing the word, is, I think, highly improbable. Between the tor and the Tavy Cleave group the hill falls back, forming, as it were, a huge amphitheatre. As the visitor passes from one to the other he will notice a reave having much the appearance of a stone row, and near it are hut circles. Other remains also occur hard by, and at the foot of the slope on the river bank are the evidences of ancient mining operations. Near the rock group is Green Gert, which is covered with velvety turf.]

Leaving the Tavy Cleave Tors we shall make our way along the side of the hill in a N.E. direction, with the defile on the R. for about ½ m., when we shall see below us the great bend of the Tavy. It is here that it receives the Rattle Brook, which flows from the N., and to this stream we descend. Crossing it we mount the slope of Watern Oke (Ex. 12), and following the course of the Tavy upward, and keeping it in view, we shall soon be led to a cluster of hut circles in the midst of a clatter. These were thoroughly explored in the summer of 1905 by the Rev. Irvine K. Anderson, Rector of Mary Tavy, who encamped here. For many weeks men were engaged in digging into the hut circles under his personal superintendence, and the work was thoroughly carried out. Flint, and fragments of pottery, charcoal, and the usual cooking-stones, were found, but no object of any exceptional interest.

On the opposite bank of the Tavy, on the slope of Knoll, a hill sometimes called Outer Standon, and erroneously shown as Watern Oke on a map made from a survey of the early part of the nineteenth century, is a large mound, apparently thrown up by the tinners. At one time they were busy here, as the extensive remains of their workings attest. The moormen do not, however, connect this mound with them, but regard it as having formed a kind of stronghold, and give to it the name of Lord Mayor's Castle. A little further up the Tavy the tribu-tary called Homer Red Lake, mentioned in Ex. 10, comes down from the S. through Red Lake Combe, and immediately below the confluence is a ford. An upright stone will be noticed on the R. bank of the river. It is a bondmark connected with the peat works at Rattle Brook Head (Ex. 12). That part of the moor between Homer and Outer Red Lake is known as the Meads.

[EXTENSION TO *Fur Tor and Cut Hill*, 5½ m. From this point Fur Tor and Cut Hill may be conveniently reached ; the former is about 1¼ m. distant ; the latter 1 m. further. We pass up the valley to the confluence of the Tavy and the Amicombe (barely ½ m), where there is a crossing-place called Sandy Ford. The Tavy comes down from Tavy Hole (R. 3) from the S., to the W. of it being Red Lake Hill, at the top of which is Brook's Head (Ex. 10) ¾ m. distant. The Amicombe flows from the N.E., and it is this stream that we must follow. To make a beeline for Fur Tor would lead us over some rather bad ground, and it is therefore far better to go up stream for about ½ m. to Amicombe Bend, where the river receives the Cut Combe Water, choosing a path either on the R. or L. bank. It is not necessary to go

Black Hill.   Fur Tor.

Amicombe Bend.   The Meads.

The Tavy.

FROM WATERN OKE, LOOKING E.

quite so far as the bend ; we may make our way up the stony hillside to the tor when we find ourselves abreast of it. Fur Tor is perhaps the grandest of the Dartmoor tors, for while there are some that rise much higher above the ground than the loftiest of the piles here, and also exhibit finer rock masses, there is none that covers so large an area, or whose surrounding are of the desolate character as those upon which this lonely tor looks down. Fur Tor is a wilderness of stone. Masses of grey rock stud the slopes that sweep down to the Amicombe and its tributary stream. On one side the rambler may wander amid innumberable lumps of granite, each a miniature tor, as in a maze. The larger masses of this tor form two distinct groups, one overlooking the great Amicombe Hill that extends away to the N., the other being E. of this, and nearer Cut Combe. We shall find the first on the brow of the hill, and shall notice that it consists of six piles of fairly large size and several smaller ones. From this we make our way across the level piece of ground, where rocks give place to grass and rushes, to the eastern group, which is the more important of the two. Here are four piles, the chief of which has a very striking appearance. On the highest part of it are three rock basins, one being so near the edge of the granite mass as to render the result of the action of the water in the wearing away of the stone visible from the ground. On the western side of this tor an immense block of granite will be observed hanging, as it were, midway between the summit and the turf, and another similar block lies on the ground near by. The time must come when this immense stone will topple over ; the tor is slowly going to ruin. Below it, on the Cut Combe side, is a spot known to the moormen as Fur Tor Wood. The name seems to point to the former existence of trees in this sheltered hollow, and the discovery a few years ago of oak buried in the peat near Little Kneeset proves that they once grew around here. (For an extended description of Fur Tor see *Gems*, Chap. II.)

Leaving Fur Tor we shall make our way to Cut Hill, the summit of which is ¾ m. distant in an E.S.E. direction, but our walk thither will extend to about 1 m., as we sweep to the R. in order to avoid descending into Cut Combe. We keep along the edge of this, which lies L. ; on our R., *i.e.*, to the S.W. and S., the ground sinks down to the upper waters of the Tavy (R. 3). A great part of this hillside consists of fen, but it does not extend quite to the edge of the combe, so that our progress throughout will be over fairly good ground. From Cut Hill, which rises to a height of 1,981 feet, a view of the solitary parts of the forest is commanded such as can be obtained from no other point throughout the length and breadth of the moor, though for wonderful glimpses of the great waste Siddaford will by some perhaps be regarded as its equal. We have already described the view from the summit of North Hisworthy (Princetown District), but this from Cut Hill is altogether wilder in its character. In the former very much that man has done is visible ; but here, except for the distant Princetown, and the enclosures of Teign Head Farm, hardly a sign of his work on the waste is apparent. Something of what lies beyond the moor is seen, notably towards the west, and where the hills part to form a passage for the West Ockment to the north, and again towards the east. But it is far away, and forms but a small part of the picture. We look upon desolation ; upon a vast wilderness, from which life is absent.

Among the tors and hills seen from this lofty spot, the following are the principal : From W. to N. : Standon Hill, Ger Tor, the Tavy Cleave Tors, and to the R. of these, on the great ridge running N. and S. beyond the Rattle Brook, Hare Tor, Sharp Tor, Chat Tor, the Dunnagoat Tors, and Great Links Tor ; Amicombe Hill, with Kitty Tor towards its northern end, and distant about 3½ m. ; quite near to us is Fur Tor, and to the R. of it, further away, Little Kneeset, and 1 m. beyond this Great Kneeset ; a little to the L. of the latter we look down the valley of the West Ockment, with Lints Tor at its head ; on the R. side of the valley we see Black Tor, below which, though hidden from us, is the Island of Rocks (Ex. 14), with High Willes, the loftiest point on Dartmoor, towering above it ; to the R. in succession we see Yes Tor, West Mil Tor, and Row Tor, about 3 m. beyond which lies the town of Okehampton. The view from N. to E. is blocked by the high ground beyond the East Dart, the upper valley of which we look down upon. L. of its source we see Black Hill, and R. of it the hill named Newtake (Cranmere routes), 4 m. beyond which we observe the summit of the great rounded mass of Cosdon. Over White Horse Hill, N.E., the distant farm lands are visible. From E. to S. : A little N. of E., and rather over 2 m. distant, is Siddaford Tor, quite close to which are the circles known as the Grey Wethers (Exs. 20, 45) ; to the R. of this tor is a fine view of the great ridge of Hameldon, 7 m. away, and to the R. of that Saddle Tor, with the frontier height of Rippon Tor ; still further R. is Buckland Beacon, and almost in a line with it, but nearer to us, Corndon Tor and Yar Tor ; Bellaford Tor, 5 m. to

5. LYDFORD DISTRICT.

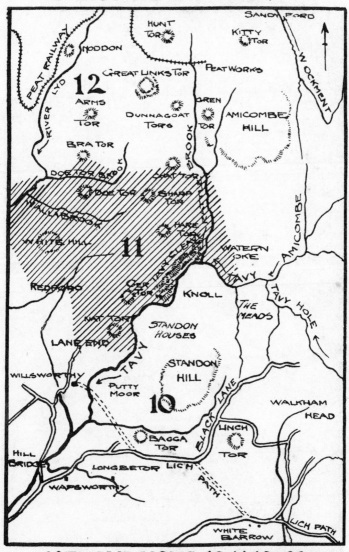

Map labels:

SANDY FORD
HUNT TOR
KITTY TOR
WOCKMENT
PEAT RAILWAY
NODDON
GREAT LINKS TOR
PEAT WORKS
RIVER LYD
12
ARMS TOR
DUNNAGOAT TORS
GREN TOR
AMICOMBE HILL
BRA TOR
DOCTORS BROOK
SHARP TOR
LIT DOCTOR TOR SHARP TOR
WALLABROOK
WHITE HILL
11
HARE TOR
TAVY CLEAVE
WATERN OKE
AMICOMBE
TAVY
REDFORD
GER TOR
KNOLL
TAVY HOLE
THE MEADS
KIT TOR
STANDON HOUSES
LANE END
TAVY
STANDON HILL
WILLSWORTHY
PUTTY MOOR
10
BLACK LANE
WALKHAM HEAD
HILL BRIDGE
BAGGA TOR
LINCH TOR
LONGBETOR
LICH PATH
WAPSWORTHY
PATH
WHITE BARROW
LICH PATH

"EXCURSIONS 10, 11, 12."
(EXTENSION TO EX. 11, ON MAP 6)

6. EXTENSIONS

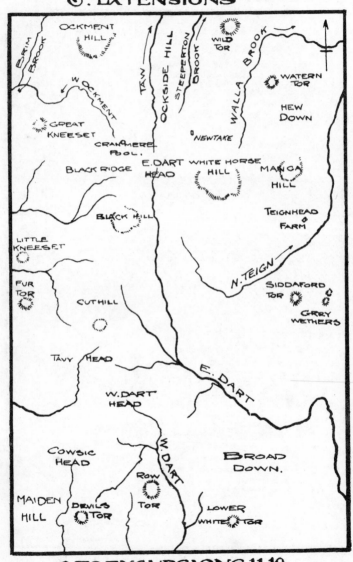

TO EXCURSIONS 11,19.

the S.E., we look down upon, as we do also upon Row Tor, near the West Dart, Higher White Tor, and the conical Longaford, above Wistman's Wood (Ex. 5); far away to the S. are Eastern and Western Whitaburrow, on the verge of Brent Moor, and the lofty Three Barrows, that looks out over the South Hams (Brent and Ivybridge District); R. of these, and very much nearer, is North Hisworthy, seen over the crest of Maiden Hill, the latter being only 2 m. away. From S. to W.: 4½ m. as the crow flies the rocks of Great Mis Tor rise against the sky S.W. by S.; to the R. and beyond it, is Great Staple Tor and Roose Tor, backed by Cocks' Tor Hill; R. of this is White Tor, above Wapsworthy (Ex. 10), and still further R. Linch Tor, and the great hill of Standon.

(As in the case of the description of the view from North Hisworthy Tor (Princetown District), the reader is directed to the index for references to the hills and tors here named).

The summit of Cut Hill is crowned with a low mound of turf, which, although rising but a few feet above the surface, is yet seen very distinctly even from a great distance. On the N. side of the hill the rain has washed away vast quantities of peat, in one place to such an extent that at first glance the visitor might be inclined to imagine it had been removed by manual labour. Below this the hill is covered with a network of gullies scooped out by the rain, some of them very deep, and this, too, is the character of the ground that extends northward over Flatters, and Black Ridge, and beyond Cranmere. On the E. side of the hill the ground is of a similar nature, and also on the S. as far as the springs of the Cowsic (Ex. 5). On the W. side, which overlooks Cut Combe, the ground is firm and covered with turf.

(The route from Princetown and Two Bridges to Cut Hill is for the first few miles over ground that has already been described (Ex. 5). The rambler may make his way from the head of the Cowsic, as in R. 3, to the Tavy, but steering due N., and trace it to its source, which is on the S. side of Cut Hill. The springs of this river are in a shallow hollow in the midst of the fen, and from this the summit of the hill is about ½ m. distant, N.N.E. Another way is by Bear Down, as in Ex. 5. If this is chosen the rambler will leave Lydford Tor L., and will steer N. with the Foxholes Water close on his R., to Row Tor, thence descending to the West Dart, E., which he will follow to its source. Or he may pass up from Two Bridges by Wistman's Wood (Ex. 5), and then follow the Dart upward. Cut Hill is ¾ m. N.N.W. of West Dart Head. Whichever way the rambler chooses the last ½ m. will be across the fen, but he will find no difficulty in making his way over it in fair weather.

The return routes from Cut Hill to Princetown and Two Bridges may be briefly described, as it is only necessary to bring the rambler to the sources of the Cowsic and the West Dart. For Princetown direct he will first make his way to Tavy Head, which can be plainly seen from the summit of the hill; it lies S.S.W., and ½ m. distant. On reaching it the stream should be kept R., and followed for about ¼ m. Here it begins to bend R., Cowsic Head, which cannot, however, be seen, being rather over ½ m. from this point L. The rambler's course now is due S. over the low ridge between the upper waters of the two streams. He is still on the fen, and the ground consequently anything but good. It is of that spongy character which renders progress over

it rather slow. But the Cowsic is not far off, and as soon as its banks
are reached firmer ground is found. The stream is followed to Travellers'
Ford, about 1 m. from its source, from which point instructions are
given for reaching both Princetown and Two Bridges in Ex. 5.
(P. T., 6½ m. ; T.B., 5½ m.)

For Two Bridges the best way is by the valley of the West Dart.
Longaford Tor, which overlooks it, can be plainly seen from Cut Hill,
¾ m. distant in a straight line. The rambler may take this for his
guide ; it lies S.S.E. of the summit of the hill, and by following that
course for ¾ m. he will be led to the springs of the West Dart. In
tracing the river downward keep it on the R. (Ex. 5). If the rambler
wishes to go by way of Bear Down he will leave the river L., and make
southward for Row Tor, 1 m. below its source. Then, still proceeding
southward, he will keep the Foxholes Water L., and make towards
Lydford Tor, 1¼ m. S.S.W. of Row Tor. This he leaves R., and steering
S. will reach Bear Down Farm, and the road near Two Bridges. The
distances by these routes are a little less than by the former.

(The route to Cut Hill from Post Bridge is described in that District
(Ex. 45), and there are also directions for reaching it in the Cranmere
Routes).

Making our way down the N. side of the hill we soon reach Cut
Lane (T. 79), and the two guide-stones already mentioned in our notice
of that ancient path. Here we turn L., and following the directions
there given, shall shortly find ourselves below Fur Tor, and between
it and Little Kneeset. On the R. bank of the Cut Combe Water,
which will be on our L. as we approach it, and close to where it receives
a little feeder from the E., we may observe the foundations of a small
structure which has much the appearance of the remains of a herdsman's hut. Little Kneeset (1,694 feet) is a fine hill of good hard
ground, covered with grass, and free from heather. It is peninsulated
by the Cut Combe Water and the feeder above alluded to on its S.
side, and by a tributary of the Amicombe on the north. This tributary, it may be well to observe, together with the lower part of the
Amicombe, is sometimes regarded as the Tavy, and thus it has been
said that this river rises near Cranmere. Little Kneeset forms a ridge,
and springs off westward from Black Hill (Cranmere Routes). When
we look at the sheltered situation of Cut Combe, and the grass on Little
Kneeset, and the slopes of Fur Tor, as well as on Amicombe Hill, we
shall hardly wonder that this part of the north quarter of the forest
has always been in favour as a pasturage ground. More than five
hundred and fifty years ago we read of the Preda de Vurtorre and the
Preda de Aunnacombe, and cattle have been agisted here ever since.

Passing out of the great combe, the entrance to which is formed by
the slopes of Little Kneeset and Fur Tor, we speedily reach the confluence of the Cut Combe Water and the Amicombe. On the L. bank
of the latter is another good stretch of grazing ground, known as
Pinswell, but our best plan will perhaps be to cross the stream, and
make our way down the R. bank. ½ m. below it joins the Tavy at
Sandy Ford, and a little further down the united stream receives
Outer Red Lake, at which point we set out on this extension of our
excursion.]

Turning from the Tavy by the peat boundary stone, we pass up
over Watern Oke in a direction rather W. of N., and at the distance

of less than a mile shall come upon a very high tumulus above the L. bank of the Rattle Brook, which has more the appearance of having been thrown up by miners than of an ancient mound. Near to this, on the bank of the brook, is a group of hut circles, and further up stream there are others. We cross the Rattle Brook at a fording-place just above where the Green Tor Water and the Scad fall into it, and make our way up the side of Rattle Brook Hill to Chat Tor, with Ker Beam on the L. Chat Tor is W. by N. of the ford, and ½ m. from it. It consists of a single mass of rock, and is shown on a Duchy map as Loaf, which, judging from its character, is probably its ancient name, *i.e.*, *Llof* (cf. Branscombe's Loaf, Ex. 13).

We pass over the ridge, bearing a little S. of W., and descend the hill to Foxhole, a combe which has been extensively streamed for tin, and which also has been the scene of more modern mining operations, as the ruins of a building will attest. Through this valley, a favourite spot with whortleberry gatherers, runs the Doe Tor Brook, its source being at the head of it, where is the spring known as Dick's Well (T. 28, Ex. 12). We strike the brook at Doe Tor Bend, where the stream suddenly changes its southern course for a westerly one. Here we cross it, and pass down the R. bank, with Doe Tor, a small pile which presents nothing remarkable, a short distance to the L. Very soon we shall reach Doe Tor Falls, a most charming cascade, hidden away in a narrow rift. Above us on the R. is Bra Tor, on which is a fine cross, about 13 feet in height, erected by the late Mr. W. Widgery, the well-known artist, in commemoration of the Jubilee of Queen Victoria, in 1887. Unlike the ancient crosses of the moor this one is not hewn from a single stone, but is composed of a number of blocks. [*Crosses*, Chap. XI.] Seen from any point this cross seems perfectly in place, but appears to the best advantage when viewed from the valley of the Lyd, below the confluence of that stream with the Doe Tor Brook. As Ger Tor has been supposed by some, but without much reason, to be a corruption of Great Tor, so there are those who similarly imagine Bra Tor to be properly Broad Tor. It is only necessary to state that an early form of the name is Brat Tor ; it appears in a document of Henry VIII's time as Brattor.

Near the entrance to Doe Tor Farm, to which a track leads, we leave the brook a little to the L., and passing down through the disused workings of Wheal Mary Emma shall reach a ford on the Lyd, where there are some stepping-stones. Just below this on the bank of the stream are the foundations of a building of the blowing-house type.

Crossing the Lyd at the ford we shall follow the track leading from it across High Down to the moor gate near the Dartmoor Inn (T. 27), to which a walk of about ½ m. will bring us. An alternative route to the village will lead us down the right bank of the Lyd. Below the point where the Doe Tor Brook falls into it we shall pass a clam where a path leads to the farm, and below this and near Doe Tor Gate Ford, is the confluence of the Lyd and the Walla Brook. Here a track runs up the hill R. from the ford, and this we follow for ½ m. to Doe Tor Gate opening on a lane (T. 27). Here there are four large granite slabs, one of them having a socket in it for the reception of the stanchion of the gate, which, however, is now hung on hinges. (See *Gate* in *Terms* Section). Passing onward we soon reach the high road, and crossing this shall make our way by Skit Lane to the village.

Ex. 12.—*The Dunnagoat Tors, Great Links Tor, The Rattle Brook, Kitty Tor, Amicombe Hill, Upper Valley of the Lyd*, 7½ m.   Add 1½ m. if from and to the village.

Starting from the gate near the Dartmoor Inn we shall follow the track already described (T. 28), passing up between Arms Tor L. and Bra Tor R., to Dick's Well, a distance of about 2 m.   Although Arms Tor (1,411 feet) does not rise to a great height above the ground, it is nevertheless rather striking in appearance, particularly when viewed from the slope of Noddon (Ex. 13), across the valley of the Lyd.   The Doe Tor Brook has its source a few yards S. of the boundary stone, but time was when the stream rose at its foot.   Ere it has gone long on its way it runs among extensive workings of the tinners, across a part of which we passed on our way from Rattle Brook Hill to the Lyd (Ex. 11).

Near Dick's Well a branch track leads R. to Rattle Brook Mine, which ceased working many years ago, the main one bearing L. at the junction, and reaching the stream a little higher up.   But we shall leave the track at the bondstone, and make our way to the two tors, about ½ m. off, N.E. by E.   These are known as Higher Dunnagoat Tor (1,845 feet) and Lower Dunnagoat Tor (1,832 feet), and overhang the Rattle Brook.   On the further side of this is Green Tor (1,774 feet), E. of which rises the Green Tor Water (Ex. 11), a tributary of the brook named, and having a course of about 1 m.   Not very far from the tor are the walls of a building erected in connection with some peat works further up the Rattle Brook, but which were only worked for a short time.   It is now known as Bleak House, a name which its situation on a bare moor at an elevation of 1,740 feet, renders very appropriate.   Mr. Richard John King says that Dunnagoat, or Dana-goat, as it is sometimes spelt, is " from the Cornish *dan*, *under*, and *coet, a wood.*"*   He takes the name to belong to a hollow.   But we incline to think it more probable that in the first syllable of the name we see the Celtic *dun*, a hill, and if the second really is *coet*, or *coed*, that this may have been derived from the former presence of trees in the valley of the Rattle Brook.   Even now in parts of it a solitary rowan, or oak, is to be met with.

Our steps will now lead us to Great Links Tor (1,908 feet), about ½ m. to the W.N.W., and which we shall find to be a grand and imposing cluster of rocks, the several piles rising to a great height above the turf. Though its form is not so suggestive of a ruined castle as is that of Hey Tor, when viewed from certain points, such a resemblance is not altogether wanting, particularly when it is seen from the slope of Gibbet Hill on Black Down (Ex. 9).   Looked at from anywhere it is striking, but perhaps creates the greatest interest when the rambler to Cranmere, from the Chagford side, or from the East Dart Valley, sees it standing up sharply against the sky as he approaches the piece of fen surrounding the pool.   For some time previously, particularly if from the Dart Valley, he has seen nothing ahead of him but dreary looking peat ridges covered with bog-grass, when suddenly the rocks of Links Tor, 3½ m. away, come into view, and lift themselves higher with each step he takes until they are fully revealed beyond the wide slope of

---

* *The Forest of Dartmoor and its Borders*.   An Historical Sketch (1856).

Amicombe. The view commanded from the tor is of a very fine character. Much of the moor is seen in one direction, and an extensive range of country which the husbandman has brought into subjection in the other. High Willes and Yes Tor (Ex. 15) are seen to the N.E., and away to the S.E., with only Amicombe between, the rocks of lonely Fur Tor (Ex. 11), crowning the great grassy hill that rises from the fen. Against the western sky the loftiest hills of Cornwall uplift themselves, and when the sun shines upon it there is a glimpse of the sea, over which the warders looked out in the old days from the walls of Tintagel. Mr. King derives the name of this tor, which he renders *Lynx*, from lynnek, or *lynnic*, *wet*, *marshy*, but we fail to see any justification for this. On one side of the tor there is a small hollow—a niche hewn by Nature in the great wall of granite. Little Links Tor is merely a small pile on the side of the hill to the N.W.

[Should the visitor wish to make his way direct to Great Links Tor he cannot do better, after crossing the Lyd, than ascend Arms Tor, from which point Links Tor is in full view ¾ m. to E.N.E. On the way he will pass a small circular enclosure.]

From Great Links Tor we strike E.N.E. to the bridge over the Rattle Brook leading to the peat works, ½ m. distant, and in view as we descend. These works were established in 1878, and the railway from Bridestowe Station for the conveyance of the peat was cut in the following year. Operations did not continue very long, nor have the endeavours to re-start them that have more than once been made, met with any success. We cross the bridge, noticing Hunt Tor (1,843 feet), a large mass of rock, on the L., and passing the peat buildings make our way E.N.E. to Kitty Tor, ½ m. distant. This tor does not rise high above the ground, but stands in such an elevated situation that its altitude is equal to, if not greater than, that of Great Links Tor. The Ordnance Map gives the height of the latter as 1,908 feet, as already stated, and the height of Kitty Tor as 1,920 feet, but I cannot say on what parts of the tors these levels were taken. Kitty Tor stands near the northern end of Amicombe Hill, which large tract of pasturage ground extends from Watern Oke on the S. to the forest boundary line, marked by Stinka Tor, on the N. On the W. it is bounded by the Rattle Brook, and on the E. by the head waters of the Amicombe and the West Ockment from Kneeset Foot to Sandy Ford. Watern Oke is really a part of the hill, and forms its southern extremity, extending from the lower waters of the Rattle Brook to Amicombe Bend (Ex. 11). A number of weird stories attach to Amicombe Hill. Fires are sometimes seen there at night, lighted, it is said, by the Evil One, who keeps watch over the men of Tavistock and Okehampton, between whom there was formerly a deadly feud. Satan, ever on the lookout for mischief, is supposed to be waiting an opportunity to stir up the old enmity.

Stinka Tor is about ½ m. northward of Kitty Tor, and is noticed in our next excursion (Ex. 13).

Leaving Kitty Tor we retrace our steps to the bridge at the peat works, or we may follow the track (T. 30) that runs close by it, to Rattle Brook Head, and Hunt Tor, on the side of Woodcock Hill. In the former case we pass from the Rattle Brook up the incline of the peat railway for about ⅓ m., where it bends R., when we leave it and steer a little N. of W., and descend towards the Lyd. If the latter route be chosen, we shall, on leaving Hunt Tor, strike W. by S., and crossing the railway also make towards the Lyd. In either case the summit of Noddon (Ex. 13), the rounded hill rising on the further side of the river, should be taken as a guide. We should strike the Lyd where a small tributary flowing from the E. falls into it, where it flows along the foot of the steep slope of Noddon. The valley here is very fine, and remains of a former day are not wanting to add interest to it. Just below the confluence, and on the L. bank of the Lyd, is a fine group of hut circles, and a small circular pound. We pass down by the river with Arms Tor above us on the L., and at the distance of ¾ m. shall reach the steps at Noddon Ford below Noddon Gate (Ex. 13, T. 29). On the hillside to the L. another group of hut circles will be found, which, from their proximity to Arms Tor, are sometimes referred to as Arms Tor Rings. ½ m. below the steps we reach High Down Ford, where we shall cross the stream, and following the track shall soon find ourselves at the gate near the Dartmoor Inn.

Ex. 13.—*Noddon, The Upper Lyd, Stinka Tor, Branscombe's Loaf, Corn Ridge, The Sourton Tors, Lake Down*, 11 m. Add 1½ m. if from and to the village.

From the Dartmoor Inn we shall proceed by the Okehampton road to Vale Down, a walk of about ½ m. On reaching the common we have on our L. Battishill Down, and adjoining this on the N. Fernworthy Down but our way will take us across the turf R. to Noddon Gate on the line of the King Way (T. 26). Passing through this we cross the peat railway at a bridge and following the old track (or another made by peat carts running parallel and very near to it) we shortly reach the corner of the enclosures on the L. From this corner a hedge runs in the same direction as our path and form the boundary of Southerly Down which is below it. Whether this hedge or the wall of the enclosures further down the hill to the W. of it is the Southerly Wall referred to in certain presentments at the Lydford Courts some centuries ago is not certain but that the inhabitants of Southerly were often ordered to repair the wall that fenced their lands against the forest and also the gate by which they gained access to the moor the entries on the Court Rolls abundantly prove. N. of Southerly Down is a small piece of common called Combe Down and the Rolls show that the dilapidated condition of the gate opening upon this was also the cause of a presentment at the Court. N. of Combe Down is Lake Down at the N.E. corner of which is a mark called the Spring Rock.

Passing a despoiled tumulus we follow the track upward with Noddon on the R. This rounded height to which the fanciful name of Plum-pudding Hill has been given is very precipitous on the E. side where it rises nearly 230 feet above the Lyd its total elevation being 1,430 feet. As we proceed we shall notice that the edge before referred to now presents a remarkable similarity to a stone row, and stops suddenly in a tiny hollow, where the track comes up from Southerly and Combe (T. 30), and crosses the King Way. Here the character of the common changes, the ground beyond this point being covered with rocks. We do not, however, proceed any further along the line of the King Way, which the peat railway here cuts into, but shall follow the track from Southerly, which passes under the line. Our next point is Lyd Head, to which the track will lead us (T. 30), but if we prefer it we may pass down to the stream and trace it to its source. In either case we again cross the railway just before the springs are reached. If we make our way by the river we shall come upon an extensive stream work, where on the L. bank is a small cave, usually spoken of as The Hut. More than one story is told in connection with it. According to these it has been a place where the " old men " used to shelter ; a smuggler's store-place ; a gipsies' haunt ; and a home of the pixies. That it was used by the " old men," or early miners, is not at all improbable.

The Lyd rises near Gren Tor, in the dip between Woodcock Hill and Corn Ridge, its source being a mire known as Tiger's Marsh, which runs up the hollow about E. by N. The stream is crossed just below its source by Lydda Bridge,* a rude structure over which passes not only the track we have followed from Southerly Down (T. 30), but also another that comes up from Prewley Moor (T. 32). Gren Tor, which is rather a striking object, though of small size, is situated close to the track S.E. of the bridge. Like Gren Tor, on the Rattle Brook (Ex. 12), 1¼ m. away, it is called by the moormen Grinny, or Grenny Tor. Our next point is Stinka Tor, which we may reach either by striking over Woodcock Hill, in a direction E. by N., the distance being 1 m., or we may follow the track for 1 m., when we shall find ourselves about ¼ m. from it. The latter will perhaps be the better plan. The track will take us close to Hunt Tor (Ex. 12), immediately after passing which we cross the higher part of the mire at Rattle Brook Head (Ex. 12), and ¼ m. beyond this, where the track turns suddenly southward to Kitty Tor (Ex. 12), we leave it, and strike N.E.

Stinka Tor, which is nearly ½ m. above Sandy Ford, on the West Ockment (Ex. 14), overlooks the deep valley through which that river runs from the forest to the Meldon Gorge, and which is noticed *post* (Ex. 14). The tor, which is small, acts as a forest bondmark, the line being drawn to the ford named in one direction, and to Rattle Brook Head in the other. In the 1609 survey of the forest bounds the tor appears as Steinegtorr, but in another document to which authority also attaches, the name is given as Steng-a-tor, or Sourton Tor, the latter having reference to its situation on the boundary line of the common lands of Sourton and Bridestowe, which is here conterminous with that of the forest. In 1699 we find it in the same form as the present day, a moorman of Lydford, named John Clement, referring to it a deposition taken in a certain suit in that year, as Stinkatorr.

Leaving this pile we make our way in a direction N.W. by N., the Ockment Valley being below us R. (Ex. 14). On the further side is High Willes, with Forsland, or Fordsland, Ledge, just below it in the foreground. Yes Tor is a short distance beyond Willes, and down the valley in advance of us are the piles of Black Tor. (These are noticed in excursions in the Okehampton District). Keeping along the brow of the hill, but not too low down, we shall, at the distance of ½ m. from Stinka Tor, reach some scattered rocks known as the Slipper Stones, opposite to Black Tor Copse (Ex. 14), and here we shall turn L. up the

---

* A corruption, in all probability, of Lyd Head.

hill. It will be noticed that the topmost stone wears the form of a huge slipper. Our course is now W. by N., and our next point the square mass on the slope of Corn Ridge called Branscombe's Loaf, rather more than ½ m. away. In the name of this lump of granite we probably see the Celtic word *Llof*, an *excrescence*, which is not an unsuitable description of it, resting as it does on the smooth turf with no scattered blocks surrounding it as in the case of the tors. (Cf. Chat Tor, Ex. 11). But the name is usually associated with a loaf of bread, and it was therefore with amazement that the baker " in along " heard the Sourton native declare that when he came out his way he would show him a bigger loaf than any he had ever seen :—" Us Sourton vokes got monstrous appetites, you knaw." Close by is a smaller lump, and the both are generally known as Branscombe's Loaf and Cheese.* Just above the rock, on the summit of Corn Ridge, is a large cairn, and on the further side of the hill ½ m. below this, in a S.W. direction, is a short level on the peat railway, where it forms an acute angle. On this the wagons were run in and stopped, while the points were shifted. The horses were then hitched to what had before been the hinder part of the truck, and the journey up the hill was resumed. Between the cairn and this spot is the peat track to Kitty Tor, which passes over Lydda Bridge (T. 30, 32, Ex. 12).

We descend the northern slope of Corn Ridge into the dip between that hill and the Sourton Tors, which are in full view N.W. Here we reach the King Way (T. 26) running nearly N. and S., very near to which we may observe a large worked granite stone. It is the half of a trough, of the kind used for pounding apples in, evidently broken in the course of being cut. Near by, and close to some shallow pits, now overgrown with turf, and which mark the site of some long-disused ice works, a row of granite posts may be seen. The spot is known as Iron Gates, and forms one of the boundaries of Sourton Common. The wider gap between two of them seems to show where the old King Way passed. The branch track that goes eastward runs out to some mine workings known as Crocker's Pits.

Climbing the slight ascent to the Sourton Tors we shall find ourselves among the scattered rock clusters covering the greater part of the hill. The principal pile, at the N.W. of the groups, is known as East Tor, that being its relative situation to the village of Sourton, which is just below it. Upon this little place we now look down, and may make our way thither if we choose by the track that crosses the railway close to the church. Not many years ago Sourton was a typical moorland village, but the presence of the railway, and the erection of one or two modern buildings, has robbed it of much of this character. In this parish of less than four hundred inhabitants there was, in 1904, one resident over a hundred years of age, and several between eighty and ninety. Our homeward way will lead us through the hamlets of Lake and Southerly to the Fox and Hounds, 1 m. beyond which we shall reach the Dartmoor Inn whence we set out.

---

* The name Branscombe occurs in another part of the county, and its derivation from *bran, a crow*, and *cwm, a valley*, *i.e.*, the crow's valley, has been suggested. But the true Celtic form would be Cwm Bran. It should be noticed that there is a combe on the hillside below this mass of rock, known as Corn Hole.

[From the Sourton tors the walk may be extended by descending the N. end of the hill to Prewley Moor, and passing under the railway (T. 32) to the high road, and turning L. to Sourton. Or the rambler may shorten it a little by striking down the hill S. by E. to the head of Withycombe Bottom, and making his way by a green path (T. 31), with that valley on his R. and Lake Down on his L., to the Lake Viaduct. This will be found a very charming walk. The sides of the valley, through which a little stream runs, are steep, and the further one partly wooded. At the bottom are a few vestiges of the old Torwood Mine. Passing under the viaduct the rambler will follow the lane by the stream to the hamlet of Lake, situated on the high road, and about 2½ m. from his destination.]

SHORTER EXCURSIONS.

S. Ex. 25.—*Brent Tor from the Manor Hotel*, 6½ m. By the Tavistock road, passing the entrance to Burnville L., and Langstone R., and on to the Herring Arms. Up the hill ¼ m. to the gate as in Ex. 9. Return past the Herring Arms to Batten's Corner, ¼ m. N.E. ; turn R. and follow road through Brent Tor village to the railway bridge by the station. Cross this, and entering on Black Down, turn L., and follow the green path parallel to the railway to the gate near Lydford Station. (The rock on the hill immediately in front of the Manor Hotel is Was Tor).

S. Ex. 26.—*Hill Bridge*, 7½ m. To Horndon Down Bridge as in Ex. 10, if from the station. If from the village the route will be to Beardon (Ex. 10), thence up the hill past Watervale to Black Down. Then over the down by the first track L. (T. 24), which is reached just before the road drops down into the hollow where a little stream passes under it. The track runs S.S.E. direct to the bridge. From Horndon Down Bridge, S.S.E. to the opening between the enclosures (see end of Ex. 10), and so to Zoar Down. To the lower L. corner of this, crossing the road on the way, and thence by the narrow lane to Lower Down, not far below which the bridge is reached (Ex. 8). The return may be by way of Hill Town, Will, Yard Gate, and Snap, as in R. 2. If from and to the station, 6¾ m.

S. Ex. 27.—*Hare Tor*, 7 m. (village). To the tor as in Ex. 11. Thence northward to Sharp Tor, and down to Foxholes, as at the end of that excursion, and home by way of High Down as there described. 6 m. (village). The return may also be made by way of the Tavy Cleave Tors, Ger Tor, and White Hill (Ex. 11). From Hare Tor we strike S.S.E. ½ m. to the first-named group, and then S.W. for about the same distance to Ger Tor, keeping on the brow of the hill instead of descending into the hollow between them. (W. of Ger Tor a track leads down to Lane End (T. 20), about ¾ m. distant). From Ger Tor the course will be N.N.W. to the wall of the Redford enclosures, which, when reached, is kept close on the L. for a short distance. The course is then due W. over the summit of White Hill to the gate at Down Lane. Thence through Skit as in R. 2.

S. Ex. 28.—*Valley of the Lyd and Bra Tor*, 5½ m. (village). **High**

Down by the gate near Skit Bridge (Ex. 11), or by that near the Dartmoor Inn. To Wheal Mary Emma Ford below Bra Tor ; cross the stream, and pass up the common with the Doe Tor Brook R., noticing the falls mentioned in Ex. 11. Ascend Bra Tor (Ex. 11), and turn N. to Arms Tor. Thence W. down the hill to the hut circles (Ex. 12) ; cross the Lyd at the stepping-stones, and pass up the hill to Noddon Gate (Ex. 13). Take the track R. to the Fox and Hounds and turn L., or strike across Vale Down from the gate to the high road.

S. Ex. 29.—*Noddon*, 7½ m. (village). By the Okehampton road and Noddon Gate as in Ex. 13. Follow the track as there described till the hill is R. (nearly ¾ m. from the gate). Then cross the peat railway and ascend it. Turn L., and down the northern slope, with the railway near by, L., to the bridge Pass under it and strike down the hill W. across Southerly Down (Ex. 13). At the bottom, between two enclosures, the track R. leads to Combe ; the L. one to Southerly. Follow the latter, passing under the railway to the high road, and turn L. Cranford Bridge is reached in a few minutes. Note the little clapper R. over the Cranford Brook in front of a cottage. Straight road home.

S. Ex. 30.—*Great Links Tor*, 6 m. (village). As in Ex. 12. Return by descending the hill W. to the Lyd, and home as at the end of that excursion.

S. Ex. 31.—*Branscombe's Loaf*, 9½ m. (village). By Noddon Gate as in Ex. 13, but instead of passing under the peat railway continue up the hill, keeping the line R. At the point where it forms an angle leave it, and climb the hill N.E. to the cairn on the summit of Corn Ridge (Ex. 13). The Loaf is just below this. Return by striking W. across the dip to the head of Withycombe Bottom (Ex. 13), and descend to Lake.

S. Ex. 32.—*The Sourton Tors*, 10 m. (village). By the Okehampton road to Higher Collaven, ⅓ m. beyond Lake, and a little over 3 m. from the Dartmoor Inn. Turn R. from the high road (T. 32) and pass under the railway ; on reaching the common the tors will be seen just above. Return by way of Sourton village, as in Ex. 13, and home by the high road ; or pass into the dip E. of the tors, and follow the King Way (T. 26) S. It soon strikes the peat railway, which is then followed to Noddon Gate (Ex. 13), from which the route will be as in S. Ex. 28. If by way of the peat railway, 9 m.

S. Ex. 33.—*The Island of Rocks*. By Noddon Gate and the peat railway, 11½ m. (village). By Lake, 12½ m. (village). (Okehampton District, Ex. 14). The first point is the dip between the Sourton Tors and Corn Ridge (Ex. 13), which may be reached by the route given in S. Ex. 31, striking L. along the King Way (T. 26) towards the dip just before reaching the point where the peat railway forms an angle (Ex. 13) ; or by the Okehampton road to Lake. In the former case the King Way must not be followed very far after it leaves the railway, as the visitor must not descend into the dip, but make his way across the northern slope of Corn Ridge ; he therefore strikes R., not, however, ascending the ridge, and maintains a N.E. course. This will lead him down the hill to the Island, Shilstone Tor being on his R. as he approaches it. If he goes by way of Lake, which is the longer, he will turn R. at the hamlet, and following the lane by the stream, pass under the viaduct. Then take the green path L. up the steep side of the common, with Withycombe Bottom (Ex. 13) L. At the head of this is the dip, and the King Way will soon be struck. Cross this, and steer N.E. by E., passing through the dip and descending the hill. Part way down Corn Hole is crossed. Care must be taken to leave the little Vellake stream well to the L., and Shilstone Tor to the R. Return to the dip, 1 m. up the hill W.S.W., from which point homeward routes are given in Ex. 13 and S. Ex. 32.

[During rifle practice that part of the moor in the neighbourhood of Tavy Cleave must be avoided by the public.]

ROUTES FROM LYDFORD.

R. 16.—To Okehampton, N.E. by N. By Road : See Route 9, 8 m. Reverse, R. 30.

[Objects passed are described in Exs. 11 to 15.]

R. 17.—To Chagford and Moreton, E. by N. *High Down, Rattle Brook Hill, Amicombe Hill, Great Kneeset, Cranmere Pool, Newtake, Hew Down, Batworthy, Teigncombe,* 14½ m. See Cranmere Routes : C.R. 5 to the Pool, thence by C.R. 12. The reverse will also be found in these routes. For Chagford to Moreton by road see that district. Reverse, R. 37.

[Objects passed described in Exs. 11, 12, 19, 20 ; and in the Cranmere Routes.]

R. 18.—To Bovey Tracey, E.S.E. by E. *Hill Bridge, White Barrow, Lich Path, Bear Down Newtake Wall, Longaford Tor, Moreton Road.* Thence (A) *via* Bellaford and Shallowford, 24 m. ; (B) *via* Post Bridge and Runnage, 25 m. Reverse, R. 44.

[Objects are noticed in Exs. 10, 5, 46, 44, 27, 26, 25.]

Hill Bridge as in S. Ex. 26. Thence to the outer end of the stroll between Bagga Tor and Longbetor, as in Ex. 10, and thence S.E. by the Lich Path (T. 18) to White Barrow (Ex. 8). Follow the Lich Path E., taking the R. branch at the fork part way down the hill. Then cross the Walkham at Sandy Ford, and the Prison Leat at the bridge. Continue on the Lich Path E. for about 1¼ m. to Travellers' Ford (Ex. 5) on the Cowsic. Cross the stream, leaving the path, and taking the wall of Bear Down Newtake for a guide, keep it on the R. This will lead over the hill to the West Dart, where the Foxholes Water (Ex. 5) falls into it. Cross the Dart, and keep E. up the hill, with Longaford Tor (Ex. 5) a little to the R. ¾ m. after passing the tor the Cherry Brook (Ex. 46) will be reached, N. of the Powder Mills. If Route A be chosen this stream must be followed downward to Higher Cherry Brook Bridge, whence the way is described in Route 5 (B) ; if B be the route the rambler will keep straight on when he crosses the brook, leaving Arch Tor, which is merely a small lump of rock, L. This will bring him to the Powder Mills leat, which a footbridge near the tor will enable him to cross. Straight on to the Moreton road, and then northward to Post Bridge, ¾ m. distant. Thence as in Route 5 (C).

R. 19.—To Ashburton *via* Two Bridges, S.E. by E. *Hill Bridge,*

White Barrow, Lich Path, The Cowsic, Two Bridges. Thence as in R. 5 (A) to Ouldsbroom Cross, and thence as in R. 6 (A), 24 m. Reverse, R. 51.

[For description of objects passed refer to Exs. 10, 5, 42, 41.]

Follow the directions given in R. 18 to reach the Lich Path. When ½ m. or so beyond the Prison Leat bridge, leave the Lich Path, and strike R., the course being about S.E. Soon the Cowsic will be reached, and this must be followed downwards, as in Ex. 5, to the road. Turn L. Two Bridges is near by. From that point see as above indicated.

R. 20.—To Brent, Ivybridge, and Cornwood *via* Hill Bridge and Princetown, S.E. round to S.S.E. *Hill Bridge, White Tor, Mis Tor, Rundle Stone, Princetown.* Thence as in R. 7. Brent, 23 m. ; Ivybridge, 23½ m. ; Cornwood, 20½ m. Reverse, R. 62.

[Objects passed are described thus : Between Lydford and Princetown in Exs. 10, 9, 6 ; from Princetown to the Plym in Exs. 2, 3, 37 ; from the Plym to Red Lake in Exs. 36, 43, 33 ; and from Red Lake to Shipley Moor Gate in Ex. 30. The route to Ivybridge includes the above to Ex. 36, and 33, 32. The Cornwood route includes those to Ex. 36.]

To Hill Bridge as in S. Ex. 26. Thence up Church Lane and turn R. On for about ⅓ m., when some steps in the hedge will be seen L. (These are noticed in R. 2). Enter the field by these, and follow the path running up across it to the hedge bordering on the common, where are other steps. Pass up over the common to White Tor (Ex. 8) S.E. by E., and distant 1 m. The next point is Mis Tor (Ex. 6), S.E. by E., and 2 m. away. But the ground above the springs of the Peter Tavy Brook being rather miry it will be well to keep to the L. of a direct line in crossing Langstone Moor (Ex. 8). The menhir will be noticed eastward of White Tor, and the stone circle (Ex. 8) on the further side of this common. Near the latter the Walkham is crossed. The next point is Mis Tor, high above the river. From here the course is S.E. by S. to Rundle Stone, over 1¼ m. distant. The wall of the New Forest enclosure (Ex. 5, 6) is on the L. of the path. From Rundle Stone to Princetown see R. 15.

[If the state of the weather is such as to render the crossing of the Walkham impossible it will be necessary to go by way of Merivale Bridge (Ex. 1). From White Tor the course is S.E. to the end of the Wedlake enclosures. These are then kept on the R., the course being S. by W., under Roose Tor, which is L., and direct to Great Staple Tor. Here the path running from Peter Tavy to Merivale (T. 14) will be struck, and must be followed L. over the ridge to the high road. Merivale Bridge is just below. The route from that place to Princetown will be found in R. 15.]

The route from Princetown to Brent and Ivybridge has already been given. See R. 7.

R. 21.—To Plympton and Shaugh, S. by E. By Road. First point Warren's Cross, thence as in R. 13. Plympton, 21½ m. ; Shaugh, 17 m. ; Cornwood, 20½ m. Reverse, R. 69.

[Objects are noticed in Exs. 10, 9, 8, 7, 40, 39, 38, 35.]

From Lydford village by Skit Steps (Ex. 10) to the road below Beardon. Turn S. to Watervale and Black Down, and follow the road over it. Pass through the village of Black Down, and by Lane

Head (Ex. 9) to Wringworthy Hill—high road the whole of the way. [From the Manor Hotel the road over the down may be reached by the Lydford Path (T. 23), passing up from the S.W.R. cottages towards Gibbet Hill, but leaving that a little to the R.] At the bottom of Wringworthy Hill turn L. opposite to the second milestone from Tavistock. Cross Harford Bridge and turn R., and keep straight up Battridge Hill, with the farm of Radge (mentioned as Raddyche in an account of the forester of the West Bailiwick of the forest, in 1502) on the R. About 1½ m. from the bridge Moor Shop (R. 1, Ex. 8) is reached. Straight on down the hill for rather over ¼ m. to Penny-come-quick. Then up the hill with Whitchurch Down on the R. to Warren's Cross, where the road from Tavistock comes in from R. From this point the route is described in R. 13.

R. 22.—To Princetown, S.E. by S. to Rundle Stone, 11 m. Reverse, R. 2. This route is the same as the first part of R. 20, q.v.

[Objects noticed in Exs. 10, 9, 6.]

R. 23.—To Tavistock, S.W. by S. By Road, 8 m. Reverse, R. 9.

[Objects noticed in Exs. 10, 9.]

To the bottom of Wringworthy Hill as in R. 21. Thence straight on by the high road, 2 m. further, to the town. An alternative route is by the road from the Manor Hotel past the Herring Arms, as in S. Ex. 25. Leave Brent Tor L. and follow the high road past Pitland Corner to the town.

OKEHAMPTON DISTRICT.

DISTANCES. By ROAD: *ASHBURTON, via* Dartmoor Inn, Black Down, Lane Head, Harford Bridge, Moor Shop, and Two Bridges, 35 m. *Via* Sticklepath, Throwleigh, Chagford, Beetor Cross, Swine Down Gate, Hemsworthy Gate, and Welstor Cross, 23 m.—*BELSTONE,* 3¼ m.—*BERRY DOWN* (for Scorhill), *via* Sticklepath, Payne's Bridge, Moortown, and Creber Pound, 8¼ m.—*BOVEY TRACEY, via* Sticklepath, Whiddon Down, Sandy Park, and Moreton, 20 m. — *BRENT TOR VILLAGE, via* Lydford, 13 m. *BUCKFASTLEIGH, via* Two Bridges (*vide* Ashburton *supra*), Hexworthy, and Holne, 34¾ m. *Via* Welstor Cross (*vide* Ashburton *supra*), 25 m.—*CHAGFORD, via* Sticklepath and Throwleigh, 10¼ m.— *CORNWOOD, via* Moor Shop (*vide* Ashburton *supra*), Warren's Cross, Huckworthy Bridge, Dousland, and Cadaford Bridge, 28½ m.—*DARTMEET, via* Two Bridges (*vide* Ashburton *supra*), 26¾ m.—*DARTMOOR INN, LYDFORD,* 8¼ m.—*DOUSLAND* (*vide* Ashburton and Cornwood *supra*), 20 m.—*DREWSTEIGNTON, via* Sticklepath and Whiddon Down, 10¼ m. To the dolmen, 8¾ m.—*EXETER, via* Sticklepath and Whiddon Down, 22 m. — *FOX AND HOUNDS,* for *BRIDESTOWE STATION,* 7¼ m. — *GIDLEIGH, via* Sticklepath, Payne's Bridge, and Throwleigh, 8½ m. *Via* Payne's Bridge and Ensworthy, about the same.—*HEXWORTHY, via* Two Bridges (*vide* Ashburton *supra*), 27 m.—*HILL BRIDGE, via* Black Down, Lane Head, and Horndon, 16¼ m.—*HOLNE,* 3½ m. short of Buckfastleigh, *via* Hexworthy, q.v.—*IVYBRIDGE,* 3 m. beyond Cornwood, q.v.— *LANE END,* for *TAVY CLEAVE, via* Lane Head and Horndon,

16¼ m.—*LYDFORD*, 9 m.—*MARY TAVY*, *via* Black Down and Lane Head, 13 m.—*MELDON HAMLET*, 3 m. — *MERIVALE BRIDGE*, *via* Moor Shop (*vide* Ashburton *supra*), 18 m. — *MOOR GATE, OKEHAMPTON PARK*, 1½ m.—*MOOR SHOP* (2 m. from Tavistock ; R. 1, 15), 15⅜ m.—*MORETON*, *via* Whiddon Down (*vide* Bovey *supra*), 13¾ m.—*PETER TAVY*, *via* Black Down and Harford Bridge, 15 m.—*PLYMOUTH*, *via* Tavistock, 30 m.—*PLYMPTON*, *via* Cadaford Bridge (*vide* Cornwood *supra*), and Niel Gate, 29½ m.— *POST BRIDGE*, *via* Throwleigh and Chagford, q.v., 17½ m.— *PRINCETOWN*, *via* Moor Shop (*vide* Ashburton *supra*), 21¼ m.— *SOURTON*, 5 m.—*SOUTH BRENT*, 5 m. beyond Buckfastleigh, *via* Welstor Cross, q.v. ; or 5½ m. beyond Ivybridge *via* Cornwood, q.v.— *SOUTH TAWTON*, 4½ m.—*SOUTH ZEAL*, 4½ m.—*STICKLE-PATH*, 3½ m.—Tavistock, 16 m.—*TAVY CLEAVE* (*vide* Lane End, and Ex. 11).—*THROWLEIGH*, 6¾ m.—*TWO BRIDGES*, *via* Moor Shop (*vide* Ashburton *supra*), 21¾ m.—*WARREN HOUSE INN*, 2 m. short of Post Bridge, q.v.—*WHIDDON DOWN*, 7 m.—*WIDECOMBE*, *via* Chagford, q.v., Beetor Cross, Heytree Down, and Natsworthy, 19½ m.—*YELVERTON*, *via* Moor Shop (*vide* Ashburton *supra*), and Plaster Down, 20¼ m. ; *via* Tavistock, 21 m.

BY RAIL : *EXETER* (L.S.W.), 26 m. ; *LYDFORD* (L.S.W.), 10 m. ; *PLYMOUTH* (L.S.W. direct), 37 m. ; *PRINCETOWN* (L.S.W. to Tavistock, thence by G.W.), 33¾ m. ; *TAVISTOCK* (L.S.W.), 17½ m. ; *YELVERTON* (L.S.W. to Tavistock, thence by G.W.), 23¼ m.

The manor of Ochmentune, the present Okehampton, was bestowed, among others, upon Baldwin de Brionys, by the Conqueror. The statement has been made that this Baldwin also bore the name of De Redvers, and was created Earl of Devon. But Baldwin de Redvers was quite a different person, and did not live until later, nor was the earldom of Devon created by William. An extensive chase belonged to the barony of Okehampton, which was a possession of the De Redvers in the thirteenth century (Ex. 6), and in the midst of this De Brionys is said to have built a castle, but nothing now remains of it. The ruin near the town, which probably stands on its site, is of a later period. William of Worcester states that it was erected by Thomas Courtenay, whose death took place in 1458, but any work that this earl may have done must have been in the nature of repairs, since it is evident that the building is earlier than his time. Some parts of the keep, which is certainly older than the rest of the edifice, have been thought to be late Norman. Among the broken walls the situation of a number of apartments can still be traced, but opinions are divided as to what they originally were. About one, however, there can be no mistake. It is a portion of the chapel, in which are the remains of three very good windows. On a stone by the side of the piscina is an inscription—*Hic V . . . . . fuit captivus belli*, 1809—which is supposed to be the work of one of the French prisoners of war who were quartered here in the early part of the nineteenth century.

There are no remains of a prehistoric time on the commons of Okehampton that call for any particular notice, though a few exist to show that man was here in a ruder age. Flint flakes have been picked up, and a stone hammer was also found in the neighbourhood a few years ago. It was of a kind of rough, hard, grit sandstone, and much weather-worn. But if the commons lack something from an anti-quarian point of view, the visitor will quickly discover that they are richly endowed in other respects.

For a considerable time a permanent Artillery Camp has been formed in Okehampton Park, and gun practice takes place during each summer on the common, the targets being placed some distance out upon the forest. From the point of view of the Dartmoor rambler this is disastrous. Firing commences on the ranges at the beginning of May, and continues until about the end of September, so that for the five months that the moor is at its best he finds himself debarred from visiting a great part of it, except at certain hours, and on Satur-days. And not only is this so, but the north quarter of the forest is robbed of what constitutes one of Dartmoor's greatest charms, its silence and its solitude. The area over which the firing takes place is very large, and the zone is marked at various points by danger boards. There is one on the Sourton Tors ; another near Kitty Tor ; one on Great Kneeset ; on the fen near Cranmere ; on Newtake Hill ; on Steeperton ; and on Watchet Hill, close to Belstone village. Boards are also placed on the roads leading to the dangerous area, and they all bear this notice :

"DANGER.

"When the Artillery are firing a Flag will be hoisted on Yes Tor ; it is then dangerous to proceed in the direction towards which this board points. It is dangerous to handle shell found on the moor."

Further notice is also issued as follows :

"A Red Danger Flag will be hoisted on Yes Tor every morn-ing when firing is to take place, and will be kept flying until firing ceases for the day. While this flag is flying it is dangerous to proceed within the firing zone.

"Flags are hoisted on Watchet Hill in order to inform the Belstone inhabitants which range or ranges are to be used, viz. :—

"A Red Flag denotes No. 1 Range ; a White Flag No. 2 Range ; a Blue Flag No. 3, or the Belstone Range ; a combination of any of these flags indicates the particular ranges to be used during the day.

"When firing is going to take place a Red Flag is also hoisted on the brow of the hill near Fitz's Well, for the special information of the inhabitants of Okehampton and of tourists arriving at the Railway Station.

"No firing takes place on Sunday, and when it can be avoided, none on Saturday. Firing is only carried out on Saturday when there has been misty or excessive wet weather during the week.

"When there is to be no firing on Saturday notices to that effect will be sent to, and posted up in, the following Post Offices on Friday afternoon :—Okehampton, Bridestowe, Lydford, Chagford, Princetown, and Belstone.

"Notices stating whether firing is going to be carried out on Saturday or not are also inserted every Saturday morning in the following Newspapers :—*Western Morning News, Western Daily Mercury, Western Independent, Western Daily Times,* and *Devon and Exeter Daily Gazette.*"

It has recently been ordered that no firing shall take place on Easter Mondays, or on Whit Mondays.

All cattle are driven off the ranges early in the day when firing is to take place, the moormen being specially paid for this work by the War Office.   Compensation is also paid to the commoners.   The firing usually ceases in the early part of the afternoon.

EXCURSIONS FROM OKEHAMPTON.

Tracks in the vicinity, Nos. 33 to 42. [The district described in these excursions is bounded on the W. by the valley of the West Ockment ; on the south by an imaginary line drawn from Great Kneeset and Lints Tor to the sources of Brim Brook and the Blackaven, thence across Ockment Hill to Steeperton Tor on the Taw, and thence by Hound Tor and Kennon Hill to Shilstone Tor on the verge of Throwleigh Common.   The district to the S. of this line is noticed in the Cranmere Routes.]

As the Okehampton Excursions are also intended for Belstone visitors, and as that village is made the starting-point for some of them, it will perhaps be well that we should briefly describe the routes between the two places before setting out on our rambles.

OKEHAMPTON TO BELSTONE. By Road. The way lies over the East Bridge and up the Bartons Hill. We then take the second turning R. and follow the lane to the railway arch near the Fatherford Viaduct. We pass under the line at the arch, shortly afterwards reaching East Lake, where the road runs up the hill R. Belstone is about 1 m. distant ; on the way one turning L. is passed, and shortly after another on the R.

By Path to Fatherford Viaduct from the Station.   Immediately opposite the booking-office entrance a narrow path runs down the bank to another, and wider one. This, which is part of an old tram-way, we follow eastward to the viaduct. The side of the hill along which the path is conducted is wooded. Across the valley is Ball Hill, its great rounded form presenting a charming picture when the furze, with which it is covered, is in bloom. We cross the East Ockment where it flows under the viaduct at a footbridge. A short distance up the lane is the railway arch mentioned above, where we turn towards East Lake.

By Halstock and Chapel Ford (T. 36). Our first point is the gate of East Hill, near Fitz's Well, on the brow of the hill, above the railway station, and to this there are two roads. One is that which leads from the town towards the station. Just before the latter is reached it passes under the railway and on to the common, up which it winds to meet the other. The latter is now the camp road, and branches R. from the station road near the foot of the hill. A short distance above the junction L. in ascending, the corner of the wall of East Down is passed, and here a track runs L. to the gate referred to, and which is only a few score yards away. (Fitz's Well, noticed in Ex. 15, is on the R.) Passing through the gate we follow the road, which runs down the side of East Hill, to the Moor Brook. (The ancient encampment on East Down is noticed in S. Ex. 40). A bridge, built by the tenant at Halstock, now crosses the brook, before which there was a ford here, with a single stone clapper for foot passengers. The clapper is still in its place, but is hidden beneath the soil placed upon it to elevate the roadway. Some years ago I took the measurements of this stone and found it to be 11 feet in length, and 1 foot thick. It was wider at one end than at the other, but about the centre its width was 2½ feet. A short distance beyond the bridge we pass Halstock farmhouse, and make our way through the yard. At the further end of this a track runs S. by the side of a field called Chapel Lands to Halstock Down, reaching it at a point known as Halstock Corner. But instead of following this track we turn L. into the field named, our path lying across it, and close to its northern edge. At the point where the track leaves the farm-yard are the remains of some low walls, much over-grown, and close by, in the corner of the field, are the vestiges of an enclosure. It is traditionally reported that Halstock was once a settlement of considerable size, its inhabitants numbering several hundred, and these ruined walls were formerly pointed out as marking a part of its site. The name of the field to which we have referred commemorates the ancient sanctuary referred to in the Forest Per-ambulation of 1240 as St. Michael's Chapel of Halstock. Little more, however, than its name now remains. Its site is marked by some grass-covered banks, on which grow two storm-stricken thorns, but there are no traces of masonry. The Rev. H. G. Fothergill, a former Rector of Belstone, left some manuscript notes to a work written about 1839, by William Bridges, entitled, *Some Account of the Barony and Town of Okehampton*, and these were printed in a new edition published in 1889. These notes contain some references to the chapel, of which Mr. Fothergill took measurements. He found it to be nine paces in length and four in width on the inside and says it was enclosed in a sort of court measuring 23 paces by 13 at the western end of which were traces of a belfry or vestry. Some years ago I also care-fully measured it, and found it to be 40 feet long, and 24 feet wide ; and the court in which it stands 90 feet by 57 feet. The foundations of what Mr. Fothergill supposed to be those of a belfry, or vestry, cover a space 30 feet by 25 feet. These are external measurements. Halstock Chapel, together with the church of Okehampton, belonged to Cowick Priory, in the parish of St. Thomas-by-Exeter, which at its foundation was subordinate to the great abbey of Bec, in Normandy. About the middle of the fifteenth century, on the resignation of the prior, Henry VI. applied its revenues to Eton College, but Edward IV. transferred the gift to the Abbey of Tavistock. The remains are in the S. part of the field, the site being marked by the two thorns. The view from the chapel is very fine, embracing towards the N. much that is seen from the brow of the hill near Fitz's Well. Across the valley eastward is the Belstone range of tors, and beyond that part of the Moor Brook Valley known as Halstock Cleave (S. Ex. 41) is seen the beautiful Ashbury Tor, from nowhere beheld to greater advantage. Close to it are the mounds of the ancient entrenchment already alluded to (S. Ex. 40).

Passing across Chapel Lands to its N.E. corner, near which we shall observe three stones curiously placed, we make our way by a narrow path down through Halstock Wood to Chapel Ford (T. 36), on the East Ockment, supposed to be identical with that mentioned in the Perambulation of 1240, and the Survey of 1609. Here are stepping-stones by which we may cross, although this is not to be done when the stream is in flood. The track runs up the side of the hill L. from the ford, and will bring us very near to Cleave Tor (S. Ex. 41), where is a stroll R. Into this we turn, and passing through a moor gate opening upon a narrow lane shall speedily reach the road coming up L. from East Lake (see *ante*), where we turn R. and follow it direct to Belstone.

BELSTONE TO OKEHAMPTON. (Reverse of the preceding, q.v., for descriptions). BY ROAD. Old vicarage gate ; straight down the hill to East Lake ; turn L. to railway arch ; cross road, and up the lane to the highway ; turn L. down Bartons Hill to the town.

Path to Station from Fatherford Viaduct. As above to the railway arch ; then down L. to the viaduct ; cross the Ockment at the foot-bridge, and follow the path, with the railway above L., to the station.

By Chapel Ford and Halstock (T. 36). Old vicarage gate ; a short distance beyond turn L. to the common ; leave Cleave Tor on R. ; descend by the track L. to Chapel Ford ; cross the Ockment ; follow path R. up through Halstock Wood to Chapel Lands ; cross this to Halstock Farm and on to the bridge over Moor Brook ; pass up with wall on L. to gate, outside which the road leads down the hill. Through the gate in the corner R. for the station ; down L. for the town.

BY ROAD TO STICKLEPATH, WITH BRANCH TO BEL-STONE. This forms the best carriage road to Belstone, 3¼ m. ; Sticklepath is situated at the foot of Cosdon, on the direct road to Exeter, and is 3½ m. from the town. We cross the East Bridge and make our way up the Bartons Hill. One mile from the bridge we pass over the railway, close to Fatherford farmhouse, which lies L. (The road R. runs down to Fatherford Viaduct). 1¼ m. further on we reach a small piece of common known as Tongue End, where a road turns up the hill R. for Belstone, close to a large parish boundary stone. (This road branches near the top of the little common ; keep R. for the village, which is about 1 m. distant). On the L. as we proceed towards Sticklepath is Combeshead Farm, well named from its situation, where, it is said, some Royalist troopers once hid themselves, and cut off the cock's head, lest his crowing should draw attention to their place of refuge.* Just beyond this a lane branches L. to Bude Farm, and here is an ancient stone, having markings on three of its sides. [See *Crosses*, Chap. XI., where also the stones at Sticklepath and Belstone are described.] About ¾ m. further on Sticklepath is reached.

Reverse.—Pass up the western road by Lady Well, leaving the school L. ; then Bude Lane is passed R. ; then Combeshead also R. ; Tongue End ; the railway bridge near Fatherford Farm ; pass down the Bartons Hill to the town.

Ex. 14.—*Meldon, The Island of Rocks, Black Tor Copse, Sandy Ford [High Willes, Yes Tor], Lints Tor, Dinger Tor*, about 11 m. With Extension to *Great Kneeset*, about 2½ m. more.

---

* Fothergill's Notes to Bridges' *Barony and Town of Okehampton.*

Our road from the town will lead us by the Union House to the northern slope of Okehampton Park. But if our starting-point be the station we pass along by the houses facing the railway to Westhill Villa, where we reach the camp road. Here a gate will give us admittance to the park, and our path will soon effect a junction with the lower one. As we proceed we have a view of the castle on the further side of the river, which flows at the foot of the hill. Parts of the ruin are hidden by the trees, but the keep is lifted high above them. On the hill-side across which our way lies are numerous ancient hollies, some of them being of considerable size. When about 2 m. from the town we draw near the Ockment, which is here spanned by the lofty Meldon Viaduct. On the further side of the stream the grey rocks of Burrow Cleave, or Cliff, draped with creeping plants, rise from amid the trees, and here a track leads up to the hamlet of Meldon (S. Ex. 34). Passing under the viaduct we notice the remains of quarrying. A vein of granulite was discovered here many years ago, which was used in the making of a certain kind of glass, and for other purposes [100 *Years*, Chap. III.] On the opposite side of the river is a deep quarry pit filled with water.

We here enter Meldon Gorge, which extends from this point to Vellake Corner. A track runs up the hill L., and after crossing a part of Black Down, reaches the Redaven (T. 33)* ; but we shall follow the one on the R. bank of the Ockment (T. 33), leaving it, however, at the point where the Redaven falls into that stream. On crossing the affluent the track ascends Longstone Hill L., a name perhaps derived from a menhir, though none exists there now (cf Longstone, Ex. 7), but we pass along at its foot. High above the W. bank of the river is Meldon Down, on which, in 1643, an encounter took place during a stormy night between the Royalists and the Parliamentarians under Major James Chudleigh, who was quartered at Okehampton at the time. Much of the down has probably since been covered with fields. We shall notice a track running down the side of it to a ford (T. 33), where also are some stepping-stones called Higher Bowden Steps (S. Ex. 35). ¼ m. beyond these we reach a little tributary stream separating Longstone Hill from Homerton Hill, the great rounded eminence we now see rising before us. This tributary is sometimes known as the Homerton Brook, but its true name is the Fishcombe Water. It has its source in a charming little hollow, where dwarf oaks grow, high up on the hill. At the point where it falls into the Ockment are the long deserted workings of Homerton Mine.

Homerton Hill is exceedingly steep, and sweeps down abruptly to a piece of level ground, around which the river makes a bend. We do not here follow the course of the latter, but pass along the foot of the hill, meeting it again further up. The high ground that rises before us is Corn Ridge, near the summit of which is Branscombe's Loaf (Ex. 13). As we pass round the base of Homerton we notice a small

* Pronounced Red-a-ven, with the stress on the last syllable. Strangers sometimes lay this on the *a*, which is wrong. The name has nothing to do with *avon, water*. It is really the *red fen* brook, the Dartmoor vernacular being responsible for the change of the *f* into *v*, and for the insertion of the *a*. Another stream in the locality is the Blackaven ; in this name the stress is similarly on the last syllable.

stream coming down from the S.W. The point where it falls into the Ockment is known as Vellake Corner, and forms one of the bounds between the commons of Okehampton and Sourton. The little Vellake rises not far below Iron Gates (Ex. 13), and one tiny feeder, dry in summer, runs into it from Corn Hole (Ex. 13). Here we leave Meldon Gorge and enter the narrow valley that extends up into the forest, where the hills on either side rise to a still greater height, and where the scenery becomes even more wild and grand than that through which we have just passed. We again welcome the river, which is to be our companion through the defile, and shall make for ourselves a path above its eastern bank. Speedily the character of our surroundings begins to change, and ere we have advanced many steps we look upon a picture not surpassed on Dartmoor for a happy mingling of the stern and rugged with that which is beautiful. Below us, in a wild glen, is the Island of Rocks [described in *Gems*, Chap. IV.] thickly clothed with low trees and bushes, a cascade at its upper end and another at its lower. Above it is a deep and narrow gorge, down which the river rushes as through a long, darkened trough. Trees grow on the steep banks, and the grey granite is partly covered with ivy and creeping plants. At its head we may make our way on the boulders to the centre of the stream, and look down through this miniature canyon, whence comes the never-ceasing roar of the waters.

[Should the visitor desire to cross the Ockment he will find one or two places either below the Island, or at the head of the gorge, where he may do so. A route to the Island *via* Meldon, and by the L. bank, is given *post*, S. Ex. 35.]

On the side of the hill above the L. bank of the Ockment is Shilstone Tor, the name being, perhaps, a corruption of *shelf stone*, or hanging stone, but not necessarily an artificially placed one. On the other side of the valley, *i.e.*, the eastern side, but further from us, and at a much greater elevation, is Black Tor (S. Ex. 36). Viewed from below the Island of Rocks this tor appears to consist of one pile only, but from the point we have now reached its triple crown is plainly seen. Passing upward we shortly reach another small island, but of a character altogether different from the former, its level surface being covered with turf and patches of heather. About 100 yards above it the river falls over a ledge of rocks, forming a fine cascade ; near by some withies are growing, and on the L. bank is a huge lump of granite partially covered with ivy. In our progress up this part of the valley we shall not fail to be struck with the number of bushes of various kinds that grow near the river, and above all shall note the presence of several dwarf oaks. By-and-bye the latter become more numerous, and then it is seen that an oak wood, similar to Wistman's Wood on the Dart (Ex. 5), fills part of the valley. It is situated below the triple tor from which it took its ancient name of Black Torre Beare, now, however, being known as Black Tor Copse. Documentary evidence exists showing that this wood was once very much more extensive than at present ; it probably stretched from the Island of Rocks into the forest. There is mention of it by the jurors of the 1609 Survey, and also in the Lydford Court Rolls of the time of Elizabeth. On the W. bank of the Ockment, above the small hollow opposite to which the higher island referred to is situated, is another and a larger one, named Hawks' Hollow. It forms a kind of huge amphitheatre, above which are the masses of granite called the Slipper Stones (Ex. 13). Its lower part is covered with some old tin workings known as Crocker's Pits.

As we make our way up the valley a hill crowned with rocks that have very much the appearance of a tower comes into view at the head of it. This is Lints Tor, and although it rises to a height of 1,605 feet, it looks almost low against the hills on either side. Passing the ancient wood, and finding for ourselves a path along the foot of the steep declivity under Forsland Ledge (Ex. 15), we reach Sandy Ford, to which the forest boundary line comes down from Stinka Tor (Ex. 13), and which is named as one of the bondmarks.

Here a boundary stone will be noticed ; it marks the line which is drawn up the hill N.E., between the forest and Okehampton Common. There is abundant evidence that this line formerly ran from the ford to High Willes, and thence to Mil Tor and Row Tor (see *Perambulation* in the *Terms* section), and consequently much that is now reckoned as forming part of the common was once within the bounds of the royal hunting-ground.

[High Willes and Yes Tor may be ascended from Sandy Ford, but the climb is a long one. The first named is nearly a mile from the ford in a N.N.E. direction, and 700 feet above it. These points are noticed in Ex. 15.]

[*Extension to Great Kneeset.* About ¾ m. above Sandy Ford is Kneeset Foot, where the little tributary referred to in R. 3 comes down from Broad Amicombe Hole. To the L., or S. of it, is Great Kneeset, which may be readily reached from the ford by tracing the Ockment upward, following the R. bank to the first sharp bend, ½ m. above the point where the tributary falls into it. From this bend, where the course of the Ockment is changed from S.S.W. to N.N.W., the summit of Kneeset is distant hardly ½ m. E.S.E., and here the river must be crossed. No tor crowns this hill, only a few small rocks nearly on a level with the ground. It is, however, well worth ascending, as it commands a fine view of the range capped by Willes (Ex. 15) N.N.W. to N. and Ockment Hill (Ex. 16) N.E. ; the Cranmere fen and Black Ridge on the E. and S.E. (Cranmere Routes) ; Little Kneeset (Ex. 11 and Cranmere Routes) and Fur Tor (Ex. 11) to the S. ; and Amicombe Hill (Ex. 12), backed by the lofty range of which Great Links Tor (Ex. 12) is the highest point, on the W. N.E. of the summit of Great Kneeset is a hollow known as Jackman's Bottom, through which a tiny feeder trickles to the Ockment. Kneeset and this hollow are mentioned in the Cranmere routes. The rambler, instead of keeping close to the river on leaving Sandy Ford for Kneeset, may take Lints Tor, which rises above its R. bank, on his way. If he does this he will cross the Ockment about midway between the bend before named, and another over ½ m. above it, called Kneeset Nose, where the river receives Brim Brook. He will find no difficulty in doing this, Kneeset being in full view from Lints Tor. It lies S.E. by S., and is about 1¼ m. distant. The return from Kneeset may be made either by way of the lower bend, W.N.W. from the summit, when the Ockment will be followed downward, or by Kneeset Nose, N. by W., in which case Brim Brook, which flows from the north, will be followed up nearly to its source, less than 1 m., when the rambler will turn up the hill L., ¼ m. to Dinger Tor. See S. Ex. 37.]

Above Sandy Ford the Lints Tor Brook falls into the Ockment, and on reaching this point we leave the river and make our way direct to the tor, which is close at hand L. After having viewed this curious pile we turn N.E. by N., and pass up the hill to the single mass of rock known as Dinger Tor, 1,810 feet. (The summit of High Willes is ¾ m. N.W. by N. See R. 15). Here we are on the line of the ancient track from Okehampton to Post Bridge (T. 34, 79, 78), that part of it running out to the tor being still used as already stated (T. 34) for the conveyance of peat. Near by a number of ties will be seen. The track, which will be struck a little way beyond the tor, runs northward between West Mil Tor L., and Row Tor R., and will bring the rambler to Moor Gate, which opens upon Okehampton Park. This part of it it noticed the reverse way in Ex. 15. From Moor Gate we follow the road across the park, taking care not to turn L., and at the distance of about ½ m. shall pass Fitz's Well, which is close to a hedge L. (Ex. 15). Just below this the road turns abruptly to the L. at a gate. If the rambler is making his way to the station he will pass through this ; if to the town, he may either take that way or follow the road down the hill.

Ex. 15.—*Yes Tor, High Willes, Forsland Ledge, Dinger Plain, West Mil Tor, Row Tor,* about 9½ m. To Yes Tor direct (*via* Redaven Ford), 4 m.

The route to Fitz's Well, which is our first point, has already been sketched (Okehampton to Belstone Routes). On reaching the brow of the hill the old cross that marks the spring will be seen R. For many years this lay on the ground neglected, but it is now set upon a mound, built of earth and stone. Tradition says that the cross was brought from St. Michael's Chapel, at Halstock, but there is probably no foundation for this. We have already stated that to this well a story similar to the one related of that on the Blackabrook, near Princetown, attaches (Ex. 6). This was told to me several years ago by the late Miss Luxmore, of Okehampton, who was joint owner of the park, and describes how a man and his wife having lost their way when riding over this part of the moor, presumably led astray by the pixies, recovered it on reaching the well, thus justifying the lady's opinion, previously expressed, that they would only do so on finding water. (*Crosses*, Chap. XI.) It is fortunate that when they reached the pool it was not as it is said to have been in the month of September, 1676, when, in consequence of the dry summer, no water was to be seen there. In this state it is not infrequently found to-day. Its name connects it with the Fitz family, to whom the manor of Meldon once belonged. Like many other wells it probably had miraculous powers ascribed to it, and was formerly visited by the youths and maidens of the neighbourhood on the morning of Easter Day.

A short distance beyond the well, at the top of the ascent, a fine view of the moor suddenly unfolds itself. To the L., in the distance, is Cosdon, and nearer to us the Belstone range. Halstock Down rises beyond the confines of the park, not far off ; and to the R. of that, in succession, Row Tor, West Mill Tor, and Yes Tor are seen ; and still further R., beyond the camp ground, Black Down. The camp occupies a considerable portion of this part of the park. There are houses and bungalows for the officers, huts for the men, and ranges of shelters for the horses. There are also a recreation room, cook houses, and numerous other offices, and when the batteries are here during summer a very animated scene is presented.

A little further on we leave the camp road, which is marked with white stones, and branch L. to Moor Gate, immediately outside which is a ford, and a footbridge over the Moor Brook. Near by, L., is a cottage, and across two fields is seen Pudhanger farmhouse. We do not cross the stream, but turn R. and follow the rough road between

Row   West Mill   Yes Tor.
Tor.   Tor.

FROM MOOR BROOK, LOOKING S.

it and the park wall, our path now being the track leading to Dinger Tor, and which has already been described (T. 34). It will lead us between Row Tor and West Mil Tor, and may be seen from the point we have now reached running up the side of the latter. One or two tracks cross our own, and just beyond Anthony Stile, where the wall turns away R., a road runs R. over the shoulder of Black Down (T. 33, S. Ex. 35). But we do not leave the Moor Brook ; we keep it on the L., and it will be our companion nearly to its source. Between Row Tor L., and West Mil Tor R., is Creaber's Hole, through which Moor Brook runs, and here we shall notice, as we pass upward, some railings enclosing a small space. It is the place where the water is taken in for use at the camp. When directly below Row Tor and Mil Tor the distant hills come into view, and we see away to the L. the Belstone range with Cosdon to the R. of it. Just here a branch track crosses the brook and runs towards Row Tor. As we climb the hill many other heights disclose themselves. First East Mil Tor (Ex. 16) is seen, very near to us, with Steeperton Tor (Ex. 17) beyond it ; then shortly after, between these two, the rocks of Wild Tor appear (Ex. 19) ; a few steps further on Hound Tor (Ex. 17), with Ock Tor (Ex. 17) below it, become visible to the L. of Steeperton. To the R. of the latter, and far away, is Newtake, partly hidden by Ockment Hill.

At the head of Moor Brook is a small mire and an old stream work, and on the E. side of this are the vestiges of another track. But we leave the stream and the track soon after passing the ford above mentioned, and strike R., under West Mil Tor, toward the foot of Yes Tor, which is now in full view, and marked by a flag-staff on its summit, our direction being about S.W. On our way we shall pass three piles of rock S. of West Mil Tor, and forming, as it were, outlying masses of it.

Crossing the Redaven (Ex. 14), here only a small stream, we commence the ascent of the tor, taking care to keep well to the R., in order to avoid the great clatter that streams from its south-eastern side.

[Yes Tor may also be conveniently reached from Okehampton Park by way of Redaven Ford, which is, indeed, rather the shorter route of the two. The track branches R. from the one just described (see also T. 33) near Anthony Stile, and running up the hill S.W. reaches a ford on the Redaven (T. 33), the distance from the stile to this point being 1 m. From here the rambler may either make straight for the tor, which is about ¾ m. S., and more than 700 feet above him, or he may follow up the stream to Redaven Dip, which is the way sometimes traversed by peat carts, as a rough track will show. When between West Mil Tor L., and Yes Tor R., he will leave the stream and ascend the hill. The distance from the town to the summit is about 4 m.]

The fine pile of rocks of which Yes Tor consists may be easily ascended ; indeed, on the W. side a path has been made by which it is possible to ride almost to the top of the tor. On the highest rock is the staff already referred to, on which the danger flag is hoisted during the artillery practice. Due W. of the rocks is a large tumulus, and there are indications of another having existed between the tor and High Willes ; flint flakes have been found near the tor. As the view from Willes, ½ m. distant S., which on the moorland side is even more extensive than that seen from this prominent height, is hereafter described, it is only necessary now to briefly indicate those points that are not to be seen from the former. Much of the in-country over which the eye ranges from this tor is hidden from the beholder on Willes. The prospect there is almost entirely a moor one ; from Yes Tor it is one of wild upland on one side and cultivated country on the other. The camp, and the roads that have been cut as approaches to it, spoil the picture presented from this tor when looking towards the north. These are altogether out of keeping with our surroundings ; they take from us that sense of loneliness which the absence of man's work imparts, and in which there is so much charm when wandering on Dartmoor. The farm lands seen in this direction do not do this to any extent, for although the cultivator's hand is there visible, his work is too far away to thrust itself prominently into the picture. Looking down into the valley of the Ockment W. we see Shilstone Tor, and the summit of Black Tor (S. Ex. 36) rising over the edge of the common ; beyond these are Corn Ridge and the Sourton Tors (Ex. 13). We also get a good view of Homerton Hill and Longstone Hill far down below us now, though seeming to rise to a great height above us as we passed up through Meldon Gorge (Ex. 14). Beyond this northern verge of the moor we look over a vast expanse of fields and woodland, with here and there a cluster of dwellings. Much of North Devon is visible, and also a great part of North-East Cornwall. Looking into the moor we see where the lonely Cranmere hides itself, though its situation can be discerned better from Willes. In a direction S.S.E. by E. the distant hills will be seen to dip behind a nearer ridge, the second one from us, the first stretching away from our feet (see *post*). To the L. of this dip is the pool, which bears S.S.E. from the tor. It might be considered rather strange that such a prominent object as Yes Tor, although on the line of the original boundary of the forest, is not mentioned in the Perambulation of 1240, or in subsequent Surveys. But this is to be accounted for by the fact that Willes, which is also on the line, and is, as we have seen, quite near to it, is mentioned as a bondmark. In a note in Bridges' *Okehampton*, setting forth the ancient bounds on Dartmoor belonging to that parish, the tor is referred to as " Eastor, *alias* Highest Tor."

Descending from this lofty station we shall make our way to High Willes, which attains an even greater elevation, being indeed, not only the highest point on Dartmoor, but in England south of Ingleborough in Yorkshire.* For many years Yes Tor was popularly supposed to occupy this position (though the moormen did not hold this opinion), but the latest Ordnance Survey shows the height of Willes to be 2,039 feet, or 12 feet higher than Yes Tor. They may be said to stand on the same hill, the dip between them being very slight indeed.

Row Tor, West Mil Tor, Yes Tor, and Willes form a range extending from Halstock Down, on the N.E., to the West Ockment on the S.W. The first three are in a line running N.E. and S.W., but Willes is due S. of Yes Tor. On the N.W. side of this range, that is to say, on the side near the cultivated lands, is that part of Okehampton Common comprising Homerton Hill, Longtone Hill, and Black Down, and also Okehampton Park ; on its S.E. side towards the forest, are Row Tor Ridge and Dinger Plain. Row Tor Ridge, which is very stony, lies to the S. of the tor so named, 'and slopes eastward to the Blackaven ; Dinger Plain, usually called only Dinger, is a continuation southward of this ridge, but is of much greater extent. Dinger Tor is placed towards its southern end, and the plain is bounded by the Blackaven and the head waters of Brim Brook on the east.

High Willes has been thought to have derived its name from Huel, or Wheal, signifying a mine, but as old workings are invariably found near streams, this is not very probable. The somewhat similar name, at least with regard to its latter part, of Brown Willy, a hill in Cornwall, has been thought to be a corruption of Bron, or Bryn, Gwili. But *gwili* means *winding*, or *tortuous*, as a path or stream, and has no bearing in the present case. The suggestion has also been made that the root is perhaps to be found in *gwylfa*, a watching place, and it certainly may well be that a look-out was once kept upon it for the beacon fires. The name appears in 1532 as Hight Wyll, and in later documents as High Willows. There is no tor on Willes, only an outcrop of rock, on the highest part of which is a small tower, said to have been built by the Ordnance surveyors some century ago. On the turf near by are the ruined walls of a little shelter.

Although the view of the moor from Willes is a very wide one, it is not so extensive as that gained from Cut Hill, and which we have already described (Ex. 11). But we nevertheless look upon a picture instinct with the spirit of Dartmoor. Incongruous features are absent ; great stretches of brown heath, with here and there a fantastically heaped pile of dark rocks, alone are seen. We cannot fail to be impressed with the silence and the solitude. To the L. as we face southward, and beyond Yes Tor, is West Mil Tor, behind which Row

---

* Ingleborough, 2,361 feet ; High Willes (the loftiest hill on Dartmoor), 2,039 feet. The Cumberland hills are much higher : Skiddaw, 3,022 feet ; Helvellyn, 3,055 feet ; Scaw Fell, 3,229 feet.

Tor hides itself. A little to the R. of these, but further away, is Halstock Down, and still further off Watchet Hill, with the track on its
side (T. 37) plainly visible. R. of this is the Belstone range, with East
Ockment Farm under it N.E. by E. Beyond the range, in a **direction**

| Cosdon. | Steeperton Tor, | Wild Tor | Watern Tor, |

E N E.　　　　　E. Mil Tor.　　　　　　　　　　　　　　　　　　　　　　S.E.

FROM HIGH WILLES.

E.N.E., rises Cosdon, the summit of which is exactly 4 m. distant in a
straight line. The rounded form of this hill is well seen from this
point. Immediately beneath it is the south part of the Belstone range,
and in front of that, and near to us, is the tor already spoken of, East
Mil Tor. To the R. of the latter, but further off, E. by N., is Ock
Tor, and beyond that again White Hill, under Cosdon, and Metheral
Hill. R. of this is Little Hound Tor, with Kennon Hill rising behind
it. E. by S. is Steeperton, the fine tor at the head of Taw Plain
(Ex. 17), with the wall crossing the ridge between the Taw and the
East Ockment (Ex. 16), and which is continued to the Blackaven,
the combe from which the East Ockment issues will be noticed to
the R. of East Mil Tor, which is covered from end to end with granite,
and between it and Steeperton. E.S.E., and 3 m. away, is Wild Tor,
with Watern Tor peeping over the ridge to the R. of it. In the foreground, and not 200 feet below us, is Dinger Plain, over the whole
extent of which we can look. The little sheet of water that we see
near the source of the Redaven is Dinger Pool, or as it is sometimes
called, the Pixies' Pool. Beyond the plain, southward, Ockment Hill
rolls away to the dusky ridge that rises against the sky, its summit
being seen to the R. of Watern Tor. R. of Ockment Hill is Newtake,
with the higher part of White Horse Hill. To the R. of Newtake is
Cranmere, which bears S.E. by S., and is 2½ m. off in a direct line.
The site of the pool may be discovered in the same manner as from
Yes Tor, but is more readily located from this hill. We look in a
direction about S.S.E., where a distant hill (which is a part of Cut Hill)
is seen to dip behind Black Hill, and to the L. of this dip, but much
nearer to us, is the pool. Its exact situation is marked by a dark cleft
in the side of the ridge. This is the hollow in which the West Ockment
rises, and the pool is at its head. (See Routes to Cranmere). R. of
the pool is Black Ridge, in a line with Dinger Tor, the latter being
only ¾ m. distant. S. of S.S.E. is Great Kneeset, 2 m. off, with Cut
Hill the same distance beyond it, and to the R. of the latter Fur Tor,

of which we have here a very fine view. Then comes the high ground near the south of the Cowsic and Walkham Head, stretching away in a long range towards the W., behind which Great Mis Tor lifts up his rocky crown in a direction W. of S., and 8 m. away. There is a dip where the western side of huge Standon drops to the unseen Tavy.

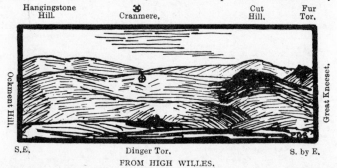

Hangingstone Hill.   Cranmere.   Cut Hill.   Fur Tor.

Ockment Hill.   Great Kneeset,

S.E.   Dinger Tor.   S. by E.

FROM HIGH WILLES.

and then White Tor rises S.S.W. Further R., and looking across the N. end of Amicombe, we see the Dunnagoat Tors, with Great Links Tor rising high above them, the most prominent of all the rock piles in the view. It is about 2½ m. to the S.W. In front of Great Links and only 1½ m. distant, is Kitty Tor. To the R. is Hunt Tor and Stinka Tor, the latter overlooking the valley of the Ockment. To the R. on the brow of the hill are the Slipper Stones, with Corn Ridge beyond, and still further away in the same direction the Sourton Tors. Beyond these there is a grand stretch of distant in-country, which completes the view.

And now we move onward to a point whence another view is presented, which, if it does not embrace such a wide extent of country, certainly possesses features which that seen from Willes cannot show. We shall make our way to Forsland Ledge, or, as one document gives it, Fosborne Ledge, though this name is never heard, a small pile of rocks ⅓ m. S.W. of Willes, and about 200 feet below it. The beholder looks from it down into the gorge of the Ockment, and upon a picture that has not many equals on the moor. The range of hills from Newtake by Black Ridge, Cut Hill, and Fur Tor to Great Mis Tor, bounds the view to the S. We look into the recesses of the moor around Cranmere, and upon the two Kneesets. Across the valley is Amicombe, and beyond it Great Links Tor, which from no other point presents a finer appearance. Away to the R. are the rocks of Black Tor (S. Ex. 36) at the foot of which is seen the shelter from which the artillery practice is watched, with the in-country over the down beyond. But the features that will arrest the attention are Lints Tor, which came into view shortly after we left Willes, and the winding Ockment far down below. The resemblance of the tor to a castle has been already mentioned (Ex. 14), and the rambler will not fail to be struck with it here. The rocks crown a rounded hill, covered with grass, on which are long lines of heather. Below it on the W. the Ockment flows the part of the stream here being that between Kneeset Foot and Sandy Ford (Ex. 14). In several parts of Dartmoor are tors bearing a resemblance to a building, or to ruins, but nowhere is the illusion so perfect as here. To the R. of the tor Kneeset Foot is seen, with the pass called Broad Amicombe Hole above it (R. 3). Great Kneeset is 1¼ m. beyond the tor; Little Kneeset is a little to the R. of this, and 1 m. further away. Forsland Ledge is about 550 feet above the river; the hill on which it is placed is very steep, and plentifully strewn with granite. Quite close to it is a small tumulus, within which is what appears to be a ruined kistvaen.

Leaving Forsland Ledge we shall make our way back towards Willes, the summit of which we keep L., and passing over the shoulder of the hill N.E. by E., shall descend to the head of the Redaven, with Dinger Plain R. This little stream runs for some distance through a shallow gully clothed with turf, where we shall find good ground. Our path will lie along the R. bank, and we shall be led through Redaven Dip, between Yes Tor L., and West Mil Tor R., to Redaven Ford, 500 feet below its source. At the ford we shall take the track R. (T. 33, 34) which will lead us direct to Moor Gate, 1½ m. distant, from which the road to the town is described in Ex. 14.

Instead of returning by way of Redaven Dip the visitor may pass over West Mil Tor and Row Tor to the road leading to Moor Gate. He will leave the Redaven at the bend under Yes Tor, about ½ m. from its source, and striking N. by E. will soon reach the first-named group of rocks, which is in full view from the bank of the little stream. The three outlying masses of which we have already spoken will be passed on the way. West Mil Tor is certainly worth a visit; the largest pile, which forms the southern part of the tor, is of a conical form, and rather striking. In the report of the commissioners relative to the boundaries of the Chase of Okehampton, in 1532, when it belonged to Henry, Marquis of Exeter, the tor is mentioned as " Milltor," but in the description of the bounds of the common lands of Okehampton as at one time recognized, and to which reference has been made, it appears as " Middle Tor, *alias* Miltor." From this it seems probable that the name is a corruption of *middle*, a word which correctly describes the situation of the tor with regard to its two companions, and that it has nothing to do with the Celtic *melyn, yellow*, as has been suggested. If this be correct another instance is supplied of a tor bearing a comparatively modern name. Under the rocks is a little shed like that at Black Tor, from which the artillery practice can be safely watched, and its results noted. Dropping down into the hollow on the N.E., and crossing the Moor Brook, the visitor will ascend Row Tor, ½ m. distant. On the stony Row Tor Ridge the wooden figures forming the targets for the artillery will often be seen. The guns, which are placed on Halstock Down, sweep this ridge and Dinger Plain. From Row Tor the visitor will pass down the hill N. to a track (T. 35) ¼ m., which he will follow for a short distance to the road leading N. to Moor Gate, which is less than 1 m. from the tor.

[The road to the town is described in Ex. 14.]

Ex. 16.—*The Blackaven, East Mil Tor, Ockment Hill, The East Ockment, Crovenor Steps, Halstock Down*, about 11 m., including summit of Ockment Hill, and return by Crovenor Steps and Moor Gate.

Our way will first take us to Moor Gate (Ex. 15), where, instead of turning R. as in going to Yes Tor, we shall cross the Moor Brook, and follow the road up the hill southward with the Pudhanger enclosures on our L. ½ m. from the brook, and soon after passing a large sand-pit, we shall strike into a track (T. 35) R., just under Row Tor (Ex. 15). Ere we have gone far we shall notice by the side of it one of the many objects of a similar character to be seen on the moor ; it is a granite trough having two compartments, one of which is broken, a flaw having probably discovered itself while it was being cut. Below us on the L. is Row Tor Combe, where there is a crossing-place on the Blackaven, known as Middle Ford. As we proceed we have a fine view of East Mil Tor, which rises boldly in front of us. Away to the L. is seen the Belstone range, with the huge Cosdon behind ; also Steeperton Tor, with Ock Tor to the L. of it, the latter, though a small pile, here show-ing itself to great advantage. Nearer to us the little Hart Tor is seen, on the common at the corner of the enclosure to which it gives name. 1½ m. from the point where our track leaves the camp road it reaches the Blackaven, which is here crossed by a clapper, known as New Bridge. Though not quite what its name would suggest, the structure nevertheless belongs to a comparatively recent period. At one time I imagined that it might have had some connection with the extensive streamwork close by ; that peat was perhaps brought over it for use there. But I now believe it to have been erected at the beginning of the nineteenth century. On the bank of the Blackaven a ruined wall will be seen extending both up and down the stream, and which marks an attempt to enclose a portion of the forest. Several years ago I learnt in the neighbourhood, on good authority, that the bridge was erected at the same time as the wall, and the latter is not ancient, as a farmer, who had lived on the verge of the common all his life, once told me that he remembered men who had helped to build it. It was a part of this wall that we were able to see from Willes (Ex. 15), the area it encloses being very large. From the bridge it runs up to the head of the stream, 1 m., where it turns eastward and is carried over the ridge to the Taw, crossing the East Ockment a short distance below its source. It then runs down the Taw to Taw Plain, and it was doubtless intended to continue it to a point on this river under Belstone Tor (Ex. 17), where a wall runs up the hill and crossing the ridge between that tor and Higher Tor, descends nearly to the East Ockment, its direction between these points being about W. A short distance below where it terminates is Crovenor Steps, where the Blackaven falls into the East Ockment, and here it is seen again, forming for a short distance part of the en-closing wall of East Ockment Farm. It is then continued up the Blackaven to the bridge. The total length of the line we have traced is about 7 miles.

The portion of this wall running down the hill from Belstone Tor towards the East Ockment, as also that part of it on the lower Blacka-ven, is known as the Irishman's Wall. The story goes that some years ago a project was formed by an Irishman to enclose a part of the moor here, and for the purpose of carrying out the work he brought a number of his countrymen to the locality. They set to work building the wall, creating no little surprise among the Dartmoor folk, and showing their contempt for the rough, damp ground over which they had to walk to their labour by going bare-footed. The men of Belstone and Okehampton said nothing, but let the work proceed. But they had, notwithstanding, no intention of allowing it to be completed. They saw that the taking in of such an immense tract would cut off their commons from the forest. Consequently, when they considered that a fitting time had arrived, they met in force and made such breaches in the wall as to render it useless. The outworks of the Irishmen having thus been carried by storm, he evacuated his position, and left the commoners victorious.

Who the Irishman was I am unable to say, but I find in the *Additions* to Risdon's *Survey*, published in 1811, that among those who are there called "improvers" of Dartmoor, Dr. Brown and Mr. Crawford are named as having not long previously to that time enclosed land on the verge of the forest near Okehampton. This statement can only have reference to the tract of land within the ruined wall, since there are no other enclosures in the forest in that neighbourhood, and thus the time of its erection can be approximately fixed, and if my informant was correct, which there is no reason to doubt, the time of the building of the bridge as well.

Where the wall runs by the Blackaven from Crovenor Steps to New Bridge it is carried nearly on the line of the forest boundary, but not actually so. The latter runs a little to the W. of the bridge, which, however, as it is near the line, is sometimes referred to as a bondmark.* Above the bridge, and on the W. side of the Blackaven, the line is carried through Curtory Clitters, and across Dinger Plain to Sandy Ford (Ex. 14), being marked here and there by a bondstone.

New Bridge is 18 feet long, and rather more than that in width. There are two openings for the water, each being about four feet wide on the lower side; the buttresses and centre pier are very thick, and irregularly built. It is about 8 feet high on its lower side, and 18 inches less than this on its upper. Looking down the stream the distant in-country is seen, backed by the high land of Exmoor.

The track by which we have reached the bridge is continued along the R. bank of the stream in a southerly direction (T. 35. See also Cranmere Routes), and climbs the hill S. of East Mil Tor. 1 m. from the bridge it is crossed by the wall just noticed, outside which it is continued for about ¾ m. to the summit of Ockment Hill, 1,856 feet, but is there more of the character of a green path.

Leaving the track at the bridge and striking almost due E. we make our way to the northern end of East Mil Tor, which rises close by. Then we turn our steps southward, passing along the ridge, from which there is a fine view of Yes Tor and the neighbouring heights Rocks extend from end to end of this ridge, which is about ½ m. long. On reaching its southern extremity we continue S. to the wall, ½ m.

---

* It is very improbable that the forest boundary line, even if it ever came this way, and there is ample evidence to show that it did not (see *Perambulation* in the *Terms* Section), would have been drawn as at present laid down. The Blackaven would form a convenient boundary, and it is difficult to imagine that it would not have been followed. As it at present stands this stream is for some distance left just outside the forest bounds; an arrangement not altogether inconvenient for the Okehampton commoners.

7. LYDFORD & OKEHAMPTON Districts.

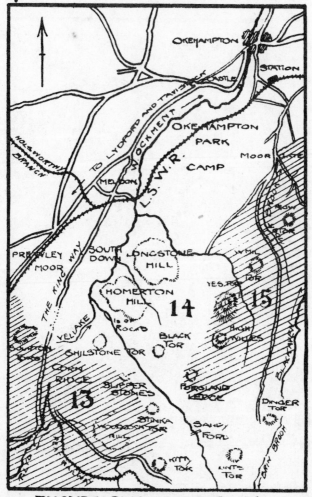

EXCURSIONS 13, 14, 15.
(PART OF EX. 13 ON MAP 5 EXTENSION OF
EX. 14 ON MAPS 5 & 6)

8. OKEHAMPTON & CHAGFORD DISTRICTS.

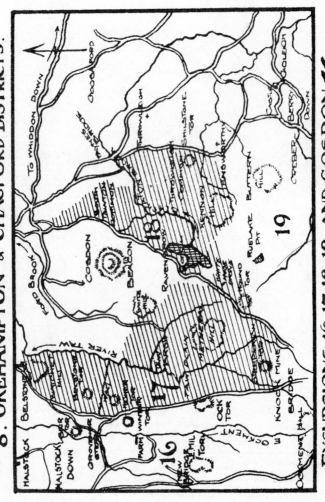

EXCURSIONS 16,17,18,19, AND COSDON.
(PARTS OF EX.19 ARE SHOWN ON MAPS 6 & 9)

distant, noticing as we proceed a small tumulus near the track which comes up the hill from the bridge on our R.

[We may extend our walk from the wall to the summit of Ockment Hill, locally known as Ockaton Hill, where we shall find the remains of a large tumulus. This hill, on which there is much broken ground, comprises that part of the moor lying between the springs of the East Ockment and the head of the West Ockment, and extends westward to Brim Brook. About ½ m. S.W. of the summit a little stream rises and flows down through Vergyland Combe to the West Ockment. This combe is noticed in the Routes to Cranmere. Instead of retracing our steps we strike N.E. for nearly ½ m., avoiding the head of the East Ockment on our L., and then N. to the wall, which we shall reach at a point ¼ m. E. of where we left it, and on the E. side of the combe in which the Ockment rises.]

At the wall we turn L., *i.e.*, eastward, and follow it for ½ m., crossing on the way a combe through which the Ockment and a couple of small feeders run. Having reached the E. side of this we turn northward, where we shall find good ground, and shall make our way down the valley, with Middle Hill on the further side of the Ockment on our L., to Skit Bottom, where are numerous remains of old mining operations known as Rithy Pits, and these extend to the enclosures of East Ockment Farm, about 1½ m. down from the wall. The river is often known in this part of its course as the Skit, and seems also to have formerly borne the name of Lede, at least in the town of Okehampton. In a journal kept by John Rattenbury, " gentleman and burgess," in the time of Charles I., the following entry occurs :—" 3 August, 1628, being Sabbath day. About four o'clocke in the afternoon, immediately after evening prayer ended att the Church of Okehampton, there being noe raine perceived to fall within or neare this towne, and the streets being then very drye, the water now called Lede, or the East water, was suddenly risen about some V. foote at the Easte bridge, running more violent than had been usually knowne, and twas conceived the water did savour and smell of some brimstone."

[As we approach East Ockment Farm we shall strike a camp road, which comes out over Hart Tor Hill and crosses the Ockment. This road we may follow L. to Okehampton Park, crossing the Blackaven at Stone Ford, sometimes called Hart Tor (or Harter) Ford, on the verge of Halstock Down. In the other direction, *i.e.*, southerly, it runs out towards Taw Head.]

We pass down the valley with the river still on our L., noticing as we proceed the bridge over which the road runs to the farm. A few score yards eastward of this bridge are the remains of a small circle, about 15 feet in diameter, which probably once enclosed a kistvaen, though nothing is to be seen of it now. A few of the stones are still standing. East Ockment Farm is situated within the area that was attempted to be enclosed by the great wall, but was only formed about 1878. As it came in the line of the artillery firing from Halstock Down a lease of it was acquired by the War Office from the Duchy. It is still let as a farm, but under certain restrictions. An under-ground shelter is provided in which those who belong to the place take refuge when firing is in progress. At the lower, or N.E. corner, of the farm enclosures is the ford known as Crovenor Steps, which has been already mentioned, and here we meet the present forest bounds, the line being drawn to this point from Dinger Plain along the Blackaven. A camp road has been made to the ford, and this we now follow up the slope westward, with the higher part of Halstock Down on our R., and the Blackaven, in which we shall notice a number of small cascades, on our L. After a walk of about ½ m. we find ourselves near Stone Ford, L., but shall follow the road R., and passing the sand-pit before referred to, shall soon reach Moor Gate. The route from this point is described in Ex. 14.

[From Crovenor Steps the return to Okehampton may be made by way of Halstock ; the walk will be found more interesting than that by Moor Gate, and the distance is about the same. On crossing the Ockment instead of following the road, we pass up the hill N.N.W. to Kelly's Corner, a little over ¼ m. distant. Here is a stone having the letter L cut upon it, and forming a bondmark of land belonging to Lydford. The small portion of the common of which this stone marks one of the bounds, though now outside the forest, is nevertheless always regarded as " forest " by those living in the locality, and there can be little doubt that it was once within the confines of the ancient hunting ground. The possession of this piece of common by the Duchy is strong evidence that the forest bounds originally ran as the old Perambulations and Surveys state. Passing onward, with the fields a little to the R., we shall shortly reach a gate in a corner of the common, where a road leads to Halstock. Near to it is Halstock Pound, R., a small square enclosure, used as the drifts principally for ponies. Entering the gate we make our way down the road, with Chapel Lands on our R. At the lower end of this field we strike the path from Belstone to Okehampton, which we have already noticed (T. 36), and turning L. to Halstock Farm, shall make our way to Okehampton in the manner described in that route.]

(FROM STICKLEPATH AND BELSTONE).

Sticklepath is pleasantly situated, and offers many advantages to the visitor. Quite near to it is the fine frontier height of Cosdon and the charming Belstone Cleave. *Stickle* is equivalent to the A.S. *Sticele, steep*. At the west end of the village is a well with the inscription :

" Lady Well. Drink and Be Thankful."

Near it on the verge of the common is an inscribed stone, and here a road runs up the valley to Belstone. The latter village is well placed for the Dartmoor explorer. Among old-time objects to be seen there are a small manor pound, and the pillars between which formerly swung the castigatory, more often spoken of as the ducking-stool.

Ex. 17.—*The Belstone Tors, Steeperton, Metheral Hill, Hound Tor, White Moor Stone and Circle, White Hill, Taw Plain, Birchy Lake*, about 8 m.

Passing up the lane near the W. end of Belstone Church we soon reach the common, where, leaving the track (T. 38) running from the moor gate to the forest, we turn aside L., to Watchet Hill, on which, as before mentioned, a danger signal is displayed when artillery practice takes place in this part of the moor. This hill forms the northern end of the ridge between the East Ockment and the Taw, which we were able to see when on our ramble to Yes Tor and Willes (Ex. 15),

On its summit is a despoiled cairn, about 112 feet in circumference, though a correct measurement cannot well be taken, as it is in such a dilapidated condition. From this point we shall proceed to Belstone Tor, nearly ¾ m. distant, in a direction almost due S., passing on the way two smaller piles, the three usually being spoken of as the Belstone Tors. On the slope to the R., and near the track, is the small circle called the Nine Stones, or Nine Maidens, noticed in S. Ex. 41 ; it is passed shortly before the first of the rock piles is reached.

Belstone Tor (1,567 feet) stands a little to the N. of the Irishman's Wall (Ex. 16), which is here carried from the Taw over the ridge nearly to the East Ockment. The whole of the ground is encumbered with lumps of granite, the clatter on the E. side of the hill descending to the Taw and covering both banks. On the S. side of the wall is Higher Tor, and on reaching this we shall bear a little to the R. to Winter Tor, a small pile close to the track which we left at the moor gate (T. 38), and near to the point where it is joined by another coming up from Crovenor Steps (T. 37, Ex. 16). On the further side of the valley W., is East Ockment Farm, of which we have here a good view. We now follow the track, and at the distance of rather over a furlong shall notice a low mound to the L. of the way ; in the centre of this is a ruined kistvaen covered with a granite slab. As we proceed along the summit of the ridge the whole of the level valley known as Taw Plain is in sight on the L. At the southern end of this is the fine hill crowned with Steeperton Tor, and peninsulated by the Taw on one side and by Steeperton Brook on the other. The latter stream rises on the northern side of Hangingstone Hill, and at no great distance from the former. The western side of the valley is formed by the ridge along which we are making our way ; on its eastern side are Metheral Hill, White Hill, and the lower slope of Cosdon. It extends northward to the clatter below the Belstone Tors, and is about 2 m. in length, and less than 1 m. in width at its widest part. The Taw runs through it, receiving the Steeperton Brook at its head, and Small Brook lower down, between which two tributary streams is Metheral Hill. Passing Ock Tor, near which, on the western slope of the ridge, are some stones placed in such a manner as to suggest a stone row, and noticing some old tin workings at the foot of the great hill we are approaching, we soon reach Steeperton Gorge, through which the Taw forces its way to the open plain below. The further side of this ravine is formed by the great flank of Steeperton, and it is so narrow as to afford little more than room for the river. Quite close to the bank we shall observe the wall spoken of in Ex. 16, and ere we have proceeded far shall meet with this as it comes up the side of the defile at right angles to the Taw.

[The wall runs westward over Middle Hill, crossing the springs of the East Ockment, and reaching the Blackaven. The visitor is here near the point where he turns towards the N. in Ex. 16, to make his way from the wall down the valley of the Skit, or East Ockment. Southward of Middle Hill is Ockment Hill (Ex. 16, and C.R.), which is bounded on the E. by the Taw ; it is noticed in the Cranmere Routes, as also is the Ridge S. of Steeperton, and between the Taw and the Steeperton Brook. This ridge, a part of which is known as Ockside Hill, terminates on the S. at the foot of Hangingstone Hill, in the neighbourhood of Cranmere.]

On leaving the wall our track descends to the Taw, here crossed by the clapper known as Knock Mine Bridge (T. 38). This is 29 feet long and fifteen feet wide, and there are four openings, the two central ones being wider than the others. The bridge was greatly damaged by a flood in 1890. On the side of the steep slope above it are the walls of a small building, one of the vestiges of the " knocked " Knock Mine.

Crossing the stream we make our way up the side of Steeperton Hill to the tor, distant ⅓ m. from the bridge, and 286 feet above it. The rocks do not rise to a great height, and are therefore not particularly striking in themselves, but the hill should certainly be ascended for the sake of the fine view to be obtained from it. Northward we look out over Taw Plain, with the Belstone range on the L. and the huge Cosdon on the R. E. by N. is Hound Tor, with Kennon Hill beyond it, the former being about ¾ m. distant. S.E. by S. is Wild Tor (i. short ; rhymes with filled), ¾ m. off. Southward is the Wild Tor Ridge and Ockside Hill, with Hangingstone Hill beyond. S.W. is Ockment Hill ; and W., and ranging round towards the N., Willes, Yes Tor, the two Mil Tors, and Row Tor. The southernmost mass on this hill is sometimes known as the Eagle Rock.

Our next point will be Hound Tor, but instead of making for it direct we shall bear a little to the R. If we shape our course S. of E. we shall strike the track running out from South Zeal (T. 41) shortly after crossing the Steeperton Brook, and turn L. into this shall soon find ourselves abreast of the tor. On the L. as we proceed is Metheral Hill, a tract sloping down to Taw Marsh, and rising in a slightly rounded form between the Steeperton Brook L. and Small Brook R. The first-named stream runs down through Metheral Hole, where are the remains of some tin workings known as White Pits. This name is found attached to several places or objects in the locality, there being White Hill, White Moor, White Moor Mead (see *post* and *Cosdon Section*), and White Works (Ex. 19). The line marking the boundary between the forest and South Tawton Common is now drawn from Small Brook Foot, on which stream there are also some mining remains, up through the middle of Metheral Hill to White Moor Stone, but as already stated it is probable that it formerly ran further to the east.

Hound Tor is a small low pile placed on a narrow ridge between the watersheds of the Taw and the Teign. It forms one of the forest bondmarks, and appears in the Perambulation of 1240 as " parva Hundetorre." The line is now drawn from White Moor Stone, less than ½ m. N.E., to the tor, and thence to Wild Tor Well, nearly ¹ m. to the S. (Ex. 19), and throughout this distance defines the boundary between the Duchy possessions and Throwleigh Common. From Hound Tor the ground slopes southward to the mire above Gallaven Ford, to which point a track comes out from Clannaborough Down (T. 42), passing between Kennon Hill, the summit of which is less than a mile distant E. by N., and Raybarrow Pool (Ex. 18). Beyond the mire, and to the R. of it, rise the rocks of Wild Tor (Ex. 19). E. by S. of Hound Tor, and not far from Gallaven Ford, is a plain piece of ground sometimes known as White Moor Mead. N. of this is White Moor, marked by the tall stone bearing that name, and to which we shall now make our way.

[For a description of other objects in the neighbourhood of this tor see Exs. 18, 19, R. 24, 25, and *Cranmere Section*.]

White Moor is a tract extending north-eastward to Raybarrow

Pool, and is bounded on the N. by Brook Hill, which is situated to the S. of White Hill. White Moor Stone stands on a flat, broken piece of ground, W.S.W. of the southern arm of the pool, and about 250 yards from it. Though now serving as a boundary mark it may still be a genuine menhir, though it is, as the same time, not at all unlikely that it originally belonged to the stone circle near by. It is a large slab about 5 feet 6 inches high, and less than 6 inches thick ; its width is about 3 feet. The circle is N. by W. of it, and very near to the South Zeal track (T. 41). It now consists of 13 stones, only one of which was erect previous to about 1897, in which year the monument was "restored." It is evident that there were formerly more stones than at present, and as we can hardly suppose that they would be carried far, it is not at all improbable that they were taken away to serve as bondstones, of which there are several in the locality. The stones are between three 2nd four feet in height.

On leaving the White Moor Circle we shall cross the track and strike N.N.W. to a group of ruined huts ½ m. distant, passing over Brook Hill, on which is a low cairn. Close to the huts we shall notice a short reave, and not far from this, in a northerly direction, is a dilapidated kist, and what appears to be a menhir lying prone on the ground. Below this group the hill, which sinks down to Small Brook, is covered with rocks, between which whortleberry plants grow in great profusion. One cluster of these granite masses near the stream is called the Flock o' Sheep. Passing down the slope in a north-westerly direction, with the stream on the L., we shortly come upon other remains. These consist of hut circles enclosed within three pounds of an irregular circular shape, the walls, or rather banks, of which are very low, and in a dilapidated condition. One of these pounds is quite near to Small Brook, which here flows through a hollow. From the smallest of them a short reave is carried towards the stream, and close to it is another running from the stream northward. This terminates very near to the Ivy Tor Water, which is about ¾ m. distant, and is mentioned in our notice of the track leading from Ford over the shoulder of Cosdon (T. 40).

In descending the side of the hill from the first group of huts we have a good view of Taw Plain, and of the distant range of hills capped by Willes, rising beyond the Belstone ridge. From this part of the moor these hills present such a different appearance from that worn by them when seen from other points as to render them at first not readily recognizable. The sides of Taw Plain very nearly approach each other at its lower, or northern end, where the Taw seems to have scooped out a channel for itself. In the days when this channel was at a higher level than at present it is probable that the plain formed the bed of a shallow lake, into which the foot of Steeperton projected. This idea will certainly be suggested to the visitor who looks upon it from the point we have now reached, or when he views it from near Birchy Lake. It is about 1,160 feet above sea-level.

Below the hut circles Small Brook runs through Taw Marsh to the Taw, the confluence being known as Small Brook Foot. The tributary may be followed to the larger stream, there being good hard ground upon its banks ; or we may strike into the green track that we shall see running towards the N. from a ford over the brook (T. 40). If we choose the former we shall pass between the two patches of miry ground of which Taw Marsh consists, and on reaching the Taw shall cross it at the first place where an opportunity offers, or follow the river down to Ducky Pool, just below which it makes an abrupt bend where there are two fords. Here it is narrow as well as shallow, and can generally be crossed without difficulty. If we follow the track it will lead us for a short distance over a smooth level piece of ground, with White Hill on the R. Then we leave it and strike towards the river, our mark being Higher Tor, on the ridge beyond. This will bring us to the fords at the bend.

[Should the Taw be in flood it will, of course, be necessary for the visitor to return by way of Knock Mine Bridge.]

On crossing the river we strike a rough track (T. 39), which we shall follow past the Irishman's Wall, and through a wilderness of stones, to Birchy Lake. It was among these masses of granite that the cottage of the old woman with the evil eye formerly stood, and where Luke Duggins shot the black cat, Pluto. The visitor will look in vain for traces of it now, for it was destroyed by the spell of a good pixy at the very moment the old woman was about to fly away on a broomstick. Birchy Lake consists of a farmhouse, and one or two other dwellings. A good road leads to Belstone, ¼ m. distant, a fine view of the Cleave being obtained on the way.

COSDON.

The huge hill of Cosdon spreads itself over the greater part of South Tawton Common. Its local name is Cosson, for which there is a certain degree of authority, as we find that both names were in use in 1609, but none whatever for Cawsand, which form appears on the Ordnance Map published in 1888. Cosson is, of course, merely the Devonshire way of pronouncing the true name, the earliest mention of which is in the Perambulation of 1240, where it is given as Cossdonne. Until the nineteenth century was well advanced this hill was thought to be the highest on Dartmoor, but there are several of much greater elevation ; its height is 1,799 feet, or 240 feet less than that of Willes. On the N. the hill is bounded by Belstone Cleave, Skaigh Wood, and the plantation above Ford ; on the E. by the enclosures running S. from that plantation nearly to the head of Cherriton Combe ; on the S. by Raybarrow Pool and White Hill ; and on the W. by the northern part of Taw Plain.

The summit of this hill is crowned with a cairn 90 yards in circumference, known as Cosdon, or Cosson, Beacon ; indeed, this name is often applied by the natives to the whole hill. About 150 yards N.E. of this cairn are the remains of what appears to have been two kistvaens encircled by a ring of slabs over 50 feet in diameter. A short distance to the N.E. are the scant vestiges of a cairn, and to the N.W. of this the remains of another, each of them being about 60 feet in diameter. Around the latter are some slabs leaning outwards, in the manner often noticed where the stone circle surrounds a tumulus. before these remains were despoiled they must have formed a striking group. But the wall builder on Dartmoor is, or was, generally a vandal ; a cairn would mean nothing more to him than a heap of material, and a kistvaen, if its sides were long, a couple of gate-posts.

The antiquities on the summit of Cosdon are not by any means the only ones on that hill that have suffered at the hands of the spoliator. We remember when there were many hut circles on its eastern side, between the peat road (T. 41) and the enclosures opposite West Week, but only the vestiges of a few are to be found there now, and it is not so many years since that the monument formerly known in the locality as Eight Rocks disappeared. This consisted of eight upright stones, forming part of what had once been a fine circle or row. From a description given to me many years ago at Whiddon Down I judge it to have been the latter. The stones stood at the northern end of the hill, on the slope above Ford. Children in the neighbourhood used to be told that when the Eight Rocks heard South Tawton bells they would be seen to dance.

Another stone row, which is situated on a little plateau on the eastern side of the hill, and not very far from the enclosures, is known as the Cemetery, and which we have mentioned in our description of the track from South Zeal and Prospect Place to the forest (T. 41). This consists of three parallel rows of stones, running from two kistvaens, and was " restored " in 1897. The kists are surrounded by a circle of low stones about 17 feet in diameter, and are placed side by side. One of them is fairly intact, but of the other only one side stone and one end stone remain, the latter serving also as an end stone to the more complete kist. Running almost due E. from this little circle is the triple row, which is about 8 feet in width at its widest part, and here some of the stones composing it are from 3 to 4 feet in height. For a distance of about 85 paces the row is well defined ; it then becomes rather fainter, and extends for another 70 paces to the track referred to. About 120 paces N. of this monument, which presents a rather striking appearance, is a reave running like the row E. and W. It is very much overgrown in places, but it can be seen that some large stones were used in forming it. This group of antiquities is situated N. of the upper end of Cherriton Combe, looking down which the tower of Throwleigh Church can be seen S.E. by E.

On the western slope of this great hill, due W. of the beacon cairn, and rather over a furlong from it, is a group of hut circles, some being of rather large size and others small. A part of this group stands within a pound about 350 paces in circumference, the wall of which is irregularly built of loose stones, and is not more than about 3 feet in height. The whole is much overgrown with heather. Below this, towards the W., is a dilapidated cairn, and the vestiges of a reave, and running southward from the head of the Ivy Tor Water is the reave mentioned in Ex. 17.

In our notice of the bounds of Dartmoor forest we have stated that Cosdon was the starting-point of the perambulators who were appointed in 1240 to view them, but from what part of the hill they set out cannot now be stated with any certainty. If the forest line then ran across Taw Plain, as it is now supposed to do, Cosdon would be altogether outside it, and there would have been no reason for mentioning it, unless it was that the point from which the perambulators set out was the foot of the hill, supposing what we now call White Hill to have been looked upon as one with Cosdon itself. But the return made under the commission (only copies of which, however, exist), shows the Perambulation to have begun at Hoga de Cosdonne, or Cosdon Hill, and as when other hills are named in the return it is clear that the summit of them is meant, it is only reasonable to suppose that such was intended in the case of the one in question, besides which the name would also lead us to that conclusion, *hoga* meaning height.* But whether the bounds viewed in 1240 included much or little of Cosdon within the royal forest, it appears certain that the crown had possessed rights over that part of the moor, and probably contended for them then, a claim which we believe has not been abandoned by the Duchy. South Tawton was ancient demesne, and King John, when Earl of Moretain, held the manor of Richard I. It afterwards came into the possession of Roger de Toeny, who apparently paid twenty shillings a year for the common, which is probably what is referred to in certain manorial records as Tawland.

The view from Cosdon is of great extent and variety. On one hand the solitary moor, with its hills rising bleak and bare ; on the other a vast panorama of wood and field happily intermingled. All the prominent heights to which our rambles from Okehampton and Belstone have taken us are in sight. Away to the S.E. by S. is the ridge of Hameldon, and to the L. of it, and further off, the twin masses of Hey Tor (Ex. 25). Between the openings in the hills, in a direction almost due S., a distant eminence rises against the sky. On this, but too far removed from us to be visible, is the cairn known as Western Whitaburrow, which marks the extreme southern point of the forest, the line being there drawn between it and Brent Moor (Ex. 30). Its distance from the summit of Cosdon is 16 m., as measured on the map. Nearly the whole of North Devon is revealed, and very much of the eastern part of the county. Northward is the stretch of cultivated country that extends to the foot of the Exmoor hills, which are seen bounding the view in that direction. Hardly a season passes but some of the red deer from that district make their way across this to Dartmoor, a journey of about 30 miles. When the weather is favourable the Bristol Channel off Barnstaple Bay is clearly discernible, and towards the S.E. the English Channel beyond the mouth of the Teign.

Few directions for ascending Cosdon Hill are necessary, the ground being everywhere easily passable, but it may perhaps be well to briefly indicate the best routes.

(A). From Belstone the first point will be Birchy Lake (Ex. 17), a short distance above which, where the enclosures on the L. terminate, the Taw(will be crossed by the natural stepping-stones in its channel, which, unless the stream be in flood, will present no difficulty. The summit of the hill is now about 1 m. distant in a direction S.E. by E. About midway up the track running out to Small Brook is crossed (T. 40), and also the Ivy Tor Water, near which the ground is sometimes rather marshy, but not sufficiently so to prove an obstacle. Between this little brook and the beacon cairn on the summit the hut circles referred to as being on the western slope of the hill will be passed. (If, on reaching the R. bank of the Taw, the rambler follows it up for

---

* The name appears in many parts of the country ; as in Morthoe and Trentishoe, in the North of Devon ; in Hawley's Hoe, the residence of a former merchant of Dartmouth ; in Plymouth Hoe ; in Humbershoe and Tatternhoe, in Bedfordshire ; and in Wivenhoe, in Essex. Alster Hohe also occurs near Hamburg.

a short distance instead of immediately ascending the hill, he will come upon the ruins of a small building, consisting of walls forming three sides of a square, and of the kind seen in connection with the tinners' workings. But many years ago we found a story current in the locality to the effect that this house was one of those in which the Irish people who settled in this part of the moor some years ago used to live, and it was then referred to as the Irishmen's House. Presumably these were employed in building the wall which has been described in Ex. 16, and according to the account we gathered they were driven away by the natives. From this ruin the course to the summit of the hill will be a trifle more eastward than the former one).

(B). From Sticklepath the hill is best approached by way of Ford, the track running to Small Brook, and already described, being followed to the common (T. 40). Soon after leaving the enclosures the branch of this path ascending the hill L. will be reached, and into this the visitor must turn. It does not go quite to the summit of Cosdon, but very near to it. Another way is by leaving this track where it enters on the common, and striking a little W. of S. to a small clatter known as Rabbits' Holt. Here is a stone about 6 feet in height, one of a line erected in 1885, to mark the boundary of certain mineral rights, and also that between what was anciently known as the manor of Zeal Toeny and the land over which the Duchy claims jurisdiction. There have been frequent disputes between the commoners of South Tawton parish and the Duchy. It is claimed by the former that they have a right to enclose, and, as will be seen, they have fenced in a good part of the side of the hill opposite Ramsleigh and West Week. The late Bailiff of Dartmoor, the representative of the Duchy authorities, sought to prevent this, and once attempted to throw down some walls the commoners had erected. But the latter were not disposed to allow their rights to be interfered with, and mustering in force repelled the invaders. On one face of the stone in question are the letters S Z, with the figure 2 beneath them, and on the other the letters D C, and a similar figure. These stand for South Zeal and Duchy of Cornwall respectively, the figure being merely the number of the stone. Another of the stones may be seen near the corner of Skaigh, to the N.W. ; and a third hard by the enclosures to the S.E. South Tawton Church is about 1½ m. from the clatter in a north-easterly direction. The summit of Cosdon is rather over ½ m. distant.

(C). From South Zeal the lane leading to the road at Prospect Place, near Ramsleigh Mine, may be followed. The Place is a row of cottages erected in 1845, as a tablet in the wall shows. Here the road is crossed, and the visitor will then pass up the narrow way to the common, as described in our notice of the track to the Steeperton Brook (T. 41). When the common is reached he will leave the track and climb the hill R. ; on the way he will see the boundary stone at Rabbits' Holt which we have just noticed.

(D). From Clannaborough Down the route will be as in Ex. 18. On reaching the Cemetery the steep side of Cosdon, which rises abruptly from the plateau on which that monument is situated, must be scaled. The course will be nearly due W., and the distance from the rows to the beacon cairn on the summit about ½ m.

(E). From Ensworthy the course will be about N.W. Cross Forder Brook, and then make up over Shilstone Hill to the Blackaton

Brook, which will be struck where the Gallaven track (T. 42) runs beside it. Keep Cherriton Combe on the R., and in about ½ m. the peat road (T. 41) will be reached. The summit of the hill is about ½ m. beyond this.

(F). From White Moor Circle the peat road (T. 41) must be followed northward to the edge of Raybarrow Pool (Ex. 18), when the visitor will strike over the common L., his course being due N. Cosdon Beacon is less than 300 feet above this point, and about ¾ m. from it.

(G). From the ford at Small Brook the summit bears a little E. of N.E., and is some 550 feet above it. The way lies over White Hill, the distance being about 1 m. The ground is good, and the visitor will find no difficulty in reaching the beacon.

Ex. 18.—*Steeperton Track, Raybarrow Pool, White Moor Circle, Blackaton Brook, Cherriton Combe,* about 9 m. (EXTENSION to *Kennon Hill, White Moor Marsh, Shilstone Tor, and Clannaborough Down,* about 1½ m. further).

We leave Sticklepath by the eastern road, and after crossing the bridge over the Taw, of which there is mention in the Lydford Court Rolls of the time of Elizabeth, shall bear R. to Prospect Place. Here we turn R. into the Steeperton track, or Peat Road (T. 41), which we shall not desert until we reach the confines of the forest, 3 m. distant. On passing the Cemetery (*Cosdon Section*) we look down upon Cherriton Combe L., where is some rather miry ground, in which a little feeder of the Blackaton Brook takes its rise. Skirting the head of this our track, which as before observed is one of the best of similar paths on the moor, gradually ascends to Raybarrow Pool, ¾ m. further on, along the western edge of which it is carried. The so-called pool is really an extensive mire, one of the worst in the moorland region, and lies between the foot of the southern slope of Cosdon and that part of Throwleigh Common known as Kennon Hill. It is considerably over ½ m. in length from N. to S., but not quite ¼ m. in breadth, except in one place. It is very probable that this swampy flat once merited its name, and that it has been artificially drained by deepening the channel of the Blackaton Brook, which flows from it on the east. No stream runs into the mire, but it receives the drainage of a large area of moorland, and in very rainy season a little water gathers in one part of it. Its elevation is about 1,500 feet. It was into Raybarrow Pool that Sampson Bow, the moorman, drove the band of sheep-stealers who once made an old building called Cosdon House their haunt. One dark night, in an endeavour to escape capture, they attempted to cross the mire, but only succeeded in getting " stugged," as the moorman said when afterwards relating the circumstance. Soon after passing the mire we come in sight of White Moor Circle on the L.

(The route to Belstone from this circle is described in Ex. 17).

Our way lies past the circle to White Moor Stone, which is about 200 yards S.E. by E. of it (Ex. 17), and thence to a bondstone ¼ m. nearly due E. This stands close beside the track leading from Clanna-borough Down to Gallaven (T. 42). Here we turn northward, and follow the path along the eastern edge of Raybarrow Mire to the point where Blackaton Brook issues from it, Kennon Hill being on our R. By crossing the little stream just below its head, and following the path to another crossing-place, we shall avoid some miry ground, but on regaining the R. bank the former will become our sole companion. It will lead us past the point where the Cherriton Combe Water falls into it, and through Blackaton Hole, a romantic hollow, at the lower end of which is a small fording-place with a footpath climbing the steep L. bank. A little way down stream is the reach known as Shilley Pool, below which water is taken from the brook for use at Ramsleigh Mine.

(This mine is worked for copper. Among others in the district we are noticing may be mentioned Ivy Tor Mine, or Belstone Consols, Copper Hill Mine, and Halstock Mine).

[*Extension from White Moor Stone over Kennon Hill.* This will not greatly add to the length of our excursion. The first point will be the bondmark by the side of the Gallaven Track (T. 42), noticed above, whence we soon reach the summit of Kennon Hill (1,573 feet), ½ m. E.S.E. of the monolith. From this hill we have a good view of the commons that slope down to the North Teign, and of some of the principal points in the north-east part of the forest. Beyond the Teign, S.S.E., is seen Shovel Down (Ex. 20), with the enclosures and trees of Batworthy to the L. of it, and further away the commons rising towards that part of the moor over which runs the road between Moorgate (Ex. 21) and the Warren House Inn (Ex. 45). Two miles away to the S.S.W. is Watern Tor (Ex. 19), and 1½ m. S.W. Wild Tor (Ex. 19), backed by the high land that stretches away to the region of Cranmere. W.S.W. is Steeperton (Ex. 17), and due W., and 4 m. distant, High Willes (Ex. 15). Kennon Hill has a smooth grassy surface, with some scattered stones about its higher part. On its western side a few remains of an older day are met with, among them being the scanty vestiges of huts of the kind usually regarded as shepherds', or herdsmen's, shelters. On this side also are some mining gerts, one of which is known as Proctor's Gully, and another as London Pit. The hill is bounded on the S. by Ruelake Pit and Rival Tor (Ex. 19); on the W. by White Moor and Raybarrow Pool; on the N. by Blackaton Brook and Shilstone Hill; and on the E. by White Moor Bottom, in which is situated White Moor Marsh, the source of the Forder Brook. From the summit of Kennon the head of this marsh is ½ m. distant, and if we follow a S.E. by E. course we shall reach it where a small hollow is formed in the steep side of the shallow valley. This grassy dell was formerly a haunt of the elves of the moor, and is still called the Pixies' Parlour.

Crossing the head of White Moor Marsh we find ourselves at the foot of Buttern Hill, which forms the eastern side of the little valley, and which is noticed in our excursions from Chagford (Ex. 19), together with Creber Pound and other objects of interest in this locality. Extending northward from this hill to Blackaton Brook are Ensworthy Hill, forming, like Buttern, a part of the common lands of Gidleigh, Shilstone Hill, and Clannaborough Down, the latter two belonging to Throwleigh Common. We pass down the hollow, with the marsh close on our L., and near its lower end shall observe the ruins of a mining hut of the usual rectangular form, and consisting of a central chamber with a smaller one on each side. On the slope are also the remains of a circle, which was apparently over 80 feet in diameter when in a complete state.   Only six of the stones are now standing, but the monument seems to have originally consisted of more than thirty.

Skirting Ensworthy Hill we shall cross the little Forder Brook where it bends R., and entering once more upon Throwleigh Common, shall direct our steps to Shilstone Tor, on the further side of a tiny feeder that comes down north-westward through Shilstone Combe. Shilstone Tor stands close to the road leading from Payne's Bridge to Creber Pound and Berry Down.   The pile, never a very large one, has unfortunately been rendered almost insignificant by the quarry-man.   There are two excavations in it from which stone has been taken, and many of the blocks composing it also show the marks of the bars used in splitting them.   But this destruction by the road-mender is not all ; it has been sought to rob the tor of its name also. It is rather amusing to read that a late antiquary " identified " this pi! with the Hound Tor (Ex. 17) of the perambulators, and to note that his fanciful idea has been accepted by another writer in sketching the bounds of the forest.   There is not the slightest proof that this tor ever bore any other name than that by which it is now known, or that the perambulators ever came within two miles of it.   But the " identi-fication " was necessary in order to support a view that the forest was much larger in 1240 than it is at present.   It was desired to show that the perambulators drew their line from Cosdon to this point, but as they have distinctly recorded that they drew it to Hound Tor, this could only be done by giving the name of the latter to Shilstone Tor. The process is a beautifully simple one, and if carried out on a generous scale it would be easy to show that every tor on Dartmoor was once within the forest.   It has also been applied in another place, as we shall see later on, where a new name has been given to a stream in order to bring it in as a boundary (Ex. 21).

Near Shilstone Tor is the entrance to the farm of the same name, noticed in S. Ex. 46.

It is not only the destruction of natural objects that has taken place on this common.   The remains of erections of an old-time people have also suffered much at the hands of roadmen and wall builders, among others what appears to have been an enclosure very similar to one existing near Sharp Tor above East Combe on the Dart (Ex. 41), although the wall was not quite of the same character.   The moormen, it is said, used to refer to it as a pound, which name, indeed, they give to all ancient enclosures of larger size than the hut circles, and by which they mean a place where cattle could be driven for shelter and protection.   No trace of this now exists, but vestiges of other remains are numerous on every part of Shilston Hill and Clannaborough Down. These we shall meet with as we make our way across the commons in a north-westerly direction from the tor.   They consist chiefly of a number of reaves and hut circles, some of the latter being of large size, but they are so much overgrown with short furze and heather, as to be undiscernible until the rambler comes close upon them.   In one place two of the reaves run parallel for a considerable distance, the space between them being about the width of an ordinary roadway. Still further N.W. there are others, while hut circles are also numerous on the down due N. of the tor.

When we have proceeded about ½ m. we shall cross the Gallaven

Track (T. 42), as it runs up over Clannaborough Down, and a short distance beyond this is Blackaton Brook. We pass onward to the little crossing-place over the stream above Shilley Pool.]

On crossing Blackaton Brook we once more find ourselves on South Tawton Common, with Cherriton Combe on the L. Our course will now be about N.N.W. from the fording-place. Not very far from the brook, and a little S. of E. of East Week (the group of thatched cottages seen across the shallow valley), are two stones, their position seeming to indicate that they once formed part of a large circle, though this is not free from doubt. On the slope of the hill R., are a number of small modern farm enclosures, near which are the remains of a few hut circles. There were formerly many more of these, but they have been destroyed by the builders of the walls. About ½ m. from Blackaton Brook we shall strike the Steeperton Track (T. 41), near the Cemetery, which we shall follow northward, and where it forks turn down the hill R. to Prospect Place, thence returning to Sticklepath by the road by which we set out.

[An alternative route from Shilstone Tor, or from Shilley Pool, is by way of Payne's Bridge. In the former case the road near the tor is followed northward to the bridge, which is 1 m. distant ; in the latter Blackaton Brook is traced downward for rather less than ½ m. The distance from the bridge to Prospect Place is 1¼ m. See S. Ex. 44 and 45.]

SHORTER EXCURSIONS.

(FROM OKEHAMPTON).

S. Ex. 34.—*Sourton Down and Prewley Moor,* 9 m. Leaving the town by way of the West Bridge the visitor will follow the Tavistock road (passing the branch L. at 2¼ m. which leads to Meldon) to a point on what was formerly a part of Sourton Down. Here on the and 3½ m. from the town, where the Hatherleigh road diverges, is a guide-stone, and a little further on, but on the L., a fine granite cross over 8 feet in height. [*Crosses*, Chap. XI.] It will be noticed that the arms are very short, and this, and the fact that it bears a Romano-British inscription, will probably justify us in supposing that it was fashioned out of a menhir. The latter, which is cut lengthwise on the shaft, is apparently to the memory of Princip. The cross has also been made to serve a similar purpose to that of the guide-stone, letters indicating the direction of Hatherleigh, Okehampton, Tavistock, and Launceston, being cut upon it. Proceeding southward along the road, past the spot where Jockey Down's House formerly stood, the rambler soon reaches Prewley Moor (T. 32, Ex. 13), and ¾ m. from the cross will pass under the railway, and make his way up the common. He will not, however, follow the track running out to Kitty Tor (T. 32), but will keep rather near to the enclosures on the L. Soon after Prewley farmhouse is passed, which is situated on the verge of the common on that side, a track will be struck near where it leaves the moor. This is the King Way (T. 26), which comes down to this point from Iron Gates (Ex. 13). Turning into this ancient path the rambler will follow it down the hill northward past Higher Bowden to Meldon, which is reached just after passing under the railway.

(The road running R. leads to Meldon Down, Ex. 14). ¾ m. beyond the hamlet the rambler will reach the road by which he left Okehampton, at a point 2¼ m. from the town.

S. Ex. 35.—*Meldon Gorge.* A, 6½ m. ; B, 8 m. ; C, *including the Island of Rocks*, 10 m. By the Tavistock road as in the preceding excursion for 2¼ m. ; then bear up the hill L. to Meldon. (A) Down the path, eastward, to Burrow Cleave (Ex. 14) ; thence by the track under the viaduct (T. 33), and through Meldon Quarry, to Higher Bowden Steps, ¾ m., the Ockment being L. and Meldon Down R. Cross the river at the steps, and turn L., following the track (T. 33) under the viaduct to Okehampton Park. Thence to the town by the path, the route being the reverse of that described at the beginning of Ex. 14. (B) From the stepping-stones down to where the Redaven falls into the Ockment. Cross this tributary, and ascend the road R., with the enclosures on the L. Keep these on that side, and follow the road eastward across Black Down. In rather over 1½ m. Anthony Stile will be reached, near which is a small building. This is the filtering-house connected with the Okehampton water supply, which is taken from the Redaven. Follow the track between the wall L., and Moor Brook R., to Moor Gate. (C) From Meldon up the road towards the railway ; take the *first* turning L. under the bridge ; thence by the lane to Meldon Down, ¼ m. distant. From the moor gate a track descends to Higher Bowden Steps (T. 33), but the rambler will keep this on his L., and not descend far below the brow of the hill. By so doing he will strike an old disused water-course, which now serves as a path, and this he will follow along the side of South Down for about 1 m., to the point where the little Vellake comes down on the R. The scenery is described in Ex. 14. A short distance above this is the Island of Rocks, whence the rambler may make his way to Shilstone Tor, on the slope of the hill to the S. From this group of rocks he will return to the Vellake, reaching it, however, a few hundred yards above the confluence. Passing up the hill, with the enclosures close to him on the R., he will soon reach the King Way where it comes down from Iron Gates, as described in S. Ex. 34. From this point he will follow the directions given in that excursion.

The West Ockment from Sandy Ford downward (Ex. 14) forms the boundary between the commons of Okehampton and those in Sourton parish. At Vellake Corner the boundary line leaves the Ockment and runs up the little stream, and is continued on to Iron Gates (Ex. 13), where, forming an acute angle, it turns back to the point where the King Way enters on the enclosed lands. A wedge-shaped tract is thus cut out of the Sourton common lands, and to account for this erratic course of the boundary line the story often attached to spots where a similar curious arrangement occurs is related. This is to the effect that the dead body of a strange man was found on the common belonging to Sourton, but the people of that parish refusing to give it burial it was interred by the men of Okehampton, and as a consequence that part of the moor was afterwards claimed by them.* A similar story is related in other parts of Dartmoor.

---

* I have referred to this in my account of the Okehampton Com-

The Glazes are said to have been lost to Brent in this manner (Ex. 31), and the parish of Shaugh thrusts its boundaries into the forest on a like pretence (Ex. 34).

S. Ex. 36.—*Black Tor*, 9 m.   To Meldon Gorge through the Park as in Ex. 14. On crossing the Redaven we shall leave the Ockment and ascend Longstone Hill L., by following the upward track (T. 33). When it bends sharply L. we leave it, and striking a little E. of S. shall soon reach the Fishcombe Water, often called the Homerton Brook. This stream we shall then follow to its source, a charming spot named Fishcombe Head, where a few dwarf oaks grow among scattered rocks, and at a considerable height above the gorge. About ¾ m. distant, in a direction S. by E., is Black Tor, consisting of three fine piles, from which there is a grand view of the deep valley of the West Ockment. This tor is seen from Cranmere Pool. Against one of the piles a small shelter is reared, for use during the artillery firing. Forsland Ledge is seen on the brow of the hill ¾ m. S.E. On leaving the tor the visitor will strike N.E., and crossing the common under Willes and Yes Tor, will reach the ford on the Redaven in about 1½ m. From that point he will follow the track to Moor Gate as described in Ex. 15. Redaven Ford is 1 m. E.N.E. of Fishcombe Head.

S. Ex. 37.—*The Blackaven and Dinger Tor*, 10 m.   To New Bridge as in Ex. 16 (T. 35). We do not cross the stream, but continue our way up the L. bank to Curtory Clitters, and on to Blackaven Head. About ½ m. beyond this, in a S.S.W. direction, is the source of Brim Brook. On reaching this we follow the little stream downward for a short distance, when we shall come upon a miners' hut on the L. bank. It is of the usual type, and is 17½ feet by 11 feet on the inside, the walls being between 3 feet and 4 feet in height. Below it, and on the same side of the stream, is another ; this is rather smaller, being only 16 feet by 7 feet, but is a better example. These buildings are 3¼ m. from Moor Gate by the route we have followed. On leaving them we strike northward, ascending the hill to Dinger Tor, less than ½ m. distant. E. of this we strike the track noticed in Ex. 15 (T. 34), and shall follow it back to Moor Gate.

S. Ex. 38.—*West Mil Tor and Row Tor*, 6½ m.   To Redaven Dip as in Ex. 15. Then strike L. to West Mil Tor, and passing over this, cross the head of Creaber's Hole to Row Tor. From thence N.E. to the track running to New Bridge, which follow N. to Moor Gate.

S. Ex. 39.—*Crovenor Steps*, 5½ m.   To Moor Gate as in Ex. 15. Then follow the camp road, with the enclosures of Pudhanger L., to Halstock Down. The road bears L. to Crovenor Steps, on the East Ockment. From this point the return may be made by way of Halstock as described in Ex. 16.

---

mons in the new edition of Bridges' book already mentioned. Mr. J. D. Prickman informs me that it used to be said that the body was discovered by a dog. Some time ago he took the trouble to search the registers of Okehampton and Sourton, but found that the only recorded burial of an unknown person related to a woman, and that there was no entry confirmatory of the story.

The Chapel of Halstock may be visited on the return route. The direct route to it from Okehampton is given in our notice of the path between that place and Belstone.

S. Ex. 40.—*Ancient Camp near Ashbury Tor*, 3½ m.   To the brow of the hill near Fitz's Well. We then enter the gate on the L. as in going to Halstock (T. 36), but instead of following the road thither we strike across East Hill, our course being a little N. of E. On the R. is Halstock Cleave, through which Moor Brook runs to join the Ockment. Passing over Heather Knoll we reach the mounds known as The Camp, which the Rev. H. G. Fothergill, who made an examination of them in 1840, thought to consist of British, Danish, and Roman remains. He considered that he found the first two periods represented by some ramparts overlooking Moor Brook, and the latter by the rectangular enclosures adjoining these on the N. Close by is Ashbury Tor, beautifully draped with climbing plants, and half hidden amid heather. The spot is altogether very charming, and the visitor should by no means omit to include it in his rambles. A fine view of Belstone West Cleave is obtained from the rocks. We may return to the hill near the station by striking over the down N.W.

(From Belstone).

S. Ex. 41.—*The West Cleave and Nine Maidens*, 3½ m.   We leave by the road running N.W. from Belstone Church, and at the distance of ½ m. shall reach the entrance to the old Belstone Rectory, L. A short distance inside the gate, and built into the wall on the R., is a stone with some curious markings, which I have elsewhere noticed. [*Crosses*, Chap. XI.]   It is about four feet high, and among the devices incised upon it is a circle enclosing a cross. Passing onward from the gate we take the first turning L., which will lead us to the common. On the brow of the hill is Cleave Tor, or Cleave Rocks, as the mass is more often called, which it will be readily seen is not of granite formation. A fine view is obtained from it of Halstock Cleave on the further side of the Ockment, and of Ashbury Tor (S. Ex. 40). Our next point will be Chapel Ford, to which the track running near the rock goes direct (T. 36), but this will not now be the route we shall follow. The valley, or West Cleave as it is called [*Gems*, Chap. V.], is worth seeing, and we shall therefore descend its steep side to the Ockment, reaching the stream a short distance below the point where Moor Brook flows out of Halstock Cleave to join it. There is a fine cascade on the river here. We pass up stream, presently reaching Chapel Ford, whence the path already described (T. 36) runs up through Halstock Woods. But we still follow the Ockment, and when we have gone a little further up the valley shall come in sight of Skir Tor. Soon after passing the higher end of the woods we reach the pile ; it is not far from the track leading from Belstone to Crovenor Steps (T. 37, Ex. 16), and opposite to a farm on the W. side of the river known as East Bowden. Striking E. from the tor into the track we follow it upwards, turning aside R. shortly before reaching Watchet Hill, to the circle called the Nine Stones, and sometimes the Nine Maidens. But as a matter of fact there are 17 of these, and thus the circle is sometimes known as the Seventeen Brothers. The circle, which is not of great size, probably surrounded a kistvaen, though no vestiges of such are now visible ;

the stones composing it are rather small. More than one story attaches to it. It is said that these lumps of granite were once creatures of flesh and blood—a band of merry maidens, who met here to dance upon a Sunday. For this wicked act they were turned into stone, and are compelled to dance every day at noon. That they do so may plainly be seen *when the conditions are favourable. Maiden* is, of course, a corruption of *maen.* On reaching the moor gate we descend the lane to Belstone.

S. Ex. 42.—*The Belstone Ridge and Taw Plain,* 6 m. Up the lane to Watchet Hill, as in Ex. 17. Thence southward along the ridge to Ock Tor, 2¼ m. from the village. Descend L. to the Taw, which will be struck at its confluence with the Steeperton Brook. Pass up the R. bank of the latter stream for about ¼ m., then turn N.E. over Metheral Hill to the source of Small Brook, which follow downward to the Taw. Down the bank of that river to the fords (Ex. 17), and thence to Belstone by the track through Birchy Lake.

(Steeperton and Knock Mine Bridge are noticed in Ex. 17).

For White Moor Circle, Wild Tor, and Watern Tor, see Ex. 17, 19.

The routes to the summit of Cosdon are given in the section dealing with that hill.

For direct route from Belstone to Throwleigh see S. Ex. 47.

(FROM STICKLEPATH).

S. Ex. 43.—*South Tawton, Oxenham, and South Zeal,* 3½ m. We take the eastern road from the village as in Ex. 18, but on crossing the bridge instead of turning R., or keeping straight on to South Zeal, shall strike into a narrow lane L. This will bring us to South Tawton, ¾ m. distant, a charming example of a Dartmoor border village, with its playstow and ancient tree. (About 3 m. distant, on the road to North Tawton, is the fine old mansion of North Week, or Wyke.)

Taking the road to the mill E., the visitor will pass this and ascend the hill to Oxenham Cross, of which monument, however, only a small fragment now remains. This stands in the hedge L. [*Crosses,* Chap. XII.] Just beyond this on the R. is the entrance to Oxenham, an eighteenth century farmhouse built on, or near, the site of the ancient mansion of that name. With the family of Oxenham was connected the tradition of the White Bird, the notice of which in Howel's *Familiar Letters* has been so often quoted. The White Bird was said to appear as a forewarning of the death of the head of the family, and sometimes of that of other of its members. There are many accounts of the appearance of this mysterious visitor between 1618 and 1873. " How Mr. Oxenham saw the White Bird " will be well remembered by all readers of *Westward Ho!* A poem has also been written on the subject.

(If the rambler desires he may extend his walk along the lane for about ½ m. beyond the entrance to Oxenham to Ringhole Copse, at the eastern end of which is a very fine wayside cross).

Turning from Oxenham Cross the visitor will strike into the lane opposite to it, and running S., which will bring him in about 1 m. to the village of South Zeal. The way now lies through the one long street of which the place mainly consists, one part of which ascends the hill north-westward. Formerly this was the coach road, but in a later time a new road was cut, and the descent into South Zeal and the climb out of it thus avoided. The latter is the one running by Prospect Place (*Cosdon Section*) to Ramsleigh Mine, where it turns abruptly to the east, and joins the Exeter road again about ¾ m. E. of the village, and not far from a little common called Firestone Ley. Most of the houses in South Zeal are covered with thatch, and have a pleasing old-world air. Part way up the hill on the L. is the Chapel of St. Mary and St. Thomas, and near it an ancient cross set in a socket-stone on a calvary consisting of three steps. A small panel will be observed on this base, in which are some faint markings. This inscription was the work of a native of the place called John Stanbury. [*Crosses*, Chap. XII.] In 1298 Robert de Toeny, then the holder of the manor, granted to the inhabitants of South Zeal the right to hold a market and two fairs annually.

Passing up the steep street the visitor will reach Zeal Head Cross, or, as it is sometimes called, Townsend Cross, ¼ m. above the chapel. This is now only a cross road, but formerly a monument of the kind indicated by the name stood here, but is said to have been destroyed by a man named John Orchard, who lived at Ford Farm. Still following the road the visitor will in less than ½ m. reach the bridge at Sticklepath.

S. Ex. 44.—*Dishcombe and West Week*, 4½ m. As in the last excursion the visitor will cross the Taw and bear L. to South Tawton village. Thence he will follow the road leading to South Zeal as far as Moon's Cross, the remains of which stand on a small open space in front of an old barn. Here the road forks, the point being a very important one. Travellers from the north would here branch off according as they were journeying along the northern or the eastern edge of the moor. Our way will lie to the L., and following the road south-eastward we shall leave the village of Zeal on our R., and ¾ m. from the cross shall pass Dishcombe, and ascend the hill to the Exeter road a little to the E. of its junction with the new one running on to Ramsleigh Mine. We cross this and enter a narrow lane, shortly reaching a gate on the R. Passing through this we find ourselves in a rough bridle-path, forming one of the means of approach to West Week. This ancient house, one of the most interesting in this part of the Dartmoor borderland, was formerly the seat of the Wyke, or Weekes, family, and also of the Battishills. There is a fine old embattled gateway, on which is carved the coat of the last-named and the date 1656. Opposite to this are the remains of an old cross placed under a tree. Readers of *John Herring* will remember that it was to West Week that the father of Mirelle was taken after the carriage accident. In full view from the house is the slope down which rolled old Cobbledick's barrel.

The way will now take the visitor past the house and by some fine old trees to a narrow lane leading down to the main road. On reaching this he will turn R., and passing Ramsleigh Mine and Prospect Place will return to Sticklepath.

S. Ex. 45.—*Cherriton Combe and Payne's Bridge*, 5½ m. To Ford as in the ascent of Cosdon, but on turning L. when leaving the little stream keep straight on, between the enclosures, instead of again turning R. up to the common (T. 41). Keep a southerly course (there are a few turnings here), and soon the peat road coming up from Prospect Place (T. 41) will be entered upon. Follow this to the Cemetery (*Cosdon Section*), and leaving it there, strike south-eastward over the common, keeping Cherriton Combe on the R. (*Cosdon Section*, Ex. 18). On reaching Blackaton Brook cross it and follow the R. bank down to Payne's Bridge, passing Shilley Pool (Ex. 18) on the way. From this part of the common the hamlet of East Week, mentioned in Ex. 18, is in full view. The road running through it goes on to Gooseford, or Goosaford as it is called in the locality, and thence to the Exeter road near the little village of Whiddon Down. L. of East Week is the farm of Middle Week, and below it, and nearer to the visitor, is Clannaborough Wood. At the head of this Blackaton Brook makes a bend ; its course changing from about N.E. to S.E.

The visitor will cross Payne's Bridge, a small one-arched structure, and follow the road northward to the entrance to West Week, whence he will return to Sticklepath by the road as in S. Ex. 44.

S. Ex. 46.—*Throwleigh*, 7½ m. Crossing the Taw the visitor will bear R. as in S. Ex. 45, and follow the road past Prospect Place and Ramsleigh Mine to the entrance to West Week. About 100 yards beyond this the road forks, the L. branch going on through East Week and Goosaford (see Ex. 45), and the R. to Throwleigh and Gidleigh, The visitor will choose the latter, and speedily reach Payne's Bridge, the route up to this point being the reverse of the latter part of the last excursion. Just beyond the bridge, and not far from a dwelling-house which is seen on the side of the hill R., the road to Throwleigh branches off L., the other running on past Shilstone to Creber Pound and Berry Down. (See *Road Distances*). Striking into this L. branch the visitor will soon reach Clannaborough Farm on the verge of the common, where he will enter upon the enclosed lands. A little further on a footpath runs across some fields R. direct to Throwleigh village ; the lane will lead the visitor through a part of Clannaborough Copse. Throwleigh Church is on the R. as the village is entered. It possesses several features worthy of notice ; there is a very fine priest's doorway, and the carving of the ribs and bosses of the roof is good. There is also a granite tomb in the north wall of the chancel, but as it bears no inscription much of its interest is unfortunately lost. The lich gate is ancient, as also is the church house near it. A few score yards eastward is an open space usually known as Throwleigh Barton Cross, in the centre of which is a granite cross standing on a low calvary of the same, formed by three steps. It was erected, as the inscription upon it shows, in 1897. Only the base, or socket-stone, is ancient. [*Crosses*, Chap. XIII.] From the gate of the churchyard a lane runs southward up the hill to Shilstone Farm (Ex. 18), on the verge of the common. This the visitor will follow, taking care not to turn L. at the southern corner of the graveyard into Deave Lane. Shilstone is rather less than ¾ m. from the village. The farmhouse, like most of the older border dwellings, is surrounded by some fine trees, and is a good specimen of the habitations of the yeomen of two or three centuries since.

From the farm the rambler will pass on to the common, where he will find himself close to Shilstone Tor, from which point he may return to Sticklepath by either of the routes described in Ex. 18 and S. Ex. 45. If the latter, *via* Payne's Bridge, the distance will be about ¾ m. less.

(THROWLEIGH TO BELSTONE).

S. Ex. 47.—*Via White Moor Stone*, 6.m. The first point will be Shilstone Farm. The rambler will strike W. by S. up over Shilstone Hill, leaving White Moor Marsh L., to Kennon Hill (Ex. 18). This he will cross to the bondstone on the Gallaven track (T. 42), and thence proceed westward to White Moor Stone. Directions for reaching Belstone from this object are given in Ex. 17, but Brook Hill and White Hill may be left a little to the R. in descending to the fords on the Taw. The straight course to these from White Moor Circle is N.W. by N.

Via North end of Raybarrow Pool, 5 m. This, the more direct route, passes exactly 1 m. N. of White Moor Stone. From Shilstone Farm the course is W.N.W. by W. Blackaton Brook is crossed at, or near, the lower ford of the Gallaven track (T. 42), and the Peat Road (T. 41) a little to the northward of Raybarrow Pool. The next point is White Hill, whence the rambler descends to the fords on the Taw (Ex. 17), leaving Taw Marsh on his L. There is no difficulty in striking a bee-line, the ground being good throughout the whole distance. Conversely the points from Belstone will be the fords above Birchy Lake ; thence E.S.E. to the summit of White Hill ; thence, following the same course, to the northern end of Raybarrow Pool ; and then bearing a trifle more E. to the Blackaton Brook and Shilstone Farm.

ROUTES FROM OKEHAMPTON.

R. 24.—To Chagford and Moreton, S.E. by E. (A) *Crovenor Steps, Fords on the Taw, North end of Raybarrow Pool, Shilstone Tor*, thence by road. *C*, 11 m. ; *M*, 15½ m. Reverse, R. 38 A. (B) *Crovenor Steps, Small Brook Foot, White Moor Stone, Berry Down*, thence by road. Distance about the same. Reverse, R. 38 B.

[Objects : Exs. 16, 17, 18, 19.]

From Belstone the route will lie (A) through Birchy Lake to the fords on the Taw, 1½ m. (B) to Small Brook Foot, ¼ m. further up the stream. In the latter case it will be well not to cross the Taw until arriving at Small Brook, and so avoid the marsh on the R. bank. The distance is about 2 m. less than from Okehampton.

From Sticklepath the road is followed to Payne's Bridge as in S. Ex. 46, thence keeping R. at the fork just beyond it to Shilstone Tor. *C*, 7¾ m. ; *M*, 12¼ m.

(A) Setting out from the town the rambler will first make his way to the brow of the hill near Fitz's Well, as in Ex. 15, and thence by the gate L. to Halstock, as described in the route to Belstone, T. 36. On reaching the entrance to Chapel Lands the road running to the moor gate near Halstock Pound is followed, from which point a short track runs S. past Halstock Corner to Kelly's Corner, where is a stone marking the boundary of land belonging to the parish of Lydford, and lying outside the forest limits as now recognized. The next point is Crovenor Steps, ¼ m. S.S.E., and the road is then followed up the hill to Winter Tor, with Higher Tor L. (Ex. 17). From Winter Tor the rambler will descend to the fords on the Taw, rather over ½ m. E. From this point the directions for reaching Shilstone Tor as given in S. Ex. 47 must be followed. Here the road will be struck, and the rambler will turn S., reaching Forder Bridge in ¼ m. Forder Brook is a small tributary of Blackaton Brook, falling into it at Blackaton Bridge, not far from the hamlet of Providence Place. Soon after crossing the brook Great and Little Ensworthy Farms are passed L. ; Buttern House is seen on the moor R. A little further on the road enters the enclosures at Moortown, and here it forks. The R. branch must be followed for ¼ m. to the entrance to Thule. Turn into this to the farm L., whence a footpath across some fields runs S.E. towards Gidleigh. This will bring the rambler to the steep hill down which he will pass for a few yards, and then turn R. The old manor pound will be seen L., and just beyond it is Gidleigh village, from which the road will be followed to Highbury Bridge, where Blackaton Brook is crossed. It then ascends to Murchington, 1¼ m. from Gidleigh, and runs down Walland Hill to Chagford Bridge. This part of the road is noticed in our account of Chagford District.

(B) To Crovenor Steps and Winter Tor as in the preceding route. Thence down the hill S.E. to Small Brook Foot (Ex. 17), and up Metheral Hill, with Small Brook L. and Steeperton Brook R., the course being the same until abreast of the source of the former, when the rambler will bend a little L., and on reaching the top of Hound Tor Ridge will pass the White Moor Circle L., and make his way to White Moor Stone (Ex. 17). The course will now be S.E. by E. across the shoulder of Kennon Hill, the head of White Moor Bottom, and Buttern Down, to the stroll above Berry Down (Ex. 19), a distance of 2 m. (Buttern Down is noticed in Exs. 18, 19). At the bottom of Berry Down Stroll, which is referred to in the Chagford District, the rambler will turn into the lane R., and passing Berry Down Farm, will descend the hill, with Gidleigh village L., to Highbury Bridge, whence he will proceed to Chagford as in the former route.

The road from Chagford to Moreton is described in the account of that district.

R. 25.—To Bovey Tracey, S.E. by E. The best route is through Chagford, following the instructions given in R. 24, 31. 22 m. Reverse, R. 46, 38. But should the rambler prefer to go by way of the moor instead of partly through lanes, the directions for doing so are here furnished.

White Moor Stone, Teign Clapper, South Teign, Bovey River, Hookney Down, Heathercombe, Heytree Cross, Swine Down Gate, Leighon, Trendlebere Down, Lower Down Cross. Distance about the same. Reverse, R. 45.

Visitors from Belstone and Sticklepath will join these routes as in R. 24, except that if the moor route be chosen those from Sticklepath will leave the road at Ensworthy, and strike S. across the side of Buttern Hill to the Creber enclosures, passing between them L., and a newtake, disconnected with others, on the hillside R. Still keeping S. Teign Clapper will be reached from this point in about 1 m.

[Objects : Exs. 17 to 24.]

For the first few miles the route will be the same as R. 24 B, but on reaching the side of Kennon Hill after leaving White Moor Stone (Ex. 17), the rambler will bear S.E., a course that will bring him in about 2 m. to the great stone circle on Scorhill Down (Ex. 19). Near this is Teign Clapper, where he will cross the North Teign immediately

below where it receives the Walla Brook.   The course is then up the hill
S.S.E. to Shovel Down, with the Batworthy enclosures L., and across
the site of the stone remains described in Ex. 20.   Beyond Batworthy
Corner, still following the same course with Kes Tor L., the rambler
will make his way to the Long Stone, 1¼ m. from the circle at Scorhill.
Thence the way lies down the hill to the South Teign.   If this cannot
be crossed here it must be followed up for a short distance to Fernworthy Bridge (Ex. 20), when the rambler will make his way back by
the road to the wall of the Metheral enclosures, and at the corner of
these, where it turns abruptly to the L. near a rivulet, will leave it
and strike up over the common, his course being due S.   He must
avoid keeping to the L. of this line, as should he do so he will strike
Metheral Bogs (S. Ex. 58).   When abreast of the head of this mire
the course must be changed to E.S.E., and followed for over 3 m. to
Heathercombe.   First the valley of the Bovey River, or as it is usually
called in this part of its course, the Hurston Water, is crossed ; then
the Princetown and Moreton road ; then (about ¾ m. further on) the
Challacombe road ; and then Hookney Down.   This should bring the
rambler to King's Barrow, a small tumulus near to which is a kistvaen
(Ex. 22).   Rather over ½ m. beyond this, the course being still E.S.E.,
is Heathercombe (S. Ex. 62), where the rambler will enter upon a lane.
This is followed past Heytree to Heytree Cross, about ¾ m., where the
rambler will turn R. into the Ashburton road.   This will lead him
along the edge of Cripdon Down and Swine Down to Swine Down Gate,
locally Swallerton Gate, 1½ m. from the cross road (Ex. 24).   Passing
through this he will turn L. and follow a narrow lane leading down
into the valley of the Becky Brook.   Hound Tor is seen boldly placed
on the hill R.   Soon after entering upon the enclosed land, a narrow
road branches L. to Great Hound Tor Farm, but the rambler will bear
R. to the stream.   There he will cross Leighon Bridge, and make his
way up the hill past the house of that name to the common, and follow
the road for rather over ½ m. to another that comes L. from Manaton.
This he will cross, and striking a little S. of E. over the down, will
descend the hill to a corner of Yarner Wood, about ¾ m. distant, where
he will find himself on the Lower Terrace Drive.   Turning R. into this
he will be led over Trendlebere Down to the east side of the wood.
Keep R. to the guide-post near one of the entrances to Yarner.   (The
house was once known as Chad Wycke).   Here the road runs along
the foot of Lower Down for nearly 1 m. to Lower Down Cross.   At
this point the rambler will turn down the hill L., and in about ¾ m.
will reach Bovey Station.

R. 26.—To Ashburton, S.E. by S. *White Moor Stone, Teign
Clapper, South Teign, Warren House Inn, Grendon Bridge, Bittleford
Down, Cockingford, Buckland-in-the-Moor*, 22½ m.   Reverse, R. 52.

Belstone and Sticklepath visitors will join this route as described
in R. 25.

[Objects : Exs. 17 to 22, 44 and 26.]

For the first 10 miles this route is identical with R. 25 (the moor
route), but when the rambler is abreast of the head of Metheral Bogs,
his course, instead of being changed to E.S.E., will lie over Hurston
Ridge and the E. slope of Watern Hill, a little E. of S.   This will bring
him in about 1¼ m. to the Warren House Inn, on the Princetown and
Moreton road.   Immediately in front of this hostelry a footpath runs

to Golden Dagger Mine, first crossing a leat and then the Walla Brook. The rambler will follow it until he has passed over the latter (less than ¼ m.) and will then turn due S. This course will take him over Soussons Common to the Post Bridge and Widecombe road at the point known as Ephraim's Pinch (Ex. 44), 1½ m. distant. About midway he will pass a group of tumuli. On reaching the road he must turn L., or eastward, and descending Ephraim's Pinch, follow it to Grendon Bridge on the West Webburn. The way then lies by Hill Head to Lower Blackaton, as in R. 5, C. Here the Broadford Brook is crossed, and the road R. is followed southward over Bittaford Down. (Pass three turnings R. See R. 33). Near the S.E. corner of this it joins the road from Ponsworthy to Widecombe. Here the rambler turns L. for a few hundred yards, and then down the hill R. to Cockingford (R. 5 A). ½ m. beyond this is a turning R. into which the rambler will strike, and will be led in 1 m. to the church of Buckland-in-the-Moor. From this point Ashburton is 3½ m. distant, the road, which is noticed in the account of that district, running in a south-easterly direction.

R. 27.—To Brent and Ivybridge, S.S.E. to S. by E. *New Bridge, Ockment Hill, Cranmere, East Dart Valley, Broad Down, Hollow Combe, Muddy Lakes, Prince Hall Bridge, Fox Tor Black Lane, Red Lake Ford, Western Whitaburrow, Shipley, Brent.* (To Ivybridge from Black Lane : *Erme Head, Green Bottom, Valley of the Erme, Harford Bridge*). To Brent, 26 m. ; to Ivybridge, 27 m. Reverse, R. 63. To Cornwood see R. 28.

Visitors from Belstone and Sticklepath will join this route at Cranmere (C.R. 10).

[Objects are noticed in Exs. 15 and 16 ; in C.R. 9 and 17 ; and Exs. 45, 46, 3, 4, 30, and 33.]

The first part of this route in described in Ex. 16 and C.R. 9, which together give directions for reaching Cranmere Pool, and in C.R. 17, which will show the way from the pool down the upper valley of the East Dart. But on reaching Sandy Hole (Ex. 45) the directions given in C. R. 17 must no longer be followed. The rambler must there leave the river and strike due S. across Broad Down for 1 m., when he will reach Hollow Combe, through which the Cherry Brook runs. He will cross this just where the great reave (Ex. 46) is seen running up the precipitous side of the hill R. to Lower White Tor, and still follow-ing a course due S., with the Powder Mills Cottages L., will in 2 m. reach the Princetown and Moreton road. This must be crossed, and a course still due S. be kept over Muddy Lakes to Prince Hall Lodge, about 1 m. distant. The rambler will then follow the road to Prince Hall Bridge, as described in Ex. 4. Passing a few hundred yards up the lane he will take the first turning R. and make his way by Moorlands to Tor Royal Newtake close by (Ex. 4). Here he will again turn due S., his point being Fox Tor, and in about 1½ m. will reach the Swin-combe River. He should strike this near the point where the Wheal Emma Leat is taken in from the stream, close to which is a ford (Ex. 3). From this crossing-place he may either make his way direct to Fox Tor, which he will see above him (with Childe's Tomb on the plain ground at its foot), or keep L. and follow up the stream towards the ruined Fox Tor farmhouse, and then ascend the hill with the tor R. Black Lane commences to the S. of the tor, and this will now form his path. (See T. 75, Ex. 3, and R. 7). On reaching the head of the great stream-work the rambler will find himself near Ducks' Pool, and on the route from Princetown to Brent, which latter is about 7½ m. in a south-easterly direction (R. 7), and to this he is referred. If his destination be Ivybridge, 8½ m. S., he will follow Dark Lake downward to the stream-work at Erme Head, from which point directions for reaching that place are given in R. 7.

R. 28.—To Cornwood, Plympton, and Shaugh. The first a little E. of S. ; the others a little W. of S. *Dinger Plain, Broad Amicombe Hole, Tavy Hole, Walkham Head, Rundle Stone, Princetown, Nosworthy Bridge, Sheeps Tor, Cadaford Bridge.* To Cornwood, 27 m. ; Plympton, 27 m. ; Shaugh, 24 m. Reverse, R. 70. This route is identical with R. 29 and R. 8, q.v.

R. 29.—To Princetown, with branch to Two Bridges, and routes from Belstone and Sticklepath, S. *Dinger Plain, Broad Amicombe Hole, Tavy Hole, Walkham Head, Rundle Stone, Princetown,* 15½ m. To Two Bridges *via* Walkham Head : *Conies Down, Lich Path, Cowsic Valley,* 14 m. From Belstone to Princetown, *via* Black-aven and Brim Brook, or *via* Taw Head and Little Kneeset, 14½ m. Belstone to Two Bridges : *Taw Head, East Dart Head, Broad Marsh, Broad Down, West Dart Valley,* 12½ m. ; from Taw Head *via* Cut Hill, 13 m. Reverses, R. 3.

[Objects : Exs. 15, 10, 6, 5, 11 ; and C.R. 2, 10, 17.]

The first point will be Moor Gate, whence the track to Dinger Plain (T. 34) will be followed as in Ex. 15, but will not be left until the rambler reaches Dinger Tor. The next point is Broad Amicombe Hole, the dip which will be seen to the R. of Great Kneeset (R. 3), but it will not be wise to make direct for it, as it may not be possible to cross the West Ockment so low down. We shall therefore strike S., and in ¾ m. shall reach Kneeset Nose, following the Brim Brook to the river, and near this shall have no difficulty in finding a crossing-place. On reaching the L. bank of the Ockment we make our way downward in a S.S.W. direction, to the bend ½ m. distant. We then leave the stream and climb the hill to Broad Amicombe Hole, ½ m., our course being altered to S.W. We now follow the infant Amicombe, which here runs due S., downward for 1 m., to where it receives the Cut Combe Water (Ex. 11, Extension), which is the second tributary flowing into it on the L. Here we cross the stream, and still pursuing a southerly course, shall pass over the shoulder of Fur Tor to Tavy Hole, ¾ m., which the rambler should reach just where the Fur Tor Brook runs into the Tavy. (Care must be taken not to keep too far up the side of Fur Tor on leaving the Amicombe, or the rambler will find himself amid a clatter, where progress will be slow ; nor must he keep too near the river, or he will get into boggy ground). If nothing is seen of the tiny Fur Tor Brook the rambler will be nearer than he ought to be to the Amicombe ; if he is higher than his line to the confluence should bring him, he will strike it shortly before reaching the Tavy. This, indeed, is as it should be, for the exact point he has to reach is ¼ m. above the confluence ; if he strikes the latter, therefore, he will follow up the Tavy for that distance. Looking back he should now see Fur Tor N.E. by N. The next point is Walkham Head (Ex. 10), but a straight course up the hill must not be followed, or the rambler will get into a bad piece of fen. (See R. 3). His line should be S.W. for about ½ m. and then he must turn due S., when he will pass over some old turf ties. and reach the stream in a little over ¼ m. This he will cross just above its first bend, and will shortly find himself on the old peat track that runs into Peter Tavy (T. 16). This passes down the shallow valley about ¼ m. from the L. bank of the stream, and must be followed for ¾ m. to the head of the Prison Leat, which will now become the rambler's guide. (See Ex. 5 and 6). It will lead him between Black Dunghill (L) and Great Mis Tor (R) to Rundle Stone (or the Prison enclosures near it), whence the road runs direct to Princetown.

To Two Bridges from Walkham Head. When rather less than ½ m. down the peat track (T. 16) the rambler must leave it and strike S.E., and in ¼ m. he will reach a ford on Spriddle Lake, where he will cross that little tributary. Soon after this, the course being the same, he will cross another rivulet in Nipper's Hole, a shallow hollow which branches from Spriddle Combe and runs up under Maiden Hill. From this point he will bear a trifle S. of S.E. and pass over Conies Down to the Lich Path (T. 18), rather over ½ m. distant. Crossing this old track he will make his way for another mile to the Cowsic, which he will strike below Broad Hole, 1 m. Two Bridges is about 2½ m. distant, the way thither being described in Ex. 5.

Belstone to Princetown. (A) *Via* Broad Amicombe Hole. This is the reverse of the branch described in R. 3. To the moor gate at Watchet Hill, and thence by the road S.W. to Crovenor Steps. Cross the East Ockment and follow the Blackaven to its source. Strike S.S.W. to Brim Brook Head, and trace that stream to the Ockment at Kneeset Nose. Here that river must be crossed and followed downward for ½ m. to the sharp bend as described above. (Another way is by Taw Head and Cranmere, C.R. 10, C.R. 1).

(B) *Via* Two Bridges. Taw Head as in C. R. 10. Then strike due S. over the fen, the plateau on the edge of which Cranmere Pool is situated being R. and Newtake (Ex. 19, Extension) on the L., to East Dart Head, the distance being under ½ m. Thence as in C. R. 2.

[Should the visitor desire to take in Cut Hill on his journey, he will leave Dart Head L. and strike S.W. by S. for ½ m. up the side of Black Hill, and then turn S. by W. The summit of Cut Hill is now about 1¼ m. distant, the way lying over Flatters, where the ground is seamed with narrow crevices. An easier way is to follow the Dart for about 1¼ m. from its source, when the summit of the hill will bear about W.S.W., and then to make for a point a little to the R. of it, crossing the Cut Hill stream, here a tiny rivulet trickling through the peat, on the way ; on reaching the top of the ridge bear L. and make straight for the summit. For a notice of the hill see Ex. 11, Extension, where also routes to Princetown and Two Bridges are given.]

R. 30.—To Lydford and Tavistock, S.W. by S.

(A) BY ROAD. (See road distances). To the fork 2¼ m. from the town ; take R. branch and pass under the railway bridge to the stone cross on the L. of the way (S. Ex. 34) ; Prewley Moor, Sourton, Lake, Southerly, Fox and Hounds. (Turn R. for Bridestowe Station), Vale Down, Dartmoor Inn. (Turn R. for Lydford). Skit Bridge,

Black Down, Lane Head, Wringworthy Hill, Tavistock.   16 m.
Reverse, R. 16 and 9 A.

[Objects : Ex. 15 to 9.]

(B) TO TAVISTOCK BY WAY OF THE MOOR. *Dinger Plain, Broad
Amicombe Hole, Tavy Hole, Walkham Head, Sandy Ford, Peter Tavy,*
18 m.   Reverse, R. 9 B.

[Objects : Exs. 15, 14, 10, 8.]

The route to Walkham Head is described in R. 29.   When the
rambler reaches the peat track (T. 16) on the east side of the Walkham,
he will follow it down to the first ford, immediately below Timber
Bridge (Ex. 10).   Here the stream is crossed, and the track followed up
the rising ground above the western bank, and through the cut between
Stooky Moor and Green Hill on the R., and Cocks' Hill on the L.   It
soon afterwards bends L. (Ex. 8, Extension), and the rambler following
it will have the enclosures above Wapsworthy (Ex. 8, Extension) on
his R.   He will then pass on by the Long Stone and Stephens' Grave,
as described in Ex. 8, to Twyste Lane, on making his way through
which his green track will lead him to the Godsworthy road.   Instructions are given in the excursion named for reaching Peter Tavy from
this point, and the road over Harford Bridge (see Road Distances) is
followed to Tavistock.

The rambler from Belstone will strike this route at Kneeset Nose.
His first point will be Crovenor Steps (T. 37), and he will then follow
the Blackaven to its source.   Thence S. by W. for $\frac{1}{2}$ m. to the head
of Brim Brook, which he will trace down to its confluence with the
West Ockment, at the Nose.

CHAGFORD AND MORETON DISTRICT.

These places are $4\frac{1}{2}$ miles apart, *via* Easton Cross, but as mentioned
post, the distance between them may be shortened by 1 mile if the road
by Great Week and Drewston is followed, which it may well be by
the pedestrian.   There is a regular road motor service between
Chagford and the G.W.R. Station at Moreton, 5 m., and also between
Chagford and Exeter, L.S.W.R.

DISTANCES : BY ROAD. *ASHBURTON, via* Beetor Cross
and Swine Down Gate, $12\frac{3}{4}$ m. from *C.* ; *via* North Bovey and Swine
Down Gate, $11\frac{1}{2}$ from *M.* *BARRAMOOR BRIDGE, C.,* $3\frac{1}{4}$; *M.,*
$3\frac{1}{4}$. *BECKY FALL, C.,* $7\frac{1}{2}$; *M.,* $4\frac{3}{4}$. *BEETOR CROSS, C.,* $2\frac{1}{2}$;
M., 3. *BELSTONE, C.,* $8\frac{1}{4}$; *M.,* $11\frac{1}{4}$. *BOVEY TRACEY, C.,* $10\frac{3}{4}$;
M., $6\frac{1}{4}$. *BRIDFORD, C.,* $9\frac{1}{2}$; *M.,* 5. *BUCKFASTLEIGH* (Ash-
burton road past Welstor Cross), *C.,* $15\frac{1}{4}$; *M.,* 14. *BUCKLAND-
IN-THE-MOOR, via* Widecombe, *C.,* 12 ; *M.,* 11. *CHRISTOW,*
C., 11 ; *M.,* 7. *CLIFFORD BRIDGE, C., via* Uppacott, $6\frac{1}{4}$; *M.,* $3\frac{1}{2}$.
CREDITON, C., 14 ; *M.,* 12. *DARTMEET, via* Two Bridges,
C., $15\frac{1}{2}$; *M.,* 17. *DREWSTEIGNTON, C.,* 4 ; *M., via* Easton, 6.
DUNSFORD, C., $8\frac{1}{4}$; *M.,* 5. *EASTON, C.,* $1\frac{1}{2}$; *M.,* 3. *EXETER,*
C., 15 ; *M.,* 12. *FERNWORTHY, C.,* $4\frac{1}{2}$; *M., via* Stiniel, $7\frac{1}{4}$.
FINGLE BRIDGE, C., $4\frac{1}{4}$; *M.,* $3\frac{1}{4}$. *GIDLEIGH, C.,* $2\frac{1}{2}$; *M., via*
Easton, 7. *GRENDON BRIDGE, C.,* $8\frac{1}{2}$; *M.,* 10. *GRIM'S POUND,*
C., $5\frac{1}{2}$; *M.* $5\frac{3}{4}$. *HEMSWORTHY GATE, C.,* $8\frac{1}{4}$; *M.,* 7. *HENNOCK,*
C., $10\frac{1}{2}$; *M.,* 6. *HEXWORTHY, C.,* $15\frac{3}{4}$; *M.,* $17\frac{1}{4}$. *ILSINGTON,*

C., 12½; *M.*, 8. *IVYBRIDGE*, *via* Buckfastleigh, *C.*, 25¼; *M.*, 24. *JURSTON GATE*, 2¾ from *C.* *LUSTLEIGH*, *C.*, 8; *M.*, 3½. *LYDFORD*, *C.*, 19¼; *M.*, 22¾. *MANATON*, *C.*, 6½; *M.*, 3¾. *METHERAL*, *C. M*, ¾ m. short of Fernworthy. *MOOR GATE*, *C.*, 3½; *M.*, 4. *NEWTON ABBOT*, *C.*, 16½; *M.*, 12. *NORTH BOVEY*, *C.*, 4¼; *M.*, 1¾. *OKEHAMPTON*, *C.*, 10¼; *M.*, 13¾. *PLYMOUTH*, *via* Princetown, *C.*, 26¾; *M.*, 28¼. *PLYMPTON*, *via* Princetown, *C.*, 26; *M.*, 27½. *POST BRIDGE*, *C.*, 7; *M.*, 8½. *PRINCETOWN*, *C.*, 12; *M.*, 13½. *SANDY PARK*, *C.*, 1½; *M.*, 3¾. *SOUTH BRENT*, *C*, 20¼; *M.*, 19. *SOUTH TAWTON*, *C. M.*, ½ m. beyond South Zeal. *SOUTH ZEAL*, *C.*, 6¼; *M.*, 9¾. *STICKLEPATH*, *via* Throwleigh, *C.*, 6¾; *M.*, 10¼. *SWINE DOWN GATE*, *C.*, 6¼; *M.*, 5. *TAVISTOCK*, *C.*, 18½; *M.*, 20. *THROWLEIGH*, *C.*, 3½; *M.*, 8. *TWO BRIDGES*, *C.*, 10½; *M.*, 12. *WARREN HOUSE INN*, *C.*, 4¾; *M.*, 6¼. *WHIDDON DOWN*, *C.*, 4½; *M.*, 6¾. *WIDECOMBE*, *C.*, 9; *M.*, 8. *YELVERTON*, *C.*, 18; *M.*, 19½. *YEOFORD*, *C.*, 11; *M.*, 13.

BY RAIL from *MORETONHAMPSTEAD* (G.W.R.) to *LUSTLEIGH*, 3½ m.; *BOVEY TRACEY*, 6¼ m.; *NEWTON ABBOT*, 12¼ m. Distances from *NEWTON* are given in the Bovey Tracey District.

Chagford had an early connection with Dartmoor as one of the Stannary towns, and it has a later one consequent upon the favour it has found with visitors to the moorland district. The parish is divided into four quarters, and there are three manors, one of them belonging to the Duchy. This is the Prince's Manor, or Manor of Great Week. The tract of land now forming Whiddon Park was purchased by Sir John Widdon in the reign of Elizabeth. In the churchyard is the grave of James Perrott, long known to all visitors to Chagford as the Dartmoor guide.

As our excursions will commence at Gidleigh, Teigncombe, Metheral, and Moor Gate, it will be more convenient to describe here the way to those points both from Chagford and Moreton, and first of all the road between the two last-named places.

Moreton to Chagford, 4½ m., *and Reverse*. Few directions are necessary. The road runs north-westward from the town, and all that the visitor need remember is not to branch R. About 1¾ m. from the town the road forks, at a point known as Half Way House, and he may choose either branch. The L. is the shorter way, but the R. is the better road. If he decide upon the former all he has to do is to maintain a westerly course. Drewston is first passed and then Great Week, his destination being reached 2 m. from the forks. The road R. will bring him in 1¼ m. to Easton Cross (straight on to Sandy Park, R. to Uppacott), where he will turn L., and reach Chagford in another 1½ m., or rather less. Conversely, the pedestrian from Chagford desiring to go by the shorter way, will pass round the east end of the churchyard, and follow the lane E. by Great Week and Drewston to the forks, where he will keep straight on for Moreton. If he chooses the other way he will pass down through the town with the Moor Park Hotel L., and taking care not to branch L. to Rushford Bridge, will make his way to Easton Cross, 1½ m., where he will turn R., and in about 1¼ m. will reach Half Way House, entering Moreton 1¾ m. further on.

Chagford to Gidleigh, 2½ m.   Crossing the Teign at Chagford Bridge, which is mentioned by the sixteenth century topographer, Leland, the visitor passes upward, and L., to Walland Hill, and thence westward to Murchington.   The way lies through this, and the visitor, turning neither R. nor L., soon begins to descend to Highbury Bridge, where he crosses the Blackaton Brook.   Less than ½ m. up the lane a turning R. leads directly to the village.   Visitors from Moreton will pass through Chagford.

Chagford to Teigncombe Down.   (A) By Yeo Bridge, 2¾ m.   (B) By Leigh Bridge, 2¼ m.   (A) Instead of descending to Chagford Bridge turn L. at the end of the town.   The road runs S.W., down as first, and then up to Waye Barton, where the family of Prous were seated in the sixteenth and seventeenth centuries, and here it forks.   Keep R. to Thorn, where a road branches L. to Collihole, the ancient Collerewe, and the moor.   Avoid this, and follow the road on to Yeo Bridge, on the South Teign, just beyond which another road runs L. to Great Frenchbere and Thornworthy.   But the way lies past the mill to a point about ½ m. further on, where North Hill Lane comes up R. from Leigh Bridge.   Turn L. to the hamlet of Teigncombe, whence the moor may be reached by way of Teigncombe Common Lane (S. Ex. 50), or by turning R. at the hamlet, and then L. to the moor gate near Brimstone Down.   (B) A shorter route to Teigncombe is by way of Holy Street and Leigh Bridge.   The visitor will pass down the hill as for Chagford Bridge, but will turn L. at the old serge factory and follow the narrow road, with the mill stream R., to Holy Street.   Passing this he will climb the hill, and soon after descend to Leigh Bridge, where he will cross the South Teign immediately above its confluence with the northern branch of that stream.   North Hill Lane must then be followed upward to Teigncombe, ¾ m. from the bridge.   Visitors from Moreton will first make their way to Chagford.

Chagford to Metheral, 3¾ m.   To the fork at Waye Barton, as in the preceding route A., or over Meldon Common, as in S. Ex. 57 ; then branch L., and at the fork on the western edge of Meldon Common keep R. to Tannaford.   (There is a guide-post here).   Avoid the turning L. just beyond this place.   The moor is entered about 1 m. further on at Tawton Gate, near Yardworthy, and the enclosures of Metheral are reached in another ¾ m.   The same point may also be arrived at by passing Waye Barton and turning L. at Thorn, whence a lane runs straight to the moor, passing Hole and Collihole.

Moreton to Metheral, 6½ m.   The Princetown, or western, road is followed past Bughead Cross, 1¼ m., to a point where it forks, ¼ m. further on.   Striking into the R. branch the visitor will make his way past Thorn (not the farm named in the preceding route), and thence to a stile in the hedge L., ⅓ m. on, where he will cross one field and reach the road again.   His next point is Batworthy, ⅓ m. (this must not be confounded with the estate of that name near Teigncombe), and less than ¼ m. beyond it he will reach the junction of the road he is following with one coming L. from Beetor Cross, which is marked by a guide-post.   A little further on the Chagford road runs off R.   The visitor must bear L., and passing between higher and Lower Stiniel will make his way to Jurston Common, through which the Bovey river runs.   He must not descend to the stream, but follow the road across the little common W., and so on to Jurston Cross, where is a guide-post. (See next Route). Taking care not to turn R. or L. he will continue on the road to the next guide-post, where he will branch L. to Corndon, which is not far off. Here, turning R., he will proceed for ¼ m. and reach the road coming up from Waye Barton, where he will turn L. and soon find himself on that part of the moor formerly known as Tawton Common, with the Metheral enclosures before him.

Chagford to Moor Gate, via Jurston Gate, 3 m. Turning R. from the High Street at the southern corner of the churchyard the visitor will pass on by the school and up the hill to Meldon Hall, the direction being due S. Here he will bear R., as also at the next fork at Higher Weddicott. He will then skirt Meldon Hill for a short distance, when the road again forks, the point being marked by a guide-post. Avoid bearing R., and keep straight on to Yellands, and thence to Jurston Cross, where is another guide-post. The way then lies S. to Jurston Bridge, on the Bovey river, a little beyond which the visitor will arrive at Jurston Farm. The road bears R., or westerly, and then abruptly turns L. and runs up the hill to Jurston Gate. Moor Gate (*i.e.*, the point so named where the Moreton road enters the moor) is about ½ m. S.E., and to reach it direct the narrow valley of the Bovey must be crossed. There will, however, be no necessity for doing this for the purpose of our excursions. The common may also be reached from Jurston by following up the stream instead of proceeding by the road. See also *Chagford to Beetor Cross.*

Moreton to Moor Gate, 4 m. Few directions are needed here, the Princetown road simply being followed. The first point is Bughead Cross, 1¼ m., where a road comes N. from Easton and Sandy Park, and goes S. to Lustleigh. The L. branch is taken at the fork just beyond it, and Wormhill Bridge over the Bovey is reached ¾ m. further on. Beyond this keep R. at the fork, and climb Worm Hlll. Less than ½ m. after passing the farm so named Beetor Cross (R. 32, 53) will be reached, where is a guide-post. Descend the hill to the point where the old stone cross stands on a bank, and then follow the road R., or westerly, for 1 m. to Moor Gate. For a further notice of this road *vide* S. Ex. 59, and *Crosses*, Chap. XIV.

Chagford to Beetor Cross, 2½ m. To the fork at Higher Weddicott, as in going to Moor Gate. Take the branch L., and follow the road past Lower Weddicott to the cross road. Then turn down the hill R., to the guide-post just below the turning R. to Stiniel. Take the R. branch at the fork, and follow the road S. to Beetor Bridge. Thence past Beetor Farm direct to the cross. The return route is given in S. Ex. 61.

Another road leads to Beetor Cross from Jurston Cross (see above). On reaching the last-named point the road running down to Langaford Bridge L., or south-easterly, must be chosen. From the bridge it goes on direct to the Princetown road, which it joins about ½ m. from Beetor Cross, L., Moor Gate being ¾ m. R.

EXCURSIONS FROM CHAGFORD AND MORETON.

The district here described is bounded on the north by a line drawn from Shilstone Tor to Wild Tor, and on the south by one extending from Heathercombe past Grim's Pound to the Warren House Inn and Assacombe Hill, and embraces Gidleigh Common, Chagford Common, the common lands of North Bovey, and part of the commons in Manaton parish, and also a portion of the east side of the forest.

[Tracks Nos. 43, 44, 45, 46, 47, and 77.]

Ex. 19.—*Creber Pound, Buttern Hill, Rival Tor, Mining Remains, Wild Tor.* [EXTENSION TO Ockment Hill and Newtake, add 4 m.] *Walla Brook Combe, Watern Tor, Manga Hill, Teign Head Farm, Battey Meres, Scorhill Circle, Berry Down.* From and to Gidleigh 2½ m. from Chagford), 11 m.

Leaving Gidleigh, which is noticed in S. Ex. 49, 50, by the road running north-eastward, with the castle on our L., we soon reach the old manor pound R., and then turn L. up the hill to Creber Pound. Just before arriving at the gate of this we shall notice the road branching R. at an acute angle to Moortown and Ensworthy (R. 24, 38). Creber Pound, though for several centuries a drift pound, is really a small piece of common separated from the open moor by enclosures. Besides the entrance by which we reach it there are two others leading up to which roads will be seen. The one on the L. is at the lower end of Berry Down Stroll, and the other at the head of the pound at Creber Farms. It is mentioned in a document of Charles the First's reign, where it is set forth that at the time of the drifts " cattle are driven to a pound called Dunnabridge Pound if they are found in the east, west, and south quarter of the forest, and if found in the north quarter of the forest to a pound called Creber Pound." Making our way up through this ancient enclosure by the road R. we speedily reach South Creber L., and North Creber R., and passing through a short stroll emerge on the open moor. Our next point is the summit of Buttern Hill (R. 24, 38), on which is a small cluster of rocks sometimes referred to as Buttern Tor, and to which also the name of the Cuckoo Stone has been given, rather over ½ m. to the N.W. We pass a newtake on the slope R. as we ascend (R. 25). This does not join any others, but a little northward, near Buttern House, there are several, as well as many old enclosures. This small farm place was built by a moorman who used to pasture cattle on the northern part of the forest at the time when Creber Pound was used much more than it is at present. A certain Jan Lake, who once haunted it, has never been seen, so the story says, since a big earthenware vessel was discovered somewhere in the vicinity. It was thought Jan has got an idea that treasure was buried on Buttern Down, which accounted for his frequent presence there, and that he abandoned his search on hearing of the finding of the urn, believing that it contained the gold he had hoped to unearth. Several hut circles exist in the neighbourhood of these enclosures on the down, but the most interesting object is a stone circle, though, unfortunately, it has been nearly destroyed. We shall find it about ¼ m. S.W. of the rocks. A green path (T. 43) coming from Ensworthy N., and running along the E. side of White Moor Bottom (Ex. 18), will be seen leading to it.

Leaving the head of this bottom, and the Pixies' Parlour (Ex. 18)

R., we strike S.W. to Rival Tor, which is about ½ m. away (T. 43). This we shall find to consist of one lump of granite, near the summit of a low hill (1,379 feet), the western side, which descends to a little feeder of the Walla Brook, being covered with grass to such an extent as almost to resemble a meadow. This feeder comes down from the mire at Gallaven (Ex. 17), ¾ m. N.W. by W., and another branch of it from Rue Lake Pit, less than ½ m. N.W. by N. Near the head of Gallaven Mire, and over the shoulder of the hill W.N.W., is a bank about 14 feet wide, and about 150 feet long, having something the appearance of a track, though I have been unable to discover any other parts of it in the same line. It runs N. and S., and passes over the boggy ground. It may have had some connection with the mining remains on the banks of the little Rue Lake, a short distance below the mire, and which are known in the locality as the White Works. Some vestiges of these we shall see as we presently make our way to Wild Tor.

Although Rival Tor, which, were it not spoken of as Rifle Tor by the moor people we might possibly be inclined to regard as being a corruption of the Celtic *Yr Eifl* (*f* as *v*), and which, indeed, means *The Rival*, is not of great height, several important landmarks are seen from it. White Moor Stone (Ex. 17) is seen standing out against the sky to the N.W., with Kennon Hill (Ex. 18) a little to the R. of it. Hound Tor bears N.W. by W., and Steeperton Tor W. by N.; Wild Tor rises across the little valley W. by S., and Watern Tor, the prominent object in all this part of the moor, S.W., the two ridges on which these stand being separated by the dip forming the entrance to Walla Brook Combe. Away to the southward Siddaford Tor (Ex. 20, 45) is seen, and S.E. the square mass of Kes Tor.

Striking W.S.W. we shall descend the grassy side of Rival Tor to a point on Rue Lake where a leat is taken from it, close to which is a little fording place. (This is the leat that runs by Scorhill Rocks and across the stroll above Berry Down). Here the stone heaps testify to the former presence of the tinner, and near to the ford is one of his curious shelters. It is of the kind which are regarded as shelters, in which it is thought the miners placed their tools when leaving the scene of their labours for the in-country. Peat cutters sometimes adopt a similar plan, and conceal their " irons " under a heap of peat. Several stones will here be observed set in the ground on their edges, above which is an overhanging rock forming a canopy, or roof. Lower down the stream is a larger fording-place with a track leading to it. This, which is not very plain in places, is the one seen at the stone circle on Buttern Hill (T. 43).

Our way now lies up the hill W. by S. to Wild Tor, rather over 1 m. distant, the Walla Brook being on our L. At the entrance to Walla Brook Combe, where the stream bends, previously flowing from the S., we reach a point known as Wild Tor Well, to which the forest boundary comes northward from Hound Tor, and crossing the stream is carried up to Watern Tor. The so-called Well is mentioned in 1702 as a mark standing on the boundary, and it is also one common to the parishes of Throwleigh and Gidleigh, which here meet on the forest line. It is about 150 yards from the Walla Brook where this is nearest to it, or twice that distance if the boundary line be followed, and which here runs S. by E. to the northern pile of Watern Tor. It has been suggested that Wild Tor Well was not on the old forest boundary but was named later as a bondmark for the purpose of making the line agree with that which the Jury of Survey had presented in 1609. There is no foundation whatever for this.

Passing up the hill W. by N. from the Well we reach Wild Tor, 1,741 feet, in ¼ m. This pile, which stands amid scattered granite, is situated on a lofty ridge rising between the Steeperton Brook on the W. (Ex. 17), and the Gallaven Mire and Walla Brook Combe on the E. Steeperton Tor, seen across the valley to the N.N.W., is about 1 m. distant. Northward the ground slopes downward towards Hound Tor. but southward it rises to the lofty Newtake Hill, which attains an elevation of 1,893 feet. This is sometimes called Hangingstone Hill, but that name is usually considered by the moormen to belong only to the N.W. side of it, where there is a small outlying pile of rock. Between Wild Tor and Newtake there are several very large cairns.

[*Extension to Ockment Hill and Newtake.* This will take the rambler through some of the more remote parts of the forest. Striking W.S.W. from Wild Tor he will, in less than ½ m., reach the Steeperton Brook a short distance below its source. He will then steer a little N. of W. over Ockside Hill to Taw Rocks, ¼ m., where that river is crossed, and still following the same course will, in another ½ m., reach the summit of Ockment Hill (Ex. 16 and Cranmere Routes). In returning he will strike S.E. to Newtake, crossing the Taw on the way, but rather further up stream than before. The summit of Newtake consists of good hard ground, on which are scattered rocks, though the hill itself is on the edge of the fen. A fragment of wall exists there, and to this it owes its present name. It is said that in the early days of Teignhead Farm its extension was contemplated, and that the formation of a great Newtake was projected that would include the top of this hill. As the founder of the place took in no less than 1,400 acres, we can very well believe that he would have no scruples about enclosing a few hundred more, and his reason for not going on with the work of robbing the commoners may possibly have been the discovery that farming operations on the Dartmoor fen were not likely to prove remunerative. The view from Newtake is very fine. To the N. is Ock Tor, with Steeperton Tor a little to the R. of it. N.E. is Wild Tor, with Cosdon rising grandly some 2½ m. beyond. E. by N. we see Watern Tor ; southward we look upon White Horse Hill ; S.W. the rocks of Fur Tor appear ; westward is Rattlebrook Hill, with Hare Tor and Great Links Tor, and the high land of Amicombe ; and R. of these are Willes, Yes Tor, and West and East Mil Tor. On leaving the hill we strike N.E., and soon come in sight of Walla Brook Combe R. Looking across it E. we see Watern Tor, but instead of making for it direct shall bear a little to the L. of it. Presently we discern a rough track climbing the side of the hill under the tor, and this becomes our point. We cross the Walla Brook and follow the path towards the tor.]

Leaving Wild Tor we pass down the granite strewn slope S. by E to the Walla Brook, and make our way by the track referred to above to Watern Tor, 1,756 feet. This pile bore the name of Thurlestone in the thirteenth century, for there can hardly be a doubt that it is the bound named as such by the Perambulators of 1240. This name is supposed to be derived from the appearance presented by the two northern piles, which, when viewed from certain points, give the idea of being one in which is a large aperture, the *thurl*, or *thirl*, stone being thus the perforated stone, the term having its origin in the Anglo-Saxon *thyrelan*, to pierce. An arched rock on the shore of Bigbury Bay, between the mouth of the Avon and Hope Cove, which much resembles this tor seen from a distance, bears the name of Thurlestone Rock, and this seems to me confirmatory of its derivation. I have a copy of a document in my possession in which the forest line is drawn to the east of the one recognized by the border commoners, and this runs to what is there called Thurston Tor, or Stone Tor. But I cannot find any other mention of Thurston Tor as identical with Stone Tor. The name of the next bondmark also helps to prove that Thurlestone was the bound to which the old Perambulators came. This is Manga Rock, ¾ m. S.E. of Watern Tor, *manga* being a Gaelic word meaning a boundary mark. We have already noticed the instance of the Saxon *hareston* (T. 44), occurring on the line, and when we find such names as these, and remember also that most of the objects forming the early bondmarks can still be identified with certainty, we shall be justified in believing that the bounds of the forest of Dartmoor have altered very little since they were perambulated in 1240.

Watern Tor, which has also been called Watern Borough, exhibits in its present name a shortened form of that by which it was known three hundred years ago, it being then referred to as Waterdontor. Thurlestone is the name attaching to the two northern piles only.

Less than ¼ m. S.E. by S. of Watern Tor is the N.W. corner of the Teignhead Farm enclosure. One wall, about 2 m. in length, comes up from the S., and another, about ½ m. long, from the E., the latter climbing the steep hill from the Teign. Not far from the corner is a gate, and passing through this we shall find ourselves on Hew Down, and close to Hewthorn Clitter. As we proceed, our course being a little E. of S., we leave Manga Rock below us L., and cross the head of a streamlet referred to in 1702 as Hugh Lake (*vide post*). Thence passing over Manga Hill, and crossing Manga Brook, we shall reach the farmhouse, about 1½ m. from the corner near which we entered the enclosure.

Teignhead Farm was taken in from the forest somewhere about twenty years before the close of the eighteenth century by a Mr. Rogers, who built the house, and lived there many years. He was succeeded in 1817 by a Mr. Dodd, and thirty years later Mr. James Endacott became the tenant. After him, in 1872, came his son—known in this part of the moor as Teignhead George—who, however, only remained there three years. Then the place was taken by Mr. John Gemmell, of Woolwell, in the parish of Bickleigh, as a summer run for cattle, and about 1878 was acquired by Mr. Lamb, of Prince Hall (Ex. 4), who placed a shepherd there, and devoted it to the rearing of Scotch sheep. But the venture did not prove very successful, and the place is again used as a summer grazing farm. There was formerly another homestead on it at Great Varracombe, called Mandles, where a son of James Endacott once lived, and brought up a large family. The place is now in ruins.

Proceeding down the rough track that leads from the house to the river we shall soon find ourselves at Teignhead Bridge, a clapper erected by Mr. Rogers. It consists of four piers with three openings, three stones being laid over each. Its length is nearly 28 feet, and its width 6 feet 9 inches.

The track by which we have reached it goes on to Fernworthy (T. 45) ; we shall not, however, cross the river and follow this, but shall make our way down its L. bank. Just below the bridge, and a little removed from the river are the remains of some tinners' buildings, and still further down a waterfall. We shall also pass a fording-place, which may possibly be the Mangersford mentioned in a presentment at a Court of the Manor of Lydford, in the 20th of Henry VI. The little tributary which we cross is Hew Lake, and the spot at which it joins the Teign was formerly known as Blackstone. It seems probable that Hew Lake is the Whoodelake of 1609, and the Woodlake of ninety years later,* although on a copy of an old map in my possession this name is given to the little stream that rises S.E. of Stone Tor Hill, and flows by the enclosures of Thornworthy into the South Teign, or Little Teign, as the river is there called. Below Hew Lake the North Teign enters a level, part of which appears on the map in question as Battey Meres, a name which may have reference to the boundary of the forest near by, or to a former lake of which the level has been supposed to be the bed, though it is possible that Battery (*i.e.*, Batworthy) mires, which I have heard the spot called, may after all be the correct form. On this level, which is bounded on the N. by the Walla Brook, the former presence of the tin-streamer is plainly shown. The ground has been worked most extensively, and heaps of debris, now covered with vegetation, extend for some distance along the bank of the Teign.

We shall, however, turn a little from the river after passing Hew Lake Foot, where the wall of the Teignhead enclosure runs up the hill, and pass round to the L. of a swampy flat, our course being northward towards the Walla Brook. When about ½ m. from Hew Lake, and ¼ m. from the nearest corner of the wall, we shall come upon a little hut, but not of the kind usually associated with the tinners. It measures only 6 feet by 4½ feet internally, the back wall being 5 feet high, and the front one rather lower. The doorway is intact, and there is a fire-place. It was probably a shepherd's or a peat cutter's shelter.

We now make our way to the Walla Brook, where we shall follow downward to its junction with the Teign. Here it is spanned by a single stone clapper, and it will also be seen that its banks are walled in the manner of those on the East Dart above Sandy Hole (Ex. 45, R. 10 B, 36 B). Immediately below the confluence is Teign Clapper, which replaces one known more than 200 years ago by that name, and which was swept away by a great flood in 1826. Quite close to this, and opposite to the corner of the Batworthy enclosures on the

---

* The sound of the *W* would disappear in Dartmoor speech, and the name be pronounced Oodlake, or Hoodlake, from which Hewlake would be a natural transition, since the native drops the *d* sound equally with that of the *w*. Hood Lake is the form given in Westcote's *View of Devon in* 1630, which, however, was not published until 1845. In the sixteenth century, and also at the beginning of the eighteenth, there is mention of a Hugh Stone, but this seems to indicate an object S. of the Teign.

other side of the stream, is the curious Holed Stone, which, in the days when everything on Dartmoor out of the ordinary was ascribed to the Druids, was regarded as having been perhaps used by them for some mysterious purpose connected with their religious rites, and was looked upon as a tolmen. And such it is in so far as it is a stone with a hole in it, but it is of quite a different character from the tolmen that is classed as a pre-historic monument. The story used to be told that people were brought here to be "christened"; probably this arose after antiquaries began to show curiosity concerning it. The hole, which is about three feet in diameter, is worn through an immense block of granite that rests in the bed of the Teign, and close to its L. bank. Many rocks with cavities worn partly through them by the action of the water may be seen on the Dartmoor streams.

On Scorhill Down, due N. of the Holed Stone, and only a short distance from it, is the fine stone circle usually known by the same name as the common. It is 90 feet in diameter, and consists of 24 upright stones, and eight fallen ones, but the vacancies seem to show that there were formerly more than this. One, which is much higher than the others, is about 8 feet in height, and another, standing nearly opposite to it, is about 6 feet. The others are lower, some being under 3 feet. There is little doubt that when the walls near by were built this monument suffered at the hands of those engaged in the work, and unfortunately it was again assailed by the vandal a few years ago, one of its stones being split for posts. This destructive work was, however, quickly discovered and stopped.

Striking north-eastward we shall make our way to Berry Down Stroll, the head of which is only ¼ m. distant. Down through this stroll we pass, and at the bottom turn R. to Berry Down Farm, or Beridon, as it is sometimes, and probably more correctly, called, when one Autumn day, in the 24th of Henry VIII., John Roo, its holder, set out to the Parliament of the Tinners on Crockern Tor. We pass the farm and make our way down the long lane to Highbury Bridge, returning to Chagford through Murchington, as in R. 24 B.

Ex. 20.—*Teigncombe Down, The Round Pound, Shovel Down Stone Rows, The Long Stone, The Three Boys, Fernworthy, Circle on Froggy- mead Hill, The Lord and the Lady, Long Ridge, The Grey Wethers, Siddaford Tor [Quintin's Man, add 2 m.], Kes Tor.* From and to Teigncombe Down (2¼ m. from Chagford,) 9 m.

Entering upon the common at the moor gate at Brimstone Down we follow the road for about ½ m., when we shall reach the object known as the Round Pound. This stands close beside the track, and in the midst of a group of remains consisting of reaves, or low banks, and hut circles, and one or two rectangular enclosures, the whole being overlooked by the prominent Kes Tor. The Round Pound is really the remains of a large hut dwelling surrounded by a wall, the space between the two being divided into half a dozen small courts, or pens, by low walls radiating from the hut to the outer rampart. Across the road, and a short distance up the hill, is another enclosure, but rectangular in form, and which is also somewhat similarly divided into pens. The hut circles on this part of the common show us that a very extensive settlement of the primitive people of the moor once existed here. And it is one of more than ordinary interest ; for, standing in proximity to these ruined dwellings, are also many sepulchral monuments, while in the immediate vicinity a vast number of flint implements, consisting of arrow-heads, knives, and scrapers, have been found. These were first discovered in 1887, on the adjoining estate of Batworthy, and were so numerous that by 1889 Mr. F. N. Budd, the owner, had collected no less than 6,400 specimens, including flakes and nodules. As many of these were of chocolate coloured chert, similar to the chert pebbles at Sidmouth, Mr. Budd was led to the belief that much of the material was brought from the further side of the Exe. The fields in which the specimens were found were evidently formed on a spot once devoted to their manufacture. Further specimens have been obtained there since 1889. The monuments referred to we shall find on Shovel Down, to which we make our way by following the track, with the enclosures of Batworthy R., to Batworthy Corner, where the walls form a sharp angle, and is carried down the hill in a north-westerly direction to the North Teign at the Holed Stone (Ex. 19). Exactly 300 yards S. by W. of Batworthy Corner is a group of stones forming the remains of three concentric circles, and if the visitor first makes his way to this he will the better be able to follow the brief description of the monuments here given. They cannot be said to be particularly striking, for the stones composing them are small, but they are interesting as furnishing examples of the circle, the row, the cairn, and the menhir. They have obtained some celebrity in consequence of being situated on a border common often visited, but the rambler who knows Dartmoor will hardly fail to remember places where remains much more striking are to be seen. Standing in the triple circle and looking northward the visitor will have before him two double stone rows, one running almost due N., and extending for about 140 yards, and the other running N. by W. for about the same distance. Now turning southward the visitor will find another row before him, also double. This runs in a direction S. by E. for 110 yards, and terminates in a dilapidated cairn, probably the former site of a kist. Having reached this point, and still looking southward, he will have yet another double row before him, although it does not start from the cairn, but some few score yards further on. Upon the line of this row stands the fine menhir known as the Longstone, to which the visitor now makes his way. This ancient monolith is ten feet in height, and forms one of the forest boundmarks, a purpose it has probably served from an early time. It seems to be either the Heigheston or Langestone of the perambulators of 1240.* It also stands at that point on the forest boundary line where the common lands belonging to Gidleigh and Chagford meet. Southward of the menhir about 220 yards is a stone that once formed a supporter of a capstone of a dolmen. This single block, and the former name of the dolmen—it was called the Three Boys—are all that remains of a monu-

---

* Among other forms of these names mentioned at various periods (though it is by no means certain that they refer to the same object), are Hangeston, Hengston, Highstone, Yessetone, Gotestone, and Yestelay. We have already referred to Hugh Stone (Ex. 19); this also appears at Fewstone ; and Heath Stone seems also to be called Gesstone, while in 1699 there is mention of an object in its vicinity, if not identical with it, called Half Stone.

ment which, were it now in a complete state, would have given us an object of antiquity such as this part of the moor now furnishes no example of, and would have lent much additional interest to these Shovel Down remains.

Striking S. from the Three Boys, but bearing a little to the L., we soon reach a small stream, a tributary of the South Teign, and shall make our way down this through Longstone Bottom, a rather marshy spot, with Thornworthy Tor on our L. When about ¾ m. from the ruined dolmen we enter a stroll formed on the L. by the enclosures of Thornworthy, and on the R. by those of Fernworthy. In this stroll, which runs down to the Teign, and not far from the left bank of the little tributary stream, a good example of a kistvaen may be seen. It was only brought to light about 1880, having previously been buried beneath a small mound. On removing the cover stone and examining this sarcophagus, some fragments of pottery and flints were discovered. In some of the examples on the moor the covering slab is missing (although this is not found to be the case where the kists are far removed from newtake walls), but usually it is seen lying near the grave. In the present instance, instead of being thrown on one side it was supported on some fragments of rock quite near to the kist, but in such a manner as not to interfere with the view of the interior. One side stone of this rude coffin is five feet long, the other being 3 ft. 7 inches at the top ; the end stones are 2 feet, and 1 foot 9 inches long respectively, the height of the whole being about 2 feet. The cover stone in 5 feet in length, and 3½ feet in width at its widest part. The circle formed by the bank that enclosed the low mound that covered the kist is 24 feet in diameter, interior measurement.

Making our way down to the Teign we shall turn R. and follow that stream upward to Fernworthy Bridge. Here close to the modern erection is a fine example of the single stone clapper. The slab forming this solid footway is rather over ten feet in length, and nearly four feet wide, and is about a foot thick. The road, which comes down to the bridge from Metheral, runs past the farmhouse to Froggymead Hill, whence a green track goes out to Teign Head (T. 45). Fernworthy is an old settlement, and formerly consisted of three farms, and is referred to in the seventeenth century as a village. It is not, however, one of the ancient forest tenements, nor is it strictly a part of the forest, although it lies within its boundaries, and is consequently in the parish of Lydford. Rather over 200 years ago it was in the possession of a Farmer Lightfoot, and the letter L cut in the stone over the doorway, and which also bears the date 1690, in all probability refers to him. The estate is mentioned by the Jury of Survey, who enquired into the bounds of the forest in 1609, so that the date on the stone evidently records some alterations, or enlargement, only. A considerable portion of the land has been enclosed within the last hundred years or so, but had previously belonged to the estate, and was defined by a tin bound. Other parts of it are Lowtons, Silkhouse, Assacombe, Brownhills, and Little Newtake, and it extends along both banks of the Teign. Fernworthy is a good example of a moorland dwelling, and like most of the Dartmoor homesteads in similar situations, is sheltered by some fine sycamores.

Passing the house, near to which we shall notice an old well, we make our way to the head of the lane, where a gate opens on Froggy

mead Hill. Here, built into the wall, is a large stone having a circular
hollow sunk in it. The rambler round Chagford will meet with many
of these stones. The hollows were intended to receive the stanchion
of a gate, one of the holed stones being fixed in the ground, and the
other placed so as to project from the wall or hedge in which it was built.
This upper stone was, of course, not secured until the gate was put
in its proper position. About ¼ m. N.W. of the gate is a good example
of the stone circle. It is not of great size certainly, the diameter being
only about sixty feet, nor do the stones rise high above the turf, but
it is in a capital state of preservation. Two or three of the stones
appear to be missing. A short distance N. by E. are the remains of a
stone row, and the vestiges of another are to be seen to the S. of the
circle. This has led to a suggestion that these rows were once connected
with the ones we have just examined near the Longstone, and also
that the latter may perhaps have been continued to the circle at Scorhill (Ex. 19). In fact, the idea has been so elaborated that a sketch
plan has been made in which the rows are shown to extend throughout
the whole of the distance from Froggymead to Scorhill. But there
is no reason for supposing that these remains on Froggymead Hill
ever formed part of the Longstone group, or that the latter were linked
up with the Scorhill circle. The existence of a cluster of antiquities
near to another of a similar character furnishes no ground for supposing them to have been connected with each other. But by means
of an imaginary plan it would, of course, be easy to show that the
whole of the antiquities in the moorland region once formed a single
group.

Turning south-westward we shall make our way to Hemstone
Rocks, situated on that part of Long Ridge known as Tom's Hill,
passing a few hut circles as we proceed. Near to us, on the L., is the
South Teign, and on the further side of that stream the slope of Assacombe Hill. Ages ago this quiet valley was the scene of the secret
meetings of a handsome youth and a fair maiden. Who or what they
were the story does not tell us, further than the lady dwelt somewhere
near by on the border of the moor, and that her lover was in hiding in
the forest, but was " kept out of his rights." (Cf. the story of
Gaveston, Ex. 2). From Hemstone Rocks, below which is Hemstone Bottom, we pass up the hill W.S.W. to the circles known as the
Grey Wethers, ½ m. distant. This name, which we find applied to
similar monuments in other parts of the country, is popularly supposed to have been derived from a fancied resemblance of the group
of stones to a flock of sheep. I have elsewhere related [*Crosses*,
Chap. XIV.] how these stones were once the object of a practical joke,
having been sold by a man named Debben to a farmer, who was a
stranger to this part of the moor, as so many grey wethers. The
bargain was struck in the Warren House Inn, and the farmer was
directed to go to the newtake near Siddaford Tor, where he would be
able to see his purchase. This he did, but unlike Bo Peep found not
only that the sheep would not come home, but also that they had got
no tails to bring behind them. The Grey Wethers consist of two circles,
the circumferences of which nearly touch each other. The northern
one is 100 feet in diameter, and the southern one about 5 feet more
than that. Many of the stones have fallen, but fortunately the greater
number of these have escaped the hand of the vandal, which is rather

to be wondered at seeing that there is a newtake wall close by. I first examined these circles in 1878, when the northern one consisted of 16 stones, of which 9 were erect, but there were indications of others over which the turf had grown. In the southern circle I counted 27 stones, of which only 7 were standing. The average height of these is about 4 feet. They are rather different in appearance from the stones that usually compose the circles on the moor, being slabs approaching a rectangular form. The circles are situated on the slope of Siddaford Tor, a pile presenting nothing of importance in itself, but commanding a most extensive view, and being a prominent landmark throughout a great part of the moorland region. It attains an elevation of 1,764 feet, and one of its rocks, a thin flattish mass, could once be made to rock, or log, with ease. It is a pity the Druidophiles were unaware of this. What a scene they might have drawn of the arch druid hurrying up from Wistman's Wood with a big bunch of mistletoe, while the other druids gathered in the "sacred" circles, and the verdant laymen waited by the logan with a beautiful childlike trust.

(About 1 m. from Siddaford Tor is a tumulus known as Quintin's Man. The name points to the former existence there of a menhir, but no such object is now to be seen. To reach it the visitor may follow the wall running north-westward from near the tor, and will cross the North Teign about midway. The tumulus is only a little over 200 yards from the wall. The return may be either by way of Siddaford or the visitor may strike E.N.E. to Teignhead Farmhouse, 1 m., crossing the tributaries known as Little Verracombe and Great Varracombe on the way. Near the latter was situated the dwelling known as Mandles, mentioned previously (Ex. 19). From Teignhead Farm the homeward route given in Ex. 19 may be followed).

(From Post Bridge to the Grey Wethers see Ex. 45).

From Siddaford Tor we shall make our way over Long Ridge, our course being N.E. In about 2 m. we shall reach the westerly arm of the tributary flowing through Longstone Bottom, and $\frac{1}{2}$ m. further on shall reach the Longstone itself. We may now either follow the stone rows, and so retrace our steps to Batworthy Corner and thence return to the moor gate at Brimstone Down, or we may reach Teigncombe Common Lane by way of Kes Tor, which we see above us to the N.E. (Routes from the two are given in S. Ex. 55).

Another route from Siddaford is by way of the North Teign. The visitor will pass through the gate near the Grey Wethers, and descend to the clapper below Teignhead farmhouse (Ex. 19), whence he will pass up the side of the hill, with the river L. Soon leaving the track he will strike N.E. to Stonetor Hill, or Round Hill, as it is also called, 1 m. from the Bridge. This is about 1 m. from Batworthy Corner, the direction being N.E. by E., and the way running over Shovel Down.

Ex. 21.—*Hut Circles near Metheral, Stone Row in Assacombe, Waters Down, King's Oven, Lakeland, Moor Gate.* From and to the moor gate at Yardworthy ($3\frac{1}{4}$ m. from Chagford), 6 m. If the return be to Moor Gate (4 m. from Moreton), the distance is about the same.

Proceeding by the road past Waye and the western flank of Meldon Common (see *Chagford to Metheral*), we enter the moor at Tawton Gate, near Yardworthy, and following the road over Yardworthy Common, shall cross the Metheral Brook, and reach the entrance to the farm of that name. The ancient track to which we have already referred as running across the forest from Chagford took a southerly line from near this point, and was carried over Hurston Ridge (T. 77). The stone marking its course, and to which we have referred, may yet be seen near the farm, and is shown on an unpublished map of the forest at King-de-stone. From this the boundary went on to Heath Stone, which has already been the subject of our remarks (T. 44. This part of Chagford Common is also noticed in S. Ex. 58). On the slope below the farmhouse at Metheral, to the N.W., and not very far from the South Teign, is an object which has been thought by some to be part of a stone row ; in fact, it is shown as such on the new Ordnance Maps, or rather, as a stone "avenue." But I altogether fail to see the true characteristics of a row in this object. It consists merely of two parallel walls, about a dozen feet apart, of stones set closely together on their edges. These fragments of wall are probably the remains of some ancient enclosures, and are precisely similar in character to some that may be seen in a newtake on the hillside above the Forest Inn, at Hexworthy, and between that hostelry and Down Ridge. But there are, nevertheless, some undoubted antiquarian objects near Metheral. In the glen below, and not very far from Thornworthy, is a good example of the miner's blowing-house, with a trough and mould-stone, which we have noticed in S. Ex. 56, and on Lowton Hill near by are some fine specimens of hut circles, one being particularly noticeable. Lowton forms a part of the old Fernworthy settlement (Ex. 20), and takes its name from a pile of rocks, anciently known as Lowton Borough. This pile we shall see in front of us as we make our way along the road past Metheral Farm gate. On reaching the corner of the enclosures we leave the road, and keep straight on towards the rocks. On and around this pile the hut circles will be seen, the striking example to which we have alluded being not far from the summit. This hut is 32 feet in internal diameter, and the stones of which its wall is built are of very large size. Running round the interior of the wall is a low bench of stones, a most unusual feature in these erections. A somewhat similar arrangement may be seen in a hut near the entrance to Erme Pound (Ex. 32), but in that case the building is a small rectangular one, of the kind associated with the tinners, whereas the present example is circular, and of another type.

Striking S.W. we cross the Lowton Brook (R. 10 B, 36 B), above the L. bank of which we shall find more hut circles. We now make our way up Assacombe Hill, our direction being about S.S.W., and shall soon look down into Assacombe, through which the brook of that name runs northward to the Teign. Our course should bring us near to a ruined farmhouse, sometimes known as Hamlyn's House, or Assacombe House, and to the L. of this, *i.e.*, a little S. of it, is a stone row running down the slope in a direction due W. It is a double row, and starts from a dilapidate circle at the eastern end, and extends for a distance of nearly 75 yards. A few years ago this row was restored, the tall stones at its higher end being set up. One of these may be regarded as a menhir.

Making our way up through the combe we shall gradually leave the little stream on the R., and pursuing a S.E. course shall pass over

Assacombe Hill to Watern Hill, with Hurston Ridge on our L. Water Hill, or Waters Down, as it is more frequently called—apparently the Waterdown Rugge, of which there is mention in the early part of the sixteenth century—rises behind the Warren House Inn. It is rather amusing to find the summit of this hill described by a writer under the impression that he was giving his readers an account of King's Oven. He tells us that it was "generally regarded as a smelting-house of the 'old men,'" but that he could not "regard it as anything but a cairn pure and simple." This certainly would not matter very much, only it was rather unkind to say that *many* before him had speculated "on the low cairn, the stone-lined trench, and the little pits." We venture to think that very few since the days of the Rev. E. A. Bray have mistaken Water Hill for King's Oven. Near the summit of the hill is a double stone row, extending for a distance of about 153 yards, its direction being S.W. and N.E. At the western end is a dilapidated cairn and a menhir. Here a stone hammer was found, which had been used as a trigging stone for one of the mono-liths.

(The neighbourhood of the Warren House Inn, or Newhouse as it is usually called there, is noticed in our account of the Post Bridge District).

Leaving the despoiled cairn on Waters Down we shall make our way down the slope eastward, and when at a distance of 350 yards from it, and about ¼ m. N. of the Warren House Inn, shall find ourselves on the site of the ancient blowing-house mentioned in the Perambulation of 1240 as Furnum Regis, and in the Forest Survey of 1609 as King's Oven. In the scanty remains that now exist it would be impossible to recognize the ruins of a smelting-house, and it is the name alone that enables us to identify the site. Down to about the second half of the eighteenth century it would appear that most of this interesting structure, which in early times was probably the centre of the tin streaming industry in this part of the moor, was standing. Later the work of destruction was completed by the erectors of some modern mine buildings near by, who supplied themselves with stone from the ruins. All that is now to be seen is a low rampart, composed of small stones, forming a circular enclosure rather over 700 yards in diameter, in the centre of which is a roughly rounded stone measuring 3 feet across, and near it a small pile of stones that seem to have had one end worked into a rounded form. These were once taken away from the circle to be used in a mine building near by, but before this was done the source whence they had been obtained became known, and they were ordered to be taken back. On the south side of the circle is a dilapidated rectangular building, but this cannot with safety be identified as part of the ancient smelting-house. Apparently it belongs to a later day than that of the circle. Nothing is known of King's Oven, for the Perambulators of 1240 merely mention it, and do not say whether it was then in use. But however this may be we shall hardly be wrong in supposing that its name was derived not from being a furnace connected with tinworks belonging to Henry III., but to a much earlier king, for there cannot be a doubt of the high antiquity of this smelting-place.

From King's Oven we shall bend our steps northward, and shall soon reach the springs of the main branch of the Bovey river, known

locally as the Husson, *i.e.*, Hurston, Water, but to which during late
years the name of the North Walla Brook has been given as being in
accordance with a certain view with regard to the forest boundary
line. It is true that the perambulators of 1240 draw the line " in
longum Wallebroke " from the north towards King's Oven, but we
cannot be sure that the Bovey was intended, and as it is nowhere else
spoken of as the Walla Brook, it is misleading to fasten that name
upon it. More than two hundred years ago the spot where this stream
rises was referred to as Bovey Combe Head.* But in support of the
contention in question the name North Walla Brook has been placed
on the Ordnance Map of Devon (XCIX., N.E.), although on the very
next sheet (LXXXIX., S.E.) the same stream is called the River
Bovey, which, indeed, it is well known to be. But the theory respecting the forest boundary only needed that the upper portion of it in
the neighbourhood of King's Oven should be labelled Walla Brook.
Presumably it was deemed necessary to add " North " to the name
in order to distinguish the stream from the Walla Brook flowing south
from King's Oven, and which becomes the forest boundary to the
East Dart. But what about the Walla Brook flowing into the Teign
at Scorhill ? By this rule, we suppose, that stream would be the
" North North " Walla Brook. The plan of arbitrarily naming objects
on the moor is a delightful one for getting over topographical difficulties.

Keeping above the L. bank of this little stream, on the further
side of which is Bush Down, sometimes spoken of as Bush Down Heath,
we shall find ourselves at the distance of about ¾ m. from its source
opposite the old workings of the West Vitifer Mine. Soon after passing
these we have below us Lakeland Farm, which appears on Owen's
plan as Lakelawne, and just beyond this, on the slope of the hill, and
about ⅓ m. N. by W. of the house, shall come upon a most curious and
interesting object. It is a circular pound 56 paces in diameter, but
the wall is totally unlike that usually found in such structures. Instead
of being composed of stones laid in courses this is formed of large
slabs set on their edges in the ground, and touching each other. On
the lower side of this enclosure, and quite close to it, are one or two
hut circles. The visitor who finds an interest in the examination of the
stone remains on the moor should certainly not fail to visit this curious
object.

From this point, if our destination be Chagford we may either
return by striking N.W. across the common to the road near Metheral,
under ¾ m., and so make our way home by the road on the side of
Meldon to Waye (S. Ex. 56, 57), or we may shorten the distance by
turning into a track just above the enclosure and following it through
Hurston and Higher Corndon, as in S. Ex. 58, to Meldon Common.
A third way is by descending to the Bovey just below the pound, and
striking the stream near a ridge of rock on its eastern bank known as
Hurston Castle. Crossing it we make our way up the side of the hill
by a track running between the enclosures to the common, and

* Combe Head, on the northern slope of Hookney Down, 2 m.
distant, where another branch of the Bovey rises, has also been called
Bovey Combe Head. This, however, seems to have arisen through
confusing the name with Cullicombe Head. (Ex. 22).

following a footpath L., or N.E., direct to Jurston Gate (see R. 4 and end of Ex. 22). If bound for Moreton this will be our course, but instead of striking into the footpath we shall keep due E. on reaching the common, which will bring us to the Chagford road. This we cross, and also the shallow valley through which runs another branch of the Bovey river, on the further side of which we climb up to the Moreton road, which we reach not far from Moor Gate (R. 4).

Ex. 22.—*Bush Down, Bennet's Cross, Birch Tor, Stone Row at Headland, Headland Warren, Grim's Pound [Hameldon Tor, Hameldon Cross, Berry Pound], Hookney Down, Shapley Common, Green Combe.* Chagford, 11½ m. ; Moreton, 14½ m.

From Chagford the way will lie over the side of Meldon Common to the moor gate beyond Jurston (see *Chagford to Jurston Gate*), and thence along the road to its junction with the Princetown highway ; from Moreton the same point will be reached by way of Moor Gate, beyond which it is situated ¾ m. Here the road, for some ½ m. onward, passes between several small groups of hut dwellings, and a reave will also be seen on the L. of it, as well as the remains of others. We make our way onward, with Birch Tor on the L., to Bennet's Cross, which will be seen on the L. of the road, ¾ m., after passing the fifth milestone from Moreton. The cross is very rudely sculptured, and is leaning considerably on one side. Its original purpose was probably to mark the track over the moor from Moreton to its western side, on the line of which, as previously observed, the present road was formed, but it also serves as a boundary mark between the parishes of Chagford and North Bovey. It is possible that the parish line determined its precise situation, and that it was set up to serve the double purpose of a guide and a bondmark. It also forms one of the tin bounds of Vitifer, as well as a bound of Headland Warren. [*Crosses*, Chap. XIV.] The letters W. B., which are graven on this cross, are supposed to stand for Warren Bounds, and similar letters may be seen on a line of bond-stones running from it. But the cross,which may have been an ancient tin bound, was known as Bennet's Cross over two centuries since, and it is worthy of note that the name of William Benet occurs in the list of jurors who attended a Tinners' Parliament held on Crockern Tor in the 24th of Henry VIII., as a representative of the Stannary of Chagford.

Leaving this time-worn object, which may yet serve something of that higher purpose doubtless intended by those who set it up, we shall strike across the common in a direction E.S.E. to Birch Tor, sometimes called Warren Tor, which is less than ½ m. distant. The extensive workings of Birch Tor Mine, once known as the old Vitifer Mines, are on our R. as we proceed, and some of these we shall cross on our way, and also pass one of the four small newtakes that are supposed to represent the aces in the suits of cards. These four aces, which are in view from the Warren House Inn (Ex. 45), were dropped by the wicked Jan Reynolds, as related in our account of the sur-roundings of Widecombe (S. Ex. 87). Among the workings of Birch Tor are some very deep gullies, which are evidently of considerable age. A curious circular shaft, cased with stone in the manner of a well, has given the name of Walled Shaft Gully to one of these artificial ravines. Another shaft of a similar kind is to be seen in Chough Gully, locally Chow, or Chaw, and so named from the rare Cornish bird associated with the spirit of King Arthur. Southward of Birch Tor Mine is the Golden Dagger Mine, briefly noticed in Ex. 44, and the visitor will not fail to be struck with the extensive operations in the search for ore of which the locality has been the scene.

Considerable mining enterprise has been shown in this district by Mr. Moses Bawden, to whom we have already referred in our notice of the White Works, near Princetown (Ex. 3).

We shall find nothing remarkable on Birch Tor, but the view from it is good. A few hut dwellings exist on its slope, and on the northern side is a cairn, but it is not of great height. Still keeping a course E.S.E. we shall direct our steps towards an artificial cleft in the ridge before us, and on reaching it shall cross it, and keeping it on our L. make our way up the hill. Here we shall come upon a triple stone row, the existence of which was recorded in 1830, but at that time the whole of the stones composing it were lying on the ground. A few years ago they were re-erected, so that the visitor has now something to look at, but whether he will be able to find any interest in what is only a late nineteenth century erection, formed out of old materials and on an ancient plan, is another matter. No real antiquarian interest can attach to such an erection as this, at the same time we are constrained to admit that re-building is preferable to allowing the stones to lie upon the turf, and this even at the risk of its being said (and it has been said) that on Dartmoor you can be supplied with stone monuments " while you wait." The row extends for about 170 yards, and at its southern end there is a menhir. Some stones near by have been thought to be the remains of other rows, of which, it is considered, there were originally eight, but the evidence of this is not very clear.

Eastward of the ridge on which we stand, which terminates on the S. at Challacombe Down, and on the further side of the valley of the West Webburn, is a wide combe running up between the lofty Hameldon, or Hamel Down, on the R., or S., and Hookney Down, on the L., or N. On one side this combe is overlooked by Hameldon Tor, and on the other by Hookney Tor, and between these piles, neither of which is of striking proportions, is the large circular enclosure known as Grim's Pound, and which is in full view and not more than ½ m. distant. To this we shall now make our way, and on reaching the valley shall pass through the old workings of Headland Mine, with Headland Warren House on the L. The situation of this lonely dwelling is hardly one that would be deemed suitable for a hostelry, but such the house nevertheless once was, rejoicing in the name of the Birch Tor Inn, and in the palmy days of the mines in its vicinity did not lack support.* The house was at one time kept by John Roberts, a noted character in this part of the moor. In Mrs. Bray's *Tamar and Tavy* there is an extract from Mr. Bray's Journal, of the 27th July, 1831, on which day he visited Newhouse. He speaks of a sign that he was told was once to be seen there on which an invitation was held out to the traveller, and which, he says, he thinks he must himself have seen when a boy. But from enquiries that I made in the neighbourhood thirty years ago of old men who had been born and had lived all their

---

* At Challacombe, 1 m. S., are the ruins of a building also said to have been a beer-house.

days on the moor, I am of opinion that Mr. Bray was misinformed, and that the sign was not to be seen at Newhouse, but at Headland. It ran thus :—

> " Jan Roberts lives here,
> Sells cider and beer,
> Your hearts for to cheer ;
> And if you want meat
> To make up a treat
> Here be rabbits to eat."

In this house for many years resided the late tenant of the Warren, James Hannaford, who died in 1899, and was buried at Widecombe, the coffin being borne over the great ridge of Hameldon. He was the son of John Hannaford, who, early in the nineteenth century, lived at Bear Down, and who died in 1868, aged 94 ; we have referred to him in Ex. 5. Several years ago an adventure befel James Hannaford, when he was crossing the common one dark night from the Warren House Inn to his home at Headland. He approached so near to the edge of one of the old shafts of which we have spoken, that the earth gave way and he fell in. Fortunately he was caught in some woodwork, and contrived to find a resting-place upon it. He could see nothing, but heard the dripping of water below. His faithful collie remained on the brink of the shaft during the whole of the night and the following day, and gave evidence by his piteous whining that he knew his master was in peril. His furious barking at length attracted the attention of a search party, and with every manifestation of delight the trusty animal led them to the shaft down which his master had fallen. James Hannaford was soon rescued from his perilous position, but exposure to the cold during that long night and day so affected him that he was ever after crippled. But he lived for many years, and never forgot that he owed his life to his faithful dog.

Climbing the further side of the valley we speedily reach the road running from the Princetown highway to Grendon, Blackaton, and Cator (R. 33). Near the spot where we strike this it is carried over a little stream called Grim's Lake, at Firth Bridge. By following up this stream we shall be led directly to the great hut enclosure we saw from the hill.

Grim's Pound is a fine example of a walled hut cluster, but is not more interesting than others on the moor, notably those existing in the valleys of the Avon, Erme, and Yealm (Exs. 29 to 34), and more-over there are some that are larger. But not one possesses so fine a rampart, and it is this feature that renders the pound so striking. It encloses a space of about four acres, the wall measuring over 500 yards in circumferance. The stones composing this are very massive, and, as a slight examination will reveal, were laid in courses. It was really a double wall that ran around this area where the huts were grouped, the space between the two being probably filled with earth. Judging from the quantity of stones these walls were carried to a height of about six feet, and upon this there is little doubt turf was piled, the plan of construction, to compare small things with great, being not unlike that of the walls of Babylon. For a long time the entrance to Grim's Pound was a disputed point, the lower break in the wall being thought by some to be the original gateway. But a careful examination proved that this was on the S.E. side, as had been shown on a plan made in 1829, and the stones being cleared away, and then placed in the positions it was imagined they once occupied, the result was the entrance upon which the visitor looks to-day. At one time a secret passage leading through the wall was talked of. My eye of faith was never piercing enough to allow me to see it. The wall, which is now a mere ring of great stones, is only about four or five feet in height ; it appears to have been about eight or ten feet in width, but the fallen blocks being iscattered this is now much greater When in a complete state such a barrier would ensure the safety of cattle against the attacks of wolves or other wild animals, and prove a protection for the settlers in a case of a foray. There are the ruins of twenty-four hut dwellings in the pound, some of them, however, being in a very dilapidated condition, and two or three small enclosures, resembling courts, may be seen on the inner side of the wall. The hut in the centre was cleared some years ago in order that the internal arrangements might be seen, and the iron hurdles placed round it to protect it from injury by cattle. [*Gems*, Chap. VIII.]

It has been suggested that Grim was the name of a viking, who, having forced his way into the heart of the moor, erected this stronghold. The name has also been considered to be a corruption of Graham, or Græme. As there is not the slightest proof that the Scandinavian rovers ever visited Dartmoor, the first suggestion is, to say the least of it, a very improbable one, nor does there appear any reason whatever for the second. By some the name has been traced to Grima, an Anglo-Saxon word for the Evil One, a derivation which at least possesses the merit of being as probable as either of the others. It has been the fashion to regard Grim's Pound as having something very mysterious about it, this, no doubt, arising in great measure from the accounts given of the pound by the older antiquaries, who, not knowing the moor well, imagined it to be almost the only thing of its kind upon it. They entered into the wildest speculations concerning it, regarding it, among other things, as a temple of the Sun, and a seat of judicature. But Grim's Pound is just what other similar enclosures on the moor are, a place of security for cattle, and one in which men could seek safety if the necessity for doing so arose. The fact of the wall being formed of blocks more massive than were usually employed for the purpose merely shows that the site chosen for the pound happened to be strewn with lumps of granite of an extraordinary size. There would, of course, be much difficulty in moving these, but we can well suppose that a large number of men were employed on the task. The Roman soldiers as we know never encamped even for a single night without digging a ditch and throwing up a rampart, and while it is certain that the neolithic men of Dartmoor, probably having no cause for haste, and working with heavy material, exhibited no such expeditiousness, there is no reason for supposing that they were a long time in building their huts and enclosures.

[Hameldon is described in the *Bovey Tracey District*, but the visitor will find in the *Shorter Excursions* which follow, directions for reaching Hameldon Cross from Hameldon Tor, and also Berry Pound. In the *Shorter Excursions* instructions are also given for reaching Grim's Pound direct from Chagford and Moreton and from North Bovey.]

Grim's Pound is situated almost entirely in the parish of Manaton, but that part of the wall below Hookney Tor is in the parish of North

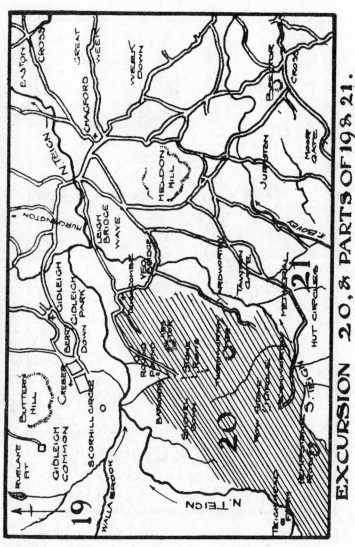

9. CHACFORD & MORETON DISTRICT.

EXCURSION 2O, & PARTS OF 19 & 21.

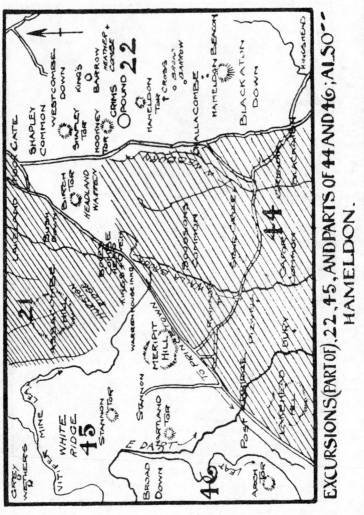

EXCURSIONS (PART OF) 22, 44, 45, AND PARTS OF 44 AND 46; ALSO "
HAMELDON.

Bovey, the little Grim's Lake acting as a boundary between the two From its head eastward the line is marked by boundary stones, and runs under King's Barrow, our next point. This is rather over ½ m. N.E. by E. of the pound. We may either make our way to it direct, or, if we prefer it, first climb the slope to Hookney Tor, whence we have a good view of Grim's Pound. The tor consists of several small piles of rock, and close to it is a cairn. The range of hills forming the southern part of Dartmoor is distinctly visible, and looking through the opening formed by Hameldon on one hand, and Challacombe Down on the other, we see far away in the distance the peak of Brent Hill rising beyond Buckfastleigh Moor, below which are the plantations of Hayford. West of S.W. South Hisworthy and North Hisworthy are seen, and W. by S. the rocks of White Tor. Siddaford is in full view W. by N.

From Hookney Tor to King's Barrow the distance is ¾ m., the direction being E. by N. The cairn here is not a large one, and as will be seen, has been opened. A little to the W. of it is a kistvaen within a circle of stones. The few rocks near by are known as King Tor. From this point we look down over the northern slope of Hookney Down and across Combe Head to Westcombe Down, on which is situated the East Vitifer Mine. At the head of this combe are some hut circles, one of them being enclosed by a low wall, and presently a somewhat similar appearance to the Round Pound at Batworthy. This we shall come upon if we make our way over Hookney Down to Shapley Tor, pursuing a W.N.W. course. It is about ½ m. from King's Barrow, and close to a path running eastward near Bennet's Cross to the north of Birch Tor, and thence to the mine above mentioned and to Westcombe, from which place there is a road to North Bovey. This seems to be the hut mentioned many years ago by Mr. Ormerod as existing near what he called Bovey Combe Head, but he is not very definite about its situation and may have meant Cullicombe Head.

Having visited Shapley Tor, 1,597 feet, we strike due W. down the slope to the road, in order to examine a few hut circles near it. These will be found on either hand, but it is the ones on its western side, or L. as we proceed northward, that will particularly claim our attention. They are situated in Green Combe, near the head of a small tributary of the Bovey, and the visitor will not fail to be struck with the massive stones of which they are formed. The huge slabs of granite of which one is built gives it quite a different appearance from the ordinary hut dwellings on the moor. When the rambler visits the Yealm, and sees the hut circles there with walls formed of stone and turf ten feet thick, and compares them with the present examples, and with others he may have observed, he will see that the ancient dwellings on Dartmoor, though all of one general plan, differ very materially in certain details.

Following the road northward we speedily arrive at the Princetown highway, where, if our destination be Moreton, we turn R. to Moor Gate, from which point we shall make our way to the town as described in R. 4. If bound for Chagford we cross the road, and also the little valley in front of us, our course being a trifle W. of N., to the road running to that town, which will lead us very shortly to Jurston Gate. We descend the hill, as in R. 4, and turn R. or E. towards Jurston

Farm, soon after passing which we cross the Bovey at Jurston Bridge. A short distance further on is Jurston Cross, where a guide-post will show us that our way lies up the hill N. Keeping Meldon Common L. we soon reach Meldon Hall, beyond which we descend the road between Padley Common and Nattadon to Chagford.

————

SHORTER EXCURSIONS.

S. Ex. 48.—*Throwleigh and Shilstone*, 8½ m. To Chagford Bridge and up Walland Hill to Murchington. Turn R. at the guide-post to Higher Murchington, then turn L. and follow the road down to the Blackaton Brook. Cross Wonson Mill Bridge (the road L. runs down to Blackaton Bridge and up to Gidleigh) and climb the hill to Providence Place, a short distance beyond which a road turns R. (guide-post), which will bring the visitor to Wonson, a small hamlet named after the manor house near by. (A footpath will be seen on the R. just after crossing the bridge, which may be followed instead of the road. It leads to a lane running by the manor house to the hamlet). Quite near to the New Inn the ancient entrance to Wonson Manor will be seen.

From Wonson the road runs north-westward to Throwleigh, ¾ m. distant. Another route to it is by way of Deave Lane (S. Ex. 46). Instead of turning R. shortly before reaching Wonson, the visitor continues onward to Cross Park Cottage, and there turns R. into the lane mentioned, which leads direct to the village. Near Cross Park Cottage is the hamlet of Forder, where may be seen a good example of the old manner of hanging gates to which we have more than once referred. From Throwleigh the road leading upward to Shilstone has been described in S. Ex. 46, and Throwleigh Common and Shilstone Tor in Ex. 18. On reaching the verge of the moor at Shilstone the visitor will turn southward, and follow the road very nearly to the Forder Brook. Here a track L. is carried down beside it to a lane, by which he will be led past Ash to Forder. Here turn R., and at the fork of the roads, where is a guide post, take the L. branch to Chapple. Beyond this Chapple Brook is crossed, and the road followed southward to Gidleigh.

Instead of turning down by the Forder Brook after leaving Shilstone the rambler may follow the road past Great and Little Ensworthy and Moortown, and reach Gidleigh as described in R. 24. The way from Gidleigh to Chagford is also given in that route.

S. Ex. 49.—*Gidleigh*, 7½ m. The road from Chagford to Gidleigh has been described. Gidleigh is a small village, consisting of a church, the ruins of an ancient castle, a manor house, a few cottages, and a modern dwelling. The church is eminently characteristic of a Dartmoor sanctuary, granite having been employed not only in the edifice itself, but also in its furnishings, the pulpit, lecterns and reredos being of this material. Not far off is the manor house, and quite near to this the remains of the castle, which is of fourteenth century date. That it was larger than has usually been supposed is proved by the discovery of the foundations of ancient walls in its immediate vicinity, but at the same time it is not likely that it was ever a very extensive building.

[*Gems*, Chap. VI.]   The remains consist of a square tower, with a lower chamber with steps leading to an upper apartment, in which is a fireplace.   At what period the Gidleys came into possession of the manor is not certain, although it was probably very early.

The manor was purchased in 1819 by the Rev. Dr. Whipham, and is now in the possession of his grandson, Mr. A. Guy Whipham, of Gidleigh Park.   This park, together with the adjoining property of Scorhill, once formed part of the ancient Gidleigh Chase.   It is briefly noticed in S. Ex. 50.   [*Gems*, Chap. VI.]

On leaving the castle the visitor will notice an old well by the roadside, just opposite to the manor house gate.   [*Dev. Alps*, Chap. IX.]   It is covered with granite slabs, and granite steps lead down to it.   The way now lies by the manor pound, which has already received mention.   Turn L. up the hill, as in Ex. 19.   Just after passing the second sharp turning in the road a gateway will be noticed R., in which the primitive method of fixing the bars between the upright granite posts is seen.   Looking across the field the visitor has a view of the Rectory.   A little further a road runs R. to this, and to Moortown and Ensworthy (Ex. 18).   A few steps more and the visitor will reach Creber Pound, and make his way up to the moor by South and North Creber Farms, Ex. 19.   On reaching the common turn L. outside the enclosures, and by keeping close to the wall the head of Berry Down Stroll is reached (Ex. 19).   The visitor will make his way down this and at the bottom may either re-enter Creber Pound and return to Gidleigh, or take the lane R. and passing Berry Down, follow it down to Highbury Bridge.

Instead of returning through Murchington the visitor will find it a pleasant walk to go by way of Leigh Steps and Leigh Bridge.   Just before Murchington is reached there is a cross road, the R. one leading towards the valley of the Teign.   Into this the visitor will turn, and it will bring him to a narrow pathway by which he will descend the hill to the steps, where he will cross the river.   Another path, running on the R. bank, leads to Leigh Bridge, immediately below which the North and South Teign unite.   Between these two points a road branches to Gidleigh Park, being carried over the North Teign at Gidleigh Park Bridge.   On crossing Leigh Bridge, which is placed in the midst of charming scenery, the rambler ascends the hill, passing near the Puggie, or Puckie, Stone—the name probably being a corruption of Pixy—which overlooks the river L.   Very soon he will descend towards Holy Street, and at the bend of the road near it will pass an old cross built into the wall.   [*Crosses*, Chap. XIII.]   The picturesque old mill that formerly stood near Holy Street, and formed a favourite subject with so many artists, has now disappeared.   The road here runs by the side of a mill stream to the old woollen factory at the foot of the hill leading to Chagford.

S. Ex. 50.—*Gidleigh Chase and Teigncombe*, 7 m.   The first point is Highbury Bridge, whence the rambler will ascend the road towards Gidleigh, but instead of turning R. to the village, will continue straight up the lane to Berry Down.   Gidleigh Chase, or that part of it now comprising the park and Scorhill, is situated on the L. as the visitor ascends ; there is no doubt that it was formerly of much greater extent, and lay open to the forest.   Just before reaching Berry Down a gate on the L. will enable him to obtain a glimpse of part of it, with a view also of Gidleigh Tor, more generally known as Prinsep's Folly. [*Gems*, Chap. VI.] On this tor are the remains of a house. This fine hill we shall see to great advantage when we reach the southern side of the river.

Passing Berry Down the visitor will make his way up the stroll. and when about ¼ m. from the bottom of it will reach an iron gate on the L. This is an entrance to Scorhill and also a church path (T. 44). The visitor will follow it to Scorhill House, a romantically situated residence, which cannot, however, boast of much antiquity. It formerly belonged to Mr. Rowe, of Berry Down, from whom it was purchased by Mr. Stark, who sold it to its present holder, the Rev. E. B. Layard. Passing the house the visitor will descend to the North Teign which he will cross where that stream forms an island, the channel on each side being spanned by a clam. As he makes his way up the side of the common in an easterly direction, a view of the chase will unfold itself L. Very soon he will reach the road near the Round Pound (Ex. 20), and may either follow this L. to the moor gate or cross it, and proceeding E. enter the short stroll leading to Teigncombe Common Lane, which, being strewn with boulders and more nearly resembling the bed of a stream than a track, has been playfully dubbed Featherbed Lane. Near the gateway at Teigncombe some holed stones similar to the one we observed at Fernworthy may be seen ; one of these has a square hole, the other a round one. Here also are the remains of a chapel, one of three formerly existing in the parish. Instead of turning R. to Yeo Bridge and following the road to Chagford through Thorn and Waye, the visitor will make his way down North Hill Lane, where he will notice another holed stone. As he descends he will have a good view of the wild chase, where oaks and hollies clothe the slopes, and also of Gidleigh Tor, which crowns a heather-clad hill rising boldly above the surrounding wood. In about ¾ m. from Teigncombe the rambler will reach Leigh Bridge, when he will have completed the circuit of the chase. From this point the road to Chagford has been described (S. Ex. 49).

S. Ex. 51.—*Scorhill Circle, Holed Stone in the Teign, Batworthy, and Teigncombe,* 8 m. To Berry Down Stroll, as in the preceding excursion. Instead of turning into the path L. to Scorhill House, the visitor will continue to the end of the stroll, and will then turn L. and follow the wall of the enclosure. This he will notice is higher and more carefully built than the ordinary newtake walls, and is also furnished with a coping. Very soon he will reach another entrance to the Scorhill grounds, where is an iron gate similar to the one in the stroll. This, however, is but very little used. A ruined farmhouse will be noticed just within the lower wall. Here the rambler turns R., and on reaching a leat, the same he saw in the stroll, and also at Rue Lake (Ex. 19), will follow it to Scorhill Tor, or as the pile is usually termed, Scorhill Rocks. Thence the leat will become his guide over Scorhill Down to the stone circle described in Ex. 19. (The circle may be reached direct from the head of Berry Down Stroll, S.W. by W., over Scorhill Hill, 1,323 feet, the distance being ½ m.) From the circle the visitor will make his way down to the North Teign to examine the Holed Stone, and the single stone clapper known as Walla Brook Bridge (Ex. 19). Crossing the river at Teign Clapper he will pass up the side of Shovel Down, with the enclosures of Batworthy L., to Batworthy Corner. The Shovel Down antiquities, which are near by, are described in Ex. 20. The return may be by way of the road N.E. past the Round Pound to the moor gate at Brimstone Down, or the rambler may strike up over the common E. from the Round Pound to Teigncombe Common Lane, as described in S. Ex. 50.

S. Ex. 52.—*Watern Tor, direct*, 11 m. To Teigncombe, either by way of Yeo Bridge, or Leigh Bridge. From the hamlet the moor may be reached by going up Teigncombe Common Lane (S. Ex. 50), or by the Gate at Brimstone Down. The next point is Batworthy Corner, S.W. of the moor end of the lane, and approached by road from the gate (Ex. 20). Watern Tor bears W. by N. from the corner, from which it is distant 2 m., and is seen rising conspicuously from the lofty ridge on which it is placed. But as to make a bee-line towards it would necessitate crossing the Teign at a point where it might not be convenient to do so, it will be best for the rambler to make his way down the side of Shovel Down, with the Batworthy enclosures R., to Teign Clapper (Ex. 19). Having crossed the Teign here he will turn L. to Walla Brook Bridge, where he will cross that stream, and thus find himself in the fork formed by the two. From this point Watern Tor bears a little S. of W., and is 1½ m. distant. As the ground is here in places rather swampy it may not be possible to follow a perfectly direct course to the tor, but the rambler will find that it will not be necessary to diverge far from it. The tor is described in Ex. 19.

Watern Tor.   Wild Tor.

FROM WALLA BROOK CLAPPER, LOOKING WEST.

S. Ex. 53.—*The Grey Wethers, direct*, 13 m. The road is followed to Metheral, as already described, and thence to Fernworthy, from which place the route is given in Ex. 20. If the return is made the same way the course to be followed from the circles is N.E. for about 1 m., when the rambler will bear R. to Fernworthy.

S. Ex. 54.—*Teignhead Farm, direct*, 13 m. This is described in Ex. 19. There is little difference in the distance between the Teigncombe route, or that by Metheral. If the rambler chooses the latter he will first make his way to the top of the lane at Fernworthy, as in S. Ex. 53 ; see also Ex. 20. From the circle on Froggymead Hill the course is a trifle N. of W., and the distance to Teignhead Bridge about 1 m. The return by way of Stonetor Hill and Batworthy Corner to Teigncombe is given at the end of Ex. 20.

S. Ex. 55.—*Kes Tor and the Shovel Down Antiquities*, 6½ m. The first point is Teigncombe, which may be reached by way of Leigh Bridge, or by the road past Waye and Thorn. The latter will take the rambler by Yeo Mill, which being near South Hill probably occupies the same site as one mentioned in a forester's account of the year 1491, in which is an entry of "6d. of new rent of John Wille, of Hille, for having a course of water from the water of Teign within the Forest of Dartmoor across the land of the Forest aforesaid, and venville, to the mill of the said John at Stouthill, within the parish of Chagford, to have and occupy the aforesaid watercourse to the aforesaid John, his heirs, and his assigns, according to the custom of the Forest, as appears on the Court Rolls."

Leaving Yeo Mill the rambler will pass through Teigncombe, and make his way up the lane to the commons, which latter he will reach very near to Kes Tor, 1,433 feet, a rock mass which has been almost constantly in view during his wanderings in the neighbourhood of Chagford. It has been suggested that the tor may have derived its name from the Celtic *kist*, *i.e.*, *chest*, which, indeed, is not improbable, as its square form certainly gives it a resemblance to such an object. Though not of great size Kes Tor is nevertheless striking in appearance, its situation contributing greatly to this. The view from it is very fine, and embraces many of the prominent hills on the eastern side of the moor, as well as a wide extent of cultivated country. Cosdon lifts up its great rounded form towards the N. (*Okehampton District*) ; the rocks of Wild Tor and Watern Tor (Ex. 19) rise from the dusky ridges westward, and beyond the latter is Newtake, overlooking the morasses of Cranmere. White Horse Hill is seen L. of this, and due S. are Hurston Ridge and Assacombe Hill. Away to the S.E. is Hey Tor, seen to the L. of Hameldon (*Bovey Tracey District*), and L. of this, but much nearer to us, the hill known as East Down, or Easdon (S. Ex. 61), placed at the head of the Widecombe Valley. Turning from the moor the visitor will look down upon Gidleigh Chase and Chagford, and will mark the entrance to the great gorge of Fingle (S. Ex. 66, 67). Far away beyond the Teign is Haldon, and looming indistinctly against the northern sky the hills of Exmoor.

There are several rock basins on Kes Tor, but one is particularly noticeable, being by far the largest on the moor. Previous to 1856 its existence was unknown, as it had been filled with earth, probably being regarded as dangerous to sheep or cattle. In that year it was discovered by Mr. Ormerod, and on its being cleared it was deemed advisable to surround it with an iron rail. Its longer diameter at the top is about 7½ feet ; the side are sloping, the diameter at the bottom being about 2 feet. It is just over 2½ feet in depth.

The Shovel Down stone rows commence close to the W.S.W. of the tor, and are less than ½ m. from it. For a description of these see Ex. 20.

On returning from Kes Tor the rambler may either strike due N. for about ¼ m., and then bear R. to the stroll at the head of Teigncombe Common Lane : or N. by W. to the Round Pound, thence following the road R. over Brimstone Down to Teigncombe hamlet.

S. Ex. 56.—*Frenchbere and Thornworthy*, 7½ m. To Yeo Bridge by Waye Barton (S. Ex. 55). On crossing this the visitor will turn up the hill L., and in about ½ m. will reach the farm of Great Frenchbere ; he will notice some holed stones built into the wall of the enclosures as he proceeds. Passing the farm he will enter upon the common, with Frenchbere Tor a little in advance of him on the R. Before reaching this he will notice a hut circle. From the tor he will bear southward to Thornworthy, in the walls of the enclosures of which are some more circular holed stones. Some of these may be unfinished millstones, left by those engaged in cutting them in consequence of the stone being found to be unsuitable for the intended purpose, and others were perhaps used by tinners, being similar to those at Riddy Pit, noticed in Ex. 2. We shall notice others in our ramble round the moor. Below Thornworthy, in the narrow glen through which the South Teign leaves the wastes through which its earlier course has led it, is the stream-work and blowing-house referred to in Ex. 21. There are in fact two mining buildings, and a good example of a trough and mould-stone. A similar story attaches to these old houses to the one related of Snails' House, in Lough Tor Hole, and which is related further on (Ex. 44). [*Dev, Alps*, Chap. IV.] On Thornworthy Down is Thornworthy Tor, less than ½ m. W.N.W. of the farm, and to this the rambler will now make his way. N.E. by N. of it, and ½ m. distant, is Middle Tor, which is worth a visit. From Middle Tor it is not far to Kes Tor, from which the routes to Chagford are given in S. Ex. 55.

The return may also be made by way of Frenchbere and Yardworthy ; the distance is very little further. From the first-named farm a path leads down to a wooden foot-bridge on the South Teign. This the rambler will follow, and crossing the river will make his way up through Yardworthy to the road. Turning L., or N.E., he may either take the R. or L. branch at the fork. The R. will lead him to the western edge of Meldon Common (he must not turn R. before reaching it), whence he will follow the road to Waye, or cross over the down as in S. Ex. 57. The L. branch will give him a better view of the narrow vale through which the South Teign runs. He will also pass Collihole, the ancient Collerewe ; the house is a good example of the moorland homesteads of a former day. Here, as in other old houses in the moorland region, some of which are to be seen in the valley of the Tavy, while others are noticed in our description of the *Post Bridge District*, the shippen, or cowshed, adjoined the living rooms, and the inmates and the cattle all entered at one door. It will be seen that the house stands on a site excavated from the side of the hill, an arrangement observed elsewhere on the moorland borders, and which was doubtless intended for shelter. Collihole now forms part of Hole Farm, which the visitor will pass a little further on. Beyond this he will reach Thorn, where he will turn R. to Waye and Chagford.

S. Ex. 57.—*Meldon, Nattadon, and Week Down*. These elevated commons are situated to the S of the town of Chagford, the summits of the first and last named being about 1 m. from the church. Nattadon is a little nearer. Meldon is reached from the Square by way of High Street (in which is the well-known hostelry, the Three Crowns, once a house belonging to the Whiddons) and the School, opposite to which is a path leading to Padley Common, a small down lying at the northern foot of this fine hill. From this point the visitor may make his way direct to the top, 647 feet above the churchyard, or 1,280 feet above sea level, where are some scattered masses of granite, and from which a fine view is commanded. Another way is by passing the School and following the road to Meldon Hall, just before arriving at which it touches the common, or by going still further on to Higher Weddicott, from which the summit is only a short distance.

Nattadon may also be reached by the same road, the visitor turning L. a little short of Meldon Hall ; or he may strike into a path at Highfield, which will also bring him to the common. This hill, the north-western slope of which is strewn with granite, attains an elevation of about 1,000 feet. On its eastern edge the path alluded to joins the road that comes up from the town by the Rectory, and at a point very near to where it enters upon Week Down, which common is noticed in S. Ex. 61.

The road on the south-western verge of Meldon Common, between Waye and Tawton Gate near Yardworthy, may be reached by striking over this hill from Padley Common in a south-westerly direction, leaving the summit L. In reversing this the rambler will leave the road at the guide-post, and, of course, strike N.E. This route may be preferred by visitors making their way to or from that part of the moor in the neighbourhood of Metheral.

S. Ex. 58.—*Warren House Inn, direct.* By the moor from C., 11 m. ; by road from *C.,* 10 m. From Moreton the route is by road only, 12½ m. By the Moor. This route will first take the rambler to the moor at Tawton Gate, which point he may reach by the road branching off at Waye (See *Chagford to Metheral*); or he may join the same road by striking up over Padley Common, as in S. Ex. 57 On entering upon Yardworthy Common, near a large newtake enclosed between sixty and seventy years ago, the rambler will turn L., with the wall of Willandhead close on that hand, and make his way due S., with Metheral Brook on his right. In 1240 this stream seems to have been called the Alber, or Aber, but the name is now lost. The perambulators of that date draw the boundary line of the forest in this part of the moor through the midst of the Turbary of Alberysheved,* and this can only have reference to the peaty ground near the head of this stream. In 1609 the jury of survey identified it as such, though the spot was then called Turf Hill, and this name it also bore some ninety years later, when, however, it was also known as Black Fen. In the earlier part of the nineteenth century it is referred to as Broadmoor Mires, but it is now generally known as Metheral Bogs. About ½ m. from the point at which the rambler has entered on the moor the wall on the L. is carried toward the S.E., so that in pursuing a southerly course he will gradually leave it. When he has proceeded about ¾ m. from the point where it strikes off he will be abreast of the head of the bogs, which should be ¼ m. R. This part of the moor is noticed in R. 25, in Ex. 21, and in T. 44, where are also are some remarks on the old track that ran over Hurston Ridge. The course will now be

---

*Among other forms in which this name appears are Alberyshede, Aberesheved, and Aberheve.

W. of S., to avoid dropping down in the valley of the Bovey, and in
a little over 1¼ m. the Warren House Inn will be reached.

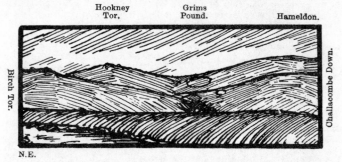

FROM NEAR WARREN HOUSE INN, LOOKING E.

No directions for the return route are needed, as the rambler will
merely steer E. of N. from the Inn, changing his course to due N.
when about 1¼ m. from it, and on reaching the road between Metheral
and Yardworthy will turn R. and make his way to Chagford as in
S. Exs. 56, 57.

The Warren House Inn may also be reached by way of the Bovey
river. The rambler will proceed for the first 2 m. or so as above
(see also *Chagford to Metheral*), but at the turning beyond Tannaford he must strike into the road L., which will lead him to Higher
Corndon, whence a lane runs down to the river. This he will follow
upwards to Hurston, and passing through the farm, reach the common
by a track running between the enclosures. A short distance to the
L. of the point at which he emerges upon it is the pound described in
Ex. 21. The rambler will now strike southward, with the Bovey, or
Hurston Water, in the valley L., to King's Oven, 1½ m. distant, and
about ¼ m. N. of his destination.

The first part of the reverse of this route will be found in Ex. 21,
where directions are given for reaching the pound above Lakeland
just referred to. On leaving this he will strike into the track 200 yards
N.W. of it, and will shortly reach Hurston, beyond which he will follow
the Bovey downward for nearly ½ m. Here, where it bends R., he
will leave it, and pass up the lane to Higher Corndon, at which farm
he turns L. and then R. and shortly reaches the S.W. corner of Meldon
Common. From this point the route is described in S. Ex. 56, 57.

By ROAD. From Chagford the way lies past the School and up
the hill due S. to Meldon Hall, as in S. Ex. 57, and thence to Jurston
Gate, as already described (see *Chagford to Moor Gate via Jurston Gate*).
This gate, which is about 2½ m. from the town, is hung between two
masses of rock, on one of which there are three basins. The road
is now followed over the common for about 1 m., when it is joined
by that coming L. from Moreton. On this hill are the Chagford Golf
Links.

From Moreton to Moor Gate q.v. The junction with the road

from Chagford is about ¾ m. further on, between which two points the road to Challacombe and Cator branches L. (R. 33). From the junction the Princetown road runs in a south-westerly direction, and this is now followed. In the valley on the R. is Lakeland, and the disused West Vitifer Mine (Ex. 21). Further on the road runs by Bush Down, with Bennet's Cross L. (Ex. 22), and shortly afterwards enters the forest, the boundary being marked by a tiny stream—the head waters of the Walla Brook, which flows S. to the East Dart. Just within the boundary is the Warren House Inn, which is noticed in Ex. 45.

(These road routes from Chagford and Moreton form the first part of R. 35).

The return by the road is given in R. 4.

S. Ex. 59.—*Grim's Pound, direct.* From *C.,* 9½ m.; from *M.,* 11½ m. From Chagford the route to the moor at Jurston Gate, as above, must be followed. About 200 yards beyond the gate the road must be deserted and a southerly course struck. (Bear a little E. of S.) This will take the rambler across the branch of the Bovey rising in Green Combe, and on climbing the slope on the further side of it he will find himself at the point where the road to Challacombe diverges from the Princetown highway. This Challacombe road must be followed as in R. 33, for a distance of nearly 1½ m., when Firth Bridge will be reached, with Grim's Pound in the wide combe L. (Ex. 22). If preferred the rambler may strike over the common L. instead of following the Challacombe road from the highway, and visit Shapley Tor and Hookney Tor *en route.*

From Moreton the visitor may reach the pound either by way of Moor Gate or North Bovey. The latter is the shorter, and the route is sketched in S. Ex. 61 and 62. The road to Moor Gate has already been described, and it is now only necessary to mention a few objects the rambler will pass. About ½ m. from the town, on the R. of the way, is an entrance gate to Lowton, where are two granite pillars. One bears the date 1720, and the other the letters I.S., and on each is an emblazoned shield. It is evident that these once formed one stone, and that the carving was on a panel, part of the moulding of which is still to be seen. At Bughead Cross, just over 1 m. from Moreton, is an old guide-stone bearing the initials of Moreton, Newton, Tavistock, and Chagford. This part of the road was once the haunt of a mysterious individual named John Fall, who seems to have been a highwayman with a penchant for frightening his victims by a kind of Spring-heel Jack performance. In ascending the hill after crossing Worm Hill Bridge, a gate hung in the primitive manner will be observed on the R. At Beetor Cross, where a road comes up R. from Beetor Farm, is another old guide-stone, and a little further on, where the road branches L. to Barramoor Bridge (R. 32, 53), the ancient stone cross, erected in all probability to mark the track across the moor on the line of which the present road runs, will be seen on the hedge L. For many years this cross served as a guide-post in a field near by, but was placed in its present situation, which there is little doubt is very near to its original site, in 1900. [*Crosses,* Chap. XIV] This spot is also known as Watching Place, and it is said that a gibbet was once erected here, the criminal whose corpse was hung upon it being the last to be made such an example of in this neighbourhood.

(The road L. runs eastward, the one to Barramoor Bridge and

Ashburton leaving it 150 yards on and running S. The former goes
E. to Hele, where is another stone cross [*Crosses*, Chap. XV.], and
passing Bowden Mill is carried over a branch of the Bovey flowing
from near Vogwell Down (Ex. 23), and reaches Yard, just beyond
which it crosses Bovey Bridge and enters the village of North Bovey).

From Beetor Cross the road to the moor, 1 m. distant, runs south-
westerly. Just before it is reached there is a turning across some fields
L. leading to a small farm named Liapa. Here the upper portion of
a fine granite cross may be seen built into the garden wall [*Crosses*,
Chap. XIV.]

On reaching Moor Gate the rambler may desert the Princetown
road and strike up over Shapley Common L. to Shapley Tor, noticing
some hut circles as he proceeds. The course is at first S.W. by S.,
with the enclosures L., but in less than ¼ m. this changed to S., and
then to E. of S. By this route Shapley Tor is about 1 m. from Moor
Gate. Hookney Tor is ½ m. S. of it, and Grim's Pound is immediately
below this. The return is given in Ex. 22.

S. Ex. 60.—*Hameldon and Berry Pound.* Add 2 m. to the distances
given in S. Ex. 59. From Chagford Grim's Pound will be the first
point, instructions for reaching which are given in S. Ex. 59. Thence
the visitor will make his way to Hameldon Tor, 1,737 feet, sometimes
called Grim's Tor, which is quite near to the pound and is seen from
it S.E. A fine view of the great hut enclosure is obtained from the
rocks. About ⅓ m. from them, S. by E., is Hameldon Cross. This is
noticed in our description of the ridge of Hameldon given in the
Bovey Tracey District, to which the reader is referred. Rather over
½ m. E. by S. of the tor, and about the same distance E.N.E. of the
cross, is Berry Pound, also noticed as above. From this enclosure
King's Barrow is ¾ m. N.N.W., and Grim's Pound rather more than
that distance W.N.W.

From Moreton the route may be by Moor Gate, as in S. Ex. 59,
or through North Bovey. For the latter see S. Ex. 61 and 62.

For the return route from the pound see Ex. 22 and S. Ex. 61.

S. Ex. 61.—*North Bovey and East Down.* *C.*, 11½ m.; *M.*, 6½ m.
The visitor from Chagford will pass up the hill S. of the church with
the rectory grounds L. to Week Down, whence a fine view is presented
of the district over which our rambles have extended. Kes Tor stands
up well between Nattadon, or Nat Tor Down, as it has sometimes been
called, R., and Meldon Hill L. Here, by the roadside, is an old granite
cross, having an incised Maltese Cross on each face. It is leaning
somewhat out of the perpendicular. This cross, together with Shorter
Cross, which the visitor will pass a little further on, I have described
elsewhere [*Crosses*, Chap. XIII.] Shorter Cross stands near the down
on the L. of the lane leading from it to Middlecott, which is the next
point. After passing this place, which consists of three farmhouses,
avoid taking the first turning L. The lane only leads to some fields, but
bend sharp to the L. just after the guide-post. Here the L. branch
must be followed to Thorn, where some holed stones will be noticed.
A very short distance beyond the farm a road branches R., or S., which
will bring the visitor to a point on the Moreton and Moor Gate road,
1¾ m. from the former place, where is a guide-post. This road must
be crossed and the lane, which is a very winding one, be followed the

general direction being S.E. A little way in is a turning to the R.; this must be passed. About 1¼ m. on is a guide-post, and here is the manor pound. The road to the village, which is close by, runs to the R. of this.

From Moreton the road bearing L. near the White Horse Hotel is followed for a few score yards, when the visitor will branch R. (The road going straight on, or S., leads into one shortly to be reached, and runs to Lustleigh). About 1 m. further one this is met at Bovey Cross, or Horse Pit Cross [*Crosses*, Chap. XV.] It comes N. from Sandy Park (S. Ex. 67, 68), and Easton, and goes to Lustleigh by way of Sanduck. Less than ½ m. beyond Horse Pit Cross is the pound mentioned above.

North Bovey has happily preserved its old restful air. Removed from the high road and the railway it is now almost as ever it was. Although not altogether typical of a Dartmoor border village, there is certainly not one that is more pleasing. The houses, one of which bears the date 1738, surround a playstow, shaded by a grove of ancient oaks. The village cross is an interesting feature. For a time this served the purpose of a footbridge, but was set up in its present situation in 1829 by the Rev. J. P. Jones, who was then curate of the parish. [*Crosses*, Chap. XV.] Mr. Jones was the author of a small book on the scenery and antiquities of Moretonhampstead, and another on the scenery in the neighbourhood of Ashburton, both first published in 1823.

North Bovey Church, which is perpendicular in style, possesses no monuments of importance. The tower has a projecting stair turret.

A new manor house has lately been built in the Week Valley by the Hon. W. F. D. Smith.

Near the village is an interesting object. It is a memorial set up by a loving hand, and stands in a field belonging to Fairbrook, which is reached by crossing the bridge near Broadmead Cottage, and turning into a gateway on the right a short distance up the lane. Beneath a large oak, on a granite block *in situ*, rests a square slab of the same, and on this is placed a small kist, the inner side and ends, as well as the cover-stone, being also of granite, and carefully worked, while the front is of white marble. On this is the following inscription :

FLORA,

The Much Loved Friend

AND

Companion of her Master.

7 July, 1834.

Surmounting the whole is a small granite obelisk. This little monument, which conveys so much to us, was erected by Captain Britten to the memory of his faithful dog.

North Bovey village is overlooked on the S.W. by East Down, or Easton Down, as it is now usually called, a fine eminence at the N., or upper end of the Widecombe Valley. It is approached by crossing Bovey Bridge and following the road towards Yard for about a furlong, and then turning up a lane L. to the down which is close by. Its length from N. to S. is about 1¼ m., and its breadth about 1 m. On its southern verge are the farms of Easdon and Barracott, N. of the former being East Down, or Easdon Tor, and N. of the latter, Easdon

Hill. The down may also be reached from the village by crossing the Bovey at the lower bridge near Broadmead Cottage, and taking the R. branch of the road at the first fork to Bowda. There are a number of hut circles upon it, and if the visitor goes by way of the lane near Yard he may meet with some of these by steering a S.S.W. course, which will also bring him to the tor crowning the hill, when he will have attained an elevation of 1,440 feet. He will first pass the disused workings of Great Wheal Eleanor, above Hourder Plantation, and continuing his way up the steep ascent, will reach a group of hut circles in about ½ m. Another group is situated to the S.E. of the tor. Just before reaching the rocks the line of stones marking the boundary between the parishes of North Bovey and Manaton is passed. The view from the summit is good, all the chief hills and tors in the vicinity being in sight. Southward is the Widecombe Valley, Honeybag and Chinkwell being on the L., and Hameldon R. (*Bovey Tracey District*). To the N.W. is Cosdon, which is seen from every lofty place on the E. side of the moor. East Down is in view from Brent Hill (*Brent and Ivybridge District*), and from the Kingsbridge road above Wrangaton Station (R. 47). Many years ago I used to be amused at hearing the landlord at the hotel of the latter place point out the hill to visitors as Yes Tor. There is a large block of granite on this pile known as the Whooping Rock, and so called according to a note in Carrington's *Dartmoor* (poem, 1826) from the noise it made in tempestuous weather, presumably occasioned by the wind rushing through some aperture. But it has also been said to have obtained this name from a custom formerly observed in the locality of taking children to the tor when suffering from whooping-cough, in order that they might be near the sheep, a belief once existing that those afflicted with that complaint would be cured if left for a time among those animals.

At Easdon Farm some sixteenth and seventeenth century silver coins were found several years ago, together with an old jack-knife, concealed within the house. An account of these was given by the late Mr. W. Pengelly in the *Transactions of the Devonshire Association*, Vol. XII. Not far to the west of Easdon is Vogwell, of which there is a very early mention. The name appears in a document found among the Exeter Cathedral archives, dealing with the boundaries of certain lands in this neighbourhood in Saxon times, but in a slightly different form. The boundary line being drawn from Lustleigh to Withecombe Head, is then said to go "from thence to Lime Stream, and so to Voghill Lake; and along that lake to Voghill's Head." That Voghill is the present Vogwell there can be no doubt.

From Easdon Farm the return to North Bovey may be by way of the hill, the course to be steered being N.N.E. On reaching the road below Wheal Eleanor turn R. to Bovey Bridge. Then passing through the village leave it by the road above the New Inn, and pass up to the pound. The guide-post here will show that the R. branch of the road —running N.E.—must be taken. Soon afterwards the Lustleigh road is crossed at Horse Pit Cross, and in another 1¼ m. Moreton will be reached.

The visitor from Chagford will, of course, take the L. branch at the pound, and in ¾ m. will cross the Moreton and Moor Gate road. He will then turn L. to Thorn, thence following the road to Middlecott and Week Down. (The guide-post ½ m. beyond Thorn will show that he has to take the road running W. and then N.W.) From Week Down the road leads down the hill direct to the town.

[If preferred the return from Easdon to Chagford may be by the way of Beetor Cross. The road running N.W. from the farm is followed for 1¼ m. to Barramoor Bridge (R. 53). Between these points a road branches R. to Langdon, after which there is a cross road, and then another road R. to Gratnar ; avoid turning into either. N. of the bridge there is another turning R. where a road runs to Hele ; this must be passed also. About ½ m. further on is a guide-post, where the road to Watching Place, or Beetor Cross, turns L. At the cross turn sharp R., or N., and then almost immediately L., and passing Beetor Farm follow the road to Beetor Bridge, where the Bovey is crossed, and thence N. to the guide-post near Stiniel. Leave this farm L., and about ½ m. further on turn L. to Lower Weddicott. Just beyond this is Higher Weddicott, where the rambler will turn R., or N., and speedily reach Meldon Hall. The way to the town lies straight down the hill, N.

S. Ex. 62.—*North Bovey to Grim's Pound*, 6½ m. Crossing Bovey Bridge the rambler will make his way to Yard, rather over ¼ m., where he will take the L. branch at the fork reached immediately *after* passing that place. ¼ m. further on is another fork, and here also he will strike into the L. branch, and follow the road to Langdon, which is rather more than ½ m. distant. Very soon after that farm is passed the Chagford (R.) and Ashburton (L.) road is reached (R. 32), and here the visitor will turn L., but will only follow it for a few score yards, when he will strike into a path R. running across some enclosures. This leads to Kendon and Heathercombe, to the first of which farms he must make his way. On crossing the branches of the Bovey that flow from near Vogwell Down (Ex. 24), close to where they unite, the path runs southward by the stream, and ¼ m. up a lane branches R. This will lead the rambler to Kendon, which is near by. This farm is one of the ancient vills, and appears four hundred years ago as the " hamelett de Kyndon," when it paid a venville rent of 1d. The lane is continued past this to the moor, which is less than ¼ m. distant. The rambler will now find himself below King's Barrow, which bears W.S.W., and which has already been noticed. On reaching this he will see the wide combe in which Grim's Pound is situated—the pound itself is about ½ m. S.W. by W. As the surroundings have been described in Ex. 22, the rambler is referred there for further directions.

If the return from Grim's Pound to North Bovey is to be made over the same road by which the rambler has approached it, he will first direct his steps to King's Barrow, as in Ex. 22, and then strike E.N.E. to the lane leading to Kendon, thence passing by the farm to the stream. This becomes his companion down to the point where it unites with another, when it is crossed, and the path running N.E. followed to the Chagford road. Here turn L., and then immediately R. up the hill to Langdon, on passing which the descent to Yard is commenced, the common being kept close on the R.

Another way of returning is by Heathercombe. Pass up the combe due E. from Grim's Pound, and in 1 m. the enclosures of this farm will be reached. A little stream which runs close to it will first be struck. On passing Heathercombe the path L., which is carried along by the side of the Bovey branch mentioned above, is followed down the valley due N. to the lane L. leading to Kendon, Vogwell Farm, R., being passed on the way. From this point directions have been given above.

S. Ex. 63.—*North Bovey to Manaton*, 4½ m. Just beyond the bridge near Broadmead Cottage a lane turns L. This must be passed, but at the fork a little way further on, the L. branch must be followed. ½ m. on Higher Luckdon is passed R., and then Lower Luckdon L. (R. 32). Just beyond this a footpath leads across some fields L. Follow this, and on reaching another road, cross it, and strike into one running S.E. This passes through Neadon (*Bovey Tracey District*, Short Excursions), ¼ m. beyond which the rambler turns R. and ascends the hill to the village, nearly ¾ m. distant.

Another way is by going through Langstone. The field path mentioned above must not be chosen, but the road followed to the farm named, where is a guide-post. Turn R., and almost immediately after strike into a path L. This runs across a field to some enclosures on the down N. of Manaton Rocks, and may be followed to the road, which climbs the hill from Neadon. Here turn R. to the village. The return is given in the Shorter Excursions in the *Bovey Tracey District*.

Cosdon. Chagford visitors will proceed *via* Shilstone Hill, and Clannaborough Down ; directions for reaching Shilstone Tor are given in R. 38 A. *Vide* S. Ex. 47 and the section on Cosdon in the *Okehampton District.*

THE BANKS OF THE TEIGN.

Although, as De la Beche has pointed out, the region bounded on the north and east by the Teign, and embracing the parishes of Moreton, Bridford, Christow, and Hennock, is geologically and geographically one with Dartmoor, it has certainly never been looked upon as forming part of it, nor is there any mention of it in connection with the forest or commons of Devon. The true eastern boundary of the moor, south of the Teign, runs through the parishes of Chagford, North Bovey, and Manaton, to Lustleigh, and the district referred to is altogether outside this. But within its confines are a number of hills and tors of a character precisely similar to those on Dartmoor itself, and although this large tract does not come within the scope of this book, it may perhaps be well to notice briefly the chief of these. To one part of this district—The Gorge of Fingle and Drewsteignton, which are near Chagford and Moreton—it will be necessary to devote a little more attention. This is therefore described in a series of short excursions.

About 1 m. from Moreton, and approached by the Exeter road, which leaves the town by way of Cross Street, where the old almshouses are situated (this runs eastward from the White Hart Hotel), is Hingston Down, the summit of which, crowned with the granite masses known as Hingston Rocks, attains an elevation of over 1,000 feet. On the eastern side of this down two roads, branching from the Exeter highway, run southward, one of them (the R. in following that course) leading to Pepperdon Down, and the other to the common on which is situated the fine Blackingstone Rock. Further E. is Laployd Down, adjoining which is Beacon Down, and S. of these the Kennick Reservoir. This is over ¾ m. in length, and communicates with the Tottiford Reservoir, the both forming the collecting basin of the water supply of Torquay. Towards Christow, which is about 2 m. from these fine sheets of water, are Clampitt Down, Kiln Down, and Inn Down, and S. of these, and between Christow and Hennock, are Waye Down and Barton Down. North-west of the village of Christow, the church of which formerly belonged to the great Abbey of Bec, in Normandy, and afterwards to Tavistock Abbey, is Bridford, anciently Bridgeford, proverbial for its remote situation, and between these two places is a pile known as Skat Tor, 948 feet, more frequently referred to as Skatter Rock. This is finely situated on the summit of Christow Common, and commands a charming view of that part of the valley of the Teign a short distance below Dunsford Bridge. About 1 m. N. of Bridford, and on a hill that sweeps abruptly down to the Teign, is Hel Tor, whence the climber to its breezy summit looks over a wide extent of East Devon, the panorama being as beautiful as it is varied. Blackingstone Rock, or Blackystone, as it is always called, is rather more than 1 m. W. by S. of Hel Tor, and about the same distance E. of Hingston. Rocks. Being well placed, and having an elevation of considerably over 1,000 feet, this pile forms another point from which a magnificent view is to be obtained. Like Hel Tor, it is seen for many miles round, but according to tradition there was a time when these tors were not to be seen at all. This tells us that on the hills on which they are placed King Arthur and the Evil One once took their stand and threw quoits at each other, an encounter in which the latter was defeated. As the quoits fell they became changed into rocks, and thus the masses that we now look upon were formed. Not far from Blackingstone is a pile of rocks bearing the name of the Druids' Altar. The reader will expect to find this, for he knows by this time that the Druids were ubiquitous. These tors are called by Risdon Blackstone and Whitstone. The present name of the latter has no connection with the British king's adversary, *hel* simply implying height.

Further south on this high land between the Wray and the Teign are other rock piles. The chief among these are referred to in our account of the *Bovey Tracey District.*

The rambler will find the walk from Moreton to Dunsford Bridge a very charming one ; the road runs to the N. of the tors just noticed. In descending towards the bridge, Woodhill, an outlying boulder-strewn eminence, is passed on the R. A lane leads from the village of Dunsford to Clifford Bridge, whence the way to Moreton is described in S. Ex. 64.

S. Ex. 64.—*Mardon Down, Clifford Bridge, and Wooston Castle.* (From Moreton). 7½ m. Following the road on the north side of the church we take the L. branch at the fork, and climb the hill to Mardon Down, about 1 m. from the town. Here we have a fine view of the eastern frontier of Dartmoor, Hey Tor rising very conspicuously to the S. On Mardon are some antiquarian remains, but they have been despoiled. About ½ m. on the R. soon after entering on the down the visitor will find some vestiges of a cairn known as the Giant's Grave, 1,170 feet, and a little to the north of this part of a stone circle, either a hut dwelling or ring of stones surrounding a cairn. ¼ m. N.E. of this is a stone pillar, six feet high, which bears the name of the Headless Cross, but whether it ever was a cross is doubtful. It has also been called the Maximajor Stone. Passing onward the rambler will descend the hill to Clifford Bridge, placed in the midst of delightful scenery at the lower, or eastern, end of the Gorge of Fingle.

[The rambler who may have reached Clifford Bridge from Dunsford, or from Fingle Bridge, on his way to Moreton, will follow the main road up the hill S. to Mardon Down, along the verge of which he will be led. The common is on the L. At the cross road where he leaves it he will keep straight on, and descend to the town, 1 m. distant.]

At the southern end of Clifford Bridge a very steep road branches from the one leading to Mardon Down, towards the W. Climbing this long ascent the rambler will, in about 1 m., reach a point where it forks, and here he takes the R. branch to the down on which is situated Wooston Castle, one of the ancient hill camps guarding the eastern frontier of the moorland region. [Others will presently be noticed, besides which there are also camps near Lustleigh and Ashburton (*Vide* those *Districts*)]. Wooston is an earthwork approaching an oval form, and is situated on a steep declivity commanding the wild Teign Gorge. Below it are cliffs, partly hidden by trees, and above it the bare down. This rises many hundred feet, and as it would here be exposed to the assaults of an enemy, supposing the latter to have forced their way to the higher ground, it was strongly fortified on this side. Here the rampart is thirty feet in height, and is protected by a deep ditch ; the other parts of it are unprovided with this additional means of security, the nature of the ground rendering such unnecessary. Some distance above this is a second ditch, and also a rampart and other outworks. The chief purpose of this fort seems to have been to guard the pass, through which an enemy might be expected to approach. The high ground behind the entrenchments would be inaccessible to him unless he could succeed in fighting his way to it.

The road by which we have approached the down from Clifford Bridge runs on by Cranbrook Castle, and through Uppacott to Easton and Chagford (S. Ex. 66), and this must be followed if the last-named place be our destination. If, however, we are returning to Moreton we leave this road immediately above the fort and strike into another running up the hill due S. This will take us past Wooston Farm to Mardon Down. Some distance to the R. is Willingstone Rock, 1,078 feet, to which a road leads soon after the farm is passed. From Mardon we retrace our steps over the road by which we left the town.

[Wooston Castle is 2½ m. from Moreton. On reaching Mardon Down from the town, *ante*, the L. branch of the road must be followed. This will lead the visitor past Wooston Farm, R., and straight down to the fort. From Chagford the way lies past Cranbrook Down. S. Ex. 66.]

S. Ex. 65.—*The Teign Gorge below Fingle Bridge.* (From Moreton). 10 m. To Clifford Bridge as in the preceding excursion. Here an angler's path will be seen running W. through the wood on the S. bank of the Teign, and this may be followed to Fingle Bridge, about 3 m. up stream. The rambler will pass below Wooston Castle, and will obtain some good views of the gorge, particularly when the fine hill of Prestonbury comes in sight. This hill, and Fingle Bridge, together with the return route to Moreton, are described in the next excursion.

S. Ex. 66.—*Cranbrook Castle, Fingle Bridge, and Prestonbury.*
M , 8½ m. ; C., 10½ m.   The first point will be Uppacott Down, and
this is reached from Moreton by leaving the town by the Chagford
road, and shortly turning R., and then almost immediately taking the
L. branch at the fork.   This will bring the rambler to Howton, where
is an open space with a seat, and two roads branching R.   (The one
bearing L. leads to Lynscott and Uppacott.   At Lynscott is an old
cross, discovered a few years ago acting as a gate-post, but now placed
under a tree on a turfy space in the lane.   [*Crosses*, Chap. XIV.]   It
probably once marked a pack-horse track running from Lynscott over
the side of Butterdon Hill, 1,154 feet, to Fingle Bridge).   At Howton
the second road R. is followed for 1¼ m., where the road coming L.
from Uppacott will be reached, the point being marked by a guide-post,
and here the visitor turns R.   (Care must be taken not to branch R.
into the lane ¼ m. from Howton).   ¼ m. from the guide-post is another,
where a turning L. leads directly to that part of Uppacott Down
usually known as Cranbrook Down, on the summit of which is the fine
hill fort called Cranbrook Castle.

This ancient encampment is reached from Chagford by following
the Moreton road to Easton, 1½ m., and then keeping straight on past
the entrance to Whiddon Park, L., up the steep Uppacott Hill.   About
1 m. from Easton is Uppacott, where a road turns R. to Lynscott,
and ½ m. above this is the guide-post where the road comes R. from
Howton and Moreton.   ¼ m. further on is another guide-post, where
a turning L. leads to Cranbrook Down.

[For Wooston Castle the visitor must keep straight on E. from
the second guide-post, leaving Butterdon Down and Willingstone
Rock R.   1½ m. from the guide-post is Wooston Down, on which the
fort is situated.   This is on the L. ; the road R. goes up by Wooston
Farm to Mardon Down and Moreton.]

Cranbrook Castle occupies a commanding position 700 feet above
the Teign, its height above sea level being over 1,100 feet (a survey
mark gives 1,104).   It is an irregular encampment approaching a
circular form, and is surrounded by a rampart of stone and turf.   On
the S. this rampart is over 20 feet in height on the inner side, while
the outer slope is more than 40 feet, and here it is also protected by
two ditches.   On the W. there is a single ditch. but none on the N.
and E., where the ground drops considerably, particularly on the N.,
where the vallum is on the brow of the precipitous scarp that rises
from the Teign.   The space enclosed is stated by Lysons in the
Devonshire volume of the *Magna Britannia*, 1822, to be about six or
seven acres in extent ; Mr. W. T. P. Shortt, who published in 1841
an essay on some remains in Devon, describes it as being about seven
acres.

The view from Cranbrook is exceedingly fine.   Cosdon uplifts his
huge form beyond the pleasant fields of Gidleigh and Throwleigh, and
stretching away from the great hill a long sweep of dusky moorland
forms the western horizon, to sink down to the farm lands where the
twin rocks of Hey Tor rise sharply against the sky.   Eastward the
beholder looks across the gorge to Prestonbury, and upon a wide extent
of cultivated country, where red earth, and green meadows and woods,
present a happy contrast to the dun hills of Dartmoor.

The road over the down near this ancient fort, formed on the line of an old pack-horse track, descends by a series of zig-zags to Fingle Bridge, in the deep ravine below. On the R. as the rambler descends he will notice at a point where a path diverges, an upright slab with an incised cross measuring 14 inches by 10 inches. [*Crosses*, Chap. XIII.] At the angles of the zig-zags very fine views of the gorge are obtained, that presented from one of these points being particularly fine, when the rambler looks up the valley and sees the folding hills that rise steeply from the banks of the hidden river, in places clothed with oak coppice, and in others showing only bold, bare scarps.

Fingle Bridge is a narrow structure of three arches, furnished with buttresses, and with recesses into which the wayfarer might turn when meeting pack-horses carrying their burdens on crooks. Below it, on the R. bank, is an old mill, and from here the angler's path before spoken of (S. Ex. 65) runs down to Clifford Bridge. Above the L. bank towers the great hill of Prestonbury, covered with heather, and crowned with its huge camp. The visitor will here find himself in the midst of some of the most charming and romantic scenery in Devon. The Gorge of Fingle is the finest thing of its kind in the Westcountry. [*Gems*, Chap. VII.]

Crossing the bridge the rambler will follow the road up through the defile, with Drewston Wood L. and Prestonbury R., to the top of the hill, where another road comes R. from Clifford Bridge and runs L. to Drewsteignton village. Here he will turn R. and enter upon a path leading to the summit of the camp-crowned height, which, though many hundred feet above the river, is yet of much less elevation than Cranbrook. That he will be more struck with the magnificent view of the gorge which he obtains from this point of vantage than with the fort itself is certain, but when, after having looked upon the folding hills, and into the depths of the narrow valley, he turns his attention to the ruins he will not fail to notice how skilfully this elevated spot was defended. The early builders of this fort took full advantage of what Nature had done for them, but there yet remained much for their hands to do. They accomplished it, and in the days when the only long distance weapons were the bow and the sling, the place must have been impregnable. The fort, which is of an oblong shape, is said, with its outworks, to cover about twenty-five acres. Descending once more to the bridge, we shall climb the zig-zags through the wood to Cranbrook Down, though the visitor whose destination is Moreton may perhaps choose the way by Fingle Mill, following the angler's path on the R. bank of the Teign down to Clifford Bridge, where he will turn R. into the road leading over Mardon Down to the town (S. Ex. 64). This way, however, will increase the distance by three miles.

From Cranbrook Down the road E. of the camp must be followed to the guide-post, where the rambler will turn R. ¼ m. on is another guide-post, and here, if bound for Moreton, he will branch L., or S.E., to Howton, 1¼ m. from this point, and thence keep straight on till he joins the road from Chagford, where he turns L. to the town, ¼ m. distant. For Chagford the visitor instead of turning L. at the second guide-post, will descend the hill to Easton, passing Uppacott and the entrance to Whiddon Park on the way. Thence straight on, S.W., 1½ m.

(The road to Drewsteignton, it has already been stated, turns L., or W., at the top of the defile between Prestonbury and Drewston

Wood, N. of Fingle Bsidge, the distance to the village from this point being not much over ½ m. To reach Sandy Park Bridge from Fingle the rambler may either find his way by the L. bank of the Teign upward to the logan under Hunts Tor (S. Ex. 67), and then climb up to the path near Combe ; or he may strike into this same path at Fingle and follow it along the side of Piddledown Common).

S. Ex. 67.—*Fingle Bridge by way of Piddledown Common.* (From Chagford). 7½ m. Leaving the town by the Moreton road the visitor will take the L. branch at the fork. ½ m. from the Moor Park Hotel, and descend the hill to Rushford Bridge, where the Teign is crossed. Just beyond is Rushford Mill, one approach to which is by a ford and stepping-stones, and here a path is carried down the L. bank of the river. This is followed for about ¾ m. to the Moreton and Okehampton road at Dogamarsh Bridge, or as it is often called, Sandy Park Bridge, from its proximity to the hamlet of that name (L.) The road is crossed, and the path still followed. This now gradually leaves the river, which a little further down enters Fingle Gorge. Passing Combe Vale, through which a streamlet runs, the rambler will reach Hunts Tor, where the scene is particularly wild. The great mass looks down upon the Teign, which here rushes impetuously over its boulder-strewn bed, to hide itself in the depths of the narrow ravine, where the folding hills rise, bare in places and in others show a covering of heather or coppice. Opposite to the tor is Whiddon Wood, as this part of the park is called, where sturdy oaks grow on the steep amid a wilderness of rocks. From this point the path runs onward over the side of Piddledown Common to Fingle Bridge, about 1½ m. down, Sharp Tor being passed on the way. Should the rambler prefer to make the river his companion, by finding a passage through the bottom of the gorge, he may either follow it from Dogamarsh Bridge, or descend to it on reaching the little vale of Combe. By doing this he will pass close to the logan, a great rock in its bed under Hunts Tor, which, having been noticed by Polwhele, who was imbued with Druidic ideas, was for long looked upon as an object once connected with mysterious rites. In 1797 he was able to move it easily ; it still oscillates, but has lost much of its former " logging " power. This route by the river, which is not of the easiest description, will lead the rambler under Sharp Tor. The scenery all the way down is exceedingly fine, and from no point is Prestonbury seen to such advantage as from the bottom of this romantic gorge. The return from Fingle Bridge is given in S. Ex. 66. (The little stream falling into the Teign above Dogamarsh Bridge is known as White Water ; very near to it is Dogamarsh Wood).

S. Ex. 68.—*Drewsteignton.* (From Chagford). 8 m. (If the return is by way of the dolmen the distance will be about 1 m. more). the first point is Dogamarsh Bridge, as in S. Ex. 67. This bridge, which was built about 1816, replaces one which an old drawing shows to have consisted of three arches, as stated by Polwhele. It was situated a little further up the stream than the present structure. Here the rambler may either make his way by the Combe path (S. Ex. 67), or he may turn L. to Sandy Park and follow the road. In the former case he will, on reaching Combe Vale, turn up the path L. by Combe Farm, in one of the fields of which is a heap of rocks called the Pixies' Parlour, where a labourer, so a story says, aided by the darkness, once caught, as he thought, one of that elfin race ; but his prize turned out to be a tame rabbit belonging to his master's little son. Above Combe Farm the rambler passes Hundred Acre Plantation, R., and soon reaches the road, where he will turn R. to Drewsteignton, 1¼ m. distant. If he chooses the road he will branch R. at the inn at Sandy Park, and in about 1 m. will arrive at the point where the path comes up R. from Combe.

The village of Drewsteignton is placed on high ground, and some fine views are obtained from several points near it, especially E. of the church. This, which has a Perpendicular tower and nave with a modern chancel, stands at the end of the village street. In a little book by the late Mr. E. Tozer, who wrote under the pen-name of "Tickler," published in 1869, the ringers' rules which hang in the belfry are given.

The name of the parish is in part derived from its former possessors, though when antiquaries believed that such things as tolmens, logans, and rock basins formed part of the paraphernalia of Druidism they gave the name quite another meaning. They gravely told us that it meant the Druids' town on the Teign.* But at a very early period it belonged to Drogo, or Dru, the second son of Walter de Ponz, and the grandson of Richard, Duke of Normandy. Walter de Ponz, who was Earl of Arques and Thoulouse, had three sons, of whom Dru was the second, and from him the family of Drew of Devonshire are descended. At the time of the Domesday Survey he had seventy-three manors in the county. The name is variously spelt in parish records, Dru, Drue, Drewe, and Drew. Drewsteignton is simply Drew's Teign town, and its connection with the Druids a dream of the dry-as-dusts of other days. In Domesday the manor appears as Teintona, and thus, as Sir William Pole observes, the place "both gave and tooke the name of the possessor thereof."†

To return direct to Chagford the visitor will follow the western road, and branch L. at the fork, to Sandy Park. Here he will not cross the bridge, but strike into the river side path, which will bring him to Rushford Mill and the bridge of that name. Crossing this he will pass up the hill to the town.

[*The Spinsters' Rock.* This dolmen is about 2½ m. from Chagford. From Drewsteignton the western road is followed as above, but at the fork the R. branch must be taken. For the next 1½ m. turn neither R. nor L. Then Stone Cross is reached just beyond Stone Farm, which lies L. The road goes on to Whiddon Down, 1½ m., but the visitor will strike into the lane L. About ¼ m. on, and near the entrance to Shilston Farm, the dolmen will be seen in a field L. (S. Ex. 69).]

S. Ex. 69.—*The Spinsters' Rock and Bradford Pool.* (From Chagford). 6 m. The way lies first to Chagford Bridge and up Walland Hill, but instead of turning L. to Murchington the visitor will keep

* Stanton Drew, a few miles south of Bristol, where are some striking stone circles, has also been claimed as a Druids' town—a Druids' stone town—and probably with as much reason as Drewsteignton has been so regarded.

† *Collections towards a Description of the County of Devon.* By Sir William Pole, of Colcombe and Shute, 1791. Sir William died in 1635

straight on to Sands Gate, where he reaches the road coming up R. from Sandy Park and running on to Whiddon Down and Oke-hampton. There are several branch lanes between Walland Hill and this point, but if it is remembered that the road runs nearly N. there will be no danger of turning into these. Cross the road at Sands Gate and enter the lane. The dolmen, which stands on Shilston Farm, will be seen R. less than ½ m. on.

With the exception of that within the gate at Dunnabridge Pound, (Ex. 42), which some will perhaps be disinclined to regard as a dolmen, this Drewsteignton example is the only one in the Dartmoor country, or, indeed, in Devon, that is not found in a ruined condition. And even this is a restoration. In January, 1862, it fell, and was re-erected during the same year, the work being completed in the November following. The expense of this was borne by the late Mrs. Bragg, of Furlong, the owner of Shilston, and it was superintended by the rector, the Rev. William Ponsford. John Ball, a carpenter, and William Stone, a builder, both of Chagford, carried out the work, an account of which is given in a paper contributed by Mr. G. W. Ormerod to the *Journal of the Royal Archæological Institute*, in 1872. It is rather humiliating to reflect that what could only be accomplished by the men of the nineteenth century with an expenditure of much labour and time, was in the " dim old days " effected by three women one morning before breakfast. According to the legend this monument was raised by three spinsters, not necessarily unmarried women, but spinners of yard—a calling which the original narrator of the story also appears to have followed. Being on their way homeward from the Yarn-jobber, and seeing the great stones lying on the ground, they diverted themselves with building the dolmen. The legend is first related by William Chapple, in 1779, who says that the monument was then known as the Spinsters' Rock.* But he derived the name from some Celtic words having much the same sound, and which he says mean an open observatory, or star-gazing place. Whether this throws any light upon the matter—other than moonshine—I am not prepared to say, but it is only right to mention that this belief that our ancient stone monuments had some astronomical signification, has lately again engaged the attention of antiquaries. Polwhele refers to another story connected with the dolmen,† and probably an older one of which the foregoing is a variant. He quotes a writer as stating that the monument was said to have been erected by three young men who came down with their father from the hills of Dartmoor, whence they brought the stones, and this it was thought had reference to the old man and his sons who descended from the mountain on which the ark had rested.

The impost, or capstone, of the dolmen is 15 feet in length, and its under surface is about six feet from the ground. Its weight is computed to be rather over 16 tons.

According to several accounts there were formerly some stone rows and circles near the dolmen. These were noticed in 1789 by the Rev. John Swete, of Oxton House, who in that year visited the spot

---

* *Description and Exegesis of the Drewsteignton Cromlech.* Exeter, 1779. The author died before the work was completed.

† *History of Devonshire.* Vol. II. 1793-1806. (3 vols.)

while on a tour into North Devon, and four years afterwards were described by Polwhele. They were also mapped by the Rev. W. Grey, of Exeter, in 1838. Some twenty years later search was made for these remains by Mr. G. W. Ormerod, but the stones had then disappeared.

On the further side of the lane that runs N. of the dolmen is Bradford Pool, said to be about three acres in extent. It is of a rectangular shape, and about 180 yards long by 40 yards wide, and is really an old mining excavation. The trees by which it is surrounded do much to conceal its artificial character, and render it a truly romantic spot. When visited by Mr. Swete the pool had been drained, but the accumulation of water in it seems to have taken place soon after that time, and was occasioned by the stopping of an adit which runs under Shilston Farm. The existence of this adit probably gave rise to the belief once prevalent in the locality that a subterranean passage ran from the pool to the Teign under Hunts Tor. Similarly the story of a secret passage formerly said to lead from Gidleigh Castle to the Teign at Gidleigh Park Bridge, seems to have been suggested by some old mining excavations near the last-named spot.

The return from the dolmen will be by way of the lane running southward to Sands Gate, where the road coming R. from Whiddon Down and going L. to Sandy Park is crossed. Keep straight on, the course being nearly S., to Walland Hill, about 1½ m., at the bottom of which is Chagford Bridge.

S. Ex. 70.—*Rushford Wood.* (From Chagford). 1½ m. The way lies over Rushford Bridge as in S. Ex. 67, but instead of striking into the river path at the mill, the road must be followed to Rushford Barton, once the seat of the Hoares, a family which settled here in the reign of Richard II. The visitor now turns L. to the wood, through which he may pass up to Rushford Tower. No antiquarian interest attaches to this ; in fact, the building is quite modern, but a fine view is obtained from it, and it also forms an interesting feature in the picture seen from Chagford. North of it a strip of turf was formerly known as the Bowling Green, and a basin in one of the rocks with which this was dotted, as the Punch Bowl. (Near Mount Flaggon, on the road to Torhill and Goosaford, is the Rushford Manor Pound, modern).

On returning to Rushford Mill the visitor, instead of crossing the bridge, may turn R. into a path by which he will be led along the left, or north, bank of the Teign to Chagford Bridge, and so make his way to the town.

ROUTES FROM CHAGFORD AND MORETON.

(The road between these two places has already been described).

R. 31.—To Bovey Tracey, S.E. from Moreton. *Hayne, Wray Barton, Wray Cleave, Kelly, Slade, King's Cross, Woolley, Atway.* From *C.*, 11 m. ; *M.*, 6½ m. Reverse, R. 46.

This is a road route, and few directions are needed. From Moreton the way lies by the Railway Station, and down the valley of the Wray, with Wray Cleave L., for 3½ m., where a road runs R. to Lustleigh. The route is then by Kelly and Slade, at each of which points there are guide-posts. At King's Cross, where is a milestone (1 m. from Bovey), the visitor must bear L. to Woolley. At that spot he will also bear L., but take the next turning R.

R. 32.—To Ashburton, S.S.E. from Chagford; S. from Moreton. *Beetor Cross, Barramoor Bridge, Heytree Cross.* (From Moreton: *North Bovey, Langstone, Hayne Down*). *Swine Down Gate, Hemsworthy Gate, Cold East Cross, Welstor Cross.* From C., 12¾ m.; from M., 11½ m. Reverse, R. 53.

[Objects : S. Ex. 61, Ex. 23 to 26.]

Although this is a road route the greater part of it lies over the moor. The visitor will pass up the hill S., having Nattadown L. and Meldon R., and make his way to Beetor Cross, 2½ m. q.v. Here the road runs L. to Moreton, and R. to Princetown, but he will strike into the one running L. below the cross, *i.e.*, S.E., and follow it for a few yards when he will turn R., and in about 2½ m. will reach Heytree Cross (Ex. 24). (This 2½ m. of road pursues a S.S.E. direction, and the turnings, all of which the rambler will avoid, are as follow : First L. to Hele ; then cross Barramoor Bridge ; Second L. to Gratnar ; Third, a cross road—L. to North Bovey and R. to Shapley and Westcombe Down ; Fourth L. to Langdon Farm and North Bovey ; Fifth, L. to Easdon Farm and Manaton ; and Sixth, R. to Vogwell, from which turning Heytree Cross is ½ m. distant). A little way beyond this cross road is the farm of Fordgate, and when this is passed the pedestrian will enter upon Cripdon Down, along the western edge of which the road runs for about ½ m. and then skirts Swine Down, leaving it at Swine Down Gate. (R. 25 and Ex. 24). On passing through the gate the rambler will turn southward, having Hound Tor (Ex. 24) on his L. About 1¼ m. on a green track across the down L. cuts off an angle of the road, and in this another, marked by a guide-post, branches westward to Widecombe. Soon after the road is regained Hemsworthy Gate is reached, through which lies the way to Ilsington and Bovey Tracey (Ex. 25, S. Ex. 82, 90). Leaving this on the L. the rambler will follow the road southward under Rippon Tor, and passing the ruins of Newhouse, on the verge of Blackslade Down R. (Ex. 26), will reach Cold East Cross, 1¼ m. Here a road comes up L. from Halshanger, and another runs R. to Widecombe (Ex. 26, R. 5), with a branch to Cockingford (R. 5, 42) and the forest. The rambler will keep to the road he has been following, its course here being about S.W., and in about 1½ m. will reach Welstor Cross, where he will turn R. into the road leading from Buckland to Ashburton, and then turn L. and follow it to his destination. (*Vide Ashburton District*).

From Moreton the road lies through North Bovey (S. Ex. 61), and joins the one just described at Swine Down Gate. Langstone is the first point from North Bovey, about 1 m. S.S.E., Aller and Higher and Lower Luckdon being passed on the way, and here the visitor will turn R. to Langstone Cross, ½ m. At both points there is a guide-post. He will here turn L., and on reaching the fork a little way down, will strike into the R. branch, which will shortly bring him to Hayne Down. Across this his road runs direct to Swine Down Gate, 1¼ m. S., Bowerman's Nose being passed on the way (Ex. 23).

R. 33.—To Brent and Ivybridge. Brent, S. ; Ivybridge, S. by W. ; with branch to Cornwood, S.S.W. To BRENT : *Jurston Gate,*

*Challacombe, Jordan, Ponsworthy, Pound's Gate, Holne, Cross Furzes,
Gigley Bridge.* From *C.*, 19 m. ; from *M.*, by Moor Gate, 20 m. ; a
nearer way from *M.* is through Widecombe (See R. 64). To IVYBRIDGE :
*Jurston Gate, Warren House Inn, Post Bridge, Dunnabridge Pound,
Sherburton Bridge, Hexworthy, Aune Head, Red Lake,* by the Erme to
Harford. From *C.*, 23½ m. ; from *M.*, by Moor Gate, 25 m. To
CORNWOOD : from Red Lake over Stall Moor, from *C.*, 22 m. ; from
M., by Moor Gate, 23½ m. Reverse, R. 64.

[Objects : Exs. 22, 27, 28, *Holne Moor* Section, and S. Exs. from
Brent. If to Ivybridge, Exs. 22, 21, 45, 44, 42, 43, 30, 32 ; and if to
Cornwood add Ex. 33.]

To BRENT. The road to Jurston Gate as already described must
first be followed, where the pedestrian will cross the valley, as directed
in S. Ex. 59, to the point where the road to Challacombe, Grendon,
and Cator leaves the Moreton and Princetown highway. Here the
visitors from Moreton will join. This Challacombe road must then
be followed, the rambler having Shapley Common on his L., and the
upper waters of a branch of the Bovey on his R. About 1½ m. on the
road crosses Grim's Lake at Firth Bridge, Grim's Pound (Ex. 22)
lying on the slope L., and Headland Warren House in the valley R.
At Challacombe, about 1 m. further down, the road forks. The
rambler must take the L. branch, which will bring him to Lower
Blackaton, 1 m. (T. 76). Still keeping southward his course for yet
another mile will be on the line of R. 26, and will bring him to Dunstone
Down, when he will turn R. (The first turning R. leads to Cator ; the
second R. is a track running down a stroll to Rowden Down ; these he
must pass). At the point where he will leave the road a track comes
down from the N.E. Route 26 runs on over Bittleford Down, but we
must now desert it and strike S. by W. down a narrow lane between
some enclosures to Jordan Mill, just before reaching which our way is
crossed by another lane. Passing the mill the visitor will proceed to
the Widecombe and Ponsworthy road, ½ m. distant, where he will turn
R. down the hill, and in another ½ m. will reach the last-named village
(Ex. 27). Passing through this little place we ascend the hill and keep
L. towards Leusdon Church, but bearing R. just before reaching it.
The way lies by Spitchwick Higher Lodge to the hamlet of Pound's
Gate, whence the road runs by the Tavistock Inn down the hill, with
Leign Tor L. to New Bridge (R. 6 A). Immediately after crossing the
bridge a path will be seen R. running through the wood close to the
Dart. This will lead the rambler up to some fields, and near to Holne
Cot, on passing which he will emerge upon a lane. A few yards L. is
a branch into which he will turn, and very speedily reach Holne
village. (*Vide* S. Ex. 96). Passing through this to Play Cross the
pedestrian turns L., and a few score yards on, when at the top of
Langaford Hill, takes the road R. This will lead him to Holy Brook
Bridge and Scorriton, just beyond which he will cross Combe Bridge
and ascend the long steep lane to Cross Furzes, taking care not to
branch L. when nearing the top. At the cross, where is an old guide-
stone, a lane comes from the moor at Lid Gate R., and two run L.,
one to Buckfast and the other to Buckfastleigh, the latter going over
Wallaford Down. The rambler will descend the side of the furze-
covered space, to a ford on the Dean Burn, and will ascend the track
leading up towards the ruined Lambs Down Farm (S. Ex. 101). **Before**

reaching it a footpath will be seen branching L. and running down to a small tributary rivulet, where is a hunting gate, and this must be followed. The path on the further side leads to a gateway where a green track comes from the moor R. This track, the direction of which is S.E., the pedestrian will follow over Skerraton Down to a lane in the corner, and entering this will proceed for ¼ m. to a turning R., which will bring him immediately to Gigley Bridge. From this point the way to Brent is described in S. Ex. 103.

To IVYBRIDGE. As in the route to Brent the visitor will first make his way to Jurston Gate, but will not then desert the highway. His road, in fact, will be the same as that described in R. 35 as far as Post Bridge. (This also applies to Moreton visitors). Then, on crossing the East Dart, he will enter the gate L. and follow the green track by Bellaford Tor to Dunnabridge Pound, as described in T. 80 and Ex. 44. [This path has lately been claimed as a private way.] On emerging from the newtakes on the Two Bridges (R.) and Dartmeet (L.) road, he will turn L. for a few score yards, and passing Brownberry, will enter a gate R. and descend to the West Dart, which is spanned by a clam just below where it makes a sharp bend. On crossing this the rambler will find himself on land belonging to Sherburton Farm ; a path leads along the hillside to the house. Below, on the L., is the confluence of the Dart and the Swincombe, marked by the plantation known as Sherburton Firs. Having reached the farmhouse the rambler will descend the road to Sherburton Bridge, whence he will pass upward to Gobbet Plain, below which is the forest settlement of Hexworthy.

[The part of this route that follows forms the reverse of the route from Ivybridge to Hexworthy. *Vide* R. 64, and *Brent and Ivybridge, and Hexworthy Districts*.]

The first part of the journey from Hexworthy is described in T. 54. This will bring the rambler to Aune Head, from which point he will follow the Avon down for about 1½ m. to Heng Lake Gully, keeping on the R. bank. (For a description of the mire at Aune Head and the upper part of the stream see Ex. 43). The gully, which is on the R. bank of the Avon, will be reached just before the river makes a rather rapid descent. It is covered with granite, and a little tributary runs through it. The visitor will make his way nearly to its head, where on the L. he will find a narrow strip of hard ground leading across Red Lake Mire. By means of this he will be able to reach Green Hill (Ex. 30) without trouble, when he will turn southward, with the mire close to him on the L. This will bring him to Red Lake, near the ford (T. 1), and he may now either follow the brook to the Erme, and crossing that stream pass downward to Green Bottom ¾ m. below the confluence, and so make his way to Harford Bridge, as described in R. 7 ; or he may cross Red Brook, and strike S. over Brown Heath to Stony Bottom, and thence proceed to Harford village. There is little difference in the length of these routes. In the latter case the visitor, after crossing Stony Bottom (Ex. 32) (which is about 1 m. from the ford over the brook, and runs E. and W., and which should be reached at a point rather over ¼ m. E. of the Erme), should endeavour to strike the track running out from Harford to Erme Pound (T. 63). This he may do if he gradually approaches the line of bondstones that he will notice on his L., which mark the boundary between Harford and Ugborough Moors, as the two intersect each other about ¾ m. southward of the bottom. At all events the stones will prove a sufficient guide, and by following up the line the rambler will be led to the dip between Three Barrows, L., and Sharp Tor, R., through which the track runs. Less than ½ m. southward of Sharp Tor it forks, and here the R. branch must be followed. Harford Church, 1¾ m. distant, may now be seen S.W., and to this the track will lead direct.

[*Brent from Hexworthy, by way of Aune Head.* From Heng Lake, *ante*, the rambler will follow the Avon downward, keeping on the L. bank, until he reaches Small Brook, over 4 m., where a bondstone will be seen close to the confluence. He will then strike up the hill S.S.E. to Shipley Tor. See Ex. 29. Or he may leave the river below him on the L. after passing Heng Lake Gully, and make his way along the brow of the hill southward to Western Whitaburrow, where he will strike the old tram-road (T. 60, Ex. 30), which he may follow to Shipley as in R. 7.]

To CORNWOOD. If his destination be Cornwood the pedestrian will follow the Ivybridge route as far as Red Lake Ford. He must then trace the stream down to the Erme, which he should cross either near the confluence, or at the ford below Erme Pound, about ½ m. lower down. From here a track runs over Stall Moor (T. 66), and this will lead him to Watercombe Waste Gate, 3¼ m. distant. Should the rambler not be able to strike this track at first his best plan will be to follow the Erme downward, keeping high above the right bank after crossing Green Bottom, ¼ m. below the fording place, as by so doing he will not fail to notice the long stone row leading to the circle described in Ex. 33. This row here runs N. and S., and is nearly parallel to the track, which is only about 200 yards W. of it. As progress is made the path becomes plainer, but the rambler cannot go wrong if he keeps well to the R. or W. of Stalldon Barrow, the high hill he sees rising before him. When the track draws near Harrowthorn Plantation and Dendles Wood it is crossed by another coming R. from the direction of Yealm Head. Here the pedestrian will keep L., and about 1 m. further on will reach the moor gate at Watercombe, from which a road leads to Cornwood, not quite 2 m. distant (Ex. 34).

R. 34.—To Plympton and Shaugh, S.W. by S.; with branch to Cornwood, S.S.W. *Jurston Gate, Warren House Inn, Post Bridge, Cherry Brook, Prince Hall Bridge, Peat Cot, Siward's Cross, Plym Steps, Hen Tor, Great Trowlesworthy Tor, Blackabrook Head, Shaugh Moor, Brag Lane End, Niel Gate.* To Plympton, 25¾ m.; to Shaugh, 21 m.; to Cornwood, 21½ m. From Moreton, 1½ m. more. Reverse, R. 71.

[Objects : Exs. 22, 45, 44, 46, 4, 3, 37, 36. If to Cornwood add 34, 35.]

By Jurston Gate, following the Princetown route, R. 35, to the entrance to the old Powder Mills, ¾ m. south-westward of the bridge over the Cherry Brook. Just beyond this the rambler will cross Muddy Lakes Newtake, L., as in R. 27, and follow the directions given there for reaching Tor Royal Newtake by way of Moorlands and Prince Hall. But when he enters that newtake he will steer S.W. by W. across it for 1¼ m., leaving Royal Hill, 1,333 feet, the highest part of it, on the L. (The rambler must be careful not to bear too much to the L. when nearing the end of this 1¼ m., or he will get among the turf ties, which will hinder his progress). This will bring him to the wall of some enclosures belonging to Tor Royal (Exs. 3, 4), which runs S. and then turns abruptly W. He will follow this to the Devonport Leat, along the bank of which is a path, which will bring him to Peat Cot, a short distance S. From this little settlement the rambler will proceed in a south-westerly direction for rather less than ½ m., when he will turn S., and in another ½ m. will reach Siward's Cross (T. 1, Ex. 2, Extension). From this point the way lies over Eylesbarrow and Higher Hart Tor to the Plym, and thence onward to Shavercombe and Hen Tor, and is described in R. 7. The direction is S. by W.

[The rambler bound for Cornwood will branch off at Hen Tor, and follow the directions given in R. 7, his way lying over Shell Top and Pen Beacon.]

If either Plympton or Shaugh is the point to be reached the rambler will not find it necessary to make direct for Hen Tor on leaving Shavercombe Brook ; it will be better for him to pass about ¼ m. below it, *i.e.*, to the W. of it, and near the ruined buildings known as Hen Tor House (Ex. 37). From this point he will strike S.W. by W., and crossing Hen Tor Brook will pass over Wiling's Hill to Great Trowlesworthy Tor, 1 m., close to which is the source of Spanish Lake. Little Trowlesworthy Tor will be seen below it, and further down, Trowlesworthy Warren House (Ex. 37). The course is now about S.W. by W., to the head of Blackabrook, ½ m. distant, the Lee Moor Clay Works Leat being crossed on the way. (There are some foot bridges over it here). Less than another ½ m., the course being about the same, will bring the rambler to the road from Dousland (R.) to Cornwood (L.), (R. 13). This he will cross, and strike W. by S. over Shaugh Moor to Brag Lane End, about 1 m. (Ex. 36). The visitor to Shaugh will turn into this as directed in R. 8. For Plympton he will turn L. and follow the road to his destination, leaving the moor at Niel Gate, as described in the same route.

R. 35.—To Princetown, S.W. By Road. *Meldon, Jurston Gate, Bush Down, Bennet's Cross, Warren House Inn, Stats Brook, Meripit Hill, Post Bridge, Gawler Bottom, Bellaford Tor, Powder Mills, Crockern Tor, Two Bridges.* (The road from Moreton runs by *Bughead Cross, Worm Hill, Beetor Cross, Moor Gate,* ¾ m. W. of which it joins the one from Chagford). From *C.*, 12 m. ; from *M.*, 13½ m. Reverse, R. 4.

[Objects : Exs. 22, 45, 44, 46, 5.]

The portion of this route from Chagford and Moreton to the Warren House Inn is described in S. Ex. 58.

Shortly after leaving the Warren House Inn we cross Stats Brook, whence the road is carried over Meripit Hill to the hamlet of Post Bridge. Crossing the East Dart close to the well-known clapper, it ascends the hill, with Lakehead on the L., and Archerton R. Soon Bellaford Tor is seen rising L., on the R. being Gawler Bottom. We cross the Cherry Brook, and passing the entrance to the Powder Mills ¾ m. further on soon reach Two Bridges. Branch L. to Princetown, 1½ m.

R. 36.—To Tavistock, W.S.W. (A) BY ROAD. *Jurston Gate, Warren House Inn, Post Bridge, Two Bridges, Rundle Stone, Merivale.* From *C.*, 18½ m. ; from *M.*, 20 m. Reverse, R. 10 A. (B) FROM CHAGFORD BY WAY OF THE MOOR. *Waye Barton, Metheral, Assacombe, White Ridge, East Dart, Broad Down, Row Tor, Devil's Tor, Maiden Hill, White Barrow, Peter Tavy,* 19 m. From *Moreton via Chagford*, as above, 23½ m. Reverse, R. 10 B.

[Objects : (A) Exs. 22, 21, 45, 44, 46, 5, 6, 1, 7, 8. (B) 21, 46, 5, 8.]

(A) By road to Two Bridges as in R. 35. Thence the road branching R. is followed to Rundle Stone, 2 m., from which point the road to Tavistock is shown in R. 1.

(B) The first part of this route is described in the notice of the road from *Chagford to Metheral*, and will take the rambler to the moor by way of Waye Barton and Tawton Gate. On leaving the corner of the enclosures just beyond Metheral the rambler must steer S.W. by W., with Lowton Rocks on his R., and in ½ m. will cross Lowton Brook. Assacombe Brook is about ⅓ m. further on. Crossing this, and shortly afterwards the Vitifer Mine Leat, the rambler will pass up the western side of the combe, with a wall on his L. running S.W. by W., and will soon find himself on White Ridge (Ex. 45). He will now steer W. by S., with the crest of the ridge L. and the leat R. for a little over 1 m., when the leat, here bending southward, will be directly in his path. He will cross it and steer W.S.W. for 1 m. to the East Dart, which it is his object to strike at the head of the pass above Sandy Hole. Care must be taken not to bear too much to the R. in passing from the leat to the river. Above the pass (Ex. 45) the Dart can usually be crossed without difficulty.

[If the visitor cares to try to cross the Dart at Sandy Hole he will steer S.W. from the leat, but the safer plan is to aim for the head of the pass. A more direct course than either of these, if the river can be crossed, is to strike S.W. from the point where the wall of the Assacombe enclosures is left, and White Ridge entered upon. 1 m. on is Lade Hill Bottom (Ex. 45), through which a small tributary runs down to the Dart. Crossing this, and still steering S.W., the pedestrian will shortly have the river on his L. and the Vitifer Leat on his R. (Ex. 45). Thence he will pass along the foot of Lade Hill, and crossing another small stream, will strike the Dart about ¾ m. from Lade Hill Bottom, and ¼ m. below the spot where the leat is taken in, and just where the river begins to bend and run towards the north. Here it must be crossed, and the course will then be W.S.W. over Broad Down for ¾ m. to the corner of the wall of Wild Banks Newtake, *vide post.*]

Having reached the R. bank of the East Dart at the higher end of the Sandy Hole pass, and just below Broad Marsh (Ex. 45), the rambler will make his way down through the pass to the hollow nearly ¼ m. below, and there he will leave the river. His way now lies over Broad Down, the course being S.S.W., to the corner of Wild Banks Newtake, which he will reach in about ½ m. He will then follow the wall for ½ m. W.S.W. to the West Dart, and crossing that river will still take the wall for his guide. This will lead him nearly to Row Tor, Whence he will make his way W. by S. to Devil's Tor, about ½ m. distant. Close to this small pile is Bear Down Man (Ex. 5). The course is now W.S.W. for 1 m. The Cowsic is first crossed, and then the southern verge of Maiden Hill, the line running a little to the N. of Conies Down Tor. This will bring the pedestrian to the Lich Path (T. 18), which must be followed westward. Immediately after crossing the Prison Leat this ancient way reaches the Walkham at Sandy Ford, and is carried up the western side of the shallow valley through which that river runs towards White Barrow. From this ford the route to Tavistock has already been described (R. 30 B).

R. 37.—To Lydford, W. by S. *Teigncombe, Batworthy Corner, Hew Down, Newtake, Cranmere Pool, Great Kneeset, Amicombe Hill, Rattle Brook, High Down.* C., 14½ m. ; M., 19 m. Reverse, R. 17.

[Objects : Exs. 20, 19, 12, 11, and in C.R. 12, 5, and in the description of the surroundings of Cranmere in the section dealing with that district.]

This route is composed entirely of C.R. 12, which describes the ground between Chagford and Cranmere, and C.R. 5, which notices that between the Pool and Lydford, and to these the rambler is referred.

R. 38.—To Okehampton, with branches to Sticklepath and Belstone, N.W. by W.

(A) *Road to Shilstone Tor, North end of Raybarrow Pool, Fords on the Taw, Crovenor Steps.* From C., 11 m. ; M., 15½ m. To Sticklepath, from C., 7¾ m. ; M., 12¼ m. To Belstone, from C., 9 m. ; M., 13½ m. Reverse, R. 24 A.

(B) *Road to Berry Down, White Moor Stone, Small Brook Foot, Crovenor Steps.* Distance about the same. Reverse, R. 24 B.

[Objects : Exs. 19, 18, 17, 16.]

(A) The rambler will first make his way to Gidleigh *via* Murchington. (See *Chagford to Gidleigh*). Thence he will turn up the hill by the little manor pound to the footpath R., which is close by, and follow it W.N.W. to Thule. On reaching the lane here turn R. to Moortown, soon after passing which the commons will be reached. The rambler continues to follow the road which skirts them, having Buttern House L. and Great and Little Ensworthy Farms R. Forder Bridge is then crossed, and from this Shilstone Tor is distant ¼ m.

(The rambler bound for Sticklepath will continue to follow the road, reaching Payne's Bridge in 1 m., whence the route is described in S. Ex. 45).

From Shilstone Tor the route to Okehampton by way of the Blackaton Brook and the north end of Raybarrow Pool takes a course a little N. of W., the stream named being crossed at, or near, the ford where the Gallaven track passes over it (T. 42). This point is about ¾ m. from Shilstone Tor (Ex. 18). Thence the line, still N. of W., runs across the common to the northern end of Raybarrow Pool, and crossing the Peat Road (T. 41) goes W.N.W. over White Hill to the fords on the Taw. This part of the route is noticed in S. Ex. 47.

(On crossing the Taw the path to Belstone through Birchy Lake, 1¼ m., runs R).

For Okehampton ascend the hill W. at the fords, to Winter Tor. ½ m., where the track leading down to Crovenor Steps (T. 37, Ex. 16) will be struck. From this point the route is given in Ex. 16.

(B) This route is the same as the preceding one as far as the turning to Gidleigh village. Here the rambler will keep straight up the hill to Berry Down Farm, and thence to the head of the stroll (Ex. 19). His course is now N.W. by W. across Buttern Down, by the head of White Moor Bottom, and over the side of Kennon Hill to White Moor Stone (Ex. 17), 2 m. from the stroll. From this point he will follow the instructions given in the route from Throwleigh, S. Ex. 47. *Vide* also Ex. 17.

BOVEY TRACEY DISTRICT.

DISTANCES. By Road: *ASHBURTON*, 7½ m. *BARRAMOOR BRIDGE*, *via* Manaton, 8 m. *BECKY FALL*, 4 m. *BEETOR CROSS*, *via* Manaton, 8¾ m. *BICKINGTON*, 3 m. *BUCKFASTLEIGH*, *via* Ashburton, 10½ m. *BUCKLAND-IN-THE-MOOR*, *via* Hemsworthy Gate, 9½ m.; *via* Ashburton, 11¼ m. *CHAGFORD*, *via* Moreton, 11 m. *CHRISTOW*, *via* Hennock and Canonteign, 5 m. *CHUDLEIGH*, 4 m. *CLIFFORD BRIDGE*, *via* Dunsford, or *via* Moreton, 10 m. *COLD EAST CROSS*, 6¼ m. *DARTMEET*, *via* Hemsworthy Gate and Widecombe, 12½ m. *DUNSFORD*, *via* Christow. 8 m. *EXETER*, *via* Chudleigh, 13 m. *FINGLE BRIDGE*, *via* Moreton, 9¾ m. *GRENDON BRIDGE*, *via* Widecombe, 10¾ m. *GRIM'S POUND*, *via* Widecombe and Hill Head, 12½ m.; *via* Moor Gate, 11¾ m. *HALSHANGER CROSS*, 6 m. *HEMSWORTHY GATE*, 5 m. *HENNOCK*, 2 m. *HEXWORTHY*, *via* Dartmeet, 14 m. *HEY TOR*, *see* Lud Gate. *HEYTREE CROSS*, 7½ m. *ILSINGTON*, *via* Brimley, 3 m. *IVYBRIDGE*, *via* Ashburton, 20½ m. *LUD GATE*, 3 m. *LUSTLEIGH*, 3¼ m. *LYDFORD*, *via* Moreton and Sandy Park, 29 m. *MANATON*, 5 m. *MOOR GATE*, *via* Manaton, 9¾ m. *MORETON*, 6½ m. *NEWTON ABBOT*, 5½ m. *NORTH BOVEY*, *via* Manaton or Sanduck, 7¼ m. *OKEHAMPTON*, *via* Moreton and Sandy Park, 20 m. *PLYMOUTH*, *via* Ashburton and Ivybridge, 31 m. *PLYMPTON*, do., 27 m. *POST BRIDGE* (the Dart), *via* Grendon Bridge, 13¾ m. *PRINCETOWN*, *via* Dartmeet, 19 m. *SANDUCK*, 5¼ m. *SOUTH BRENT*, *via* Ashburton, 15¾ m. *SWINE DOWN GATE*, *via* Owlacombe Barrow and Leighon, 6 m. *TAVISTOCK*, *via* Two Bridges and Rundle Stone, 25½ m. *TWO BRIDGES*, *via* Dartmeet, 17½ m. *WARREN HOUSE INN*, *via* Moor Gate, 12 m. *WELSTOR CROSS*, 7¾ m. *WIDECOMBE*, *via* Hemsworthy Gate, 6¾ m. *YELVERTON*, *via* Princetown, 25 m.

By Rail: (G.W.R.) *To MORETON*, 6¼ m. *To NEWTON ABBOT*, 6 m. *From* Newton Abbot to Ashburton, 18 m.; Brent, 15½ m.; Buckfastleigh, 15½ m.; Cornwood, 23½ m.; Exeter, 20¼ m.; Ivybridge, 21 m.; Plymouth, 32½ m.; Plympton, 27¾ m.; Torquay, 5¾ m.; Totnes, 8½ m.

Bovey Tracey takes its name from the river on which it is situated, and the family which formerly possessed it. The Bovey was once also known as the West Teign. Though not a suitable base from which to explore the wilder parts of Dartmoor, it is well placed with regard to that corner of it comprising Ilsington Common, part of Manaton Common lands, and Lustleigh, while the Widecombe valley can also be conveniently reached from it.

HAMELDON AND THE WIDECOMBE VALLEY.

Before starting on our excursions from Bovey it will be well to
describe the great hill of Hamel Down (or Hameldon, as it is more often
called), together with the valley of Widecombe, in case the visitor
should desire to extend his rambles that far. These are also conveniently reached from Ashburton or Post Bridge, and the routes
from those places will be given when we come to describe that part of
the moor in their vicinity. The way to the northern end of Hameldon
from Chagford and Moreton has already been shown (R. 33, S. Ex. 59,
60).

Hameldon occupies the central portion of the lofty ridge extending
from Shapley Common on the north to Bittleford Down on the south,
a distance of 5 m. This central portion is about 2½ m. in length, and,
at its widest, 1½ m. in width, the ridge here rising between the valleys
of the East and West Webburn. It is bounded on the north by the
combe in which Grim's Pound is situated (Ex. 22), and may be said
to terminate in the opposite direction near the Church Way, which
crosses the down from Blackaton to Widecombe (T. 76). Overlooking
the combe, as already stated (Ex. 22), is Hameldon Tor, 1,737 feet in
height, and this elevation is nearly maintained by the ridge for a
distance of 1¼ m., when, at Hameldon Beacon (surface level, 1,695 ;
bench mark, 1,697) the ground begins to drop towards the S. The
rambler who takes the trouble to scale this huge rounded ridge will
find himself well rewarded, for though he may not, as the moormen
say, be able to see the whole of Devon from it, it is certain that he will
look over a good deal of the county. Though the western foot of
Hameldon is some mile and a half outside the forest, the greater part
of the ancient hunting-ground is nevertheless visible, as well as much
of the belt of common land encircling it. In fact, there are few
prominent heights in the moorland region that cannot be seen from this
hill, while from whatever point it is itself viewed it forms a conspicuous
feature in the scene.

About ⅓ m. S.S.E. of Hameldon Tor is Hameldon Cross, and
between these a reave runs from a small bog on the western slope of
the hill (from which a rivulet dribbles into the Webburn) across to
another little stream on its eastern side. This reave was said by the
Rev. J. P. Jones, to whom we have referred as the author of a little
book on the scenery in the neighbourhood of Moreton, published in
1823, to have been traced to Waydon Tor (by which is meant White
Tor, called on the moor Whitten Tor), and this can still be done,
although there are several breaks in it. It is briefly noticed in Ex. 46,
which describes that part of the moor in which White Tor is situated.
The stream on the eastern side of the hill forms the boundary between
the common lands of Manaton and Widecombe, and this is drawn
from its head to Hameldon Cross, the space between the two being
marked by a couple of bondstones, the lower one being called Blue Jug,
and the other the Grey Wethers Stone.* This line also forms the

---

* Among other bondstones on this ridge may be mentioned
Hameldon Old House and Aaron's Knock. Another mark is named
Two Crosses, and these were formerly cut on the turf. The late
Mr. Robert Dymond, owner of Dunstone Manor, intended to erect a

northern boundary of Natsworthy Manor, one of the six in the parish of Widecombe, and which in the sixteenth century, appears among the vills bordering the east quarter of the forest as North Werthiehed, and also as North Worthied. On the Widecombe side of the little stream, which runs through a hollow, is the enclosure known as Berry Pound, to which reference has been made in our Chagford excursions (S. Ex. 60). The area covered is very much smaller than that occupied by Grim's Pound, and the vallum is low and not of great width. It is about ½ m. W.N.W. of Higher Natsworthy.

Hameldon Cross consists of a granite slab rather over four feet in height and about two feet in width, rudely fashioned into the form of the sacred symbol, and probably has never served any other purpose than that of a boundary stone. Like other manorial bondmarks on this hill it bears its name (or rather, in this instance, the initials of its name) and the letters D.S., which stand for Duke of Somerset, the former owner of Natsworthy, and the date 1854, in which year the marks were set up or renewed. [*Crosses*, Chap. XVI.] Less than ¼ m. S.E. of the cross is Broad Barrow, to which the boundary line runs, and is thence continued due S. to Single Barrow, which is not far off. This tumulus was opened in 1873 by the late Mr. C. Spence Bate, and was found to consist of earth with the exception of a low hedge of stones which encircled it, and a low cairn in the centre. About six feet from the latter a small heap of burnt human bones was discovered, together with some fragments of charcoal, and a flint flake. From Single Barrow the boundary runs a little E. of S. to Two Barrows, which are close to the corner of the wall surrounding Blackaton Down. This wall is carried down the hill westward to the Webburn, more than 500 feet below, and here forms a boundary of Manaton parish, Blackaton Down, as well as Hameldon, being in Widecombe. One of these barrows was also opened by Mr. Spence Bate, in the year preceding that of his investigation of Single Barrow. He found it to be formed like the other, and it also yielded burnt human bones and charcoal. But the chief object of interest was the bronze blade of a dagger, and the amber pommel of the same, inlaid with small pins of gold. This is now in the Museum of the Plymouth Institution. The boundary between the manors of Natsworthy and Blackaton is now marked by the wall which runs S.E. by S. for ¼ m. to the large tumulus known as Hameldon Beacon, over which it is carried.†

The view from this elevated spot is exceedingly fine. Many of the hills with which our wanderings have made us familiar are in sight, as well as a number of others yet to be visited. North Hisworthy, on the other side of the forest, and which we ascended from Princetown (*Princetown District*) is plainly seen to the W.S.W., and to the right of it, a little S. of W., the granite cap of Mis Tor. Cut Hill rises from the recesses of the north quarter W.N.W., and from this the eye ranges over a great extent of moorland to Cosdon, the summit of

---

mark at this point, but was undecided whether it should take the form of a cross with two pairs of arms, or two separate crosses. We had some correspondence on the subject, but unfortunately his death put an end to the project.

† A stone chair preserved in a garden near Crediton is said to have been brought there from Hameldon about seventy years ago.

which bears N.W. by N. Nearly due S. is Brent Hill, and to the right of it, S. by W., and a dozen miles away, the Eastern Beacon, which looks far out over the South Hams from its frontier station on Ugborough Moor (Ex. 32). Eastward, on the further side of the Widecombe Valley, are the tors of Honeybag and Chinkwell, and beyond them Hound Tor, Hey Tor, and Rippon Tor.

The wall now runs south-westward for about ¾ m. to the head of a little stream that falls into the Broadford Brook, a tributary of the West Webburn, but the limit of Natsworthy Manor is marked by bondstones, the line extending from the beacon E.S.E. for ¾ m. to Bag Park Plantation. About 1 m. S. of these stones the Church Way crosses the down, running S.E. from the head of Gore Hill to the top of Church Lane, which leads down to Widecombe Green. Southward of this is Dunstone Down, and still further south, Bittleford Down, where the ridge terminates.

The fine group of rocks known as Honeybag Tor is the northern-most of a range extending for about 2½ m. southward, others being the equally striking Chinkwell Tor and Bonehill Rocks, with many minor piles hereafter mentioned. The high land from which these rise forms the E. side of the deep Widecombe valley, the head of which is a little to the N. of Honeybag, where the branches of the East Webburn meet. This stream, which was anciently called the Niprell, runs through it, as also does a road, the latter coming down from Heytree Cross (R. 32). The valley is here very narrow, and the scenery of a romantic character. A short distance below the confluence of the Webburn branches is the entrance to Bag Park, and below this Wide-combe Manor House, not far from which the road crosses the stream and runs near its right bank. Below Bonehill Rocks, and about 1½ m. from its head, the sides of the valley fall back, and here, about its centre, and on slightly rising ground, is the village which for many centuries has been closely connected with the forest, and which is known as Widecombe-in-the-Moor.

In our notice of the Lich Path (T. 18), we have spoken of the application made to Bishop Bronescombe in 1260 by the dwellers in the ancient tenements of Babeny and Pizwell within the forest to be allowed to pay their tithes to the parson of Widecombe, that being the church to which they mostly resorted, in consequence of their own parish church of Lydford being at such a distance. And until the mission chapels at Huccaby and Post Bridge were built, in 1868-9, the forest men of the Wallabrook Valley attended Widecombe Church. They were, however, compelled to go to Lydford occasionally, for it was there that the Forest Courts were held, but beyond this it is probable that they felt less interest in that place than in Widecombe. At the present day it is likely that even this is diminished, though they are periodically reminded by the visits of the rate-collector that such a place exists.

Besides Natsworthy, which four hundred years ago was set down in a forester's account as a hamlet, there were five vills in Widecombe parish, namely, Sherwell and Grendon, the two Cators, or, as the forester gives it, the " hamlett de North Catrowe " and the " villat de Higher Catrowe," and another the name of which does not appear in the account.

No inhabited district in the whole of the moorland region has better preserved its primitive aspect than the Widecombe Valley and the hill country about it, and the visitor who desires to look into an old-fashioned land, free from what are erroneously called "improvements," will here find much to delight him. Open moor, rocky heights, clear streams, and shady lanes, invite him to wander, and he will not go far without stumbling upon something to remind him of a by-gone day. On the commons he will find relics of the stone man; on their verge, or hidden away in some combe, that interesting feature of the Dartmoor border parishes, the substantially built farmhouses of a couple of centuries or more ago; in the hamlets the upping-stock, reminiscent of the time when the pillion was in vogue; the broken crosses that tell of Time's ravages, or the vandal's hand; walls of grey granite straggling along steep hillsides and enclosing crofts in which boulders are hardly less apparent than pasturage; rude bridges and solitary cots; the tiny manor pound; and much else that is "quaint and curious."

Widecombe Church, which has been someti.nes called the Cathedral of the Moor, is a large building in the Perpendicular style, and possesses a handsome tower, over a hundred feet in height. At the corners of this are double buttresses, diminishing in size as they ascend the stages, of which there are three. The top is battlemented and ornamented with four crocketted pinnacles, each surmounted with a cross. According to tradition the church was built by tinners, who, having been particularly successful in their ventures in the locality, adopted this course of showing their thankfulness for their good fortune, and the presence of the alchemical symbol of three rabbits on one of the bosses of the roof (which also appears at Chagford and in other moorland churches) has been thought to support this. It is, of course, quite possible that those who came into the Webburn valleys to seek tin should have re-built, or assisted to re-build, the church, which was not only attended by the parishioners of Widecombe, but also by those who dwelt in the south-east corner of the forest, where many of the streamworks were, and although it is unwise to place too much credence in tradition, it is sometimes found to have a foundation in fact. The size of the church is readily to be accounted for when it is remembered what district it was intended to serve, but the beauty of the tower, which far surpasses that of any other in the moorland district, certainly points to its having been erected in circumstances other than the ordinary, and thus we may not unreasonably suppose the story to be true. It is also not improbable that the forest men joined with the tinners in furthering the work. On Sunday, the 21st October, 1638, Widecombe Church was the scene of an occurrence of a kind which, though not unknown in other border villages, is happily one that is rare. While the service was proceeding the vicar, the Rev. George Lyde, being in the pulpit, a sudden darkness fell, and speedily a terrific thunder-storm broke over the building, doing considerable damage. Four persons were killed, and sixty-two injured, either by the lightning or falling masonry, large stones being hurled from the tower into the body of the church. An account of the storm appeared the same year, two tracts on the subject being published in London, and it was also commemorated in some lines written by Richard Hill, the village schoolmaster, as well as in others by the Rev. George Lyde, and these have since been printed. Hill's lines were painted in black letters on boards and fixed in the chancel, but, presumably having become decayed, were replaced by the present ones, which bear the date 1786. It was there that I first saw these wooden tablets, but when the church was restored in 1874 they were removed, and fixed against the wall in the basement of the tower, where they may now be seen. Opposite to them is a fragment of one of the old black letter boards, which came to light in a neighbouring cottage a few years ago. At the foot of the lines are the names of the churchwardens in 1786—Peter and Sylvester Mann. This name has existed in the locality for many centuries, and it is still found there. In the Court Rolls of the 10th of Henry VI., 1432-3, Robert Manna is mentioned as having taken land of the Lord of the Forest ; in 1579-80, Anthony Man, of Wydecomb, surrendered the moiety of a tenement at Babeny, then held by Leonard Man ; and in 1702 Richard Man is named as one of the forest tenants at Dunnabridge.

There are three stone crosses, or rather the remains of them, at Widecombe. Just without the churchyard gate is the base of one, but the cross itself is gone, and a small yew is now growing in the place it occupied. Very near to the south porch is a cross standing in a socket stone. The upper part of this one, which it will be seen has been restored, was formerly built into the churchyard wall. The third cross stands in the vicarage garden, where it was placed many years ago, but its original site was on the green at Dunstone. *Vide post.* [*Crosses*, Chap. XVI.] Another relic of an older day is the well, over which is raised a curious little edifice of granite. Close to the churchyard gate is a row of ancient almshouses, and on the opposite side of the road, the Old Inn. Behind the former is the green, a fine open space, whence a good view of the church tower is obtained. In the churchyard wall, and quite close to a gate at the back of the houses, is a small circular stone, 21 inches in diameter, and having a round hole through its centre. It is apparently a quern. On the north side of the green formerly stood the home of the Fitz Ralphs, of which a description has been left us in some verses by Richard Hill, the author of the lines commemorative of the great storm. This was North Hall, or as they have it locally, Narral, but the sole vestiges of it are some grass-covered mounds. In Hill's day, however, this moorland mansion was still standing, though, as he says, it was then much decayed. He describes it as being at one time surrounded with " moats of standing water," but only the ruined banks were then to be seen.

" And when the family within would walk into the town,
Or else return, a draw-bridge firm they presently let down ;
And at their pleasure drew it up to keep the household safe.
This house did anciently belong to Raph, the son of Raph."

In the thirteenth century Robert Courtenay granted certain privileges to the burgesses of Okehampton by charter. Among the names of those by whom this was attested occurs that of Ralph, son of Ralph, who was probably a representative of this Widecombe family ; as also, it is supposed, was Richard Fitz-Ralph, made Archbishop of Armagh and Primate of Ireland by Pope Clement VI., in 1347.

John Gerrard, the author of a book of poems published in 1769, was for some time curate of Widecombe. He does not, however, appear to have been a native of Devon.

From 1815 until his death in 1860 the Rev. James Holman Mason was vicar of Widecombe. He was a parson of the old-fashioned type, and many stories are yet related concerning him. Soon after his institution to the parish he was appointed a deputy rider and master forester of Dartmoor. [*Hundred Years*, Chap. V.] At the manor house lived his niece, Mrs. Drake, or Lady Drake, as she insisted on being called, who is still well remembered for her eccentricities.

Widecombe has been called the cold country, and like every other place in the Dartmoor region, at certain times it must be confessed its climate is anything but genial. I have been on the top of Hameldon when the hill was hard gripped by the hand of Winter, and darkness was coming on, and was made painfully aware of it. In the in-country it used to be said when snow was falling that Widecombe folks were picking their geese. It has, however, been suggested that " Widecombe " in this case is merely a corruption of " widdicote," meaning the sky, and it is possible that a confusion of terms led to the former belief that Widecombe was a very cold place. The comparison of falling snow with feathers was made a very long time ago. When the Scythians said the air was filled with them, Herodotus was at no loss to understand what was meant.

In September falls the great event of the year in this moorland parish. It is then that Widecombe Fair is held, and forest folk and men from the in-country for miles around flock to the village, as on a certain day (Tom Pearse havin' lained he's grey mare) did " Beel Brewer, Jan Stewer, Peter Gurney, Peter Davy, Dan'l Whiddon, Harry Hawk, Old Uncle Tom Cobbleigh and all." Then for a brief space unwonted sounds are heard ; the voices of buyer and seller, and the laughter of the reveller, break the quietude. But the next rising sun looks down into the valley to see it again in repose, in which state it continues till, another twelve months having passed, the day of business and festivity comes round again.

EXCURSIONS FROM BOVEY TRACEY.

The district described in these excursions is bounded on the N. by a line drawn from Lustleigh Cleave through Manaton to Heytree Down ; on the W. by the ridge of Hameldon ; and on the S. by a line running from Dunstone to Chittleford, Blackslade Down, and Hemsworthy Gate, to Bag Tor Down. In the Shorter Excursions a few places near the town of Bovey Tracey are also described, and in the Excursions from Widecombe directions are given for reaching the chief objects of interest in that locality.

[Tracks in the vicinity : Nos. 48 to 52.]

Ex. 23.—*Lustleigh, Lustleigh Cleave, Little Silver, Manaton, Bowerman's Nose, Becky Fall, Trendlebere Down*, 13 m. from and to Bovey Station. From Lud Gate and Ilsington about 1 m. more.

For the purpose of visiting the romantic valley known as Lustleigh Cleave, and the district around Manaton, where so much that is interesting is to be found, we shall first make our way to the village of Lustleigh, which is charmingly situated in the valley of the Wray. Should the visitor prefer the walk through the lanes instead of taking the train at Bovey (the distance by railway is 2½ m.), he will cross the line at the station and follow the road for about ½ m. to Five Wyches Cross, where he will turn R. ¼ m. on is a footpath across some fields R., and into this he will strike, and skirting Lodge Wood, and crossing a road (running R. to Wilford Bridge), will be led by it to Pullaford Farm. This he will pass through, and follow the lane to New Bridge on the Bovey.

Visitors at Lud Gate will take the Bovey road to the fork beyond Owlacombe, 1½ m. from the hotel, añd then branch L. across Lower Down to the guide-post, there turning R. to New Bridge.

Visitors at Ilsington first make their way to Narrowcombe, where they will turn L. and pass up the hill to the guide-post on the verge of the common, where they will reach the road from Lud Gate to Bovey. Here they turn R. to the fork beyond Owlacombe and follow the directions just given.

Immediately beyond New Bridge is Packsaddle Bridge, which spans the Wray. The former the visitor will cross, but not the latter, the road to Lustleigh turning L. between the two. A little way on this forks, the point being marked by a guide-post. If it should be desired to go to the cleave direct the L. branch must be followed ; for Lustleigh village the R. branch will be chosen. (By the L. road the down will be reached in ¾ m. Pass the first cross road ; then the entrance to Pethybridge Farm ; then a second road, and continue W. to the common. From this point a footpath runs across it to another leading down to a footbridge on the Bovey below Wanford Wood, ¾ m. distant).

Lustleigh, like Bovey Tracey, is outside venville, and has played no part in Dartmoor history, but it has its place among the parishes that go to form the moorland region, nevertheless, and contributes in no slight degree to its beauties. The village is small, but has a pleasing appearance, not only on account of its delightful situation, but for the manner in which the cottages are dotted about. The church possesses several features of interest, among them being a Norman font, two ancient monumental tombs, and an inscribed stone of the Romano-British period. One monument is supposed to be the effigy of Sir William Prouz, and another is generally believed to be to the memory of Sir John Dynham and his wife, though there is much doubt about this. In 1483 the office of Master Forester of Dartmoor was granted to Sir John.

The Rev. William Davy, who was curate of the parish at the latter end of the eighteenth century and during the first quarter of the nineteenth century, was the compiler of a work which he called *A System of Divinity*, and which consisted of 26 volumes of nearly 500 pages each. Not being willing to incur the risk of having it printed, he purchased a font of worn-out type, made a press, and set up and printed the whole work himself. When it was completed he presented a copy to his diocesan, when the bishop remarked that he could not be supposed to notice every *trifle* that appeared in print. But William Davy is remembered to-day, while the bishop is forgotten ; posterity did not regard the result of fifty years' labour as a trifle.

Not far from the station is a block of granite, which it is not unlikely formed the pedestal of a cross. It is known as the Bishop's Stone, and tradition relates that Bishop Grandisson once dined upon it. The carving on the side, of which, however, only traces are now to be seen, has been said to represent the arms of that prelate. But there is reason for supposing that it was once a bondmark to some lands connected with the See of Exeter, and it may have obtained its name in that connection. [*Crosses*, Chap. XV.] Another curious object in this locality is a rock at the rectory on the road to Sanduck called the Parson's Brown Loaf, but which, it appears, once bore the name of the Map Stone, and this has been given to the villa near by.

In order to reach the common we shall turn up a lane near the smithy, which in about ½ m. will bring us to Ellimore. Just beyond this we turn R., and proceeding for a short distance towards Hammerslake turn L., and shall speedily find ourselves, close to Sharp Tor, the summit of which is about 200 feet above us. From this pile of rocks we have a fine view of the cleave, by which term is now comprehended the romantic valley from above Foxworthy to Hisley Wood, though there is good reason to believe that in this case the word *cleave* is a corruption of cliff. (cf. Tavy Cleave, Ex. 11). At all events, there is documentary evidence showing that the hill was once known as Bortor Down and Bovey Combe Cliff, and Bovey Combe is still found here, a cottage above Hisley Wood being called by that name. On the tor is a logan bearing the name of the Nutcrackers, one which is applied to most of the moving stones on the moor, and on the slope are one or two other " logging " rocks. A little to the S.E. of the tor is a small circular enclosure, and there are vestiges of another a short distance N.W. on land belonging to South Harton Farm, while at the N.W. end of the ridge, near Hunters Tor, is an ancient hill camp. This, and another at Water Hill, on the ridge on the further side of the valley, form part of the chain of forts referred to in our notice of the encampments above the gorge of the Teign (S. Exs. 64, 65, 66). Some miles further S. are Place Wood Camp, Boro Wood Castle, Holne Chase Castle, and Hembury Castle, all of which are briefly noticed in our account of the Ashburton District.

The valley of Lustleigh Cleave is formed by the ridge situated between the Wray and the Bovey, and the steeps rising from the latter to the farms land of Manaton. One side of it—that on which we stand —is bare common, the other is clothed with woods. At the lower end of the valley this further side takes the form of a peninsulated ridge, at the eastern extremity of which the Bovey and the Becky Brook unite their waters. This is known as Hound Tor Ridge, or Hound Tor Wood, its higher slopes forming Water Hill, on which is situated the encampment just referred to. On the further side of this ridge the Becky comes down from Hound Tor Combe, the valley here being formed by the wood and East Down, as the common below Trendlebere Down is called. N.W. of Sharp Tor is a rock called Harton Chest, and just beyond this the fine entrance to South Harton Farm. A little further on the highest part of the ridge is reached, 1,063 feet, and beyond this, and about 1 m. from Sharp Tor, is the Lustleigh Camp. Quite near to it is Hunters Tor, from which the hills drops down to the enclosed lands at its N.W. extremity. A spur of it runs a short distance northward of the camp, and this is known as North Harton Down. Not far from Hunters Tor is Peck Farm, a name borne by some old mining remains near by, these being usually known as Peck Pits. In the *Shorter Excursions, post,* we have again noticed the cleave (S. Ex. 75 ; *vide* also *Gems*, Chap. IX.)

It has already been stated that a number of paths cross the down forming the steep side of the cleave (T. 48), and one of these leads from near Sharp Tor to crossing-places on the Bovey. This we may strike by making our way southward from the tor, and then shall follow it R. Our next point is Manaton, the church of which we have been able to see from the tor nearly due W., and 1½ m. off, but we do not make our way direct to it. Instead of doing so we follow the path down the hill, avoiding the branches L., and passing some rocks called the Foxes' Yard (L. of the path and ½ m. from the tor) shall be led to Horsham Steps. This curious crossing-place is formed by a number of boulders lying so closely together that unless the river be in flood it is possible to walk from one bank to the other with ease. In fact, the stream is not seen, as it finds a channel for itself under the huge lumps of granite. Below the steps it falls into a fine pool known as Horsham Bay, and then sweeps round the wooded height of Horsham Cleave, which is crowned with a pile of rocks. From these natural stepping-stones a path climbs the hill on the further side of the stream to Horsham Farm, whence a lane runs to Manaton, but instead of following this we pass up the L. bank of the river, under the crags of Ravens' Tor, which rise from the hillside R., some 300 feet above us, to Foxworthy. First we pass the disused Foxworthy Mill, and proceeding along a narrow track shall speedily reach the farm. Here we turn L. to Foxworthy Bridge, a clapper spanning the Bovey, on the bank of which just below is the mass of granite known as the Round of Beef, and shall find ourselves in one of the loveliest nooks in the whole of Devon. Close to us on the R. is the thatched cottage called Little Silver, which, placed amidst a congeries of moorstone, and embosomed in trees, adds much to the romantic character of the scene. The name Silver is found attached to several places in the county, and much ingenuity has been exercised in regard to its meaning. The last syllable may possibly be a corruption of *ford*, and may refer to a crossing-place on a stream, or to a road or path, but the meaning of *sil* is not apparent. It may, however, be pointed out that in Domesday Silverton appears as Sulfreton, and in old documents we have such a place-name at *Sulhford*. Hence it has been suggested that the first syllable of the name was originally *sul*, and perhaps had some connection with the Anglo-Saxon word for plough, which implement is even yet spoken of on the moor as a sull.

Leaving the charming scene we make our way up a steep and narrow path, through the wood called Neadon Cleave, on emerging from which the path will lead us across some fields to a lane, which will shortly bring us to another, where we turn L., and shall speedliy find ourselves at Manaton. The chief feature of this Dartmoor village, and one that is particularly pleasing, is its spacious green. This is bordered with trees, and around it the houses are grouped. At its higher, or northern end, is a small inn, the Half Moon, and behind this is the tor called Manaton Rocks, which, instead of rising bare and stern from the heather, springs, as it were, from masses of foliage where the light quivering leaves of the quickbeam contrast delightfully with the dark green of the glistening holly. The view of Lustleigh Cleave from this cluster of rocks is remarkably fine. In another direction, S. by E., we see Hey Tor, and S.W. by S., beyond the little valley of the Hayne, the great stone which Nature has rudely moulded into a semblance of the human form, and to which has been given the name of Bowerman's Nose.

In the churchyard is the base of a cross, but the cross itself is gone. It was removed many years ago by a former rector on account of a custom the country-people had of carrying corpses brought for burial round it thrice. His influence over his flock does not appear to have been sufficiently powerful to enable him to dissuade the people from continuing the practice, and so he removed the cross, and either destroyed or buried it. Search has been made for it, but without any satisfactory result. [*Crosses*, Chap. XV.] Great damage was done to the church by lightning on the 13th December, 1779.* It is Perpendicular in style, and was restored in 1865. The doorway is formed of four huge granite stones, and a similar one is seen at Lustleigh. An enclosure formerly existed near the village which was described in a paper read before the members of the Plymouth Institution in 1830, and was conjectured by Colonel Hamilton Smith to have given name to the place, *maen-y-dun*, the stone enclosure (*dun*, a hill, or hill-fort), but it was unfortunately destroyed in 1849. It was of an elliptical form, and consisted of a wall formed of stones from four to six feet high set on their edges. Its diameters were 100 feet and 138 feet.† A fragment of an ancient wall is still to be seen at Town Barton Farm, but whether this is a part of the enclosure in question seems to be rather doubtful.

A short distance S. of Town Barton is Hayne Cross, and making our way thither we turn R. to Hayne, whence a path will lead us to Hayne Down, on which, about ¼ m. from the enclosures, we perceive the weather-beaten Bowerman's Nose. This curiously-shaped pile, which the imaginations of former antiquaries turned into a rock idol, is really part of a tor, the other part having gone to ruin and now forming the clatter below it. It consists of five layers of granite, and rises to a height of nearly forty feet. In the Notes to Carrington's *Dartmoor*, 1826, it is stated that a person named Bowerman lived at Hound Tor, near by, in the Conqueror's time, by which we suppose some sort of connection between that individual and the rock is suggested. But it has also been thought that Bowerman may be a corruption of *vawr maen*, the *great stone*. This derivation is, however, open to the objection that the words would not fall in this order, but that the *great stone* would be referred to by Celts as *maen vawr*, the noun coming first, so that we might rather expect to find the term corrupted to Minevower. But there is more than one " nose " on Dartmoor, or " nawze," as the moormen say, as we shall see by-and-bye, and most, if not all, of these names are modern. It is possible that this of Bowerman's Nose may also be of no great antiquity, though we cannot say that such is the case. About ¼ m. S.E. of Bowerman's Nose is another tor (1,300 feet), the two being connected by a reave,

---

* Dr. Croker (*The Eastern Escarpment of Dartmoor*, 1851) refers to this, and gives an extract relating to it from the parish register.

† This is stated by Dr. Croker to have been situated in a field called Hookaway. He says it was partly destroyed in 1849, and almost wholly so in 1850, only six stones being then left standing. The above measurements were taken by the Rev. Samuel Rowe, who visited the enclosure in 1828.

and near this is a kistvaen. A little W. of S. of the second tor, and
less than ¼ m. from it, is a small group of hut circles, just inside a newtake, but they present nothing remarkable.

[W. of Bowerman's Nose is a road running southward to Swine
Down Gate (R. 32, from Moreton). Should the visitor choose he may
follow this, and on passing through the gate turn L. by the wall and
descend by Great Hound Tor Farm to Leighon Bridge, as in R. 25,
and so make his way to Bovey as therein directed.

We shall return from the down to Hayne Cross, either by way of
Hayne or through Southcott, which latter lies under the southernmost
tor in an easterly direction. At the cross we keep straight on to Deal,
where we pass over the Hayne Brook, and then turning R. shall follow
the road to the Becky, which we reach immediately above where the
Hayne falls into it, and close to New Bridge. Here we cross the
last-named stream at a foot-bridge, and after passing over two others,
shall reach Becky Fall, a spot beloved by all visitors to this part of the
moor.

Although Becky Fall may not on ordinary occasions fully realize
the expectations of those who look to see a cascade, it can never be
disappointing, for the beauty of its surroundings more than com-
pensates for the lack of a volume of water. But viewed at the time
of a summer freshet the fall in very fine, for then the little river, nut
brown and flecked with foam, comes down with a roar, and dashes
impetuously over the rocks that fill its channel. From the top of the
falls to the bottom the drop is from 70 to 80 feet, and having rolled
and tumbled to the foot of this boulder-strewn steep, it runs along
merrily under Hound Tor Wood to meet the Bovey as it comes from
Lustleigh Cleave. Then the united stream flows on between Rudge
Wood and Pullabrook Wood, and having passed under New Bridge
receives the Wray, and thence, knowing only the name of Bovey, the
waters runs to the great plain of the Heathfield, where they are lost
in the Teign.

Returning to New Bridge we cross it, and thence follow the road
over Trendlebere Down, known as the Lower Terrace Drive. By the
side of this is a stone row with a small cairn at one end of it, but most
of the stones are fallen. The road will take us along the foot of
Yarner Wood, from which part of it we have a fine view northward
of Lustleigh Cleave. Having passed the wood we reach a guide-post
just beyond which the road forks. The L. branch will take us to
Five Wyches Cross, about ½ m. from Bovey Station ; the R. to Lower
Down Cross, ½ m. from the former. *Vide* R. 25. On reaching the
common from New Bridge, Ilsington and Lud Gate visitors should
turn R., and ascending to the Higher Terrace Drive make their way
S. to Yarner Wells. Instructions for reaching their destination from
that point are given at the end of Ex. 24. Yarner Wells are noticed
in Ex. 25.

Ex. 24.—*Lower Down Cross, Leighon, Swine Down Gate, Jay's
Grave.* [EXTENSION to *Cripdon Down, Natsworthy, and Bonehill
Down.*] *Hound Tor, Grea Tor, Hound Tor Combe, Black Hill, Yarner
Wells,* 12½ m. ; with Extension, 16 m. from and to Bovey Station.
From Lud Gate, 4½ m. less ; Ilsington, 2 m. less.

Setting out from the station the visitor will take the road to the moor as in Ex. 23, but instead of turning off at Five Wyches Cross he will continue straight up the hill to Lower Down Cross, nearly ½ m. further on, where he will turn R. by the school. In about 1 m. he will reach a guide-post, where a road runs up the hill to the lower Yarner Lodge. This he will leave on the L., and striking into the Lower Terrace Drive will speedily be led by it to the edge of Yarner Wood. The drive, which is carried along the lower part of the wood, gradually ascends to a point where the hill. on the L. becomes very steep, and here, 300 feet above the guide-post, it leaves it and turns towards the north. The visitor will now forsake the road, and climb the hill L., his course being a trifle S. of W., and in a little over ½ m. will reach the Higher Terrace Drive at a point about ¼ m. N. of Yarner Wells.

Visitors from Lud Gate and Ilsington will reach this point by way of the Wells, as directed in Ex. 25 and in S. Ex. 79.

Crossing the drive the rambler will bear W., with the summit of Black Hill L., and soon afterwards bending R. will strike the road running down to Leighon (S. Ex. 79), which will lead him past the house to the bridge over the Becky Brook. Crossing it he will turn L. a few yards below, and will soon come in sight of Great Hound Tor Farm. This he will leave on the R., and pass up the steep and narrow lane leading to Hound Tor Down, on reaching which he will obtain a remark-ably fine view of Hound Tor, or rather one part of it. The huge rocks are seen cresting a height immediately above him, and sharply defined against the sky. Proceeding upward, with the wall of some enclosures R. and Hound Tor Down L., the visitor will soon reach Swine Down Gate, or as it is locally called, Swallaton Gate, close to which is a cottage. Passing through this he will take the L. branch of the road at the fork immediately within it. (The R. branch runs over Hayne Down, passing very near to Bowerman's Nose, less than 1 m. distant, Ex. 23, to Langstone, North Bovey, and Moreton, R. 53). The road we now follow skirts Swine Down, the enclosures of Hedge Barton being on the L. About ¾ m. from the gate a path runs off L. between the estate named and Heytree, and here we shall notice a small mound, with a head and footstone. It is the burial place of a suicide, and is known as Jay's Grave. Kitty Jay, as she used to be spoken of, is said to have been a young unmarried woman, who many years ago hung herself in an outbuilding belonging to Canna, a farm not far from the foot of East Down (S. Ex. 61), and in accord-ance with the barbarous custom of the time, was interred at this cross-way. More than forty years ago Mr. James Bryant, of Hedge Barton, caused the grave to be opened, when human bones, including a skull, were discovered, and declared on examination to be those of a female. The date of the unfortunate woman's death is unknown, as no one then remembered the occurrence. Mr. Bryant had the bones placed in a box and re-interred on the spot where they had been found, and raised the mound and set up the stones that now mark it.

From this point the road runs northward, with Cripdon Down R. and the Heytree enclosures L., to Heytree Cross, Easdon Farm, Beetor Cross, and Chagford, and has already been described in R. 53. Cripdon Down, which presents nothing remarkable, is a small common to the W. of Hayne Down. At its northern end, near Cripdon Farm, are a few hut circles, and close to a path running across it to Blissmoor Farm there is a small pool, around which Ned Hacker once saw—or declared that he saw—the pixies dancing, and was so delighted with their antics that he remained for a considerable time on the down looking at them. But when it afterwards transpired that Ned had spent the whole of the evening at the Half Moon, at Manaton, the good folks of Natsworthy, where he was employed, were rather disposed to doubt the accuracy of his story.

[EXTENSION *to the eastern side of the Widecombe Valley.* Instead of returning direct to Hound Tor Down the visitor may extend his walk so as to embrace the tors overlooking the valley of Widecombe, and for this purpose will turn into the path running W. from Jay's Grave. This, which is known as Heytree Common Lane, will lead him by a small plantation to Heytree Down, a common to the S. of Vogwell Down, and on which there is a group of hut circles. These will be found on its western side, near a track. Vogwell Down, which is even smaller than Heytree, lies to the S. of the farm bearing the same name, and is partly surrounded by plantations, S. Ex. 61, 62. Our way lies along the southern verge of Heytree, with Hameldon rising before us, to it S.W. corner, close to Natsworthy, and ¾ m. from the grave at the crossway. Here we strike the road coming from Heytree Cross and running southward to Widecombe, and shall turn into it L. Passing Higher and Lower Natsworthy we follow this road for about ½ m. from the latter, when we shall turn L., between a plantation and some enclosures, to the common. Above us are the rocks of Honeybag, to which we shall climb, and thence make our way southward across Bonehill Down. The road runs on below the tors for a considerable distance, joining the Ashburton road rather less than 1½ m. S. of Swine Down Gate, which shortly afterwards unites with the one leading from Widecombe to Hemsworthy Gate. From Honeybag Tor we have a fine view of the upper part of the Widecombe valley, and of Hameldon, a wide extent of moorland and cultivated country being also visible. The derivation of its name is not clear, but it may be worth while to note, if only as a curious circumstance, its similarity to *hunne-bed,* a name given to ancient burial monuments situated chiefly in the province of Drenthe in the Netherlands. To the E. of the tor, and close to it, is Goodlays Plantation, belonging to Hedge Barton, and the house is also quite near. Proceeding southward we make our way to Chinkwell Tor, the next height, 1,504 feet, before reaching which we pass one of a line of manorial boundary stones, standing at a point called Slades Well. Another boundary near by is known as L. Corner. On this part of the down there are several hut circles, and on the tor we shall also fine some reaves, which appear not unlike parts of rectangular enclosures, while the summit is crowned with a dilapidated cairn, much overgrown. From this lofty point we have another grand view ; in fact, during our progress over the down we have around us a wonderful panorama of rock and hill, of wood and field. Southward of Chinkwell is another pile of rocks, to which the name of Sharp Tor is sometimes given, and still further south is Bel Tor, 1,319 feet, on which we shall find two or three rock basins. Near it a footpath runs to Hedge Barton, and this we shall cross, as well as a road running over the common towards Hound Tor Down, and also a continuation of the one which we left below Honeybag. Soon we reach Bonehill

Rocks, 1,227 feet, a fine pile near the southern end of Bonehill Down,
and having climbed it, and looked down upon Widecombe village,
nearly 500 feet below, we pass up the ascent eastward tò the Chagford and Ashburton road, to which a walk of a ¼ m. will bring us.
Here we turn L., and on passing the corner of the Hedge Barton
enclosures shall find ourselves on Hound Tor Down. The road runs
on for ¾ m. to Swine Down Gate, with the wall of Hedge Down, which
is now enclosed, on the L., but we shall ˙strìke over the common R.
towards Hound Tor.]

Retracing our steps from Jay's Grave we shall again pass through
Swine Down Gate, and make our way to Hound Tor, which is close by.
This tor, certainly one of the finest on the moor, consists of three main
piles, rising to a considerable height above the ground. Around these
are many smaller masses of granite, the tor covering altogether a large
area. The view which the visitor will obtain from it will well repay
him for any trouble he may have taken to reach it. It is one of border
scenery, and of far-off farm lands. He does not look into the desolate
parts of the moor, the wildness of its recesses being altogether hidden
notwithstanding that a great extent of it is visible ; but he sees it
where its sterness is softened down to a mood more fitting to welcome
the woods and fields that press against its slopes. A short distance
S. of the tor is a ruined kistvaen. Little of it now remains, many of
the stones of which it consisted having been taken away more than
thirty years ago for road material. [*Gems*, Chap. X.]

Leaving Hound Tor we shall descend the side of the combe which
bears its name to Grea Tor, crossing on the way the path running S.
towards Holwell (T. 50). Grea Tor, which is not quite ½ m. S.E. of
Hound Tor, is one of the most beautiful on the moor, and is draped
in a similar manner to Manaton Rocks and Hucken Tor (Ex. 23, 1).
Springing from the crevices of the grey rocks, that rise like a stately
tower from the turf, are ferns and whortleberry plants, and the graceful
quickbeam, partly shrouding them as perchance they did long ago
when a maiden walked with her lover here at eventide. Then a time
arrived when she came alone to the tor, for the youth had been called
away to the wars. Summer followed summer, and at length the
maiden's visits ceased, and the tor knew her no more. She rested
in the quiet churchyard of Manaton, while her lover slept in a foreign
land.

Passing down the Hound Tor Combe, we cross the Becky and
ascend the hill, with Smallacombe Rocks R. and Leighon Tor L., our
course being about E. The last-named pile is on the slope of Black
Hill, and over the southern edge of this we pass, and descending its
steep eastern side shall reach Yarner Wells, 1 m. from the combe.
From this point the return to Lud Gate will be by way of the Higher
Terrace Drive. If bound to Ilsington the visitor will leave this ¼ m.
beyond the Wells, and follow a narrow moor road branching from it L.
This will bring him to the guide-post below Owlacombe Barrow, where
he will take the road to the village, turning R. shortly before reaching
it at Narrowcombe. For Bovey the visitor will pass down the hill
N.E. from the Wells, with Yarner Wood close to him on the R. In
little over ½ m. he will reach the Lower Terrace Drive, and turning into
this R. will reach the town as in the preceding excursion, or R. 25.

(The road route from Hound Tor is given at the end of R. 25).

Ex. 25.—*Yarner Wells, Black Hill, Leighon Tor, Smallacombe Rocks, Holwell Tor, Saddle Tor, Bag Tor Down, Hey Tor,* 11 m. from and to Bovey Station. From Lud Gate, 5 m. less; Ilsington, 2½ m. less.

The road leading upward from the station to the moor will be followed as in the preceding excursions, and as Yarner Wells is his first point the visitor may again turn R. at Lower Down Cross, and make his way by the Lower Terrace Drive to the foot of Yarner Wood, and then, keeping this close on the L., pass up the common to the Wells. Or he may keep straight up the hill instead of turning at the Cross, for another 1¼ m., when he will reach the common near Owlacombe. Here he will leave the road, and turning R. strike over the edge of this above Yarner Wood, and passing Yarner, the residence of Mr. Justice Eve, will soon reach a narrow road, which a little further on runs into the Higher Terrace Drive, about ¼ m. from the Wells. This is the path referred to in Ex. 24 as being the direct one from the last-named point to Ilsington.

Visitors from Ilsington reach the common soon after passing Narrowcombe, as in Ex. 23, and crossing the main road at the guide-post on its verge, will take the narrower one just mentioned, which runs up the hill in a north-westerly direction. On the R. is a line of bondstones, which extends from near the guide-post to the Becky, in Hound Tor Combe, one part of it marking the boundary between the parishes of Ilsington and Bovey Tracey, the other the boundary between Ilsington and Manaton. These stones, like most others that serve a similar purpose on Dartmoor, bear names, the third which the visitor will pass after leaving the road being called Prince Albert, and the one next to it being generally referred to as Owlacombe Barrow, though no tumulus now exists there. A little beyond this the visitor will cross the line, and the next stone will therefore be on his left. This is known as Old William, the one still further up the hill being Old Jack. Beyond this is Victoria, and the next marks the point where the parishes of Ilsington, Manaton, and Bovey Tracey meet, the line between the last two running down the hill direct to Yarner Wells, rather over ¼ m. distant, N.E. by N. The Ilsington and Manaton line then runs on to the Prince of Wales bond-stone, then to Hole Rock, and thence to the Becky. Above the point where it strikes this little stream the latter becomes the boundary, and two or three stones are found on its bank. There is one at Long Pool, under Smallacombe Rocks, and another further up which is known as Duke Stone. The line then runs on to Hawkeswell, near the head of the Becky, and thence to Seven Lords' Land, which is noticed further on (S. Ex. 82).

Visitors from the Moorland Hotel at Lud Gate will proceed to the Wells by way of the Higher Terrace Drive.

The tract of moorland lying to the S. of the line drawn from Owlacombe to the Becky, and extending beyond Rippon Tor to the enclosures of Mountsland and Horridge, is situated in the parish of Ilsington, and its northern portion is usually spoken of as Ilsington Common. This consists of two parts, the northernmost forming Hey Tor Down, and that to the S. of it Bag Tor Down, and over these our present excursion will extend. That part of the Ilsington common lands lying still further S. and comprising Horridge Common, on which

Rippon Tor is situated, and Mountsland Common are noticed in the Ashburton Section, and to this visitors desirous of exploring that part of the moor are referred.

At Yarner Wells, where is a cottage on the edge of the wood, a little stream rises in a romantic hollow and runs down the steep hillside, one portion of it being conducted to the old Yarner Copper Mine, and another to the fish pond near the lower Yarner lodge. The spot lies immediately under the steep brow of Black Hill, the summit of which, though only $\frac{1}{4}$ m. distant, is some 300 feet higher, its elevation being 1,339 feet. To this we shall now make our way, following a N.W. course, and on reaching it shall find it to be crowned with a tumulus. The view from this point is very fine, and embraces the lower valley of the Becky with Manaton and Lustleigh Cleave, and in another direction Hound Tor with the moorlands beyond. A little W. of S. of the summit, and near Leighon Tor, is a group of three tumuli, a number found together in many parts of the moor. S. of the tor is the boundary line just described, which here runs from Prince of Wales Stone westward to Hole Rock, and this we cross on our way to Smallacombe Rocks, a large cluster of granite masses placed, like Leighon Tor, on the slope forming the eastern side of Hound Tor Combe. Above it, on the E., is a group of hut circles, some of them being good examples, and on one of the outlying piles to the S.W. is a rocking, or logan, stone, about which, however, there is nothing very striking. Proceeding southward we pass the head of a rivulet which falls into the Becky at Long Pool, and just beyond this shall notice a small pound, near the branch of the tramway running to the deserted granite quarry below. Crossing the tramway we direct our steps to Holwell Tor, where the rock masses rise from an extensive clatter. The lower part of this is not more than about 100 feet above the Becky, and some 400 yards from it, but its higher part is twice that distance from the stream. In the combe, just below, is Holwell Cottage, and above it the farm of that name, while rising beyond this is Holwell Down, over which the Chagford road runs from Hemsworthy Gate to Hedge Barton. On the lower side of the clatter is a small pound and some hut circles.

On the hill about $\frac{3}{4}$ m. S. of Holwell Tor is Saddle Tor, and to this we shall now direct our steps, passing on our way another branch of the disused granite tramway. This was constructed by Mr. George Templer, of Stover, well known in the earlier part of the nineteenth century for his scholarly attainments and his prowess in the hunting field, as well as for his efforts to advance the interests of his county. His father having previously constructed a canal from Newton Abbot to Teigngrace, Mr. Templer conceived the idea of connecting it by means of a tramway with the moor. He carried out his project, and the road was opened in September, 1820. It is interesting as being the first line constructed in Devon. It was very skilfully planned, and the wagons ran on grooved blocks of granite, which took the place of rails. Over it was conveyed the stone quarried near Hey Tor, and which was shipped at Teignmouth. It was used for the arches of London Bridge, and also for the columns of the British Museum library, as well as in other important buildings. The quarries have, however, ceased to be worked for many years. [*Hundred Years*, Chap. III.]

Saddle Tor is the central of the three frontier piles that form such conspicuous objects when viewed from the neighbourhood of Kings-teignton, the others being Rippon Tor, ½ m. distant in a S.W. direction, and Hey Tor, ½ m. N.E. It overlooks the head of Hound Tor Combe, which extends to the foot of the hill on which Rippon Tor is placed, a distance of more than 2 m. above Leighon Bridge. Close to it a foot-path climbs over the down, cutting off a bend in the road, which here runs westward to Hemsworthy Gate, rather over ½ m. away. Risdon speaks of this pile as " a noted place called Saddletor," from the hills near which he says the Loman, or as we now call it, the Lemon, "fetcheth her fountain." The nearest stream to the tor is the Sig, which rises on Bag Tor Down, about ¼ m. S. of it, and to this we shall now make our way. It falls into the Lemon (the springs of which are near Lud Gate) just below Sigford, and immediately after having received the waters of the Langworthy Brook.

Descending from the tor we cross the road and presently come upon a track that branches from it further R. (T. 49), and this we shall follow L. It will lead us along the bank of the stream, which flows through a shallow hollow to Bag Tor Woods, but we desert it on nearing the tor these are named after, and making our way to the latter which we see on the L. There is nothing remarkable in the rocks themselves, but the spot is worth visiting for the picture of a retired border nook there presented. The stream is lost in the woods below, in one part of which is embosomed the ancient house called after the little tor, and the former home of the Fords. This is noticed in S. Ex. 81. On leaving Bag Tor we strike into a track running close to it, and following it N.W. shall be led over the side of Pinchaford Ball to the road under Hey Tor, from which we may readily reach the rocks.

This well-known tor, rendered by its shape and situation the most conspicuous on the moor, consists of two huge masses of rock rising from the highest part of the down, and attains an elevation of 1,491 feet. The name it bears may be the Anglo-Saxon *heah*, meaning *high*, or merely a corruption of the English word, as in the case of the tor above Tavy Cleave, referred to in our description of the Lydford district (Ex. 11). The moormen, in accordance with their habit of duplicating the final syllable when naming the tors, usually speak of it as " Heyter Tar," and as " Heyter Rocks," and this seems to have misled the writer of a brief account of the moor published many years ago. He calls it Athur Tor, or Solar Tor, deriving, we suppose, the latter name from the former, and evidently regarding it as a place where sacrifices were once offered to the sun god. We may smile at this, but deriva-tions no less far-fetched are suggested to-day. We have the case of *Yr ynys Tor*, that is the island tor, offered as the probable original of the thirteenth century *Ernestorre*, a name which it is sought to fasten upon Yes Tor, for the reason that it looks like an island when its summit is seen rising from a seat of mist. The Hundred of Hey Tor apparently takes its name from these rocks, although they are not within it, and it has been said that the Hundred Court was formerly held there, but on what grounds we are unable to discover. In the north-eastern rock steps have been cut, and these are furnished with an iron hand-rail, so that it is easily ascended. Dr. Croker, writing in 1851, alludes to this as " the unsightly stair step to enable the enervated and pinguitudinous scoins of humanity of this wonderful nineteenth century to gain its summit." The twentieth century visitor is, of course, of quite a different stamp, but he will probably argue that since the steps are cut he may as well use them. On the summit is a rock-basin, but Nature has not been so happy in the formation of this one as in some she has scooped out on the moor. The view from this lofty station is magnificent, and if the visitor takes the trouble to climb to the top of the south-western pile there will be nothing to obstruct it. A great part of South Devon lies, as it were, at the feet of the beholder. The estuary of the Teign, with the Channel off Teignmouth, is plainly visible, a wide stretch of the latter, indeed, extending from Portland westward, being in view. Eastward the rock masses on the high land in the neighbourhood of Hennock and Bridford are seen, and moorward, with great Cosdon conspicuous to the N.W., the brown hills of the ancient forest.

From Hey Tor we shall descend to the Moorland Hotel. Close to this, southward, the road forks: L. to the Rock Hotel at Hey Tor Vale ; R. towards Pinchaford Farm, bearing L. at the cross roads below it, to Ilsington. Bovey visitors will follow the road running eastward, reaching the confines of the moor in about 1 m. ; thence down the hill with Colehays Plantation R. to Lower Down Cross and Five Wyches Cross, and on to the line near the station—a descent of nearly a thousand feet.

SHORTER EXCURSIONS.

S. Ex. 71.—*John Cann's Rocks, Bot Tor Rock, and Hennock*, 6 m. The visitor, starting from Bovey, will leave the town by the Moreton road, passing the old cross at Atway, and $\frac{1}{2}$ m. beyond will take the R. branch at the fork, and enter Lower Aller Lane. A few hundred yards further up turn R. at the cross-road, and soon the woods, on the verge of which John Cann's Rocks are situated R., will be reached. With these two traditions are connected. The road goes on to Furseleigh Cross, near which some Roman coins were found in 1837. This point may be reached from Bovey by turning into Fursleigh Lane immediately opposite to Cross Cottage. The rocks are less than $1\frac{1}{2}$ m. from the town.

For Bot Tor, or Bottor Rock, the visitor will follow the road running E. from Fursleigh Cross to Five Lanes, $\frac{3}{4}$ m., when the first turning L., close to the entrance to Hazelwood, must be taken. This is Beacon Lane, and it will lead him direct to the rock, which will be seen on the L. of the way. From this fine pile, the upper mass of which is sometimes referred to as Bottor's Nose, a wide and varied view is presented. On one side is seen the valley of the Teign, and Chudleigh, with the heights beyond ; and on the other a grand view of the hills of Dartmoor. The rock attains an elevation of 800 feet, being about 700 feet above Bovey Bridge near the Dolphin Hotel. Quite close to Bot Tor farmhouse, just below, is a field called Brady Park, in which an interesting object once existed. It consisted of a small pound, 77 feet in diameter, with a wall about 3 feet high and 4 feet thick. The hollows in the base of Bot Tor Rock were formerly the haunt of the pixies, who have often been heard singing by the good folks of Hennock when making their way homeward late at night. As the rambler will probably not choose such a time for his visit to the rock it is unlikely that he will be so favoured, but since the locality does not lack warblers of another kind it will doubtless be to the accompaniment of sounds not less pleasant that he will continue his walk to that village. This he will do by passing up Beacon Lane for a short distance, and entering a gate on the R., whence a path will lead him along the verge of a little common directly to it.

Hennock is a small village occupying a commanding situation, being only about 200 feet below Bot Tor. Running W. from Hennock is a road known as Bell Lane, and this we shall follow for ½ m. to Chericombe Head, where is a guide-post. We strike into Bowden Lane S., and shortly afterwards turning L. shall pass on by Lower Bowden to Furzeleigh Cross. Continuing straight down the hill with Furzeleigh Plantation R., we soon reach the fork, where we branch R. to Cross Cottage, or L. if our destination be that part of Bovey near the church.

S. Ex. 72.—*Shap Tor Rock*, 4 m. Passing up by Cross Cottage and Atway, we branch L. at the first fork, and speedily reach Woolley, where we bend R. to the first milestone, at King's Cross. Then, still following the Moreton Road R., for about 200 yards we arrive at a point where a road runs L. to Plumley, and a footpath R. to Northcombe. It is recorded that several stone circles once existed at Plumley, but they were destroyed more than fifty years ago. They were in all probability hut circles, and during the work of demolition eight bronze celts were found, four of them being piled up against one of the stones and the others lying near. Following the footpath to Northcombe, we shall make our way from that farm by another path, which runs up the hill through Northcombe Copse to Shap Tor Down, which we reach immediately below the rock. The view from this is very fine, particularly that towards Lustleigh. In returning from the down we may follow the road leading from its S.E. corner to Shap Tor Farm, and thence to the road under Higher Bowden, a point reached in the return from Hennock, as described in the preceding excursion, q.v. Here we turn R. to Furzeleigh Cross.

Shap Tor Rock is rather over 1 m. W. by N. of Bot Tor, and the two may be very well included in a single excursion. From Shap Tor the visitor will proceed as above, but when he reaches the road under Higher Bowden will turn L., then R., to Chericombe Head, and then make his way through Beacon Lane to the rock, which he will see R.

S. Ex. 73.—*Lustleigh and the Cleave, via Woolley and Ashwell Lane*, each 3¼ m. The visitor will leave the town as in the preceding excursion, but on reaching Woolley instead of turning R. will keep straight on through Ashwell Lane, which will lead him down to the railway. On crossing this he will find that the road forks, the L. branch being carried over the Bovey at Wilford Bridge and going up to the road under Lower Down (Ex. 23), the R. one running up the valley between the river and the railway. This we shall follow, and soon after shall cross the latter again. About this point we have on our L., but on the further side of the line, the confluence of the Wray and the Bovey. A little way on we turn L., and once more crossing the railway, shall reach Packsaddle Bridge, where we pass over the Wray and immediately turn R. From this point we proceed as in Ex. 23, which gives directions for reaching either Lustleigh Cleave or the village.

(Visitors from Lud Gate and Ilsington will reach this point as in Ex. 23).

If the rambler is making his way to Lustleigh Station he will not turn L. and cross the line to Packsaddle Bridge, but will keep straight on past Knowle, and under Knowle Wood, to Wrayland, just beyond which a road L. will lead him directly to it.

From Lustleigh several of the rock-piles on the high land eastward of the Wray may be conveniently visited. By crossing the railway at the bridge near the station and taking the second turning L. to Wrayland Barn he will find a footpath that will lead him up to the Moreton road under Tin Copse. It crosses the road, and running up through the copse, skirts Tinhill Copse, immediately above which is Bullaton Rock (1 m.) To reach Elsford Rock (1½ m.), the first turning L. after crossing the Lustleigh railway bridge must be followed. This will lead the rambler to Kelly Cross, where is a guide-post (R. 31, 46), and here he will turn L. Proceeding for a few score yards he will enter a lane R., and passing up through Greathill Copse, will soon reach Elsford Cottages. Beyond these is Elsford Farm, and the road running from Hennock *via* Poolmill Cross to Pepperdon Down. Elsford Rock is a short distance W. of the farm. Between Elsford Farm and Pepperdon Down a road runs R., *i.e.*, N. by E., to Moor Barton. On this farm several interesting objects were discovered many years ago in a large cairn. On the tumulus being opened a kistvaen formed of six stones was exposed ; there was also a copper spear head with two pegs by which it has been secured to its staff, a glass bead, and a small amulet of stone.

The road running S.E. from Kelly Cross goes on to Slade Cross, ¾ m., as described in R. 31, from which point Shap Tor Rock is about ¾ m. distant, E. by S., but there is no direct path to it. A road goes N.E. from Slade Cross to Poolmill Cross, ¾ m., where the road to Hennock, 2 m., runs R.

S. Ex. 74.—*Sanduck and around the Combe (from Lustleigh),* 4½ m. The Bishop's Stone near Lustleigh Station has already been noticed (Ex. 23), and the probability of its having once served as the base of a cross remarked upon. In addition to this there are three other stone crosses in the parish [*Crosses,* Chap. XV.], and these the visitor may see on a walk round the combe that runs up towards Sanduck Grove. (The routes to Lustleigh from Bovey, Lud Gate, and Ilsington, have already been given). Leaving the village by the school we pass up by Mapstone and South Hill towards Higher Combe, 1 m., and immediately before reaching the road leading to it L., in a small field on the R. called Cross Park, is one of the objects referred to. It consists of the upper part of a granite cross, and this is fixed on a rock. Passing Higher Combe Cross (*i.e.*, the branch road) L. and proceeding on our way for about a mile we reach Sanduck, where the road bends L. Here on the R. is another cross, which was discovered in 1901 in the foundations of a farmhouse burned down in that year, and soon after passing this we turn L., or southward. (About ½ m. to the west is Barnecourt, which Risdon speaks of as Barn House Barton, " the ancient possession of a race of gentlemen so called.") Very soon we pass North Harton R., and then the road forks. Here we take the R. branch, and skirt the combe on the opposite side of which we made our way upward from the village. Less than ½ m. from the fork a private road branches R. to South Harton (Ex. 23), and here we shall find a cross built into the wall. It had been split to form a pair of gateposts, but the parts were fitted together and it was placed here for preservation. Still following the road we pass Hammerslake, and ¼ m. beyond turn L. to Ellimore, and descend to Lustleigh by the path by which we left it on setting out for the cleave (Ex. 23).

S. Ex. 75.—*Lustleigh Cleave from Hisley Wood upward (from Lustleigh)*, 5 m. (Visitors from Bovey may reach the lower end of the cleave as in Ex. 23 or S. Ex. 73, making their way first to the road between New Bridge and Packsaddle Bridge (2¼ m.) as therein directed. The point for which visitors from Lud Gate and Ilsington will first make is a footbridge on the Becky a short distance above its confluence with the Bovey. This they may reach either by way of Yarner Wells, as described in S. Ex. 78, or by Reddiford Down. In the latter case they will follow the instructions given in Ex. 23, but on reaching the guide-post at the bottom of the slope under Yarner Wood will make their way along the Lower Terrace Drive N.W. for a short distance, and then leave it for the track that runs straight on down the hill to the bridge. On crossing the Becky a path will lead them round Riddy Hill to the Bovey, and upward to the footbridge under Wanford Wood. This point in 2 m. from Yarner Wells).

Leaving Lustleigh at its southern end we shall make our way past Rudge to the cross road reached in Ex. 23 between New Bridge and the down, where we continue straight on to Lower Hisley. Higher Hisley is close by on the R., and a short distance in advance are Gradner Rocks, on the edge of Hisley Wood, which the rambler may visit, as this will only necessitate his retracing his steps a little way. From Lower Hisley a lane branches W. to Boveycombe, and this we shall now follow past that cottage to the common. We are here quite near to the Bovey at the lower end of the down, and shall follow the river upward to its higher end. Passing Hisley Wood we have on the L., but on the further bank of the river, and consequently in the parish of Manaton, as the latter here forms the boundary of Lustleigh, Woodash, some of the trees of which cover the lower slope of the down on this side as well. Above there is a footbridge, where a path coming down from near Hammerslake crosses the stream and climbs the hill to the hamlet of Water, a little over ½ m. from Manaton. On the R., and high above us, is Sharp Tor. Passing up stream we skirt Wanford Wood, to which succeeds Water Cleave, where is another footbridge, just below the Foxes' Yard R. Still further up the stream is Horsham Cleave, with the curious Horsham Steps, described in Ex. 23, at the foot of the wooded steep. Above this is Neadon Cleave, between the woods of which and the grove at Foxworthy the Bovey comes down from Foxworthy Bridge. This and Little Silver, close by, are noticed in the excursion just named, and if we make our way to those objects we may regain the common by the road just above Foxworthy Farm. If we do not turn aside we leave the Bovey just above the steps, and passing Ravens' Tor on the slope shall strike northward, with the rocks sometimes called Foxworthy Tor L., to Hunters' Tor, barely ½ m.

distant. Having examined this, and the camp close by, to which Hunters' Path leads, we return by way of the summit of the ridge, keeping quite near to the enclosures L. Soon we pass the fine entrance to South Harton, where is a small plantation, and still keeping the wall of the enclosed lands L. shall make our way by Harton Chest R. to Sharp Tor (Ex. 23). Here we are near Hammerslake, which we passed on our way from the stone cross at the gate of the private road to South Harton to Ellimore (S. Ex. 74). Leaving Sharp Tor we make for a corner of the down below it to the N.E., where a short lane will take us to the road, where we turn R. and then L. to Ellimore, and descend to Lustleigh (S. Ex. 74, Ex. 23).

S. Ex. 76.—*Manaton via Pethybridge, Wanford Wood, and Water* (*from Lustleigh*), 5 m. The route to Manaton by way of Foxworthy Bridge has been sketched in Ex. 23, but there are more direct ways of reaching that village. The visitor may cross the Bovey at Horsham Steps and pass through Horsham Farm, or he may cross at the foot-bridge under the Foxes' Yard, and follow the path up through the wood either to the same farm R., or to Water L. But the most direct route is by way of the footbridge under Wanford Wood, and this he may reach by going through Ellimore as in Ex. 23, and taking the L. path on the S. side of Sharp Tor, which will lead him straight down the hill to it, or he may gain the same point by way of Pethybridge. If he decide upon the latter he will follow the lane to Ellimore for about a couple of hundred yards and then turn into a path L., which will lead him through the wood to the farm named. Just beyond this he will enter on a road, and turning R. will keep straight on to the common. (He is now at the point where he enters it in Ex. 23, if going direct to the Cleave from New Bridge). The path across the down is now followed to the bridge, ¾ m. distant, and immediately above the trees that are seen at the foot of the down a little in advance (S. Ex. 75). Crossing this the rambler will have the guidance of a path up the tree covered steep, Woodash being L. and Wanford R., and this will bring him to a narrow lane that will lead him to the hamlet of Water, ½ m. from Manaton.

The return routes to Lustleigh are here briefly sketched. *Via Foxworthy Bridge.* Leaving the village green near its northern end we follow the road for a short distance and take the second turning R. This will lead to a footpath running across some fields, and down through a wood, where it is rather steep in places, to the Bovey, close to Little Silver, L. (Ex. 23). Cross Foxworthy Bridge and turn R. to Foxworthy Mill, just beyond which is a green path leading up the side of Lustleigh Cleave to Sharp Tor (S. Ex. 75). *Via Horsham Steps.* Leave the village as before, but take the first turning R. to Horsham Farm. From there a path runs down through the wood to the steps, and is continued on the further side of the Bovey up the side of the down to Sharp Tor (S. Ex. 75). *Via Footbridge below the Foxes' Yard.* To Horsham Farm as in the preceding ; thence by the lane to Letchole Plantation, and down by the narrow path through Water Cleave to the bridge. The path then runs up the hill, with the Foxes' Yard L., to Sharp Tor (S. Ex. 75). To reach this bridge by way of Water the visitor will leave Manaton at the southern end of the green, where he will turn L. by Town Barton, again branching L. at Wrayland to the hamlet. close to which is the plantation named above. *Via Footbridge below Wanford Wood.* To Water as above. Then, instead of taking the path through Letchole Plantation, follow the lane down the hill to Wanford Wood, through which, with Woodash R., the footpath alluded to in the route just given from Lustleigh descends to the Bovey. On crossing that stream pass up the hill, and at the first fork of the green path take the R. branch and follow it to the road branching from the upper corner of the down. Take the second turning L. (only about 300 yards on) to Pethybridge, from which farm a path leads to Lustleigh as before described.

S. Ex. 77.—*Manaton to North Bovey*, 2 m. distant ; *and Lustleigh to North Bovey*, 3¾ m. distant. The reverse route (to Manaton) has already been given (S. Ex. 63). We leave the village near the northern end of the green, the rectory grounds being L. Soon after passing the second turning R., which leads down to Foxworthy Bridge, we reach a turning L., where a path runs across a little common below Manaton Rocks. We keep near to the enclosures R., and presently shall be led between these to a field, across which the path runs to the road at Langstone (R. 32, 53). This point may also be reached by following the path along the S. side of the churchyard to a road which will bring us to Langstone Cross (R. 32, 53), where we turn R.

From Langstone we proceed by the road to Lower Luckdon, to which place we may also make our way by another route. This, which will increase the distance a little, will take us down the hill from Manaton (instead of turning L. to the little common), near the bottom of which a lane runs R. to Little Silver and Foxworthy Bridge (Ex. 23), but we turn L. to Neadon. Here, on the L. of the way, we pass an ancient building now belonging to the farm, but which is said to have been formerly a chapel. On passing this we strike a road running R. to Barnecourt (S. Ex. 74) and Wray Barton, the latter being on the road from Bovey to Moreton (R. 31, 46). We turn neither R. nor L., but crossing the road enter on a path that will take us across three fields to Lower Luckdon. From this place we keep straight on, with Higher Luckdon L. (R. 32, 53) to Aller, soon after passing which we cross the Bovey, and reach our destination.

Lustleigh to North Bovey via Little Silver, 3¾ m. distant. This is a most delightful ramble. The visitor will make his way by Ellimore to Sharp Tor, and thence down the side of the cleave to Foxworthy Bridge, as described in Ex. 23. Crossing the bridge he will turn R. by the charming Little Silver, whence a walk of about ¼ m. along the edge of the wood will bring him to the road leading to Neadon, just where it comes down L. from Manaton. From this point the directions are given above.

In returning to Lustleigh the path from North Bovey past Neadon, as described in S. Ex. 63, must be followed, when the rambler, instead of turning up the hill R. to Manaton, will keep onward to Little Silver, from which point the way over the down to Sharp Tor and Ellimore is shown in S. Ex. 76, 75.

S. Ex. 78.—*Round Yarner Wood.* Bovey Station, 7½ m. ; Lud Gate, 5½ m. ; Ilsington, 6¾ m. A ramble round Yarner Wood and over Trendlebere Down, besides disclosing many other beauties, will also afford a fine view of Lustleigh Cleave. In setting out from Bovey the road to the moor will be followed as in Ex. 23. On leaving the railway the visitor first passes Parke, where in the early years of the nineteenth century lived the noted George Hunt Clapp, better known as "Councillor" Clapp. We remember hearing many stories in our younger days of the strange sights said to be formerly witnessed in the grounds on moonlight nights. Horses without heads, the gossips said, used to haunt Parke Walk, and startling sounds were heard there by the frightened peasant. Continuing on our way upward we shall shortly pass Five Wyches Cross (Ex. 23), and Lower Down Cross (Ex. 24), where the Hey Tor tramroad, noticed in Ex. 25, crossed the road. On our L. is Colehays Plantation, which extends up the hill for about a mile, and soon after passing the head of this we enter upon the moor. Here we turn R. as in Ex. 25, our way lying along the higher side of Yarner, which we have already referred to as being the residence of Mr. Justice Eve. The judge is a lover of Dartmoor, and his great hobby is "caravaning" upon it. When on one of his tours amid its hills he lives and sleeps in the van, and does his own cooking. No better way of seeing the moor can be imagined, provided it is combined with bog-trotting.

Having reached Yarner Wells, to which point visitors at Lud Gate and Ilsington will make their way as described in Ex. 25, we shall turn down the hill R., gradually leaving Yarner Wood as we descend. Here we have a good view of Lustleigh Cleave, beyond the wooded Hound Tor Ridge. Our way takes us over East Down, which extends to the Becky, Trendlebere Down being on our R. under Yarner Wood. On reaching the stream, which we should do not far from the camp on Water Hill (Ex. 23), marked by Water Rock, we turn R., and trace its course downward. On the further bank is Hound Tor Wood, the peninsulated ridge which it covers terminating in the heathery Riddy Hill. At the foot of this the Becky falls into the Bovey, the scene of their meeting being of the most romantic character. Just above it, on the further bank, are Gradner Rocks (S. Ex. 75) rising on the higher edge of Hisley Wood. Below this the united stream makes a bend and then flows on between Rudge Wood L., and Pullabrook Wood R., to its confluence with the Wray. Our path will take us past the weir to the verge of the last-named wood, and here we shall find ourselves on Reddiford Down, and just below the northern edge of Yarner Wood. This wood, as we have already seen, is situated on the side of a steep hill, and is in view from the railway between Bovey and Lustleigh. It is about 1¼ m. from E. to W., and ¾ m. from N. to S. Yarner Copper Mine, now disused, is near its S.E. corner, and the grounds of Yarner are on its southern, or higher, side. One elevated point in it is known as Yarner Beacon. Following the road over Reddiford Down we shall soon reach the guide-post, and here the visitor who is returning to Bovey will continue onward to the fork, where he will either branch L. to Five Wyches Cross, or keep straight on along the edge of Lower Down, which is really a part of Reddiford Down, to Lower Down Cross, from either of which points he will turn L. down the hill (R. 25). If bound for Ilsington or Lud Gate the visitor will strike into a footpath at the guide-post running up over the down, which will bring him to the road near the higher end of Colehays Plantation. Passing the fork where a road branches R. to Yarner, he will soon enter on the moor, and on reaching the guide-post the road L. must be taken for Ilsington. (In following this take either the first turning R. for Trumpetor and Loothorn Cross or the second R. at Narrowcombe). For Lud Gate keep straight on with the common R.

S. Ex. 79.—*Becky Fall and Manaton ; branch road to Leighon.* Bovey Station (to Fall and back) 9 m. ; Lud Gate 5 m. ; Ilsington 7½ m. ; Manaton 1 m. beyond the Becky. From Bovey the road to Lower Down Cross is followed as in Ex. 24 and R. 45. There turn R. into the Lower Terrace Drive which passing under Yarner Wood leads direct to New Bridge about ¼ m. above the fall (Ex. 23). From Lud Gate visitors simply follow the Higher Terrace Drive to Becky-ford Bridge which is only a very short distance above New Bridge, while those from Ilsington if not proceeding *via* Lud Gate will follow the instructions given in Ex. 25 and reaching the down either by way of Trumpetor or Narrowcombe, will strike over it and join the drive at Yarner Wells. The Manaton road runs up the hill from the bridges over the Becky to the cross road between Water R. and Deal L., and passing Wrayland enters the village by Town Barton (*vide* Ex. 23). The name of the little river appears not only in the fall and the higher bridge, but also in Beckyford Farm, Becky Cottage, and in Beckhams, the latter being on the edge of Deal Copse, in which the fall is situated. Visitors will find the walk to Becky Fall by the Higher Terrace Drive, making the return by the Lower Drive, or *vice versa*, a very enjoyable one. A return route is given in Ex. 23.

Leighon Bridge. About ½ m. N. of Yarner Wells a road branches westward from the higher Terrace Drive, under Black Hill, and leads down through Leighon to the Becky, which it crosses at Leighon Bridge (R. 45). This, which is a clapper of one opening and furnished with parapets, is situated in the midst of charming surroundings. Just below it the road turns L. to Hound Tor Down (Ex. 24), and by follow-ing this for a short distance, and then turning R. at Great Hound Tor Farm, the rambler will be led past Southcott to Hayne Cross, from which point the return route by way of Becky Fall is given in Ex. 23. The homeward route direct from Leighon Bridge will be found at the end of R. 25. The bridge is about 1¼ m. from Yarner Wells by the road.

S. Ex. 80.—*Hey Tor, Pinchaford Ball, and Hey Tor Vale.* Bovey Station, 9 m. ; Lud Gate, 2½ m. ; Ilsington, over Pinchaford Ball 3¾ m. Hey Tor is 3¾ m. from Bovey Station, and is approached by the road described in Ex. 25 and S. Ex. 78, the points being Five Wyches Cross (keep straight on, L. fork) ; Lower Down Cross (straight up the hill, leaving the road running by the school R.) ; a fork nearly 1 m. further up the hill (take the L. branch, and the down will be reached rather over ¼ m. on). The road now skirts this with the enclosures close on the L., and passing Shot Plantation, also on that side, reaches Lud Gate. Here, at the Moorland Hotel, the Dartmoor coaches always stop to afford those who may desire to visit the tor an opportunity of doing so. A broad green path leads to the rocks from the road close to the hotel.

Visitors from Ilsington will reach Lud Gate by turning R. at the cross ½ m. W. of the Hey Tor Hotel, and passing up the hill, and taking the L. branch of the road at the fork above Pinchaford. (The R.

branch also goes to Lud Gate, by way of Hey Tor Vale). But a much shorter way to Hey Tor is to keep straight on instead of turning up the hill R. at the cross referred to, when a walk of a few hundred yards through a narrow stroll will bring the visitor to the common. From this point Hey Tor is only ¾ m. distant, W.N.W.

For a description of the tor the visitor is referred to Ex. 25.

Descending the southern slope of the hill on which Hey Tor is situated, the road is speedily reached just where it makes a bend, and here a track runs from it southward (T. 49). This the rambler may follow to Bag Tor, the route being the reverse of that sketched in Ex. 25, but should he not wish to extend his walk that far he will see it as he crosses Pinchaford Ball. This he will do by leaving the track near some hut circles R., about ¼ m. from the road, and striking eastward. Below him R., in the little valley of the Sig, and near the boggy spot called Bag Tor Mines, is the tor. He also looks down upon Mill Wood, one part of which is known as Crownley Parks, and upon Hinds Ground near it. Descending the eastern side of the ball he enters the narrow stroll below Pinchaford Farm mentioned *ante*. From this point the Ilsington road turns down R., while a footpath L. will lead to the Pinchaford lane, which comes from the road running up to Lud Gate. Just above this is the fork before referred to, and if the visitor chooses to bear R. he will pass through Hey Tor Vale, as we have already stated. When the Hey Tor quarries ceased to be worked the season of prosperity enjoyed by this little hamlet came to an end. But of late there has been some renewal of this, though not, as formerly in consequence of stone being sent away from the neighbourhood, but because of the fact that it is there. The Rock Hotel at Hey Tor Vale bears a name that will constantly remind the visitor of this. Lud Gate is within ¼ m. of the hamlet.

S. Ex. 81.—*Ilsington.* (2½ m. distant from Bovey Tracey Station ; *with route to Ashburton*, 5½ m. further). Occupying an elevated and pleasant situation on the border of the moor, and placed in the midst of delightful scenery, the village of Ilsington has naturally grown into favour with the visitor, and since the opening of the Hey Tor Hotel has become a much frequented summer resort. From Bovey Tracey Station the rambler will make his way towards the town, having Pludda on his R., but only for a short distance. Immediately opposite to the Dolphin Hotel the Newton Abbot road runs S., and into this he will turn. Passing the first branch, a few score yards on R., he will strike into the second on that side, and will very soon reach Ashburton Bridge, where the road is carried over the railway. Just beyond this it forks, and here he will take the R. branch and keep straight on. The turning R. leads to Challabrook, and near this the Hey Tor tram-road (Ex. 25) crossed the road. The next fork is known as Brimley Corner, where again the R. branch must be followed past Chapel Cross, which is marked by a guide-post, and where a road comes down from Chapel Farm and Lower Down Cross (Ex. 24). William Ellis, who several years ago wrote an interesting account of various places in the neighbourhood of Bovey, says that the farm obtained its name from the former existence of a chapel there. He states that all traces of the building had been lost, but that during the formation of a leat some stones were found that were thought to have belonged to it. The chapel stood in a lovely little dell through which ran a sparkling stream. Passing upward through Brimley Lane the rambler will speedily arrive at Lower Brimley, beyond which he will pass through Higher Brimley, and reach Woodhouse Cross, where is a guide-post. Here a road comes down R. from Narrowcombe and the common, and descends the hill towards the Newton Abbot road. The rambler will turn neither R. nor L., but continue onward, passing Woodhouse R., to the village.

The village of Ilsington is small, and like Widecombe, Manaton, Shaugh, and others in the Dartmoor borderland, was once the scene of a remarkable accident, not, however, resulting from the warring of the elements, but from the banging of a gate. On the 17th September, 1639, the day being Tuesday, a woman passed through the west gate of the churchyard, over which was an old building that had not long before been converted into a schoolroom. The gate was a heavy one, and the woman, letting it swing back to close of itself, went on her way. She had not gone half-a-dozen yards before the building collapsed, but strange to relate not only were no lives lost, but the injuries sustained were most trifling. An account of the accident may be seen in the register, together with the names of those who were in the room at the time.

The church is chiefly Perpendicular. In the churchyard is the seventeenth century tomb of Thomas Ford, of Sigford, on which is a curious Latin chronogram, giving the date of his death. The Fords were settled very early in this parish, one of that family being John Ford, the dramatist, and the friend and acquaintance of most of the poets of his day.

In the latter part of the seventeenth century Bag Tor was in the possession of Sir Henry Ford, who was knighted by Charles II., in whose reign he was twice Secretary of State in Ireland. The property was sold by him to Mr. Tothill, from whose descendants it was afterwards purchased by John, first Lord Ashburton. East of the church, and on the R. of the road leading up to Narrowcombe, are some vestiges of a manor house built by Sir Henry, but which, it is said, was never completed. On a part of the site of this the present school is built. The manor of Ilsington was early in the possession of the Beaumonts, and afterwards belonged to the Dinhams. At the death, in 1477, of John, Lord Dinham, it was divided among his representatives, and portions of it passing through the Arundells afterwards became the property of the Fords. The Act for enclosing Ilsington Common was obtained in 1809.

According to Vicars the Royalist soldiers after their defeat at Bovey, in January, 1646, retreated to Ilsington, and sought refuge in the church. They were, however, pursued by Cromwell, and were forced to quit the building.

Natives of this parish were formerly known as Ilsington Greybacks. In 1727 William Candy left some lands to trustees, with directions that the rents should be applied to the purchase of clothes for men who had served their apprenticeship to farmers in the parish. The clothes were made of a cloth known as Parson's Grey, the shirt being of a rough material called Dowlais, and so the name of Greyback became attached to an Ilsington man. A copy of Mr. Candy's will hangs in Ilsington Church. In 1663 Miss Jane Ford, of Bag Tor, left property to be invested for the purpose of schooling poor children, and in 1804 Mr. Hale, of Ilsington, left money for the benefit of the aged poor.

Bag Tor is 1½ m. from Ingsdon, and is situated on the road running to Ashburton *via* Halshanger Cross. From the church the way lies past the vicarage and the hotel to Loothorn Cross, where the L., or S., road is followed to the Wesleyan burial ground, which point may also be reached by the lower road from the village. This must be kept L., and also Honeywell, which is passed immediately after. The next point is Burchanger Cross, where the Bag Tor road runs straight on, and then winds round a little piece of common below Burchanger Brake, a wood being on the other side of it. Very speedily it drops down to the Lemon, which it crosses in one of the most delightful nooks on the borders of Dartmoor. [*Gems*, Chap. XI.] Immediately below the bridge is the picturesque Bag Tor Mill, and above it the little river comes down through a wooded hollow from the moor. (A path running through Crownley Parks will lead the rambler thither, and he will reach it below Pinchaford Ball, with Bag Tor L. S. Ex. 80). ¼ m. further on, where a road branches L. to Sigford, is the entrance to Bag Tor R., which is pleasantly placed on the edge of Bag Tor Wood. This point is also reached in our rambles from Ashburton, q.v. The road to that town runs on to Westabrook, where it crosses the Sig, and thence to the hamlet of Mountsland, just beyond which it is carried over the Langworthy Brook. Then passing Halshanger R., it reaches Halshanger Cross, where the Newton Abbot road comes up L., or from E., and goes on by Cold East Cross to Pudsham Down and Cockingford Mill, and from there over Bittleford Down to Cator and Grendon Cot, and the forest. (These places are noticed in Ex. 26, R. 42 and Ex. 44). The Ashburton road runs on to Rushlade and down to the Yeo, which river it reaches under Whiddon Wood, and bears it company through the narrow valley nearly to Rewlea Cross. From this point the road goes southward to the town, the centre of which is about ¾ m. distant. (For a fuller notice of the route from Rushlade onward see the end of Ex. 26 ; the return route will be found partly at the beginning of Ex. 26, and partly in S. Ex. 89.)

The roads from Ilsington to the moor have all been noticed in our excursions. One runs W. from Loothorn Cross direct to Pinchafor Ball (S. Ex. 80) ; another branches from this shortly before the down is reached, and goes northward to Lud Gate ; a third goes N. from Loothorn Cross through Trumpetor and Middlecott to Smallacombe, being joined at the former place by one leaving the village by the lane opposite to the vicarage, and running up by the Sanctuary field ; and a fourth goes E. of the church northward to Narrowcombe.

The route to Bovey Tracey having already been given the reverse way it is only necessary to name the chief points here. The road runs eastward from the village S. of the church to Woodhouse Cross, and thence to Higher Brimley and Lower Brimley. From this hamlet the direction is E. by N. The town is reached soon after the railway is crossed at Ashburton Bridge.

S. Ex. 82.—*Widecombe-in-the-Moor via Hemsworthy Gate.* (7 m. from Bovey Tracey Station). The way lies up the hill to Hey Tor

Down and Lud Gate (3¼ m.), and is described in Ex. 25, and S. Ex. 78. From Lud Gate the road is followed to Hemsworthy Gate, and this part of the route may be reached by visitors from Ilsington either by way of the first-named place or by striking westward over Pinchaford Ball (S. Ex. 80). On leaving Lud Gate the road ascends towards Hey Tor, the rocks rising on the R. (Ex. 25, S. Ex. 80), on the L. being Pinchaford Ball, with Bag Tor in the hollow below it, near Mill Wood (Ex. 25). It then leads us over a level part of the ground, where the turf is exceptionally smooth, towards Saddle Tor, over which we may make our way by the footpath that we shall see branching R. (Ex. 25). In advance is the lofty Rippon Tor, noticed in Ex. 26, and as we draw nearer to it we shall not fail to observe the reave running down the N.W. side of the hill. Eastward the view of the country beyond Newton and Kingsteignton, with the estuary of the Teign, is remarkably fine. Between Saddle Tor and Hemsworthy Gate the road skirts the head of Hound Tor Combe. Hound Tor itself is 2 m. distant, but the long combe to which it gives name, and which extends upward from near Becky Fall, has its termination here. Standing near the scanty vestiges of the old Hemsworthy Mine the rambler is within a very short distance of the source of the Becky, and as he looks down the combe, beyond the lower end of which the fine hill forming the eastern side of Lustleigh Cleave is seen to great advantage, his view embraces the whole course of the stream. Immediately below, on the R. bank of it, is Hemsworthy Farm, and beyond this, lining the whole side of the valley, the grey clatters that have fallen from the tors that rise half-ruined from the slope, while above them Hey Tor, placed in a more secure situation, proudly uplifts his solid granite bosses, as yet hardly touched by the hand of Time. On the L., or W., side of the Combe is Holwell, with Haresfoot Mires below it, and beyond it, on Holwell Down, the little pile sometimes known as Holwell Rocks. Passing onward we arrive at Hemsworthy Gate, or White Gate, as it is often called locally, where we find ourselves on the Chagford and Ashburton road (R. 32, Ex. 26). About 200 yards N. of the gate, and quite close to the wall is a hut circle bearing the name of Seven Lords' Land, being, it is said, a bondmark of seven manors.

Hey
Tor.

Saddle
Tor.

Leighon Tor.

Smallacombe
Rocks.

Holwell Tor.

FROM HOLWELL DOWN, LOOKING E.

[Visitors to Ilsington or Lud Gate will find the walk round Hound Tor Combe a very enjoyable one. Making their way first to Hemsworthy Gate they will follow the Chagford road over Holwell Down as in R. 53, and on reaching the entrance to Hedge Barton strike R. across the common to Hound Tor. Then descending the hill on the N. side of the tor the road to Leighon and Yarner Wells will be struck, and this must then be followed as described in R. 25. The walk may be extended from Hound Tor Farm so as to embrace Becky Fall and Becky Ford, from which latter spot the Higher Terrace Drive runs to the Wells and Lud Brook. *Vide* end of Ex. 23, 24.]

Rippon Tor.   The Nutcracker.

FROM HOLWELL DOWN, LOOKING S.

The rambler will turn R., or N.W. at Hemsworthy Gate (5¼ m. from Bovey Station), and following the Chagford road for ½ m. will branch L. at the guide-post. A walk of a few score yards will bring him to the top of Widecombe Hill, where Tom Pearse found his old grey mare " makin' 'er weel," and here a wide view of the forest is disclosed. More than 500 feet below, but as yet unseen, and a mile away, is the East Webburn. It flows almost in the shadow of the Cathedral of the Moor, which we now begin to discover, and is there spanned by Northway Bridge. To this the rambler will now descend, and having crossed it will speedily enter Widecombe Town.

EXCURSIONS FROM WIDECOMBE.

S. Ex. 83.—*Bonehill Down*, 4 m. ; the way by Widecombe Hill is further. Having in our notice of Hameldon and the Widecombe valley described the tors on the down that form the E. side of the northern end of the latter, it will not now be necessary to do more than describe the routes by which they may be reached from the village. Of these there is a choice of three. The rambler may either make his way by the road up the valley to the turning below Isaford ; he may go by Widecombe Hill ; or by the farms that take their name from the down on which the tors stand. The first route will lead him by the manor house, ¾ m. from the village, and soon after passing this he will cross the Webburn.* Beyond the bridge are Stouts Cottages, near which a path runs through the plantation R. to the common, and further up is the entrance to Bag Park, L. Above this, on the same side, a road leads to Pitton, and 300 yards on is the turning R. to the down under Honeybag Tor. From this point, which is 1½ m. from Widecombe Green, the route will be as sketched in the Extension to R. 24. This will take the rambler along the range of tors to the road S. of Bel Tor, by which he may make his way through Bonehill, R., direct to the village ; or he may continue S. to Bonehill Rocks, and thence steering the same course reach Widecombe Hill.

The second route will take him across the green on the N. side of the church to Northway Bridge, and thence up Widecombe Hill for rather over ½ m., when having passed the enclosures he will turn L. over the common to Bonehill Rocks, ½ m. off. Just beyond this group the road comes up L. from the Bonehill farms, and he will find himself on the route now to be described.

FROM HALF-WAY UP WIDECOMBE HILL, LOOKING N.

The third route, which is the best, will lead the rambler to North-way Bridge, but instead of passing over it he will turn L. and cross the Webburn a little higher up. From this point the verge of Bonehill Down is ¾ m. distant, and 400 feet above the stream. The road runs up through the Bonehill farms, and on the common being reached the rambler will be close to the rocks bearing that name. The road R. goes on to the top of Widecombe Hill ; the track running straight up over the down goes to the corner of Hedge Down where it joins the Chagford road ; the footpath L. of it leads to Hedge Barton ; and the track L. runs to the turning below Isaford, with a branch path to the road near Stouts Cottages.

Our way will now lie N. to Bel Tor, on which there are some rock basins, and thence to Sharp Tor, Chinkwell, and Honeybag, the ramble being the reverse of that described in Ex. 24. On the R. of the visitor, as he proceeds northward, is Hedge Barton ; on the L. the Widecombe valley ; and before him, and beyond the range he

---

* This is Widecombe Town Manor. There are five others in the parish : Natsworthy, Dunstone, Blackslade, Blackaton, and Spitch-wick.

is traversing, the commons of Heytree, Vogwell, and Cripdon (Ex. 24), backed by the lofty East Down (S. Ex. 61). It was in this neighbourhood that a certain land-owner once received an unexpected reply to a question put to a native to whom he was unknown. Chancing to meet an old woman he began talking about the place as though he were a stranger, and was told that one of the estates belonged to Mr. Blank, but that he did not live there continuously. Desirous of learning what kind of reputation he had as a landlord he asked her what sort of a man Mr. Blank was. " Can't tell 'e, sir," replied the woman, " Never seed 'n as I knaw by. But us cal'n ole darnin' needle." From Honeybag Tor the rambler will descend the western side of the hill to the track, and so reach the lane at the turning below Isaford (Ex. 24). [From this point Higher Natsworthy is ¾ m. distant ; Berry Pound (*via* Natsworthy) under 1½ m. ; Heytree Cross, 1¾ m.] Turning L. when the lane is reached the visitor will make his way down the valley to the village.

[The visitor may extend this excursion by going up the valley to Higher Natsworthy, and returning by way of the side of Hameldon. A path runs from Natsworthy in a south-easterly direction nearly to Hameldon Beacon, and this the rambler will follow for about ½ m., when he will leave it and strike S. His way will now lie along the slope of the great hill, about ¼ m. above Bagpark Plantation. A walk of rather over 1 m. will bring him to the enclosures of Kingshead, with those belonging to the manor house below on the L. A path across one of them will lead to the steep lane that comes down from Kingshead, by which he will descend to the road ¼ m. from Widecombe Church. This extension will add nearly 2 m. to the ramble.]

S. Ex. 84.—*Hameldon Beacon and Natsworthy*, 5½ m. WITH EXTENSION *to Hameldon Cross and Grim's Pound*, 7 m. Leaving the green by the road running up the valley, the rambler will pass the first turning L. (the old Church Way, T. 76) and take the next on that side, which is only a very short distance further on. This is the steep lane by which the visitor was directed to descend from the common in the preceding excursion. Passing upward the path there referred to will be seen R., and turning into this, with Kingshead Farm higher up on the L., he will cross the field and reach the down. From this point Hameldon Beacon is about 1 m. distant, or 1¾ m. from the village. The course to be steered is N.W. by N., and when the rambler is nearing the summit of the hill he will come in sight of the wall of Blackaton Down. This he will keep L., and follow it to the Beacon, which has been already described in the section on Hameldon.

[If it be desired to extend this ramble to Hameldon Cross, or Grim's Pound, the wall must be followed to Two Barrows, whence the course will be northward to Single Barrow and Broad Barrow, from which last-named tumulus Hameldon Cross is only a very short distance N.W. The whole of these objects, and their bearings, are noticed in the section just referred to. Hameldon Tor is N.N.W. of the cross, and less than ½ m. away. From this pile the rambler will look down upon Grim's Pound, which, by this route, the most direct one, is 3 m. from Widecombe. A description of Grim's Pound is given in Ex. 22, and its surroundings are also noticed in S. Ex. 59, 60, and 62. From the pound the return to Widecombe will be by

way of Berry Pound and Natsworthy, the way being described in S.
Ex. 60.]

To return from Hameldon Beacon *via* Natsworthy the rambler
must steer N.E. by E., and should strike the path mentioned in the
preceding excursion as running from that place towards the beacon.
At Natsworthy the road to the village is reached. (Extension Ex. 25.
The road below it is described the reverse way at the beginning of
S. Ex. 83).

S. Ex. 85.—*Blackaton Down, Challacombe, Grendon Bridge, Lower
Blackaton, Langworthy,* 6 m.   Our way will first take us over the ridge
southward of Hameldon Beacon to the top of Gore Hill, to which point
we shall have the guidance of the Church Way (T. 76). This ancient
path commences at what is now known as Church Lane, the first turning
on the L. from the road leading up the Widecombe valley from the
green.   We follow it to the down, the point where it emerges on this
being appropriately named Church Lane Head, and thence north-
westward across the turf as in R. 42, C. q.v.   Passing the Hatchwell
branch L., and Kingshead Corner R., we speedily reach Gore Hill.
Here we leave the old path to the forest, and follow the one that goes
on to Challacombe (T. 47).   We do not therefore descend Gore Hill,
but continue our north-westerly course, with the enclosures L.   Very
soon we enter upon Blackaton Down, the wall of which comes down
the steep side of the common from Hameldon Beacon.   Our path is
a well-defined one, and runs along the higher part of the small irregular
enclosures that here creep up the steep from the valley of the Broadford Brook.   ¾ m. on we reach another wall of Blackaton Down—the
one that descends from Two Barrows—and here our path runs into
the road that comes up from Lower Hatchwell.   Following this northward for about ½ m. we reach Challacombe (2½ m. from Widecombe),
which consists of a farm and a couple of cottages.   Headland Warren
House, mentioned in Ex. 22, is 1 m. further up the valley, but we do
not now make our way thither.   We turn here, but instead of retracing
our steps to Lower Hatchwell, we shall follow the road that we see
running down by the side of the West Webburn, and which leads
onward to Grendon and Cator (Ex. 44).   The lonely house on the R.
as we proceed is Soussons (Ex. 44), and soon after passing this we
reach Grendon Bridge.   This is the road by which the coaches from
Widecombe pass up the valley, the one running up from Lower Hatchwell not being suited to such traffic.   We are now again on the line of
the old Church Way, and shall follow it eastward from the bridge, as
in R. 5 C, over Hill Head and past Lower Blackaton and Lower Hatchwell, to the point where it begins to climb Gore Hill.   There we leave
it, and shall follow the road R. for about ½ m. to the second turning L.
at Langworthy, and speedily regain the common ½ m. from Church
Lane Head.   We shall reach the path there by striking a little S. of W.

S. Ex. 86.—*Dunstone Down, Rowden Down, and Jordan Ball,* 5½ m.
Leaving the village by the Ponsworthy road we take the first turning
R. and pass up the hill towards Southcombe, our way lying over
the track already described (T. 52).   We reach Dunstone Down
at Southcombe Gate, and shall find our way over it clearly marked
by the path.   A little way on we leave the broader track and take
the footpath leading down the slope to the stroll by which Rowden

Down is approached, the direction being W.S.W. (R. 42 B.) On reaching the latter we shall make our way to the summit, which is known as Rowden Ball. Here is a small tor, and near to it is a dilapidated cairn, much overgrown, with a hollow sunk in the centre, from which stones appear to have been taken. It seems to have been formerly surrounded by a circle of stones and a low bank, but only parts of these now remain. Joined to it is an enclosure of an oblong form. Near the northern edge of the down is Rowden Farm, on the road leading to Lower Cator ; from its western verge a track leads to Broadford Farm, on the brook of that name, which falls into the West Webburn immediately below it ; and from its southern side the path which we deserted in order to examine this despoiled cairn runs down between the enclosures to the little common known as Jordan Ball. The air of semi-wildness worn by this part of the moor is very charming. Heathery downs delightfully intermingle with little irregularly shaped crofts, many of them very ancient, and which speak of a time when the early farm settlers forced their way into these upland vallays. To the path last mentioned we now direct our steps, and descend the side of Jordan Ball to the Webburn, just before reaching which we pass the entrance to East Shallowford. Built into the wall on the L. of this is a large stone of the kind formerly used for hanging gates, and of which several examples have been noticed. (Ex. 20, S. Ex. 59). In its centre the circular hollow that received the stanchion will be seen. Just below is the shallow ford on the West Webburn which gives name to this farm and to the neighbouring one on the further bank of the stream. Here there is a clapper of three openings, and crossing over this we pass up to West Shallowford, immediately above which the road from Ponsworthy, Pound's Gate, and Dartmeet, *via* Lock's Gate Cross, L., runs onward to Cator and the forest, R. (R. 42 B).

Descending to the stream we shall again cross it, and make our way down by the L. bank to Jordan Mill, and the hamlet of that name.* From near this a footpath runs across some fields to Bittleford Farm, where is a fine old granite doorway bearing the date 1706. Having reached this we shall follow the road that leads from it to Bittleford Down, and striking N. shall make for our next point, Wind Tor, which is rather over ½ m. distant. Here we turn E. and cross the turf to Higher Dunstone, where we reach the Widecombe road. We turn L. towards the village, but a few score yards on shall leave the road at the turning R. in order to visit Lower Dunstone, which is close by. On the green is a large block of stone having a hollow on its surface, and in this, it is said, the chief rents were deposited when the manor courts were held here in the open air, as was formerly the case. The late Mr. Robert Dymond, the owner of the manor, revived this old usage about thirty years ago. In this connection it is interesting to notice a custom formerly observed in some parts of Sweden by the peasantry of throwing small pieces of money into the rock basins as they passed them, and in which it has been thought a relic of the superstitious

---

* If we adopt the moorman's pronounciation of the name of the hill in the norfhern part of the moor, already visited—Kennon, near Throwleigh (Ex. 18, 19)—it is possible to agree with the statement that Canaan and Jordan are both to be found on Dartmoor.

veneration in which they were held might be traced. The manor of Dunstone was bestowed by the Conqueror on Ralph de Pomeraie, and remained in that family for at least two centuries. Returning to the road we shall make our way back to Widecombe.

S. Ex. 87.—*Venton, Blackslade Down, Foale's Arrishes, Tor Hill, and the Ruggle Stone*, 4 m. Opposite to the Old Inn a road runs easterly along the south side of the open space in front of the churchyard gate. This we shall now follow, and crossing the Webburn at Venton Bridge, just below which is a manorial bondmark called Hennaford Stone, shall reach the Ruggle Stone Inn, and may if we choose make our way direct to the logan on the verge of the common near by from which it takes its name. Or we may turn L. at Venton, a little further on, and keeping close to the enclosures, on that hand, be very speedily led to it. (Another route is by way of Widecombe Hill : about ¼ m. from Northway Bridge the limits of the enclosed land on the R. will be reached, and here the rambler must turn in that direction, again turning R. at the second corner, when he will see the rock just below him ; it is only ⅓ m. from the road). As our present excursion will bring us to this object we defer our remarks concerning it, and shall therefore pass through Venton, where on the little green we shall notice an upping-stock formed by steps cut in a large granite boulder. and follow the road to Chittleford. Here are two very good examples of the granite porches of the seventeenth and eighteenth centuries, one exhibiting the date 1686 and the other 1741. Passing up the hill we very shortly reach a gate L. where a path runs across a field to a lane leading past Blackslade, the seat of the late Mr. Robert Dymond, to the commons. (The road goes on by Scobetor to Pudsham Down, and crossing the Ruddycleave Water runs up the side of Buckland Common to Cold East Cross, R. 32, Ex. 26). On passing Blackslade, which appears in Domesday as Blacheslach, the down of that name is reached at the foot of the stroll below Tunhill Rocks (R. 5 B). The gate of Tunhill Farm is in the further corner of the stroll, and running from it is the old track we have already described (T. 51). This we now follow up the hill R., and in rather less than ½ m. shall reach a fine example of a kistvaen, discovered several years ago buried beneath a cairn. It will be seen to the L. of the track. Here it was that the wicked Jan Reynolds once entered into a compact with a stranger, who turned out to be the Prince of Darkness, and failing to keep it became his victim. Seven years after the meeting Jan was discovered indulging in a nap in Widecombe Church on a Sunday afternoon, and it was the appearance of Satan there to claim him that occasioned the great thunder-storm to which we have already referred. Jan was borne away on the fiend's black steed, when some cards that he held in his hand were dropped on the moor, and are now to be seen, in a transformed state, near the old Vitifer Mines. (Ex. 22).

We strike S. from the kistvaen to Whittaburrow, a cairn which we see on the hill a short distance off. The E. side of this hill descends to the Ruddycleave Water, here generally called the Blackslade Water, and which rises near by in Blackslade Mire. This part of the moor is noticed in Ex. 26. Returning to the Tunhill road, we cross it, leaving the kistvaen R., and make our way to Tunhill Rocks, a rather striking pile rising on the verge of the down. Thence we shall direct our steps eastward to a cluster of hut circles, about ½ m. distant, and in a line between us and Hemsworthy Gate, to which they are near. Some of these ruined dwellings are placed within small rectangular enclosures formed by low reaves, and bearing the name of Foale's Arrishes. These remains are partly covered with vegetation, and there is little about them likely to detain the ordinary visitor, but they possess an interest for the antiquary. Although this example of huts within enclosures such as these is not altogether unique on Dartmoor, the arrangement is one that is not usually seen. (A description of the common between the slope on which these remains are situated and Rippon Tor, S.E., as well as of the tor itself, will be found in Ex. 26).

A short distance northward of Foale's Arrishes is Top Tor, or, as the natives call it, Tapter. That part of the common immediately around it is usually referred to as Tor Hill, the other piles that contribute to the appropriateness of the name being Pil Tor, W. of the Arrishes, and Hollow Tor, to the N.W. of that, but they are neither of them very large. Hollow Tor, a little northward of which is a bond-mark known as Shovel Stone, should be the last to be visited, and from there the rambler will strike W. down the hill to the Ruggle Stone, ½ m. distant. When we draw near the walls of the enclosures we bear a little to the R., and speedily arrive at that object. The Ruggle Stone is a huge mass of granite resting on the rocks in such a manner as to slightly log, though it used to be said that it could only be set in motion with the aid of the church key. It is about 22 feet in length and 16 feet wide. Close to it is another "logging" stone, but one of a different character. It resembles a large slab, and is not more than half the length of the other. The weight of the larger rock has been computed to be about 115 tons.

Having brought our wanderings over this part of the Widecombe Commons to a close we shall now return to the village, which we may do either by way of the Ruggle Stone Inn, or by turning northward to the road and descending to Northway Bridge.

Ponsworthy, Leusdon, Pound's Gate, and other places near the southern end of the Widecombe valley, are noticed in our Ashburton Excursions.

ROADS OUT OF WIDECOMBE.

To Natsworthy and Heytree Cross ; S. Ex. 83. This is also the Chagford, North Bovey, and Moreton road.

To Bonehill Down and Swine Down Gate ; S. Ex. 83 ; R. 53.

To Bovey Tracey, via Widecombe Hill and Hemsworthy Gate ; R. 5 A.

To Ashburton, via Cold East Cross ; S. Ex. 87, to Chittleford ; up the hill to Pudsham Down ; descend to the Ruddycleave Water ; up the hill to Cold East Cross ; turn R. as in R. 32.

To Buckland ; S. road from the village for 1 m. ; turn L. at guide-post to Cockingford ; up the hill to Stone Cross ; turn R. and keep straight on.

To Ponsworthy and Dartmeet ; S. road from the village ; turn neither R. nor L. Ponsworthy is reached in 2¼ m. ; thence as in R. 42 A.

To Grendon Cot (branches to Cator) : S. road from the village for rather over 1 m., passing the turning to Cockingford. Then turn R. to Bittleford Down, and keep R. At guide-post continue N. for 1 m. when turn L. to Lower Hatchwell ; thence over Hill Head.

ROUTES FROM BOVEY TRACEY.

R. 39.—To Ashburton, S.W. *Leverton, New Inn, Bickington,* 7½ m. Reverse, R. 54. The route *via* Ilsington is given in S. Ex. 81 ; this is about 8 m.

This is a road route. The pedestrian will cross the railway at Ashburton Bridge, as in S. Ex. 81, and will bear R. at the first fork. ¼ m. on, at Brimley Corner, he will strike L., the direction of the road now being about S. When it begins to bend westward he must leave it for another running L. through Leverton. About 1 m. beyond this the Exeter and Plymouth highway will be reached, the New Inn standing near the junction of the roads. Here the visitor will turn R., and passing through Bickington, 1½ m. S.W., will reach Ashburton in another 3 m.

R. 40.—To Brent and Ivybridge, S.W. *B.,* 15¾ m. *I.,* 20½ m. For points and directions *vide* R. 39, 47. Reverse, R. 65.

R. 41.—To Plympton and Shaugh, S.W. by W. *P.,* 27 m. S., *via Ivybridge and Cornwood,* 29 m. For points and directions *vide* R. 39, 47, 55, 56, 57. Reverse, R. 72.

The first part of this route is the same as R. 39, 47, which give directions for reaching Ivybridge. Thence the road to Plympton is described in R. 55, and that to Shaugh in R. 57. Should the visitor desire to make his way over the moor to Shaugh, he may either branch off at Buckfastleigh or Brent. In the former case he must consult R. 48, which gives the necessary directions, while R. 56 describes the way from Brent. Distance from Buckfastleigh across the moor to Shaugh, *via Shipley and Three Barrows,* 14½ m. ; from Brent, *via Owley and Harford,* 12 m.

R. 42.—To Princetown, W. by S. (A) *Hey Tor Down, Hemsworthy Gate, Newhouse, Pudsham Down, Cockingford, Ponsworthy, Dartmeet, Hexworthy, Swincombe.* P.T., 16½ m. ; T.B., 17½ m. T.B., *via Dunnabridge from Dartmeet,* 16 m. (B) *Hemsworthy Gate, Blackslade, Dunstone Down, Rowden Down, West Shallowford, Bellaford Bridge, Cherry Brook, Two Bridges.* T.B., 15½ m. P.T., 17 m. (C) *Hemsworthy Gate, Widecombe, Gore Hill, Grendon Bridge, Runnage, Post Bridge, Two Bridges.* T.B., 16½ m. ; P.T., 18 m. Reverse, R. 5. Route A is the most convenient.

[Objects : Exs. 25, 26, 27, 44, 46, 5.]

(A) Ascending the hill leading to the commons from the station, we pass Five Wyches Cross and Lower Down Cross (Ex. 24), and 2 m. from our starting-point shall reach Hey Tor Down (S. Ex. 82, Ex. 25). Still following the road we make our way past Shot Plantation and Lud Gate (L.), afterwards leaving Hey Tor and Saddle Tor R. 2 m. from Lud Gate we reach Hemsworthy Gate, 5¼ m. from Bovey Station. Passing through this we turn L., following the road with Rippon Tor L., and when just beyond the ruined enclosures of

Newhouse, R. (Ex. 26), shall leave the road and strike S.W. down the side of Yarder to the bridge over the Ruddycleave Water. Crossing this we mount the hill, having enclosures L. and Pudsham Down R. At the first fork we keep L. ; at the second we bear R., and descend to Cockingford Mill on the East Webburn. This stream we cross, and pass up the hill to the Widecombe (R.) and Ponworthy (L.) road. (This point may be reached from Hemsworthy Gate by way of Black-slade, as in B. *post*, the rambler turning L. on striking the Widecombe and Ponsworthy road, which he will do immediately after passing through Lower Dunstone). We turn L., and in about 1 m. shall arrive at Ponsworthy. Here a steep lane branches R., and making our way up this we presently reach Sherberton Common at Lock's Gate Cross. Here two lanes runs northward, and the road also forks towards the south. We take the right hand one of the latter branches, and make our way over the common, with some enclosures R., our course being a little S. of W. At Ouldsbroom Cross, 1 m. from Pons-worthy, a road runs R. to Sherwell and another L. to Pound's Gate, but we keep straight on, and descend the long steep hill to Dartmeet. Passing up Hart Hole Lane we soon reach a gate, L., where the road runs down to Huccaby, and goes on to Holne. From this point we may either continue straight on, and follow the road past Dunnabridge Pound (Ex. 42) and Prince Hall Lodge (Ex. 4) to Two Bridges, or make our way across the moor. The rambler bound for Two Bridges should keep to the road, but if Princetown be his destination he will shorten the distance by about 1½ m. by adopting the latter course. If he decide upon this he will pass through the gate, and just beyond Huccaby (this is R., St. Raphael's Chapel L.), will cross the West Dart at Hex-worthy Bridge, and climb the hill to the Forest Inn. The way then lies over the bit of common by the side of that hostelry to the Gobbet and Sherburton road.* Here he will turn R., and proceeding for about 300 yards will enter the gate in the corner of the enclosure L. From this point we shall follow the Princetown and Hexworthy track (T. 8), which is well defined throughout. If will first lead us to another gate, and thence down the side of the hill, with the enclosures called the Arrishes R., to Swincombe Ford and the Fairy Bridge (Ex. 4).

[Two Bridges is reached from this point by passing through the short lane leading from the further bank of the stream to Swincombe Newtake, and following the somewhat imperfectly marked track that runs over it in a north-westerly direction to Prince Hall Bridge (T. 10). There the West Dart is crossed, and the road leading by the house to the Dartmeet and Two Bridges highway is followed. There turn L., and in 1 m. the last-named place will be reached.]

Crossing the stream we turn L. and follow the track W. imme-diately in front of Swincombe farmhouse (T. 8), and speedily reach Tor Royal Newtake, or the same point may be gained by passing at the back of the house. Hence the way lies by Cholake Head, the Crock of Gold, Bull Park, and Tor Royal Lodge, as in Ex. 4. The distance from Hexworthy to Princetown by this route in 4½ m.

---

* This leads to the forest holding noticed in Ex. 42, which is not connected with the common named above.

(B) *To Hemsworthy Gate as in A*. Thence the visitor will strike W. by S. across the common to Pil Tor, ½ m., passing Foale's Arrishes (S. Ex. 87) on the way. These he will leave L. From the tor he will make his way to Tunhill Rocks, ¼ m. W.S.W., and thence down the narrow stroll below. In the left hand bottom corner of this is the road leading to Blackslade, which is close by ; the road in the corner R. goes to Tunhill Farm, also quite near. Passing in front of Blackslade we shall make our way down the path through the fields to the lane, and descend to Chittleford. Here we turn L., and almost immediately afterwards R., and ¼ m. on cross the East Webburn at Dunstone Bridge, thence passing through the hamlet of Lower Dunstone (S. Ex. 86), to the Widecombe and Ponsworthy road. (If it is now desired to follow route A, the rambler will turn L., and in about ½ m. will find himself at the head of the road coming up L. from Cockingford Mill, from which point the directions given in that route must be followed). Turning L. we proceed southward for about 100 yards, and then take the turning R. to Higher Dunstone, on the verge of Dunstone Down. Striking across the common in a westerly direction, and passing close to Wind Tor, we gain the road running up towards Lower Blackaton in about ½ m., and follow it N.W. We pass the first turning L., where a lane leads to Dockwell and Jordan Mill, but turn down the next on that side, which is a stroll extending to Rowden Down (S. Ex. 86). We keep close to the walls on the L. and shortly, when near the southern extremity of the little common, pass into a lane between some enclosures and follow it down the side of Jordan Ball to the clapper on the West Webburn (T. 52). Crossing this we pass up by West Shallowford to the road running along the foot of Corn Down, and leading from Lock's Gate Cross above Ponsworthy, L., to Cator and Bellaford Bridge R. (Ex. 44). We cross it and climb the hill, our course being a little N. of W. Descending the W. side of the ridge we strike the Walla Brook about midway between Babeny L. and Riddon R. Should the stream be in flood we shall have to make our way to one or other of those places in order to cross it, but usually this can be easily done at the point we have reached. On gaining the R. bank we are in the forest, and have now to pass over Riddon Bridge to Bellaford Bridge, 1½ m. distant. (If we cross at Riddon our course will be N.W. by W. ; if at Babeny our way will lie between the newtakes to the southern part of the ridge, and thence N.N.W., with the East Dart not far below us L. ; the course from the point on the bank of the stream first reached is N.W.) Bellaford Bridge is on the old Lich Path (T. 18), and on reaching it we follow that track to the Princetown road. If will lead us up by Bellaford Farm and across the side of Lakehead Hill, with the wall of that extensive newtake close to us on the L. throughout the way. On reaching the road at Higher Cherry Brook Bridge we turn L. and follow the instructions given in R. 35. Two Bridges is 2 m., and Princetown is 3½ m. distant.

(C) Our first point will be Hemsworthy Gate, *vide* A. Here we bear R. to the fork of the road a short distance on, where is a guidepost. We take the L. branch as in S. Ex. 82, and shortly after commence the descent of the steep Widecombe Hill. At its foot we cross the East Webburn and speedily find ourselves in the village, which is rather over 1½ m. from Hemsworthy. From the church the road

running N.W. must be followed for a short distance, when the rambler
will turn L., and make his way up the steep lane to the common
(S. Ex. 85). He is now on the ancient Church Way (T. 76), which runs
from Widecombe to Post Bridge. On the common it is a plainly marked
green track, the direction of which is about N.W. Soon after leaving
the fields R. there is a branch L. to Hatchwell, but this must not be
followed. In ¾ m. from the point at which we enter on the down we
reach the corner of an enclosure, and keeping this L. shall turn into a
narrow way between rough granite walls, 150 yards further on. This
is Gore Hill, and it will lead us down to Lower Hatchwell, where we
cross the Broadford Brook. We now climb the steep ascent by Lower
Blackaton, and passing Hill Head, descend to Grendon Bridge. Crossing the West Webburn we follow the road westward to Ephraim's
Pinch (Ex. 44), and thence to Runnage Bridge, where the Walla Brook
is crossed. The road then goes on to the Princetown highway, nearly
1 m. distant, where we turn L. The directions given in R. 35 must now
be followed. Two-Bridges is 4½ m. from the point where we emerge
on the high road, and Princetown 6 m.

R. 43.—To Tavistock, W. by S. R. 42 A, Bovey to Princetown,
and R. 1, Princetown to Tavistock, from this route. 25 m. Reverse,
R. 11.

From Hemsworthy Gate to the junction of the Cockingford and
Ponsworthy roads the route through Blackslade may be followed, see
R. 42 B. If the rambler does not cross the moor by way of Hexworthy,
but follows the road from the gate above Huccaby to Two Bridges,
he will, of course, not touch Princetown, but will go direct from the
last-named place to Rundle Stone. For directions as to this see
R. 36 A.

R. 44.—To Lydford, W. by N. (A) *Via* SHALLOWFORD AND BELLA-
FORD BRIDGE : *Lower Down Cross, Hemsworthy Gate, Blackslade,
Dunstone Down, Rowden Down, Shallowford, Bellaford Bridge, Cherry
Brook, Longaford Tor, Bear Down Newtake Wall, Lich Path, White
Barrow, Hill Bridge, Down Lane*, 24 m. (B) *Via* WIDECOMBE AND
POST BRIDGE : *Hemsworthy as above, Widecombe, Gore Hill, Grendon
Bridge, Runnage Bridge, Post Bridge, Princetown Road, Arch Tor,
Longaford Tor*, thence as above, 25 m. Reverse, R. 18.

[Objects : Exs. 25, 26, 27, 44, 46, 5, 10.]

(A) *Via Shallowford.* This route is identical with R. 42 B, as far
as the bridge over the Cherry Brook on the road between Post Bridge
and Two Bridges. Here the rambler will strike north-westward
across the head of Gawler Bottom, with the Cherry Brook and old
Powder Mills L. When he has passed the latter, that is to say, when
about ½ m. from the road, he will turn towards Longaford, which rises
prominently on the ridge to the W., his direction now being W.N.W.
In ¾ m. from the brook the tor will be reached. The rambler must
leave it L. and descend to the West Dart, which he will strike at Wistman's Wood Ford, or where the Foxholes Water joins the river, just
above it (Ex. 5). Here the wall of Bear Down Newtake is carried over
the hill in front, running westerly from this point. The rambler will
follow it, keeping it L., and in about 1 m. will reach Travellers' Ford,
on the Cowsic (Ex. 5). He will now find himself on the Lich Path
(T. 18), which he will follow W. In 1¼ m. the Prison Leat is reached,

and just beyond it Sandy Ford, on the Walkham. The old path then ascends the western side of the shallow valley, where it is joined by the peat track from Walkham Head to Peter Tavy (T. 16), and then passes close to White Barrow, which is seen L. (Ex. 8, Extension). When the hill is crossed the peat track bends L., and the traces of the Lich Path are lost for a time. The rambler should now strike a little N. of W. down the slope to the wall of Longbetor Newtake, when this must be kept L. Very soon he will enter the stroll formed by this and other enclosures of Longbetor Farm on one hand, and those belonging to Bagga Tor Farm on the other. He will cross this stroll, and keeping the wall of South Common (the largest of the Bagga Tor enclosures) R., will find himself again on the line of the Lich Path (on this part of which the later Black Lane was formed, T. 19). His course is now due W. In less than ½ m. he will reach the end of the stroll, and passing through a gate will still follow the track, with Bagga Tor R. Ere he has gone far he will notice another gate L., where he will leave the down, and make his way by the road for about ½ m. nearly to Wapsworthy Bridge (Ex. 8), where he will enter a gate R. and follow a path across three fields to Hill Bridge, on the Tavy. From this point the way to Lydford by Hill Town, Yard Gate, Forstall Cross, and Down Lane has already been described (R. 2 A).

(Another route from the common near Bagga Tor may be followed, but not when the Tavy is in flood, as the river has to be crossed at some stepping-stones. Instead of passing through the gate on the L. to the road, the rambler should still follow the ancient track as it runs down the hill, past Brousen Tor Farm to the Bagga Tor Brook, which he will cross at Bagga Tor Clapper (Ex. 10), and then leaving the path, which runs on to Standon Farm, will strike N.W. to Willsworthy Ford, or Standon Steps, as the crossing-place is more often called, ½ m. distant, and less than that above Cataloo Steps, where the Bagga Tor Brook falls into the Tavy. Having gained the further bank of that river, the rambler will pass upward to Willsworthy, as in Ex. 10. The path to Forstall Cross from Willsworthy Pound by way of Willsworthy Brook and Yellowmead is noticed in that excursion.

(B) *Via Widecombe and Post Bridge.* This route is the same as R. 42 C to the ninth milestone from Moreton, on the Princetown road, and rather over ½ m. S.W. of Post Bridge. Here the rambler will leave the road and strike nearly due W. towards Arch Tor, the small mass of rock seen on the hillside across Gawler Bottom, and about ½ m. distant. Just below it is the Powder Mills Leat, which must be followed downward to a footbridge. Crossing this, and still steering W., the way lies over Cherry Brook and the ridge beyond it, to a point a little northward of Longaford Tor. When this is reached the rambler will be on the line described *ante.*

R. 45.—To Okehampton and Belstone, N.W. by W. The more direct route is through Chagford ; see R. 46 and R. 38. 22 m. Reverse, R. 24 and R. 31. The following is the moor route :

Lower Down Cross, Trendlebere Down, Leighon, Swine Down Gate, Heytree Cross, Heathercombe, Hookney Down, Bovey River, South Teign, Teign Clapper, White Moor Stone, Taw Plain. Distance about the same. Reverse, R. 25.

[Objects : Exs. 24 to 17.]

From Bovey Station the rambler will pass up the hill as in the preceding routes, but will turn R. at Lower Down Cross (rather less than 1 m.), from which point to Swine Down he will find the route described in Ex. 24. It will lead him by the Lower Terrace Drive past Yarner Wood, beyond which he will cross the slope of Black Hill to the Leighon road, and descend to the bridge below that place ; thence, passing Great Hound Tor Farm, he will climb the hill to Hound Tor Down, and be led direct to Swine Down Gate (R. 25, 32, 53). He will enter this and take the road L., which will lead him along the edge of Swine Down and Cripdon Down to Heytree Cross, 1½ m. from the gate. Here he must turn L., and passing Heytree will, in about ¾ m., reach a short lane leading by Heathercombe (S. Ex. 62) to the common. From this point the course will be W.N.W. for over 3 m., which will bring him to the head of Metheral Bogs on the common lands belonging to the parish of Chagford. First he will reach King Tor (Ex. 22), ½ m. from Heathercombe, and passing over Hookney Down will cross the Challacombe and Grendon road 1 m. further on, and ¾ m., beyond this the Princetown and Moreton road, whence he will descend to the Bovey river, ½ m. below (Ex. 21). About ½ m. beyond this the rambler will find himself at the head of the Metheral Bogs. Keeping this mire on his R. he will strike due N., and in another ½ m. will reach the road running out to Fernworthy, which farm is in full view (Ex. 20), and which will bring him to the South Teign. (See R. 25 for remarks on crossing this stream.) At the corner of the Fernworthy enclosures eastward of the house he will take a northerly course, and passing the Long Stone 1 m. up, and keeping Kes Tor R., will make his way to Batworthy Corner, his course being due N. from the menhir. Here he is near the antiquities noticed in Ex. 20. His course is now N.N.W. to the North Teign, the path being close to the wall of Batworthy enclosures, which are R. Crossing the river at Teign Clapper, close to the holed Stone (Ex. 19), he will make his way over Scorhill Down past the stone circle which he will see on the slope before him. Hence a walk of 2 m., the course being N.W., will bring him to the shoulder of Kennon Hill, near White Moor Stone, from which point the route is the same as R. 38 B, which will also show the way to Belstone.

If bound for Sticklepath the rambler will steer N. from Scorehill Circle, and make his way over the down, with Berry Down Stroll and Creber R. (Ex. 19), to the detached newtake on the side of Buttern Hill, ¾ m. He will pass below this, and bearing a little to the R., will soon reach Ensworthy, where he will strike the road running on to Shilstone Tor (Ex. 18), from which point the directions given in R. 38 A must be followed.

R. 46.—To Moreton and Chagford, N.W. *Atway, Woolley, King's Cross, Slade, Kelly, Wray Cleave, Wray Barton, Hayne, Moreton* ; thence to Chagford. To Moreton, 6½ m. ; to Chagford, 11 m. Reverse, R. 31.

This is a road route. The way lies by Cross Cottage and Atway, as in S. Ex. 72. About ½ m. beyond the latter the visitor will bear L. to Woolley, whence he will keep R. to King's Cross, 1 m. from Bovey. Still bearing R. his next point will be Slade, where is a guide-post, and another further on at Kelly Cross. From this point he will bear N.W., and will soon reach a milestone marking $3\frac{3}{4}$ m. from Bovey and from Moreton, where a road turns L. to Lustleigh. The way still runs N.W., with Wray Cleave R.

(For the route between Moreton and Chagford see beginning of *Chagford District*).

ASHBURTON DISTRICT.

DISTANCES. BY ROAD: *AUSEWELL CROSS*, 2 m. *BECKY FALL*, *via* Rewlea Cross, Halshanger Cross, and Lud Gate, $8\frac{1}{4}$ m. *BICKINGTON*, $3\frac{1}{4}$ m. *BOVEY TRACEY*, $7\frac{1}{2}$ m. *BRENT*, see South Brent. *BUCKFASTLEIGH*, 3 m. *BUCKLAND-IN-THE-MOOR*, $3\frac{1}{2}$ m. *CHAGFORD*, *via* Welstor Cross, Swine Down Gate, and Beetor Cross, $12\frac{3}{4}$ m. *COCKINGFORD MILL*, *via* Buckland, $5\frac{1}{4}$ m. *COLD EAST CROSS*, *via* Welstor Cross, $3\frac{1}{2}$ m.; *via* Halshanger Cross, $3\frac{3}{4}$ m. *CROSS FURZES*, *via* Buckfastleigh, 6 m. *DARTMEET*, 8 m. *DEAN*, 4 m. *DEAN BURN* (Gate near Warn Bridge), $4\frac{1}{2}$ m. *DEAN PRIOR*, $4\frac{3}{4}$ m. *EXETER*, 19 m. *GRENDON BRIDGE*, *via* Cockingford and Bittleford Down, $8\frac{1}{2}$ m. *GRIM'S POUND*, *via* do., $10\frac{1}{4}$ m. *HALSHANGER CROSS*. $2\frac{1}{2}$ m. *HEMBURY CASTLE*, *via* Gallant le Bower, or *via* Dart Bridge, $4\frac{1}{2}$ m. *HEMSWORTHY GATE*, *via* Welstor Cross, $4\frac{3}{4}$ m. *HEXWORTHY*, *via* Dartmeet, $9\frac{1}{2}$ m.; *via* Holne Moor Gate, $8\frac{1}{2}$ m. *HEY TOR*; The road runs within $\frac{1}{4}$ m. of the tor, and this point is the same distance from Ashburton, viz., $6\frac{1}{4}$ m., whether it is approached by way of Halshanger Cross and Lud Gate, or by Welstor Cross and Hemsworthy Gate. *HOLNE BRIDGE*, 2 m. *HOLNE CHASE LODGE*, $2\frac{1}{2}$ m. *HOLNE MOOR GATE*, 5 m. (Reservoir $\frac{3}{4}$ m. further). *HOLNE VILLAGE*, $4\frac{1}{2}$ m. *ILSINGTON*, *via* Halshanger Cross and Bag Tor Mill, $5\frac{1}{2}$ m.; *via* Owlacombe Cross and Sigford, 5 m. *IVYBRIDGE*, 13 m. *LEUSDON*, *via* Pound's Gate, $5\frac{3}{4}$ m. *LID GATE* (for Buckfastleigh Moor), 7 m. *LUD GATE*, *via* Rewlea Cross, Halshanger Cross, Bag Tor Mill and Pinchaford, $5\frac{3}{4}$ m. *LYDFORD*, *via* Two Bridges, 27 m. *MANATON*, $9\frac{1}{4}$ m. *MORETON*, *via* Welstor Cross, Swine Down Gate, Langstone, and North Bovey, $11\frac{1}{2}$ m. *NEW BRIDGE*, $3\frac{1}{2}$ m. *NEWTON ABBOT*, 8 m. *OKEHAMPTON*, *via* Dartmeet, Two Bridges, and Moor Shop, 35 m.; *via* Chagford, 23 m. *PLYMOUTH*, *via* Ivybridge, $23\frac{1}{2}$ m. *PLYMPTON*, *via* Ivybridge, $19\frac{1}{2}$ m. *POST BRIDGE*, *via* Grendon, $11\frac{1}{2}$ m. *POUND'S GATE*, *via* New Bridge, $4\frac{3}{4}$ m. *PRINCETOWN*, *via* Dartmeet, $14\frac{1}{2}$ m.; *via* Holne Moor, 16 m. *SCORRITON*, *via* Holne, 5 m.; *via* Buckfastleigh, 6 m. *SOUTH BRENT*, $8\frac{1}{4}$ m. *SWINE DOWN GATE*, 7 m. *TAVISTOCK*, *via* Dartmeet and Two Bridges, 21 m. *TOTNES*, 8 m. *TWO BRIDGES*, *via* Dartmeet, 13 m.; *via* Holne Moor, $14\frac{1}{2}$ m. *WELSTOR CROSS*, 2 m. *WIDECOMBE*, *via* Buckland and Cockingford, $6\frac{3}{4}$ m. *YELVERTON*, *via* Princetown, $20\frac{1}{2}$ m.; *via* Cornwood, 24 m.

BY RAIL: *ASHBURTON* is the terminus of a branch line running from the main line of the G.W.R. at *TOTNES*, $9\frac{1}{2}$ m. The intermediate stations are *BUCKFASTLEIGH*, $2\frac{1}{4}$ m. from *ASHBURTON*, and *STAVERTON*, $5\frac{3}{4}$ m. *NEWTON ABBOT*, *via TOTNES*, $18\frac{1}{4}$ m. *BRENT*, do., $16\frac{1}{4}$ m., q.v. for stations W.

The pleasing situation of Ashburton, which is surrounded by hills,

" 11. BOVEY TRACEY DISTRICT. "

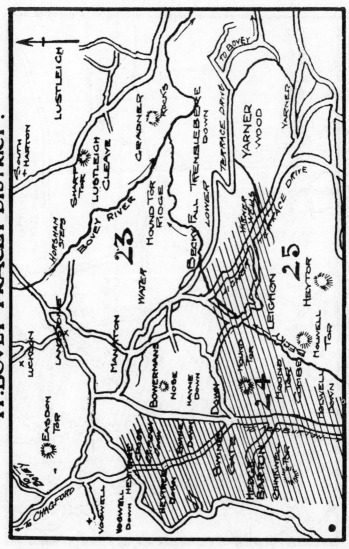

EXCURSIONS 23, 24, & PART OF 25. (FOR W. OF WIDECOMBE VALLEY SEE MAPS 10 & 13.)

12. ASHBURTON DISTRICT.

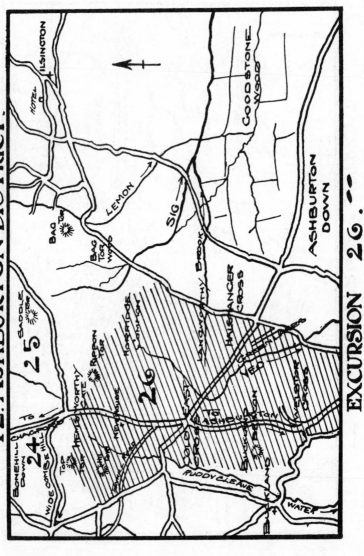

EXCURSION 26.

renders it a favourite place of sojourn with the visitor. The main road from Exeter to Plymouth runs through it, and forms the thoroughfares called East Street and West Street, in the latter of which the church is situated. These streets are crossed at their junction by another thoroughfare, the southern part of which is called S. Laurence Lane, and leads to the railway station ; the other part is North Street. The moor is approached by way of the last-named.

EXCURSIONS FROM ASHBURTON.

The area over which these excursions extend is bounded on the N. by a line drawn from Bag Tor Wood to Hemsworthy Gate, and thence to Blackslade and Dunstone, being that which forms the southern boundary of the Bovey District ; on the W. by the road running from Dunstone through Ponsworthy to Sherberton Common, thence to the Gorge of the Dart below Mil Tor, and down that river to New Bridge. The rambles also include Holne Chase and the Buckland Woods, as well as Holne village, Hembury, and Buckfastleigh.

[Tracks 49, 51, 52.]

Ex. 26.—*Valley of the Yeo, Rushlade Common, Halshanger Common, The Nutcracker, Rippon Tor, Newhouse, Foale's Arrishes, Whitaburrow, Pudsham Down, Ruddycleave Water, Buckland Beacon,* 9½ m.

Leaving Ashburton by way of North Street we soon reach Great Bridge, at the end of the town where the road to Buckland and Holne turns L. over the Yeo. We do not cross that stream here, but at Barnsey Bridge, a little further on, our course being northerly. Very soon we reach Pitt Farm, where our road bends R. to Rew Cross. We take the L. branch, and in less than ¼ m. reach Rewlea Cross, where we keep straight on to Lurgecombe Mill, and again meet the Yeo. Our road now runs up a narrow valley, with very steep tree-covered sides, Boro Wood being on the L. and Whiddon Scrubbs on the R. ½ m. from the mill we cross Waterleat Bridge, and leaving the Yeo pass up the hill to Rushlade. We turn R. at the farm buildings into the road that runs on by Halshanger, but shall only follow it for about 150 yards. We then turn L. into an approach to the moor called Green Lanes, a kind of narrow stroll running between the enclosures and leading to Rushlade Common. On reaching the latter we strike the road coming up from Halshanger Cross R. (S. Ex. 88), and which is carried along the verge of the down close to the plantation known as The Belt, with the enclosures of Welstor L. This will lead us to Water Rushes, where the Yeo comes down from Halshanger Common. The road runs on to Cold East Cross (R. 42, 53), and thence by Pudsham Down and Dunstone Down to Blackaton and the forest (S. Ex. 86, 85), but we leave it on crossing the stream, and enter the gate R. Just within this is a mire, which, however, we shall avoid by striking northward. (The Summer House, described in S. Ex. 89, is situated on the further side of the Yeo, due E. of the gate). Passing up the slope, and bearing a little to the L., *i.e.*, W. of N., we at length reach a dilapidated wall, through one of the many breaks in which we shall make our way, and keeping it R. continue the ascent of the hill. This wall runs upward towards Rippon Tor, and it will shortly bring us to an outlying pile on which is a curiously-poised stone that once moved with very slight pressure, but has now nearly lost its logging power. It is about 1 m. from Water Rushes, and stands in a corner formed by the wall we have followed and another coming up from near Newhouse L., which place it overlooks. (This second wall, which is carried over the hill in a direction from N.W. to S.E., separates the two commons of Halshanger and Horridge, and also marks the boundary between the parishes of Ashburton and Ilsington). The logan is known as the Nutcracker, and seems to be the one mentioned by Polewhele as existing between Widecombe Church and Rippon Tor.* He says : " It is called the Nutcrackers, having been the resort of the common people during the nut season, for the purpose of cracking their nuts." That the author in question should have believed that the country people took the trouble to bring nuts to Rippon Tor in order to crack them is certainly surprising, but that he did not tell us the Druids did likewise is much more so. But he may have suspected that these ancient seers preferred to crack jokes, and that the only nuts they cared anything about were chestnuts. A hundred yards S.E. of the pile, but on the other side of the wall, is a low cairn.

In the corner formed by the two walls we shall notice a gate, and passing through this shall make our way to Rippon Tor, which we see just above us. This fine height attains an elevation of 1,563 feet, and is a conspicuous object from numberless points on the moor, while its frontier situation renders it equally so from the lowlands. The view from it is similar to that gained from Hey Tor, but is more extensive towards the S.W. (Ex. 25), where Brent Hill and the Eastern Beacon, instead of being partly hidden, fully reveal themselves. (*Brent District*). Westward, towards Princetown, a great stretch of forest is seen, with North Hisworthy rising against the sky (*Princetown District*), and extending from it towards the north a long range of dusky moor. To the S. and S.W. a considerable tract of cultivated country is seen, embracing much of the South Hams ; the estuary of the Teign forms a striking feature eastward ; while woodlands and fields roll away further east, and to the north, till the moor again fills up the scene. At the foot of the hill, to the N., the long Hound Tor Combe is seen to great advantage, with Lustleigh Cleave at its further end, and the tors that rise on either side of it (Ex. 23, 24, 25). We are too far off to discern the pixies on Holwell Lawn, even should the hour be propitious for their gathering there, as gossip used to say was sometimes their wont, but we may possibly see a buzzard circling round Hey Tor. The late Prebendary Wolfe, who had a residence at Leighon (Ex. 24), once observed as many as thirteen of these birds settling down upon the rocks near the house, and knew of several instances of their nesting in this valley. He was also able to speak of ravens breeding there. The golden eagle, it is said, was

---

* Polwhele's *Historical Views of Devonshire*, 1793. The mention of Widecombe Church might be thought to point to the Ruggle Stone (S. Ex. 87), but equally so the mention of Rippon Tor points to the rock in question. Moreover, the name given by Polwhele is that by which this logan has long been known.

seen in this part of the moor by two ramblers when on their way from Rippon Tor to Hey Tor in May, 1891.

Rippon Tor consists of a number of scattered piles of rocks, though none of them are striking. But the visitor will, nevertheless, be well rewarded for making the ascent, for besides the magnificent view the spot is full of interest. Here the dwellers in the huts that stud the slopes in the vicinity of the hill brought their honoured dead for burial (as they did to other elevated situations on the moor), and here in a later day, but one, perhaps, remote from us, the stone-hewer came to fashion the symbol of Christianity. Three cairns may be seen here one of them, which is formed among the rocks on the summit, being 90 yards in circumference, and quite near to it, and almost covered with turf, is a kistvaen. A large reave runs from this cairn down the hill in a north-westerly direction towards Hemsworthy Gate, 270 feet below, and rather less than ½ m. away, and from thence is continued for some distance over the common. About 30 yards N.N.W. of the summit of the tor is one of the most curious of the stone crosses of Dartmoor. It is cut in relief on a block of granite only slightly raised above the ground, and it has been suggested that this was done in the belief that the holy symbol would free the spot from any heathen superstitions that may have attached to it. However this may be, it seems hardly probable that this cross was ever intended to be set up, seeing that it would have been an easier task fo fashion one for such a purpose from a smaller and more shapely block. The length of this cross is 6 feet 8 inches. [*Crosses*, Chap. XVI.] Under the cairn, and about 30 yards from the cross, is an unfinished mill-stone, and another may be seen close to an overhanging rock on the great reave. The former is 4 feet in diameter, and the latter 5 feet. (cf. S. Ex. 56, 105 ; Ex. 29).

Bidding adieu to this elevated spot, we descend the hill westward with the wall L., and at the bottom shall reach a gate opening on the Ashburton and Chagford road (R. 53). On passing through it we shall notice by the side of the way a flat rock which forms a bond-mark of Ashburton parish. On its surface is the letter A with the date 1793, the characters being rather large and deeply cut. Here we are close to the scanty remains of Newhouse. These consist only of a few low walls marking the site of a dwelling, and some enclosures near it with a dozen weather-beaten thorn bushes. Newhouse was formerly an inn, but did not suffer extinction, as will readily be imagined, in consequence of being kept open during prohibited hours ; it was burnt down. In the days when the woollen manufacture at Chagford was in a flourishing state wagons from the factory there often passed this way, while much lime was also formerly carried over the road from Ashburton to the neighbourhood of the former town. In the morning the farmers' men who came to fetch this would drive at a rapid pace over the down in order to reach the kilns as early in the day as possible, and thus avoid being kept waiting for their load. Then they would get on their way and waste at Newhouse the time they had saved by being early at Ashburton. It was quite a common thing, at certain times, to see a large number of carts drawn up in the road near this solitary inn while their drivers quenched their thirst within.

The Ashburton boundary line crosses the road, and runs north-westward from the flat rock to another mark about 150 yards distant, an upright stone called Grey Goose Nest, and one of a line running about S.W. and N.E. To this we now make our way, and on arriving find ourselves at the northernmost point of Ashburton, with Ilsington on our R. and Widecombe in front of us, the stone marking the meeting-place of the three parishes. Crossing the line (which runs S.W. to Blackslade Ford less than ½ m. distant, and N.E. to Stittleford's Cross, ¼ m. away, and close to Hemsworthy Gate. S. Ex. 82, 90) we enter upon Blackslade Down, and leaving Blackslade Mire L., shall follow an old reave running up the slope N.W., and be led directly to the enclosures known as Foale's Arrishes. These have been already briefly noticed in S. Ex. 87. They are formed by a number of small reaves, much overgrown, which intersect each other at right angles, and in the spaces thus formed there a few hut circles. These also occur on the outside of the low walls. It was at Foale's Arrishes that a certain villager once decided to settle, and though his neighbours tried to persuade him to remain where he was, set out one day with the avowed intention of erecting a shelter on the spot, and passing the remainder of his days there. But like Cyrus, who, as Persian legends say, having gone into retirement, suddenly disappeared, the labourer was never seen again. Whether he was spirited away by the pixies, or fell a prey to the Evil One, who is said to take an airing occasionally on Tor Hill, on the slope of which the Arrishes are situated, nobody could say ; all that was certain was that the neighbourhood knew him no more.

About ¼ m. S.W. of these enclosures is the ancient grave near Blackslade, sometimes referred to as the Tunhill kistvaen. This is noticed in S. Ex. 87, as also are the tors on this part of the moor. We make our way to the kist, our line being very nearly the same as that described in R. 42 B, and on reaching it find ourselves on the old Tunhill Road (T. 51).

[This road runs down the stroll W. and forks ; the R. branch going to Tunhill, the L. to Blackslade. From the latter a road runs to Chittleford and on to Dunstone. *Vide* R. 42 B.]

From the kist we may either cross the road and strike southward to the fine cairn known as Wittaburrow, and then turn R. to a track running by the side of the enclosures, and so reach Pudsham Down, or we may follow the Tunhill road L. as far as Blackslade Ford, and then take the Blackslade Water for our guide. In either case Ruddycleave Bridge will be our next point. The former route will lead us by the track N. of Wittaburrow southward to the road that comes up R. from Chittleford and Widecombe, past the entrance to Scobetor (Scobetor Rocks are within an enclosure near the house). This we follow across Pudsham Down to a guide-post, where we join the road coming R. from Stone Cross and Cockingford (R. 5 A). Turning L. we descend the hill with the enclosures of Ruddycleave R. to the bridge.

If we follow the Tunhill road we reach Blackslade ford in about ¼ m., close to which, on the R., is a small cairn. On the L. one of the walls belonging to the old enclosures of Newhouse comes down the hill. Just below the ford is a tiny rivulet on the R. called William's Well, and from this point the wall of the enclosure R. forms both the boundary of Blackslade Manor and of Widecombe parish. A few trees will be noticed at Burrow Corner, where the wall turns up westward.

Choosing a path on the I. bank of the Ruddycleave (the Blackslade Water mentioned above is merely that part of the same stream nearer its source) we shall now follow it downward, and at the distance of $\frac{1}{4}$ m. from the ford shall reach the bridge, which is of clapper construction.

[The Tunhill road runs from the ford up the side of the common sometimes called Yarder,* in a south-easterly direction to the Chagford and Ashburton highway, which it strikes about $\frac{1}{2}$ m. S. of Newhouse (T. 51). If the rambler decides to return that way he will, on reaching the road, turn R., and passing over Dry Bridge, soon arrive at Cold East Cross. The latter point he may also gain from Ruddycleave Bridge by following the road up the hill E.S.E. for about $\frac{1}{2}$ m. A few hut circles will be seen close to the road soon after leaving the bridge. From Cold East Cross the return to Ashburton may be made by way of Green Lanes or Welstor Cross (R. 32). The former, which is the more direct, will be the reverse of the route by which we reached the commons. Take the L. branch and follow the road, which the wall L. to The Belt (*ante*), and near the end of this strike R. through the stroll to Rushlade. Thence down the valley S., as in S. Ex. 81, reaching the Yeo at Waterleat Bridge. This stream will then become the rambler's companion to Lurgecombe Mill, whence he will continue S. past Rewlea Cross to the town.

For Welstor Cross take the road R. at Cold East Cross, and follow it S., passing along the eastern verge of Buckland Common, with the enclosed land and Higher Plantation L. At Welstor Cross, where is a guide-post, bend L. and descend the hill to Rewdown Cross, marked also with a guide-post. Keep straight on to Rewlea Cross, and then turn R. to the town, or the corner may be cut by taking the footpath across the fields R. a few score yards beyond Rewdown Cross, and which reaches the road at Pitt Farm and Tucking Mill. Another way, from Welstor Cross, the distance being about the same, is by striking R. at that point to Ausewell Cross, which is close by, and then turning L., as the guide-post will show. The way runs down the hill past Druid (L) to Water Turn, where the road L. must be taken. Keep onward S.E. (there are guide-posts here) to Headborough, $\frac{1}{4}$ m. beyond which is Great Bridge, on the outskirts of the town.]

From Ruddycleave Bridge we shall strike southward over the common, gradually leaving the stream, which runs down the valley R., and make our way to Buckland Beacon, 1 m. from the bridge. This is noticed in S. Ex. 92, to which the visitor is referred. After having looked upon the fine view commanded from this rock, we strike eastward to a gate in the wall, and crossing Welstor Common to another gate, reach the road and turn R. to Welstor Cross. The route to the town from this point has been described above.

Ex. 27.—*Buckland-in-the-Moor, Cockingford, Bittleford, Ponsworthy, Leusdon, Lizwell Meet, Spitchwick, Pound's Gate, Leigh Tor, New Bridge,* 13$\frac{1}{2}$ m.

---

* So named from the remark of a visitor at Newhouse, who, on being shown the largest of the enclosures, observed that the individual who formed it had not been particular to a *yard or* two, but had helped himself freely to the common land, and wondered he had not taken in the piece of common in question.

(The commons above Pound's Gate, described in Ex. 28, may also be included in this excursion by turning R. at the Upper Plantation after leaving Leusdon and passing through Uppacott to Bel Tor, or by striking into Dr. Blackall's Drive above Leigh Tor).

We shall first make our way by North Street to Great Bridge, as in the preceding excursion, where we turn L. to Headborough. A little beyond this is Holne Turn (guide-post), where the Tavistock road runs L., one branch of it passing through Holne and Hexworthy, the other crossing New Bridge and going through Pound's Gate and Dartmeet. We continue straight on to Water Turn, where is another guide-post, and just before reaching it shall notice the road running R. to Druid. Keeping R. we pass up the hill between Highgrove and Higher Ausewell, the latter being on the L., and skirting the Druid Plantations R., shall soon reach Ausewell Cross. [If preferred the rambler may make his way to this point by Rewdown Cross, as in S. Ex. 92.]

The guide-post at Ausewell Cross will show the visitor that he must continue straight on for Buckland—that is, about N.W. The road here runs downhill, Ausewell Wood being on the L., and some enclosures bordering Welstor Common on the R. At the entrance to Ausewell Cottages L. the boundary line between the parishes of Ashburton and Buckland crosses the road (S. Ex. 92), and on passing this we have Combe Wood L. and Buckland Common R. Rather over ½ m. further down we reach Southbrook, immediately below which the Ruddycleave Water (Ex. 26) issues from the moor between Birch Wood on its R. bank, and Bagley Wood on its L., and on reaching this we find ourselves in one of those delightful dells which make the Dartmoor borderland so beautiful. Crossing the stream, which comes white flashing from the green hollow above the bridge to lose itself amid the thick woods below, we pass up the little village, if such a tiny place may be so described, of Buckland-in-the-Moor.

This ancient border settlement occupies a pleasing situation on the higher part of a tongue of land peninsulated by the Webburn, the Dart, and the Ruddycleave Water, the steep hillsides to the E., W., and S. of it being clothed with woods, while a number of moor farms cover the rising ground to the N., extending in that direction to Pudsham Down. There is no doubt that it deserved its adjunct in early times, but much land has been won from the waste, and many bare slopes have been covered with trees, since it was first named, so that it can now hardly be said to be in the moor. The manor formerly belonged to Roger de Bockland, a man of great worth and wealth, one of who successors, William de Bockland, was Sheriff of Devon, and also of Cornwall, during the first five years of the reign of Richard I. It was given to Tor Abbey in the thirteenth century, afterwards coming to the Ercedeknes.* In the sixteenth century it was in the possession of the Woodleys, one of whom, Ralph Woodley, died in 1593, and is commemorated by a black marble tablet in the church, and later became the property of the Bastards, to which family it now belongs.

Raffe Carsleghe, of this parish, who died in 1547, left his body to

---

* In the early part of the fourteenth century, the forest having reverted to the crown in the person of Edward II., Thomas le Ercedekne was appointed Constable of Lydford Castle and Custos of Dartmoor.

" holy buriall within the churchyard of St. Peter, of Bucland-in-the More," and bequeathed " one yeo sheep " to the " head store within the said church," and another to " the store of Our Lady." It was by the discovery (by Mr. Charles Worthy, in 1888) of the contemporary copy of Carsleghe's will at the District Probate Reigstry, that the dedication of Buckland Church was ascertained, this being unknown previous to that year. It is a daughter church to Ashburton, and is a small structure with the low tower so characteristic of the moorland border churches, and has a stair turret on its southern face. The screen is elaborately carved and illuminated, and is said to have been brought from Buckfastleigh Church. The circular font is Norman, and exhibits the ziz-zag ornament and cable moulding.* Ruddycleave Farm, about 1 m. distant (Ex. 26), has pertained to the church from a very early period, the rental being devoted to its repair and the payment of the clerk and sexton. Outside the churchyard gate is the octagonal base of a cross, from the centre of which a sycamore is now growing, and on the wall close to the gate are the mutilated remains of the object which probably once surmounted it. Another cross may be seen built into the wall at Buckland Court opposite, between the higher gate and the entrance doors. [*Crosses,* Chap. XVI.] The ancient church, shaded by a grove of fine trees, the picturesque cottages, the sylvan surroundings, and the glimpses of distant hillsides where fields climb up to meet the moor, form a delightful picture, to which the tranquillity resting over all lends a further charm.

[The road to Buckland Bridge and New Bridge is noticed in S. Ex. 92.]

Turning into the Widecombe road with the church L., we take the L. branch at the fork close by and make our way to Higher Pudsham, with Great Lot Wood in the valley of the Webburn below us. From Higher Pudsham we pass on to Stone Cross, 1 m. from Buckland, and turn L. down the hill to Cockingford. (R. 42 A). The name of this place, which consists only of a farm and a mill and a smithy, is suggestive of the old-time punishment of the ducking-stool, and it is indeed not improbable that here viragos and scolding wives were once brought unpleasantly acquainted with the curative properties of the waters of the Webburn. Crossing Cockingford Bridge we pass up the hill to the road coming R. from Widecombe (R. 42 A), where is a guide-post. Turning L. we soon reach another guide-post, where we keep straight on and speedily arrive at Bittleford. Here two or three cottages will be seen on the L. ; the farm being on the R. The house seems to have been rebuilt in 1706, which date may be seen on the porch. A short lane leads from it to Bittleford Down (S. Ex. 86), and here was probably the gate named in the Court Rolls of the time of Elizabeth, where an entry of the 4th May, 1587, has reference to the ruined state of Bittleford Yeat.

Resuming our walk we soon cross the road coming R. from Jordan (S. Ex. 86), and running L. to Lizwell, and descend the hill to Pons-worthy, where we cross the West Webburn. The bridge which we may well imagine gave name to this little place was, in all probability, a clapper ; the present one is a small one-arched structure, and can

---

* The church was pulled to pieces in 1907 in order to be " restored," when the screen was removed to Ermington for renovation.

apparently boast some antiquity, a stone at the eastern end of the northern parapet bearing the date 1666. The hamlet, consisting of a few farmhouses and cottages and a smithy, occupies a secluded situation in a narrow valley, but though so near to the moor betrays few signs of it. It is placed in the midst of very fine scenery, and a short walk in any direction will bring the visitor to some interesting point. Lizwell Meet, where the two Webburns unite their waters, one of the beauty spots of the Dartmoor borderland, is about 1 m. distant, and may be reached by a path branching from the road near the E. end of the bridge and running through Cleave Wood along the L. bank of the stream, or it may also be approached from Leusdon. [*Gems*, Chap. XIII.] In another direction the high land of Corn Down, which commands extensive views of the forest, may soon be gained. The road to it runs up westward by the smithy to Lock's Gate Cross (R. 42 A), where it enters upon Sherberton Common, above which the down is situated. This part of the moor is noticed in our excursions from Hexworthy (Ex. 41).

Leaving this retired hamlet by the S. road we pass up by Sweaton Farm to Leusdon Common, and just beyond Sweaton Plantation take the L. fork at the branch. This will speedily bring us to the church of St. John the Baptist, built in 1863 by the late Mrs. Larpent, which serves the needs of the inhabitants of this part of the extensive parish of Widecombe. [100 *Years*, Chap. IV. It takes the place of the Chapel of St. Leonard, which formerly existed at Spitchwick, near by. A cross is erected to the memory of the generous donor. The pulpit was placed in the church by Mrs. Stone in commemoration of her husband, Mr. John Stone, of Leusdon Lodge, who died in 1899. He took considerable interest in the welfare of the parish, and was a great lover of the moor. Passing onward with Leusdon Lodge R. we bear L. to Blackaton Down, which we reach immediately above the tor of the same name. The outlying pile below the enclosures L. is usually known as Logwell Rock.

[The turning R., close to Leusdon Lodge, leads to Lower Town Farm, where an old cross that formerly stood on the common near Ouldsbroom (Ex. 41), now serves as a gate-post. *Crosses*, Chap. XVI.]

From Blackadon Tor we look down upon the woods that conceal Lizwell Meet, which is only about 300 yards from the main pile, and upon the narrow valley of the East Webburn, through which the stream comes down from Cockingford. It flows between Lizwell Wood, W., and Great Lot Wood, E., and is spanned by a footbridge under Lizwell Farm.

Returning from the down we again pass the church, and then bend L. to Leusdon Common, from which the view is exceedingly fine. We look across the Webburn valley upon the little church of Buckland, which is seen rising amid the trees that thickly clothe the sides of the hills, and beyond it to the Beacon lifting itself above them. More to the R. is the gorge which marks where the Dart pursues his devious course round the wild Holne Chase, his waters being hidden by the dense woods. ½ m. further on, at the end of what is called the Upper Plantation, we reach the road coming down from Sherberton Common R. (R. 6 A), where we turn L., and a few score yards further on shall come upon the entrance to Spitchwick. In the 17th century this manor belonged to the Bourchiers, Earls of Bath, and in the earlier part of the eighteenth century was in the possession of the Rev. John Wotton. Subsequently it became the property of Dr. Blackall, and was bought by its present holder, Mr. F. P. T. Struben, in 1901.

Our road to Ashburton has already been sketched in R. 6 A. Just below the lodge it makes a bend, and here on the R. is a small oblong pound. Near to it is the entrance to Lake Farm, the date on which is 1661, a very good example of an ancient moorland homestall. A little further on we reach the hamlet of Pound's Gate, where is a post office, and a wayside house of entertainment called the Tavistock Inn, from its situation on the road from Ashburton to that town (Ex. 28). Less than ½ m. beyond this we enter again upon the commons at New-bridge Hill, with the rocky ridge of Leigh Tor, or, as it is sometimes called, Long Tor, on the L. The road branching R. at the corner of the enclosures was made by the late Dr. Blackall, and is usually known as Dr. Blackall's Drive (Ex. 28, S. Ex. 95). The view from Leigh Tor, or indeed from any point on this part of the down, is very fine, and embraces the greater part of Holne Chase and the Buckland Woods. One of the piles of the tor has had the fanciful name of the Batch Loaves bestowed upon it, and another is called the Ravens' Rock.

[If it should be desired to return to Ashburton by way of Buckland the rambler will make his way down by the side of the tor to the road below it, and then turning L. will follow the directions given in the *Holne Chase Section* and in S. Ex. 93. This will increase the distance by 1 m.]

Turning into a green path L., which crosses the road here and again part way down the hill, we shall follow it to the foot of the steep descent, where we turn R., and skirting New Bridge Marsh, shall soon reach the structure of that name on the Dart (Ex. 28 and *Holne Chase Section*). Crossing this and passing the Holne Chase Lodge L. we ascend the hill, with Kinghurst Down Wood R., and having reached the summit, 507 feet, almost immediately commence the descent to Holne Bridge, about 300 feet below, and 1 m. distant. When this is reached we cross the Dart and follow the road to Holne Turn, 1¼ m. further on ; roads branch off at Horsehill and Hele Cross, but these points are marked with guide-posts. From the Turn we proceed as in Ex. 26.

Ex. 28.—*Holne Bridge, Chase Hill, New Bridge, Pound's Gate, Sherberton Common, Bel Tor, Dr. Blackall's Drive, Mil Tor (Sharp Tor,* Hexworthy District), *Gorge of the Dart,* 12 m.

This excursion will take us over that part of the moor situated between Pound's Gate and the Dart below Mil Tor, at the southern end of Widecombe parish. We shall enter upon the commons at New Bridge, 3½ m. from the town, retracing our steps over the road described at the end of Ex. 27.

[If preferred the rambler may make his way to the foot of New Bridge Hill by the Buckland road, as described in Ex. 27 and S. Ex. 92.]

Our first points will be Great Bridge, Headborough, and Holne Turn, as in Ex. 27. We then branch L., and passing the turnings at Hele Cross and Horsehill (guide-posts), shall reach Holne Bridge, 1¼ m. from the Turn. Hence we pass up Chase Hill, having North Park Wood, belonging to the Holne Park Estate, L., and the woods of Holne Chase R. Near the top of the hill, and again at its summit, a road branches L. (guide-posts), but these we pass and descend to New

Bridge, a structure of three arches, and having pointed buttresses. In places it is covered with ivy, and like most of the bridges in the Dartmoor country, presents a picturesque appearance. Crossing this we have in front of us a wide level, on the side of the steep slope beyond which is New Bridge Hill Cottage. Hannaford, once the seat of Sir Robert Torrens, and now the property of Mr. Bolitho, is L. of this. Further L., on the other side of the Dart, is seen the hill on which the village of Holne is situated, with Holne Cot near the summit, and R. of it, and still higher, the Vicarage (S. Ex. 96). According to peasant tradition the level was formerly a favourite gathering-place of the pixies, and many stories concerning the little people were once related in the locality. [*Pixies*, Chap. II.] Turning R. we make our way along the edge of New Bridge Marsh L., and at the end of it shall strike into the green path noticed in Ex. 27, which will lead us to the top of the hill above Leigh Tor, whence we follow the road to Pound's Gate.

[If the rambler goes by way of Buckland he will turn R. shortly after passing the foot of Leigh Tor, and climbing the side of the common with the rocks near him R. will soon reach the road, Ex. 27.]

The Tavistock Inn at Pound's Gate figures in local legend. It was at this hostelry that the Evil One, in the form of a dark horseman, stopped for refreshment when on his way to Widecombe on the afternoon of the dreadful thunderstorm in 1638, and paid the hostess with money that afterwards turned into dried leaves. [See the section in the *Bovey Tracey District on Hameldon and the Widecombe Valley*, and *Pixies*, Chap. II.]

Passing through the hamlet we shall notice the upping-stock, or mounting-block, near the post-office, and the pound on the L. of the way just beyond it, and which we have already mentioned (Ex. 27). Above this the road runs R. over the common to Leusdon and Ponsworthy (Ex. 27), but we shall keep straight up the hill, and passing the Wesleyan Chapel and Lower Uppacott, where is an approach L. to Lower Tor (*post*), shall soon reach a point where the road forks. The branch R. runs along the lower edge of Sherberton Common, and under Sherberton Farm to Lock's Gate Cross, but we continue to follow the Tavistock road L., which will speedily bring us also to Sherberton Common (Ex. 41). On this part of it, however, we shall find nothing to detain us.

During our progress from Leusdon Common to the point we have now reached a grand view has gradually unfolded itself, though it has necessitated our turning to look back upon it. Its main features are the same as those we noticed on our way from Leusdon to Pound's Gate (Ex. 27), but it is much more extensive. The view of the tors on the commons eastward of the Widecombe valley is particularly fine, and a wider range of country westward is visible.

The road we have hitherto followed forms part of R. 49 A. to which the reader is referred for a description of its continuation, as we now desert it. On the L., within a farm enclosure, is Bel Tor, which, although only a small pile, is sufficiently interesting to call for notice. A gate in the wall will enable the rambler to reach it. On the surface of a logan, curiously poised and appearing as though it would topple over at any moment, is a rock basin measuring 38 inches by 32, with shelving sides, and to this a tradition attaches. It used to be said that good fortune would await anyone seeing the reflection of the rising sun in the water collected in it. As health is more to be valued than wealth, and as early rising is conducive to the former, there is perhaps more truth in this than might at first appear. Two other rocks forming part of the tor are very strangely shaped, and on a pile

Combestone Tor.   Sharp Tor.

Holne Moor.

FROM BEL TOR, LOOKING W.

below them there are two other rock basins, one being 21 inches in diameter and 5 inches deep ; the other is smaller. In neither of these basins is there any appearance of the notch sometimes found on the edges of similar cavities.

At Bel Tor Corner, 1,148 feet, quite near to the pile, a road runs southward. This is Dr. Blackall's Drive (Ex. 27, S. Ex. 95), and we shall follow it between the walls of the farm enclosures to the common from the steep side of which Mil Tor looks down upon the Dart. Just before this pile is reached a track turns L. to Lower Tor, another of the many good examples of moorland farms in this neighbourhood. The porch bears the date 1707. The view from the point we have now reached is exceedingly fine. Below us the Dart courses through a deep and narrow gorge, on the further side of which are the rocks of Bench Tor, 560 feet above the river, and beyond it the wide expanse of Holne Moor (*Brent District*), backed by the dusky slopes that hide the solitary parts of the south quarter of the forest. Near to us on the R. is the bold pile of Sharp Tor, uplifting itself from the brow of the hill, and with its almost mountainous outline forming perhaps the most striking feature in the view. Below it is the winding gorge, and this we trace far downward to the L. This ravine is seen to great advantage from the road between Chase Gate and Holne village (S. Ex. 96), and is noticed in our excursions from Hexworthy.

If proof were needed that the formation of rock basins is due to natural causes Mil Tor, or Mel Tor, as it is sometimes called, would supply it. The disintegration of the granite here in process strikes the visitor at once, and when he climbs to the uppermost rock and finds four of these basins on its surface it is only what he might expect to see there. The largest is 32 inches by 20, and 6 inches deep, the next in size being 18 inches by 14, and 4 inches deep, and at the edge of each of them is a notch, or little channel, where the water has run off when falling rain has kept the basins full. The other two are smaller, and only one of them has a notch. Around them are a number of small

hollows, the rock altogether being of a very friable nature.   One large
mass which has fallen from the tor is split in two parts.   I first noticed
this in 1878, when it had not long been on the ground.

[Mil Tor Wood is below this fine pile.   Some interesting remains
east of the tor are noticed in the *Hexworthy District*, where also the
gorge is more fully described.   Sharp Tor, on the further side of the
combe W., down which flows the little Simon's Lake, also falls within
the limits of that district.   Ex. 41.]

Returning to Dr. Blackall's Drive we follow it S.E., with the
farm enclosures on our L., passing on the way an ancient pound, the
wall of which is in ruins.   About ¾ m. from the tor is Brake Corner,
where the road is carried round under Aish Tor, 922 feet, a small pile
of no particular interest.*   The visitor may now either follow the drive
to the main road, which he will reach a short distance from Pound's
Gate at the point noticed in Ex. 27, and make his way to New Bridge
as there directed, which will shorten the excursion by about ½ m. ; or
he may leave the drive when it begins to bend to the L. and descend
the steep side of the common nearly to the Dart, some 500 feet below.
If he decide upon this he will strike about S., and noticing the enclosures
of Hannaford will keep them close L.   Some way down the walls
form a sharp corner, below which, on the R., is a part of the river
known as Hannaford Stickles.   Still further down is Deadman's
Corner, and passing close to this the visitor will bend L. and soon strike
a track coming from Lower Hannaford, which he will follow to New
Bridge, ½ m. distant.

Routes to the town from New Bridge are given in Ex. 27.   New
Bridge to Ashburton, 3½ m. ; New Bridge to Buckland village, 2 m. ;
Buckland village to Ashburton, 3½ m.

HOLNE CHASE AND THE BUCKLAND WOODS.

The course of the Dart through the gorge below Sharp Tor and Mil
Tor, noticed in the preceding excursion, and also in the excursions
from Hexworthy, is S. of S.E.   At Wellsfoot Island, S. of the Hannaford enclosures, it turns towards the E., and about ¼ m. further on
again turns, and runs northward under Cleave Wood to New Bridge,
½ m. from the second bend.   In this part of its course the river sweeps
round the southern end of Widecombe parish, to which indeed it acts
as a boundary from Walla Brook Foot below Babeny to its confluence
with the Webburn.   On passing under New Bridge it pursues a north-
easterly course, afterwards turning on itself and flowing southward to
Holne Bridge, the distance covered by its windings being 3¼ m., although
these bridges, as we have already seen, are only 1½ m. apart.   The area
enclosed within this great loop forms the wild tract of heather and
wood known as Holne Chase, which has thus the Dart for its boundary
on three sides and the road between the bridges on the fourth.   Being
thus partly surrounded by water the name has been thought to be a

---

* Near by is Aish Farm, and another not far off is called Leigh
Tor.   But it is likely that in these instances the farms did not derive
their names from the tors, but that the reverse was the case.

corruption of *holm*, an island, and that the parish of Holne, in which the chase is situated, was called after it, but early forms of the name do not seem to support this view. It sometimes appears as Hole, which is the local pronounciation to-day, though this is usually broadened into Hall.* The length of the chase from N. to S. is over a mile, its average breadth being about ¾ m. Near its northern extremity, where it is less than ½ m. wide, is an ancient camp about 550 yards in circumference. This is one of those to which we have elsewhere alluded (S. Ex. 64) as existing on the eastern confines of the moor, others in the immediate neighbourhood being Place Wood Camp, Boro Wood Castle, and Hembury Castle, noticed further on. But Holne Chase Castle, as this camp is called, though resembling the others in construction, differs from them in not being a hill camp. It is only about 150 feet above the river, and is surrounded by higher ground on all sides.

The manor of Holne, which includes the chase, is said to have belonged to the Barony of Barnstaple, which was one of the possessions of Judhael, of Totnes, at the time of the Domesday Survey. It subsequently passed to the Audleys, and to the Bourchiers, Earls of Bath, from whom it descended to Sir Bourchier Wrey. Holne Park, south of the chase, and now separated from it by the road running up from Holne Bridge (R. 49 A), is mentioned in a suit, in 1631, as having been leased in the time of Henry VIII. to Thomas Prideaux, of Ashburton, for seventy years. This also came with the chase into the possession of Sir Bouchier Wrey. The properties are now owned by the Hon. Richard Dawson.

For abouf ¾ m. below New Bridge the Dart flows between Holne Chase and the common on which Leigh Tor is situated (Ex. 27). This then gives place to Park Wood, belonging to Spitchwick, soon after passing which the river receives the Webburn, here crossed by Buckland Bridge. From this point onward the steep hillside rising from the L. bank is clothed with trees, Hardridge Wood, Greypark Wood, Combe Wood, and Ausewell Wood, following each other, the three former being in the parish of Buckland, and the latter in the parish of Ashburton. They are usually known collectively as the Buckland Woods, and it is between these and the chase that the Dart runs from Buckland Bridge to Holne Bridge.

We have already stated (Ex. 27) that the manor of Buckland became the property of the Bastards. In the early part of the nineteenth century the representative of the family purchased the manor of Ausewell, which adjoined the property, and planted fir and other trees on the heathy land of which much of it consisted. In a note by the editor of the 1811 edition of Risdon's *Survey of Devon* the area thus covered is said to have been 700 acres. The present owner is the Rev. W. P. Bastard.

By the courtesy of their owners Holne Chase and the Buckland Woods are open to the public orf Tuesdays, Thursdays, and Saturdays,

---

* Derivations have also been suggested from *hol*, a hollow, cf. *holt* ; and from *holline*, holly—the latter being the most probable. According to a note in Carrington's *Dartmoor*, a tract near the chase was formerly known as Holly Chase, but I cannot find from any other source that this was so.

from May to October ; notices of the precise dates are posted at the entrances to the drives, and furnished to the principal hotels in the neighbourhood. To the chase both carriages and pedestrians are admitted, but carriages only may enter the drives. Two of these are carried along the wooded hillside, and a third runs near the river. It is the latter that the excursions coaches are permitted to use, and they enter at Buckland Lodge, which is reached from Buckland village by a steep descent (S. Ex. 92). But we propose to first visit Holne Chase and then crossing the Dart at New Bridge, make our way to the lodge by the road following the course of the river, and describe the coach run from that point.

Before setting out, however, it will be well to briefly notice the higher Buckland Drives. These are reached by way of Ausewell Gate, the first point being Water Turn, the way to which has already been described (Ex. 27). Here the gate L. is entered. A short distance beyond this the way forks, when the R. branch is followed. Further on the way again forks, the two branches forming the drives. These run parallel for some distance under Ausewell Common, the lower of the two passing quite close to Raven Rock mentioned hereafter. Above this is the cluster bearing the name of the Ausewell Rocks, though often called in the locality Hazel Tor.* These rocks are scattered about a small open space covered with heather, on the highest part of which, 1,041 feet, are two cairns. The view from this part of the woods is exceedingly fine. The higher of these two drives goes onward to Ausewell Cottage ; the other, keeping at a lower level, runs across Combe Wood ; beyond this they unite and reach the public road at Southbrook, not far from the bridge over the Ruddycleave Water, noticed in Ex. 27.

[Holne Bridge is 2 m. from Ashburton ; the length of the Holne Chase Drive from Holne Bridge to the New Bridge Lodge is 3 m. ; thence across New Bridge and down to Buckland Lodge, 1¼ m. ; the lower drive through the Buckland Woods from Buckland Lodge to Holne Bridge, 2 m. ; the circular drive is thus over 10 m.]

We shall enter Holne Chase at the gate near Holne Bridge, the road to which has already been described in Ex. 28. That there has long been such a means of crossing the Dart at this spot is shown by an entry in the registers of Bishop Stafford, dated August, 1413. A bridge that had previously existed here having been washed away, it was directed that the archdeacons should give notice of an indulgence to all the faithful who should contribute to the re-building of it. Thus by enabling some people to get over certain little difficulties others would be helped to get over the river. The *arch*deacons were very appropriately chosen. Crossing this picturesque structure, which consists of four arches, we enter the gate on the R., and following the drive for about ½ m. shall reach the main one that comes L. from the lodge on Chase Hill. Here we turn R., and passing the grounds of Chase House soon reach the wilder part of this ancient domain. As already stated, Holne Chase is partly encircled by the Dart, and carried very near to this is the drive we are now following. As we progress the objects on the Buckland side come into view, and are seen to

---

* The name also appears as Awsewell and Hazwell.

considerable advantage, but are described as we reach them in returning.

High up on the R., opposite Chase House, is Cleft Rock, and ½ m. further on Raven Rock, which presents a fine appearance from this part of the chase. A little further on our road runs quite near to the vallum of Holne Chase Castle, L. Some interesting relics were found in the chase in 1870. They consisted of about a dozen flat iron bars, and were discovered below the surface under a small heap of stones, placed on a large flat one. For long they were thought to be either unfinished swords, or pikes, but it has lately been suggested that they were " currency bars " of the Britons, notwithstanding that Cæsar says this people used brass or iron rings as money. But we understand this difficulty has been removed by arguing that the reading of the passage in which this statement occurs is incorrect ; that instead of " rings " we should read " bars." Unfortunately, we are unable to appeal to Cæsar to tell us what he really did write, but we read " rings " in our younger days, and that " bars " our reading anything else now. An account of the find by that well-known antiquary, the late Mr. P. F. S. Amery, of Druid, was read before the members of the Devonshire Association in 1906.

On passing below the camp there is a good view of the rock known as the Lovers' Leap on the northern side of the Dart. A little further on, and immediately below us, is Eagle Rock, under which the Dart makes its great bend. Here our road bends, too, and presently again leads us quite near to the castle, on the western side of which we now find ourselves. Across the river we see the charming combe through which the Ruddycleave Water descends foaming to the Dart, and as we advance the meeting-place of the Dart and the Webburn comes into view. Continuing on our way we notice the Spitchwick Lower Lodge on the further side of the stream, with Park Wood, which stretches nearly up to Pound's Gate, covering the side of the hill above it. The highest point of Chase Wood, which, however, is not much over 600 feet, is on our L., and near this are some remains of Chase Mine. Adits are also found in other parts of the wood, and a leat will be seen that formerly belonged to it, but this is now used for the purpose of conveying water to some fish-rearing ponds. Passing onward we soon reach the lodge near New Bridge, on the road described in Ex. 28.

[The excursion coaches usually stop here for a short time when on the return journey from Buckland to Ashburton, to enable tourists to visit the chase. It is a good plan to walk through it and meet the coach, which goes by way of the public road, at the foot of Chase Hill. Should the visitor decide upon this he will pass the objects just noticed in the following order. About ½ m. from the lodge, Spitchwick Lower Lodge across the Dart L. ; Chase Wood R. ; ¼ m. on confluence of the Dart and Webburn L. ; ¼ m. further, Ruddycleave Water L. ; Holne Chase Castle R. ; ¼ m. Eagle Rock close L., with bend of the Dart ; Lovers' Leap across the river L. ; ½ m., Raven Rock, high amid the trees L. ; ½ m., Cleft Rock L. ; Holne Chase House R. ; straight on for the lodge on Chase Hill ; or turn L. for the gate at Holne Bridge.]

Turning R. at the lodge a few steps bring us to New Bridge, which we cross and follow the road R., as in Ex. 28. Very soon we approach the river at a bend called New Bridge Hill Corner, where it suddenly turns towards the E., and again bends northward at Higher Corner Pool. Here on the L. is the steep road leading up to Pound's Gate, but we keep on past Deeper Marsh with the Dart R. We shall not have proceeded far before we notice an ancient circular enclosure on the R. of the way. This is sometimes referred to as Leigh Tor Pound, and also at Deeper Marsh Pound. Near this are several islands, and just below them another bend in the river, at what is known as the Lower Corner Pool, where there are more islands. Before reaching the latter we pass under Leigh Tor, a short distance beyond which is Spitchwick Lower Lodge L. About ¼ m. further on we find ourselves at Buckland Bridge, in the midst of a charming scene. It is thrown over the Webburn immediately above the confluence of that stream and the Dart ; on one hand is seen the narrow valley through which thĕ tributary comes down, and on the other the meeting-place of the waters, the last-named forming the subject of some lines by Keble. (The two Webburns are noticed in the *Excursions from Widecombe*, and in Ex. 27). Crossing the bridge we speedily arrive at Buckland Lodge, where we leave the road we have been following. This climbs up through the wood L. to the Higher Lodge at Buckland village, rather over ¾ m. distant, and 500 feet above us (Ex. 27, S. Ex. 93).

As we have already stated it is the lower one of the three Buckland Drives over which the excursion coaches go, and they enter at the lodge we have now reached. For about ¼ m. the road runs along the edge of Hardridge Wood, with the Dart close on the R., and then Warren Bridge is crossed, where the Ruddycleave Water (Ex. 26, 27) comes down through a ferny hollow to fall into the larger stream. Now we are in Greypark Wood, from which we look across the chase to the steeps beyond it, where the Raven Rock, a mass of grey, thrusts itself out from its leafy environment. Ere we have gone far from the bridge we reach that part of the river where it changes its course. Hitherto it has been flowing towards the north ; we now see its waters running in a southerly direction. At the bend is the fine Eagle Rock, which we passed in the chase ; a fitting natural outwork to the ancient encampment on the slope above it. Here we see it draped with ivy and other plants, and the graceful quickbeam, to give the mountain ash its moorland name.

When we begin to set our faces southward we approach the most striking rock mass in this winding valley. It is known as the Lovers' Leap, and the story attached to so many rocks of a similar character, not only in England, but in other countries, is related in connection with it. But whether this was formerly a spot to which despairing lovers in general made their way in order to throw themselves, Sappho-like, into the waters, or whether it was so named from a particular pair of lovers, we cannot say, since tradition is silent on the subject. This fine rock projects itself from the steep hillside, and the Dart makes a bold sweep round it. It rises almost perpendicularly from the waters to a considerable height. In places its sides are covered with creeping plants, and small trees and bushes grow from the clefts. The drive here deserts the river for a short distance, and is carried above the rock, In passing this an upright iron bar may be seen, which was placed here to mark the spot on which the Prince Consort stood when he visited the woods, by George Sparks, a former well-known whip of Ashburton, who drove his Royal Highness on that occasion.

Leaving this striking scene we pass down the valley with the Dart again for our companion, and speedily come in sight of a great crag on the hillside some 400 feet above the river. This is the Raven Rock, but it is hardly seen to such advantage here as from the points from which we have already beheld it. One part of this mass used to be known as the Duke's Nose. Viewed from a certain spot the rock presents a rude resemblance to the human face in profile, and in this, as in the case of the Rock on Roborough Down (*Yelverton District*), imagination has been able to detect the features of the Duke of Wellington. This rocky pinnacle looks down upon a part of the Dart marked by the Long Island in its channel.

During our progress along the bank of the river we have been able to obtain many good views of the chase, and shall have noticed that it is of a wilder character than the woods on the Buckland side, and this will again become evident as we pass on through Ausewell Wood. About ½ m. from the Raven Rock, and when opposite to Holne Chase House, we pass the Cleft Rock, which is about 200 feet above the drive, and here near the river are the remains of a building that show that in days gone by men were attracted to this wood by something besides the scenery. Within the scanty vestiges of a blowing-house is a cavity about four feet deep, which seems to have been a furnace. It is oval in shape, and measures 4 feet by 2 feet 9 inches. Quite near to this are the ruined walls of another small building, and there are also the remains of a leat and a large heap of slag. These ruins were discovered buried beneath debris by Mr. P. F. S. Amery.

In some far away time the channel of the Dart was here much higher than it is at present. This is shown by a bed of gravel above the left bank, a little below the point we have now reached.

On leaving Ausewell Wood the drive passes across two fields to the gate opening on the public road near the northern end of Holne Bridge. The way to the town is described at the end of Ex. 27, the points passed being Holne Turn and Headborough.

(Near the southern end of Holne Bridge, where Chase Hill makes a very sharp bend, is the lodge at the entrance to Holne Park).

SHORTER EXCURSIONS.

[The route to Bag Tor Mill and Ilsington is described in S. Ex. 89, and this connects the *Ashburton* and *Bovey Districts*. S. Ex. 96 shows the route to Holne Moor, and connects *Ashburton* with the *Brent District*. Other links between these districts are formed in the usual manner by the excursions and routes.]

S. Ex. 88.—*Place Wood Camp, Halshanger, and Boro Wood Castle*, 5 m. Opposite to the Golden Lion Hotel a branch from East Street leads to Roborough Lane. This is crossed by the road coming L. from the Terrace Walk, formed in the earlier part of the last century by Lord Clinton, and the point may also be gained from Great Bridge by following that delightful promenade, which commences there. Proceeding northward Langstone Cross is soon reached (guide-post). ¼ m. N. of this the road skirts Woodencliff Wood L. At a little distance on the R. is Place Wood, and between this and the road are the remains of an ancient hill fort. These are not extensive, and when in a complete state the camp was apparently not more than 300 yards in circumference.

[The camp may be reached by a footpath from Great Bridge. This runs under the Terrace Walk, afterwards crossing the road close to Cuddyford Bridge. which spans the Yeo. The path then runs northward to the road at Woodencliff Wood. Cuddyford is suggestive of an ogre who was formerly said to haunt this part of the Yeo, one Cutty Dyer, the terror of children in the days of our grandfathers.]

Following the road from the camp N. the visitor will be led between Higher and Lower Brownswell to Ashburton Down, a little over 1½ m. from the town. The down, most of which is now enclosed, is on the R. Here is a guide-post, and another at Owlacombe Cross, a short distance further on. At the second the visitor will turn L., and in about ½ m. will reach Halshanger Cross. The road going straight up the hill soon enters on the common near the Belt (Ex. 26), but this must not be followed. Turn L. to Rushlade, and pass down the hill, as in Ex. 26, to Boro Wood R., which is reached soon after crossing Waterleat Bridge. At the lower end of the wood, not far from Lurgecombe Mill, there is a gate opening into it. A path runs from this very nearly up to the old camp which takes its name from the wood. It is altogether a much finer example than the other, and is nearly ½ m. in circumference. From Lurgecombe Mill the way to the town is described in the excursion just named.

S. Ex. 89.—*The Commons of Horridge and Halshanger*, 8½ m. With route to Ilsington, 5½ m. from Ashburton. The first point is Rushlade (Ex. 26). The visitor will then continue straight on N. past Halshanger Cross to Langworthy Bridge and Mountsland. Just beyond the latter is the hamlet of Horridge. where a gate L. gives access to Horridge Common. On entering we shall bear westward for a short distance, when we shall strike a group of hut circles, and about 300 yards N. of these shall find another group. Bearing a little W. of N. we ascend the hill with Bag Tor Wood below us R., and when we have reached the western edge of this shall look down over Bag Tor Down N. (Ex. 25, S. Ex. 80). N.E. across the little valley is Bag Tor, and to the R. of it Mill Wood and Crownley Parks ; northward are seen Saddle Tor and Hey Tor.

The road to Ilsington runs on from Horridge to Westabrook, and thence by the entrance to Bag Tor to Bag Tor Mill. Just beyond this is Burchanger Cross, from which the village is about 1 m. distant. The route is described the reverse way in S. Ex. 81, and the points named are noticed in the *Ilsington District*.

[Bag Tor Down may be reached from the Ilsington road by following it to Westabrook, instead of turning into the common at Horridge. A path which passes through Bag Tor Wood to the down runs from Westabrook courtyard, but as it is not a public one, it will be necessary to obtain permission to go that way.]

Turning S., but bearing a little W., we shall pass down the hill to the source of the Yeo, ¾ m. from Water Rushes (Ex. 26). This stream rises just within the confines of Horridge Common, and crossing the end of Mountsland Common, enters Halshanger Common, the boundary of which is here marked by a wall running S., and to this point we shall follow it.

[If it be desired to embrace Rippon Tor and the Nutcracker (Ex. 26) in this excursion the visitor will pass up to the former from the western corner of Bag Tor Wood, from which it is distant ¾ m. N.W. On leaving the tor turn S. to the gate close to the logan, and then passing through one of the gaps in the wall strike S.E. for about ¾ m. to the Yeo, which will be reached near the point where it enters Halshanger Common.]

Crossing the Yeo we strike due S., having for a short distance the wall on our L., and in ½ m. shall reach the small ruined building known as the Old Summer House. This is now a mere shell, circular in shape, and 9½ feet in interior diameter. There is a chimney, the remains of a window, and a doorway. The view from the old house is remarkably fine, for though it is not by any means on the highest part of Halshanger Common it is yet so happily placed that it commands many striking objects in the surrounding country. Haldon, with the distant farm lands beyond it, is seen north-eastward ; the estuary of the Teign, presenting all the appearance of a lake, E. by S. ; Torquay, Ashburton, Buckfastleigh, and Dean, from S.E. by E. to S. by W., with the South Hams extending from the valley of the Dart westward and to the sea ; Brent Hill and Ugborough Beacon Rocks rise up S.S.W. ; and thence northward stretches a tract of wooded and semi-wild country, backed in places by the moor.

The gate at Water Rushes is a little over ¼ m. due W. of the Summer House, but it will be better for the visitor to strike N. of that line, as the ground is boggy near the Yeo. By keeping higher he will reach that stream above the mire, and crossing will make his way down the R. bank to the gate. Form this point the route to Ashburton is described in Ex. 26, the way lying by the Belt and through Green Lanes to Rushlade, and thence through the valley of the Yeo.

S. Ex. 90 —*To Hemsworthy Gate*, 4¾ m. from Ashburton. This point, which is named so frequently in the excursions in the *Bovey District*, is reached by way of Rushlade (Ex. 26) and Cold East Cross (R. 5), or by Welstor Cross (S. Ex. 92, R. 53). From the cross the Chagford road (R. 53) is followed northward to the gate, 1¼ m. distant. Here the boundary of Widecombe parish, marked by stones, comes up from the S.W. (Ex. 26) to a bondstone in the wall, known as Stittleford's Cross. A small incised cross will be seen on its face, together with the initials R.M. [*Crosses*, Chap. XVI.] The boundary line then runs N.W. by N., being marked by the wall, and a short distance beyond Seven Lords' Lands (S. Ex. 82) turns abruptly E. to Hawkeswell at the source of the Becky Brook (Ex. 25). The route to Widecombe from Hemsworthy Gate, which passes near the Ruggle Stone, is shown in S. Ex. 82, 87.

S. Ex. 91.—*To Widecombe*, 6 m. from Ashburton. *The route for Hameldon and Grim's Pound.* The first point is Cold East Cross (See Ex. 26 ; guide-post). Then take the road N.W. down to Ruddycleave Bridge. At the guide-post on Pudsham Down just above this turn R. ; ¼ m. on the road bends L., and leaving Scobetor L. descends the hill to Chittleford ; pass through this to Venton (S. Ex. 87), a short distance beyond which is the Ruggle Stone Inn (the logan of that name is on the common R., and quite near) ; cross Venton Bridge to the village. For routes to Hameldon and Grim's Pound from Widecombe see S. Ex. 84.

S. **Ex.** 92.—*Buckland Beacon, Buckland-in-the-Moor, and New Bridge*, 10 m. As the route to Ausewell Cross, which is close to Welstor Cross, our first point, has already been sketched in Ex. 27, we shall now make our way to the latter by way of Rewdown Cross, and for this purpose shall first proceed to Pitt Farm, a short distance N. of Great Bridge. Here a footpath L. will take us to the road a little E. of the cross, which is marked by a guide-post. Taking the R. branch we pass up the hill with Druid a short distance L., and Boro Wood Castle in the wood above us R. (S. Ex. 88), and noticing the Druid Plantations L., in which is an old copper mine, shall shortly reach Welstor Cross. The road runs L. to Ausewell Cross, but we shall keep R., or northward, and speedily reach the commons, which are here enclosed by a wall L. In this, however, there are three gates, and on reaching the first we enter and pass up the slope W., with the Rifle Range R., to Welstor Rock. In front of us is another wall, in which there is also a gate, and on passing through this we shall find ourselves close to Buckland Beacon. This small group of rocks attains an elevation of 1,282 feet, and though presenting nothing striking in itself, should by all means be visited on account of the particularly fine view commanded from it. The wooded valley of the Dart to the S.W., with the meanderings of the river, at once arrests attention. On the L. of this part of the picture, nearly due S. and only 1 m. distant, the Ausewell Rocks are seen rising amidst the trees (*Buckland Woods* Section); due W., and the same distance from us, is the tower of Buckland Church, with Leusdon Church on the further side of the valley (Ex. 27). Beyond the Ausewell Rocks, and over 3 m. from them, is Buckfastleigh Church (S. Ex. 98), and still further away to the S.S.W. the conspicuous Brent Hill (*Brent District*). Rising against the sky to the L. of Buckland Church is the dull sweep of Holne Moor, W.S.W (*The Moors of Holne and Buckfastleigh ; Brent District*), with North Hisworthy above Princetown (*Princetown. District*) far away to the R. of it, and almost due W. Thence the eye ranges northward until it rests on lonely Cut Hill, N.W. by W., 10½ m. away as the crow flies (Ex. 11) ; the low mound of turf on its summit, which is seen from so many parts of the moor, can readily be distinguished. N. by W. Hameldon lifts up his great rounded form (*Hameldon and the Widecombe Valley* ; S. Ex. 84) ; north-eastward is the high land of Haldon, seen away to the R. of Rippon Tor (Ex. 26), which rises N.E. by N. less than 2 m. from us. Further to the R. is the Channel, with the coast line from Beer Head, near the mouth of the Axe, to the estuary of the Exe. From Exmouth we trace the coast downward to the Bolt Head and Bigbury Bay, when intervening hills hide it from view. Lying snugly in the valley S.E. by S. is the town of Ashburton.

The wall to the E. of the Beacon forms the boundary between the parishes of Ashburton and Buckland-in-the-Moor. This line descends the steep hillside to the Dart, which it reaches immediately above the Lovers' Leap. Early in the reign of James I. these two commons were the subject of a suit in the Exchequer, the dispute having reference to this part of them. We keep the wall L. on leaving the Beacon, and passing a bondstone in it called the Grey Mare, and a spring known as Stidwell, which forms another mark, descend the steep pinch, with some small enclosures L., to a gate opening on the road from Ausewell

Cross to Buckland. Here we turn R. and make our way to the village as in Ex. 27.

[Should the visitor not desire to include Buckland in his walk he will turn L. on reaching the road, and follow it to Ausewell Cross, ½ m. Thence the return to the town is as given at the end of Ex. 26. This will shorten the distance by 4 m.]

Buckland has already been noticed in Ex. 27, and it only remains to speak of the road running from it down to the Webburn and onward to New Bridge. This leaves the church on the R., and descends a very steep hill, with Hardridge Wood L. Great Lot Wood (Ex. 27) covers the side of the valley R., and through this there was formerly a drive to which the public were admitted. It was closed in consequence of the road being greatly damaged by a flood. At the bottom of the hill is Buckland Lodge, and near it R. the bridge over the Webburn, noticed in the *Holne Chase* Section. Crossing this our road will lead us by the river past Spitchwick Lower Lodge R., and under Leigh Tor (Ex. 27). A little further on the Dartmeet road turns up the hill R. (Ex. 28), but we pass onward, keeping the river L., and soon reach New Bridge.

We may now retrace our steps, and return *via* Buckland, as in the *Holne Chase* Section and S. Ex. 93, or proceed direct to the town by way of Chase Hill, as in 6 A and Ex. 27. The former will be the longer route ; see end of Ex. 28.

S. Ex. 93.—*Round Holne Chase and the Buckland Woods by the Public Road*, 9 m. Fine views of the Chase and woods are obtained from the public roads that encircle them. The visitor will first make his way to Holne Bridge and over Chase Hill to New Bridge, as in Ex. 28. From this point he will proceed to Buckland Lodge, following the directions given in the *Holne Chase* Section. He will then ascend the hill between Hardridge Wood R. and Great Lot Wood L. (S. Ex. 92) to Buckland village, noticed in Ex. 27. From the church the visitor will follow the road running S.E., and crossing the Ruddycleave Water and passing Southbrook will reach Ausewell Cross in about 1½ m., the way being the reverse of that described in Ex. 27. It was on the commons near here that a hearse and four horses were seen moving slowly over the snow on the night that Colonel Bastard died. People said that the steeds were spectral ones, and indeed there were a certain few who could vouch for it that spirits were at the bottom of the matter, These latter were jovial fellows who had some acquaintance with the coast.

The route to the town from Ausewell Cross is described in Ex. 26. Part way down the hill Higher Ausewell is passed R., and further from the road is Ausewell Down (*Holne Chase* Section), Just below, but on the L., is Highgrove, and a little further removed, Druid, the residence of Mr. John S. Amery, to which we have already referred.

S. Ex. 94.—*Dartmeet*, 8 m. from Ashburton. The way lies by Holne Bridge and New Bridge, through Pound's Gate to Sherberton Common, the route given in Ex. 28 being followed to Bel Tor Corner. From that point R. 49 A will show the way. (It is noticed in the *Hexworthy District*).

S. Ex. 95.—*The Gorge of the Dart and Dr. Blackall's Drive*, 9½ m. These have already been noticed in Ex. 28. The directions given in that excursion will be followed until the visitor reaches New Bridge. He will then turn L and make his way past the fish pond (where the road runs up R. to Hannaford) to the common near Wellsfoot Island, at the second bend of the Dart. Turning northward, with the enclosures R. and the river L., he will enter the gorge, and make his way past Hannaford Stickles to a part of the river in which there are several islands. (These are noticed in our description of the gorge in the *Hexworthy District*, to which the visitor is referred should he desire to make his way further up this fine ravine). Turning from the Dart the visitor will climb the steep hillside R. to Dr. Blackall's Drive, which he will strike where it winds below the little pile of Aish Tor. Here he will turn R. and either follow the drive to the road, or make a short cut to the latter down the hill R., leaving the Hannaford enclosures on that side. The return route *via* New Bridge is given in Ex. 27 and R. 6 A. See also end of Ex. 28.

S. Ex. 96.—*Holne and Holne Moor Gate*, 10½ m. The visitor will follow the road to Holne Bridge as described in Ex. 28 and ascend Chase Hill, passing the lodge R., to the fork, where is a guide-post, ¾ m. from the bridge. Here he will branch L., and just beyond a second guide-post will reach Chase Gate. 300 yards further on is a third guide-post, where the R. branch must be chosen, and passing Green Down L. the visitor will shortly reach a fourth post, where the road turns L. to Holne village, which is close by. There is a fine view of the Dart gorge after passing Chase Gate. Holne is a small border village of very pleasing appearance. Most of the cottages have little gardens in front of them, and when the flowers are in bloom a charming picture greets the eye of the visitor. There is an old-fashioned inn, with a wide porch and parvise room, and a large open space in front of it. The church, which belonged to Buckfast Abbey, is situated near it on rather higher ground, and is late decorated. There is a particularly fine screen, and a good pulpit. In the lower panels of the former is a series of painted figures of saints. a list of which may be seen by the visitor. In the churchyard is a cross, which was restored some years ago, and also the grave-stone of Edward Collins, one time landlord of the village inn, who died in December, 1780. The lines it bears have repeatedly appeared, but have evidently been copied by the various writers who have given them from a source other than the stone. At all events, I have never seen them given exactly as they appear upon it, and, indeed, it would now be difficult to decipher all the words. Many years ago, however, I was able to do this, and the rendering in my book on the stone crosses of Dartmoor (Chap. X.), and which is here reproduced, may be relied upon as being correct :

> Here lies Poor Old Ned,
> On his last Mattrass bed,
> During life he was honest and free ;
> He knew well the Chace
> But has now run his Race
> And his Name was COLLINS *D'ye fee.*

. . . . . Dec^r., 1780. Aged 77.

The Ram Feast, or Holne Ram Roasting as it came to be termed, had several years ago degenerated into a mere meaningless feature in a village festival, being held in connection with steeplechases and sports of a kindred nature. But many years ago we knew those who remembered when it was observed with something like its original simplicity. The feast took place on old Midsummer Day, when early in the morning a party would set off to the moor, and the first ram that could be caught was taken to a field called Play Park, close to the village, and in which it has been said a menhir used to stand. There the animal was killed and roasted. That this rude custom was a survival of a religious celebration there is little doubt, but those who observed it in later times were ignorant that it once had a meaning. Latterly the ram, which was provided beforehand, was roasted on Green Down.

Instead of returning to the road where we left it at the guide-post we shall pass up N. of the church, and regain it a little further on. Here we find ourselves at the lodge at the entrance to Holne Cot, which is pleasantly situated on the hillside a short distance below. The road to the house also leads to a fisherman's path by the river which runs up through the gorge to Dartmeet, and is open on Mondays, Wednesdays, Fridays, and Saturdays, from the 1st March to 30th September. Turning L. we pass onward to where our road is joined by another coming up L. from Langaford Hill (*post*), and here is the entrance to Holne Vicarage R. This will always possess a peculiar interest as being the spot where Charles Kingsley was born, though the present is not the actual house. That was taken down and rebuilt in 1832, thirteen years after Kingsley's birth, which event took place while his father had temporary charge of the parish.

Passing up the hill the visitor will reach Holne Moor Gate in ¼ m. Just before he comes to it he will notice a gate R., belonging to Stoke Farm, where he should pause for awhile to look upon the view commanded from it. Certainly there is no finer one throughout the Dartmoor borderland. All the prominent heights over which our rambles from Ashburton have extended are seen, together with Hameldon and the rocky crests on the eastern side of the Widecombe valley, while the picture of the Buckland Woods and Holne Chase is superb.

(The Ashburton visitor has been brought to this point in case he should desire to include Holne Moor in his rambles. This is described, together with Buckfastleigh Moor, in a section included in the *Brent and Ivybridge District*. See also R. 49 B. and C).

From Holne Moor Gate the visitor may return to Ashburton by retracing his steps over the Holne Bridge road, following the instructions given in R. 6 B, or he may go by way of Buckfast as shown in R. 6 C. The latter route will take him first to Play Cross, and down Langaford Hill, thence past Hawson Farm L., near the gate of which is a cross built into the wall (*Crosses*, Chap. X.) Just beyond this is Brook R., and Hawson Court L. The way then runs down the hill to Burchetts Lodge, soon afterwards climbing up the cross-roads known as Hockmoor Head, rather less than ½ m. further on, where is a guide-post. Here the rambler will turn L., and at the distance of about ⅓ m. will turn R., almost immediately afterwards again turning L. At this point, which is called Fritz's Grave, there is a guide-post. The way then runs up past the Grange, just beyond which a road branches R. Pass this and take the next turning R. through Buckfast to Dart Bridge. Cross this and follow the high road to Ashburton.

as in R. 66. This will add about 1½ m. to the ramble. (For Buck-fastleigh keep straight on from Hockmoor Head. At the next fork the L. branch leads to the church and the town ; the R. branch direct to the town).

The visitor may vary the route to Holne by following the road to New Bridge, but this must not be crossed. Just before it is reached a path will be seen L. leading up through Cleave Wood (R. 33), which will bring him to the fields close to Holne Cot. On the way he will obtain some good glimpses of the Dart, passing Salters Pool and the Horseshoe Falls. Above the Cot he will reach the road near Holne village.

S. Ex. 97.—*Hembury Castle and Buckfast*, 9 m. As in the preceding route the visitor will first make his way to the fork near the top of Chase Hill, and pass on by Chase Gate. At the fork, 300 yards beyond this he will strike L. over a little open space bearing the name of Gallant le Bower, whence there is a remarkably fine view of the Widecombe valley N. There is a guide-post where it is entered, and another a little further on. At the second one follow the road S.E., and in about 1 m. Hembury Castle, 4½ m. from Ashburton, will be seen L. This ancient hill fort is situated on high ground between the valley of the Dart E., and the Holy Brook, a tributary of the former. On the E. side the ground is very steep, and covered with the coppice known as Hembury Woods, and this also clothes the sides of the camp. In the Dart, at the foot of the hill, is Black Pool Island, and just below this the river changes its southerly course to an easterly one. Lysons computed the area of Hembury to be about seven acres. There is a very strong rampart, with wide and deep ditches, and an inner mound on its western side. Tradition speaks of it as a Danish camp. It has been remarked by Mr. R. J. King that there is scarcely an earthwork throughout the county to which the Danes have not been linked, and this he regards as a proof of the strong impression made by their attacks. On the other hand Mr. Thomas Wright, in a paper on the *History of the English Language*, considers that much more has been ascribed to the Danes than they have any claim to. The story goes that it was taken from them by a stratagem. Some women of the neighbourhood allowed themselves to be captured and conveyed to the camp, and rising in the night when the occupants were sunk in a deep sleep induced by the fumes of wine, slew them, and admitted their com-patriots. Some oval stones and a bronze celt were discovered here many years ago.

On leaving Hembury the visitor will descend the steep road to Holy Brook, and crossing this will speedily reach Fritz's Grave, where he will turn L. to Buckfast.

Very few remains of the Abbey of Buckfast now exist. Just before reaching the hamlet the visitor will pass the Grange, where the abbey barn may be seen, and a part of the abbots' lodgings, consisting of a tower, is also standing. It is said to have been founded by Cynewulf King of Wessex, in 760, but while there is no satisfactory evidence of this there is some that it was founded prior to the time of Alfred. It was established for Benedictine monks, and afterwards re-founded for Cistercians, in 1137, or in 1148. The Cistercians, as we have before remarked, were great traders, and those of Buckfast (early forms of which name were Bucfestre and Bulfestra) were dealers in wool (T. 1). In 1236 they were admitted to the Guild Merchants of Totnes. The last abbot prior to the Dissolution was Gilbert Doune, who was appointed in 1535, and three years later, on the 24th February, 1538, surrendered the abbey to the Commissioners of Henry VIII. For 365 years the abbey had no existence, and then, on the 24th February, 1903, the first abbot of a revived order of Benedictines was installed.

It was in 1882 that the site of the old abbey was purchased on behalf of the community of monks now residing there. The foundations of the old buildings were unearthed, and a new abbey erected upon them, so that the modern structure is similar in design, as far as it possibly can be, to the older one.

There is a tradition that the apparition of a certain Sir William Kingdon, who had been a benefactor to the abbey, used to appear on the night of the 3rd July in the church, on the spot where he had been buried, and that the monks came to believe that he had been guilty of a crime that troubled his soul.

Buckfast Abbey had a close connection with Dartmoor, for Holne Moor, or perhaps it might be more correct to say a part of it, as well as Buckfastleigh Moor and Brent Moor, belonged to it. (*Brent District*).

On leaving Buckfast the visitor will make his way to Dart Bridge, and return to Ashburton by the high road as in R. 66.

S. Ex. 98.—*Buckfastleigh*, 7 m. The way to this town is shown in R. 47. Buckfastleigh has long been celebrated for its manufacture of serge, the woollen industry having probably existed here since the days of the Cistercians at Buckfast (T. 1, S. Ex. 97). A market was granted to the abbot in 1352, and a fair, to continue for three days, in 1459. A market and a fair were also granted to " the Abbot and Convent of the house and Church of the Blessed Mary of Buckfast," to be held in the manor of Kingsbridge, which belonged to the abbey. The church is situated on a hill, apart from the town, and is approached on one side by a road and on another by a flight of steps, 195 in number. The tower is surmounted with a spire, the only example in the Dartmoor country. Tradition states that it was intended to erect the building on a site nearer to the town, but that the Evil One removed the stones as fast as they were placed in position to the hill on which it now stands. (cf. *Brent Tor and Plympton*). In the churchyard are the remains of an ancient building, and an old cross said to have been brought from Dartmoor. [*Crosses*, Chap. X.] The hill on the side nearest Buckfast has been extensively quarried.

If the visitor ascends to the church by the steps he must look for them shortly after entering the town. They will be seen on the R. of the road. On leaving the church he will follow the road W., and taking care not to turn R., will be led directly to the higher part of the town. The return to Ashburton will be as in the preceding excursion.

The route to Buckfastleigh from Holne Moor Gate has been given in S. Ex. 96. In going to the gate the visitor will leave the town at its northern end, and make his way up by Bilberry Hill to Hockmoor Head. Thence keep straight on with Hawson Court R., and Brook L. The ascent of the steep Langaford Hill has next to be made ; at Play Cross the village of Holne is close by R. Keep straight up the road to the gate. Carriages should either turn L. just after passing

Hawson Farm and go through Scorriton, or R. at the foot of Langa
ford Hill.

ROUTES FROM ASHBURTON.

R. 47.—To Brent and Ivybridge, S.W. *Dart Bridge, Buckfast-
leigh, Dean (old road to Brent through Harbournford), Whiteoxen,
Palstone* (branch R. for *Brent*), *Brent Bridge, Wrangaton, Bittaford
Bridge.* Brent, 8¼ m. ; Ivybridge. 13 m. Reverse, R. 66.

[Objects : Ex. 32, seen from near Wrangaton.]

This is a road route, and few directions are needed. The visitor
will leave the town by way of West Street and Pear Tree Cross. The
road then runs southward to the Dart, which is crossed at Dart Bridge
(S. Ex. 96, 97). Passing through Buckfastleigh (S. Ex. 98) the visitor
will soon reach the little village of Dean, where the old coach road,
which runs through Brent, branches off. (This is a rather nearer
way to that village than the new road, and is much more interesting.
The rambler will pass up the long, but not steep, hill to Clampit's
Stile, and shortly after passing this will descend upon the hamlet of
Harbournford, where the Harbourn is crossed by a footbridge. Brent
is 2 m. further on. This road is noticed in our description of the Brent
District).

The new road runs about S. from Dean, and for the first mile is
quite level. Dean Prior Church (S. Ex. 100) is then passed, and shortly
afterwards the road runs under Whiteoxen Arch. Beyond this it
passes the grounds of Marley, and when these are left behind the
country becomes more open, and Brent Hill is seen not far to the R.
About 1¼ m. further on a farm will be noticed close to the road L.
This is Palstone, and ¼ m. beyond it is a cross-road, where the visitor
bound to Brent will turn R. The road to Ivybridge shortly afterwards
passes through Brent Mill and over Brent Bridge, and 1½ m. further
on reaches Wrangaton. 1¼ m. beyond this is Bittaford Bridge, where
the Lud Brook is crossed, and from which Ivybridge is 2 m. distant.

R. 48.—To Plympton and Shaugh, S.W. by W. For points on
the road to Plympton, 19½ m., see R. 47, 55 ; on the way to Shaugh,
17½ m., the following are the points from Dean onward :—*Warn Bridge,
Gigley Bridge, Yolland, Shipley Bridge, Zeal Bridge, Hickley Plain,
Three Barrows, Stall Moor, High-house Waste, Pen Beacon, Emmett's
Post, Shaugh Moor.* Reverse, R. 73.

[Objects : Exs. 29, 30, 31, 32, 33, 34, 36.]

The route to Plympton consists of R. 47 and R. 55, q.v.

Routes to Shaugh are given from Brent and from Ivybridge,
R. 56, 57 ; the former is the more convenient for the rambler from
Ashburton. But in case a route going deeper into the moorlands
should be desired the following is furnished. It will be well, however,
not to choose it if the streams are likely to be in flood, as the Erme
and the Yealm have to be crossed.

The rambler will branch R. from the Ivybridge road at Dean, as
in the preceding route, but instead of following the wide road that
leads to Brent, will strike into a lane R. close by some cottages, and in
about ½ m. will be led into another lane, when he will turn L. Passing
over Warn Bridge at the lower end of the valley of Dean Burn

(S. Ex. 100) he will pass up the hill W. by S., leaving the hamlet of Dean Combe L. Turning neither to the R. nor to the L. he will, at the distance of 1½ m. from the bridge, reach a lane running at right angles to the one he is following (see R. 33, and S. Ex. 103). Here he will turn L., and proceed for a few score yards, when he will turn R., and descend to Gigley Bridge. At the top of the lane beyond the bridge is a small green, with a gate opening upon a stroll, R. This he will pass through, and descend the stroll, at the further end of which is Dockwell Gate. He will not go quite so far as this, however, but will enter a gate L., and follow the track (T. 59) to Yolland Farm. Passing the fine grove of trees and through the yard the further entrance gate will soon be reached. Just beyond this the rambler must turn R. at Yolland Cross, and in ¾ m. will pass through a moor gate, and find himself at Shipley Bridge (S. Ex. 106). This he will cross, and turning L. will once more enter upon a lane at Shipley Gate, with Zeal Farm R. Just beyond the farmyard he will cross Zeal Bridge, and enter a gate R., and passing through two fields will reach a hunting-gate, and gain the moor. His course will now be up the steep side of Hickley Ridge to Hickley Plain and Red Brook, due W. He will only follow up the stream for a short distance, his course still being W., and his mark the lofty Three Barrows. This he will reach soon after crossing the Bala Brook Head track (T. 61). From Three Barrows the frontier height of Pen Beacon is plainly seen W., but though this is on his route the rambler must not make for it direct. He will steer W. by N., and crossing the Blackwood Path (T. 63) descend the steep side of the hill to the Erme. His mark should be a gully on the further bank, and about ½ m. above the wall of Piles Newtake (Ex. 32, 33). Down this runs a small stream, and near where it falls into the Erme that river can generally be crossed. On climbing the west bank of the river he must steer due W. across Stall Moor, with Pen Beacon in full view. He will cross the track running out to Erme Pound (T. 66, Ex. 33) and the branch leading towards Yealm Head. The Yealm (1½ m. from the Erme) should be crossed a short distance above Dendles Wood. Then the rambler will pass over Dendles Waste and Hawns to Broadall Lake (T. 67). The way then lies over High-house Waste, which is bounded on the west by a small stream. Pen Beacon (R. 7, 59 ; Ex. 34) is just above this, and on reaching it, or the slope below it, the course must be changed to W. by N. This will bring the rambler to the Lee Moor Clay Works leat, the left bank of which he will follow upwards to the head of the storage reservoir belonging to the works. Passing to the other side of this he will strike S. by W. and speedily reach the Cornwood (L.) and Dousland (R.) road. Crossing this to Emmett's Post he will steer due W. for 1 m. over Shaugh Moor to Brag Lane End, close to Shaugh village.

R. 49.—To Princetown and Two Bridges, W. by N. (A) *Holne Bridge, New Bridge, Pound's Gate, Ouldsbroom, Dartmeet, Dunnabridge Pound.* T. B., 13 m. ; P. T., 14½ m. (To P. T. *via* Hexworthy and Swincombe, 13½ m.) (B) *Holne Bridge, Holne Village, Saddle Bridge, Hexworthy.* P. T., *via* Swincombe, 12½ m. ; T. B., 13½ m. (C) *Holne Village,* as before, *Ringleshutts, Aune Head, Sand Parks, White Works.* P. T., 13½ m. ; T. B., 14 m. Reverse, R. 6.

[Objects : Exs. 27, 28, 41, 42, 43, 3, 4.]

A is a road route ; the others are over the moor for a part of the way, C passing through some of its wilder parts.   If the start be made from Buckfastleigh B or C should be chosen, and the way will lie first to Holne Moor Gate, as described in S. Ex. 96.

(A) Holne Bridge is the first point, whence the rambler will make his way up Holne Chase Hill, and then, keeping R. down to New Bridge, as in Ex. 28.   Crossing this he will follow the road up the hill with Leigh Tor R. (a narrow path cuts off some of its windings), and in 1 m. will reach Pound's Gate.   Passing through the hamlet he will keep L. to Uppacott, and soon gain the commons, whence is a magnificent view (Ex. 28).   The moor farm close to which he will pass is Ouldsbroom, and just beyond this he will strike another road coming from Ponsworthy R., at Ouldsbroom Cross.   Here he will turn L. and descend the long hill to Dartmeet.   Directions from this point onwards will be found in R. 42 A.

(B) To Holne Moor Gate as in S. Ex. 96, or if from Buckfastleigh as at end of S. Ex. 98.   Thence the rambler will follow the road past the new reservoir, and on by Hangman's Pit (*Holne Moor* Section) to Combestone Tor Hill, at the foot of which he will cross the Wo Brook and enter the forest.   About 1 m. on he will reach Hexworthy, and is referred to R. 42 A for a description of the way from that place.

(C) Holne Moor Gate is the first point, *vide supra.*   A few score yards beyond this a disused road branches L., the spot being marked by an upright stone.   Striking into this the rambler will be led to the long deserted Ringleshutts Mine.   The termination of the road is reached soon after the springs of the Wennaford Brook are crossed. and here a deep gully named Ringleshutts Gert (*Holne Moor* Section) runs up the hill, its direction being E. and W.   This must be followed to its head, when the rambler must bear S.W.   This will soon bring him to Sandy Way (T. 56), here only a green track, which he will follow westward to Aune Head Mire.   (This bears W. by S. from the head of the gert).   Leaving this swampy spot L. he will strike N.W. for about ¼ m., following the track if he can discover it, but it soon grows indistinct here, and then strike W.   This course will speedily bring him to a branch of the Swincombe river, which he will trace downwards to the enclosures of Fox Tor Farm (Ex. 3), where he will cross, and make his way down the side of Sand Parks, with Childe's Tomb L. and the stream R.   Near the confluence of this branch with another that flows eastward is a ford, and here he will cross the latter stream.   From this point, if his destination be Two Bridges, he will pass through the hunting-gate as described in Ex. 3, and make his way due N. over Tor Royal Newtake to Moorlands, 1½ m. distant. Turning R. he will pass this, and then turn L. to Prince Hall Bridge, as in R. 63 (see also Ex. 4), making his way by the house to the lodge. Here he will turn L. to Two Bridges, to which a walk of 1 m. will bring him.   Should the rambler be bound to Princetown he will pass up the valley from the ford under Fox Tor, with the stream L. and the newtake wall R., to White Works, whence he will cross the hill to Peat Cot and make his way to his destination by Castle Road (T. 7), or by the South Hisworthy Tor path (Ex. 3).

R. 50.—To Tavistock, W. by N.   R. 49, Ashburton to Princetown, and R. 1, Princetown to Tavistock, form this route.   *Via* Dartmeet and Two Bridges, 21 m. ; *via* Holne, Hexworthy, Swincombe, and Princetown, 20 m. ; *via* Holne, Aune Head, and Princetown, 21 m. Reverse, R. 12.

R. 51.—To Lydford *via* Two Bridges, N.W. by W. *Holne Bridge, New Bridge, Pound's Gate, Ouldsbroom Cross, Dartmeet, Hexworthy, Gobbet Plain, Swincombe, Prince Hall, Two Bridges, Cowsic Valley, Lich Path, White Barrow, Hill Bridge, Down Lane,* 24 m. Reverse, R. 19.

[Objects : Exs. 27, 28, 41, 42, 5, 10.]

The first part of this route, *i.e.*, from Ashburton to Two Bridges, is described in R. 49 A. From Two Bridges the way lies up the Cowsic valley for about 2 m., when the rambler must bear N.W. by N., and in about ½ m. will strike the Lich Path (T. 18). This he will follow westward, crossing the Prison Leat and the Walkham at Sandy Ford, from which point the way to Lydford is shown in R. 44. Another way from Two Bridges is described in R. 2 B.

The road route from Dartmeet to Two Bridges is noticed at the beginning of the *Princetown* Section, and in Ex. 42.

For the route from Buckfastleigh to Holne Moor Gate see end of S Ex. 98.

R. 52.—To Okehampton, N.W. by N. With branches to Belstone and Sticklepath. *Buckland-in-the-Moor, Cockingford, Bittleford Down, Grendon Bridge, Warren House Inn, South Teign, Teign Clapper, White Moor Stone, Taw Plain,* 22½ m. Reverse, R. 26.

[Objects : Exs. 26, 44, and 22 to 17.]

The road must be followed to Buckland Church as in Ex. 27, 3½ m. Thence the way lies for 1½ m. to Cockington, turning L. at the second cross-road. (The first turning L. is merely an entrance to a farm). From Cockingford ascend the hill W. and turn L. into the road leading from Widecombe to Ponsworthy. A few hundred yards on is a road R. Into this the rambler must also turn, when he will shortly reach Bittleford Down, and take the N.W. road over it. ¾ m. on, after passing a road leading to Jordan Mill L., this runs due N. Then another turning is passed L., leading to Cator, and about 1 m. further on the Broadford Brook is crossed at Lower Blackaton. Passing up the road W. the rambler will reach Hill Head, whence he will descend to Grendon Bridge, where he will cross the West Webburn, and follow the road to Ephraim's Pinch (Ex. 44). Mounting the short hill he will leave the road and strike due N. for 1½ m., passing over Soussons Common. He will then cross the Walla Brook and mine leat to the Warren House Inn (Ex. 21, 45). Behind the inn is Water Hill, and N. of that Hurston Ridge. The way lies over these, the course being a little W. of N. to the head of the Metheral Bogs, about 1¼ m. distant. From this point the route is the same as in R. 45.

R. 53.—To Chagford, N.N.W., and Moreton, N. *Welstor Cross, Cold East Cross, Hemsworthy Gate, Swine Down Gate.* (To Moreton : *Hayne Down, Langstone, North Bovey*). *Heytree Cross, Barramore Bridge, Beetor Cross.* To Chagford, 12¾ m. ; to Moreton, 11½ m. Reverse, R. 32.

[Objects : Exs. 26, 24 ; S. Exs. 61, 77.]

This is a road route throughout, but passes over much of the moor

The first point will be Welstor Cross, to which the rambler will make his way as in S. Ex. 92. He will then turn L. and follow the road N.E. At the distance of about 1½ m. Cold East Cross is passed (this point may also be reached by way of Rushlade, see Ex. 26), and 1¼ m. further on, Hemsworthy Gate (S. Ex. 90). Rippon Tor rises on the R., between these two points, and the scanty remains of Newhouse are seen close to the road L. Just beyond Hemsworthy Gate a green track runs over the common R., which will bring the rambler to the road again. From this point Swine Down Gate (R. 45), to which he must now make his way, is about 1¼ m. distant. Hound Tor rises on the R. Passing through the gate a road will be seen running R. This is the one the visitor bound for Moreton will follow. See *post.* For Chagford we keep straight on, with the hedge L. and Swine Down R. Cripdon Down succeeds the latter, the hedge being still L. Then we leave the commons, and passing Fordgate Farm, shall reach Heytree Cross, 1½ m. from Swine Down Gate. We keep on northward, and ½ m. from the cross road shall pass the turning L., where the lane leads to Vogwell. The next turning R. is the road running to Easdon Farm and Manaton ; then comes a road R. to Langdon Farm and North Bovey ; then a cross road—R. to North Bovey and L. to Westcombe Down ; then a road R. to Gratnar ; then, just after crossing Barramore Bridge, another R. to Hele. A little further on the rambler turns L. when Beetor Cross is reached. Chagford is 2½ m. from this point, and the route thither is described in S. Ex. 61.

To Moreton from Swine Down Gate. The road runs N. over Hayne Down, passing close to Bowerman's Nose, for 1¼ m. It then goes on to Langstone Cross, about ½ m., where is a guide-post. Here the visitor turns R. to Langstone, ½ m., where there is another post. Bovey is about 1¼ m. distant. He turns L., and passing between Higher and Lower Luckdon will soon reach the village. The road to Moreton is described in S. Ex. 61.

R. 54.—To Bovey Tracey, N.E. *Bickington, New Inn, Leverton,* 7½ m. Reverse, R. 39.

A road route. The visitor will quit Ashburton by way of East Street. 3 m. from the town he will pass through Bickington, and 1½ m. further on will reach the New Inn. Near here he will leave the highway and turn L. to Leverton, 1 m. Just beyond this he turns R. to Brimley Corner, where he must take the second road R., and in about ¼ m. will reach Ashburton Bridge, ½ m. S. of Bovey Station.

BRENT AND IVYBRIDGE DISTRICT.

(These places are five miles apart ; see R. 47, 66)

DISTANCES. By Road : *AISH RIDGE,* B., 1½ m. ; I., *via* Wrangaton, Pennaton Bridge, and Aish, 6¾ m. *ASHBURTON,* B., 8¼ m. ; I., 13 m. *BOVEY TRACEY,* B., 15¾ m. ; I., 20½ m. *BUCKFASTLEIGH,* B., 5¼ m. ; I., 10 m. *CADAFORD BRIDGE, via* Cornwood, B., 12¾ m. ; I., 7¾ m. *CHAGFORD, via* Buckfastleigh, Welstor Cross, Swine Down Gate, and Beetor Cross, B., 20¼ m. ; I., 25 m. *CORNWOOD,* B., 8 m. ; I., 3 m. *CROSS FURZES, via* Harbournford, Dean Combe, and Wallaford Down, B., 7 ; I., 12 ;

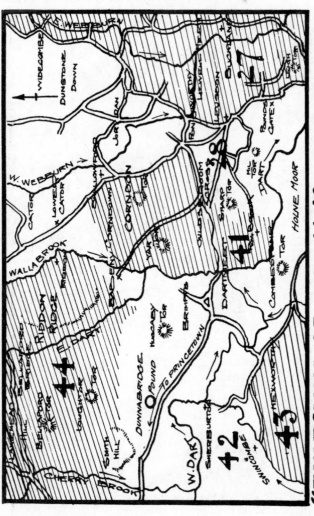

● ● 13. ASHBURTON & HEXWORTHY DISTRICTS

"EXCURSIONS 27, 28, 41, 42, AND PARTS OF 43, 44."

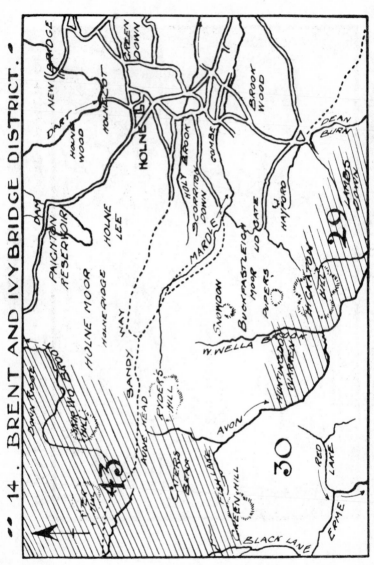

" 14. BRENT AND IVYBRIDGE DISTRICT. "

EXCURSIONS (PARTS OF) 29, 30, AND PART OF 43 "

via Skerraton Down (over turf), $2\frac{1}{2}$ m. less. *DEAN*, new road, B., $3\frac{3}{4}$ m.; I., 8 m.; old road, $\frac{3}{4}$ m. less. *DEAN BURN* (gate near Warn Bridge) *via* Harbournford and Dean Combe, B., $3\frac{3}{4}$ m.; I., $8\frac{3}{4}$ m. *DOCKWELL GATE*, B., $2\frac{3}{4}$ m.; I., $7\frac{3}{4}$ m. *EXETER*, B., 26 m.; I., 31. *GIGLEY BRIDGE*, B., $2\frac{3}{4}$ m.; I., $7\frac{3}{4}$ m. *HARBOURNFORD*, B., 2 m.; I., 7 m. *HARFORD CHURCH*, B., 7 m.; I., $2\frac{1}{2}$ m. *HEXWORTHY*, *via* Buckfastleigh, B., $12\frac{1}{4}$ m.; I., $17\frac{1}{4}$ m. *HOLNE VILLAGE*, *via* Buckfastleigh, 4 m. short of Hexworthy. *LYDFORD*, *via* Cornwood, Cadaford Bridge, Dousland, Huckworthy Bridge, and Moor Shop, B., 29 m.; I., 24 m. *MORETON*, *via* Buckfastleigh, Welstor Cross, Swine Down Gate, Langstone, and North Bovey, B., 19 m.; I., 24 m. *OKEHAMPTON*, as for Lydford, q.v., B., $36\frac{1}{2}$ m.; I., $31\frac{1}{2}$; *via* Chagford, q.v., B., 30 m.; I., 35. *OWLEY GATE*, B., $2\frac{1}{2}$ m.; I., *via* Wrangaton, $5\frac{1}{4}$ m. *PLYMOUTH*, B., 16 m.; I., $10\frac{3}{4}$ m. *PLYMPTON*, 5 m. short of Plymouth. *POST BRIDGE*, about 4 m. beyond Two Bridges, q.v. *PRINCETOWN*, *via* Dousland, B., 21 m.; I., 16 m.; *via* Hexworthy, B., $20\frac{1}{2}$ m.; I., $25\frac{1}{2}$ m. *SHIPLEY BRIDGE*, B., $2\frac{1}{2}$ m.; I., $7\frac{1}{2}$ m., or *via* Wrangaton, Pennaton Bridge, and Aish, about the same. *TAVISTOCK*, *via* Dousland, B., $21\frac{3}{4}$ m.; I., $16\frac{3}{4}$ m. *TOLCH MOOR GATE*, B., 10 m.; I., 5 m. *TOTNES*, B., 7 m.; I., 12 m. *TWO BRIDGES*, *via* Dousland, B., $22\frac{1}{2}$ m.; I., $17\frac{1}{2}$ m.; *via* Hexworthy, B., 19 m.; I., 24 m. *WRANGATON STATION*, B., 2 m.; I., $3\frac{1}{4}$ m. *YELVERTON*, *via* Cadaford Bridge and Greenwell Down, B., $16\frac{1}{4}$ m.; I., $11\frac{1}{4}$ m.

By Rail: Brent and Ivybridge Stations are on the G.W.R., and are $5\frac{1}{2}$ m. apart; *WRANGATON* (from which the Eastern Beacon is readily reached) is situated between the two. *NEWTON*, B., $14\frac{1}{2}$ m.; I., 20 m. *PLYMOUTH*, B., 17 m.; I., $11\frac{1}{2}$ m. *TOTNES*, B., $6\frac{3}{4}$ m.; I., $12\frac{1}{4}$ m. The railway distances from these to other stations near the moor are shown in the table at the commencement of each District.

The two chief streams of southern Dartmoor have already received mention in our routes, as well as in the section descriptive of the old tracks on the moor (R. 7, 33; T. 1, 54, 56, 65, 75). These are the Avon and the Erme, the one rising in the forest near Ryder's Hill, and the other on its border line under Green Hill. They both discharge their waters into Bigbury Bay, the former near Bantham, its embouchure being marked by the interesting Borough Island, and the latter at Mothecombe, about 4 m. below the village of Ermington. On leaving the moor the Avon runs through a narrow valley to the little market town of South Brent, while the course of the Erme after bidding adieu to the commons is through the romantic Stowford Cleave to Ivybridge. From either of these places the visitor may conveniently explore the interesting south quarter of the forest and the extensive moors which here form its purlieus.

The parish of Brent has always had a connection with the forest of Dartmoor, although it does not appear among the foresters' account as one of the ancient vills, nor does any estate or hamlet within it. In the south bailiwick we find the ville of Helle (Holne); the hamlet of Stourton in the parish of Buckfastleigh (Scorriton); the vill of Shiridon, in the parish of Dean (Skerraton); and the vill of Vvbirough (Ugborough); but there is no mention of any others. Brent Moor, the verge of which is over two miles from the village, extends to the forest boundary, and the two are conterminous for some distance.

THE MOORS OF HOLNE AND BUCKFASTLEIGH.

[As Holne Moor and the adjoining Buckfastleigh Moor may be con veniently reached either from Ashburton, Brent, or Hexworthy, it has been thought well to describe them in a separate section. But they are included in our *Brent and Ivybridge District*, as that compre-hends the commons extending from the Dart and the Wo Brook to the Pen Moor ridge, westward of the Yealm, and includes besides these two moors those of Dean, Brent, Ugborough, Harford, and Cornwood, as well as a part of the south quarter of the forest. Ashburton visitors will reach Holne Moor as described in S. Ex. 96 ; those from Hex-worthy will enter upon it at Saddle Bridge, following the instructions given in R. 6 B ; while from Brent and Ivybridge the way lies first to Skerraton Down, and thence to Water Oke Corner, as in S. Ex. 101 ; or to Cross Furzes and Lid Gate, as shown in S. Ex. 102 ; or R. 64 may be followed to Play Cross, whence the road L. ascends to the moor gate (S. Ex. 98). Holne Moor is also crossed by R. 6, C, Prince-town to Ashburton, and by T. 2, 55, and 56 ; T. 55 and 57 cross Buck-fastleigh Moor.]

Commencing our brief survey at Holne Moor Gate we make our way north-westward by the Hexworthy road over Sholedon, having some enclosures R. These comprise the four farms known respectively as Fore, Middle, Scale's, and West, Stoke, always called in the neigh-bourhood Stock. On the L. a little way removed from the road is the Shanty, a dwelling erected within recent years. We shall also notice on that side a road branching L. and marked by an old stone. This leads to the deserted Ringleshutts mine, just beyond which it connects with Sandy Way (T. 56). Soon after crossing Holne Moor leat for the second time we come in sight of the Paignton Reservoir, and here we desert the road and strike across the side of Ricketts Hill R. to Bench Tor. This consists of several piles, two of them being named in an old deed North Bench Tor and South Bench Tor respectively, which overlook the Gorge of the Dart (Ex. 28, 41). Another is known as the Eagle Rock. Cf. Lug Tor, Ex. 41. Immediately below it is White Wood, and on the further side of the river Mil Tor Wood, which climbs the steep slope under the tor of that name. Sharp Tor is seen to the L. of the latter, with the solitary Rowbrook Farm below it. These or other prominent heights are in view from any part of the road between Holne Moor Gate and Hexworthy, and the rambler finds something to delight him throughout the whole of the way. When he begins to lose sight of the tors above the gorge the lands of the forest settlers disclose themselves, with Bellaford rising proudly from the midst of the long lines of grey walls that spread over the heath like a net-work. Descending from the tor we cross the dam at the lower end of the reservoir, and make our way up the hill to rejoin the old road, a great part of which is now far beneath the surface of this artificial lake.

The Paignton Reservoir, which was opened in 1907, is formed in a valley usually known as Wennaford Bottom, and is supplied with water by the Wennaford Brook, which rises not far above it, and a short distance northward of Ringleshutts Mine. Near its head are some open workings now overgrown with vegetation, in the midst of which a few trees flourish. The road formerly crossed the stream at Wennaford Bridge, a small one-arched structure that stood a short distance above the present dam. It formed an interesting feature in what was altogether a charming scene, and though the construction of the reservoir has, like the formation of the one at Burrator (Ex. 39), given us something like a lake to look upon, it has only substituted one attraction for another, and it is not at all certain that the moor has gained by the change. Wennaford Brook was formerly crossed by the track running from Horse Ford to Holne village, and Buckfast (T. 2) at Workmen's Ford, not far below its source. Many years ago, having reason to believe that a cross once existed near this passage on the stream, I made search for it. In this I was unsuccessful, but met with some reward by the discovery of a stone that may have formed the base of a cross, though I was rather disposed to regard it as a mould-stone. Another worked stone was once to be seen near the Dart under Bench Tor ; it had a circular hole in its centre, and appears to have been of the kind we have noticed on Rippon Tor and in other places on the moor (Ex. 26, S. Ex. 56). The Wennaford valley above the bridge has been extensively streamed, but the workings are now in great part hidden by the water.

| Yar Tor. | Corndon Tor. | Sharp Tor. | Hameldon. | Chinkwell Tor. | Bel Tor. | Mil Tor. |

Road to Rowbrook.

FROM HOLNE ROAD, W. OF RESERVOIR, LOOKING N.N.E.

On the W. side of the lake, and not far from the dam, are the vestiges of some farm enclosures which are apparently very old. But the visitor will pass much more ancient memorials as he makes his way onward, for hut circles are found on each side of the road, and on the L. a number of long reaves. Below, on the R., but hidden from sight, is the pixy-haunted Langamarsh Pit, with the lonely farm of Rowbrook on the hillside above it, and, further up the stream, the pool known as Langawell. About ½ m. from the dam a track branches R. near a tumulus. This runs to Combestone Farm, about 1 m. distant. In local parlance it is Cumston, and appears two hundred years ago as Comberstone. Continuing on the road we reach in about another ⅓ m. a bend where the Wheal Emma leat runs quite close to us L., and here we shall notice a hollow running down to the Dart R. The work of the tin-seeker is abundantly evident, but grass and heather now cover the heaps he cast up, and the mountain ash grows in the sheltered nooks that these form. The spot is known as Hangman's

| Mil Tor. | Top Tor. | Pil Tor. | Hey Tor. | Rippon Tor. | Buckland Beacon. |

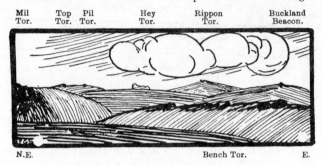

N.E.   Bench Tor.   E.

FROM HOLNE ROAD, W. OF RESERVOIR.

Pit from an unfortunate circumstance that happened here about eighty-seven years ago. A moorman who lived at Round Hill, near Two Bridges, was returning from Brent Fair, where he had changed his horse for another, and finding, it was supposed, that he had the worst of the bargain, was so troubled at what he had done that on arriving at the hollow he determined to take his life. He was found hanging from one of the trees amid the stone heaps, and on being cut down the body was taken to a barn at Hexworthy. Many years ago I heard a story in the neighbourhood to the effect that about the time when it was thought he must have committed the rash act his wife imagined she saw him approaching the door of their house.*

Soon after passing the hollow we reach Combestone Tor R. (100 *Years*, Chap. X.) whence the track to Dockwell Gate runs southward (T. 55). Near this track are several low cairns. The remains of one are still to be seen close to the highway. I remember when it was nearly intact, but in 1878 it was broken up for road material. Just beyond the tor another track leads to Combestone Farm.

Before us is Combestone Tor Hill, one of the steepest on the moor. At its foot is Saddle Bridge, which replaces an old structure taken down nearly forty years ago in consequence of becoming unsafe. It stood just above the present bridge, and being covered with ivy wore a very picturesque appearance. It used to be said, but with what truth we know not, that it was here the Prince Consort killed his first trout on Dartmoor, when on one of his visits to Princetown. The spot is a very romantic one. The Wo Brook, which here acts as the forest boundary, comes tumbling over the rocks, its banks overhung with the mountain ash. (This stream is also noticed in the

---

* It was in Hangman's Pit Bottom that Lovey Lee hid the Malherb amphora as related in Eden Phillpotts' *American Prisoner*.

excursions from Hexworthy). Having descended the hill we shall
notice just before reaching the bridge a rectangular enclosure L.,
and also some hut circles, and below these we shall turn up the valley,
with the brook R., and the enclosures of Slade on its further bank.

Bella- ford Tor.	Lough Tor.	Brimpts Plantation.	White Ridge.	Challa- combe Down.	Water Hill.	Yar Tor.

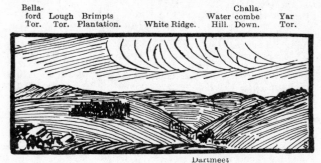

Dartmeet
Bridge.

FROM COMBESTONE TOR, LOOKING N.

At the distance of about ½ m. we reach Horse Ford, where the track
coming from the W. over Down Ridge crosses the stream (T. 2).
This runs E. up the side of Horn Hill to Horn's Cross, near to which
it is intersected by the Dockwell track (T. 55). A short distance N.
of this point, which was formerly known as Stascombe Telling-place,
is a low cairn. [*Crosses*, Chap. X.]

A little above Horse Ford, which is paved with flat stones, on one
of which is the letter H., denoting Holne, the Holne Moor leat is taken
in from Wo Brook, and above this the Wheal Emma leat (Ex. 3) is
carried over the stream. The latter, which is of much more recent
construction than the other, was cut in 1859. About ¼ m. further up
is Dry Lakes, a hollow on the L., in which are several old trees, and up
this we shall make our way S., following in the steps of the Perambulators of 1240 and 1609, who draw the line from the Wo Brook to Ryder's
Hill, or as they called it Battyshull, or Knattleburroughe.* On reaching
Dry Lakes Head we still keep S., with Holne Ridge L., and speedily
cross Sandy Way (T. 56), the bound here being known to the moormen
as Fieldfare, or Filfer Head. Ryder's Hill, the ancient Knattlebur-
rough, is less than ⅓ m. from the track. The hollow seen L. just before
we gain its summit is the head of the Mardle Combe, the extreme
upper end of it being known as Bourne's Pit, and the part immediately
below that as Rounder's Hole, and here are bond-stones called by

---

* "Ascendendo usque ad la Dryeworks, et ita ascendendo usque ad
la Dryfeld ford, et sic inde linealiter usque ad Battyshull." *Perambulation of* 1240. "Ascendinge to Drylake, al's Dryewoorke, and from
thence ascendinge by Drylake unto Crefeild fford or Dryefeild ford
and from thence to Knattleburroughe, wch. they take to be the same
that is called in the old records Gnatteshill." *Survey of* 1609. Other
forms of the names are Corfield Ford and Cattyshill.

those names. They mark the line between Holne Moor and Buck-fastleigh Moor, which is drawn from Bourne's Pit to Petre-on-the-Mount, a bond stone on the summit of Ryder, as the latter hill is always called by the moormen. Below Rounder's Hole the Mardle acts as the boundary between these two moors.

Ryder's Hill attains an elevation of 1694 feet, and commands a wonderful view of South Devonshire and the Channel. On a clear day it is possible to see the Isle of Portland and the Lizard Point, the horizon of sea between these two points being broken only in one place. There is a small cairn on the summit, but it is very much dilapidated. On this are two stones, a rough one about two feet high having the letter H. cut on it, and another more carefully worked and about four feet high with the letter B graven upon it. These represent Petre-on-the-Mount and Petre's Bound Stone.

The line between the forest and Buckfastleigh Moor runs S.E. to West Wella Brook Head, where is another bond-mark called Wella Brook Stone. Thence it is carried down through the deep workings of Wella Brook Gert past Higher Huntingdon Corner to Huntingdon Wall, whence it turns north-eastward up Gibby's Beam, a narrow trench cut through the hill from the Wella Brook to Snowdon Hole (T. 58, 55). But we shall leave the line at the bond-stone, and strike L. to Snowdon, which is quite near by. On this hill there are four cairns, the stones composing which are covered with moss. They are in a line running about N. and S. The southerly one is 80 yards in circumference; the next 52; the third, 45; and the northern one only 20 yards. Turning S. along the brow of the hill we cross Gibby's Beam, and make our way south-eastward to Pupers, the piles of which we seen on the hill before us. There are three of these, known re-spectively as Inner Pupers, Pupers Rock, and Outer Pupers. The word is a corruption of Pipers, and the usual story of men being turned into rocks for playing and dancing on a Sunday is related of these masses. On Outer Pupers the letter B is cut on the face of the rock. From Inner Pupers two reaves branch off, one of them running S.S.E. down the side of Pupers Hill to Water Oke Corner, a distance of nearly 1¼ m., and marking the limits of Buckfastleigh Moor.*

We now turn down the hill N.W. by Black Bush to Snowdon Hole, ⅓ m., and after passing this shall notice the vestiges of some ancient enclosures on the smooth turf close to the rocks. Below the hole the ground is very miry, and here is the source of the Snowdon Brook, as well as of another little stream that runs towards Lid Gate. As we make our way onward under Snowdon, our course being northerly, we have the Mardle below us R. At the head of Scea Wood, which is visible, is Chalk Ford, whence a track runs from the stream over Scorriton Down. Not far above this the Wheal Emma Leat falls precipitously down the side of the steep hill to empty its water into the Mardle. Eastward of the leat is the Holy Brook, which runs through Gibby's Combe to Mitchel Combe. A little further up stream the round hill known as Nap will be noticed. On this are four cairns,

---

* This reave is crossed by the Huntingdon track (T. 57), which is marked by a few stones, the one near the reave bearing the name of Kit's Stone. The rocks crowning the hill are sometimes known respectively as Higher, Middle, and Lower, Pupers.

one of them being very large, but the stones of which they are formed, and which are mixed with earth, are small, and much overgrown with vegetation. The ground around them is plain.

On reaching Hapstead Ford a short distance below Mardle Head, we may either cross the stream and make our way N. to the head of Ringleshutts Gert, or pass down the R. bank for ¼ m. to Mardle Ring, an ancient enclosure with a hut circle in its higher part. In the former case the gert will be followed E. to the remains of the old mine house whence the road already alluded to will conduct the rambler to Holne Moor Gate. In the latter we shall, after examining the enclosure, which is in a rather ruinous state, cross the stream work through which the Mardle here runs, and make our way N.E. up the hill towards Holne Lee, noticing three cairns just after crossing Sandy Way. From these the summit of Ryder bears W. of W.S.W. On our right are Two Hills and Whithedges, the latter being near where Sandy Way enters between the enclosures at Lane Head, and runs down the hill above Gibby's Combe Wood to the hamlet of Mitchell Combe. (At the head of Gibby's Combe is a point on Scorriton Down known as Sitting Down End, where it is usual for refreshments to be served when the bounds of the Manors of Buckfastleigh and Holne Bozom are viewed). Passing over Holne Lee we notice a couple of cairns about ½ m. E.N.E. of the three already referred to, and just beyond these shall reach the Ringleshutts road, where we turn R. to Holne Moor Gate.

Among other remains on Holne Moor may be mentioned several long reaves which intersect each other, some cairns and a small pound. These are situated on Holne Ridge, N. of the head of Ringleshutts Ger. On Buckfastleigh Moor there is a group of hut circles near the Snowdon Brook and Mardle.

Holne and Buckfastleigh Moors were anciently claimed by the Abbot of Buckfast as part of his manors, but the men of Devon always contended that they were part of the Commons of Devonshire. One of the manors was given to the abbey by Richard Bauzan, whose name still survives in Holne Bozom.

EXCURSIONS FROM BRENT.

Tracks in the vicinity Nos. 1, 55 to 62, 75.

Ex. 29.—*Dockwell Gate, The Longstone, Antiquities on Brook Hill and Hickaton Hill, Huntingdon Warren* [Extension to Heng Lake, add 2½ m.] *Huntingdon Cross, Remains on the Avon, Long-a-Traw, Shipley Tor,* 13 m.

Leaving the town by the western railway bridge we pass the entrance to the vicarage L., and ascending Splatton Hill shall soon reach Lutton Green. About 1 m. beyond this, northward, is Gingaford Cross, reached soon after a lane turns L. to Yolland, and about 300 yards further on the spot by the roadside L. known as Bloody Pool. Here some bronze spear heads were found in 1854. [*Crosses,* Chap. II.] ½ m. N. is a small open space (R. 48) from which a stroll, entered at the further end of it, leads to Dockwell Gate. We pass down this, and having gained the commons shall find ourselves on the green path running to Combestone Tor (T. 55). Built into the wall on the R., not far from the gate, is a circular stone of the kind we have noticed in other parts of the moor (Ex. 2, S. Ex. 56, Ex. 26, S. Ex. 105), one of several to be found in this locality. It is 3 feet 10 inches in diameter, and about 10 inches thick. The hole in its centre is 5 inches in diameter, and the same in depth, going only half way through the stone. Near it is another partly fashioned into a circular shape.

We speedily desert the track and turn R., and keeping near the wall of the enclosures shall soon reach Dockwell Brake. Within this is a pound, forming part of a group of remains on the slopes of Dockwell Hole, the name of the hollow below us. In this pound is a circular stone similar to those we have just noticed. Having viewed this ancient enclosure we shall make our way to the Harbourn, which has one of its springs in the hollow and another just within the verge of Dean Moor, on the E. side of it. This stream, which is referred to by Leland, who says " Harbertoun water cummith out of a well spring," serves as the boundary between the parishes of Brent and Dean for about 3 m. from its source. Crossing the stream close to the brake in order to avoid the mire we shall proceed for a short distance up its eastern bank, and then re-cross it under Parnell's Hill. Here we shall find another pound, across which are two rows of stones, with the remains of hut circles in the south-west corner. A couple of hut circles will also be seen outside the wall. Above this is a third enclosure, but the wall is very imperfect, and the two hut circles within it in a very ruinous state. Not far from Harbourn Head is the menhir known as The Longstone. This is 3 feet 9 inches wide at its base, and tapers to 1 foot at the top, the thickness throughout being 13 inches. Its height is 8 feet, and it is leaning considerably out of the perpendicular.

On Parnell's Hill, a short distance W. by N. of the menhir, and in view from it, are two cairns, and to these we now make our way. One is 78 yards in circumference ; the other measures 5 yards less. They are 23 yards apart, of no great height, and covered with grass. N.N.W. of these, and on the further side of a slight depression, is another, of similar character, but smaller, measuring only 35 yards in circumference. The view from this point is exceedingly fine. S.S.W. are the Ugborough Beacon Rocks, with the cairn-crested ridge running northward from the pile ; N. of this rises the lofty Three Barrows, whence the eye ranges R. by Knattaburrow, Eastern and Western Whitaburrow, to Huntingdon Warren, and Ryder, the latter bearing N.W. Far away beyond this Water Hill, above King's Oven (Ex. 21) ; to the R. of which is Hameldon and the Widecombe valley, with the tors that overlook it, and still further R. Rippon Tor. Much nearer to us in this direction is Yar Tor, above Dartmeet, Corn Down Tor, Sharp Tor, and the Buckland Woods. Eastward is a fine stretch of cultivated country backed by Haldon, and to the R. of that elevated land the estuary of the Teign. Beyond is the Channel, which bounds the view round towards the W., where the Ugborough Beacon Rocks rise against the sky.

Striking westward we cross the grassy track running from Combestone Tor to Dockwell Gate (T. 55), having on our R. Water Oke Plain, and make our way over the northern part of Small Brook Plain to Grippers Hill. Descending the western side of this at Waterfoot Clatter, we reach the confluence of the Avon and the Brock Hill stream. We cross the latter, which here comes down through a rocky hollow where it forms a number of small cascades, and in which are a few dwarf trees, and passing up the slope, with the little stream below us R., shall presently come upon a group of remains of a very interesting character. A rectangular enclosure will be seen, the lower wall of which is about 100 yards from the Avon, and in this are several small courts together with the walls of buildings. These appear to be the erections of mediæval tinners, but were evidently formed on the site of remains belonging to pre-historic days.* The upper wall of the main enclosure forms part of an ancient pound, containing several hut circles, one of a series on Hickaton Hill, the side of which is often spoken of as Brock Hill. In no part of the moor can pounds and hut circles be better studied than here. Some of the finest examples of primitive dwellings may be seen, and the remains being at some distance from modern enclosures they have not suffered at the hands of the spoliator.

Passing up the hill we shortly come upon another pound through which passes the Abbots' Way (T. 1), as named in our section on the ancient tracks. This old path, which comes up from Brock Hill Ford R., is here very clearly defined.† A few score yards to the N. is another and much larger pound, the circuit of the wall being 825 yards. This is ten feet wide in some places, and from 3 feet to 4 feet high. The pound is divided into parts, and it is indeed possible to regard it as being several distinct pounds close together, and having portions of their walls in common. One of the entrances to the enclosures is very perfect, and in some of the hut circles the door jambs are still erect.

The Brock Hill Water, which has been streamed throughout its whole length, comes down from Brock Hill mires, and above the ford several tinners' buildings may be found, and are curious on account of their unusually small size. Near its head, where the Hayford leat is taken from it, the stream bends to the L. as we ascend, this higher part of the hollow bearing the name of Crad Hole. On the slope at the head of this is Crad Hole Ring, a pound 260 yards in circumference, and containing four hut circles. N. of it is Pupers Hill, with the rocks crowning its summit. If the stream be not followed up the rambler may reach this pound by striking over the hill N.W. by N. from the enclosures above Brock Hill Ford.

Proceeding north-westward up the slope we soon come in sight of Huntingdon Warren House, on the further side of the West Wella Brook. A house and a newtake existed here before the close of the seventeenth century, but there is no mention of the place by the jury of survey who passed this way in 1609. W. of the house, and on the highest part of Huntingdon Hill, is a fine cairn 76 yards in circumference,

---

* The Hickaton circles and other remains here noticed as existing on this hill were fully described by me in the *Western Antiquary*, Vols. VIII., IX.

† The Abbots' Way is here carried along the side of the hill, descending to the West Wella Brook, which it crosses at Huntingdon Ford, and immediately after crosses the Avon at Avon Ford. The old posts of Huntingdon Gate will be seen not far from the cross, near the confluence of the two streams. Further up the Wella Brook s another ford where a track leads to the warren house, and also a rude bridge.

which is usually known as Huntingdon Barrow, but is sometimes referred to as the Heap o' Sinners. Less than ⅓ m. southward of this, on the slope overlooking the Avon, are three pounds, one of them, the easterly one, being very small. Little shelters, formerly used by the warreners, have been constructed in the walls.

Eastern Whitaburrow.   Western Whitaburrow.   Huntingdon Warren.

FROM HICKATON HILL, DEAN MOOR, LOOKING S.W.

Extension to *Heng Lake.* Instead of descending to the Wella Brook and tracing it downward to Lower Huntingdon Corner, the rambler may extend his walk by keeping R. towards the long disused Huntingdon Mine, and crossing the track (T. 57) leading to a ford below, reach a little river higher up, the rocks on the summit of Pupers being R. Still further up the tiny T Gert Stream comes down L. and above this is Wella Brook Gert, where some very deep open workings will be seen. At the head of this is Higher Huntingdon Corner, whence the boundary of the warren runs over the hill in a south-westerly direction. We shall not, however, proceed quite so far, but soon after reaching the workings shall strike off L. at a track leading to T Gert, and taking a wall which here runs parallel to the boundary, but S. of it, for our guide, shall follow it S.W. for about ¾ m. to the Avon. Here, looking up stream, we have a good view of the Cater's Beam ; its rounded form is clearly defined against the sky to the L., or W., of Aune Head. We turn L. and make our way down the river to Heng Lake, which flows out of the gully of that name on the R. (R. 33). Below this is Broad Falls, where the Avon enters Higher Bottom, and passing downward on the L. bank we shall find in this hollow a good example of a blowing-house, with a mortar-stone lying on the turf near it. The ruin is 24½ feet in length, and nearly 15 feet in width, on the outside ; at one end the wall is about 6 feet high. On the brow of the hill above it is a little shelter, which was built by a former warrener, and not far from this is the spring called Broady Well. Below the hollow on the R. bank is Stony Gert,* and still further down Huntingdon Clapper, which, although not boasting of any antiquity, is yet more than ordinarily interesting on account of its remote situation. It consists of two openings, but unfortunately

---

* In this locality was formerly a mine called Wheal Dorothy. It is not improbable that the workings seen here represent it.

the stone over the western one was displaced by a flood a few years ago, and now lies in the bed of the stream. The late warrener, Pearse, used to cross by means of a plank. On the R. is Fernside, and part way up this slope, a little further down than the bridge, is a small stone circle, apparently of the kind usually found enclosing kistvaens, but its real nature cannot very well be determined, as the stones are much overgrown. Below this the Avon bends L., and here the Buckland Ford Water, which is crossed by the Abbots' Way, falls into it (T. 1). This old path is carried up the hill by the side of Piper's Beam, whence it goes on to the Cross Ways (R. 7). Below the bend the Avon runs under Bush Meads to Huntingdon Cross, and here we meet the Wella Brook, which, coming down from the great gert, it gives name to and flowing below the warren house, forms throughout its length a boundary of the forest.

Although we know that Huntingdon Cross was standing in 1557 (see Ex. 31), there is no mention of it in the survey of 1609, which, however, is hardly to be wondered at seeing that the Wella Brook forms the forest boundary, and that the point given by the perambulators of 1240 was the confluence of that stream with the Avon. This was followed by the jury of survey of nearly four hundred years later. But the jurors who presented the forest bounds at Lydford Castle in 1786, though naming the same line, make mention of the cross also. It is likewise named in a certificate respecting some tin bounds at Huntingdon, dated 1759. It is about 4½ feet in height, and stands just within the limits of the forest. On the slope eastward is Biller's Pound 280 yards in circumference, but the wall is very low. This adds another to the number of similar objects existing on the hill rising between the Brock Hill stream, the Avon, and the Wella Brook. Below it are nine hut circles.

Making our way down the L. bank of the Avon, and noticing as we proceed abundant evidence of the former presence here of the tin streamer, we shortly come upon the ruins of a building. It is situated about 40 yards from the stream, from which a water-course can be traced. It was probably a tin-mill, or place where the ore was crushed. Below this, and quite near to the bank, are some upright stones, called the Three Brothers, which have something of the appearance of a portion of a stone row, but they more probably formed part of a reave which runs from the lowest of the enclosures we have already noticed on the Brock Hill Stream. Very soon this little feeder is reached, and we shall observe that where it pours its waters into the Avon it is confined within banks roughly faced with stones. (On the R. bank of the Avon, and rather over ½ m. below the cross, is a pound divided by interior walls into three, in a manner similar to the one on Brock Hill. Within it are several hut circles).

Proceeding down the Avon, with Gripper's Hill, L., and Leaman's Mead R., we shortly reach Fall Rocks, where a cascade is formed, and here the L. bank is very steep. Not far below this point we come upon Gripper's Pound, a small enclosure in the midst of a clatter. In shape it is not unlike a horse-shoe, and the wall, which is about three feet high, is 160 yards round. There are the remains of two or three hut circles within it, and others, connected by low reaves, are to be seen between it and the river. A small erection, which is evidently comparatively modern and formed out of one of these primitive dwellings, bears the name of the Blackman's Holt. Both pound and huts are in a ruinous condition, but their situation lends an interest to them. They stand in what is certainly the most charming spot on the moorland Avon. The side of the hill is strewn with rocks, amid which the heather grows and tall ferns flourish, while a few thorn bushes also find shelter here.*

At the foot of the hill the river makes a couple of bends, and below the second enters a miniature canyon, where it is pent up between walls of solid rock. It was over this that the daring John Dill leaped his horse when pursued by the farmers, from one of whom he had "borrowed" the animal without going through the form of asking whether he might have it, for the purpose of conveying certain goods that had been quietly landed by night from a village near the coast into the interior. It will be seen that the valley in which this is situated is apparently closed in both at its upper and lower ends. This formation has given to it its name of Long-a-traw, literally "long trough," which object it may be said to resemble. But the canyon is a "long trough," too, and it is therefore not unlikely that the name originated from this, but it is the valley that is generally understood by the name in the neighbourhood.

Below the canyon Small Brook falls into the Avon, and close to the confluence is one of the bond stones marking the line between Dean Moor and Brent Moor, and which is carried over the hill to Dockwell Hole. On passing this we gradually leave the river, our course being S.S.E., and make our way up the steep to the western edge of Dockwell Ridge, which is noticed in S. Ex. 105. Looking across the valley W. we have a good view of the fine hut settlement on Ryder's Plain known as The Rings, and also of Black Tor, on the hill at the southern end of Long-a-Traw. As we proceed we shall notice some small enclosures and several hut circles on the common. Presently we come in sight of Brent Moor House in the defile R., and soon after reach Shipley Tor (S. Ex. 105). Here we enter the hunting-gate near the rocks, and descend to the road coming L. from Yolland Cross (R. 48), and turning R. speedily find ourselves at the moor gate near Shipley Cottage. Our nearest way to Brent is by the path through Didworthy, as in S. Ex. 105. If we cross Shipley Bridge and take the road past Zeal we must follow the instructions given in R. 7.

Ex. 30.—*Shipley, The Rings, Eastern and Western Whitaburrow, Petre's Cross.* [Extension over Green Hill: *Red Lake Ford, Stone Row, Black Lane, Ducks' Pool, Brown Heath,* add 5 m.] *Knattaburrow Hill, Old Hill, Red Brook, Zeal Bridge,* 12 m.

Our present excursion will embrace that part of Brent Moor bounded by the Avon on the E. and Red Brook on the S., and, if the extension be included, a part of the south quarter of the forest. The

---

* The valley of the Avon is probably the "Avena" of the fourteenth century. In an account of the Bailiff of Dartmoor *temp* Edward III., there is an entry of "6s. 11d. received of 83 beasts agisted at Avena, outside the forest, this year (1354) at 1d. a head, of divers tenants of the lord venville, there being at night only for having that easement." Those who were not tenants of the lord also used to agist there, and paid 1½d. per head.

first point will be the moor gate at Shipley (S. Ex. 106), and to this we have the choice of two routes ; we may go by way of Aish, or through Lutton and Didworthy. In either case we cross the western railway bridge, and follow the lane past the vicarage gates to the foot of Splatton Hill. Here, if we choose the Aish route, we keep L. to Lydia Bridge, and crossing the Avon climb the hill to the hamlet, taking care not to turn L. (Soon after passing over the bridge, and a little way up the hill, a gate opening on a footpath will be seen R. The visitor may enter here, and crossing some fields regain the road on the side of the hill above Penstave Copse). From Aish the road must be followed to the river, on the bank of which it runs for some little distance. The Didworthy Sanatorium is seen on the further side of it. Leaving Badworthy L. and Didworthy Bridge R., we keep straight on, and soon after passing the foot of Diamond Lane L. (S. Ex. 108), shall cross Red Brook, or Bala Brook as this part of the stream is sometimes called, at Zeal Bridge, and noticing Zeal Farm L. shall speedily reach the moor gate.

Should we decide upon the Didworthy route, we make our way up to Lutton Green as in Ex. 29, but instead of crossing it shall pass down the road L. to Wash Gate, and follow a narrow bridle-path up to a field. We cross the lower side of this, and also another, with Shipley Tor in full view in advance, and making our way through the yard at the back of the Sanatorium, gain a lane which will lead us to Didworthy Bridge, L. On crossing this we turn R. and follow the road to the moor gate as just described.

Entering upon the moor we turn up by the wall L., but gradually leaving it, make our way northward across the side of Zeal Hill, with the old naphtha works about 200 yards below us R., and here we have a fine view of the valley above Shipley Bridge, with the tor of that name on the opposite steep. [*Gems*, Chap. XVI.] By following this course we shall be led to an ancient enclosure, 360 yards in circumference, the wall of which is composed of very large blocks of granite, though in one place these are much scattered. Within this pound there are fourteen hut circles, the whole of them being placed across the upper portion of it. There is one lower down, but that is situated on the outside of the wall. Above this pound is a second, and near by the vestiges of three others. The visitor must not mistake the mounds on this part of the hill for barrows. They are really old rabbit shelters, and are known as Zeal Burrows—or " burys," as the moor people call them—and mark the site of a former warren.

Northward of this group of remains Black Tor, over 1,100 feet, rises above the defile E., in which Brent Moor House is situated. To this we make our way, and on reaching the rocks shall look down upon Long-a-Traw, a name which we shall be ready to acknowledge is appropriately borne by the valley through which the Avon here comes down, for seen from this point it may certainly be likened to a long trough (Ex. 29). Keeping along the brow of the hill we shall, at the distance of rather less than ½ m. from the tor, come upon two more enclosures, and a few hut circles, but they are very small. They are plainly to be seen, when the sun is shining upon them, from the summit of Brent Hill. Close to them N. is a little stream, on which may be noticed a few specimens of the mountain ash, and on crossing this we shall find ourselves close to what is certainly one of the most interesting of the pounds to be found on Dartmoor. This ruined settlement, which occupies a commanding situation on Ryder's Plain, is known as The Rings. It is of considerable length, measuring no less than 380 yards from end to end. Its southern portion, where is its greatest breadth, is 120 yards across, and its northern 105 yards. It is narrowest near its centre, where it measures 76 yards across. The circuit of the wall is 975 yards, and although this, as in similar enclosures on the moor, has fallen, its lower courses can in places be seen, and these show it to have been about ten feet thick. Extending across the whole length of this enclosure, and immediately within the upper wall, is a row of small courts, and a few are also to be seen in the lower part of it. These are about thirty in number, and some of them appear to be of later date than the pound itself. One of them is obviously so. This, which will be found towards the N.E. end, is similar in plan to the tinners' Houses near the streams. It measures 19 feet by 8 feet on the inside. One of the courts is 42 feet by 36 ; another 33 feet by 28 ; while a detached one, which is roughly circular in shape, is about 38 feet in diameter ; all internal measurements. It is these courts that render the pound so interesting, for although one or two are sometimes to be seen within the enclosing wall, as, for instance, at Grim's Pound, they are not to be found in such numbers in any other part of the moor. Something similar, but on a much smaller scale, occurs in the Half Ring, on Red Brook, in this locality, and is noticed in Ex. 31. There are a number of hut circles within The Rings, one of them adjoining a corner of the building we have spoken of as resembling a tinner's house. A particularly striking example will be found near the centre of the pound ; in this the wall is composed of two concentric rows of stones. It seems probable that this enclosure after being vacated by its original builders was again occupied, perhaps at a much later period, and that some of the courts at least were then added. It is certain that the " tinners' House " formed no part of the early settlement. There are three entrances to the pound ; one at each end, and one in the upper wall towards the north.

(N. of The Rings, or Brent Rings as they are often called, and close to the wall, are Ryder's Rocks, an extensive clatter covering much of the hillside, and N. of this is the steep Zeal Gully, through which a little stream runs down to Apton's Marsh and into the Avon. This joins just above Viger's Corner, the higher bend on the river under Gripper's Pound (Ex. 29), close to which is Ryder's Ford. At Long-a-Traw Corner, the next bend downward, there is another crossing-place).

On leaving The Rings we shall proceed N.W. over Zeal Plains, keeping along the brow of the hill, and at the distance of 1 m. shall reach Eastern Whitaburrow, 1,539 feet.* To this fine cairn, according to the perambulators of 1240, and the jurors of 1609 and 1786, the forest boundary came up from the confluence of the Avon and Wella Brook. But it is now regarded as being altogether outside the forest, the boundary being carried up the Avon to the Buckland Ford Water, and thence up the hill to Western Whitaburrow, which was indeed claimed as the line between Brent Moor and the forest so early as

---

* Pronounced White-a-burrow, and often without the *a*.

1557. (See *Perambulation* in the *Terms* Section). Eastern Whitaburrow is a very fine example of an ancient burial heap. It consists entirely of stones, and is 90 yards in circumference at its base, and 12 yards in height. Huntingdon Warren and Hickaton Hill (Ex. 29) are commanded from it, while there is a good distant view. North-eastward the Buckland Woods are seen, with the lofty Rippon Tor beyond, and still further away the heights of Haldon. The Channel bounds the prospect southward until it is lost behind the Beacon Rocks, on Ugborough Moor. In the opposite direction Great Mis Tor is seen about N.W., and to the R. of it, beyond the dusky ridge extending westward from Aune Head, the hills of the north quarter of the forest. S.E. by S. is the town of Brent, and this great stone heap can readily be discerned from the eastern railway bridge there. The hillside N. of Eastern Whitaburrow, at the foot of which the Avon runs, is known as Bush Meads, which there is evidence to show is a corruption, or contraction, of Bishop's Meads. In a sixteenth century document this tract is referred to as " Bishop's Mead, otherwise Busshe Mead," so that we not only learn from this the true name, but also that over three hundred and fifty years ago *bishop* became *bushop* (pronounced *booshup*) in the Devon vernacular as it does to-day.

From this lofty burial heap we shall direct our steps westward to Western Whitaburrow, noticing Bush Pits, the remains of former mining operations which extend along the brow of the hill, as we proceed. The ground is sometimes rather marshy near the object we are approaching, and it may therefore be necessary to keep a little to the R., at the same time taking care not to descend the hill.

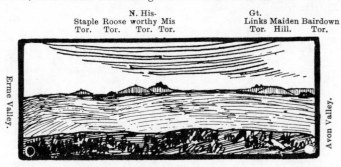

FROM PETRES CROSS. LOOKING N.W.

Western Whitaburrow forms the extreme southern bondmark of the forest, according to the limits now recognized. In our *Cosdon* section we have mentioned this cairn as being visible from that hill the northernmost point of the forest boundary line. If the visitor to Whitaburrow looks in a northerly direction he will see a small mound on the ridge about 2½ m. distant. This marks the situation of Aune Head, the morass at the source of the river being also distinguishable. Beyond this the openings between the hills through which the East Dart and the North Teign flow, permit him to see the rounded form of Cosdon, 16 m. distant. It bears a little W. of N. from this point Looking in the opposite direction Three Barrows will be seen, 2 m. S. (Ex. 31) ; Pen Beacon, with Shell Top overlooking it, about 4 m. W.S.W· (Ex. 34) ; nearer to us, and extending from S.S.W. to W., the long range of Stall Moor (Ex. 33) ; Erme Head, 2 m. W.N.W., and nearly 6 m. beyond it, North Hisworthy, N.W. (*Princetown District* and R. 58), with Great Mis Tor to the R., and still further away (Ex. 6) ; from this fine tor a distant range extends R. to Cut Hill, 11 m. N.N.W. (Ex. 11), to the R. of which, N. by W., is seen Siddaford Tor (Ex. 20) ; further R. is White Ridge, 10 m. N. (Ex. 45), over the western slope of which is seen the far-away Cosdon. Quite near to us is Huntingdon Warren (Ex. 29), and looking across this in a north-easterly direction we have a view of Rippon Tor and Hey Tor. Western Whitaburrow is generally referred to as Petre's Cross from the former existence on the cairn of a cross forming a bondmark of Sir William Petre's manor of Brent, where it abutted on the forest (Ex. 31).* This was partly destroyed about 1847 by the workmen employed at the turf ties at Red Lake Mires, but a portion of the shaft may still be seen. [*Crosses*, Chap. II.] The men, who mostly lived at or near Brent, built a house on the cairn, the foundations of which are still observable, and here they remained during the week. Dried heather and straw formed their bedding, and when their supplies of food were running short, or they desired a change of diet, they made incursions into Huntingdon Warren. Men who worked there have told me of the large number of rabbits they have seen prepared for dinner or supper. In view of this fact we can quite understand the necessity of the little watch-house of the warrener above Higher Bottom, of which we have already spoken (Ex. 29). The Whitaburrow house was slated, but when work at the ties at Red Lake Head ceased and the place was deserted, the roof was taken off by the late Mr. Meynell, the owner of the manorial rights of Brent Moor, and the materials removed. Whitaburrow is 63 yards in circumference, but its original height cannot be determined, as the stones were cleared from the centre where the house stood, but it does not appear ever to have been of great height. The altitude of this hill is given as 1,575 feet, but that of the bench mark on the shaft of the cross, which stands on the cairn, is 1,580 feet.

North-eastward of the cairn is a bondstone on the brow of the hill, sometimes called Little Petre. From this the forest line descends nearly to Buckland Ford (T. 1), and thence to the Avon.

[EXTENSION over Green Hill to Ducks' Pool, add 5 m. Close to Whitaburrow is the old Zeal Tor tram-road, already noticed (T. 60),

---

* Sir William died in 1571. He left one son, John, who was advanced to the dignity of a Baron of England by the title of Lord Petre of Writtle in Essex, in 1603. It was Robert, seventh Lord Petre, who provided Pope with the idea of *The Rape of the Lock*, by stealing a lock of hair from the head of his beautiful cousin, Arabella Fermor. The famous Father Petre, who acted as confessor to James II., belonged to a branch of this family. The late Lord Petre died in December, 1908 ; his elder brother had been domestic prelate to the Vatican. The present lord is a minor.

and over which the peat from the ties ¾ m. N.W. was conveyed to the works at Shipley. From the former there is a stiff ascent to this point, but on passing the cairn there is a level for some distance, and then for a greater distance a descent to its termination. If we extend our ramble to Green Hill this old tram-road will become our path for a little way, as in R. 58, which route we shall follow to Dark Lake. ⅓ m. from the cairn we reach the Crossways, just beyond which, at the bottom of the descent, and on the R. of the road, a great wooden press formerly stood, and near this the wagons were loaded. At the Crossways we turn L. into the Abbots' Way (T. 1), and follow it to Red Lake Ford, having as we proceed the mire below us R., and Brown Heath L. It is this part of the old monks' road that the moorman generally refer to when they speak of Jobbers Path (See T. 1, 61). On nearing Red Lake a bondstone, sometimes called the Outer U Stone, will be noticed on its bank, and one or two others will be seen on the slope of Brown Heath, L. These form the end of the line running out from the dip between Three Barrows and Sharp Tor (Ex. 32), and mark the boundary between Ugborough and Harford Moors. If the clay works recently started in this retired part of the moor do not interfere with the purity of its waters, the rambler will acknowledge that Red Lake is most suitably named. It certainly appears to be of that hue, though unlike the river of Adonis, in Phœnicia, which the marl of Lebanon stained red at the time of the spring floods, it is not really so. The water is perfectly clear ; it is only the pebbles in its bed that are coloured. Heaps of stones thrown up by the tinners here line the banks of the stream ; the large rock standing in the midst of the workings, some little distance below the crossing-place, is called the Cracker Stone.

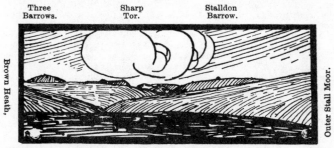

FROM GREEN HILL. LOOKING S.S.E.

From Red Lake Ford we follow a north-westerly course across Green Hill, and in a little over ½ m. shall reach a grass-covered gully, known as Middle Mires, though except in winter it is dry, In that season a rivulet rises in the lower part of it, and there it has been streamed ; below this are Dry Lake Rocks. The ruins of a small rectangular miners' hut may be seen on its bank, not far above where it joins the Erme. This little feeder has been not in-appropriately called Dry Lake, though it is occasionally referred to as Middle Brook, but its true name is Hux Lake (Ock ?). Carried across the upper end of the gully is the stone row noticed in Ex. 33. which runs out from Stall Moor to the higher part of Green Hill, 1,553 feet, ½ m. R., where it terminates in a ruined kistvaen.   This hill affords the best pasturage in this part of the moor, and is probably identical with the " preda de Irm " named in an account of John D'Abernon, Constable of Lydford Castle and Custos of Dartmoor in the reign of Edward III.

Still proceeding N.W. we shall in less than ¼ m. reach Stony Hole, the extensive stream work on Dark Lake, and from which Black Lane runs N. (T. 75).   As mentioned in our description of this track a rivulet flows into Dark Lake, or the Wollake, to give the stream its old name, at the head of the working. It comes in from the L. in ascending, and near here are the remains of a miners' building, to which the name of Ducks' Pool House has been given.   This is of the usual type, but of small size, being only 8 feet 9 inches long by 5 feet 6 inches wide on the inside.   A fire-place and the ruins of a chimney are to be seen.   Following the rivulet upward L., we shall be led direct to Ducks' Pool (T. 75), now emptied of water either by the stream having worn its channel down to the level of the bottom of the tarn, or by artificial means.   This hollow bears a resemblance to Cranmere in more ways than one.   It is still called a pool, though containing no water ; it is in a remote situation in the midst of the fen ; and has been associated with the heron, or crane.   The latter appears in the name of the more northern hollow, and in the present case in Crane Hill, above the head of the Plym, which source is only a short distance to the N.W.   But whether the name is derived from the bird is open to question ; it may possibly be a corruption of a word meaning something quite different.   (cf. *Cranmere* Section).   The name which this hollow now bears may have reference to wild ducks ; at all events, the valley of the Erme near Stony Bottom, about 2 m. distant, was once much frequented by those birds.

We shall now return to the stream work, from which we have a view of the hills above the Erme valley, the principal being Three Barrows and Sharp Tor, with Butterdon Hill and the Western Beacon beyond (Ex. 32), and on its western side the great mass of Stalldon Barrow (Ex. 33).   Making our way down the workings we notice that the piles of stones are in many instances faced with a dry wall.   Near the lower end we shall come upon two tinners' houses similar to the one already described, but larger.   One measures 19 feet by 8 feet, on the inside ; the other 13 feet by 7 feet.   Below the site of the streaming operations the Wollake enters a glen, on the eastern side of which are some masses of granite called Black Rocks, and having traced its course partly through this, we shall find on the R. bank the remains of what there is documentary evidence to show was once a tin mill, or place for crushing the ore, even were signs wanting that such was the case.   In a forester's account of the time of Henry VIII. there is an entry of 3d. having been received as rent from " Richard Coole and Thomas Hele, for a mill called Wallack Mill, and two acres adjoining in the Forest of Dartmoor."   Behind this little building is a ruined wall, which makes a semi-circular sweep on the hillside, and is continued on the L. bank of the stream.   This, it will be seen, encloses a space of about two acres, which there can be little doubt is the parcel of land named by the forester.   That the building was a mill is shown by the

15. BRENT & IVYBRIDGE DISTRICT.

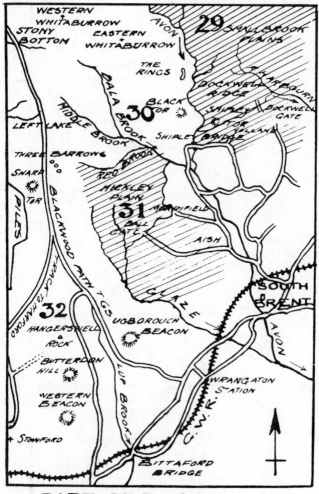

PART OF Ex. 29, 30 ;"
Ex. 31 & 32.

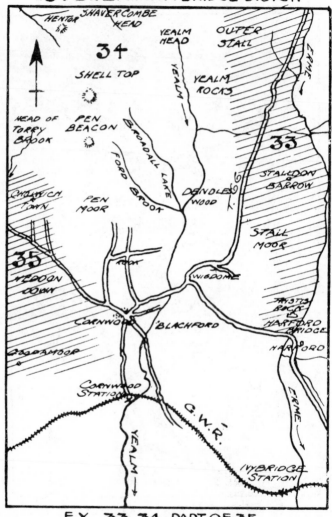

EX. 33, 34; PART OF 35.

remains of a water-course leading to it. On the inside it measures 17 feet by 7 feet. Within the wall, on the L. bank, is another erection, 18 feet by 8 feet, but no doorway is to be seen.*

Below these remains the Wollake runs on through the rocky hollow to the Erme, flowing past what is now generally referred to as Erme Pits Hill, R., but which is probably the same that was known in the seventeenth century by the name borne by the stream, and on which there are several deep excavations. John Webster, the author of *Metalographia* (1672), obtained some information about the mining in this locality from one Thomas Creber, a tinner, of Plympton. He learnt that " the hills where they get tin ore, near that place where he lived, are called Yelsbarrow and Woolack." The former, though now spelt Eylesbarrow, which is a near approach to its ancient form, is always pronounced as Webster spells it.† The working just described, as well as those at Erme Head near by, give a good idea of the different means employed by the tinners in their search for ore. Streaming was the earlier mode ; the sinking of pits a more modern practice. Erme Head is noticed in Ex. 33.

A short distance from the confluence of the Wollake and the Erme (the tributary is here the larger stream), the former is crossed by the Abbots' Way (T. 1), at Black Lane Brook Ford. This old track runs along the foot of Green Hill, close to the Erme, and is seen again at Dry Lake Ford, less than ½ m. further E. As we make our way over it we have Horton's Combe across the river, R., and on passing the last-named ford shall notice another combe also on that side, which the moormen call Knocking Mill. These are described in Ex. 33. Here the valley of the Erme is seen extending southward, between Stall Moor R., and Brown Heath and Quickbeam Hill, L. Keeping near the Erme we soon reach Red Lake Rushes, below which we shall find a little fording-place close to the confluence of the two streams. We cross here, and strike up over Brown Heath E.S.E. to Western Whitaburrow, 1¼ m. distant.

Should the visitor desire to include Erme Pound and the antiquities near it (Ex. 32) in this ramble he may do so without increasing the distance very much. In such a case he will keep near the Erme on crossing Red Lake, his course being S. The pound is only about ¼ m. down the valley. Western Whitaburrow, which, however, is not in sight, bears E. from it, and E.N.E. from the lower end of Stony Bottom. But it will be the better plan not to return thither, but to follow the bottom to its head, and leaving Whitaburrow ½ m. L. strike E.S.E. to Knattaburrow Pool.]

Turning from the cairn from which we have had such an extensive view of the moor, we make our way S. along the tramroad, and at the distance of ½ m. shall notice that it is crossed by a reave running N. and S. This, which is sometimes referred to as Meynell's Bank, was thrown up some years ago when an attempt was made to enclose Brent Moor, but which was resisted by the commoners. Should the rambler

---

* A more detailed account of this old mill was given by me in the *Western Antiquary*, in 1889, and also of the stream works in this part of the moor.

† The name has also been spelt Ailsborough, and there are several other renderings.

desire to make his way back direct to Shipley he will follow the tram-road as in R. 7, walking on the edge of it when he reaches that part upon which the bog has encroached.   This will take him by the pits of the deserted Brent Moor Clay Works R., an undertaking started about 1872, but which had a very short existence.   These, which will be seen at the head of a streamwork, are sometimes referred to as Petre's Pits, but this merely on account of their being in the vicinity of Petre's Cross.   One of the pits is named Hill's Pit, and another Hall's Pit, from two of the adventurers, who may consequently be said to have left something besides their money on the moor.   Further down, where the tramroad bends R., is Broad Rushes L., which extends to Ryder's Plain, and with that tract separates Zeal Plains from Zeal Hill. On the R. of the rambler is Bala Brook Heath, and here, on rather miry ground, are a number of hut circles within enclosures.   Bala Brook, which rises at the workings referred to above, is one of three streams that run, when united, under Zeal Bridge, and fall into the Avon.   The others are Middle Brook and Red Brook.   Between Bala Brook and Middle Brook is Knattaburrow Hill, and between Middle Brook and Red Brook is Old Hill ; southward of the last-named stream is Hickley Ridge and Plain.   The banks of all have been worked for tin, and the name of the principal one, Bala Brook, there is very little doubt has reference to this, *bal,* signifying a mine, and being in use among miners in the West at the present day.   On the L. bank of this brook, and near its confluence with the middle stream, are the remains of one of those little buildings which seem not inappropriately to have been named caches (see *Terms* Section).   Near Broad Rushes a mile-stone will be seen by the side of the tramroad, and further on another marked " $\frac{1}{4}$." Here the rambler may leave the path and strike L. over Zeal Hill to Shipley.

If we decide to return by way of Knattaburrow and Rde Brook we shall, on reaching the bank before referred to (from which a distant view of Plymouth is obtained) follow it across Whitey Mead, the depression between the head of Stony Bottom, R., and the source of Bala Brook, L.   On reaching its termination we shall notice that the Brent Moor boundary is marked by upright posts.   This line extends nearly to Three Barrows, and runs roughly parallel to the one we have already noticed on Brown Heath.   The area between these lines forms a part of Ugborough Moor, which is here very narrow ; the tract to the west of the latter is in Harford parish.   We shall follow the boundary line S. for $\frac{1}{4}$ m., when we shall find ourselves close to Knattaburrow Pool, L.   This is probably an old claypit, but its irregular shape conceals to a great extent its true character, and it has consequently the appearance of a natural tarn.   In this respect it is certainly more interesting than the better-known Crazy Well Pool.*   Knattaburrow, which is a fine cairn and well placed, will be seen a short distance off S.E., and to this we now make our way.   Here we strike the track leading from Ball Gate to Bala Brook Head, and which, as we have already stated (T. 61), is sometimes called Jobbers' Path (in fact, it is so named on the Ordnance Map), but incorrectly.   Jobbers'

---

* Knattaburrow Pool is sometimes spoken of as Petre's Pits Pool the name being taken from the cross in the vicinity.

Path is really the Abbots' Way, and elsewhere I have brought forward evidence to show that the name is found upon that path at several points between the Avon and the western side of the moor (*Crosses,* Chap. IX.)* The track is question runs to the Zeal Tor tramroad, which in turn touches the Abbots' Way at the Crossways, as we have seen, and it is this connection which has probably led to the name having been given to it. Much confusion has arisen from the loose manner in which names have been sometimes applied to places and objects on Dartmoor. Lakehead Hill, near Post Bridge, has been turned into Naked Hill, and I have before me an account of a run with the fox hounds in which a ruined building, bearing the name of Snails' House (derived from a story attaching to it) is referred to as Mr. Snell's house. I could give a number of similar instances.

Follow the track S.W., we soon reach the head of the combe down which Middle Brook runs, and which is known as Petre's Pits Bottom. In this are the ruins of a building, in which it used to be said that the horses employed at the Red Lake Peat Works were stabled. It now goes by the name of Petre's Pits House, and sometimes as Uncle Ab's House. Below the higher part of the hollow Middle Brook bends a little to the L., and flows between high banks covered with the debris of old mining operations, as well as of more recent ones, as a comparatively modern building and wheel pit will show. Passing the combe the track goes on over Red Brook Ball, as the higher part of Old Hill is called, to Red Brook Mires, ½ m. S., which it crosses at Higher Ford, but we shall now leave it and bear L., our course being S.E. by S., for 1 m. This will bring us to Lower Ford, which is situated on Red Brook, about the middle of its course, and at a point where the stream turns rather abruptly to the L. Among the mining remains on Red Brook are a few small buildings, and near the ford is a shallow granite trough. (Further N., on the other side of Old Hill, is another crossing-place, also known as Lower Ford. This is on Middle Brook, and just beyond it is Bala Brook Ford ; they are both near the confluence of the two streams named).

Tracing Red Brook downward we shall speedily be led to one of those little beauty spots that are found occasionally in some out-of-the-way corner of the moor. This is Henchertraw, where the stream is shut in between high banks, approaching closely to each other, and covered in places with moss. Heather grows no their edges, and from their sides mountain-ash trees spring, the tremulous leaves hanging over the tiny cascades formed by the brook as it forces its way through this miniature canyon. [*Gems,* Chap. XVI.] Below this the waters run into the united Bala Brook and Middle Brook, and here on the R. bank is the interesting hut enclosure called the Half Ring, to which we have already referred. The wall, which is 204 yards from end to end, and about 4½ feet in height, describes the greater part of a circle, but does not appear ever to have formed a complete one, the river being probably deemed a sufficient protection on one side. Within it are four hut circles in a fairly good state of preservation, and the vestiges of

---

* In a proclamation naming the bounds of Erme Plains the boundary is said to run from " Petre's Cross, and so on to Abbots' Way, otherwise Jobbers' Path, and from thence to Red Lake Head." See Ex. 32.

others. In the higher part of the enclosure there are several small courts, similar to those we have already noticed at The Rings, on Ryder's Plain. Close to the stream on the opposite bank is another enclosure, in which there are also hut circles.

Passing downward we soon reach a small plantation, close to which is a hunting-gate. From this a path running near to the Bala Brook will lead us across two fields to the road at Zeal Bridge (T. 73). Here we turn R. to Didworthy, or Aish.

[For the direct route to Western Whitaburrow from Shipley see R. 58 and S. Ex. 107.]

Ex. 31.—*Diamond Lane, Hickley Plain, Three Barrows, Hobajon's Cross* [EXTENSION to *Erme Pound*, add 5 m.], *The Rowe Rew, The West Glaze, Stone Rows, Fallen Dolmen, Ball Gate, Coryndon Ball, Aish Ridge*, 8½ m.

Our first point will be the Shipley road, near Didworthy Bridge, which we may reach either by way of Lutton or Aish, as in Ex. 30. Thence we proceed towards the moor, and in ¼ m. shall find ourselves at the foot of Diamond Lane, which runs up to the commons L. This bridle track, of which we have already spoken (T. 59), will now become our path,' and though it is steep and rugged, it is probable that we shall make better progress than did the coach and four which, according to local tradition, was once driven up here [*Crosses*, Chap. XVI.] Near the head of the lane the rambler will notice a granite trough, apparently an unfinished one ; objects such as this were usually cut on the spot where a stone suitable for the purpose was found, and were often, for some cause or other, never completed. The ancient track goes on between two newtakes, when the common is reached, but we shall strike up the slope R., and on gaining the head of the short stroll, turn L. and make our way over Hickley Plain, our course being a little N. of W. In 1½ m. from the newtake corner we shall reach the summit of the hill known as Three Barrows, which rises to a height of 1,521 feet, and forms an important landmark in this part of the moor. It derives its name from a group of three large cairns, the centre one of which stands on the crest of the eminence. These are on the great reave which we have already noticed in the *Terms* Section ; in fact, the centre one is actually placed upon it, as it were ; the southernmost is close to it ; and the northernmost only a few yards removed from it. This reave, which is referred to in the sixteenth century as " a long conger of stones called Le Rowe Rew," comes up the hill S. from above East Glaze Head, where it presents the usual appearance of a bank of turf. North of the cairns its character is different. Here it may be likened to a causeway, though it is difficult to see how it could ever have served the purpose of a road, as has been suggested, since it is only continued for a short distance.

In 1871 the late Mr. Spence Bate, while engaged in some antiquarian investigations here, found the mutilated head of a cross. This in all probability was the remains of one of four set up in 1557 by Sir Thomas Dennys and others who had been appointed to survey the bounds of Brent Moor, which was then in the possession of Sir William Petre. The commissioners certified that they had erected these as follows :—One on the middle cairn at Three Barrows ; another at Western Whitaburrow, which we have already noticed (Ex. 30) ; a third at Buckland Ford, of which I have never been able to discover any traces ; and a fourth at Wella Brook Foot, at the corner of Huntingdon Warren, which is still standing (Ex. 29). On the old map of Dartmoor now in the Albert Memorial Museum at Exeter, and which it seems probable was prepared in connection with this inquisition on the Brent Moor boundary, a cross is shown southward of Three Barrows, standing on a calvary, and bearing the name of Hobajon's Cross. As no cross is now to be found on the spot indicated, it is possible that it was removed by the commissioners to Three Barrows. [*Crosses*, Chap. II.] But the name is now attached to an object about $\frac{1}{3}$ m. N. by W. of the centre cairn—a small pile of stones on the boundary between the parishes of Brent and Ugborough. This is also a bondmark of that tract of moor known as Erme Plains, which, though partly in the parish of Ugborough and partly in Harford, is within the manor of Ermington. But I do not find that in the proclamation read at the time of perambulating the bounds of Erme Plains any mention of Hobajon's Cross is made. The point in question is there referred to as " a small heap of stones near Left Lake Head, at the end of the ridge of stones which proceeds north-west from the middle borough of Three Boroughs." (See Ex. 32).*

[EXTENSION to *Erme Pound and the Brown Heath Antiquities*, add 5 m. Erme Pound may be readily reached from Three Barrows, from which it is distant $2\frac{1}{4}$ m. The rambler will proceed down the " ridge of stones " to the " small heap," whence the boundary of Brent Moor is marked by a row of posts running N., the same which we saw at Meynell's Bank (Ex. 30). This, however, must not be followed. Instead, the rambler will strike down the hill L. towards the row erected on the line between Ugborough Moor and Harford Moor, and at the distance of a few hundred yards will strike the Blackwood Path (T. 63), into which he will turn R. This will lead him to a ford immediately below Left Lake Mires, and shortly afterwards to the U Stone, where he will cross the boundary line. The path runs on W. of the latter, and nearly parallel to it, to a ford on Hook Lake in Stony Bottom, and not far from the hut enclosures referred to in Ex. 30, and described in Ex. 32. These will be found L. soon after crossing the stream. This part of the moor, which is particularly interesting from an antiquarian point of view, is noticed in the last-named excursion.]

The view from Three Barrows embraces a great extent of moor, on one hand, and of cultivated country on the other. It overlooks the frontier heights in this part of Dartmoor, being nearly 300 feet higher than Ugborough Beacon Rocks, and considerably more than 400 feet higher than the Western Beacon, above Ivybridge. Much of the Erme Valley is in sight, but due W., where it is formed by this conspicuous height and the lofty down crowned with Stalldon Barrow it cannot be seen. To look upon that part of it the rambler must descend the hill for a little way. On this side, below the line of the

---

* Among other forms of this name are Threberis, Tryberie Boroughs, Triborough, and Tre Boroughs. Hobajon's is always Hoppyjone's with the moormen.

Harford boundary stones, there are several groups of hut circles, some of the examples of these ruined dwellings being particularly good.

Turning from the three huge piles of stones we shall follow the reave down the hill S.S.E. for about ¼ m., passing on the way a small tumulus of the kind usually heaped over a kistvaen. The boundary line of Brent Moor goes on to East Glaze Head, but we shall leave it and continue S.S.E. to West Glaze Head, and follow that stream for nearly ½ m. to Glascombe (*i.e.*, Glaze Combe) Corner. At its source scattered stone heaps covered with moss, and a shallow gully, attest the former presence here of the tinners, and on the way down we notice other objects reminiscent of them. The stream at first runs through a rather wide and flat bottom, having low banks, but soon these approach each other and form a hollow. In this, at the head of a marshy spot, is a cache, not unlike the one we have noticed on Rue Lake, near Rival Tor (Ex. 19), in being partly the work of Nature. This little secret store place is nine or ten feet long and about three feet high. About twenty yards from it is a granite trough. Further down, and not far from Glascombe Corner, a very extensive working commences, and at the head of this, among the heaps of debris, is a mould stone. Part of this working is within the farm enclosures which are now reached, the wall having been carried through it. At the corner there is a ford where the track from Buckfast to Plympton crossed the stream (T. 59). This we shall notice is roughly paved.

[Should the rambler desire to return by way of Owley, which route will take him down the valley of the Glaze, he will follow the instructions given in S. Ex. 110. The valley itself, and also Ugborough Beacon, are noticed in S. Ex. 111.]

Turning eastward we make our way along the ancient path with the wall of the enclosures close to us R., and shall shortly come upon a group of pre-historic remains which, if not particularly striking, is yet of more than ordinary interest to the antiquarian visitor. It consists of eight parallel rows of stones ; one running westward from a low tumulus, and seven seemingly being connected with a small circle, of which only a part now exists. The rows, which extend for about a hundred yards, are incomplete, and the stones composing them are small, but their number is unusual, and it is this feature that will attract the attention of those who are interested in such monuments. Perhaps these remains may properly be regarded as forming two monuments ; one consisting of a single row, the other of seven.

Passing onward we soon reach the East Glaze, at Glascombe Upper Plantation, where there is another ford. This stream is now regarded as forming the western boundary of the parish of Brent, but it has been said that formerly this extended to the West Glaze. In a document dated 1812, in which the acreage of the commons and waste lands of the manor of South Brent are set forth, there is an entry referring to the Glazes, which is stated to consist of over sixty-four acres, and to be situated "between Easter and Wester Glazes." Another entry refers to Glascombe, which, according to the document, was "formerly said to be in the parish of South Brent." It is further stated that it "now pays rates and taxes to Ugborough ; said to be lost from Brent by a man who was found dead on the spot and buried by the charity of the inhabitants of Ugborough, and is in measure 42a., 1r., 38p." This story, which we remember to have heard many years ago, is a counterpart of the one related in connection with Sourton Common (S. Ex. 35 ; cf. also Ex. 34), and is also met with in other places. It would appear, however, that the existing bounds of Brent Moor in this locality, are the same as those recognized in the sixteenth century, for a document of the date 1557 draws them from " a certain valley or place where and in which two waters called Les Glases run together into one " to Glaze Head, and thence by the reave running up to Three Barrows (Ex. 31).

Making our way by the wall we soon draw near Ball Gate, and here, on the L., close to a despoiled cairn, of which little now remains, is a ruined dolmen. It is unfortunate that this should have fallen, or perhaps have been intentionally overthrown, as examples of this kind of monument are rare on Dartmoor. The supporters show that it was not of great height, but its surroundings must have rendered it very striking, particularly when the cairn near it was intact.

Northward of these remains is Brent Fore Hill, or, as it is some-times called, Homer Hill, meaning the hill nearest the Brent in-ground. Still further N. is Hickley Plain, over which we passed on our way from Diamond Lane to Three Barrows.

Passing through Ball Gate and the little drift court (see *Court* in *Terms* Section) we enter upon Coryndon Ball, and follow the road over this with Treeland Down on the further side of the wall L.,* as in S. Ex. 109, where the way over Aish Ridge is described.

From Ball Gate we may also return by way of Merrifield, as shewn in S. Ex. 108.

[A rather more direct route from Brent to Three Barrows, 4 m., is *via* Aish and Ball Gate, S. Ex. 110 ; from Wrangaton, 4 m., by Peek Gate and the Glaze, S. Ex. 111 ; from Ivybridge, 4½ m., by Addicombe and Hangershell Rock, Ex. 32 and S. Ex. 115.]

SHORTER EXCURSIONS FROM BRENT.

S. Ex. 99.—*Brent Hill*, 3 m. This fine hill of trap rock attains an elevation of 1,017 feet, and commands extensive views of the South Hams and South-eastern border heights of the moor. It may be reached by way of Lutton (Ex. 29). Turn R. on reaching the green and pass up through a narrow lane to the down. Soon after entering upon it the rambler will observe a little gate in the wall above. Pass through this and turn L., and keeping near the wall, make for the summit. This part of the down is known as Beara Common. Shortly before reaching the top a rampart and ditch will be seen, the hill having formerly been fortified on this side (cf. Brent Tor, Ex. 9). The other side was naturally protected, being there very steep and rocky. Of the little building which once crowned this conspicuous height only a fragment now exists. This has already been noticed in our *Terms* Section (see *Beacon*). From no hill on the moorland borders is the view more varied than from this one. Southward there is a fine

---

* On this down are several hut circles which are sometimes **referred** to as the Pixies' Rings.

panorama of field and woodland, with farmsteads and towers of village
churches. The valley of the Avon can be traced for many miles ;
glimpses of the Channel off Torbay and westward of the Bolt Tail are
obtained ; the higher part of Torquay is seen, and several landmarks
on the coast, with Berry Head and the Bolt Head. S.W. is Ugborough
Beacon, with the moor extending from it northward ; the valley above
Shipley is seen N. by W. ; beyond it rises Eastern Whitaburrow, and
to the R. of this Huntingdon Warren house is seen peeping over Dockwell Ridge. Away to the N. is Hameldon, and between it and Challacombe Down, W. of it, the break in the huge hill in which Grim's
Pound is situated is plainly discernible. R. of Hameldon are the
lofty tors above the E. side of the Widecombe valley, and when the
sun is shining on it the tower of Widecombe Church clearly reveals
itself. N. by E. is Rippon Tor, with the bosses of Hey Tor looking
over the shoulder of the hill it crests, and below it the woods of
Buckland. To return strike down the hill due E. to a gate opening
upon a bridle path. Turn R. to the high road, and passing Leigh
Cross descend to the village.

(The crags on the W. side of Brent Hill are best seen by turning
L. on entering upon the down above Lutton. If this route is followed
the visitor may make his way to the summit by the grassy slopes
between the piles. Another way to the summit is by the steep path
E. of Underhill Farm).

S. Ex. 100.—*The Valley of Dean Burn*, 12 m. With road to Dean
Prior Church and Buckfastleigh. For the first 3 m. the way lies along
the old road to Buckfastleigh. Cross the eastern railway bridge
and ascend Leigh Cross Hill. Keep L. at the fork. Note the bridle
path leading to Beara Common L. just beyond. Straight on to Harbournford Cross, then down the hill to Harbournford hamlet, where
there is a footbridge, built clapper fashion, over the Harbourn (Ex.
29). Ascend the hill passing Dean Cross and Clampits Stile, to a
plantation, where the road forks.

(The lane R. leads to Dean Prior, the way to which by the new road
from Brent is shown in R. 66. Here Herrick was vicar from 1629 until
1647, when he was deprived of the living, but he returned to it after the
Restoration, and died here in 1674. The road going straight on leads
down to the new road at Dean ; Buckfastleigh is about 1 m. further).

The road L. is the one we must follow, leaving the plantation on
our R., and just after passing this must again turn L., and then almost
immediately R. The lane will take us down to Dean Combe, beyond
which we reach Warn Bridge on the Dean Burn. Close to this is a
gate where we gain access to the narrow valley named after the stream,
and which extends upwards to Lambs Down and Cross Furzes. The
scenery throughout is of a romantic character. The sides of the
vale are wooded, and in places grey crags thrust themselves from
amid the foliage, while the stream forcing its way through its rocky
channel forms more than one fine cascade. [*Gems*, Chap. XV.] The
sound of falling water tells the visitor that he is near one of these ere
he has advanced far into the wood. This is the spot where one
Knowles, a weaver, is condemned to do penance in the form of a black
hound, according to a tradition gathered in the neighbourhood by
Richard John King, an authority on Devon folk-lore and antiquities.

The basin into which the water falls is known as the Hound's Pool ; further up is Pan Pool, and this also has its story. Passing up the valley under Dean Clatters, and noticing Skerraton Farm high up on the side of a combe L., the visitor will draw near Larkham Wood and reach the termination of the path, when he will find it his best plan to climb the side of the valley R. to Wallaford Down. Over this he will make his way northward to Cross Furzes, where he will turn down L. and cross the Burn. From this point the homeward route is shown in R. 33 and S. Ex. 103. Cross Furzes and Lambs Down Farm near by, are noticed in S. Ex. 101. and also is Skerraton Down, from which there is a fine view of the valley.

S. Ex. 101.—*Cross Furzes and Scorriton Down*, 14 m. With road to Holne. By the Lutton road to the little green beyond Bloody Pool, as in Ex. 29. Thence down the lane R. to Gigley Bridge, which spans the Harbourn. On the L. are the enclosures of Dockwell Farm and Reddacleave Farm, and in the valley R. Higher and Lower Thynacombe Woods, past which the stream flows on to Zempson Bridge and Harbournford. Pass upward from the bridge and turn L. Avoid the lane R., which leads by Dean Combe to Buckfastleigh and Ashburton (R. 73). This is marked by a guide-stone showing the direction of the last-named town, and also that of Totnes, Plympton (or Plymouth), and Tavistock. Continue onward to Skerraton Down, and leaving the road, follow the green track which runs up over it.

[By striking across the down, near the hedge R., the brow of the hill forming the western side of the valley of Dean Burn will be speedily reached, and a fine view of that romantic glen obtained. On the R., overlooking Dean Wood, but unseen, is Skerraton (S. Ex. 100), the ancient Sciredun, once held, together with lands in Shipley, by David, by the serjeantry of two arrows when the king hunted on Dartmoor. It was afterwards similarly held by Roger Mirabel, but being forfeited by him was given to Walter Medicus, and in 1275 was in the possession of John Boyvile, who married Dionisia, the daughter of Medicus. Skerraton appears in a forester's account of 1502 as " Shiridon in parochia de Dene," and then paid a venville rent of 7d.]

The track leads to a gate at the higher part of the down opening on to Dean Moor, and from this goes onward by the wall of Lambs' Down to Water Oke Corner, from which point the reave referred to in the section on *The Moors of Holne and Buckfastleigh* runs up the hill to Pupers. If the visitor is driving to Cross Furzes he must pass through this gate, and turning R. to another enter upon Lambs' Down, the way then running in front of the ruined farm.* But the pedestrian will leave the gate L. and pass across the higher side of the down near the wall, and will shortly afterwards descend to a little feeder of the Dean Burn stream. Pass through the hunting-gate and up the narrow path. Here is a fine view of the valley. Close by are the ruined walls of Lambs' Down Farm, locally Lemson Farm. The track now descends to the Burn, where is a fording-place, and a single stone clapper 11 feet

---

* The down is usually referred to as Lambs' Down Waste in order to distinguish it from the farm. Just above Cross Furzes on the Dean Burn is Lower Ford, and still further up is Higher Ford, and Forder Farm.

8 inches long, 3 feet 7 inches wide at its centre, and about 10 inches thick. At its western end the date 1705, followed by the script letters G.R., is cut upon its surface, and about the middle of it near its edge is a later one—1737, preceded by the letters B.D.A. From the bridge we ascend the side of Cross Furzes, a small open space where several roads cross (T. 1). The first on the R. runs S.E. across Wallaford Down, a common between the Dean Burn valley S. and King's Wood N., and thence by Wallaford Cross to Buckfastleigh. The next on that side runs about E. down the hill between King's Wood R. and Brook Wood L. to Hockmoor Head, on the road from Buckfastleigh to the moor. The one running N. from the higher corner is the Scorriton and Holne road ; and the other bearing L., or N.W. from the corner goes on past the entrance to Hayford to Lid Gate, which opens on Buckfastleigh Moor. Note the guide-stone near the corner with the initials of Brent, Tavistock, and Ashburton. Following the road running N., the rambler will descend to Two Oaks, ½ m., and take the L. branch at the fork, and ½ m. further on will cross the Mardle at Combe Bridge. About ¼ m. beyond this is the hamlet of Scorriton, where a road turns L., or W., up the hill to Scorriton Down.

[From Scorriton, where is a small inn called The Tradesmen's Arms, the Holne road runs to Holy Brook Bridge, near which a lane leads L. to Michelcombe, a small hamlet. (The Holy Brook comes down from Gibby's Combe Wood through Michel Combe, which gives name to this little place). On crossing the bridge keep R. up the hill. At the top turn L. to Play Cross, and then R. to the village.]

The rambler will make his way to the down as above, passing Clarke's Barn Plantation immediately before he reaches it. Here he will follow a track for a short distance W., which will lead him to Chalk Ford, on the Mardle (T. 56), which stream enters Scae Wood just below. (For a notice of the objects in this locality see the Section on *The Moors of Holne and Buckfastleigh.* Above the ford the Wheal Emma leat will be seen rolling down the hill into the Mardle, from which the water is again taken above Combe and conducted to the mine. Turn S. up the hill on crossing the footbridge, keeping the enclosures close L. Pass the stroll leading to Lid Gate, and also Hayford Plantation, L., and about ¾ m. further on Water Oke Corner will be reached. Here the rambler may turn eastward, and keeping the wall L., make his way to Skerraton Down, on entering upon which he will follow the instructions given in R. 33 and S. Ex. 101 ; or he may bear S. and strike the green path running to Dockwell Gate (T. 55). This path leaves Parnell's Hill L., and descends to the head of Dockwell Hole, (note the bond-stone called The Goose, R.), where it is a plainly defined track, and can be readily followed to the gate. Pass up the wide stroll to the little green, whence the way to Brent is shown in S. Ex. 103.

S. Ex. 102.—*Cross Furzes and Pupers*, 13½ m. To Cross Furzes as in the preceding excursion. Strike L. from the higher corner up the lane to Lid Gate, with Hayford L. On emerging on the moor the rambler will find himself at the foot of Pupers Hill, the rocks on its summit being about ½ m. distant. These are noticed in the Section on *The Moors of Holne and Buckfastleigh.* Having visited them the rambler may follow the reave extending S.S.E. from Inner Pupers, *i.e.*, the eastern pile, down the hill to Water Oke Corner. Here he may

choose his homeward route as in the last excursion. The most direct
route to Pupers from Brent is by way of this corner, which may be
reached as directed in S. Ex. 101, or S. Ex. 104.

S. Ex. 103.—*Dockwell Hole and Skerraton Down*, 8 **m.** **Dockwell**
Gate is the first point ; see Ex. 29. (From here Shipley Tor is ¾ m.
distant L., the way to it lying along by the wall outside the enclosures).
Turn R. soon after passing through the gate, and descend the slope to
Dockwell Hole, as directed in Ex. 29, where the remains near Harbourn
Head are noticed. A track goes eastward from Harbourn Head Ford
to a gate in the wall of Skerraton Down, whence a road runs by the
side of it to the lower corner, S., at which it is entered upon from
Gigley Bridge, as described in S. Ex. 101. This the rambler may
follow, or he may strike across from the Long Stone to the gate further
N., at the higher part of the down, as noticed in the same excursion.
In either case his point will be the lower corner. On leaving the down
here follow the lane and take the first turning R. to Gigley Bridge, as
directed in R. 33. On crossing the bridge pass up the lane to the little
green, and bear L. Exactly ½ m. on, and just after passing Blood.
Pool R., is Gingaford Cross (guide-post). Here take the R. branch.
A short distance further on the road again forks, the R. branch going
on past Downstow to Yolland and the moor. Take the L. branch,
and ¾ m. on Lutton Green will be reached. Continue on the road, and
at the foot of Splatton Hill keep L. to the village, with the vicarage
grounds R.

S. Ex. 104.—*Huntingdon Warren* direct, *via* Dockwell Gate and
Water Oke Plain. The Warren House is 6 m. from Brent. To Dockwell Gate as in Ex. 29. Thence the way will lie over the Combestone
Tor track, with Dockwell Hole at the bottom of the slope R. On
passing the head of the hollow Parnell's Hill is R., and Small Brook
Plains L. A straight line to the Warren House would take the rambler
to Brock Hill Ford and over Hickaton Hill, but the better way is to
continue on the green track over Water Oke Plain to a little fording
place on the leat, ½ m. N.W. of Water Oke Corner. (The route to this
point *via* Gigley Bridge is shown in S. Ex. 101). Huntingdon Bridge,
in front of the house, is 1 m. distant W. by N., and the ground is good
throughout the way.

[The warren may also be reached from Shipley (Ex. 30, S. Ex. 106).
If the L. bank of the Avon be chosen it should be followed up to Lower
Huntingdon Corner, and the Wella Brook be crossed at Huntingdon
Ford ; if the rambler proceeds by the R. bank (S. Ex. 106) he will
cross the river at Avon Ford, which is close to the other.]

A return route from the warren is given in Ex. 29.

S. Ex. 105.—*Yolland, Dockwell Ridge, and Shipley*, 7 **m.** To
Lutton Green as in Ex. 29. Straight on N. for about ¼ m., when a gate
L. must be entered and the footpath followed over some fields. Cross
the lane at Over Brent Farm and another field, then turn R. into a
second lane ; follow it for a few score yards and turn up the hill L.
At Downstow Cross. ¼ m., a lane turns L. to Didworthy Bridge. Here
note the view : northward Shipley Tor, westward Ugborough Beacon
Rocks, and southward Brent Hill. A little further on is Yolland
Cross. Enter the gate and follow the road past the farm and the fine

grove near it (R. 73). A short distance beyond this leave the path and strike L. across Yolland Waste to a hunting gate, Yolland Warren being L. On passing through the gate Dockwell Ridge is reached. Under this name is comprehended that part of the Brent common land situated on the E. side of the Avon, and consisting of 374 acres, the northern boundary of which is marked by the line of posts extending from Dockwell Hole to Small Brook Foot. Turn L. to Shipley Tor, ½ m. westward. Shortly before this is reached a circular stone, 3 feet 10 inches in diameter, and 10 inches thick, will be seen built into the wall. It is similar to the one we have already noticed near Dockwell Gate (Ex. 29) and the same size, but the hole in its centre is only about 2½ inches deep. This wall cuts across Shipley Tor, and another runs down the hill S. from the rocks at right-angles to it. On the W. side of the latter is Black Brake, and on the lower side of this, there are more of these circular stones. (These may be reached by passing through the hunting-gate near the tor to another gate R., a little way down the hill. Just above this, one of them, in a partly finished state, may be seen in the wall, and below the gate but on that side of the wall facing W., is another. The others are further down ; one is on its face, and partly built upon, and another, which is also on its face, is hidden among scattered rocks and bushes. These were probably intended for mill stones, and not for crushing ore. I have known those who remember when it was customary to go to the moor to cut stones for the corn mills, and that this had been done for a long period is most likely).

From the hunting-gate we pass down the hill S. to the road (R. 33) where we turn R. to the moor gate. The return from Shipley Bridge to Brent is given in Ex. 29. If the rambler chooses the route *via* Didworthy he need not cross the bridge from the point he has now reached, but may make his way to that place by a pleasant footpath. Close to the gate is another, L. ; this he will enter, and the path will lead him across some fields to the one opening on the yard at the back of the Sanatorium. The wooded Didworthy Bottom (noticed in the next excursion) is kept R.

S. Ex. 106.—*Shipley Bridge and Long-a-Traw,* 9 m. To Shipley *via* Lutton and Didworthy, or *via Aish,* as in Ex. 30. If *via D*idworthy the rambler may take the field path from that place to Shipley, as in the last excursion. He will cross the lane on leaving the yard of the Sanatorium, and passing up by some cottages will soon reach the fields, over which he will follow the path with Didworthy Bottom L.

[A private path runs through the woods from Didworthy Bridge to Shipley. This is carried along the L. bank of the Avon, and from it a view of the confluence of that river and Red Brook, or Bala Brook, is obtained (Ex. 30), the picture being a very charming one. It also passes close to a rocky canyon known as Zeal Pool, at the head of which is a cataract, and still further up a series of beautiful cascades. Just below the latter the path approaches quite near to the river. [*Gems,* Chap. XVI.]

From Shipley the road running eastward by the enclosures of Shipley Cottage should be followed for about ¼ m., when a gate will be reached L., from which a hunting path leads to the tor (R. 64). A track runs N. from the latter over Stone Heath, and parallel to it, and near to the wall, is another, but neither goes very far out. By follow-ing the line of these the rambler has a good view of the narrow valley below, with Brent Moor House and Brent Moor Cottages close to the river. Keeping near the decayed boundary hedge L. he will pass above the two clatters that stream down into the river, known as Woolholes and Higher Woolholes, in which Reynard sometimes finds a shelter. Near the point where the hedge turns down the hill some small pounds containing hut circles will be noticed, and further E. on Dockwell Ridge are several low reaves. Here the rambler will descend to Woola Plain on the L. bank of the river at the lower end of Long-a-Traw (Ex. 29), where is a deserted granite quarry. He will now make his way upward, noticing Long-a-Traw Islands as he proceeds. Not far from this, on a part of the plain called Peathy's Path, are the faint vestiges of a hut, or building of some sort. In front is Gripper's Hill, and between it and Small Brook is Itifer Bottom, which runs up to Small Brook Plains. This part of the moor, including the canyon through which the Avon flows, is noticed in Ex. 29. Crossing the river either immediately below the canyon, or at Viger's Corner a little way above it, the rambler will make his way down the R. bank. (The Rings are on the brow of the hill above him, Ex. 30). Ere he has pro-ceeded far it will be necessary to leave the river, as near it is Black Tor Mire, but when opposite to the granite quarry, and under Black Tor, he may again approach it, and will then follow the road down its R. bank. The little building near where he strikes it was once a smithy connected with the quarry, and not far from this, and close to the path, there was formerly a rock to which the name of Hobbs' Nose was given, from its fancied resemblance in form to the nasal organ of a certain quarryman of that name who once worked there. Just below Brent Moor House a granite pedestal will be noticed on a rock R. This was erected to the memory of a little daughter of Mr. Meynell, who formerly resided here. The river here runs over a solid bed of granite. A little further down, R. of the way, and below Stone Hollow, is the Hunter's Stone, a rock bearing the names of four fol-lowers of hounds well known on Dartmoor in a former day—Treby, Trelawny, and Bulteel being graven on its sides, and on the top Carew. This memorial was the work of Mr. C. A. Mohun-Harris, who lived at Brent Moor House for a time. Not far below there is a fine water-fall. Passing the buildings originally erected as a naphtha factory, and afterwards repaired and utilized by the Brent Moor Clay Company (T. 60), the rambler reaches Shipley Bridge. For routes to Brent see Ex. 29, S. Ex. 105.

S. Ex. 107.—*Western Whitaburrow direct.* This cairn is 5 m. from Brent. To Shipley as in Ex. 30. Then by the old Zeal Tor tramroad as shown in R. 58.

S. Ex. 108.—*Hickley Ridge, Henchertraw, and Merrifield,* 6½ m. To Zeal Bridge and through the gateway L. as in Ex. 31. On reaching the common keep near the river to the Half Ring, and then follow up Red Brook L. to Henchertraw (Ex. 30). Just above this strike S.S.E. over Hickley Plain to Merrifield Plantation, ¾ m., which keep L. Near to this is the grave of Quicksilver, a hunter belonging to Mr. Calmady, which dropped dead here when being ridden by his owner after the

Dartmoor hounds about thirty years ago. Enter the gate below the plantation, and follow the path past Merrifield Farm to Badworthy Brook, where turn up the hill R. to Binnamore Cross. Turn R. to Aish.

S. Ex. 109.—*Merrifield, Brent Fore Hill, and the East Glaze,* 6½ m. To Aish and on by the Shipley road, or by the pathfields entered above Lydia Bridge, as in Ex. 30. ½ m. beyond the hamlet Binnamore Cross is reached. Turn L. and descend the hill with Staddon Plantation on that side, to Badworthy Brook, where a track leads L. to Treeland. On passing over the brook turn L. up across the fields past Merrifield to the common. Strike W.N.W. over Brent Fore Hill to some rocks known as Sharp Tor, not far from East Glaze Head, which is ¾ m. S.E. of Three Barrows. This stream rises in a marsh, on the lower side of which vestiges of the operations of the old tinners are observable. Following it downward a small working is soon reached, and a little removed from the L. bank is a gert over 100 yards in length, and about 15 feet deep. Below the working a leat is taken from the stream, and here, but on the opposite bank, is a hut circle. Still following the Glaze the rambler will speedily reach Glascombe Upper Plantation, where he will turn L. to Ball Gate. Here is the fallen dolmen and ruined cairn noticed in Ex. 31. Passing through the gate, as in that excursion, the rambler will follow the road by the side of Coryndon Ball R. to the plantation of the same name. The road will lead him down by the side of this to a stroll at the end of which is a gate. Pass through this and up the hill to Aish Ridge. Then leave the road and strike L. up over the common by the gravel pit following the green path to the gate at its eastern corner. From here a lane runs down the hill to Aish, ½ m. distant. (Another, leading to some fields, branches from it ; on reaching this keep R.)

S. Ex. 110.—*Aish Ridge, Coryndon Ball, Glascombe Bottom, Owley,* 6½ m. To Aish as in Ex. 30. Avoid the first turning L., but take the next on that side at the higher part of the hamlet, and follow this up to the down. Thence across this westward to Aish Ridge Plantation. Keep this L., and descend the hill to the gate. Pass through the stroll, and up the narrow lane with Coryndon Ball Plantation L. Thence the road runs straight on to Ball Gate. Coryndon Ball is an enclosed down, extending about ½ m. from N. to S. and the same from E. to W. It is bounded on the W. by the East Glaze, and on the slope above that stream there are some small pounds and hut circles ; there are also some stones having something of the appearance of a row. At Ball Gate the rambler will turn L., his route being the reverse of that described in Ex. 31, to which he is referred for notices of the objects passed. This will bring him to Glascombe Corner, ½ m. distant. (Three Barrows is 1¼ m. distant N.W. by N. See Ex. 31 ; Ugborough Beacon Rocks 1¼ m. S.S.E. See S. Ex. 112). Turning L. he will trace the West Glaze down the valley, passing the great stream work mentioned in Ex. 31. This is succeeded by Glascombe Lower Plantation, below which is Glaze Meet. The objects in this valley, which is usually referred to as Glascombe Bottom, being noticed in the following excursion it is unnecessary to describe them here. Near Glaze Meet is a fine pound through which the rough track running down from the corner will take us. Below the pound this crosses the little tributary called the Scad, and soon after leaves the commons at Owley Gate. It then runs for a short distance between the enclosures to Owley where the rambler will turn L. to Owley Bridge, and crossing the Glaze will ascend the hill to Bulhornstone Cross. Here is a circular stone similar to those noticed near Shipley (S. Ex. 105) ; it was originally intended to be used at Owley Mill. The road L., or N., runs up to Aish Ridge ; the one R. runs S. to Broad Moor and Pennaton Bridge ; but the rambler will keep straight on N.E., and will soon reach the road below Aish, where he will turn R. to Lydia Bridge.

S. Ex. 111.—*The Valley of the Glaze*, 8 m. Crossing Lydia Bridge the rambler will ascend the hill towards Aish, and turn L. below the hamlet. A few yards on he will turn up R. and follow the road past Bulhornstone Cross to Owley Bridge (S. Ex. 110). Thence he will pass up to Owley, where he will turn R., and in less than ½ m. will reach the moor gate. On his L. is Owley Corner, to which a track comes out from Peek Gate (S. Ex. 112), and is the one by which visitors from Wrangaton will reach this point (Ex. 31). The road the rambler has been following from Owley now becomes a rough track. About 200 yards from the gate it forks, the L. branch running past the source of the little Scad up the hill to Spurrell's Cross, whence, marked by small stone heaps, it goes on to Harford Gate (T. 62, 59 ; the R. branch running a short distance up the valley. The latter he will follow, and not far on will cross the Scad, near where it joins the Glaze. At that point there is a ford on the latter, from which a private road runs up the hillside between Coryndon Wood R. and Skitscombe Wood L. to Coryndon Farm. Soon the rambler's road begins to climb a slope, and before him he sees grey stones and ferns and thorn bushes. When he reaches these he will find himself at the wall of an ancient pound of a more than ordinarily pleasing character. The vegetation which has partially covered the vallum though not increasing its interest from an antiquarian point of view, certainly does so from the standpoint of the picturesque. In places moss covers the stones, and amid them sturdy thorns and a holly are growing, while ferns are everywhere abundant. A thorn bush has also found shelter in the wall of one of the two dilapidated hut circles within this enclosure. The vallum is 422 yards around, and some parts of it now cover a space of ten or eleven feet in width. It is intact except for a few breaches where tracks have been carried through it. One of these is that by which we have reached the pound, and this crosses it and goes on to Glascombe Corner, from which Three Barrows is 1¼ m. distant. (See S. Ex. 110, Ex. 31). The surroundings are of a romantic character. Eastward there is a steep descent to the Glaze, which here partly hides itself in a wooded hollow, the acclivity above the further bank being clothed with trees. In other directions rise the bare slopes of the moor, with the rocks of Ugborough Beacon crowning the hill to the south, about 1 m. distant. Passing down to the river E. the rambler will make his way up its R. bank, and very speedily find himself at the meeting-place of its two branches. On the peninsula which these form is Glascombe Lower Plantation, and on leaving this the united streams flow for a short distance below Newland's Brakes, which stretch upward to Coryndon Ball. (S. Ex. 110). Glaze Meet is one of the beauty spots of Dartmoor. Here are great boulders of granite, some with coats of moss, ferns and heather, and sturdy hawthorns, a charming cascade, and a dark pool over which trees spread their branches. This is the Wishing Pool, and it is said that those who leap across it, and while doing so loudly express a wish, will obtain what they desire. In the plantation, and near to the confluence, are two heaps of moss-covered stones, not unlike the ruined basements of huts, but their true nature cannot be determined. They are only interesting as perhaps being the remains of a building shown on the old map of the moor to which we have alluded in Ex. 31 as existing on this tongue of land in the sixteenth century. (On the same map Glaze Bridge, lower down the stream, appears as Glaas Bridge).

Leaving this delightful spot the rambler will proceed up stream for about ½ m , when he will leave it and strike up the slope westward, or a little N. of W. This course will bring him to a stone row, which is of rather exceptional interest, in being single at one end, the N.E., and double at the other. From this he will proceed westward to the brow of the ridge, and then turn S. to the cairn on Glascombe Ball, 1 m. N.W. of Ugborough Beacon. This is known as Glas Barrow, and is nearly due W. of the pound on the glaze, but 400 feet above it. These ancient burial mounds abound on this part of the moor ; on the summit of every hill between the West Glaze and the Erme they are found in groups, and are also scattered on the lower slopes. Less than ¼ m. S. of Glascombe Ball is Spurrell's Cross, where the Black-wood Path (T. 63) and the track from Owley to Harford (T. 62) inter-sect each other, but of the monument which once marked the spot only a fragment now remains. [*Crosses*, Chap. III.) A short distance westward is a single stone row running approximately N. and S., and starting from a small cairn, another cairn being near it. It is rather over 120 yards in length, but most of the stones have fallen.*

Turning eastward into the Owley path the rambler will follow it down the hill to Owley Gate, whence he will return to Brent as in the preceding excursion.

S. Ex. 112.—*Ugborough Beacon*, 8 m. The summit of this hill is 3 m. from Brent, *via* Owley and Peek Gate, and 1½ m. from Wrangaton Station, *via* Wrangaton Gate. The first point will be Owley as in S. Ex. 111, but instead of there turning R. to the moor, the rambler will follow the road for about ¼ m. further, when he will reach Peek

---

* This row is referred to in my book on the crosses of the moor (1st Edition, 1884). When the late Mr. R. N. Worth was preparing a paper on the stone rows of Dartmoor for the Devonshire Association (1892) he wrote to me about the Butterdon row, noticed later on (Ex. 32), and in my reply I happened to mention that eastward there was another running parallel to it, referring to this row near Spurrell's Cross. He states this in his paper, but the description he gives is that of the one on the slope of the West Glaze, which we have spoken of above, S. Ex. 111. These rows were named by me to the Ordnance Surveyors in 1883 in response to an enquiry relative to the stone remains in this locality.

Gate, between the plantations of that name.* The rocks on the summit of the Beacon Hill are more than 530 feet above this gate, and over ½ m. from it W. by S.

[The visitor from Wrangaton should enter upon the common at the gate of that name. From the station bridge he will follow the Ivybridge road for a few score yards and then turn R. into Green Lane. This will shortly bring him to Marwood's Cross, where is a guide-post. Here he will cross the old highway, which runs L. past Wrangaton to Bittaford, and R. past Glazebrook to Brent Bridge, and make his way up the lane to Wrangaton Gate, ¾ m. from the station, at which point the Blackwood Path commences (T. 63). The rocks are ¾ m. N.W. by W. Other gates opening on this part of Ugborough Moor, are Shute Gate, a little to the N. of the last-named, and Leigh Gate further W. Shute Gate is close to Deals Brake, and at the head of Deals Bottom ; Leigh Gate mentioned in the sixteenth century as Laye Yeat, is W. of Knowle Plantation, which abuts on the golf links. On a kind of sketch plan of the moor appended to the document *Instructions for my Lord Prince, temp.* Henry VIII. South Steeryton Yeatte appears opposite to what may be taken to be the venville lands of Dean and Ugborough. It is probable that this gate was to be found nearer the former place than the latter. There is also early mention of Eston Gate in this neighbourhood, but this cannot be identified. Leigh Gate is the most convenient for visitors from Bittaford Bridge. The golf links at the foot of this hill may be approached by either.]

The tor crowning this fine frontier eminence consists of several distinct piles, neither of them being of great height, yet forming a rather striking group. They are sometimes spoken of as the Beacon Rocks, though more often as Ugborough Beacon, and sometimes as the Eastern Beacon. But the ordnance map gives the name of Ugborough Beacon to one of the piles only—the westernmost one, round which a cairn 84 yards in circumference has been built—and applies the name of the Eastern Beacon to another cairn 178 yards S.S.W. of the former. (This one is so dilapidated and overgrown with grass that I found it difficult to take a correct measurement of it, but it is about 48 yards in circumference). On what authority these cairns were so named I do not know, but if the hill ever was a station on which signal fires were lighted, it is highly improbable that there were two within a few yards of each other. It is, however, very doubtful whether this hill was a signalling station. I have elsewhere brought forward some evidence to show that in this instance the word *Beacon* is probably a corruption of *Pigedon, i.e.,* Peek Down. [*Crosses*, Chap. II.], and have also referred to the subject in the *Terms* Section (see *Beacon*). One of the masses of granite, it will be seen, is nicely balanced on a very small base, and another, on the northern pile, overhangs and forms a rude canopy, beneath which is a seat of such convenient proportions as almost to lead one to suppose that the work of Nature has been supplemented by that of man. Perhaps it was here that a certain

---

* Shown as Picke Yeat on the old map in the museum at Exeter referred to in Ex. 31. The farm of East Peek is between Peek Gate and Cheston.

Mr. John Elliott—Lord Elliott, as he was afterwards called—once took his seat, when he came, as it used to be said, to this lofty spot to look down upon Brent, which manor he was then contemplating the purchase of, and which he subsequently acquired.   The seat seems to have escaped the notice of former antiquaries, otherwise it is nearly certain they would have told us that it was the chair of an arch-druid.   A fine view is obtained from the rocks, the elevation of which is 1,233 feet. The village of Brent is seen E.N.E., and Ugborough S.S.E., together with many places in the South Hams, the whole of which district is visible.   Much that is commanded from Brent Hill (S. Ex. 99) the visitor looks upon here, and westward sees other objects, among them being the great rounded Kit Hill on the further side of the Tamar.

(To the S.S.W. of the cairn to which the name of the Eastern Beacon has been attached, and 135 yards from it, are two others, 25 yards apart.   The larger is 94 yards in circumference, the other being 70 yards, and both are much covered with vegetation.   A short distance down the hill, in the midst of some old workings, is a small mound, but its real nature is not apparent).

Turning from this fine group of rocks the rambler will make his way down the slope of Beacon Plain, his course being a little N. of W. This will bring him to a shallow gert in which the Lud rises, and to which the name of Main Head has been given.*   Here there are two small mounds of earth, each enclosed by a low stone wall, but they present nothing remarkable.†   From this spot Spurrell's Cross is about ½ m. distant N. by W. (S. Exs. 111, 113), and is approached by the Blackwood Path (T. 63).   Into this, which runs near the L. bank of the little stream, the rambler will now turn, and following it southward by Creber's Rock, will soon reach the golf links.   He will leave it here L. if making his way to Leigh Gate ; for Wrangaton he will follow it to the enclosures ; and for Peek Gate will leave it on the R. and strike northward towards the plantations close to it.   If he is bound for Brent he will there turn L. to Owley, whence the road is described in S. Ex. 110.

(The route from Brent to Holne Moor and Hexworthy is given in the *Routes* Section (see *post*).   Reverse, T. 55.   The route to Aune Head and Hexworthy will be found in R. 64 ; Reverse R. 33).

EXCURSIONS FROM IVYBRIDGE.

Delightfully situated on the Erme, one of the most beautiful of the Dartmoor rivers, the large village of Ivybridge extends itself into four parishes, and these meet at the structure which gives the place its name.   On the E. side of the river is the parish of Harford to the

---

* The Lud leaves the moor just above Bittaford Bridge, and flowing past Ludbrook falls into the Erme below Ermington.

† These mounds are evidently not particularly old, nor do they seem to partake of the character of mining remains.   In 1861 there was a military encampment on this part of the moor, and it is possible that the mounds were thrown up for some purpose by the soldiers.

N. of the bridge, and Ugborough to the S. of it ; on the west side Corn-wood to the N. and Ermington S. The first three each embrace a considerable portion of the moor, and extend to the forest, the latter does not touch the waste, but, as we have already seen (Ex. 31), the lord of the manor of Ermington, possesses certain rights upon Erme Plains, which tract of moor lies within the bounds of Harford and Ugborough, and thus the bridge may be regarded as the centre of four places having a connection with Dartmoor. The present lord of the manor of Erming-ton is Mr. F. B. Mildmay, M.P., of Flete. In spite of its modern sounding name Ivybridge has long been so called, for Risdon speaks of one Alfred de Ponte Hedera, to whom a grant of land here was con-firmed by Sir John Peverell, lord of Ermington, in Edward the First's time. The bridge was formerly very narrow (the visitor will probably be inclined to think it is not much other now) being only of sufficient width to admit of a packhorse crossing it. This structure still exists (though it is probably not the original one) as may be seen from the rocks in the stream under it, where the mark between the older and the added portions is plainly visible. The bridge is situated immediately in front of the London Hotel.

Ivybridge Church, being a modern structure, possesses no features of particular interest. Neither does the old church it replaces, though this is certainly a picturesque object. Its dismantled walls, and the low tower, thickly covered with ivy, will be seen close by, and give the impression of the ruin of an ancient building, and yet it is only of comparatively recent date. But the visitor with a taste for ecclesi-astical architecture will find something to reward him when he makes his way to the fine church of Ugborough, or to Ermington Church, with its curious bent spire, while Harford and Cornwood, though much smaller, are good examples of moorland churches.

Ivybridge is placed amid scenery of a charming character. The Erme, with its deep pools and cascades, the wooded valley of Stowford Cleave, the moor hills that look down upon it, the pleasant pastures on the south and east and west, all make up a picture that will delight the rambler who fixes upon this village as a base whence to explore the southern part of Dartmoor.

Ex. 32.—*The Western Beacon* [*Ugborough Beacon*] *Butterdon Hill, Sharp Tor* [*Three Barrows*], *Erme Plains, Antiquities on Brown Heath, Erme Pound, Mining Remains on the Erme, Piles Copse, Butter Brook, Addicombe Slaggets,* 14 m.

Our starting-point will be the old bridge from which we shall pass up the hill with the extensive paper mills of the Messrs. John Allen and Sons, L., and soon after crossing the railway reach Stowford. Of the ancient mansion very little now remains. This formerly belonged to Matthew de Ivybridge, as Risdon calls him, whose daughter brought it to the Dymocks. It afterwards came to the crown, and was purchased by Adam Williams, whose descendent, Thomas Williams, was Speaker of Parliament in the time of Elizabeth. There is a brass to his memory in Harford Church. John Prideaux, who became Bishop of Worcester, was born of humble parents, in a cottage at Stowford. He is also commemorated by a brass in that church. Turning R. behind the house we pass up a lane to the commons, and then strike eastward to the Western Beacon, which is about ½ m. distant, and nearly 400 feet above the moor gate. (This may possibly be Stonorde Yeat, of which there is early mention). The view from this fine border height, the southernmost of all the Dartmoor eminences, is one of great beauty. The estuary of the Erme is in full view, and we are placed so high above it (1,088 feet) that it looks quite near. The West Pigedon of an older day, it forms a conspicuous landmark from numerous points in the South Hams. Eastward rises East Pigedon, now represented by the hill crowned with the Beacon Rocks (S. Ex. 112). Most of the tor has been destroyed by quarrymen, and the six cairns that are to be seen here has been despoiled. One of these was placed on the rocks, but very little of it now· remains. The foundations of a small square building are to be seen upon it. It is not possible to obtain a correct measurement of all of these cairns, but one of them is 85 yards in circumference, and another· 67 yards.

A line of boundary stones runs N. to Butterdon Hill, ¾ m., and this we shall now follow. About mid-way is Black Pool, through which the line passes, the eastern part of it thus being in Ugborough parish and the western in Harford. This pool, which is very shallow, is oblong in shape, and 95 yards in circumference. A dilapidated cairn may be seen close to on the S.W.

[If the rambler desires to visit Ugborough Beacon from this part of the moor he will find it the better plan to branch off here, and not ascend Butterdon Hill. The summit of the Beacon Hill is just over 1 m. from the pool, and the course to be steered is N.E. by E. The way lies N. of Cuckoo Ball Corner, and Lud Brook is crossed about mid-way. The rocks to which the name of Claret Tor has been given will also be passed. The beacon is noticed in S. Ex. 112.]

Cairns.   Ugborough Beacon.

Cairns.

FROM BUTTERDON HILL. LOOKING N.E.

Continuing on our way we pass the Long Stone, as the first boundary pillar N. of the pool is called, and then climb up between the scattered rocks to the summit of Butterdon, 1,204 feet. Here there are three cairns, while others are found on the slopes near by. These three are nearly in a line running N.E. and S.W. The N.E. one is 92 yards in circumference ; the middle one 80 yards ; and the other 50 yards. Close to the centre cairn are the foundations of three small comparatively modern enclosures. W.N.W. is Weatherdon Hill, the summit of which is only ⅓ m. distant. On this there are two cairns, 115 yards apart, one 79 yards in circumference, and the other 62 yards. They appear to have been opened ; at all events hollows have been made in them. Between the two hills there is another cairn, 53 yards in circumference.

Stalldon Barrow.	Sharp Tor.	Three Barrows.	Eastern Whitaburrow.

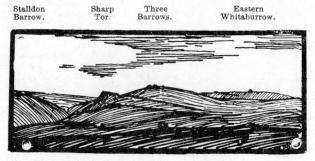

Piles Hill. Hangershell Rock.

FROM BUTTERDON HILL. LOOKING N.

About 43 yards N.E. of the north-eastern cairn is a stone circle 35 feet in diameter, enclosing a cairn the diameter of which is about 20 feet. Only eight stones are now to be seen, and these have all fallen but two, which are in a slanting position. From this circle a stone row extends northward for a distance of 1,791 yards, and this has been adapted as the boundary between the moors of Ugborough and Harford. We shall now follow it, and when at a distance of 640 yards from the circle, with Hangershell Rock, noticed in S. Ex. 114, L., shall reach a small grass-covered cairn R. On this a small shelter has been formed. I remember when some horse races were held here, and the course can still be seen near this tumulus.* It is connected with a track that comes up from the in-country southward of the Western Beacon. (On the E. side of the ground the course touches the Blackwood Path (T. 63). About ⅛ m. N. of the tumulus the stone row crosses the path from Owley to Harford (T. 62), which, however, is here not very clearly defined. Spurrell's Cross is less than ¼ m. E., and a little nearer to us than that point is the stone row we have already noticed (S. Ex. 111, T. 62), which runs parallel to the one we are following. A little further on we cross a depression extending upwards from the source of Butter Brook, and in this are eight rifle butts, four on each side of the shallow hollow. These are of granite and were erected when the soldiers were encamped near here in 1861 (S. Ex. 112). The cairn on Glascombe Ball (S. Ex. 111) is ¼ m. R., or E. of this point.

Still following the stone row we pass up the slope N., and soon arrive at its termination, which is marked by a small pillar about 3½ feet in height, set in the centre of a circular pavement 6 feet

---

* This was about forty years ago, and the meeting was attended by a large number of people from the neighbouring parishes.

9 inches in diameter. On its W.S.W. face is an incised cross 7 inches high and 5½ inches across the arms. On the old map of Dartmoor, to which we have several times referred, Hobajon's Cross, noticed in Ex. 31, is shown as standing in this row, and I have elsewhere suggested that this stone with the incised cross may not improbably mark the place it occupied [*Crosses*, Chap. II]. From this point the Ugborough and Harford boundary is marked in the same way as it is S. of Butterdon Hill, that is, by a row of posts, and this, which we have already noticed, we shall follow, and on Piles Hill shall strike the Blackwood Path (T. 63), which comes up R. from Spurrell's Cross. Here we see a cairn L., and on the further side of this is the branch path which enters on the moor at Harford Gate (T. 63). A little way on is another cairn L., and just beyond this the two tracks unite. Some distance below us L., is Piles Gate, at the S.E. corner of Higher Piles, which we shall pass on our homeward route.

Leaving the track we strike L. to Sharp Tor, a solid mass of rock placed on the brow of a steep hill and overlooking Piles, the higher wall of which enclosure is carried along the side of the declivity below it. Close to the tor is a large cairn. The summit of Three Barrows is about ½ m. distant (Ex. 31). Making our way northward we shall strike the track again, and soon pass Piles Corner, where the wall turns downward to the Erme. Immediately inside it are some hut circles, and a noted fox holt known as The Dungeon, where, so Mr. C. A. Harris tells us in his *Foxhounds of Devon*, a well-known master, deeming the occasion demanded it, once thundered forth the Epistle to the Danmonians.

Our track will lead us below Three Barrows and Hobajon's Cross, which are noticed in Ex. 31, to the long-deserted Left Lake clay pits, and on passing over the brook at Left Lake Ford we find ourselves on Erme Plains, of which tract of moorland we have already spoken. This comprises Quickbeam Hill and Brown Heath, though on the Ordnance map the name is attached only to a narrow stretch of level ground through which the Erme flows, this flat, we presume, being considered the only justification for calling any spot near here a plain. (See that word in the *Terms* Section). The first recorded perambulation of the bounds of this tract took place in 1603, and subsequently it was customary to view them once in every seven years. When this was done a proclamation was read at certain points on the Erme giving notice of the perambulation, and setting forth the rights belonging to the manor of Ermington. The tenants have the right of pasture, and the lord the right of free fishery, not only where the river bounds the tract in question, but from its source to the sea, and also the right to all wreckage found in the river, or as far from its mouth seawards "as an umber or tar barrel can be seen."

Passing onward we cross the Ugborough boundary line, and make our way along the lower side of Quickbeam Hill, with several groups of hut circles below us L. In about 1 m. we reach Belter's Ford on Hook Lake, in Stony Bottom, less than ¼ m. below the line, one of the pillars in which, near the hollow, bears the initial letter of Ugborough, and is known as the U Stone. The bottom has been streamed throughout, but the heaps thrown up by the tinners are now in great measure clothed with plants, and the spot is a favourite one with whortle-berry gatherers. At its head are some deep pits, and the scanty vestiges of a mining hut. On crossing it we are on Brown Heath, where is one of the most interesting groups of remains on the moor. These consist not only of relics of prehistoric times, but also of those of mediæval days. The cluster comprises three pounds forming a large hut settlement, a stone row, and kistvaens, as well as an old drift pound with accompanying buildings, and vestiges of tinners' operations, which include a blowing-house with a mould-stone.

The track which we have followed to this point now bends L., and running through the southernmost of the hut enclosures, again turns and goes N. along the L. bank of the river to Erme Pound. It is here not very clearly defined, but by turning in the direction named the visitor will speedily arrive at the ruined wall. On the side nearest Stony Bottom this makes an inward sweep, so that the enclosure, which measures 338 yards in circumference, is irregular in shape. The stones composing the wall are now scattered over a width of about 11 feet ; the entrance appears to have been on the northern side. In the western part of the pound a wall runs across it N. and S., thus cutting off a portion of it, and about the middle of this wall is a small hut circle, 10 feet in interior diameter. Immediately without the wall on the N.W. the basements of two other dwellings are to be seen. Two walls there run out from the main one for a short distance, and the two huts being placed between these, and being connected with a piece of wall about 12 feet long, act as a third side, and thus a small court is formed. The larger of these huts has a very perfect basement. Its diameter is 16 feet ; the other is 12 feet. Another hut circle, about 21 feet in diameter, will be seen N. of the enclosure, and in this is a low curved wall, which, however, does not run entirely across it, the part that appears to be wanting being probably the doorway leading into what may have been an inner apartment.

On the E. side of this lower enclosure a wall runs out from the main vallum for a distance of about eight yards, and from this, but at a right angle to it, a double stone row runs up the slope for a distance of 170 yards, and terminates in a small circle 30 feet in diameter, enclosing a ruined kistvaen. At its lower end some of the stones in this row, which is about five feet wide, are from 3 feet to 4 feet high, but most of them are small. Near its upper end it passes quite close to a hut circle, and above this it is nearly obliterated. Ten stones remain erect in the circle, one of them being 5 feet high and 3 feet wide ; two others are fallen, and some are missing. The best view of the row is obtained from this point, where the beholder looks down the slope and sees it throughout its length.

This circle is placed close to the wall of another enclosure, 126 yards from the lower one, and forming a particularly fine example of an ancient hut pound. It is 426 yards in circumference, and the wall, which is formed of very large stones, is about 5 feet in height and of considerable width. In places these are seen lying in courses. On the northern side is a block 9 feet long, which has its ends supported by two others, a hollow being formed beneath it. Near this the wall is imperfect for a distance of about 30 feet, the stones perhaps having sunk, the ground being here rather boggy. There appears to be an entrance on the S.E., and another on the S., and here a wall runs across the pound. Close to this is a hut circle, and there is another in the middle of the enclosure. Outside the wall, but connected with it by two smaller ones, is a hut circle 22 feet in diameter, a small court being thus formed in a similar manner to the one seen in the lower pound.

Thirty yards N. of this enclosure the visitor will come upon the third, in which, however, there is nothing particular to note. The wall now resembles a low reave, and near it are what appears to be the remains of a kistvaen. It closely adjoins Erme Pound, formerly used for estrays, and which possesses a peculiar interest as being the only things of its kind in the purlieus of the forest, and throughout Dartmoor with the exception of Dunnabridge Pound, above West Dart (Ex. 5, 42)* The wall of each stands on the line of an ancient circumvallation, as even a slight examination is sufficient to reveal, and although there are many instances of newtakes having been formed on the sites of hut enclosures, these are the only pounds whose walls are reared on such primitive foundations. When Erme Pound was built the stones of the older enclosure, the line of which it followed, would, of course, be used, but it is probable that recourse was also had to the wall of this higher one. Other later enclosures were also formed here, for in an account of the forester of the south quarter of the time of Henry VII. there is an entry of 1½d., " being new rent of Thomas Rawe, John Beare, and others for one acre of land on the common of Devon lying neare to Yerme next Erme Pound and Quyocke Beinefote [Quickbeam Foot] to hold to them according to the custom of the forest of Dartmoor."

The view from the higher part of these hut groups, which extend upward for about ⅓ m. from the foot of the slope, and are appropriately known as Erme Pound Rings, embraces the most solitary parts of the extensive southern border commons. It is a scene of desolation. Not even a tor is visible ; only long stretches of heath with the great ridge of Stalldon rising high to the south. The Erme pursuing its course through the long valley alone gives life to the picture. But the seclusion of this part of the moor endows it with a certain charm, while the remains of an older day found here on every hand give to it an exceptional interest. The visitor who enters the Erme valley where the cultivated country gives place to the moorlands, and passes up through it till he reaches the spot where the river rises, will find something to attract him throughout the whole of the way.

We shall now proceed to the pound, which is connected with the enclosure last noticed by some old walls. It is situated on the side of the hill, the lower, or western, part of the wall being at its foot, and on

---

* The statement that has been made that " there are several other enclosures in this neighbourhood, of which most appear to have served a purpose similar to that of Erme Pound," this purpose being the securing of cattle at the drifts, is incorrect. The only enclosures in the neighbourhood of the pound are those described above, which nobody ever supposed to be drift pounds—that is, nobody who had visited the spot, which the writer of the statement is question had not. Nor would anyone who knew much about Dartmoor suppose that more than one drift pound would be found in any locality. As a matter of fact there were only four or five for the whole of the moor. The manor pounds near the border villages are of quite a different character.

the brink of the river. In shape it is roughly circular, and is 345 yards in circumference. The gateway, which is 8 feet wide, is on the S.S.E., and here the wall is 6 feet thick. It is from 4 feet to 4½ feet in height, being at its lowest on the higher side, where the ground is covered with rocks. The lower part of the pound is fairly clear of granite. Four hut circles exist within it, with vestiges of others, and tiny courts may be seen adjoining them, but the remains are in a very ruinous state. Outside the gateway, but near to the pound, are the walls of a curious little building 22 feet long by 12 feet wide. A low stone bench, or seat, 15 inches high and 22 inches wide, runs round its interior. Further down is another, which is rather larger, but this has no bench. In this a gable is still standing, and it will be noticed that the doorway is protected by a kind of passage. These buildings were probably erected as shelters for those attending the drifts when the pound was in use. They stand in a small clatter.

[About ¼ m. above Erme Pound the river receives Red Lake (Ex. 30, R. 64). W. of the pound is the stone row running over Stall Moor, and noticed in Ex. 33. S. of it is a ford, where the track coming out from Watercombe Waste (T. 66) crosses the river. Should the rambler desire to make his way down the R. bank of the Erme, he may cross it at this ford, or he will find a place where he can generally do so at the foot of Stony Bottom. Directions for this route, which will lead him down to Harford Bridge and past the church, are given in Ex. 33.]

Leaving Erme Pound we pass down with the river R. to the point where Hook Lake falls into it, and very near to this shall find a good example of a blowing-house. It is 27 feet in length by 17½ feet wide. and like a good many of these buildings stands against a bank. A watercourse may be seen leading to it, and where this is taken from the Erme are the remains of a weir. Lying within the entrance is a granite block in which there are two tin moulds, one in a complete state, the other partly destroyed. It is interesting to find a notice of this stream work in the seventeenth century. In a lease of the date 1661 it is described as " a certain Tynnwork called, or known, by the name of Hooke Lake, situate within the parishes of Brent and Ugborough, and within the jurisdiction of the Stannary Courts of Plympton and Ashburton." Hook Lake, it may be explained, rises on Brent Moor, and then crosses Ugborough and Harford Moors, which are here merely narrow strips of land running out to the forest. Opposite to the confluence of Hook Lake and the Erme is Green Lake Bottom, noticed in Ex. 33. (For the route to Brent from this point see Ex. 30).

Passing down the valley by Quickbeam Foot, and noticing on one hand the evidences of mediæval mining, and on the other those of the presence here of man in times still further remote, as shown by the ruined huts on the slope of the hill L., we shall, when about 1 m. below Hook Lake, come upon some ruined walls where these evidences are combined. At the lower end of a circular enclosure containing huts, and within a few yards of the river, is a small rectangular building of the type erected by the tinners. Just beyond this we cross Dry Lake, and almost immediately afterwards Left Lake, which forms the southern boundary of the tract over which the Ermington manorial rights extend. Still continuing to follow the Erme, we at length pass

Crooked Oak, and find ourselves at the wall of Higher Piles. On the hillside L. all the way down to this point, hut circles and small pounds are numerous.

[The rambler who does not care to scramble through the rocky enclosure below, but who is content to view the ancient oak wood known as Piles Copse from a distance, may here turn up the hill, and on arriving at the higher corner of the newtake will turn R., and keeping close to Piles Wall pass under Sharp Tor. On reaching the corner at Piles Gate, where the wall is carried down the hill W. by the side of Piles Brook, he will leave it and strike due S. till he reaches the branch of the Blackwood Path (T. 63), which he will follow to Harford Gate.]

Entering Higher Piles Newtake we shall pass down by the stream finding a path through the oak wood, or between it and the river, along the bank of which it extends for about ⅓ m. The trees are not of the size of those in Wistman's Wood (Ex. 5); they more nearly resemble those at Black Tor Copse, on the West Ockment (Ex. 14). But there is evidence that the wood is of considerable age, and thus an additional interest is lent to it. It is figured on the old map of Dartmoor now in the museum at Exeter. ¼ m. below it we shall come upon an ancient enclosure, and a little further on shall cross Piles Brook and enter Lower Piles, up across which we shall make our way through a wilderness of granite to Lower Piles Corner, S.E. Here are a number of hut circles, and low walls arranged in such a curious manner as to render it difficult to understand the plan of the cluster.

Outside the newtake and not far from the corner, is a kistvaen near a dilapidated hut circle. This kist is about 3 feet deep, and is placed in a partly demolished circle, of which only seven stones are now standing. The cover stone is missing, and the northern end of the kist is composed of several small stones instead of one slab like the other end and sides. Striking due S. we soon reach Harford Gate, into which the rambler may turn and make his way to Ivybridge past Broomhill and Lukesland, as in Ex. 33.* If he desires to return by way of Addicombe he will continue S. keeping the wall R., and just before reaching Butter Brook will notice some very fine hut circles. Crossing the little stream he will leave Tor Rocks, a very interesting pile, R., and still pursuing a southerly course will soon reach the wall of the Combeshead enclosures, where a track will lead him across Addicombe Slaggets to the moor gate (T. 64). (Opposite Addicombe are two ancient enclosures which are noticed in S. Ex. 114). From the moor gate the rambler will make his way by the lane to Stowford, and thence follow the road down to the village.

Ex. 33.—*Harford, Tristis Rock, Stalldon Barrow, Stall Moor Circle, Erme Head, Valley of the Erme, Harford Bridge, 17 m.*

We shall first make our way up the hill to Stowford, as in Ex. 32, but instead of turning R. to the common shall follow the lane past Lukesland and Broomhill to Harford, one of the most delightfully situated hamlets on the moorland borders. (Near Broomhill the rambler may desert the road and strike over some fields R. to the

---

* This gate appears as Harford Yeat in the sixteenth century. Lukesland stands near the site of a house formerly known as Lukesland Grove.

church, crossing the Butter Brook a little way below Tor Rocks, by a single stone clapper). Descending to Harford Bridge, placed at the head of the wooded part of the beautiful valley which extends upwards from Ivybridge, we cross it and enter a gate R. Here we are on the track which runs up by the Erme under Stalldon Barrow (T. 65), which, however, we shortly leave and climb the side of Hall Newtake L. towards the enclosures of the ancient farm of that name. This was once the residence of Colonel Chudleigh, father of Elizabeth Chudleigh, whose absurdities, as Macaulay observes, Horace Walpole made it his serious business to record, and who afterwards became Duchess of Kingston. The scanty ruins of Hall Pleasure House are just within the plantation on the verge of the down. They are surrounded by a wall which encloses a space of about an acre in extent. On the further bank of the river is Bullaven, the enclosures belonging to which extend nearly to Lower Piles (Ex. 32). Our way will take us to Tristis Rock, or Hall Tor, as it is sometimes called, whence we have a good view of Stalldon, with Sharp Tor and Three Barrows on the other side of the deep Erme valley.

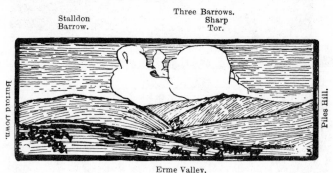

Erme Valley.

FROM TRISTIS ROCK. LOOKING N.

Not far from the rock is a single stone row which starts from a ruined circle and runs N. for a distance of 400 yards, and consists of 112 stones. This we shall follow to Burford Down, and then crossing Yadsworthy Waste, where are a number of hut circles, shall pass upward to Stalldon Barrow. A good view of the moor opens up as we proceed, particularly that part of it lying between the Erme and the West Glaze, the prominent heights on which are Ugborough Beacon, Butterdon, Weatherdon, and the Western Beacon, and on the slopes of these and on the ridges between them many of the cairns that stud that part of the moor are seen clearly defined against the sky.

Stalldon Barrow is really a cairn, but the name also attaches to the lofty hill which it crowns. This hill is situated near the southern extremity of Stall Moor, which may be said to extend from the enclosures of Yadsworthy to Erme Head, a distance of 4 m. Its northern portion, that is the part the more remote from the cultivated country, is known as Outer Stall. This moor is mentioned in the Court Rolls of the forest *temp* Edward IV. as " the land of Stealdon."

The cairn is 60 yards in circumference, but is not very high. On the S.W. side the stones have been removed, and used in the erection of a little house on the summit. Of this only three walls now remain, but they are very substantially built. The story goes that a child was once found on Stall Moor, and was adopted by some good people

| Ugborough Beacon. | Hangershell Rocks. | Butterdon Hill. | Weatherdon Hill. | Western Beacon. | Tor Rocks. | Tristis Rock. |

Erme Valley.

FROM SOUTHERN SLOPE OF STALLDON BARROW. LOOKING S.S.E.

in the neighbourhood. and given the name of Hillson. As a son of the hill this was certainly a very appropriate one, but as though further to justify it, the foundling betook himself to Stalldon Barrow when he grew up, and built a little house there. Here he dwelt and earned a living by making eight-day clocks, and one version of the story says that the first ever seen in the neighbourhood was made by him. Mr. W. Hillson, of Wakeham's Rook, not far from Cornwood village, has had one of the clocks over forty years ; it formerly belonged to a family named Mumford, of Great Steart, in this parish. " I cannot tell how the truth may be ; all I can vouch for is that the little house on the cairn has long been known as Hillson's Hut. About five-and-thirty years ago I heard it stated that a rain gauge was once to be seen here."

On the slope of this hill to the N.E. are some ancient remains, and others occur on the N.W. side of it. To the latter we now make our way, and shall come upon the first of these objects when about 125 yards from the cairn. This is a circular enclosure 22 yards in diameter, the wall being formed of small stones and covered with grass. Outside this wall is a hut circle, but there are none within it. Further on, and nearly ¼ m. N.W. of the Stalldon cairn, are two others, one enclosed in a circle 30 feet in diameter, of which only a few of the stones remain. Both cairns are covered with vegetation. From these remains a single stone row runs S. for a distance of about 460 yards. Some of the stones are large, but few of them are standing.

Proceeding in the same direction, that is, about N.W., we soon strike the track running out to Erme Pound (T. 66), and this we shall follow R. About ¾ m. on we cross Bledge Brook, a little tributary of the Erme,* and just beyond this shall reach the circle sometimes known as The Dancers, and also as Kiss-in-the-Ring. This is 54 feet in diameter, and consists of 26 stones, of which three are fallen. The average height of these is 2½ feet, but there is one 5 feet high. From this circle a single stone row runs northward for a distance of over two miles, terminating in the ruined kistvaen we have already observed on Green Hill (Ex. 30).† The groups of hut circles above the eastern bank of the Erme, noticed in Ex. 32, are here plainly visible, as also are Erme Pound Rings, also described in that excursion. Looking down the valley between Stalldon Barrow R. and Sharp Tor and Three Barrows L., the Western Beacon is seen 4½ m. distant in a straight line. On the slope towards the river, and 123 yards from the circle, is a hut enclosure 320 yards in circumference. This is divided into three parts by low walls, and contains the basements of several ancient dwellings. The whole is in a very ruinous state. Southward, and also on the slope, is another decayed enclosure with hut circles. The Erme Islands in the river form a striking feature in the picture seen from these remains.

From the circle we follow the row northward, and shall notice that the stones composing it become smaller as the distance from the starting-point increases. When rather over ¼ m. from this we pass a mossy cairn 23 yards to the L., or W., of the row, 44 yards in circumference, but not very high. R. of the row is a small pound with hut circles. Just beyond this we reach Green Bottom opposite Stony Bottom (Ex. 32), in which is an old stream work. It is noticeable that the row crosses the latter, and it would thus appear as though the mediæval tinners (for it was they who laboured here, as the ruins of two small rectangular buildings in the combe attest) had such reverence for pre-historic monuments that they did not disturb the row, or where they were compelled to do so, carefully set up the stones again upon their rubble heaps. The circumstance is rather difficult to understand. The row crosses the Erme over ¼ m. N. of the bottom (Ex. 32), and then runs straight to Red Lake, which it also crosses, and ascends Green Hill, where there is a considerable break in it.‡

---

* I have heard Ranny Brook (mentioned *post*) spoken of as Bledge Brook, but from careful inquiry I find the name really belongs to the stream in question.

† I have always striven to be correct in taking my measurements of objects on the moor, some of which I obtained between thirty and forty years ago, but I cannot pretend to such nicety as this : I read that the Stall Moor Row was measured in 1880 and found to be exactly 11,239 ft. 8 ins. in length ! This monument was figured in a paper by the late Mr. C. Spence Bate read before the Devon Association in 1871, and a plan of it was made in 1880 by the Rev. W. C. Lukis, in which year I also briefly described it in the second volume of *The Antiquary*. Nine years later it was " discovered " by a writer during a flying visit to Southern Dartmoor.

‡ In the *Terms* section we have noticed various suggestions that have been made as to the uses or meaning of the stone rows, and among these it will be seen that an astronomical signification has been claimed for them by some. This seems to be the favourite theory just

[The following routes from Ivybridge cross Green Bottom : R. 59, to Princetown ; R. 62, to Lydford ; R. 63, to Okehampton ; R. 64, to Hexworthy and Chagford (if by the R. bank of the Erme) ; and R. 64, from Cornwood to Hexworthy and Chagford.]

From the head of Green Bottom we strike N.W. by N. over the hill to Horton's Combe, passing the head of Knocking Mill on the way, This latter is a combe running down to the Erme, its lower end being nearly opposite to the point where Dry Lake falls into that river.* In winter a rivulet flows through it, but there is no stream in the summer and it is consequently difficult to see how mining operations could have been conducted here, but that they were the stone heaps, now covered with moss, that extend throughout the length of the combe clearly show. At its head are the remains of two small mining buildings, which, like the workings, are clothed with moss. A little way down the combe another runs from it towards the S.W., the lower end of it being on the brink of the river just above Erme Pound. This also has been worked, though no stream runs through it. Between these two combes is Stinger's Hill, at the eastern foot of which is a small strip of ground known as the Meadow. Horton's Combe is so called from having formerly been the spot in which a Cornwood farmer of that name was in the habit of collecting his cattle. It is sometimes known as Hortons' Ford Bottom, and the stream that runs through it as Hortons' Ford Brook. By continuing our N.W. course for another ½ m. we may pass above Erme Pits to the springs of the Erme, or we may keep more to the R. and reach the river where it is yet only a rivulet below the pits.

---

at present according to a report issued by the Board of Education in January, 1909, giving the result of the enquiry of the Solar Physics Committee as to the origin of British stone circles. The report states : " An investigation as to the astronomical origin of the ancient stone monuments which are scattered up and down the country, more especially of those situated in Cornwall, Devon, South Wales, and Aberdeen, has led to the general conclusion that these circles, crom-lechs, avenues, etc., were erected as observatories for the determination of time and season by the observation of the sun and stars. The results of the investigation indicate that the dates of erection lie between 2000 B.C. and 800 B.C." From this it would appear that star-gazing was indulged in nearly forty centuries ago and is still practised. Meanwhile we may content ourselves, if we can, with the solution now offered until such time as another is brought forward. It may be well to note in this connection that in some parts of Scotland stone circles are still erected. A ring of slabs is placed round the peat stacks, which are formed where the peat is cut, to prevent them from being thrown down by cattle, or from falling. When the peat is carried away the stones are allowed to remain, and in a short time present the appearance of an ancient monument.

* Or Hux Lake ; see Ex. 30. In 1502 there is mention of Hertes-lake or Hurtlake in connection with Whitepytte, both on the Erme. It is probable that this refers to Hook Lake, Ex. 32, and not to Hux Lake. Other forms of Erme are Arme, and Irm. In 1468 we have Sedilburgh Hill and Dertstream Hill, " between the rivers Erme and Aune," but these cannot now be identified.

[The following points are within easy reach of Erme Head : Ducks' Pool (Ex. 30) ¾ m. N. ; kistvaen on Green Hill (Ex. 30) 1 m. N.E. ; Red Lake Ford (Ex. 30, R. 7) 1¼ m. E. by S. ; Erme Pound (Ex. 32) 1¼ m. S.E. by E. ; Yealm Head (Ex. 34) 1½ m. S.S.W. ; Broad Rock (Ex. 34) ½ m. N.W. The Abbots' Way (T. 1) passes here, crossing the infant stream at Erme Pits Ford in the midst of the great tin work, and again at Erme Head Ford immediately below where it oozes from the mire, and goes on N.W. to Broad Rock. The perambulators of 1240 mention a bound in this part of the moor which they call Grymsgrove, and this the jurors of 1609 considered to be Erme Head. The next point named in the 1240 perambulation is Eylesbarrow, but in 1609 the line was carried first to Plym Head, and it is this line that is now regarded as the boundary. It runs from near Erme Pits Ford to Erme Head Stone, N.W., on which is the inscription " A Head," the older form of Erme being Arme (which is still used by the moormen), and then abruptly turns westward to Broad Rock, which is near by.]

As we have already seen (Ex. 30), the mining remains in this locality are extensive, and afford examples of streaming and also of open workings. Of the latter Erme Pits, by which name the excavations on the Cornwood side of the stream are generally distinguished from those on Erme Pits Hill, are the largest and deepest. These probably represent the Armed Pit mentioned in 1672 as yielding a particular kind of ore called zill tin. The remains of two little buildings of the usual mining type may be seen in these pits.

Passing down through the stream work, where we shall notice a great slab of granite called the Table Stone, we find for ourselves a path along the R. bank of the Erme, and in about 1 m. shall reach the point where Red Lake falls into it. The river, which will be our companion as far as Harford Bridge, here bends R. We pass along the Meadow, and when opposite Erme Pound shall strike the Stall Moor stone row, and shortly after come upon the track leading from the pound to Watercombe (T. 66). Just below this we reach Green Bottom, from which point downward the bank is covered with the debris of the tinners, among which we shall notice the remains of some of their buildings, one being of more than ordinary interest in possessing a double wall. Bledge Brook is crossed on the way. When opposite Dry Lake (mention in Ex. 32, where the L. bank of the river is described) the rambler should turn aside to the rocky hollow R., the entrance to which is marked by a few mountain ash trees. It is really the work of the miners, but is now so draped with plants that it might well pass for that of Nature. Immediately below Dry Lake is Left Lake (both on the E. side of the stream), and soon after passing the latter we shall come upon a little tributary. A short distance up the hollow R. through which this flows is the best example of a miners' cache to be found on Dartmoor. It is on the L. bank of the little stream, and quite close to it. The entrance is on the higher side, and until this is seen there is nothing to indicate its nature, for in approaching it up stream it has the appearance of a grass covered mound. It is known as Downing's House, and sometimes as the Smugglers' Hole (see *Cache* in *Terms* Section), and a story is related of its having been a place of concealment for contraband spirits. A short distance above it is a little crossing place on the stream, sometimes referred to as Tinker's Bridge. On the hill northward of the cache is a cluster of hut circles.

Still keeping near the Erme we pass over Tom's Plain, where we shall strike the track coming up the valley from Harford Bridge, 2 m. further down, and shall follow it thither (T. 65). It will lead us through the pass in which the ancient oaks of Piles Copse find shelter (Ex. 32), and above which Sharp Tor rises on one hand and Stalldon on the other, the relative situations of which may be supposed to be similar to those of the two mountains chained together by Riquetti. Thence our way will lead us below Burford Down where are pound-like remains, to Hall Newtake, where we emerge on the road.

Turning L. we ascend the hill to Harford Church, and keeping R. shall make our way past the hamlet to Broomhill, ¾ m. from it. Thence the lane will lead us by Lukesland L. and Erme View R. (the latter overlooking the romantic Stowford Cleave) to Stowford House, whence we shall pass down to the village.

Ex. 34.—*New Waste, Stall Moor Gate, Antiquities on the Yealm* [EXTENSION TO *Yealm Head, Langcombe Bottom, and Broad Rock,* add 4 m.], *Broadall Lake, Pen Beacon* [*Shell Top,* add 1 m.], *Rook Farms,* 7½ m. from and to Cornwood.

Our starting-point will be the moor gate at Watercombe, which we may reach either by way of Harford Bridge, saving about ½ m., or from Cornwood. If we choose the former we shall pass over Burford Down as in Ex. 33, and when about 1 m. from the bridge shall turn L. at the end of the Yadsworthy enclosures, and steering W.N.W. shall arrive at the gate, or the track near it, in another mile. If we go by way of Cornwood we follow the instructions given in S. Ex. 119 for reaching that village, and shall then take the road running N.E. from the open space in front of the inn. This will bring us to the Vicarage Bridge, on the Yealm, ¼ m. beyond which we turn L. at Tor, and then almost immediately bend R. At the fork a little further on, where a road runs R. to Yadsworthy, we keep L., and soon reach the gate near Watercombe Farm. Here we enter on New Waste, often called Watercombe Waste, and follow the track northward, and crossing Redaven Lake, with Redaven Gulf R., pass through Stall Moor Gate and gain the open common.* This track, which is the one described as running over Stall Moor to Erme Pound (T. 66), we follow from the point we have now reached for ½ m., when we shall leave it to examine the fine enclosure below us on the L. This is of considerable size, and contains a large number of hut circles. In shape it approaches an oval. On the S.E. side a wall is carried out from the main one with a semi-circular sweep, thus forming a smaller pound. A small stream flows through the larger enclosure and falls into the Yealm in Dendles

---

* New Waste Gate, which opens upon the lane, is the true moor gate, as the waste has not been enclosed more than 80 or 90 years. It may possibly be the one referred to at Lydford Castle in 1479 as Abbot's Gate, for allowing which to be ruinous, to the nuisance of the country, Walter Abbot and another were fined. It is described as "the gate of the Moor at Staledon," *i.e.,* Stalldon. That part of the moor E. of the waste is sometimes known as Steart Ridge.

Wood. This wood, with the bare hill of Hawns on the further side of the valley, which, together form the well-known Hawns and Dendles, is in full view from the pound.

[Stalldon Barrow crowns the hill E., and is about 1 m. distant. It is also about 1 m. from the gate near Redaven Gulf, from which it bears N.E. by E. Ex. 33.]

Close to the hut enclosure a track comes up from between Dendles Wood and Harrowthorn Plantation. This we leave R. and strike N. to a little affluent of the Yealm known as Ranny Brook which flows from the E., and on crossing this shall at once come upon an extensive hut settlement, situated with regard to the river and its tributary like the one on Brown Heath (Ex. 32), and is also placed on a slope. The settlement consists of two pounds, roughly circular in shape, within and without which are a number of ruined huts. The pounds are joined together, and the wall that is common to both being of smaller proportions than the main one, they have more the appearance of a single pound divided into two parts. Regarded in this way the enclosure is 635 yards in circumference. On the S.S.W. is an entrance formed by two large slabs about four feet high, one of which is in a slanting position, and there are other openings. Three little huts of the type known as behive huts, that is, having domed roofs, and which were probably used as shelters for shepherds or herdsmen, have been formed on the ruins of the wall. In the larger of the divisions there are 16 hut circles, some being good examples, and in the smaller division five hut circles. One of these is 21 feet in diameter, and the stones of which its wall is composed are laid in courses. Between the pounds and the tributary huts are numerous—one has the door jamb in a very complete state—and there are also appearances of a reave. Above the pounds, that is N. of them, there a few more hut circles, and these are of a character unlike those usually found on the moor. The basement wall instead of being formed of slabs set on their edges, or, as is more rare, of stones piled on one another, is composed of earth with stone facings, this being, in one example, quite ten feet thick. About 30 yards S.S.E. of the larger pound is a kistvaen in a circle 13 feet in diameter, but much overgrown.

From this ruined settlement of the early men of the moor, we descend westward to the Yealm, here flowing through a romantic glen, into which it falls from a considerable height in a series of cascades. On the L. bank is a blowing-house in a very decayed state, and within it two mould stones, one of which is broken. By following the river upward and crossing it near Yealm Rocks we shall find the ruins of another building, and in this tin was also smelted, as is proved by the granite mould lying within it. This is about ¼ m. above the former. The course of the Yealm on the moor is but a short one, for 1½ m. below its source trees begin to line its banks, and about ¼ m. lower down it enters Dendles Wood. But this moorland part of it is, nevertheless, full of interest. Above the wood is a great streamwork, and at the head of that the hollow through which we have now traced it, while to this succeeds a scene of wildness and desolation. The river separates the two divisions of the common lands of Cornwood : the tract to the E. of it forming Stall Moor, as noticed in Ex. 33, and that to the W. forming Pen Moor.

[EXTENSION TO *Yealm Head, Langcombe Bottom, and Broad Rock :* add 5 m. if the return be made to Yealm Rocks ; if the rambler returns direct to Pen Beacon *via* Shell Top, add 4 m. Passing upward we leave the source of the Yealm, less than ¾ m. distant, and 500 feet higher than where it is joined by Ranny Brook below Yealm Steps, on the R., in order to avoid the mire. We soon draw near the summit of the ridge running N.E. from Shell Top, and along which the Cornwood boundary is carried. This ridge, although so high, is very marshy, but the ground presents no real obstacle to the pedestrian. (In R. 59 the line is drawn from Yealm Head to Broad Rock direct, the marsh being avoided by keeping a little to the R., but we now follow another course). We strike N.N.W. over the ridge, and in less than ½ m. shall reach firmer ground. Then we turn due N. and make our way for ½ m. along the upper slope of Langcombe Hill to Langcombe Bottom, which we should strike about ¼ m. below Langcombe Head. Here, on the R. bank of the stream, is a good example of a kistvaen, standing in a small stone circle. The covering slab has fallen, or has been thrown, into it. The late Mr. Spence Bate considered that this ancient tomb may have been the Grymsgrove of the perambulators of 1240 (Ex. 33), but, as it appears to me, without any better reason than that *grove* may have meant *grave*. Had there been a few trees in the locality it is possible that the name might have retained the form in which we have received it from the perambulators. But there are no trees within several miles of Erme Head, while a number of graves are to be found not far from it. By the change of a single letter one of these could be fixed upon, and so the ancient bound became Grim's Grave. By the suggestion that Grim may have been a chieftain, the founder perhaps of Grim's Pound, the idea was made interesting. But that is all that can be said for it. I see no reason for believing that the jurors of 1609 were wrong when they supposed the Grymsgrove of the " auncient recordes " to be identical with Erme Head. At the same time they certainly appear to have been so in carrying the line from that place to Plym Head. By so doing the common lands of Shaugh Parish are made to run, as it were, into the forest. We have already noticed the occurrence in two localities (S. Ex. 35, Ex. 31) of the story of land having been claimed by a parish on the ground of having given burial to a stranger found dead within the bounds of another which had refused to do so. The story is also met with in this part of the moor, and though probably having no more truth in it than the others, at least points to some encroachment, or altering of boundaries here. The man was found, so the tale runs, lying on the moor at the head of a combe, about ½ m. below Broad Rock, and not far from some scattered granite known as Little Gnats' Head. The combe, down which trickles a small feeder of the Langcombe Brook, bears the name of Deadman's Bottom.

Leaving the kistvaen we strike N.E. by N. over Broad Mead, and in ¾ m. reach Broad Rock, to which we have referred in Ex. 33 and in R. 59. This object is important not only as a bond mark, but also as indicating the point where the Abbots' Way branched (T. 1). It is only 11½ feet long by 7½ feet wide, and not being more than 3 feet high, cannot be seen from a distance, but I remember when a pole standing by the side of it made it a very convenient landmark. On its surface is this inscription :

BB.
BROAD ROCK.

The initials stand for Blachford Boundary, the stone here defining the limits between that manor and the forest.

| Petres Cross. | Erme Valley. | Three Barrows. |

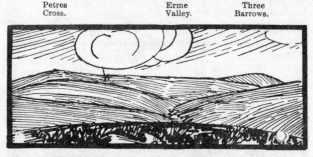

FROM BROAD ROCK. LOOKING S.E.

The view eastward embraces Green Hill, Brown Heath, and Three Barrows. Over the ridge beyond Red Lake Mires the cairn in Huntingdon Warren is seen due E., and to the R. of the mires the Abbots' Way where it approaches Red Lake Ford. R. of Brown Heath is Stony Bottom and Quickbeam Hill, S.E. Turning toward the W. only the heath on which the beholder is standing is seen, but when he has walked a few yards from the rock in that direction, an extensive view suddenly unfolds itself.

| Yelverton. | Sheeps Tor. | Hart Tor. | Peak Hill. | Sharp Tor. Leather Tor. |

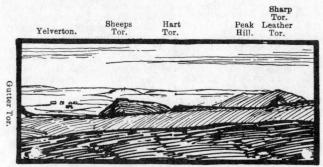

Gutter Tor.

FROM NEAR BROAD ROCK. LOOKING N.W.

Sheeps Tor, Lether Tor, and Sharp Tor are prominent objects to the N.W., beyond which is a fine range of country, backed by the Cornish hills. More to the R. of the picture North Hisworthy and Mis Tor are seen uplifting their forms against the sky.

(From Broad Rock Plym Head is ¾ m. N. ; Ducks' Pool ¾ m. N.E. ; Erme Head over ¼ m. S.E. ; Langcombe Head over ½ m. S. by W. ; Plym Steps 1 m. W. ; and Plym Ford 1 m. N.W.)

The Abbots' Way descends the hill from Broad Rock to Plym Steps, passing the head of Deadman's Bottom, on the side of which is a hut settlement, about midway down. The Tavistock branch goes towards Great Gnats' Head, below which it reaches Plym Ford.

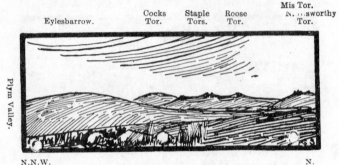

	Cocks Tor.	Staple Tors.	Roose Tor.	Mis Tor. N. ...sworthy Tor.
Eylesbarrow.				

Plym Valley.

N.N.W.   N.

FROM NEAR BROAD ROCK.

The boundary between Cornwood and Shaugh is carried southward to Shell Top, running along the ridge, as we have already observed. It affords no guidance as the bondmarks are few, and the ground being marshy in places, it will be better to keep on the brow of the hill westward of it, unless the rambler prefers to retrace his steps to Yealm Head. In either case he will first return to the kistvaen by the Langcombe Brook, and then if he decides upon the former route will strike S.W. He will pass below Shavercombe Head, but must take care not to descend the hill too much, but keep some distance above Hen Tor (R. 7, Ex. 37). Bearing L., or S.S.W., Shell Top, 2½ m. from Broad Rock, will be reached. A few rocks crown its summit, and round them a small cairn has been built. But the rambler who climbs this lofty height is not likely to bestow his first thoughts upon objects such as this ; his attention will be attracted by that which is seen from it. One of the finest views to be obtained from any Dartmoor border height is spread before him. From the giant hills that look down upon the waters of the Walkham in the north, to the woods and green fields of the western part of the South Hams in the opposite direction, the eye ranges over a succession of beauties. A striking feature is formed by the rivers that fall into the sea near Plymouth, which are seen embosomed amid hills, one of them being the little stream that we have lately traced to its source.

S.W. of the cairn, and about ¼ m. from it, is an enclosure with hut circles. ½ m. below that is the wall of Cholwich Town Waste. On the farm of that name. (Ex. 35) in a field called Great Hill, is a fine single stone row, over 230 yards in length, with the remains of a circle at the N.E. end. In the wall on the slope above is a large stone that may once have served as a menhir.

Shell Top rises to a height of 1546 feet. About ½ m. S. of it is Pen Beacon, 1407 feet. A reave connects the two, and this we shall follow down to the lower height (R. 7).

Leaving the Yealm we make our way south-westward to Broadall Lake, the upper part of which is generally referred to as Broadall Gulf. This we should strike near the point at which it enters the enclosures, where are a number of hut circles. We pass upward with the wall L. to the higher corner of High-house Waste, which is close to the head of a little stream. Thence we follow a reave up the hill to a pound 250 yards in circumference, and containing eight hut circles, one, which is nearly in the centre, having a wall about six feet thick. Above this are several reaves, which in places cross each other. One goes westward, and seems to be connected with a longer one coming up the side of the hill from the Plym. Another runs upward to Pen Beacon, and to that point we make our way. On this is a barrow 72 yards in circumference, but not of great height. On its S. side a little shelter has been built, and on the W., a few yards from it, are the ruins of a small rectangular building. Shell Top is ½ m. N. by W.

1 m. S.S.E. of Pen Beacon is West Rook Gate, and to this we shall now make our way, and follow the road thence by the Rook farms to Heathfield Down and Cornwood village, as in R. 7. The return to Ivybridge will be by way of the road running S.E. from the inn, and will lead us by Moor Cross to Houndle Hill, soon after which we pass Fardel, R., and in about 1½ m. reach Dame Hannah Rogers' School, where we turn down R. to the village.

SHORTER EXCURSIONS FROM IVYBRIDGE.

S. Ex. 113.—*The Lud Brook*, 6 m. Following the Brent highway (R. 66) for 2 m. the visitor will reach Bittaford Bridge, where a road turns L. under the viaduct, and runs past the hamlet up to the common. (Another road passes under the viaduct very near to the Horse and Groom Inn : this is the old coach road noticed in S. Ex. 112, and by following it to Leigh Cross, a short distance beyond the entrance to the Plymouth Borough Lunatic Asylum, at Blackadon, and then turning L. the visitor is led to the commons at Leigh Gate and the Golf Links, ¾ m. from the summit of Ugborough Beacon, as described in S. Ex. 112). Blackadon Farm was formerly known as Blacket. On reaching the moor above Bittaford by the lane running by West Peek the rambler will strike N., with Cuckoo Ball R., and at Cuckoo Ball Corner will turn R. to the Lud (S. Ex. 112). This little stream may be traced to its source, and the return be made by way of Butterdon Hill, ½ m. S.W. of it, whence a green track may be followed S.W. for 1 m. to the moor gate at Quarry Pit Plantation. Thence by the road down the hill past Stowford to the village. Between Ivybridge and Bittaford is the hamlet of Filham. From this a road runs up to the moor. Fyllam Yeat (gate) receives early mention. Further on is a second turning, L., to the moor, and then a third. The latter leads to Cantrell Farm and Cantrell Gate, or Cantrel Yeat as it appears in the sixteenth century. Near it are the remains of a stone row about 50 yards in length, and running westerly from a low tumulus. It appears to have been double, though only a few stones are now standing.

S. Ex. 114.—*The Western Beacon, Butterdon, and Hangershell Rock*, 5½ m. The visitor will first make his way past Stowford to the gate at Quarry Pit Plantation, and will then pass upward to the Western Beacon, as in Ex. 32. It is interesting to note that the source of the Erme, which stream flows so far below the visitor, is over 260 feet above this lofty point. The line of bond-stones referred to in Ex. 32 comes up the hill from behind Stowford, where is a boundary rock having the letters H U cut upon it, denoting Harford and Ugborough. This line is followed N. by Black Pool to Butterdon, as directed in the excursion just named, whence the visitor makes his way N. by the ancient row to Hangershell Rock, which is not far to the L. of it, and about ¼ m. on. The view from this point is particularly good. I remember when a little grave was to be seen close to the rock, with a headstone bearing the following inscription :

" In memory of Tiny, a faithful and affectionate little terrier, who died at Lukesland, March 19th, 1875, aged 12 years.

> My little dog lies buried here,
> Stranger stop and drop a fear ;
> And as you pass this little grave,
> One small request I of you crave—
> Let no hand nor foot of thine
> Despoil this little Tiny's shrine.   S.F.M."

Near the rock a green path will lead the visitor S.W. past Weatherdon Hill, ¼ m. distant (Ex. 32). Less than ½ m. S. of the summit of this hill, and near Addicombe, are two ancient pounds, the larger of which is divided by a wall running across it. It is 165 yards in circumference. There are also a few hut circles, but the remains are very much decayed. Crossing Addicombe Slaggets S. to the moor gate the visitor will descend the hill as in S. Ex. 113.

S. Ex. 115.—*To Three Barrows direct* (4½ m. from Ivybridge), 9 m. To the moor gate as in Ex. 32. Thence N. across Addicombe Slaggets, and up the green path with Butterdon R. and Weatherdon Hill L. Thence past Hangershell Rock to the stone row. Follow this N. to its termination, when the bond-stones will form a guide. These lead past Sharp Tor L., about ½ m. beyond which the cairn crowned hill rises R. See Ex. 32.

S. Ex. 116.—*Piles Copse* (4¼ m. from Ivybridge), 8½ m. Harford Moor gate is the first point, and this the visitor may reach either by way of Harford as in Ex. 33, from which place he will turn up the hill by the church, or he may go by way of the gate at Quarry Pit Plantation as in Ex. 32. Should he choose the latter he will pass over Addicombe Slaggets, keeping near the enclosures L. About ¾ m. from the gate, at Combeshead Brake, the wall is carried westward towards Tor Rocks, which rise above the southern bank of the Butter Brook, and which the rambler should visit. The direct course is N. to Butter Ford at the corner ¼ m. distant, close to which are some fine examples of hut circles. Harford Gate is just beyond this. Here three tracks start ; one being the Owley Path (T. 62), another the branch of the Blackwood Path (T. 63), which runs up to Piles Hill, and the third, which is carried along by the wall, going to the gate of Lower Piles, ½ m. N. The rambler will follow the last-named. Outside the gate of Piles is the kist noticed in Ex. 32, and inside it the curious hut circles also mentioned in that excursion, which embraces Piles and the copse. The latter is 1 m. N., and the way to it lies through the newtakes, Piles Brook being crossed midway.

S. Ex. 117. *Stowford Cleave*, 5½ m. The beautifully wooded valley through which the Erme flows from Harford Bridge to Ivybridge bears the name of Stowford Cleave, and justly takes high rank among similar spots in the Dartmoor borderland. We have elsewhere remarked on the word *Cleave*, Exs. 11, 23. The visitor may enter this close to the viaduct below the station, where he will find a path that will take him up the valley by the R. bank of the river. When this is lost Harford Church comes in sight, half hidden amid trees, and the hills begin to reveal themselves, the picture being as fine as anything the fringe of the moor can show. [*Gems*, Chap. XVII.] Crossing a field a lane is reached where the visitor turns R. to Harford Bridge. Thence the return route is by the church as in Ex. 32.

S. Ex. 118.—*Henlake Down and Hangher Down*, 4 m. A road leads up through the wood from the viaduct near the station. Following this the visitor will be led to Henlake Down and Pithill Farm. From the down there is a fine view, which, however, is greatly extended when Hangher Down is reached. A track in the higher corner of Henlake leads to this. On the summit is the Round Plantation, a conspicuous object in the neighbourhood. A track runs over the common, going northward to the road between Harford Bridge and Cornwood. N.W. of the Round Plantation a road leads down to Moor Cross (S. Ex. 119).

S. Ex. 119.—*Cornwood and Hawns and Dendles*: with road to Lutton. (Cornwood village is 3 m. from Ivybridge, and 1 m. from Cornwood Station (G.W.R.); the entrance to Hawns and Dendles is at Combe, 1½ m. from Cornwood village). The Cornwood road, as stated in Ex. 34, runs up the hill with Ivybridge church R. to Dame Hannah Rogers' School, where it turns L. About 1½ m. on it passes Fardle, the former home of the Raleighs, though not the birthplace of Sir Walter. The chapel is in a good state of preservation. Passing over Houndle Hill the rambler will reach Moor Cross, where is one of the entrances to Blachford.

(The road running L. is the one which the rambler is directed to take for Lutton, R. 57. After crossing the Yealm, which is close by, he will pass the first turning R. and at the next cross road on the ridge, will keep straight down the hill to Piall Brook, and will then pass up the hill and bend R. to Lutton, a hamlet where is a small hostelry called the Mountain Inn. Below the bridge over the Piall Brook is Slade Hall, the residence of Mr. J. D. Pode. Here an ingot of tin was found in 1879. It measured 14 inches by 8 inches, and was about 3 inches thick, its weight being 51½lbs. I mention this because I have seen it stated that the tin ingots were of a cubic form. The rambler on Dartmoor who has examined the blowing-houses there will know better.).

From Moor Cross we make our way to Cornwood, which is sometimes locally spoken of as Cross. Here on the open space in the centre of the little village is a fine Latin cross, erected in 1902 to the memory of Frederic Rogers, Lord Blachford, and of Georgiana, his wife. [*Crosses*, Chap. IV. and Addenda.] On one side of this space is an entrance to Blachford, and on the other the gate of Delamore.

(A road branches R. from the one leading to the station a short distance from the village. This runs on past Lutton and through Sparkwell to Old Newnham and Plympton Station).

From the cross we take the road running N.E. as in Ex. 34, and on crossing the bridge over the Yealm near the vicarage turn L. and follow the path by the river. Soon we bend R. and here there is a road L. leading to Wisdome Mill. We pass this and take the next turning L., and then again bend R. and pass up by Sweet's Wood to Combe L. Here we enter Hawns and Dendles. This charming spot seems to have derived its curious appellation from the names of two owners of the lands that form it. The existence of one of these, however, a Madame Hawns, rests only on tradition ; that of the other has the authority of title-deeds, in which the name appears as Daniels. Hawns and Dendles is a wooded valley through which the Yealm flows on quitting the moor, and in which it is joined by Broadall Lake, the confluence being between Fernfires Wood S. and Dendles Wood N. The tract of land between these streams is divided into two parts, the western one being called Hawns, and the eastern Dendles Waste. The cascades on the Yealm are fine, and there are some delightful glimpses of the surrounding moor. [*Gems*, Chap. XVIII.] At the northern end of the higher path on the W. side of the valley a gate opens on to Combe Waste, between the woods and Harrowthorn Plantation. The path is continued on the moor, and is the one referred to in Ex. 34 ; by following this Yealm Falls and the Yealm Rings or Yealm Circles, as the pounds are sometimes called, may readily be reached. The public are admitted to Hawns and Dendles on Monday, Wednesday, and Saturday in each week, by the courtesy of the owner, Miss Deare.

S. Ex. 120.—*Stone Circle on Stall Moor, and Erme Pound*, from Cornwood, $10\frac{1}{2}$ m. The distance is from and to Cornwood village. The Ivybridge visitor will find it very interesting to go to Erme Pound by this route, and return by way of the L. bank of the Erme and Harford as in Ex. 32, or by the R. bank as in Ex. 33. The moor gate at Watercombe is the first point. Thence the Stall Moor track should be followed northward (T. 66). The circle called the Dancers will be seen R. near by $2\frac{1}{2}$ m. from the gate (Ex. 33). The ford on the Erme is about $\frac{3}{4}$ m. further on, and Erme Pound is just above it (Ex. 32).

S. Ex. 121.—*Pen Beacon and Shell Top* from and to Cornwood village, 6 m. ; add 6 m. if from Ivybridge. The way lies first to Heathfield Down, $\frac{1}{4}$ m., which is approached by the road running N.W. from the cross (R. 56). On reaching this little common take the road over it R. to the enclosures and pass up the lane, branching R. at the first fork ; the L. branch leads to Newpark Waste under Rook Wood.

Passing West Rook L., and Middle Rook R., the rambler will make his way up to West Rook Gate, between Broker's Plantation L., and Hillson's Brake R., and here he will enter on the moor. This part is usually spoken of as Rook Tor, but nothing more than some scattered stones are to be seen there (cf. Clay Tor, Ex. 8). Pen Beacon is ½ m. N. by W., and Shell Top, 1 m. in the same direction. These are described in Ex. 34. On returning from the beacon the rambler may steer S.E. by S., that is, a little to the L. of the line struck in ascending, which will bring him to East Rook Gate, with Hillson's Brake R. and Ford Waste L. About ½ m. down the hill a lane branches L. to Hele Cross and Wisdome Mill, and another R. to Wakeham's Rook and East Rook. He may return by way of the latter, or keep straight down the hill for another ½ m. and then turn R. to the village.

The district covered by the excursions from Brent and Ivybridge is deficient in tors, and is less wild than the northern part of the moor, as the rambler over it will have seen. But he will also admit that there is ample compensation for this. The borders are here particularly interesting, while the south quarter of the forest and the venville commons abutting upon it are far more rich in pre-historic remains than any other part of the great waste.

ROUTES FROM BRENT AND IVYBRIDGE.

(To Hexworthy and Post Bridge : See R. 64, Reverse, R. 33. The Dockwell track (T. 55) also furnishes a route to Hexworthy : *Dockwell Gate, Water Oke Corner, Pupers, Hapstead Ford, Head of Ringleshutts Gert, Combestone Tor, Saddle Bridge*). [Objects : Ex. 29, and Holne Moor Section.]

R. 55.—To Plympton, W.S.W. and W. *Brent Bridge, Wrangaton, Bittaford Bridge, Ivybridge, Lee Mill Bridge, Lyneham Inn.* From Brent, 11½ m. ; from Ivybridge, 6½ m. Reverse, R. 74.
[Objects : Ex. 32.]
This is a road route ; few directions are needed. The way from Brent to Ivybridge has been shown in R. 47. Thence the high road is followed past Cadleigh Park, Lee Mill Bridge, where the Yealm is crossed, Smithaleigh, and the Lyneham Inn. Just beyond the sixth milestone from Plymouth a road branches L. to the town of Plympton ; the main road goes on to Ridgway, whence a road also leads L. to Plympton, immediately opposite the George Hotel. If the visitor is bound for Plympton Station he will not enter the town, but will pass down through Ridgway.

R. 56.—Brent to Shaugh. W. by N. *Owley Gate, Spurrell's Cross, Harford, Cornwood, Piall Bridge, White Hill Corner, Wotter,* 12 m. Reverse, R. 75.
[Objects : S. Exs. 111, 112 ; Exs. 32, 33, 34, 35, 36.]
The way lies by the hamlet of Aish, and Bulhornstone Cross to Owley Gate, as in Ex. 111. Here we are on the Harford track, already described (T. 62), and after following it for a short distance we shall find its character alters. It becomes a wide, green path, and will lead

us up the hill N. of Ugborough Beacon to Spurrell's Cross; Its course is nearly due W., and is marked by low heaps of stones not far apart. West of the shattered cross [*Ancient Crosses*, Chap. III.] the path runs on the line of the track leading from Buckfast to Plympton (T. 59), which was carried up the hill N.E. from Glascombe Corner. After passing the head of Butter Brook L., Harford Gate is soon reached. The way then lies down the lane to the church, where we turn R. and descend to Harford Bridge (Ex. 33, S. Ex. 117). Thence the road passes upward with the ancient farm of Hall R. ½ m. beyond the gate of this homestead, just after passing Hall Cross the road forks. The L. branch is known as Reddapitt Lane, and runs by Blachford to Cornwood, being a shorter way than the other. But it is not a public road, and therefore the R. branch must be followed. In rather over ½ m. we reach Tor, where we turn L., and passing Wisdome and crossing the Vicarage Bridge, shall proceed direct to the village.

(Here the visitor from Ivybridge will join this route. See R. 57).

From Cornwood our way will take us N.W. over the side of Heathfield Down to Piall Bridge, which we shall cross, and still following the road shall in about ½ m. reach Quick Bridge. We pass up the hill with Cholwich Town R., to Tolchmoor Gate (Ex. 35), and crossing the Torry at Tolchmoor Bridge shall speedily find ourselves at White Hill Corner, where is a guide-post (Ex. 36). Here we turn L., and passing Boringdon Cottages R. shall make our way up a narrow road by Shade Cottages, also R., which will bring us to the commons. Passing along the side of Stewarts Hill, R., and by the Wottor Waste Clay Works R., we continue to follow the road under Collard Tor Cottage to Beatland Corner (guide-post). Here we cross the road from Plympton to Cadaford Bridge, and soon arrive at Shaugh village.

R. 57.—Ivybridge to Shaugh, N.W. by W. *Houndle Hill, Moor Cross* [*Lutton, Heddon Down, Crownhill Down, Portworthy, Niel Gate*, 9 m.], *Cornwood ;* thence as in R. 56, 8½ m. Reverse, R. 76.

[Objects : Exs. 34, 35, 36.]

Passing up by the church we turn L. to Fardle, Moor Cross, and Cornwood village, as in S. Ex. 119. From Cornwood the way is described in R. 56.

Another way is by Lutton, but the former is the better one. Turn L. at Moor Cross as shown in S. Ex. 119, and on reaching Lutton pass up to the common and strike W. by N. It may not be possible to keep a direct line, as there are a number of clay pits in this part of the moor. The point to be reached is the northern end of Hooksbury Wood, at the western foot of Crownhill Down, 2½ m. from Lutton. Here are cross roads and a guide-post. Take the road running down westward to the Torry, keeping the wood L. On crossing the stream the road goes up the hill to Portworthy, about ¼ m. beyond which turn R. and follow the road N. to Niel Gate, 1 m. Turn L. to the village at Beatland Corner, ¼ m. N.

R. 58.—Brent to Princetown, N.W. *Shipley, Western Whitaburrow, Red Lake Ford, Ducks' Pool, The Plym, Siward's Cross*, 12 m. To Two Bridges, add 1½ m. Reverse, R. 7.

[Objects : Exs. 30, 32, 33, 37, 3.]

The first point will be Shipley, to which we may make our way either by the hamlet of Aish, or by Wash Gate and Didworthy, as in Ex. 30. On passing through the moor gate near Zeal we leave the road, turning up L. by the wall of the enclosures, with the deserted naphtha works on the R. For the next 3 m. we shall have the guidance of the old Zeal Tor tramroad (T. 60), but as it here goes L. around Zeal Hill, it will shorten the distance a little if we strike up over the common in a N.W. direction, taking care, however, not to keep too much to the R., when we shall meet with it again. About 2 m. from Shipley this old tramway passes the long-deserted Brent Moor Clay Works, which are seen L. Just before reaching these it will be found that the path has been encroached upon by the bog, and can no longer be followed. Here we must keep it a short distance on our L. and further on we shall find that it becomes a hard path again. It is almost better to walk along its side here as the cutting is encumbered with loose stones. 2½ m. from Shipley Western Whitaburrow is reached (Ex. 30), and from here North Hisworthy above Princetown is in full view to the N.W. ; to the R. of it is Great Mis Tor (Ex. 6). 2 m. away W.N.W. is Erme Head, marked by a large stream work, and ½ m. R. of this our way lies. From Whitaburrow onward the tramroad descends, and ⅓ m. from it we reach the Crossways (Ex. 30). Here we turn L. into the old Abbots' Way (T. 1), which we shall follow to Red Lake Ford. On crossing the stream we must steer N.W. over Green Hill to Stony Hole, a great stream work on Dark Lake, or, as it is also called, the Black Lane Brook, passing Middle Mires on the way.

[From the stream-work the rambler may follow Black Lane (T. 75) to Fox Tor, and crossing the ford below it (Ex. 3) make his way to White Works, and thence to Princetown by Castle Road (T. 7). See R. 7.]

Crossing the stream-work, our course being W.N.W., and leaving Ducks' Pool R. (Ex. 30), we descend to the Plym. On the slope are the scattered rocks of Great Gnats' Head, above which is a cairn, (about ¾ m. below the pool), and by keeping these near us L. we shall strike the river at, or near, Plym Ford. The ridge running N.E. from Eylesbarrow now lies between us and Siward's Cross, our next point, and in passing over this we must keep a N.N.W. course. The house near the cross is seen as we make our way down the northern side of this ridge. The way from the cross to Princetown is described in the extension to Ex. 2. The course is W. of N., and a branch of the Abbots' Way is followed throughout the distance (T. 1). The walls of the enclosures must be kept R., care being taken when those belonging to Nun's Cross Farm are passed, to keep straight on to the corner of another enclosure. Beyond this South Hisworthy Tor. Princetown is entered by way of Ivybridge Lane (T. 6). The distance to Two Bridges may be shortened by about 1 m. by bearing R. when Nun's Cross enclosures are passed, and steering N.E. for ½ m. to Peat Cot. Here cross the Devonport leat ; leave it L., and strike due N. towards the outer corner of the Tor Royal enclosures, or follow up the leat and leave it when near the wall, See R. 34. From the corner the course is N.E. over Tor Royal Newtake to the steps over the Blackabrook S. of Round Hill farmhouse. See Ex. 3, T.B. to Peat Cot.

R. 59.—Ivybridge to Princetown, N. by W., with route from Cornwood, N. *Harford Bridge, Valley of the Erme, Green Bottom.*

Erme Head, The Plym, Siward's Cross, 12½ m. **From Cornwood:**
Pen Beacon, Shell Top, Shavercombe, Hart Tors, Siward's Cross, 9½ m.
To Two Bridges, add 1½ m.   Reverse, R. 7.

[Objects: Exs. 32, 33, 34, 37, 3.]

Starting from the bridge we pass up the hill to Stowford, and make our way on by Lukesland to Harford, and thence to Harford Bridge, as in Ex. 33.   Entering the gate at the W. end of this we follow the track running up the R. bank of the Erme (T. 65), and passing under Stalldon Barrow reach Tom's Plain.   Here we lose the path, but continue our way up the valley to Green Bottom, rather over ¼ m. below Erme Pound, which is on the opposite bank.   (The Erme valley is described in Exs. 32, 33).   We now leave the river and strike up over the hill N.W., as in Ex. 33, and in 1½ m. shall pass Erme Head R., and ¼ m. further on shall reach Broad Rock on the Abbots' Way (Ex. 34, T. 1).   Our next point is Plym Ford, 1 m. N.W.   The branch of the Abbots' Way leading to it is not very plainly defined, but the ground is good, and by following a N.W. course down the hill by Great Gnats' Head, which should be kept R., the ford will be reached.   From this point the way is described in R. 58, where also the route from Nun's Cross to Two Bridges is shown.

From Cornwood the route to Shell Top as given in S. Ex. 121 must be followed.   The rambler will then strike W. of N. down the hillside, but on approaching Hen Tor, 1 m., must leave it about ¼ m. below him.   He will thus avoid the marshy ground on the top of the ridge.   The course is now a little E. of N., the Plym being in sight in the valley L.   Very soon the Snavercombe Brook is crossed, near a tumulus ¼ m. above Shavercombe Falls, and 1 m. further on the Plym at Plym Steps, when the course is changed to due N., and the slope ascended with Lower Hart Tor R., and Higher Hart Tor L.   When a little to the R. of Eylesbarrow, a cairn marking the bounds of the forest, the track coming up from Siward's Cross should be struck (T. 6).   Should it not be seen the same northerly course must be followed down the hill, and the cross will be reached in about 1 m.   The path from the cross to Princetown is described in the extension to Ex. 2 and in R. 58.

Another route from Cornwood is by way of Stall Moor, but it is longer.   The rambler will cross the Vicarage Bridge and at Tor turn L. and then R. to Watercombe Waste Gate as in Ex. 34, and thence to Stall Moor Gate, from which he will follow the track running near the Stall Moor Circle out to Erme Pound (T. 66).   Just before reaching the Erme he will cross Green Bottom, when he will leave the track, and follow the directions given in the former part of this route, *i.e.,* Ivybridge to Princetown.   Or he may take the L. branch of the track after leaving Stall Moor Gate, and following this to the Yealm trace that stream nearly to its source.   Thence, keeping a little to the R., to avoid the mire, he will strike northward for 1½ m. to Broad Rock, coming in sight first of Erme Head.   See *ante.*   The route from Yealm Head to Langcombe Bottom given in Ex. 34 may also be followed, when the brook can be traced downward to Plym Steps.

R. 60.—Brent to Tavistock.   For points and objects see R. 58, 1, which compose this route, 19½ m.   Reverse, R. 13.

R. 61.—Ivybridge to Tavistock. This route is composed of R. 59, 1, where points and objects are named, 20 m. Reverse, R. 13.

If the visitor goes by road the way will lie through Cornwood, R. 57, and thence to White Hill Corner, R. 56. From this point he will follow the road N.W., passing Lee Moor House R., and shortly after Blackaton Cross [*Crosses*, Chap. IV.], and descend the hill, with Saddlesborough L., to Cadaford Bridge. Thence he will proceed as in R. 68, passing over Marchants Bridge, through Dousland (Ex. 39), and Walkhampton, over Huckworthy Bridge (Ex. 40), to Warren's Cross and Whitchurch Down. Reverse, R. 13.

[Objects : S. Ex. 119, Exs. 34 to 40, 7.]

R. 62.—To Lydford. From Brent, N.W. ; from Ivybridge, N.N.W. ; from Cornwood, N.N.W. *Shipley, Western Whitaburrow, Red Lake Ford, Ducks' Pool, The Plym* (From Ivybridge : *Harford Bridge, Valley of the Erme, Green Bottom, Erme Head, The Plym*), *Siward's Cross.* (From Cornwood : *Pen Beacon, Shell Top, Shavercombe, Hart Tors, Siward's Cross*), *Princetown, Rundle Stone, Mis Tor, White Tor, Hill Bridge.* From Brent, 23 m. ; from Ivybridge, 23½ m. ; from Cornwood, 20½ m. Reverse, R. 20.

[Objects : Between Shipley and Red Lake, Ex. 30 ; Red Lake to the Plym, Exs. 33, 43, 36 ; Plym to Princetown, Exs. 37, 3, 2 ; Princetown to Lydford, Exs. 6, 9, 10. The route from Ivybridge does not include Exs. 30, 43, but adds Ex. 32. The Cornwood route leaves out Exs. 30, 32, 33, 43.]

This route is composed of R. 58, 59, 2, q.v. The visitor is also referred to the Reverse (R. 20) for some hints relative to crossing the Walkham between Princetown and Hill Bridge.

R. 63.—To Okehampton. From Brent, N.N.W. ; from Ivybridge, N. by W. With branch to Belstone. *Shipley, Western Whitaburrow, Red Lake Ford, Black Lane* (From Ivybridge : *Harford Bridge, Valley of the Erme, Green Bottom, Erme Head, Black Lane*), *Fox Tor, Prince Hall Bridge, Muddy Lakes, Hollow Combe, Broad Down, East Dart Valley, Cranmere, Ockment Hill, New Bridge.* From Brent, 26 m. ; from Ivybridge, 27 m. Reverse, R. 27.

[Objects : Exs. 33, 30, 4, 3, 46, 45, 16, and 15.]

From Brent the directions given in R. 58 must be followed for the first 7½ m., which will bring the rambler to the stream work on Dark Lake, and quite close to Ducks' Pool (Ex. 30). From Ivybridge the route to Erme Head, 8 m., is given in R. 59 ; on reaching the stream work at that place the rambler must follow up Dark Lake for about ½ m., when he will reach the old workings near Ducks' Pool. Black Lane, which runs W. of N., will now become his path (T. 75, Ex. 3, R. 7), and in about 1 m. he will come in sight of Fox Tor, below which is Child's Tomb (Ex. 3). On passing this L. he will descend to Stream Hill Ford on the Swincombe river, ½ m. distant, and crossing the latter will proceed due N. over Tor Royal Newtake (Ex. 3, 4) for 1½ m., when he will turn R. to Moorlands. Passing this he will turn down the lane L. to Prince Hall Bridge, and follow the road by the house to the lodge on the Two Bridges L., and Dartmeet road R. Muddy Lakes Newtake, in front of the lodge, must then be crossed, the course being due N., when the rambler will reach the Princetown and Moreton road close to the old Powder Mills gate. Entering this he will still keep a course due N., with the Powder Mills Cottages R., and in 2 m. will reach Hollow Combe, where he will cross the Cherry Brook under Lower White Tor, which rises from the steep hill L. Another mile, the course still being N., will take the rambler over Broad Down to Sandy Hole (Ex. 45), on the East Dart. From this point the directions given in C.R. 1a for reaching Cranmere must be followed, and from that spot C.R. 9 and Ex. 16 will show the way to Okehampton.

If the rambler is bound for Belstone he will, on reaching Cranmere, make his way down the Taw as described in C.R. 10, or he may, leaving the pool L., strike direct from East Dart Head to Taw Head. The direction is due N., and the distance ½ m.

R. 64.—To Chagford and Moreton. From Brent, N. ; from Ivybridge, N. by E. ; from Cornwood, N.N.E. From Brent : *Gigley Bridge, Cross Furzes, Holne, Pound's Gate, Ponsworthy, Jordan, Challacombe, Jurston Gate, C,* 19 m. ; *M.* (by Moor Gate) about 1 m. further : but a more direct way from Ponsworthy would be through Widecombe thence by Heytree Cross and North Bovey. From Ivybridge : *Harford, Valley of the Erme to Red Lake Foot, Aune Head, Hexworthy, Sherburton Bridge, Dunnabridge Pound, Post Bridge, Warren House Inn, Jurston Gate, C.,* 23½ m. ; *M.* (by Moor Gate), 25 m. From Cornwood : *Watercombe Waste and Stall Moor Gate, Stall Moor, Red Lake Foot ;* thence from Ivybridge *vide supra. C.,* 22 m. ; *M.* (by Moor Gate), 23½ m. Reverse, R. 33.

Objects : S. Exs. from Brent, *Holne Moor* Section, and Exs. 28, 27, 22. If from Ivybridge, Exs. 32, 30, 43, 42, 44, 45, 21, 22 ; if from Cornwood commence with Ex. 33.

From Brent : The way lies through Scorriton, directions for reaching which are given in S. Ex. 101. Thence pass up the hill to Holne, crossing the road from Buckfastleigh to the moor just before arriving at the village. Pass on by the Church House Inn, and on reaching a road running E. by W. cross it and enter the field at the stile L. Follow the path past Holne Cot, and down through a wood with the Dart L. to the road close to New Bridge (Exs. 27, 28), which cross and ascend to hill to Pound's Gate (Exs. 27, 28). At the further end of the hamlet we turn R. after passing the Spitchwick Lodge, and leaving Leusdon Church R. descend to Ponsworthy. When ½ m. up the hill beyond Ponsworthy turn L. to Jordan Mill, and crossing a narrow lane keep N. by E. to Dunstone Down, where turn L. Passing a stroll leading to Rowden Down L., and a short distance beyond that a road running to Cator L., we follow the road for 1 m. to Lower Blackaton (S. Ex. 85), from which point we continue northward up the valley to Challacombe, 1 m. (S. Ex. 85). Thence onward between Grim's Pound R., and Headland Warren House in the valley L., for 2½ m., to the Princetown and Moreton road. Turn R. for Moreton. Cross the little valley N. for Chagford, and reaching the road follow it to Jurston Gate. See R. 4.

From Ivybridge : The first point is Harford (Ex. 33). The second is Green Hill, which may be reached either by way of the R. bank of the Erme, or by going over Sharp Tor and Quickbeam Hill. In the former case the rambler will follow the directions given in R. 59 for reaching Green Bottom. Here he may cross the river, or at the ford just above (T. 66), or still proceeding up the R. bank, find a crossing-place at Red Lake Foot, and pass upwards towards Red Lake Ford, with the stream R. If he goes by way of Sharp Tor he will pass up the lane with the church L. to Harford Gate, and bearing L. will follow the green track running N.W. to Piles Hill (T. 63), his mark being Sharp Tor, which on passing he will keep L. The way now lies through the shallow dip between this tor and Three Barrows to Stony Bottom, as in Ex. 32, 3¼ m. from the moor gate. The course is now N. over Brown Heath to Red Lake Ford, 1 m. The hut enclosures noticed in the excursion named are on the slope L., and the line of bond-stones between Harford and Ugborough Moors R. Crossing Red Lake at the ford we still steer N., having Green Hill L. (Ex. 30) and Red Lake Mires R. By keeping near to the latter the rambler will strike the hard path running through the marshy ground to Heng Lake Gully (Ex. 29), and so reach the Avon. The way lies up this stream, the R. bank being traced to its source, 1½ m. (Ex. 43). From Aune Head the track running N. must be followed to Hexworthy (T. 54). This is not well defined near the mire, but by proceeding W. of N. for about ½ m. the head of the Wo Brook will be seen R. The track runs down the hill near the L. bank of this stream, and when it turns sharply toward the E., still goes N. over Down Ridge. It runs to a gate in the wall of a newtake through which it passes, and reaches the road below immediately behind the Forest Inn.

[The part of this route just described forms the route from Ivybridge to Hexworthy referred to in R. 33. The way from Heng Lake Gully to Brent was there sketched; the reverse is here given. The first point is Shipley (Ex. 30), whence the old tram road (T. 60) may be followed as in the route to Princetown as far as the Crossways (R. 58). Thence strike N. by E. over the old peat workings, keeping the valley of the Avon in sight R. to the gully, ¾ m. Or the Avon may be traced from Shipley upward as directed in S. Ex. 104, to Lower Huntingdon Corner, and thence followed to the gully, 1¼ m. further up. From that point see directions *ante*.]

From the Forest Inn the way lies over Gobbet Plain, to which the road above the inn leads westward ; or it may be reached by the road running down in front of the inn and turning L. up the slope. Descending to Sherburton Bridge on the Swincombe river the rambler will pass up to the farm, where he may obtain permission to go through the enclosures to the clam on the West Dart, near Sherburton Firs. Crossing this he will climb the hill northward to the road coming R. from Dartmeet and going L. to Two Bridges. On the L. is Brownberry, and opposite to it Dunnabridge Pound (Ex. 5, 42). Pass the gate of this and turn R. by the wall, and follow the green track through the newtakes and over the side of Bellaford Tor, to Post Bridge (T. 80, Ex. 44). The way to Chagford and Moreton from that place is given in R. 4.

(The visitor from Cornwood enters upon the moor at Watercombe, and will follow the track over Stall Moor to the ford on the Erme above Green Bottom (T. 66, S. Ex. 120), and may either cross here or at Red Lake Foot, a little further up stream. See *ante*.

R. 65.—To Bovey Tracey, N.E. For points and objects see R. 66, 54, of which this route is made up. From *B.*, 15¾ m. ; *I.*, 20½ m. ; Reverse, R. 40. Road throughout.

R. 66.—To Ashburton, N.E. *Bittaford Bridge, Wrangaton Station, Brent Bridge* (L. *for Brent*), *Palstone, Whiteoxen, Dean* (OLD ROAD *from Brent through Harbournford*), *Buckfastleigh, Dart Bridge.* From *I.*, 13 m. ; *B.*, 8¼ m. Reverse, R. 47.

[Objects : Ex. 32 ; seen from near Wrangaton Station.]

A road route. From Ivybridge the first point is Bittaford Bridge, 2 m. (S. Ex. 113) ; 1¼ m. beyond this is Wrangaton Station. About 1 m. further on, at the Carew Arms, a road branches R. to Totnes. Keep straight on, crossing the Glaze, and shortly afterwards the Avon at Brent Bridge. Road L. to Brent. Continue on past the London Inn. The cross-road a little way up is the point where the rambler from Brent joins this route, leaving the village by the Avonwick road ; but he would do better to proceed by the old road through Harbournford to Dean, as in S. Ex. 100. ¼ m. from the cross-roads is Palstone, R., and 1¼ m. beyond this the road forks, the R. branch leading to Totnes. Keep straight on down the hill with the grounds of Marley R., and the farm L. Thence pass under Whiteoxen Arch, or Dry Bridge, as it is sometimes called. A little further on is Dean Church (S. Ex. 100), and 1 m. beyond is Dean village, where the old road from Brent comes in L. Pass through Buckfastleigh, about 1 m. on, and thence as in S. Ex. 97, 98.

PLYMPTON AND SHAUGH DISTRICT.

[The village of Shaugh is about 5 m. from Plympton Station (G.W.R.), by road *via* Niel Gate, and 2½ m. from Bickleigh Station (Launceston Branch, G.W.R.), by road *via* Shaugh Bridge.]

DISTANCES : BY ROAD. *ASHBURTON, via* Ivybridge, *P.*, 18¾ m. ; *S.*, 22 m. *BICKLEIGH, P.*, 5 m. ; *S.*, 3 m. *BOTTLE HILL GATE*, 2¾ m. from *P. BOVEY TRACEY, via* Ivybridge, *P.*, 26¼ m. ; *S.*, 29½ m. *BROWNEY CROSS, P.*, 3 m. ; *S.*, 1¾ m. *CADAFORD BRIDGE, P.*, 6 m. ; *S.*, 1½ m. *CHAGFORD, via* Dousland and Princetown, *P.*, 26 m. ; *S.*, 21½ m. *CORNWOOD, P.*, 5½ m. ; *S.*, 6 m. *DOUSLAND, P.*, 9½ m. ; *S.*, 5 m. *EXETER*, 40 m. from *P. GEORGE HOTEL*, Tavistock Road, *P.*, 4 m. ; *S.*, 5½ m. *HEXWORTHY, via* Princetown, 20½ m. ; *via* Ivybridge, 23 m. *IVYBRIDGE, P.*, 5¾ m. ; *S.*, 9 m. *LEE MOOR CROSS, via* Beatland Corner, *P.*, 6¼ m. ; *S.*, 3 m. *LUTTON*, 4½ m. from *P. LYDFORD, via* Dousland, *P.*, 21½ m. ; *S.*, 17 m. *MORETON*, 13½ m. beyond Princetown. *OKEHAMPTON, via* Dousland, *P.*, 23½ m. ; *S.*, 19 m. *PLYM BRIDGE*, 2 m. from *P. PLYMOUTH, P.*, 5 m. (or about 4 m. to the outskirts of the town) ; *S., via* Bickleigh, 10 m. *POST BRIDGE*, 5 m. beyond Princetown. *PRINCETOWN, via* Dousland, *P.*, 14 m. ; *S.*, 9½ m. *SOUTH BRENT, P.*, 12 m. ; *S.*, 14 m. *SPARKWELL*, 3 m. from *P. TAVISTOCK, via* Plym Bridge and George Hotel, 14 m. from *P.* ; *via* Dousland, 10½ m. from *S. TWO BRIDGES*, 1½ m. beyond Princetown. *YELVERTON, via* Cadaford Bridge and Greenwell Down, *P.*, 9½ m. ; *S.*, 5 m.

BY RAIL (G.W.R.) *PLYMOUTH*, 4¾ m. (Marsh Mills, on the Launceston Branch, is 1 m. from Plympton Station ; this is the station for Yelverton and the Princetown Railway, Tavistock, and

Lydford). For *SOUTHERN DARTMOOR—CORNWOOD*, 4½ m. ;
IVYBRIDGE, 6¾ m. ; *WRANGATON*, 10 m. ; *BRENT*, 12¼ m.

Although Plympton is somewhat removed from the moor, there
was early a connection between the two. As stated in the *Terms*
Section it was one of the four Stannary towns. The barony of Plympton was bestowed by Henry I. upon Richard de Redvers, to whom has
been attributed the building of the castle, of which little more than
fragments of the keep now remain. Baldwin de Redvers, the son of
Richard, granted to the burgesses of Plympton common of turbary
for all necessary fuel for their houses on his commons forming part of
the moor, and a right of way through Lea Wood for their carts, and this
was confirmed by his daughter, Isabella de Fortibus (Ex. 6).

A Saxon monastery seems to have existed at Plympton, but was
suppressed in 1121 by Bishop Warelwast, who founded in its stead a
priory of Augustine Canons. This was so richly endowed that at the
Dissolution it was the wealthiest foundation in the county. A few
remains of it exist to the south of the churchyard, and fragments are
also discoverable in other places near by.

The parish church of Plympton St. Mary stands in a low situation
near the Torry Brook, and, as already stated, has attached to it a
similar legend to that we have noticed as being connected with the
churches of Brent Tor and Buckfastleigh (Ex. 9, S. Ex. 98). The story
says that Crownhay Castle, on the outskirts of Ridgway, was selected
as a site for it, but this not being pleasing to the Evil One, he removed
the stones from it to the spot where the building now stands. The
Stannary town and the castle are not, however, in this parish, but in
the adjoining one of Plympton Maurice, or as it is also called, Plympton
Earl. This ancient town is memorable as being the birthplace of Sir
Joshua Reynolds, and it was also in or near it that Sir George Treby,
the eminent lawyer and judge, was born.

EXCURSIONS FROM PLYMPTON AND SHAUGH.

[Tracks : 68 to 71.]

Ex. 35.—*Newnham, Crownhill Down, Ridding Down, Tolchmoor
Gate, Quick Bridge, Heddon Down, Sparkwell*, 12 m. ; this is from and
to Plympton Station. Shaugh visitors reach Crownhill Down by way
of Niel Gate, Portbury, and Hooksbury Wood, as in R. 76.

Passing through Colebrook we keep R. near the railway, and
follow the road running E. for ¾ m. to the foot of West Park Hill,
where we turn L. to Loughtor Mill. About ¼ m. R. is Old Newnham,
which, in the time of Edward I., was the seat of Simon de Plympton.
It afterwards came into the possession of the Strodes, one of the members of which family, Richard Strode, we have already referred to as
having been confined in Lydford Castle by order of the Tinners' Court,
held on Crockern Tor (see *Stannaries*, in *Terms* Section). Another was
William Strode, one of the five members whom Charles I. attempted
to seize. The sweet tone of the tenor bell hanging in Plympton St.
Mary Church tower is traditionally said to be owing to a lapful of
silver having been thrown by Marie Strode into the metal from which
the bell was cast. This was in 1614. Keeping R. on passing Loughtor

Mill we ascend the hill by Holly Wood, and turn L. just beyond one of the entrances to Newnham Park, in which is the mansion that took the place of Old Newnham. This was built about two hundred years ago. As we proceed we have a view of the deer park in the valley of the Torry, L. At the fork shortly reached we take the R. branch, and pass upward through Bottle Hill Mine to the common.

[The L. branch goes on to a moor gate and runs down the side of a part of Crownhill Down, usually referred to as Pits, to the cross roads at the N.E. corner of Hooksbury Wood, mentioned in R. 57. From this corner one road goes up the valley to Coleland Bridge, another straight on to Fernhill, above which is Higher Lee Wood, and a third to Portworthy.]

On our R. as we pass up through the mine is the rounded hill known as Hemerdon Ball, a conspicuous object from the vicinity of Plympton Station. Hemerdon, on the southern slope of this hill, is the seat of the Woollcombes, and not far from this is the hamlet of the same name. Here, in Henry the Third's reign, dwelt Alexander de Hemerdon, castellan of Plympton Castle, and one of the witnesses to the charter granted by Baldwin to the burgesses. At the time when an invasion of England by Napoleon was deemed not improbable, troops were encamped on Hemerdon Ball.

From Bottle Hill Gate we make our way along the verge of Crownhill Down with the wall R., and when this recedes towards Drakeland Corner shall keep straight on towards another corner, where is a ruined building, known as Horniwink Here we leave the enclosures and strike over the down a little E. of N. By so doing we shall avoid the numerous clay pits on this part of the common, some of which belong to the Smallhanger Clay Works, and others to the Heddon and Broomage Works. There is little to interest the rambler here beyond the view of the moor which he obtains. We have already referred to the paths on this down (T. 68) ; these have been chiefly made by the clay workers, and run in every direction. Passing one or two barrows we at length arrive at the enclosures of Crownhill Down Cottage, which we keep R., and shortly afterwards reach Broomage Farm, where, besides the farmhouse itself, there are also a couple of cottages. Here, keeping the wall R., we pass Crownhill Tor, a small mass of rock of no great height above the turf, L., and bearing a little to the R. shall find ourselves near Broomage farmhouse. Here we strike N. to Tolch Moor Gate, 5 m. from Plympton. (On the other side of this the road descends to Tolch Bridge, which is quite near. Below this the Torry flows under Knowle Wood, on its L. bank, and enters Torry Combe).

Here we turn R., our next point being Quick Bridge, nearly 1 m. S.E. The wall L. bounds the land belonging to Cholwich Town, the stone row to which we have referred as existing there (Ex. 34), being less than ½ m. N.E. from the gate. The present farmhouse was formerly a residence of the Cholwich family, and is an interesting example of the old border dwellings. The kitchen possesses a particularly wide hearth. An immense granite trough is to be seen here, which may have been used for brewing purposes, but more probably for salting meat in. A site very near the house is pointed out as that on which the chapel stood. The last member of the family who lived here is said to have died in prison, but in what circumstances the story does not tell us, and whether there is any truth in it I have not been able to discover. The form of the name under which Polwhele refers to the family is Cholditch. They had a considerable estate in the parish of Chudleigh ; the last notice of the family in the registers of that place is the burial in September, 1727, of Thomas Cholwich. According to Lysons Cholwich Town belonged at the time he wrote, 1822, to Mr. J. B. Cholwich, of Farringdon House, near Exeter. In the Additions to Risdon, 1811, it is stated that Oldstone, in the parish of Blackawton, also belonged to this representative of the family.

Proceeding down the road we shall notice the lane leading to the house L. In this, a short distance from the gate, and on the R., is an old cross now doing duty as a gate-post [*Crosses.* Chap. IV.] A little below this lane we may observe the ancient entrance, but this is not now used. A branch of the Piall Brook runs near the house, and on the further side of this is Holmbush Waste and Nelder Wood, and above these Parkland Plantation, on the verge of the moor below Pen Beacon (Ex. 34). Quick Bridge spans the Piall Brook, called in the neighbourhood the Pall Brook, which comes down from Broomage Waste, on the hill above Broomage Wood, and on crossing this we desert the road. This runs on to Piall Bridge, and past Heathfield Down to Cornwood (R. 75), but we shall climb the hill R. Our course will now be S.S.W. over Heddon Down to the enclosures L. The clay works must be kept some distance R., and the plantation on the brow of the hill L. In 1 m. Heddon Gate will be reached, where a road runs down to Gorah Cottages. This we follow, and turning R. at the cottages make our way to Sparkwell, 1 m. Here there is a small inn called the Treby Arms. A short distance from the village, and near the verge of the common, is Goodamoor, the seat of the late General Phillipps-Treby. Mr. Paul Ourry Treby, once so well-known in the hunting-field, and whose name will long be remembered by Devon sportsmen, formerly resided here, and sixty years ago was one of the four Deputy Foresters of Dartmoor. In the opposite direction, that is, southward of the village, is Beechwood, anciently called Moor ; the present residence was built in 1797. As we make our way by West Park Hill to Colebrook we pass Hemerdon and Old Newnham.

Ex. 36.—*Hawks' Tor, Collard Tor, Stewart's Hill, White Hill Corner* [EXTENSION TO *White Hill Yeo*, add 1½ m.], *Blackaton Cross* [EXTENSION TO *Cadaford Bridge*, add 1½ m.], *Saddlesborough*, 5¼ m. from and to Shaugh.

[In the section dealing with the ancient tracks on the moor we have described one that formerly ran from Plympton to Tavistock (T. 69), on the line of which the present road is formed. Along this we shall now make our way from the ancient place that, according to the old rhyme, was a borough town when Plymouth was non-existent, to the village of Shaugh, as the monks did when they went from their priory to visit their church there. We follow the road described in R. 67, leaving it when we reach Beatland Corner, ¼ m. after entering upon the moor. Here we branch L. by Beatland and Bunghill Plantations, and skirting the Bowling Green, a level piece of turf L., shall enter upon the enclosed lands and speedily find ourselves in the village.

Shaugh is a typical border settlement, with its sturdy-looking granite church, its unpretentious inn, its ancient cross and tiny manor pound. Its full name is Shaugh Prior, its adjunct being derived from its connection with Plympton Priory, to which it was given by Roger de Novant. Behind it is the rock-strewn steep of West Down, crested by Shaugh Beacon, from which a fine view of the Plym valley and the Dewer Stone is commanded, with Roborough Down to the N.W. In the White Thorn Inn there was formerly a peat fire, which was kept continually burning. We remember seeing it in 1873, when it had not been suffered to go out for forty years. Near the door the upping-stock will be noticed. Shaugh Bridge, at the foot of the hill E. of the village, has long been celebrated as one of the beauty spots of the moorland borders. It is associated with Carrington, the poet of Dartmoor, who tells us that he often lingered near it. On the Dewer Stone Hill his name with the month and year of his death, is cut upon a rock, and in Shaugh Church is a tablet to his memory, placed there by his son, Mr. W. M. Carrington, in 1871. Carrington died at Bath, and was buried in the churchyard at Combe Hay, a few miles from that city. On his granite tomb is the following :

"Sacred to the memory of the Poet N. T. Carrington,

Who died the 2nd of September, 1830, aged 53 years."]

A little to the E. of Shaugh Church is an old cross standing in a socket-stone built into the hedge [*Crosses*, Chap. V.], and here we turn R. to the common, where we shall desert the road and keeping close to the enclosures L. be led to Huxton Corner, or as the spot is sometimes called, Windmill Hill. Crossing the road we strike up over Shaugh Moor to Hawks' Tor, which is not much more than ¼ m. distant. This is a small pile, but a very curious one. One end of a large slab of granite rests on what is the main part of the tor, its other end being supported on a boulder standing on the lesser and lower part of the tor, a kind of small chamber thus being formed beneath it. There is some reason for supposing this arrangement to be artificial, though it is difficult to see what the object could have been intended for. It has been suggested that it was a dolmen. Polwhele, writing in 1793, says that several had supposed it to be such, though he was not of that opinion.*

Less than ½ m. southward of Hawks' Tor is Collard Tor, near which is the cottage of the same name, with its small enclosures formed on the slope of a rock-strewn hill, and to this we shall now make our way. Below it is the road running from Shaugh to White Hill Corner, which is noticed in R. 75. Near the foot of the Collard Tor Cottage enclosures a narrow strip of common runs down towards the Torry, which is known as The Rut. Eastward of it, under Wotter, is Higher Lee Wood, which is probably the wood referred to in the grant made to the men of Plympton by Baldwin de Redvers, already mentioned. The parish of Plympton does not include much of the common land that goes to make up Dartmoor (though the greater part of Crownhill Down is situated within its boundary), so that the permission to supply themselves with peat from other commons would be of value to the people of Plympton. Eastward of Collard Tor are two single stone rows, fourteen stones standing in one, and ten in the other.

* *Historical Views of Devonshire.* Vol. 1, Section IV.

Passing these we make our way over Wotter Common to Wott er Brook, here a tiny stream, and crossing it shall reach what is known as the Roman Camp, but which is supposed to be a disused reservoir, and of modern date. It is situated on the side of Stewarts Hill, and close to the road. The latter we now follow eastward, with Black Alder Tor R. Below this, but not in sight, is White Hill Tor, sometimes called Torry Combe Tor, from its situation. The moor people often speak of this valley as Terracum ; I have seen the name written Tor-y-cwm, the idea, I suppose, being to give it a Celtic appearance ; as Torrycomb it was known more than 400 years ago, when there is a reference to the pinfold there. It is now the centre of a great clay industry, of which we see abundant evidence on every hand. The Lee Moor Clay Works of the Messrs. Martin Bros. are by far the largest of any in the district. Quite a settlement has been formed here, their employees numbering about 400. There is a church mission room, a Wesleyan Chapel, and a reading room. One of their large pits is about 40 acres in extent, and of great depth. Following the road past the cottages of the employees we shall be led to White Hill Corner (R. 75, 56, 61), where there is a guide-post : Meavy, 4¼ m. ; Sheepstor, 4½ m. ; Cornwood, 3 m. ; Ivybridge, 5½ m. ; Shaugh, 3 m. ; Bickleigh, 5½ m.

Shell   Pen
Top.   Beacon.

Clay Works.

FROM WHITEHALL CORNER. LOOKING E.

[EXTENSION TO *White Hill Yeo*, add 1½ m. If the rambler cares to do so he may trace the Torry to its source. It rises at a spot known as White Hill Yeo, a little to the E. of Pen Beacon (Ex. 34), and about 1 m. distant. There is, however, little to reward him, unless he desires to see the great clay pit we have referred to, for the formation of which it was found necessary to divert the Torry. Striking E. over the common he will soon reach this, and will then cross the little stream and make his way up its L. bank with Cholwich Town Waste R. On reaching Torry Brook Head, near which are the vestiges of some ancient pounds, he will bear R. around the leat where it makes a bend, and then keeping it close L. trace it upwards to the reservoir or Big Pond, as it is called (R. 48). On the R. as he proceeds is the hill known as Hexton, where is a stone called the Hanging Rock, and also one or two cairns. It is possible that this name points to the former existence of a dolmen here, though it would not be safe to conclude that such was the case (cf. Shilstone Tor, Ex. 14). Turning L. at the pond the rambler will pass over the side of Grey Hills to Blackaton Cross.]

From White Hill Corner we make our way along the road N.W. (R. 67), and passing Sunderland Cottages R. shall soon reach the enclosures of Lee Moor House. Beyond these we enter again upon the open moor, and here, close beside the way, shall find an interesting object. This is Blackaton Cross, often called the Roman, or Roman's Cross, a name also sometimes attached to a similar relic near Sheepstor, and to others in the neighbourhood. Only the head and the socket-stone belong to the original monument. It was furnished with the present shaft, which was cut for a window-sill at Lee Moor House, and set up by the late Mr. Phillips, who resided there [*Crosses*, Chap. IV.]

| Cocks Tor. | Peak Hill. | Sharp Tor. | Lether Tor. | Sheeps Tor. | Mis Tor. | | N. Hisworthy Tor. |

Ringmoor Down.

Trowlsworthy Warren.   Leggis Tor.

FROM BLACKATON CROSS. LOOKING N.

There is a good view from the cross. Far away to the N.W. is seen the peak of Brent Tor (Ex. 9); to the R. of this Cocks' Tor and Great Mis Tor (Exs. 8, 6) reveal themselves; nearer to us are Lether Tor, Sharp Tor, and Sheeps Tor (Ex. 39); while beyond Grey Hills and Blackaton Slaggets, and only 1 m. distant, are the piles of Trowls-worthy.

Proceeding along the road for a few score yards we shall notice that it is crossed by a green path running E. and W. Here we turn L. to Emmett's Post, which stands on a mound near by. This serves as a bond-mark between the lands of Lord Morley and Sir Henry Lopes. The boundary runs northward to the road, where is another bond-stone, having the initial L. on its northern face and M on the southern, and thence goes north-eastward to the Blackabrook.

[EXTENSION TO *Cadaford Bridge*, add 1½ m. From Emmett's Post the way lies N. to the bond-stone, whence the road is followed to the bridge. A short distance from the stone, and L. of the road in descending, is a small pound containing hut circles, but it presents nothing remarkable. Beyond this the Shaugh Lake Clay Works are passed L. Away to the R. is Leggis Tor (Ex. 38), above the R. bank of the Plym, with Trowlsworthy Warren House above the L. bank, and beyond it Hen Tor (Ex. 37). Very soon we draw near to the river, which becomes our companion till we reach the bridge. This is noticed

| Leggis Tor. | | Trowlsworthy Warren House. | Hen Tor. |

Plym.   E.

FROM NEAR CADAFORD BRIDGE.

post. In returning to Shaugh the rambler takes the R. branch S. of the bridge, as in R. 8. On the L. of the road the ruins of an old farm house will be noticed. This, so the story tells us, was once the abode of Merry Ann and Merry Andrew, a couple who always viewed the bright side of things. Just above this the rambler, looking up the valley of the Plym N.E., will see Ditsworthy Warren house with the path running down to the river, 2 m. away (Ex. 37). Passing the entrance to Dunstone Farm R. he will soon reach Shaden Plantation, probably a corruption of Shaugh Down, the name of the parish being sometimes pronounced Sha; formerly this was generally so.* Here, close to some hedge steps, whence a path runs through Shaden Brake towards the village, is the upper portion of an old cross. A socket-stone to be seen near Beatland Corner perhaps belongs to it, and indicates its original situation. Adjoining the brake is Shaden Moor, which extends to North Wood and West Down. A short distance beyond the cross is Brag Lane End.]

From Emmett's Post we shall direct our steps westward over that part of Shaugh Moor known as Saddlesborough, probably the Chechilburgh of an earlier time (R. 48). Here the ground drops considerably from what is the highest part of the common, 996 feet,

---

* Old forms of the name are Schagh (1291); Shawe (1505), at which time the venville rent was 7d.; and Shagh and Shaye about the middle of the sixteenth century. In our younger days we invariably heard the natives speak of the village as Sha Town. A story used to be told of a tourist who met a countryman near the Dewer Stone and asked him the way to Shaugh. The man replied that he did not know of such a place, but on the stranger remarking that it was a village with an inn called the White Thorn, exclaimed : " Aw, you main Sha Town ; way, that's where I live to."

towards the N., and the brow of the hill is covered with scattered rocks. On the slope below is a small pound, with two or three·hut circles near it. Still maintaining a westerly course, we shall pass down the hill to Brag Lane End, and follow the road to the village.

Trowlsworthy Tors   Shell Top.   Pen Beacon.

Hen Tor.

E.   Plym.   S.E.

FROM CADAFORD BRIDGE.

Ex. 37.—*Trowlsworthy, Hen Tor, Shavercombe, Plym Steps, Calves Lake Tor* [EXTENSION TO *Plym Head*, add 2¼ m.] *Evil Combe, Thrushel Combe, Ditsworthy Warren, Cadaford Bridge,* 13 m. from and to Shaugh. (With direct route to Thrushel Combe *via* Trowlsworthy Warren, 4 m. from Shaugh).

Turning L. at the cross E. of the church we speedily reach the common at Brag Lane End, whence we strike eastward over Shaugh Moor, our way being the reverse of that described at the end of Ex. 36. On reaching the highest point of Saddlesborough we shall bear L. and descend the side of Whit Hills to the road, reaching it about ¼ m. below Blackaton Cross. Still following the same course we strike across Grey Hills to the Blackabrook, meeting on the way with abundant evidence of the tin-seeker's former presence here. His deep open workings, in which dwarf trees are growing, cover the ground for some distance, extending down the banks of the little tributary to the Plym. On the slope of the further side of this stream, and between it and the Trowlesworthy Tors, is a fine group of antiquities, consisting of examples of dwellings and burial monuments, and these we shall now briefly examine on our way up the valley of the Plym. From Blackabrook Head we strike E.N.E., and in less than ¼ m. shall come upon a double stone row intersected by the Clay Works leat. It runs about N. and S., and is 142 yards in length. At its northern end is a stone circle, known locally as the Pulpit, and consisting of eight stones ; this is 23 feet in diameter. W. of this circle, but on the other side of the leat, that is to say, on the lower side of it, are the remains of another, and from this also a row extends. This, however, is a single one, and is not more than about 85 yards long. Its direction is E. and W. Crossing the leat by one of the numerous footbridges here we make our way along its bank north-westward, and soon reach a couple of pounds containing hut circles. The entrances to these enclosure have each been partitioned into two by walls built in the form of the letter X, the point where the arms cross being in the centre of the opening. It has been thought that this masking and narrowing of the entrances was designed for protection. But if these walls had been carried to a sufficient height to render such an arrangement effective. they would have fallen in a confused heap, and would not have preserved the form of a cross, or letter X. It is probable that they are later additions to the pounds, and were never more than about half the height of a man. The hill on which these remains are found has been a warren for centuries, and it may well be that the pounds have been utilized at some period either as traps, or for other purposes not now understood. At all events, no such arrangement is seen in any other pound on Dartmoor. According to the *Additions* to Risdon (1811) Trowlsworthy Warren was granted by Baldwin de Redvers to Sampson de Traylesworthy before 1272. A Simon de Travailesworth was one of the witnesses in 1291 to the deed of Isabella de Fortibus, Countess of Devon, to which we have more than once referred (Ex. 6). In 1560 the warren came into the possession of the Woollcombes. For a long period only one name has been associated with it as tenant. The present occupant is Richard Lavers, who is 89 years of age, and succeeded his father here. The ruined building near the pounds appears to be of comparatively modern date. On the common are a number of hut circles, and others are seen lower down near the warren house. A small tor close by is locally known as Shadyback Tor ; this there can be no doubt is the Shearaback Tor referred to in 1828 by H. E. Carrington, son of the poet, as being situated two miles E. of Shaugh village.

[To reach Trowlsworthy Warren house direct from Brag Lane End, and also Ditsworthy Warren, near which are the Thrushel Combe antiquities, the visitor will follow the road N. to Shaden Plantation, where he will leave it and strike N.E. over the common. The way lies across Whit Hills and through the Shaugh Lake Clay Works to the road coming down R. from Lee Moor House (Ex. 36), the distance being about 1 m. Care must be taken not to keep too much to the L. ; but the visitor will hardly do this, as the house soon comes into view. Near the bottom of the hill a rough track branches from the road, and this, which is carried over the Blackabrook by a single stone clapper, leads direct to the house. Pounds and hut circles will be noticed L. when drawing near to it. Leaving it R., and ascending towards the tors, the antiquities just noticed will be met with on crossing the leat. If the rambler is bound for Ditsworthy he must not keep quite so much to the R. on passing the house. He should strike the leat a little further N. than in the former case, and follow it where it is carried along the side of Round Hill to Spanish Lake, which stream it crosses in a delightful little dell. The view of the valley from Round Hill is very fine ; Leggis Tor is seen on the further side of the Plym (Ex. 38). On crossing Spanish Lake keep on the higher side of the leat and along the side of Willings Hill direct to Ditsworthy, which is in full view. The leat will be met again where it passes Hen Tor Brook, and just below this, L., and close to it, are some pounds with hut circles. The way now lies to the clam spanning the Plym below the house, just before reaching which the leat is crossed. From the clam a track leads up to the house, from the grassy hill behind which one of the

Thrushel Combe menhirs can be seen.   The combe is about $\frac{1}{2}$ m. distant, and the way to it lies over the side of Eastern Tor (see *post* and
Ex. 38).

We shall now make our way from the Trowlsworthy antiquities
to the tors that rise above them.   The lower one is Little Trowlsworthy
Tor, and from this an old wall, broken down in many places, extends
northward towards the Plym.   Great Trowlsworthy Tor, which is
rather higher, 1,141 feet, is close by (R. 71).   Here a moorman of my
acquaintance once found some coins which he described to me as
"base guineas."   Naturally deeming them to be of no value he took
no care of them, and they were unfortunately lost.   The disused
quarry that will be seen here was once worked for red granite.   The
huge cylindrical block lying on the ground was intended for the base
of a monument.

From Great Trowlsworthy Tor we shall strike north-eastward to
the head of Spanish Lake, and over Willings Hill to Hen Tor, 1 m.
This tract forms Willings Walls Warren, and the stream that bounds
it on the E. is sometimes called Wall Brook, or Walla Brook, though
it is more generally known as Hen Tor Brook, from the proximity of
its source to that pile.   The latter thrusts itself from out the side of
Hen Tor Hill, and a clatter streams from its foot.   Some rocks northward of the pile bear the name of Little Hen Tor.   As the ground rises
behind Hen Tor the ascent to its summit is easy, and from here a good
view of the valley is commanded.   The most conspicuous object is
Ditsworthy Warren house, with the clam spanning the river, less than
1 m. distant.   Below the tor are the ruined walls of the enclosures of
Hen Tor Farm, mixed up with those of pounds of an early date.   A
number of hut circles will also be seen, some being fairly good examples.
In the second half of the eighteenth century this farm was in the
occupation of a man named Nicholls.   When he relinquished it Nature
resumed her sway, and the fields in which it is said as many as ten
oxen were employed in ploughing, soon became a part of the moor
again.   As the years went by the dwelling, still known as Hen Tor
House, also fell into decay, but enough remains to show the passer-by
who may not know its history that the man who erected it was certainly
not a jerry-builder.

Leaving Hen Tor we shall cross the side of the hill to the Shavercombe Brook, our course being N.N.E., or from Hen Tor House, N.E.
by N.   Just before the stream is reached we shall come upon a kistvaen
within a small circle, not, however, in a very good state of preservation,
though none of the stones have been removed.   Shavercombe Head
is $\frac{1}{2}$ m. distant.   Between this and Broadall Head a bronze dagger
was found, about four feet below the surface, by a man employed at
Ditsworthy Warren whilst cutting peat in the summer of 1892.   It
was shortly afterwards secured by Mr. H. P. Hearder, of Plymouth,
who still has it in his possession.   Broadall Head is 1 m. S.S.E. ;
Yealm Head $\frac{3}{4}$ m. E.S.E., and Langcombe Head 1 m. N.E. by E.
(Ex. 34).   Shavercombe is one of those delightful little valleys which
the rambler on Dartmoor meets with occasionally, where a mountain
ash or an oak find shelter, and where ferns grow abundantly.   As we
make our way downward its beauties speedily begin to reveal themselves.   Ere we have gone far the stream falls over a high rock forming

a charming cascade when rains have swollen its volume. Below this and quite close to the deep combe, is the tiny Shavercombe Tor, and near it a small pound with hut circles. Having gained the R. bank of the brawling little stream we strike northward over Giant's Hill, to Plym Steps, where the Abbots' Way crosses the river at a ford, as already stated (T. 1). Although its name would lead the visitor to suppose that stepping-stones existed here none are to be seen.

[At this point the Langcombe Brook falls into the Plym, and of this we have already spoken (Ex. 34). At its foot is an old leat an other mining remains. A little way up, and not far from the L. bank is a kistvaen. Still further up the feeder from Deadman's Bottom comes in on the other side, and above that is another kistvaen. This has been noticed in Ex. 34. From Plym Steps to Broad Rock the Abbots' Way is a well-defined track.]

Passing upward we emerge from the gorge through which the Plym runs between the ford and Shavercombe Foot, and gradually leaving the stream L. shall make our way to Calves Lake Tor, a small pile $\frac{1}{2}$ m. distant. Very near to this on the S.E. is a kistvaen, the covering slab of which has been raised, and now hangs partly over the open grave. If the visitor does not care to extend his ramble to Plym Head he will now make his way to the river and cross it near where the little Calves Lake falls into it.

[EXTENSION TO *Plym Head*, add 2$\frac{1}{4}$ m. The rambler will strike N.E. by E., and when about $\frac{1}{4}$ m. from the tor will cross the Tavistock branch of the Abbots' Way between Broad Rock R. and Plym Ford L., but it is not here very plainly defined. $\frac{1}{4}$ m. further on Great Gnats' Head is passed L. (Ex. 34), and soon after the broken ground in which the river has its source will be reached. The stream issues from a fissure in the peat, and does not rise in a swamp as is often the case. Northward of Plym Head is Crane Hill, which we have already mentioned in connection with Ducks' Pool, $\frac{1}{2}$ m. S.E. (Ex. 30) ; N.W. of Crane Hill is Hand Hill, on the N. slope of which is Wheal Anne Bottom (Ex. 3) ; N. of it is Stream Hill, which descends to the edge of Fox Tor Mire ; and E. of it is Black Lane (T. 75). Beyond that is Cater's Beam, which extends nearly to the Avon. Not far below its source the Plym receives the little Crane Lake. Calves Lake is 1$\frac{1}{4}$ m. below the source of the Plym if the stream be followed, and this the rambler will probably prefer to do in returning.]

Having crossed the Plym at Calves Lake Foot we find ourselves close to another little tributary, which comes down from Evil Combe. In this combe is a hut of the sort usually called beehive huts (cf. Ex. 33), but it is partly in ruins. This stream is probably identical with the Plymcrundla mentioned in the charter of Isabella de Fortibus, referred to in Ex. 6. This, which is of the date 1291, sets forth the boundaries of the lands given by the Lady Amicia, mother of Isabella, to found the abbey of Buckland, and the boundary is conterminous with that of the forest from the Walkham below Mis Tor to the Plym. It is set forth as running from Siward's Cross (Ex. 2) to "Gyllesburgh [*i.e.*, Eylesbarrow] et Plymcrundla ad Plymma." Crundle is a word signifying a spring, or well. That the forest boundary (which is usually drawn in the opposite direction) ran from Erme Head, that is, Grymsgrove, to the head or foot of Calves Lake, and thence up Evil Combe to the two cairns on the summit of Eylesbarrow, 1,491 feet can hardly be doubted. *Ivel* is a name implying *little water*. Some bounds in this part of the moor were described by one Anthony Torr, of Bishop's Tawton, in 1702, but incorrectly. He mentions among others Wood-lake (Wollake), Fox Tor Head (R. 7), Reddicliffe Head, Stevon Head (Strane), and Harborlake Head under South Hisworthy.

As we make our way down by the Plym through the great stream-work we pass under Lower Harter Tor. This is not a very large pile, but is, nevertheless, striking on account of the massive blocks of which it is composed. The ground around it is strewn with granite. Higher Harter Tor is about ¼ m. N.W. of this, and like it is not large. Its elevation is only 1,349 feet, but a very fine view is gained from it. Among other eminences in the vicinity that are seen are Sheeps Tor, Down Tor, and Combe Tor, while peeping over a ridge of moorland is the distant summit of Brent Tor. The tumuli on Eylesbarrow are about ½ m. N., midway between being the disused Eylesbarrow Tin Mine, with the ruins of a house built here many years ago by Mr. Deacon, well known in his day as an enthusiastic follower of hounds. On the hillside westward of the mine are several fine examples of hut circles.

About ½ m. below Evil Combe we reach Plym Steps, very near to which, on the slope R., is a pound containing three hut circles, and outside it a small cairn. Here we meet a little stream which falls into the Plym just opposite to where the Langcombe Brook joins that river, and is crossed by the Abbots' Way as that old path descends to the ford. I have found this rivulet to be usually dry during summer.

(Eylesbarrow is passed in R. 67, which runs from this point to Siward's Cross. From its summit that ancient monument is 1 m. N.N.E.; Plym Ford ¾ m. E. by S.; Evil Combe ½ m. S.E.; Plym Steps 1 m. S. by E.; Head of Thrushel Combe ¾ m. S.W. by S.; Head of Dean Combe ¾ m. W. by S.; Down Tor 1¼ m. W.N.W.; and the springs of the Newleycombe Lake 1 m. N.N.W.)

Climbing the western bank we leave the old monks path, which was utilized in later times by the tinners, and continue on our way down stream, keeping above the gorge L., with Giant's Hill, and Shaver-combe Down above it, on the further side. In about ¾ m. we reach the little lateral valley of Thrushel Combe. Here, near its head R. is a blowing-house, which although of modern date, is interesting as being the last place in which tin was smelted on Dartmoor. Mr. William Burt, in his preface to Carrington's poem, states that 100 blocks were coined here during the Michaelmas quarter, 1824. Lower down, at Mill Corner, on the Plym, is a more ancient blowing-house. Thrushel Combe is locally called Drizzle Combe, and this name has been generally adopted, and figures on the Ordnance map. But on the copy of an old map in my possession, which I have every reason to believe to be authoritative, the valley is shown as Thrushel Combe, and there can hardly be a doubt that this is the correct name. It is easy to under-stand how it would become Drizzle Combe in the Dartmoor vernacular.

The group of antiquities in this combe was first described by Mr. R. Hansford Worth in a paper read before the members of the Plymouth

Institution, in 1889, but was mentioned some years before that date by the late Mr. C. Spence Bate in a discussion at a meeting of the Devonshire Association. When Mr. Worth noticed these remains the menhirs lay upon the ground, but his paper had the effect of calling attention to them, with the result that in the summer of 1893 they were set up. The group is situated to the E. of the stream that runs through the combe, and in approaching it from Plym Steps we first come upon a small pound, close to which is a cairn. Below this are other cairns, and three stone rows and menhirs, the whole extending for about ¼ m. As these cairns may more properly be regarded as the termination of the group, it will be fitting that we commence our examination of it at the lower end of the combe. Here is a menhir, from which a row of stones, not of great height, extends for a distance of over 160 yards, its direction being a little N. of E. By the side of this is another line of similar stones, but incomplete. At its eastern end is a kistvaen, the mound by which it was once covered, being nearly 20 yards in circumference. Between 50 and 60 yards eastward of this kistvaen is another menhir, certainly the finest on Dartmoor, and from this also a single row of stones extends. This line, which is not very complete, terminates in a barrow about 30 yards in circumference, and surrounded by a circle of twelve slabs. Running roughly parallel to this last row, and northward of it, is another, which, like its companions, also starts from a menhir and terminates in a barrow. It is about the same length as the one first noticed. The circumference of the barrow is about 30 yards, and it is surrounded by slabs, as also is another barrow near to it. This latter with the two other terminal tumuli forms a line running W. of N., and pointing to a tumulus as some distance off, on which is a kistvaen, and about 100 yards south-eastward of this is a stone circle. E. of the three barrows is the small pound already mentioned. Not very far from the barrow at which the first row ends is the fine cairn known as the Giant's Basin. Like many of these great stone heaps on the moor, there is a depression in its centre, and in this is probably seen the resemblance to the article the name of which it bears. Mr. Worth took the measurements of the three menhirs while they lay prostrate. The tallest of these was 17 feet 10 inches ; the one at the lower end of the group 12 feet 6 inches ; and the third 9 feet 5 inches.

(Carriages can approach very near to these remains by the road from Sheepstor ; if from Cadaford Bridge or Meavy it is not necessary to go into that village ; the green track running from Ringmoor Cot to Ditsworthy (T. 71) is suitable for driving, or the road branching from near the Cot may be chosen. This joins the road from Sheepstor about ¾ m. eastward of that place. From Cadaford Bridge the route sketched *ante* is a good one for the pedestrian, or he may go by the R. bank of the Plym. While here he should not omit to visit Shaver-combe. From Princetown the route to Newleycombe Lake below Kingsett has been described (Ex. 2). From that point the rambler will climb the side of Down Tor, leaving it R., and strike S.E. to Combeshead Tor. This he will leave L. and descend to the lower end of the gorge just below, where the Narrator Brook makes a bend towards the W. From this point the blowing-house near the head of Thrushel Combe is ½ m. distant S. by E. Or he may pass close to

Down Tor and strike S. to the moor road between the enclosures. This will lead him to Deancombe Farm, below which he will cross the stream and follow the path up the valley to the foot of the gorge below Combeshead Tor).

West of Thrushel Combe are two rock piles, the northern one being known as Whittenknowles Rocks, and the other as Eastern Tor. On the former among the masses of stone there are a number of hut circles, and also the remains of rectangular buildings, while on the latter is a small enclosure. Below this tor is Ditsworthy Warren house. This warren was always referred to in our childhood's days as Ware's Warren, being occupied, as it still is, by a family of that name. This extends a considerable distance up the valley, and includes Willings Walls and Hen Tor on the other side of the Plym within its boundaries. A road leads from the house down to the clam, which is raised high above the river on stone buttresses, and another runs up the side of the hill to Ringmoor Down (Ex. 38). We descend the slope between these, and reaching Meavy Pool, where a little feeder falls into the river, shall find a path on the R. bank of the latter, which we shall follow down the valley. This will lead us below Leggis Tor R., where are some hut circles (Ex. 38), past Trowlsworthy L., and across Brisworthy Burrows to the road close to Cadaford Bridge. It may interest the rambler by the Plym to know that an authority has stated that gold has been found on its banks. But—and this is the unfortunate part of it—" in too small quantities to justify mining researches."

Crossing the bridge we strike into the R. branch where the road forks, and make our way to Shaugh as in Ex. 36. For Yelverton see the *Dewer Stone* Section which follows.

THE DEWER STONE AND CADAFORD BRIDGE.

A road runs from the village of Shaugh down the hill to Shaugh Bridge, whence it goes on to Bickleigh. The present bridge replaces an old structure which was so much damaged by a flood in 1823 that it was found necessary to demolish it. Immediately above it is the confluence of the Mew (Ex. 2) and the Plym, the latter a Celtic name derived by Baxter from *pilim, to roll*. This stream comes down through the wooded valley on the E. side of the Dewer Stone Hill, which is peninsulated by the two, and this part of it is sometimes erroneously called the Cad. There is no authority for such a name whatever, and it would probably never be heard now had it not been adopted by the fishing association having control of this part of the river as a means of distinguishing it from the part below the bridge. It first appears in 1804 in Howard's poem on Bickleigh Vale. Cadaford Bridge further up the stream is locally spoken of as Cadover; this was thought to mean a bridge over the Cad, although existing records showed that the river had been known as the Plym for more than five centuries before that date. In the charter of Isabella de Fortibus, 1291, the river is called Plymma from its source downward, and the confluence is thus referred to, " locum ubi Mewy cadit in Plymma." The bridge, probably then a clapper, is called in the same charter " ponte de Cada worth." This name it doubtless taken from the Saxon *worthig* close by now called Cadworthy, and which was apparently formed on the site of a British battle—*cad* being a Celtic word meaning a *conflict*, or *strife*. Just before reaching Shaugh Bridge the Plym flows past the Dewer Stone, a fine mass of rock rising almost perpendicularly, from its brink. In its name we probably see the Celtic *dwr*, *water*, and this its situation amply justifies [*Gems*, Chap. XIX.] A fine view of the rock is obtained from West Down, on the R. of the road in descending from the village. Below the bridge the Plym sweeps onward to the wooded Bickleigh Vale, where it encounters fresh beauties, and finally meets the tidal waters at the head of the Laira estuary.

Above the confluence the Plym is spanned by a clam, and from this a path leads upwards to the summit of the hill which forms the southern extremity of Wigford Down, an extensive common in the parish of Meavy. Here there is a good view of the valley ; the northern side is covered with oak coppice, and from this grey crags thrust themselves. Near the stone this leafy covering forms the Dewer Stone Wood ; above this is Common Wood ; and still further up Cadworthy Wood, between each being a depression on the hillside. Facing the higher one on the S. side of the river is North Wood, which stretches from the bank upward to Shaden Moor ; opposite to the two others is the bare slope of West Down. About sixty years ago there was a strike of wool-combers in Plymouth, and many of the men found work in these woods at rinding, or " ripping," as it is often called, that is, felling the young trees and stripping them of their bark. Among them were two, a father and son, who, unable to procure lodgings, walked from and to their home in Plymouth every day for a week. On the northern side of the Dewer Stone Hill is Blacklands. Some years ago a quarry was opened here, but operations were not continued very long. A reave which seems to have encircled the summit of this peninsular hill, and the remains of two others that run across it, point to its having once been fortified.

The ramble from the summit of the Dewer Stone Hill to Cadaford Bridge and down the valley of the Plym is a good one, though the latter part of it may necessitate some scrambling over rocks and through undergrowth The visitor will proceed N.E. along the brow of the hill till he arrives at the enclosures of Cadworthy Farm, and if he does not keep too near to these he will come upon a kistvaen standing in a circle of stones. Further on there is another, and not far from it, on the highest part of the down, a small pound. Below these, to the N., are the hedges of some old enclosures that the down has claimed again for its own.

Keeping the Cadworthy enclosures R. the rambler will descend to Cadaford Bridge, noticing the upper part of an old cross set upon a mound as he proceeds [*Crosses*, Chap. V.] When the moorman calls the bridge Cadover he is nearer to the old form of the name than are those who accept the modern one of Cadaford.

[R. 13 shows the way from Cadaford Bridge to Cornwood and Ivybridge ; R. 8 to Shaugh and Plympton. In Ex. 36 the road·to Shaugh is more fully described. For Yelverton pass up the road northward and turn L. at the top ; thence the way lies above Durance R. along the side of Wigford Down ; on crossing Greenwell Cert, about 1 m. on. the down of that name is entered upon, with Catstor Down on the other side of the wall R. ; leave the road and keep the hedge R. to the moor gate ; thence by the lane down the side of Callisham Down R. to Gratton Bridge ; up the hill to Yelverton.]

From Cadaford Bridge the rambler will make his way down the L. bank of the river, and passing below Dunstone Farm will cross the tiny Dunstone Brook and enter North Wood. In this is a fine cascade, and below it a deep pool. On emerging from the wood the rambler will find himself at the foot of West Down. He will continue to follow the river until he is nearly abreast of the Dewer Stone, when he will leave it and make his way up the side of the down to Shaugh Hill and follow the road leading upward to the village. If bound for Shaugh Bridge he will keep nearer to the stream when approaching the Dewer Stone.

ROUTES FROM PLYMPTON AND SHAUGH.

R. 67.—To Princetown, N.N.E. *Niel Gate, Cadaford Bridge, Ringmoor Cot, Sheepstor, Narrator Farm, Nosworthy Bridge, Roundy Farm, Crazy Well Pool, Cramber Tor, Hart Tor,*   P., 12 m. ; S., 8½ m. To Two Bridges, add 1½ m. Reverse, R. 8.

[Objects : Ex. 36 between Niel Gate and Cadaford Bridge ; thence Exs. 38, 39, 2.]

Passing through Colebrook we turn L., and when the lane forks take the R. branch. This will lead us over the hill, on the further side of which we cross the Lee Moor tramroad,* and shortly afterwards arrive at Browney Cross [*Crosses,* Chap. V.] Here is a guide-post, and a road branching L. to Bickleigh. (Shaugh, 1¾ m. ; Cadaford Bridge, 2½ ; Plympton, 3½ ; Ridgway, 3½ ; Bickleigh, 2 ; Roborough, 3). We keep straight on as in Ex. 36, to Niel Gate, where we enter upon the common, and turning neither R. nor L., shall reach Brag Lane End in ¾ m., where the visitor setting out from Shaugh will join this route. A short distance further on we pass Shaden Plantation L., and soon arrive at Cadaford Bridge. Crossing this we ascend the hill with the Wigford Down Clay Works L., and at the top bear round to the R. (The road L. leads to Hooe Meavy and Yelverton). We speedily turn L. to Lynch Down, and then leaving the road strike into a footpath running northward over the common to Ringmoor Cot, ¾ m. Brisworthy Plantation is first on our R. and then Ringmoor Down, Lynch Down being L. Immediately beyond the Cot a road runs R. (T. 71) ; we follow the main one L., which will lead us down the hill between some enclosures to the Sheepstor Brook. Soon after crossing this we turn L., in the village, and about 200 yards on shall turn R., or northward, to Park Cottage, where a way leads R. up to the common. On reaching this we bear L., and skirt it to its northern verge, having the walls of the enclosures close to us L. There is a footpath over this part of the common, and in one place it will lead us between the enclosures

------

* Here, on the L., is Brixton Farm, where are the remains of an ancient entrenchment known as Boringdon Camp. It is sometimes referred to as Castle Ring, though this name is more often applied to the ruined keep at Plympton.

and a detached newtake. About ¾ m. from the point at which we entered upon the down is Narrator Farm, and this we pass through and follow the road to the Dean Combe Brook (Ex. 39). This we cross at a ford, and reaching another road turn L. to the clapper over Newley-combe Lake. Crossing this we leave Nosworthy Bridge L., and turn R. to the ruined Nosworthy farmhouse, and make our way by a rough road running up between the enclosures for rather over ½ m. to another coming up L. from Lether Tor Bridge (T. 2). This we follow eastward with Kingset Farm R., and speedily reach the common near the ruins of Roundy Farm (Ex. 2). About ¼ m beyond this is a gully on the L. of the track, which we trace upward to Crazy Well Pool (Ex. 2). Northward of the pool, and at a much greater elevation, is the Devonport leat, and just here there is a bridge over it (T. 3). From this our course is N. to Cramber Tor, beyond which we descend to the Hart Tor Brook, where is a ford. Hart Tor we leave a little to the L. Our course is about N. from the brook, and ¾ m. from it, we reach the road above Devil's Bridge Hill. Princetown is close by.

Visitors from Ivybridge and Cornwood choosing this route to Princetown will join it at Cadaford Bridge. (See R. 57 for road from Ivybridge to Cornwood ; R. 56 Cornwood to White Hill Corner ; and R. 61 from the corner to Cadaford).

R. 68.—To Tavistock, N.N.W. *Niel Gate, Cadaford Bridge Marchants Bridge, Dousland, Walkhampton, Huckworthy Bridge, Warren's Cross, Whitchurch Down.* P., 15 m. ; S., 10½ m. Reverse, R. 14.

[Objects : Exs. 36 to 40; 7.]

This is a road route throughout, and few directions are needed. R. 67 shows the way to Lynch Down *via* Cadaford Bridge. On reaching this down the rambler will continue to follow the road with the enclosures L., and ¾ m. on will descend Lynch Hill, at the foot of which he will cross the Mew at Marchants Bridge. Leaving the village of Meavy L. he will pass up to Yennadon Down and follow the road to Dousland (Ex. 39). Here he will cross the Plymouth and Princetown road, and make his way down the lane to Walkhampton. Passing through the village he will take the road N. to Huckworthy Bridge, ½ m. (Ex. 40), where he will cross the Walkham. A little way up the steep lane he will branch R to Huckworthy Common (T. 69), and keeping the hedge L. will be led to an old stone cross placed where the road forks [*Crosses*, Chap. VIII.] The R. branch runs to Sampford Spiney and Ward Bridge (Exs. 1, 7). The rambler will take the L. one, and 1¼ m. on will pass over the N.E. corner of Plaster Down, and after again entering upon the enclosed land will emerge once more on the commons at Warren's Cross (Ex. 7). Here the way to Tavistock lies over Whitchurch Down L. Directions are given in R. 1.

R. 69.—To Lydford, N. by W. *Niel Gate, Cadaford Bridge, Marchants Bridge, Dousland, Huckworthy Bridge, Warren's Cross, Moor Shop, Harford Bridge, Black Down, Skit.* P., 21½ m. ; S., 17 m. ; from Cornwood, 20½ m. Reverse, R. 21.

[Objects : Exs. 36, 38, 39, 40, 7, 8, 9, 10.]

The rambler from Cornwood will join this route at Cadaford Bridge. The first part of it, *i.e.*, as far as the road to Lynch Down, is the same as R. 67 ; thence it is identical with R. 68 as far as Warren's Cross. From that point the road must be followed N. to Pennycomequick, where a little stream crosses the road, and thence to Moor Shop (Ex. 8). The rambler keeps straight on, and in 1½ m. reaches Harford Bridge, on the Tavy (Exs. 8, 9), and crossing it soon finds himself on the Tavistock and Okehampton high road. Turn R. up Wringworthy Hill to Black Down, 2½ m. (Ex. 9). Soon after entering on the common four granite posts will be seen R. of the road. Here the track branches L. to Lydford Station, and the Manor Hotel (T. 23), whence a road runs to Lydford village. This may also be reached by following the highway past Beardon, 2¼ m. further on. There, close to the seventh milestone from Tavistock, is a gate from which a path leads by Skit Steps to the village (Ex. 10). The Dartmoor Inn is ¾ m. beyond this gate on the main road.

R. 70.—To Okehampton, a little E. of N. *Cadaford Bridge, Sheepstor, Nosworthy Bridge, Princetown, Rundle Stone, Walkham Head, Tavy Hole, Broad Amicombe Hole, Dinger Plain, Moor Gate. P.,* 27 m. ; *S.,* 24 m. ; from Cornwood, a little W. of N., 27 m. Reverse, R. 28.

This route is made up of R. 67 and R. 3, q.v.

R. 71.—To Chagford and Moreton, N.E. by N. With route from Cornwood, N.N.E. *Niel Gate, Brag Lane End, Shaugh Moor, Blackabrook Head, Great Trowlsworthy Tor, Hen Tor* (FROM CORNWOOD : *Rook Gate, Pen Beacon, Shell Top, Hen Tor*), *Plym Steps, Siward's Cross, Peat Cot, Prince Hall Bridge, Cherry Brook, Post Bridge, Warren House Inn, Jurston Gate, P.,* 26 m. ; *S.,* 21 m. ; from Cornwood, 21½ m. To Moreton, 1½ m. further. Reverse, R. 34.

[Objects : Exs. 36, 37, 3, 4, 46, 44, 45, 22. If from Cornwood prefix Exs. 34, 35, and S. Ex. 121.]

The visitor starting from Cornwood should follow the directions given in R. 59 for reaching Hen Tor, where he will join the preesnt route. If from Plympton those for reaching Brag Lane End, as given in R. 67 should be followed, and here the rambler from Shaugh will join. The course is then E. by N. over Shaugh Moor, and across the Cornwood road, to Blackabrook Head, as in Ex. 37. (The visitor from Plympton may shorten the distance a little by striking up over the common N.E. by E. from Niel Gate to Hawks' Tor, which he will leave L., and still following the same course make his way to Emmett's Post. 1 m. further on. Blackabrook Head is then ½ m. N.E.) From the source of the tributary the rambler will ascend the hill to Great Trowlsworthy Tor, ½ m. N.E., crossing the Clay Works leat by one of the footbridges here, and will thence strike across Willings Hill to Hen Tor House, a little below the pile of that name, keeping very nearly on the line of route sketched in Ex. 37. [From this point the way onward to Siward's Cross is described in R. 59). About ½ m. N. of Siward's Cross the rambler will bear R., his course being north-easterly, and in ½ m. he will reach Peat Cot (Ex. 3). He will here cross the Devonport leat, and leaving it L. will strike about N. towards the enclosures of the estate of Tor Royal. By so doing he will avoid some rather bad ground near the springs of the Strane, R. 34. [This stream joins the Swincombe below the White Works (Ex. 3). Above its L.

bank is a small pile known as Strane Tor.]   When nearing the outer corner of the enclosures the course must be altered to N.E. by E. The summit of Royal Hill must be kept a little to the R. (end of Ex. 3), and Cholake Head, which is due N. of this, L.   About ¾ m. further on the gate at Moorlands will be reached.   Pass through this and turn L. down to Prince Hall Bridge, thence up by the house to the lodge, and across Muddy Lakes Newtake to the Moreton road as in R. 63.   Turn R. and follow the directions given in R. 4.

R. 72.—To Bovey Tracey, N.E. by E.   For points and objects from Plympton, 27 m., see R. 74, 66, 54.   E.N.E. from Shaugh, 29 m., *via* Cornwood and Ivybridge, R. 75, 76, 66, 54.   Reverse, R. 41.

R. 73.—To Ashburton, N.E. by E.   For points from Plympton, 19½ m., see R. 74, 66.   E. by N. from Shaugh, 17½ m. ; points : *Shaugh Moor, Emmett's Post, Pen Beacon, High-house Waste, Stall Moor, Three Barrows, Hickley Plain, Zeal Bridge, Shipley Bridge, Yolland, Gigley Bridge, Warne Bridge, Dean ;* thence as in R. 66.   Reverse, R. 48.

[Objects : Exs. 36, 34 to 29.]

The route from Plympton consists of R. 74, 66.

From Shaugh : to Ivybridge by R. 76, or to Brent by R. 75, and thence as in R. 66, the latter being the better way ; or the moor route may be taken as here described, provided the state of the weather does not render the crossing of the rivers doubtful (see R. 48).

From Shaugh village to the common by Brag Lane.   Strike E. to Emmett's Post, 1 m., and cross the Cornwood road to the Clay Works reservoir.   Cross the leat at the northern end of this and follow it eastward for about ½ m.   Pen Beacon (Ex. 34) now bears E. by S., and is 1 m. distant, and directly in our line of route.   If the rambler cares to go over it he will descend its eastern side (the course there being due E.) to the north-western corner of High-house Waste, close to the source of Ford Brook.   Should he not desire to make the ascent he will pass about ¼ m. S. of the summit, and then strike north-eastward to the corner.   Keep the wall R.   Cross Broadall Lake where it comes from Broadall Gulf, and so down to Yealm Steps.   Here leave the wall, and pass up the source of Ranny Brook, nearly ½ m. E.   From this point steer E. by S. for about 1 m. over Stall Moor, crossing on the way the track to Erme Pound (T. 66).   This will bring the rambler to Downing's House Brook.

(Another way from below Pen Beacon to Downing's House, of which the reverse is given in R. 48, is by steering a little N. of E. and passing over High-house and Dendles Waste to the Yealm, which is crossed about ½ m. below Yealm Steps.   Keep the same N. of E. course across Stall Moor to the brook.   In either of these routes Stalldon Barrow must be kept well to the R.)

Three Barrows, S. of E., is the next point, but a direct route should not be struck.   Follow the brook to the Erme, which can usually be crossed without much difficulty where the tributary falls into it.   The summit of Three Barrows is not now in sight, and care must be taken not to keep too much to the R. in ascending.   Steer E. by S.   The climb is a stiff one, and the distance not much short of a mile.   The Blackwood Path (T. 63) is crossed shortly before the three cairns are reached (Ex. 31). From this lofty hill the course is nearly due E. for 1½ m., the bend of Red Brook, on Hickley Plain, being passed close L. The point to be reached is a small plantation at the foot of Hickley Ridge, and close to Bala Brook. Here is a hunting-gate whence a path leads across two fields to a lane (Ex. 30). The rambler turns L. over Zeal Bridge, and passing Zeal Farm again reaches the moor at Shipley. Here he will cross the Avon, and keeping the wall L. enter a lane. About ¾ m. on is Yolland Cross, whence it makes a sharp bend R., and here he will enter the gate L. to Yolland Farm, as in S. Ex. 105. Passing this he will follow the green track across the level with the hedge R. (this is part of T. 59). Reaching a stroll, with Dockwell Gate L. (Ex. 29), he will turn R. and make his way to the head of it, and passing through the gate there will turn down the lane L. to Gigley Bridge, just beyond which he will again turn L. Almost immediately a lane branching R. is reached, and into this he will strike, and passing down the hill E. by N., will, in 1½ m., reach Warn Bridge, near the gate where a track runs up the Valley of Dean Burn (S. Ex. 100). The hamlet of Dean Combe is passed just before reaching this; it lies a little in on the R. A short distance beyond the bridge he will turn R., and speedily reach the village of Dean, from which place he will proceed as directed in R. 66.

R. 74.—To Ivybridge and Brent. *The Lyneham Inn, Lee Mill Bridge, Ivybridge, Bittaford Bridge, Wrangaton Station, Brent Bridge. I., 6½ m.; B., 11½ m. Reverse R. 55.*

[Objects: Ex. 32, seen from near Wrangaton.]

From the George Hotel the main road is followed eastward, the Lyneham Inn and Smithaleigh being passed between that starting-point and Lee Mill Bridge, on the Yealm, 3½ m. Thence the road goes by Cadleigh Park to Ivybridge, 2 m., from which place the Brent road is described in R. 66.

R. 75.—Shaugh to Brent, E. by S. *Wotter, White Hill Corner, Piall Bridge, Cornwood, Harford, Spurrell's Cross, Owley Gate, 12 m. Reverse, R. 56.*

[Objects: Exs. 36, 35, 37, 33, 32, S. Ex. 112, 111.]

To the common by the road R. at the stone cross. Follow the road past Beatland Corner, where the Plympton and Cadaford road is crossed. Beyond Collard Tor is Wotter, and less than a mile from this the road turns down by Shade Cottages, and then passing Boringdon Cottages L. goes on to White Hill Corner. Here the rambler will turn R. to Tolchmoor Bridge, and soon after descend the hill, with Ridding Down R. and Cholwich Town L., to Quick Bridge (Ex. 35). From here the road runs to Piall Bridge, Heathfield Down, and Cornwood village, whence the way to Ivybridge is shown in R. 76. For Brent turn L. to the Vicarage Bridge and Tor, where turn R. to Harford Bridge, 2½ m. Thence up to the church, and L. to Harford Gate, whence the green track running east over the common is followed (T. 62). In tracing this keep Butter Brook R.; ½ m. a little N. of E. from the head of this is the shattered Spurrell's Cross [*Crosses*, Chap. III.] near which the Buckfast track branched off (T. 59); from this the source of the Scad, 200 feet below, bears S. of E., ¼ m.; rather less than ½ m. due E. is Owley Gate (S. Ex. 110). From this the way

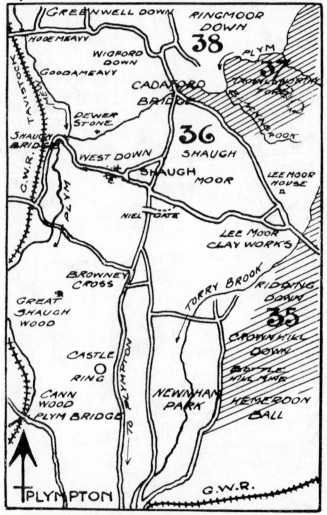

EX. 35, 36; PARTS OF 37, 38.

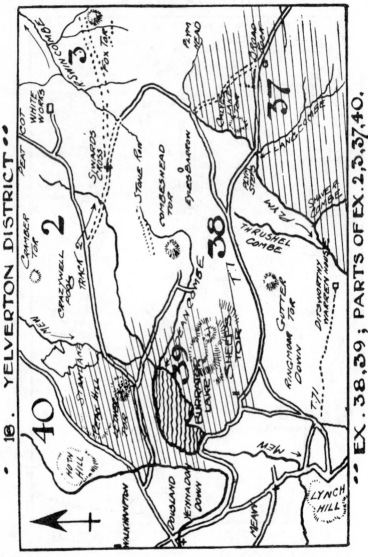

18. YELVERTON DISTRICT "

" EX. 38, 39 ; PARTS OF EX. 2, 3, 37, 40.

lies through the lane between the enclosure walls to Owley, and L. to the Glaze; thence up the hill to Bulhornstone Cross, about ¾ m. beyond which Aish is reached. Turn down the hill R. and cross Lydia Bridge to the village.

R. 76.—Shaugh to Ivybridge, S.E. by E. The points are the same as in the preceding route as far as Cornwood; thence the way lies by Moor Cross and up Houndle Hill. If the way over Crownhill Down be chosen the points are as follows: *Niel Gate, Portworthy, Hooksbury Wood, Crownhill Down, Heddon Down, Lutton, Moor Cross. Via* Cornwood, 8½ m.; *via* Crownhill Down, 9 m. Reverse, R. 57.

[Objects: Exs. 36, 35, 34.]

To Cornwood as in R. 75. Keeping the inn R. follow the road to Moor Cross and Houndle Hill, and past Fardle to Dame Hannah Rogers' School, as in S. Ex. 119. Down by the church to the village. If by way of Crownhill Down and Lutton (see R. 57) take the road to Beatland Corner and Niel Gate. At the fork ¼ m. down take the L. branch. Over ½ m. on cross the Lee Moor Railway, and ¼ m. beyond that turn L. to Portworthy. Cross the Torry, and keeping Hooksbury Wood R. go on to the guide-post on the verge of the common. From this point the way lies E. by S. over Crownhill Down and Heddon Down to Lutton, 2½ m. (see R. 57). From Lutton descend the hill southward towards Slade Hall, but before this is reached turn L. to the Piall Brook. Thence over the ridge, keeping straight on at the cross road, and down to the bridge over the Yealm. Just beyond this is Moor Cross, where the road runs R. to Ivybridge (see *ante*).

YELVERTON AND DOUSLAND DISTRICT.

DISTANCES (from Yelverton). BY ROAD: *ASHBURTON, via* Two Bridges, 20½ m.; *via* Cornwood, 24 m. *BICKLEIGH*, 4 m. *BOVEY TRACEY, via* Two Bridges, 25 m. *BUCKLAND MONACHORUM*, 2½ m. *CADAFORD BRIDGE, via* Greenwell Down, 3½ m. *CHAGFORD, via* Two Bridges, 18 m. *CORNWOOD, via* Greenwell Down, 8¼ m. *DARTMEET*, 12½ m. *EXETER*, 31½ m. *HEXWORTHY*, 12¾ m. *IVYBRIDGE, via* Cornwood, q.v., 11¼ m. *WHITE HILL CORNER, via* Greenwell Down, 5¾ m. *LYDFORD* (Dartmoor Inn), 8 m. short of Okehampton, q.v. *MERIVALE BRIDGE, via* Moor Shop, 7 m.; *via* Princetown, 9 m. *MORETON*, 19½ m. *NIEL GATE*, 5¼ m. *NOSWORTHY BRIDGE*, 3½ m.; *OKEHAMPTON, via* Huckworthy Bridge and Moor Shop, 20¼ m.; *via* Tavistock, 21 m. *PLYMOUTH*, 9 m. *PLYMPTON, via* Niel Gate, 9½ m.; *via* Roborough and Plym Bridge, 9 m. *POST BRIDGE*, 11 m. *PRINCETOWN*, 6 m. *ROBOROUGH*, 3¾ m. *SAMPFORD SPINEY*, 3½ m. *SHAUGH, via* Cadaford Bridge, 5 m.; *via* Bickleigh and Shaugh Bridge, 7 m. *SHEEPSTOR VILLAGE*, 4 m. *SOUTH BRENT, via* Cornwood, 16¼ m. *TAVISTOCK*, 5 m. *TWO BRIDGES*, 7½ m.

BY RAIL: (G.W.R.) *BICKLEIGH*, 3¼ m. *EXETER, via* Plymouth, 63½ m.; *via* Tavistock (L.S.W. from T.), 47½ m. *HORRABRIDGE*, 1 m. *MARSH MILLS*. 7 m. *PLYMOUTH*, 11 m.

PRINCETOWN, 10½ m.   *TAVISTOCK*, 5¾ m.   In the **Princetown table** Exeter *via* Plymouth is given as 63½ m., it should be 74 m.

From the latter part of the fifteenth century till the middle of the eighteenth century the ancient family of Elford was seated at Longstone, near Sheepstor village.   One of their possessions, on the verge of Roborough Down, was called Elford Town, and is mentioned in the thirteenth century as Elleford.   In the speech of the country people this became Yelver Town, or Yelverton, and when some years ago houses sprang up on the verge of the common, and a name was required by which to distinguish the locality, it was decided that no better one could be given to it than Yelverton.   When we first knew Roborough Down the only houses in this part of it were the Rock Hotel, the cottage which stands by the roadside some 200 or 300 yards in its rear, and the Buller's Arms, at Leg o' Mutton Corner ; the latter stood opposite to the present Yelverton Hotel.   One of my earliest recollections is a walk from the cottage referred to past Roborough Rock to that part of the down between the entrances to Bickham and Maristowe, to which I was taken by my father, to see some military manœuvres. This was in 1854, and among the troops was a Highland regiment, which shortly after left England for the Crimea.   For several years Roborough Down remained as I first knew it ; then a few houses were built on the Horrabridge road, and at length with the opening of the Princetown railway came the development of the present residental neighbourhood.   Another possession of the Elfords was Crapstone, near the village of Buckland Monachorum.   This they obtained by purchase from the Crymes, the family to which we have referred as probably having been the possessors of Roundy Farm, on Walkhampton Common (Ex. 2).   The last of the Elfords of Longstone died in 1748.   Bickham, which had been bought by a branch of the family, was later the residence of Sir William Elford, who represented Plymouth in Parliament.   He died in 1837.   In the early part of the nineteenth century Elford Town was in the occupation of Mr. G. Leach, and subsequently in that of Mrs. Davy.

Roborough Down, on the verge of which the residences forming Yelverton are situated, extends from the sixth milestone from Plymouth to about the tenth, the continuation of the common, which makes a north-westerly sweep to the Tavy forming Buckland Down. Its name is supposed to be derived from an earthwork, or " borough," and appears in the thirteenth century as Roburg and Rugheburgh, and in later times as Rowborrough.   The hundred is also named from this earthwork.   Among the possessions of Buckland Abbey at the time of the Dissolution were certain perquisites of the Hundred Court, and the rent of the down, which amounted to twenty shillings.   On the slope between the eighth and ninth milestones is Roborough Rock. It is shown on an eighteenth century map of Devon as Ullestor Rock, but early in the nineteenth was scarcely ever called by that name.   It consists of two bosses, with a connecting portion of some length and of much less elevation, the whole forming one mass.   On the northern side of the eastern boss a rude resemblance to the human face in profile may be traced when seen from the road.   In my early days this was always called the Duke of Wellington's Nose.   The view from near the eighth milestone, a little southward of the rock is particularly fine.

The grouping of the tors above the Walkham valley at once strikes the observer as its chief feature. On the extreme L. is the bold Cocks' Tor Hill, and next to it the fantastically-shaped rocks of Staple Tor. To the R. of these the Walkham comes down from the recesses of the

| | White | Pu | Staple | Merivale | Mis |
| Cocks Tor. | Tor. | Tor. | Tor. | Quarry. | Tor. |

N. Roborough Rock.　　　　　　　Vixen Tor.

FROM NEAR ROBOROUGH ROCK.

moor, and above the cleft is seen the granite crown of Mis Tor. R. of it is North Hisworthy, from which the dusky Yennadon sweeps towards the giant form of Sheeps Tor, which rises grandly beyond the vale where the little village of Meavy, with its ancient church, nestles among the trees.

Though no part of Roborough Down is without interest, for delightful views are commanded from every point, its northern end is

		Hollow Tor.				
Slope of		Inga	N. Hisworthy		Peak	Lether
Mis Tor.		Tor.	Tor.	Dousland.	Hill.	Tor.

King Tor.

FROM NEAR ROBOROUGH ROCK.

the most charming and romantic. Here, near where the Tavy and the Walkham mingle their waters, are precipitous slopes, clothed in places with coppice, and in others with tall bracken, through which wind green paths. The confluence of the two streams is known as Double Waters, and just above it is a clam over the Walkham, whence a path leads up to a rugged pile of rocks, and over West Down. From the down a road runs to Tavistock, 2 m., passing Walreddon, the ancient mansion of the Courtenays, which is quite close to the verge of the common. It is of middle sixteenth century date, though some parts

Lether   Down   Sheeps
Tor.   Tor.   Tor.   Eylesbarrow.

Yennadon Down.   E.

FROM NEAR ROBOROUGH ROCK.

are said to be earlier. The road goes on to Rix Hill and Brook Lane, and joins the Tavistock main road opposite to the entrance to the cemetery. Overlooking the Walkham above the confluence are Buck Tor, and the crag known as the Raven Rock. Below the confluence is the Virtuous Lady Mine, which name is supposed to have reference to Queen Elizabeth. It is this part of the down to which we have referred in our introductory remarks as being not far from the Tamar. On the Walkham above West Down is Grenofen. Here a bridge spans the river, the steep track leading down to it on the south, and which forms the approach to it from the neighbourhood of Buckland Mona-chorum, being known as Sticklepath.

On the E. side of the southern part of Roborough Down, and not far from Hooe Meavy Bridge, on the Mew, is the hamlet of Clearbrook. The road runs eastward up the hill to Greenwell Down, a branch near the bridge going N. to the village of Meavy. This road reaches the common at Shady Combe, the name given to the lower part of Green-well Gert where it has been planted with trees. This gert, which is so much overgrown with heather and ferns as almost to conceal its artificial character, extends over the hill to Catstor down. The road runs very near to it across Greenwell Down, and on leaving it is carried along the northern verge of Wigford Down to Cadaford Bridge (*Dewer Stone* Section, *Plympton* District). On Greenwell Down it is crossed by another coming from Urgles Farm, S., and running north to Gratton Bridge and Yelverton (*post*). Urgles is approached from Roborough Down by a road branching from the one that leads from the Plymouth and Tavistock highway to Clearbrook; this crosses the Mew at Good-a-Meavy Bridge. Opposite to the gate at Urgles is the socket stone of a cross [*Crosses*, Chap. VI.] From this point the summit of the Dewer Stone is about 1 m. to the south.

The visitor has the choice of two roads from Yelverton to Cadaford

Bridge ; he may go either by way of Greenwell Down, or through the village of Meavy. Between the road leading to the station from the down and the Rock Hotel is Meavy Lane. This is followed to the fork, and if the first-named way is decided upon the rambler will take the R. branch, and pass down to Gratton Bridge, on the Mew. This was rebuilt in 1887. A short distance beyond it a road crosses it, coming L. from Meavy and running R. by Olderwood Plantation to Hooe Meavy, and here is a guide-post : Hooe Meavy, ¾ m. ; Roborough, 4½ m. ; Horrabridge, 3¼ m. Tavistock, 7¼ m. Meavy, ¾ m. ; Walkhampton, 2½ m. ; Lovaton, 1 m. ; Sheepstor, 2¼ m. The way now lies up the hill, and is the reverse of that sketched at the end of the *Dewer Stone* Section. The Sheepstor road branches L., a little way up, and crosses Callisham Down, where is a pile bearing the name of Callisham Tor. This down is kept L., and soon the gate opening on to Greenwell Down is reached. From this the way lies over the turf with the hedge close L. to Greenwell Gert, the narrow lane leading to Catstor Down being passed on the way. By the roadside near the gert is the base of a cross [*Crosses*, Chap. VI.] From this there is a good view of the Burrator Gorge, beyond which the tower of Princetown Church is seen. [For the Dewer Stone Hill the rambler should strike S. from this point over Wigford Down, the view from the higher part of which is very fine. The whole of south-west Devon is seen, and much of East Cornwall.] Several old trees will be observed on the down, and a little further on the old farm enclosures noticed in the *Dewer Stone* Section. These are R. of the road ; Durance is L. Shortly the road coming from Lynch Down will be seen, and this must be followed R. down to the bridge.

If the Meavy route to Cadaford be chosen the L. branch at the fork in Meavy Lane must be followed. This will bring the rambler direct to the village, Church Ford (which bore the same name in the time of Edward I.) being passed on the way. Meavy is a small, but pleasing, border village. On the green, near the church gate, is an ancient oak, which, though showing only too plainly the havoc of years, yet spreads its boughs and puts forth its green gleaves over the cross below. After being lost for over a century the shaft of this cross was discovered by a former rector, the Rev. W. A. G. Gray, and once more set up on its old pedestal. Only the head is new work. The way lies along the lower side of the green, and turns R. near the little disused pound to the river which it crosses at Marchants Bridge.*
Just beyond this is Marchants Cross, which is one of the most important in the Dartmoor district [*Crosses*, Chap. V., VII.] In the charter of Isabella de Fortibus, 1291, it appears as Smalacumbacrosse, and then formed one of the bondmarks to the lands given by her mother to Buckland Abbey, in 1280. But that it was erected long before that time there can hardly be a doubt. It stands on the main track from Tavistock Abbey to the South Hams, from which branched the one going to Plympton Priory. In my early days several traditions used to be related concerning it. It was said that it marked the grave of a suicide, and also that wayfarers about to cross the moor would kneel before it and pray that they might not run into danger during the

---

* Below this is Marchants Ford and stepping-stones.

journey. The road branching L. is on the line of the Abbots' Way
the R. one runs to Cornwood and Plympton. From this point the way
to Cadaford Bridge is shown in R. 13. The rambler ascends Lynch
Hill R. and follows the road with the enclosures on that hand till he
meets the one coming from Greenwell Down, when he will turn L. to
the bridge.

Dousland, like Yelverton, was called into existence by the railway.
It is not so many years since that it was represented by a single roadside
hostelry, named the Manor Inn, but which was generally referred to as
Dousland Barn. It forms a capital base for moorland explorations
Quite near to it is Yennadon Down, a fine, elevated common, from
which delightful views are commanded. Dousland is rather over 1 m.
from Yelverton.

EXCURSIONS FROM YELVERTON.

The area over which these excursions extend embraces Ringmoor
Down, Sheeps Tor, Dean Combe, and Peak Hill. Many of the objects
in the neighbourhood are described in the excursions from Plympton,
Princetown, and Tavistock. These may be joined as follows : *Plympton*, Ex. 36 at Brag Lane End, near Shaugh, and Ex. 37 at Cadaford
Bridge ; *Princetown*, Ex. 1 at Peak Hill, and Ex. 2 at Lether Tor
Bridge ; *Tavistock*, Ex. 7 at Sampford Spiney. The centre of the
Princetown District is reached by the high road, and the Hexworthy
District by T. 2.

[Tracks 1 to 4, 13, 69, to 74.]

Ex. 38.—*Brisworthy, Leggis Tor, Ditsworthy, Whittenknowles Rocks,
Thrushel Combe* [EXTENSION TO *Dean Combe*, add 3¾ m.], *Gutter Tor,
Ringmoor Down*, 11½ m. From and to Dousland, 10 m.

Our first point will be the southern corner of Lynch Down, which
we may reach by either of the two routes just sketched. (Visitors
from Dousland will take the route by Marchants Cross and Lynch Hill,
reaching the first-named by the road along the side of Yennadon and
following it down to the river). At the corner of Lynch Down, where
the main road makes an abrupt angle, a narrow farm road will be
noticed, and this must be followed to Brisworthy, and thence to Ringmoor Down, which is close by. Brisworthy was one of the ancient vills,
and appears in 1505 as Brightesworth, when it paid a venville rent of
two shillings. On emerging on the down we shall notice on the R. a
stone circle, which is a fairly good example of this class of monument
as it exists on the moor at present. Keeping near to the enclosures R.
we shortly reach a corner formed by the walls where the little Leggis
Lake comes down from Leggis Mire. This seems to be identical with
the Yaddabrook mentioned in the charter of Isabella de Fortibus.
Here we enter the warren (there is a gate near the higher corner) called
after Leggis Tor, the pile in its centre, though not infrequently the
reverse is found to be the case, for the former being sometimes spoken
of as New Warren the tor is occasionally referred to as New Warren
Tor. From the tor, which is rather interesting, we look down upon
the Plym. Between Leggis Tor and the river are some large enclosures
containing hut circles. Through these runs the path from Ditsworthy

to Cadaford Bridge. Some ancient walls will be seen mixed up with the rocks on the tor, and here also is a ruined kistvaen. Not very far distant is a single stone row, the existence of which was first recorded by Mr. R. Hansford Worth.

Proceeding north-westward to the gate in the higher corner of the warren we again enter on the down and turn N.E., and in little over ½ m. shall reach a gate on the track leading from Ringmoor Cot to Ditsworthy (T. 71). Here we have a fine view in the direction of Plymouth. Looking over the distant town we see Penlee Point and Cawsand Bay, Mount Edgcumbe, and Maker Heights. From the higher ground a little to the W. Staddon Heights and the Breakwater come in sight, and moorward the tower of Princetown church. From here we descend to Ditsworthy Warren house, noticed in Ex. 37. (If the rambler prefers it he can make his way to the house direct from Leggis Tor by striking north-eastward towards the river). From Ditsworthy we pass on northward over Eastern Tor, which is covered with short turf, and is of no great height, to Whittenknowles Rocks, both of which objects are noticed in Ex. 37, as also are the antiquities at Thrushel Combe, which are seen on the further side of the little stream to the E. (The direct way from Yelverton to Ditsworthy and Thrushel Combe is by Marchants Cross. Thence L. to Ringmoor Cot ; pass in front of the Cot and either take the R. branch at the fork, or strike E. over the down. In the latter case the track (T. 71) can be followed to Ditsworthy, or an E. by N. course taken to Gutter Tor, from which Whittenknowles Rocks are not far distant.

[EXTENSION TO *Dean Combe*, add 3¾ m. With route to *Eyles-barrow*. From the Thrushel Combe stone rows pass up to the blowing-house near the head of the little valley, and then strike N. by W. (For Eylesbarrow, ¾ m. distant, the course is N.E.) About ½ m. from the blowing-house the head of Dean Combe is reached. The Dean Combe Brook, or Narrator Brook as it is also called, comes down through a gorge E. of Combeshead Tor (Exs. 2, 39). At the bend of the stream where it changes its course from S. to W. is an excavated chamber. It is a little way from the L. bank, and is approached through a dyke, or trench. The doorway is only about 3 feet in height, and from this a low tunnel leads to the chamber. The latter is about 9 feet by 8 feet, and nearly 10 feet high. It was first described by Mr. Robert Burnard, in the *Transactions of the Plymouth Institution*. On the other side of the stream, and nearer the farmhouse is another, called by the farmer the Potato Cave from the use to which he has put it. The other is generally regarded as having been a place of concealment for a still, as also is a third near by. That they were formed and used by the tinners there is little doubt. A walk down Dean Combe (see also Ex. 39) will take the visitor through one of the most charming valleys on the moor. [*Gems*, Chap. XX.] On passing Combeshead Farm the Cuckoo Rock high above the N. side of the valley will be seen. Midway down is Dennicombe Ford, where is a small single stone clapper. The farm of Dean Combe is seen near by. From here the road runs on to Middleworth before reaching which a fine grove of trees is passed. Above this, R., is Snappers Tor. Below Middleworth, just before the Newleycombe Lake is reached, turn L. to Narrator Farm, and on gaining the common turn L. and pass along the side of Yellowmead

Down, with Sheeps Tor R. and the enclosures above Rough Tor Plantation L., the course being S.E. by E.　Not far from this are some rocks
known as Rough Tor, and nearer the Plym a pile called Click Tor.
½ m. on the enclosures of Yellowmead Farm will be reached.　Keep
them R. and change the course to S.E.　¾ m. further on the road
formed on the line of the Abbots' Way will be reached.　Cross this,
and make for Gutter Tor, which rises close by it.]

Leaving Thrushel Combe we shall make our way back to Whittenknowles Rocks, and thence to Gutter Tor, W., keeping Gutter Tor
Mire, in which the Sheeps Tor Brook rises, L.　This tor is placed at
the north-eastern corner of Ringmoor Down, and viewed from some
parts presents a bold outline.　From here our course will be W. by S.
over Ringmoor Down to Ringmoor Cot, a little over 1 m. distant.
An early form of the name of this down is Rydemoor.　The old
tradition of buried treasure which is related of so many places is attached
to Ringmoor Down.　It used to be said that if this could be discovered
" all England might plough with a golden share."　We have not the
least doubt of it.

From Ringmoor Cot we shall descend Lynch Down to Marchants
Cross, and soon after turn L. to Meavy and Yelverton.　Dousland
visitors will keep straight up the hill.

Ex. 39.—*Burrator Lake, Sheeps Tor, Nosworthy Bridge* [EXTENSION
TO Dean Combe, add 3¼ m.], *Lether Tor, Peak Hill, Dousland*, 10 m. ;
½ m. further by Burrator.　From and to Dousland, 8 m. ; about the
same by Burrator.

In making our way to Sheeps Tor we may either go by Marchants
Cross and Ringmoor Cot, as in the preceding excursion, or by Dousland
and the Burrator dam.　At the Cot there is a guide-post : Cadaford
Bridge, 2 m. ; Shaugh, 3½ m. ; Meavy, 1 m. ; Roborough, 6 m. ;
Sheepstor, ¾ m. ; Burrator, 1 m.　The L. branch at the fork will take
us by Portland Lane to the village.　From Dousland the visitor will
make his way to Yennadon and there branch L. into the road running
along the side of the hill with Burrator Gorge R.　On the hill above, L.,
are the Yennadon Crags.　The road is carried over the dam to Sheepstor
village.　On approaching the dam the view of the lake, and the hills
grouped round it, is particularly fine.　This sheet of water, which the
Mew, the Hart Tor Brook, the Newleycombe Lake, and the Narrator,
or Dean Combe Brook, contribute to form, is 116 acres in extent,
and was opened in September, 1898, by the Mayor of Plymouth, Mr.
J. T. Bond, as a storage reservoir in connection with the town water
supply.　The head weir of the old leat, which was cut by Sir Francis
Drake (not, it is at present said, for the purpose of conveying water to
Plymouth, but to supply some mills which he owned with power), is
now below the surface of the lake.*　The old building on the point of
land that juts out from the southern shore is Longstone, the ancient
seat of the Elfords.

Sheepstor is a small moorland village, and takes its name from the

---

* Some stepping stones that formerly existed on the Mew are also
covered.　These are referred to in an Anglo-Saxon document naming
some bounds in this locality as the Cleaca.　It appears not unlikely
that the term *clapper* is derived from this word.

huge pile that rises from the hill above it, but this, as an early form
of the name proves, has nothing to do with sheep. The dedication of
the church is unknown, but there is some reason for supposing it to
have been dedicated to St. Leonard [*Crosses*, Chap. VII.] Over the
door of the south porch is a curious carving with the initials J.E., and
the date 1640. This in all probability refers to John Elford, who was
the lord of Longstone in the first half of the seventeenth century. He
was the husband of four wives, to one of whom there is a monument
in the church. Another, Mary Gale, who was his third wife, is commemorated by a slab in the church of Widecombe-in-the-Moor. In
the churchyard is the tomb of Sir James Brooke, Rajah of Sarawak,
who formerly resided at Burrator. It is of red Aberdeen granite.
There are the remains of two crosses near by, as well as one in a field
overlooking the Burrator Gorge [*Crosses*, Chap. VII.] Near the
church is the old bull ring, a feature that few of our moor villages can
now show. In August, 1908, the iron ring to which the bulls were
tethered was found a foot below the surface in the Vicarage field.
We have already referred to the ancient privileges pertaining to the
manor of Sheepstor (see *Beacon* in *Terms* Section) Professor Newton,
F.R.S., has stated that the sparrow is never seen in Sheepstor. I am
prepared to state that neither is the pixy seen there, and further that
even his former home is disappearing.

This we shall see, or what is left of it, on reaching the common by
the lane running eastward by the church. If we look straight up
the stony hillside towards the tor we shall perceive a dark looking
cleft close to the ground, and making our way up to it shall find ourselves at the threshold of the Pixies' Cave. A few years ago this little
chamber was capable of holding several persons, but latterly the rocks
have gradually moved forward, and it is now much smaller than it was.
It is not advisable to endeavour to enter it Tradition says that one
of the Elfords found refuge here during the Civil War, but there is
nothing to support the story further than that about a century ago
some paintings were to be seen on the rocky walls of the cave, which
it is said were the work of the concealed man. Several pixy stories
also attach to it, but the evidence in favour of these is even slighter
than that respecting the fugitive. At the east end of the tor the rocks
rise perpendicularly, and here, on the summit, is what is known as the
Feather Bed. There is a fine view from all parts of this hill ; on the
west the beholder looks down upon the Burrator Lake. Sheeps Tor
is one of the largest of the Dartmoor tors. On leaving this lofty
height we shall descend the northern side of the hill to Narrator Farm,
and passing through the yard shall make our way with the lake L. to
the Narrator Brook, which we cross and speedily reach the Newleycombe Lake close to Nosworthy Bridge.

(To reach Thrushel Combe from Sheeps Tor strike eastward from
the pile to the Yellowmead enclosures. Keep these R. From the
northern corner of them the combe is 1¼ m. distant south-eastward).

[EXTENSION TO *Dean Combe*, add 3¼ m. From the clapper over
the Newleycombe Lake the road runs up the valley to Middleworth
(It is into this that the rambler comes from Narrator, and, if he intends
visiting the combe, he will then turn R. instead of L. to Newleycombe).
Before reaching Middleworth Snappers Tor is seen on the side of the

hill L. Beyond the farm and the grove of beech trees is a little common. Here the view is good. Looking down the valley a bit of the Burrator Lake is seen, and a part of Yennadon and Peak Hill, while Lether Tor shows to great advantage [*Gems*, Chap. XX.] Near Dean Combe Farm turn down R. and cross the stream. Just beyond this there is a fine view of the valley. The Cuckoo Rock is seen on the hill L. Combeshead Farm is ½ m. further up. The return may be made by way of Combeshead Tor (Ex. 38) and Down Tor. Follow up the stream towards the former, which rises L. Thence strike N. to the stone row (Ex. 2), and from that W. to Down Tor. A little W. of this is a stroll leading down to Middleworth, whence the road is followed to Nosworthy Bridge.]

Nosworthy Bridge is a small one-arch structure spanning the Mew immediately above the confluence of that stream and the Newleycombe Lake (Ex. 2). We take the road running up over the common westward, and on reaching Lower Cross Gate near Vinneylake Farm, L., shall notice the object which gives it its name. This is an old cross built into the wall. Passing up to Cross Gate we find ourselves on the road between Lowery Cross and the common above Kingset, with the pile of Lether Tor above us. (Here turn L. for Yennadon Cross and Dousland). To climb to the summit of Lether Tor, 1,250 feet, will well reward the rambler. Not only is the tor itself worth visiting, but the view from it is particularly good. Should he do this he will then turn north-westward to Sharp Tor, where he looks down upon that part of Walkhampton Common between Peak Hill and Princetown. The enclosures of Stanlake are below. The western wall of the northernmost of these, near Black Tor, is built on a stone row. The latter is, however, very distinct in places. From Sharp Tor we make our way N.W. to the road, which we strike near the stone rows by the pond, described in Ex. 1. Here we turn L. and descend Peak Hill, and passing Yennadon Cross shall soon reach Dousland.

S. Hisworthy
Hart   Tor.   Gramber
Tor.   Tor.

Sharp Tor.   Riddick   Lether
                             Hill.   Tor.

FROM SUMMIT OF PEAK HILL.   LOOKING N.E.

(Lether Tor and Sharp Tor are readily reached from Peak Hill.

On entering upon the common above Peak Hill Plantation (Ex. 40) strike up over it R., or due E., to Lowery Tor. The summit of the hill, 1,311 feet, is a little to the N. of this).

Hen Gutter Shell   Pen   Trowlesworthy
Tor.   Tor.   Tor.   Beacon.   Tors.

Sheeps Tor.   Sheeps Tor
                                     Village.

FROM THE SUMMIT OF PEAK HILL.

Ex. 40.—*Peak Hill, Ward Bridge, Sampford Spiney, Plaster Down, Huckworthy Bridge, Walkhampton,* 10½ m. From and to Dousland, 8½ m.

The beautiful valley of the Walkham is described in Exs. 1, 7. From Yelverton and Dousland it is reached by way of Walkhampton, whence the road leading to Huckworthy Bridge (R. 68) is followed for a short distance, the first turning R. being taken. This lane will bring us to the cross roads near Whithill Farm, and Ward Bridge, 1¾ m. To this point we shall now sketch the route by way of the moor, which, however, is longer.

The road from Yelverton to Dousland runs past the Rock Hotel. At the fork about ½ m. beyond it branches R. (the L. branch goes to Walkhampton). Dousland is ¾ m. further on. From here the road to the moor runs up the hill N.E. (At Yennadon Cross above Dousland

Brent Barn Cox Staple   Roose White Great Links   Mis
Tor.   Hill. Tor. Tors.   Tor.   Tor.   Tor   Tor.
                                         Hare Tor

Vixen Tor.   Inga Tor.   King Tor.
FROM POND ON PEAK HILL.   LOOKING N.

Plantation a road branches R., and a little way on it forks : L. to Lowery, R. to Sheepstor).   We keep straight up the hill, with Blindwell Plantation R., and pass under the railway.   Just beyond is Peak Hill Plantation, and here we reach the common.*   (For Peak Hill R. see Ex. 39).   Following the road for about ½ m., with Horn Hill L., we reach the pond named in the preceding excursion, and to which the rambler was brought from Princetown in our first.   The route sketched

Foggin	N. Hisworthy Tor.	
Tor Hollow		Princetown
Quarry. Tor.	Leedon Tor.	Church.

N.E.

FROM POND ON PEAK HILL.

in the latter (Ex. 1) we shall now follow, making our way down L. to the railway and past Routrendle to the cross-roads near Withill.

[The Walkham valley cannot better be seen than by following the road northward to Merivale Bridge, passing Okel, or Hucken Tor, on the way as described in Ex. 1.   From Merivale the rambler should strike over the common towards Vixen Tor, and keeping it L. cross the little valley through which the Beckamoor Combe Water runs, and follow the track to Sampford Spiney, T. 13.   From Merivale Bridge the road runs up to the Rundle Stone as described in Exs. 1, 6, where it is noticed.   But reference to it here appears to be necessary in consequence of some statements made in a paper that appeared in the *Transactions of the Devon Association*, 1908.   The writer of that paper, which is, unfortunately, misleading, found a disused gate-post, and supposed it to be the Rundle Stone.]

From the cross roads we shall descend to Ward Bridge, and thence make our way to Sampford Spiney as described in R. 7.   From this delightful little place the visitor may return to Huckworthy Bridge by the road direct (turning R. soon after he leaves it and keeping the valley L.) ; or, he may extend his ramble by proceeding along the road running north-westward from the lower side of the green.   This will bring him to the down under Pu Tor (Ex. 7), along the side of which he will keep with the hedge L., and so reach Plaster Down.   Here he

* A former moor-gate here seems to have borne the name of West Pyke Yeat, and another that existed somewhere near that of North Dickenton Yeat.   A moor-gate in Meavy parish receives early mention as Hart Yeat.

will turn L. and crossing the first road he comes to (R. 13) will make his way over the side of the common for nearly ¾ m. Now he is near the road R. where it runs past Fullamoor Corner, and goes S. down the hill to Horrabridge, 1¼ m. distant. Close by is the Grimstone leat, which is taken from the Walkham, under Mis Tor. Turn L. down into the valley, and passing Brook climb the hill to the cross-road. A short distance to the L. is the old cross on the verge of Huckworthy Common, to which we have already referred, R. 13. [*Crosses*, Chap. VIII.] It stands on a small mound and marks the point where the road to Sampford Spiney, N.E., diverged from the old Tavistock track (T. 69).

Passing down the side of the common with the hedge close R. we soon regain the road, and very speedily reach Huckworthy Bridge, where a charming scene is presented. From here the road to Walkhampton is followed. At the time of the Domesday Survey the duty of providing accommodation for the king and his suite for one night whenever he came this way attached to this manor. The Dousland visitor will pass up by the smithy L., and the rambler from Yelverton make his way by the road running southward to Roborough Down.

ROUTES FROM YELVERTON AND DOUSLAND.

To PRINCETOWN, N.E. by E. By road *via* Dousland and Peak Hill. See *Princetown District*.

To TAVISTOCK, N.W. By road *via* Bedford Bridge and Grenofen Hill, or through Horrabridge and Whitchurch. From Dousland Horrabridge may be reached by way of Walkhampton and Knowle Down, or R. 68 may be followed.

To LYDFORD, N. By road through Horrabridge and over Plaster Down to Warren's Cross. From Dousland Warren's Cross is reached as in R. 68. Thence R. 69.

To OKEHAMPTON, N. by E. To Warren's Cross as for Lydford. Thence R. 69 to the Dartmoor Inn; thence R. 9. R. 9 describes the route from Wringworthy Hill onward more fully.

To CHAGFORD, N.E. by E. To Princetown as above. Thence R. 4.

To BOVEY TRACEY, E.N.E. Yennadon Cross; R. to Lowery Cross; take the L. branch and follow the road by Lowery Stent and Cross Gate to Lether Tor Bridge, and thence to the common. Follow the track to Siward's Cross, with Newleycombe Valley R. (T. 2). From Siward's Cross to White Works, and down the Swincombe to Swincombe Ford. Thence as in R. 5. Or, to Princetown and then as in R. 5.

To ASHBURTON, E. by N. To White Works as above. From there as in R. 6c to Holne Moor Gate, and thence as in R. 6B.

To BRENT, E.S.E. Road to Cadaford Bridge; L. branch to White Hill Corner, 2¼ m. From there as in R. 75. *For IVYBRIDGE*, S.E., branch off at Cornwood, as in R. 76.

To PLYMPTON, S. by E., *and SHAUGH*, S.S.E. By road *via* Cadaford Bridge. On crossing take the R. branch. First turning R. for Shaugh; straight on for Plympton.

HEXWORTHY DISTRICT.

DISTANCES. By Road : *ASHBURTON, via* Holne, 8½ m.;
via Dartmeet, 9½ m. *BOVEY TRACEY, via* Dartmeet, 14 m.
BUCKFASTLEIGH, 7½ m.; to Station, 8¾ m. *CHAGFORD.*
15¾ m. *DARTMEET,* 1½ m. *HOLNE,* 4¼ m. *IVYBRIDGE, via*
South Brent, 17¼ m. *LYDFORD, via* Moor Shop, 19 m. *MORETON,*
17¼ m. *OKEHAMPTON, via* Post Bridge, 26 m.; *via* Moor Shop,
27 m. *PLYMPTON, via* Princetown, 20½ m.; *via* Ivybridge, 23 m.
POST BRIDGE, via Two Bridges, 8¾ m. *PRINCETOWN,* 6¾ m.
RUNDLE STONE, 7 m. *SHAUGH, via* Dousland, 16 m. *SOUTH
BRENT, via* Buckfastleigh, 12¼ m. *TAVISTOCK, via* Two Bridges
and Rundle Stone, 13 m. *TWO BRIDGES,* 5¼ D. *WARREN
HOUSE INN,* 11 m. *WIDECOMBE,* 6½ m. *YELVERTON, via*
Two Bridges and Princetown, 12½ m.

Nearest Railway Stations : *ASHBURTON,* 8½ m. *MORE-
TON,* 17¼ m. *PRINCETOWN,* 6¾ m.

Hexworthy is one of the old forest settlements, and originally
consisted of five holdings (see *Ancient Tenements* in the *Terms* Section).
One form of the name is Hextworthy, and in 1344 we find Robert de
Hextenworth referred to as a holder of land in the forest. In 1379
there mention of Bysouthexworthi, which was probably one of the
tenements. The present form of the name as used by the moormen
is Haxary.

The area over which these rambles extend is not large, much of
the district having already been noticed in the excursions from Princetown, Ashburton, and Brent, besides which it has also been crossed by
a number of routes. The visitor will, however, be able to lengthen
his walks if he desires to do so by connecting the present excursions
with others previously described as here indicated.

In Ex. 41 that part of the district east of the Dart between Babeny
and Rowbrook is noticed ; this abuts on the ground covered by Ex. 28.
Ex. 42 embraces the part between the East Dart and the Swincombe
river, and abuts on Exs. 44, 5, 4. Ex. 43 takes in that between the
Swincombe river and the Wo Brook, and abuts on Exs. 3, 29. Holne
Moor is described in the *Brent and Ivybridge District.*

Excursions from Hexworthy. [Tracks : 2, 8, 10, 53 to 56, 75,
80, 81. Routes passing through the district : 5a, 42 ; 6abc, 49 ; 27, 63 ;
33, 64.]

Ex. 41.—*The Forest Inn, Huccaby, Dartmeet* [*Gorge of the Dart,*
3½ m. from Dartmeet to Wellsfoot Island], *Babeny, Corndon Tor, Yar
Tor, Sharp Tor, Dartmeet Hill, The Coffin Stone,* 8 m.

From the Forest Inn at Hexworthy the beholder looks upon one
of the finest scenes on Dartmoor, though it is not quite as it was when
we first knew it, when in the little settlement across the combe only
rough granite walls and thatch were to be seen. In the valley the West
Dart comes sweeping round a low promontory on which are some old
farm enclosures known as The Byes. Huccaby Farm stands on the
further bank, and above this are the Brimpts Plantations, and beyond,
the crests of Corndon Tor and Yar Tor.

From this comfortable little hostelry the rambler will follow R. 5a
down the hill towards the river, passing Jolly Lane Cot, the last of the

dwellings to be erected under the old custom of building a house between sunrise and sunset, and thereby claiming the land on which it stood, and also the enclosure that could be formed round it. [*Hundred Years*, Chap. I.] Across the river is Huccaby House, the residence of Mr. Robert Burnard, F.S.A., whose researches on Dartmoor have thrown

Brimpts. Corndon Yar Dartmeet
Tor. Tor. Hill.

FROM FOREST INN, HEXWORTHY.

much light on the subject of its pre-historic antiquities, as well as upon its ancient mining.   Mr. Burnard may be regarded as the pioneer of spade work among the rude stone remains, and both singly and in conjunction with the Rev. S. Baring-Gould, and the Rev. Irvine K. Anderson, of Mary Tavy, has done good service in this direction.

Hexworthy Bridge takes the place of a clam, but it is probable that the forerunner of the latter was a clapper. Here the road runs over the Marsh, as it is called, towards St. Raphael's Chapel. An old track (T. 2) is carried from this to Week Ford, at Wo Brook Foot. By following it the Piskies' Holt may be reached. Its situation is marked by four sycamores [*Pixies*, Chap. I.] Below it the West Dart flows through Huccaby Cleave, often called Cleave Combe, or, as the moormen say, Clay Combe. On the L. as we proceed is Huccaby, an ancient tenement. The final syllable is sounded by the moor folks so as to rhymn with *my*, and the name may possibly have some relation to the Byes on the other side of the river. Older forms of it are Hokecaby and Hookerby. We pass up the hill and turn R. at the gate. A little further on L. is Brimpts Gate. This is one of the ancient tenements, and in 1307 is referred to as Bremstonte. Three hundred and twenty years later it appears as Brymst, and still later. in 1702, as Brimpston. Thence our way takes us down Hart Hole Lane to Dartmeet. Looking up stream the woods and plantations of Brimpts are seen clothing the hillside L. On the R. is Yar Tor. Close to the bridge on this side the remains of a clapper will be seen. This was destroyed by a flood in 1826. About twenty years ago it was partly "restored," but some of the stones have been again displaced. Below the bridge is the confluence of the two Darts. On the hillside S. is Combestone Farm (see *Holne Moor* Section in the *Brent District*) ; on the L. is Dartmeet Hill.

[*The GORGE OF THE DART*, 3½ m. from the bridge to Wellsfoot Island. To trace the Dart through the deep valley below Dartmeet

Bridge will reward the rambler.   He should make his way down by the
L. bank.   (On the R. bank there is a fisherman's path from Holne Cot
upward, which is open on certain days as stated in S. Ex. 96).

On leaving the bridge there is a fine view of Huccaby Cleave,
through which the West Dart comes down to meet the eastern branch.
On our L. is Dartmeet Hill ; R. the tongue of land on which are the
enclosures of Combestone Farm, and below this, on the same side, is
Combestone Wood.   Below Combestone Island the river bends L. or E.
Under Rowbrook Farm, L., is that part of the valley known as Langamarsh Pit.   Here, close to the stream, is Lug Tor, sometimes called
Lucky Tor, and also the Raven Rock.   It is a mass of granite draped
with ivy, and resembles a ruined castle.   Some times it is spoken of as
the Eagle Rock.   (cf. Bench Tor, in the *Holne Moor* Section).   Close
to it is Black Pool and a couple of small islands, and a little stream that
flows from East Combe.   A short distance below this the Wennaford
Brook comes in from S., and not far up the valley from which it issues
is the dam at the lower end of the Paignton Reservoir.   (*Holne Moor*
Section in *Brent and Ivybridge District*).   Now the Dart sweeps northward round the promontory on which Bench Tor is situated R.
Below the tor is White Wood.   Opposite to the extremity of the
promontory Simon's Lake falls into the river, and here are the boulders
known as the Broad Stones.   To " heer the cry o' the Brad Stones "
is a sign of coming foul weather.   A little further down
below Mil Tor L., is Mil Tor Wood, near the lower end of which is
Mil Pool, and a miry spot known as Stony Marsh.   Under Bench Tor,
but on the L. bank is Hockinston Tor, and close to it Hockinston
Marsh.   Below Sharrah Pool is Sharrah Pool Marsh, at the head of a
group of three islands, Bel Pool, Little Bel Pool, and Long Island.   At
the lower end of the latter is a fine waterfall.   Here on the R. bank is
Ford Newtake.   Half-a-mile further down, and under Holne Wood, is
that part of the river called Hannaford Stickles, not far below which, at
Wellsfoot Island, the Dart bends E. and emerges from the gorge.
Below the next bend its course is N. under Cleave Wood R. to New
Bridge (Exs. 27, 28).

From Bel Pool Island the rambler may climb the steep hill to
Dr. Blackall's Drive, N.E. (S. Ex. 95).   Here he will turn L. and follow
it north-westward to Bel Tor Corner (Ex. 28), and there again turning
L. will make his way by Ouldsbroom to the head of Dartmeet Hill,
and descend to the bridge.   Distance from and to Dartmeet, if the
ramble does not extend beyond Bel Pool Island, 6 m.]

From Dartmeet Bridge we follow for a short distance the path
running up the valley under Yar Tor to Sherwell (T. 53).   Across the
stream some portion of the ancient sylvan honours of Brimpts is seen.
A number of oaks were felled here some years ago for ship timber,
though they were not used for that purpose.   On the brow of the hill
is the clump of trees to which the name of The Seven Sisters has been
given.   Below may be seen the ruins of Dolly's Cot.   To this retired
spot a certain moorland benedict brought his newly-wedded wife, in
order to place her out of the reach of those who admired her rather
more than he cared for.   This was in the days when Sir Thomas
Tyrwhitt was master of Tor Royal (Ex. 3), and some of the guests at
his bachelor house parties seem to have been attracted by the " beauty "

of the moor. I find it quite recently stated that the " First Gentleman in Europe " was one of the guests, and that he made love to Dolly. It is unfortunate that what is nothing more than an idle story should be stated as a fact. As is well known George IV. was a friend of Tyrwhitt's but there is no evidence that he was ever at Tor Royal, or even on Dartmoor, either as Prince Regent or King. In 1788 the prince came to Plymouth to see his brother, the Duke of Clarence, off on a voyage, but Tor Royal was not then built, and it does not appear that His Royal Highness came into Devonshire after that date.

We leave the path over Yar Tor Down under the tor and follow the Dart up to Babeny, where the Walla Brook comes into it. Over the latter, not far above the confluence, is a very interesting clapper. This consists of three openings ; the stone over the eastern one is 7 feet 4 inches long, and 3 feet 10 inches wide ; that over the centre opening is 9 feet 10 inches long, but much narrower ; and the third 5 feet 9 inches in length. Above Babeny is Mill Hill, which forms the southern slope of Riddon Ridge, over which we have already conducted the rambler (R. 5, 42b). In 1302 or 1303 the holders of the tenements in the forest built a mill at Babeny at their own cost, the king supplying the timber, which was felled in his wood. At this mill each tenant had to do service, as appears from an account of the prince's manors of the 22nd March, 1344. Babeny has been mentioned as one of the " villages " the inhabitants of which petitioned Bishop Bronescombe in 1260 to allow them to pay their tithes to the church of Widecombe, which they attended, their own being so far away (see T. 18). It is sometimes called White's Babeny, and a similar prefix is borne by a ruined farm in the locality. This is White's Slade, on the L. bank of the East Dart opposite Lough Tor Hole Farm (Ex. 44).*

Turning eastward we climb the hill between the enclosures to Sherwell, one of the ancient vills. In Edward the First's time there is mention of a Hamlin de Sherwell, who held land at Dunnabridge.

Thence we make our way to the summit of the lofty Corn Down, ½ m. E., where are several fine cairns. Southward is Corndon Tor, and still further S. Sherwell Down, or as it is often called, Sherberton Common (Ex. 28). Sherwell, by the way, is always Sherell on the moor. Here, near the Babeny road, is a double stone row, with appearances of a third line between the others, and not far off is another double row. S.W. of Corndon Tor, but on the western side of the Babeny road, is the kistvaen known as Money Pit. One of the side stones and one end stone remain, as well as the covering slab, which is of a lozenge shape. This kist is enclosed within a circle, of which nine stones are standing ; it is 12½ feet in diameter. Between Corndon Tor R. and Yar Tor L. there is a fine view of the eastern side of the forest, with the ancient enclosures of Riddon Farm on the further side of the Walla Brook valley. In the opposite direction Sharp Tor, with its bold outline, is the chief feature in the scene, while beyond is Holne Moor and the distant in-country. From Yar Tor, which is quite close

---

* In the time of James I. we have mention of a reave, as *le rewe*, in this locality. It is named in connection with Wenford Lake, which forms one of the boundary points of the manor of Spitchwick. Wenford Gate (Vennyfer Yeat) is mentioned in Elizabeth's time.

to the kist, N.W., the view is much extended. But apart from this the tor should be visited, as although not rising high above the turf, some of the piles are very striking.

From Money Pit we make our way to Sharp Tor, passing Ouldsbroom Cross L. Here formerly stood the stone cross which we have spoken of as now serving as a gate-post at Lower Town Farm. [*Crosses,* Chap. XVI. See also Ex. 27.] There is mention of John, of Ollesbrom in the fourteenth century, and that is probably the correct form of the name. Keeping the farm enclosures L. we strike across the common to the tor, which we shall find to consist of two separate piles rising from a large conical base, the southernmost being the larger and higher. There is a rock basin on this, but not a particularly good example. Mil Tor to the S.E. we have already noticed (Ex. 28). E. of this are a number of reaves forming rectangular enclosures, and a fine hut circle, the wall of which is about five feet thick. It is constructed, of very large stones, one of them being 9 feet long and over 5 feet wide. It is this hut to which we have referred as probably resembling the small enclosure formerly existing near Shilstone Tor (Ex. 18). Reaves and hut circles are found on other parts of this common.

On the side of the hill from which Sharp Tor rises is the solitary farm of Rowbrook. This moorland dwelling, with the wild valley below it, is the scene of the story of Jan Coo, which I gathered many years ago from the late Mr. Richard Cleave, of Hexworthy, and which I have related in my *Tales of the Dartmoor Pixies,* Chap. VII. (1890). The farm is approached by a track branching from the road at Bel Tor Corner (Ex. 28), and is carried down the side of the combe through which runs the little Simon's Lake.

On leaving Sharp Tor we strike N.W., with the ruined cottage at the head of East Combe below us L., and shall regain the road at the top of Dartmeet Hill. On each side of this are a number of reaves,

| Sharp Tor. | Holne Moor. Bench Tor. | Paignton Reservoir. |

FROM THE ROAD AT TOP OF DARTMEET HILL. LOOKING DUE S.

and on the R. many scattered hut circles. A little way down a green track will be seen L. By following this we shall be led to an object long associated with an old custom. This is known as the Coffin Stone, but it really consists of two blocks of granite. Here the bearers rest the coffin when a corpse is being borne from this part of the moor to

Widecombe for burial. On the surface of the stones several initials and small crosses are incised [*Crosses*, Chap. XVI.] Near here, but on the other side of the road, is a small enclosure with a hut circle at one end of it. Descending to the bridge we shall return to Hexworthy as in R. 42.

Ex. 42.—*Huccaby Tor, Stone Row, Lough Tor, Dunnabridge Pound, Sherburton, Swincombe,* 6½ m.

Our first point is the gate above Huccaby, as in the preceding excursion, and here we turn L. with Snider Park Plantation R. A short distance on is Huccaby Cottage, whence a track runs northward to Post Bridge (T. 81). Here we enter upon the commons, but instead

Combestone Tor   Holne Ridge.   Down Ridge.

S.E.   Huccaby.   S.

FROM THE ROAD NEAR HUCCABY COTTAGE.

of following the track shall strike L. to Huccaby Tor, which, however, presents nothing remarkable, and thence N.W. to the wall of some enclosures on the sides of the little combe down which Cocks' Lake runs on its brief journey to the Dart. Here we strike N. and make our way to the scanty remains of the old Brimpts Mine buildings. Not far from these is a fallen menhir, from which runs a double stone row, and near by are vestiges of other monuments. Still proceeding northward, but keeping the wall R., we shall soon reach Lough Tor, close to which we come upon the rectangular enclosure known as Lough Tor Pound. The gateway is on the side nearest the tor, and the walls are high. This the moormen used to speak of as a "sheep measure." Its capacity being known, when it was filled with these animals there was no need of counting them to ascertain their number! North and east of the tor, from which there is a fine view of the moor, the ground drops steeply down to that part of the East Dart valley bearing the name of Lough Tor Hole—the Lafter Hall of the moormen—and here is the farm also so called (T. 81, Ex. 44).

Turning from the pile we strike S.W. for about ½ m. to the track leading from Post Bridge to Dunnabridge (T. 80), and follow it to the latter place, keeping the wall R. We have already noticed Dunnabridge Pound in the section on *Crockern Tor*, in the *Princetown District*, and have referred to the story of the so-called Judge's Chair. This object will be seen immediately within the gate; there is little doubt that it is really a dolmen. The wall of the pound, like that of Erme Pound (Ex. 32) is built on the line of a more ancient enclosure. That sepulchral monuments were erected on, or close to, the walls of such is proved by the existence of the kistvaen at the end of the stone row on Brown Heath (Ex. 32), the circle enclosing which touches the vallum of a large hut pound. Close to this interesting object at Dunnabridge a slab will be seen in which are several circular holes, but it is now broken along the line of these. It appears probable that this once formed the side of the sepulchral chamber. In many examples of enclosed dolmens similar holes are found. If, however, the visitor should not agree with this opinion, he may amuse himself by supposing that disturbers of the peace during the time of the drifts were put to sit beneath this stone canopy, and their legs secured in these holes, since we find the reave of the manor of Lydford laying out a certain sum in 1620 for the repair of the pound walls, gate, and *stocks* at Dunnabridge. The enclosure has long served as a drift pound. In 1342 there is mention of it in an account of the bailiff of Dartmoor, where the sum of threepence is shown as having been expended for a lock for the gate (see *Pound* in *Terms* Section). Eastward of the pound, on Dunnabridge Moor, is another circular enclosure, the wall of which is much overgrown.

The bridge near the pound has been built during recent years. When Mr. Bray visited the place, in 1831, he was surprised at finding no bridge there. In this connection it is well to remember that in the earlier forms of the name the final syllable is *brig*, and not *bridge*. Across the road is Brownberry, one of the ancient tenements which now belongs to the poor of Brixham. Quite close is Dunnabridge Pound Farm. Near the bridge is a track leading to a gate. This runs on to Dunnabridge Farm, which, like Brownberry, was one of the old forest holdings, but is now the property of the Duchy. Here, over a water trough in the yard, is the large flat stone referred to in the Section on *Crockern Tor*. That this was brought from the tor there is good reason to believe. It was by confusing Dunnabridge Farm with Dunnabridge Pound that led, in all probability, to the report that the dolmen was brought from there. The farm is not far from the Dart, over which, but higher up the stream, are some stepping-stones, by means of which Little Sherburton is reached from this side.

To the R., or N., of the road running westward to Two Bridges is the farm of Smith Hill. The house stands on the R. bank of Cherry Brook, which is there spanned by a clapper. On Smith Hill, between Cherry Brook and the Moreton road, a small feeder takes its rise, and is sometimes called the Smith Hill Brook. Below this, at Cherry Brook Bridge, is another feeder, the Muddy Lakes Brook, which has its source in the newtake bearing that name.

If the condition of the Dart be suitable the rambler may proceed by Dunnabridge Farm to the steps, and thence to Little Sherburton, from which he will pass up S. to Swincombe Newtake. If this cannot be done he will descend from near Brownberry to the clam and make his way up to Sherburton, as in R. 33, and will readily get permission to follow the lane running westward from the house to the newtake named. Here, on the R., in the corner of the enclosure abutting on the newtake, are the remains of a circle consisting of ten stones. A reave runs from it down to Little Sherburton.

Striking S. over Swincombe Newtake we shortly reach Swincombe Ford, and thence make our way to Hexworthy, as in T. 8.

[The estate of Sherburton, which is one of the old forest tenements, is situated on a tongue of land round which the West Dart makes a

Bellaford
Tor.

Lough
Tor.

Dunnabridge
Pound.

FROM SWINCOMBE NEWTAKE. LOOKING N. BY E.

bold sweep, its course being northerly on the W. side and southerly on the E. The ground rises rather steeply from the river in places. There were formerly three tenements here called Sherborne, " or lying in Sherborne." This form of the name is found as early as 1360 ; in Queen Elizabeth's time it appears as Shurbora. There is mention also of Sherborne Wood in 1358 ; Sherborncroft in 1416 ; and Sherborne Foot about 1521. The names of Sherling, Shirebourne, and Sherlond are also met with, and they appear to refer to the same place.* On the N.W. side of the estate, close to the river, are traces of a former building, and the spot used to be known as Broom Park. Below the house at Sherburton the Swincombe runs down to the Dart, and over this the road is carried by means of a clapper of two openings (R. 33). This was originally only of sufficient width for packhorses. Advantage has been taken of a rock to serve as a foundation for the centre pier. The imposts are supported by stones placed in the manner of brackets. A short distance below this is the confluence of the streams, the spot, which is a charming one, being marked by the plantation known as Sherburton Firs. This may be reached from Hexworthy by passing through the enclosures N. of the hamlet. Below this is Timber Pool, so called from an oak tree brought down by a flood, and which remained there for some time ; near it is the patch called Black Furzes, which s probably the Blackfursses mentioned in a bailiff's account in 1350 The road from Sherburton Bridge to Hexworthy runs over Gobbet Plain.]

---

* Previous to 1301, in which year he is described as a " fugitive," Joel Bird held a ferling of land " at Sherling, in Dartmoor." In 1307 Walter Dernelof held half a ferling and four acres " at Shirebourne, in the King's waste of Dartmoor " ; and in 1349 Abraham Elyett paid rent, sixpence, for two acres of land " in Dunbridgeford," and one

Ex. 43.—*The Swincombe Valley, Deep Swincombe, Ter Hill, Aune Head, The Wo Brook, Down Ridge, Saddle Bridge, Week Ford,* 6½ m.

For a short distance we follow the route to Princetown (R. 42, T. 8). This will take us by the road above the Forest Inn nearly to Gobbet Plain, where we turn L. through the gate, and make our way along the lower side of the stroll with the Arrishes R. Just above where we enter the newtake, and on the higher side of the Wheal Emma Leat, is the Long Newtake. This is formed on the site of an ancient pound, and contains a number of hut circles. A little further on we shall desert the track, which runs down to Swincombe Ford and the Fairy Bridge, and strike L. by some hut circles. From one of these the door jambs have been removed—thirty years ago the pits in which these stood could be plainly seen—and appear to have been carried to the enclosure below, where the two gate-posts have all the appearance of such stones. The Swincombe valley extends from Sherburton Firs to Siward's Cross, and in the lower part of it hut circles are numerous. Whether it be the combe of Sweyne, or the combe of swine, I am not prepared to say, but if any should incline to the latter view they may perhaps consider that there is some evidence in favour of such a derivation in the name of a little mining hut in Deep Swincombe, which the moor people usually call the Pigs' House ! Deep Swincombe is a small lateral combe that we presently reach, and from it a little stream issues to fall into the river at Swincombe Ford. On reaching it we shall pass upward, and just above the leat shall find this curious hut. The hollowed stone in front of it so nearly resembles a pigs' trough that the name given to the place seems not inappropriate. To a sharp pointed stone not far off the name of Swincombe Point was given by Will Mann, formerly of Hexworthy.

On leaving the combe we strike up the hill W. of S., and in rather less than 1 m. shall reach Mount Misery, the name which has been given to the higher corner of Fox Tor Newtake.* Here is an old cross, and the head of another. A short distance eastward on Ter Hill—Terrell, as the moormen call it—are tw oothers (T. 2). The easternmost one, which is a very fine cross, was taken to Sherburton many years ago by the late Mr. Richard Coaker, who desired to preserve it there, but was brought back by him when he learnt that the Duchy authorities were averse to its removal. [*Crosses*, Chap. X.]

Leaving the summit of Ter Hill, 1575 feet, L., we strike S.E. by S. to Aune Head Mire, nearly 1 m., having the source of a branch of the Swincombe R. and the springs of the Wo Brook L. If we keep a little to the R., that is, more S., we shall come upon Sandy Way, and this will lead us directly to the head of the mire (T. 56). At the N.W. corner of this, and near the path, are the remains of a small rectangular

---

parcel of land " upon Sherlond, which he took of the lord to hold for the term of his life.''

* The name of Fox Tor attaches to several objects in this valley from this newtake up to Fox Tor Gulf and Fox Tor Combe. In the newtake are one or two kists to which I called the attention of the Ordnance Surveyors many years ago. Others will be found on the further side of the valley in Tor Royal Newtake (Ex. 3), and in May's Newtake adjoining it.

building of the kind associated with the tinners. Also close to the path, and not far from the mire, is the large boulder known to the moormen as Luckcombe Stone. On reaching the verge of the swamp, which is of considerable extent, we shall find that we can pass down on its western side (R. 33, 64) and reach the point where the Aune, or Avon, flows from it. On each side of the rivulet the ground is hard for a few feet, so that it can be traced to the spot where it wells up up in the centre of the morass. A short distance down stream, and on its W. side, is another mire, which bears the name of Little Aune. Extending south-westward from the swamp is Nakers Hill, which is really a flank of Cater's Beam. The latter drops to the river at a point rather less than ½ m. from the head of the mire, and is peninsulated by the Avon and Fish Lake. At the foot of the Beam, that is to say, along the bank of the Avon to its confluence with Fish Lake, is an old stream-work, in which the stone heaps are much overgrown with vegetation. Some little distance from the L. bank, and not far above the confluence, are the ruins of two tinners' buildings, placed so closely together as to leave only sufficient room for a man to pass between, and in this narrow passage, which was in all probability, covered in, are the entrances. Fish Lake rises in the midst of the fen, its source being usually referred to as Fish Lake Mire, but before reaching the Avon runs through some hard ground which extends down by that stream to Heng Lake (Ex. 29), between which and the confluence is another stream-work (R. 64). A branch of Black Lane (T. 57) runs westward from Fish Lake Head across the fen. East of the Avon below its springs is Ryder's Hill, the summit of which bears S.E. by E. from the head of the mire. On this is Petre's Boundstone, described in the Section on *Holne Moore.*

Almost due N. of Aune Head is the source of the Wo Brook, which in the first part of its course runs N. between Ter Hill on the W. and Skir Hill on the E. It then turns and flows S.E. to Hooten Wheals, from which it runs N.E. past Dry Lakes, when it again turns and pursues a northerly course to the West Dart. Its name is probably the Saxon *wog, crooked,* or *serpentine,* which well describes it. From a short distance below its source to Hooten Wheals it runs through Skir Gut, or Gert, though the valley below Skir Ford is often called Henroost Gully. We strike a little E. of N. from Aune Head to the summit of Skir Hill (on the moor simply called Skir), from which a fine view of the eastern side of Dartmoor presents itself. On the R. we soon notice a rocky hollow into which we turn, and shall follow the little stream that runs through it down to the Wo Brook at Hooten Wheals. About ¼ m. L., or W., of this is a kistvaen. Hooten Wheals is an old tin work, but is now, like Henroost, a part of the mine started here within recent years. On the further side of the Wo Brook, that is, above the northern bank, is Down Ridge, across which pass two tracks, one running out to Aune Head (T. 54), and the other being a part of the monks' path from Buckland to the E. side of the moor (T. 2). The latter is marked by two crosses, which show its direction where it approaches Horse Ford [*Crosses,* Chap. X.] On the N. slope of Down Ridge, close to the gateway where the Aune Head track enters upon it, are the remains of a large stone circle.

We turn R. and follow the Wo Brook down to Dry Lakes, where the forest boundary runs up the hill past Wellaby Gulf to Petre's

Boundstone, and on crossing this ancient working shall find ourselves on Holne Moor. Just below, we also cross the Wheal Emma Leat, and reach Horse Ford. This is paved, and on the side nearest the venville common the letter H., denoting Holne, is cut on one of the stones. Above, R., on Horn Hill, is Horn's Cross (*Holne Moor* Section). Keeping near the Wo Brook we make our way down to Saddle Bridge, whence the road runs below the enclosures known as Slade direct to Hexworthy.

The old track across the forest (T. 2) can be plainly seen on the R. bank of the Wo Brook below Saddle Bridge. This crosses the West Dart, into which the Wo Brook falls, at Week Ford, immediately above the confluence. The rambler should on no account omit to visit this spot. It is one of the most delightful little nooks on the moor. Dwarf trees, ferns, moss, and heather, grey boulders, and rippling water all combine to form a charming picture. Below its meeting-place with the Wo Brook the Dart runs through Huccaby Cleave to Dartmeet, passing Clay, or Cleave Brake, and the deep Otter Pool. At Week Ford is an old blowing-house, in which an oak is now growing. The building is called Beara House in the locality, and is also often referred to as The Mill. There are some stones here with hollows sunk in them, which probably once served as mortars. On the hillside just above is a hut circle to which a gable end has been added at some later time. It used to be told in the neighbourhood that here the old men hid their tools at the time when dragons haunted the valley. Just above this the visitor will gain the Hexworthy road.

On the down not far from the Forest Inn is Queen Victoria's Cross. This, as the inscription upon it will show, was set up in 1897 to commemorate the Diamond Jubilee of her late Majesty.

To Aune Head direct, see T. 54.

POST BRIDGE DISTRICT.

DISTANCES. By Road : *ASHBURTON, via* Grendon Bridge, 11½ m. *BOVEY TRACEY, via* do., 13¾ m. *BUCKFASTLEIGH, via* do., 14 m. *CHAGFORD,* 7 m. *DARTMEET,* 8½ m. *GRENDON BRIDGE,* 3 m. *GRIM'S POUND, via* Grendon Bridge, 4¾ m. *HEXWORTHY, via* Two Bridges, 8¾ m. *HOLNE, via* Hexworthy, 13 m. *IVYBRIDGE, via* Dousland, 21 m. *LYDFORD, via* Moor Shop, 17½ m. *MORETON,* 8½ m. *NORTH BOVEY,* 7½ m. *OKEHAMPTON, via* Chagford and Throwleigh, 17½ m. *PLYMPTON, via* Dousland, 19 m. *PRINCETOWN,* 5 m. *RUNDLE STONE,* 5½ m. *SHAUGH, via* Dousland, 14½ m. *SOUTH BRENT, via* Hexworthy, 22½ m. ; *via* Princetown and Dousland, 26 m. *TAVISTOCK,* 11½ m. *TWO BRIDGES,* 3½ m. *WARREN HOUSE INN,* 2¼ m. *WIDECOMBE, via* Grendon Bridge, 8 m. *YELVERTON,* 11 m.

NEAREST RAILWAY STATIONS : *ASHBURTON,* 12 m. *MORETON,* 9 m. *PRINCETOWN,* 5 m.

The comparatively modern settlement of Post Bridge has grown up in the midst of a group of ancient forest holdings, and its name is derived from the clapper spanning the East Dart, which flows at the foot of the slope on which the place is situated. I have heard inhabitants of Dartmoor refer to the old tracks as post-roads, and the clapper in question being on the most important of these, the forerunner of the present highway from Plymouth and Tavistock to Chagford and Moreton, would no doubt be spoken of as the post-bridge. Indeed, we know that this was so some two hundred years ago. In Owen's edition of *Britannia Depicta*, a book to which we have already referred (T. 44), and which was published in 1720, the bridge is mentioned. On a plan showing the track across the forest from Chagford to Tavistock the East Dart is marked, though not named, and where the road crosses the river are the words, " Post Stone Bridge, 3 Arches." A road branching " to Withecomb " is shown, and a small building is figured, the latter being marked, " A House call'd Merry Pit." This, as its situation shows, was intended for Higher Meripit. The example set by the so-called " improvers " of Dartmoor in the neighbourhood of Two Bridges was followed in other places, and Post Bridge was one of them. Land was enclosed, and a residence was commenced at Stannon, about 1 m. from the high road, but this was only partly completed, and was afterwards turned into a cottage ; the lodges at the entrance are still to be seen. Attention, had, however, been directed to the locality, and houses were built there for the men employed at the mines near the upper waters of the Walla Brook and the Webburn. A Wesleyan Chapel was erected, and later, in 1868, the Mission Chapel of St. Gabriel. The little place gradually grew, and has now become a favourite summer resort. There are good postal facilities and telegraphic communication.

The clapper, which is situated only a few yards below the present county bridge, which takes the place of it, is the finest example of these interesting objects on the moor. It is 42 feet 8 inches long, and consists of three openings, and the buttresses and piers are formed of large blocks of granite carefully fitted, and dry laid. The upper ends of the piers are roughly pointed, in order to offer as little resistence as possible to the rush of water during a freshet. These, which rather more than 2 feet thick, project about 18 inches on each side of the roadway. The latter is formed of four immense slabs, one being laid over the western opening, one over the eastern, while two span the centre water-way. The two former are each 15 feet 2 inches in length, one being 6 feet 9 inches in width and the other 6 feet 5 inches. The two centre slabs are smaller, but each is over 12 feet long. They vary in thickness from about 8 inches to 1 foot. The height of the bridge from the bed of the river to the top of the centre stones is 8½ feet ; the ends are a little lower, as the roadway is slightly arched. When we first knew the clapper the northernmost of the centre slabs lay in the bed of the stream. In 1874 I learnt from an old man whom I met on the spot that it had been intentionally thrown off about fifty years before that time. Enquiries which I afterwards made in the locality resulted in several versions of the cause of its overthrow being given me, but later on I discovered the facts, and the man who displaced the stone. I also found that my aged informant was right as to the time when it was thrown down. This was not done in a mischievous spirit. The intention was to throw off the slabs in the hope that they would fall on their edges, and by resting against the buttresses form, as it were, a wall across the river. The water was to find its way between them.

The object of all this was to prevent ducks from going too far down stream ! Fortunately the first stone that was thrown off fell on its face instead of its edge, and the project was abandoned. It is only fair to state that this was done by a very young man, and that he afterwards regretted it. He lived to see it replaced. This was done in 1880, at the instance of the Duchy authorities, the work of lifting the stone into its former place on the piers being executed by the Messrs. Duke, of the Tor Granite Quarries, at Merivale. But the slab does not quite occupy its original position. It is now, as an inhabitant once said to me when speaking of it, " upside down and inside out."

The neighbourhood of Post Bridge, like the Hexworthy District, has been partly described in excursions from other centres, and has also been crossed by several of our routes. The area that has still to be noticed is therefore not large, but the rambler can, of course, be extended by linking them with those to which we have referred.

Ex. 44 embraces that part of the district southward of the Prince-town and Moreton road, extending from Bellaford Tor to the Warren House Inn, and this abuts on ground noticed in Ex. 42, S. Ex. 85, and Ex. 22. In Ex. 45 that part of the district northward of the road from the Warren House Inn to the East Dart is described ; this abuts on Ex. 21, 20, and S. Ex. 58. In Ex. 46 is noticed the district north of the road between the East Dart and the Cherry Brook, which abuts on Ex. 5   Grim's Pound, which is noticed in Ex. 22, may be reached by road *via* Runnage, Grendon Bridge, and Challacombe, 4¾ m., or by Bush Down and Shapley Common, 5½ m., or by the pedestrian from the Warren House Inn, as described in Ex. 45.

EXCURSIONS FROM POST BRIDGE.

[Tracks : 18, 44 to 47, 76, to 81. Routes passing through the district : 4, 35 ; 5bc, 42 ; 10, 10b, 36 ; 18, 44 ; 25, 45 ; 26, 52 ; 27, 63 ; 33, 64 ; 34, 71.]

Ex. 44.—*Lakehead Hill, Bellaford Tor, Bellaford Bridge, White's Slade, Riddon Ridge, Cator Common, Soussons Common, The Warren House Inn,* 10 m.   (1½ m. less if the return be made *via* Runnage Bridge).

Near the W. end of the bridge, and on the S. side of the road, is a gate opening on the enclosed Lakehead Hill, and from this an old track leads by Bellaford Farm and Lough Tor Hole to the road above Huccaby (T. 81), another path running up the slope more to the R. and going past Bellaford Tor to Dunnabridge Pound (T. 80).* Entering this we shall make our way to the ruined building which we see near the bank of the river. This was erected as a dwelling-place for miners, and is locally known as The Barracks. Mr. Robert Burnard discovered a mould-stone here, and also learnt that a blowing-house formerly stood on the spot, and that the tinners in this part of the moor used to bring

---

* In the *Tracks* Section it was stated that this path, T. 80, had lately been closed. We are pleased to be able to say that it is again open to the public. In the hunting reports the hill it crosses is usually referred to as Naked Hill. It should be Lakehead Hill as above.

their ore here to be smelted. The mould may be seen just in front of the ruin. Another, which was subsequently found here is close to the wall of a little outbuilding at the S. end of the yard. The visitor will notice that certain garden flowers, the lilac and geranium, still haunt the decayed walls.

Leaving this spot we shall make our way S. over Lakehead Hill, on which are several objects of antiquarian interest. Not far from the Princetown road R. is the pound known as Kraps Ring, which contains several hut circles. The fallen wall covers a space about 12 feet wide, but on the N. side it is not quite perfect. It is placed between two others, but these have been so despoiled that little more than low banks, hardly traceable in places, now remain. At the lower end of the northernmost pound is a dilapidated kistvaen. Near Kraps Ring, on the S.W., is a fine hut circle, 23 feet in diameter, and close to it another about the same size, though not in such a good state of preservation. but yet having the door jambs erect. Higher up the hill are some sepulchral remains. Among these is a circle of slabs, of which a few seem to be missing, 19 feet in diameter, and a kistvaen in a good state of preservation. About a furlong S.S.E. of this is another, but much dilapidated. Only the two side stones of the kist remain, but these are each nearly 6 feet long. The gate of Bellaford Newtake is about midway between this and Bellaford Tor, which bears S.W. by S. A short distance from the kist is a cairn, and a ruined kist within a double circle ; some of the monuments have been restored. The remains of stone rows are seen in connection with these ancient graves.

White Ridge.   Water Hill. Meripit Hill.   Birch Tor.

Post Bridge.

FROM LAKEHEAD HILL. LOOKING N.E.

Passing through the gate in the wall of the newtake, by the side of which runs the ancient Lich Path (T. 18), we make our way to Bellaford Tor, noticing as we go the vestiges of a large enclosure and the remains of two hut circles. Bellaford (1½ m. from P. B.), is a fine cluster of rocks, and forms a very prominent feature in the view from any elevated point in the central parts of the forest. On the summit is a small rocking-stone, and another, a thin slab, is to be found on the slope between the tor and the gate below it, S.E. (This gate is in the corner of the newtake, and on the track leading to Dunnabridge Two granite posts are to be seen in the wall close to it, in which are notches for bars, similar to others that have been noticed during our rambles. But these posts are higher than is usually the case, and, it has been thought, belonged to a drift gate, an idea which the proximity of Dunnabridge Pound and Lough Tor Pound renders probable. A gold coin was found on the tor by a young man of the neighbourhood about 1870, but I could not discover its nature further than that it was of ancient date. The view from the tor is good. The plantation seen N.E. is called the Cranery. Once a year, in April, the great Dartmoor picnic is held on the rocks, the occasion being the last day (Friday always) of the Dartmoor Harrier Week. Then " old Bellavur " becomes the centre of a scene of animation. Hundreds of spectators, some driving, some on foot, cover the slopes, while hounds, horses and riders engage in the chase around it.

Our next point is Bellaford Bridge. This may be reached by crossing the head of Cranery Bottom E., and descending to the Dart, and following it upward, but there is no public path that way. This bottom appears to have been formerly called Bellaford Combe, and there is a newtake there now of that name. In the Lydford Court Rolls of the seventh of James I. the little stream flowing from this combe is referred to as " Torrente de Beltaburr combe, Anglice Bellavur combe lake."

Retracing our steps we once more enter upon Lakehead Newtake, and turning R. into the Lich Path pass over the crest of the hill and descend towards the farmhouses. There are two of these, Bellaford and Lake, both being ancient tenements.

Bellaford Bridge is about 1¼ m. below Post Bridge. The most direct way to it from the latter is by the path running past The Barracks (T. 81). On the lower side of it is a clapper of three openings, but unfortunately the stone that spanned the centre one is missing. It was thrown off intentionally, and, as in the case of the displaced stone at Post Bridge, I discovered many years ago who it was that did this. [Dev. Alps, Chap. IV.] A stream falls into the Dart close by. This is known as the Dury Brook. It rises above Lower Meripit, and about 1 m. below that farm passes Dury, which latter is situated to the N. of the road running eastward from the bridge. Both these are ancient tenements. In 1689 Dury was held on lease by John Tickell, whose son Jonathan was vicar of Widecombe. We may follow the road to the Walla Brook, where it leaves the forest, or we may make our way down the L. bank of the Dart to White's Slade, ¾ m. below Bellaford Bridge. We have already referred to this place (Ex. 41), which is situated opposite to the farm. of Lough Tor Hole. Neither of these are forest tenements. Lartercombfoote and Larterhole are mentioned about 1609 ; this is the moorman's way of speaking of the spot to-day. In 1702 these appear as Laughter Combe and Laster Hole, and are given as the names of newtakes.* White's Slade has long been a ruin. It is generally spoken of as Snails' House, and to it attaches a story similar to the one related of a blowing-house on the South Teign, to which we have referred in S. Ex. 56. [Dev. Alps,

---

* Among other newtakes named in that year are Bradrings, Winford, Broad Oak, Cocks Lake, Dead Lake, and Holeshead.

Chap. IV.] This tells us how two spinsters who dwelt here aroused the curiosity of the few gossips in the sparsely populated neighbourhood by their mysterious way of living. They never did any work in the garden, nor had they any cattle, and no food was ever seen to be taken to the house. Yet they always presented a buxom appearance. At length it was discovered that they subsisted on black slugs, which they gathered on the moor. The secret being out the women pined and died, and the dwelling fell to ruin. Near by are some hut circles.

[For about 1¼ m. below Bellaford Combe Lake the Dart pursues a straight course through the valley, or " hole," the farm to which the latter gives name being about the middle of this. The river then bends slightly and flows under Little Newtake Plantation and Brimpts Northern Wood. It then turns southward to Dartmeet. The Walla Brook comes down from the N. and runs into the Dart by the wood named. A short distance above the confluence the Walla Brook is spanned by the interesting clapper noticed in Ex. 41, and a little further up is Babeny. The latter is about 1 m. S.E. White's Slade. Nearly 1 m. N. of Babeny is Riddon, an ancient tenement, the holder of which in the time of Elizabeth was more than once presented at the Lydford Court, as indeed other tenants not infrequently were, for not keeping a certain gate and walls in repair, and also for not appearing to serve the queen. This farm and Babeny are noticed in R. 5b, 42), which crosses Riddon Ridge between Bellaford Bridge and Corn Down. Rather less than 1 m. N. of Riddon is Pizwell Bridge. This spans the Walla Brook to which the road comes from Bellaford.]

Leaving White's Slade we shall make our way over Riddon Ridge, our course being N.E. by N., and in 1 m. shall reach Pizwell Bridge, which is a clapper of three openings, but of comparatively modern construction. Crossing the stream we shall leave the road which runs onward past Cator (S. Exs. 85, 86) to Corn Down, along the eastern foot of which it is carried by West Shallowford and Corndonford to Locks' Gate Cross (R. 5a), and turning L. by Pizwell Cottage and the plantation, shall make our way northward over Cator Common. On the R. or E., are the plantations known as the Grendon Strips, and our way will take us to the northern end of the one nearest to us. As we approach this point Pizwell, referred to in 1260 as a village, as we have already seen (T. 18), will be observed L. Of all the ancient holdings on the moor none is perhaps so interesting as this small group of farms. The buildings with their thatched roofs probably present the same appearance as they did some centuries ago. In 1300 the name appears as Pishull. A few years later we find an entry in the account of John de Tresympel, custodian of the forest, concerning " one clawe of land containing 8a. land at Pishull." This refers to the addition of a newtake, and it is stated to be the duty of the holder, John Renewith, to manure it in the following year. In 1346 another enclosure was made there by John French. This name frequently occurs in the various records of the forest, and is still found there. Immediately below the dwellings is Pizwell Ford.

Near the corner of the strip of plantation R. is a double circle, which, were it not so overgrown, would be very interesting. The outer one, which is 45 feet in diameter, consists of granite slabs, partially hidden by heather and furze. The inner one, which is almost entirely hidden, is about 20 feet in diameter. In the centre is a hollow in which there may once have been a kist. This circle is about ¼ m. S.S.W. of the gate across the road between Runnage Bridge, W., and Grendon Cot, E., and which is placed near the foot of the hill known as Ephraim's Pinch. The story attaching to the latter was first related to me by Mr. Edward Coaker, formerly of Hexworthy. A man named Ephraim laid a wager that he would carry a sack of corn from Wide-combe to Post Bridge, a distance of five miles, without dropping it. On reaching this hill, after accomplishing three-and-a-half miles of his journey, he found the *pinch* too much for him, and was obliged to throw his burden upon the ground.

[S. of the road between Ephraim's Pinch and Grendon Cot, E., is the Grendon estate (S. Ex. 85); N. of it is Soussons Warren, the warren house, a solitary dwelling, being in view.* A path leads to it from below the gate, and there is another from Runnage Bridge. A path also leads from the house to Challacombe, ¾ m. from it (T. 47, Ex. 22, S. Ex. 85). S. of the road between Ephraim's Pinch and

Bellaford
Tor.　　　　　　　　Lakehead Hill.　　　　　　Bairdown　Longaford
　　　　　　　　　　　　　　　　　　　　　　　Tor.　　　Tor.

Pizwell.

FROM SOUSSONS COMMON. LOOKING W.

Runnage Bridge, W., is Grendon Common and Cator Common, over which we have made our way, and across the former a track runs from the corner of the plantation to Pizwell. N. of the road is Soussons Common, which extends nearly to the Warren House Inn. Not far from the road, on the N., and about midway between the " pinch " and the bridge, is a very perfect circle. It is 27 feet in diameter, and in all probability once enclosed a kist, though only a hollow is to be seen in the centre now. There are 22 stones, varying in height from 2 feet

---

* Whether this is a corruption of an old name or of a comparatively modern one is not certain. South Sands has been suggested as one from which it may have been formed, but does not commend itself to us. Thirty years ago I heard the common spoken of as South Stone Common. I possess a map on which it is shown as South Shute Com-mon. The affluent of the Webburn draining by Scudely Bogs seems once to have been known as Shute Lake. Further south, and nearer the Walla Brook, are Langlake Mires.

downward a few being no more than one foot high. They are placed from one foot to 2½ feet apart, and only one appears to be missing. Runnage Bridge is a clapper, but like the one near Pizwell Cottage, is of comparatively modern date, and is furnished with parapets. There are three openings. At the W. end of the bridge a track runs L. by the Walla Brook to Pizwell, whence it goes on to Dury ; the lane leading to

Birch Tor.   Challacombe Down.   Hameldon.

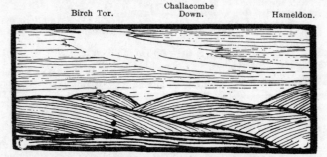

FROM SOUSSONS COMMON. LOOKING N.E.

these farms is a little further on. Close by is the entrance to Runnage, N. About midway between the bridge and the highway at Higher Meripit, a road branches L., or S.W. This goes to Post Bridge by way of Lower Meripit, reaching the highway at the Wesleyan Chapel.]

Turning L. from the corner of the plantation into the Runnage road, which is on the line of the old Church Way (T. 76), we speedily come in sight of the circle just described, and if the visitor does not propose to return direct to Post Bridge he may strike northward from it over Soussons Common, which is in the parish of Manaton. On the L. is Runnage, which is named as an ancient tenement in conjunction with Warner. The latter, however, does not now exist, but some scanty ruins northward of the farm go by the name of Walna Buildings, and no doubt indicate its site. About ¾ m. N. of the circle are the tumuli referred to in R. 26, and a little beyond these, on the R., is the Golden Dagger Mine, and just here we enter upon the common lands of North Bovey.* Bearing L. we follow the Walla Brook upward to the point where it is crossed by a footpath coming from the mine. This we follow L. to the footbridge over the leat, as directed in R. 26 52, and speedily gain the road at the Warren House Inn. Thence our way to Post Bridge is by the road over Meripit Hill (R. 35), which is noticed in our next excursion.

Ex. 45.—*Meripit Hill, Warren House Inn, Waters Down [Assa-*

---

* These barrows were examined a few years ago, and the result communicated to the members of the Devonshire Association in a Report by Mr. Robert Burnard. In two of them various objects were found. These consisted of charcoal, burnt bones, including a small piece of a human skull, some fragments of bronze, a flint arrow-head, and a small sherd of pottery.

combe, add 1 m.], *White Ridge, Lade Hill Bottom* [*Sandy Hole*, add 2 m.], *The Sheepfold, Stannon*, 7½ m. (With route from the Warren House Inn to Grim's Pound and Hameldon).

From the bridge our way lies up the hill through the village. Opposite to the church of St. Gabriel we shall notice the lodges at the entrance to Stannon, in one of which formerly dwelt an old woman who was known as the Witch of Dartmoor. A little further up a road branches R. by the Wesleyan Chapel, and leads by Lower Meripit to the Runnage road (Ex. 44). This forms a part of the old Church Way. Lower Meripit is one of the ancient forest tenements, and appears on the Court Rolls of the time of Elizabeth as Merepitt. In a list of Dartmoor tenants in 1344 is the name of William de Meriput. Higher Meripit is not one of those tenements, but it is, nevertheless, an ancient holding, there being in existence a lease of it from William French to Walter French and John French, dated the 10th May, 1555. The old house was unfortunately burnt down in 1907. Meripit was one of the old dwellings in which a common entrance served alike for the inmates and the cattle. The former occupied one end of the house, while to the latter was apportioned the other. The parts were separated by a wall, though it has been said that in dwellings of this kind such was sometimes deemed superfluous. In some of the ancient houses in this neighbourhood it can be seen that a similar arrangement formerly existed. Cf. Collerewe, S. Ex. 56. Passing upward with this L. we gain the commons just above where a road branches R. to Runnage. (Ephraim's Pinch and Soussons Common, noticed in Ex. 44, are reached by this road, or by the one through Lower Meripit).

Our road now passes over Meripit Hill, from the higher part of

| Bellaford Tor. | S. Hisworthy Tor. | Princetown Church. | N. Hisworthy Tor. |

FROM MERIPIT HILL. LOOKING S.W.

which we have a view of the forest between this point and Princetown. Descending the hill we reach Stats Bridge, whence a path runs across the common L. to Stannon, 1 m. W. This passes close to Coal Mires, in which name we probably see an allusion to the peat, which, as will be noticed, is cut in this locality. Crossing Stats Brook, which is sometimes regarded as being the Walla Brook instead of its tributary, and the Vitifer Mine leat (taken from the Dart near Sandy Hole, and which we have several times met on our rambles, T. 79, R. 10b), we ascend the hill towards the Warren House Inn. The ruins seen L. of the road are the remains of Wheal Caroline.

The Warren House Inn, which was formerly known as Newhouse, takes the place of a building that once stood on the other side of the road. On a tablet in the wall is the inscription : " I. Wills, Septr. 18, 1845." The statement has been made that the house now non-existent was one of the oldest on the moor, but apparently with no better grounds than the opinion of a former tenant of Bear Down Farm, as related by the Rev. E. A. Bray. As the forest tenements are the most ancient buildings on Dartmoor this is, of course, incorrect. No house is shown as existing here in Owen's *Britannia Depicta*, 1720. The old house was generally regarded as being the scene of Mrs. Bray's story of the corpse which was " salted in " in order to preserve it until the disappearance of the snow that covered the moor permitted of its removal for burial. The late Mr. Richard Cleave, of Hexworthy, gave me several particulars respecting the story, for which there certainly seems to be some foundation, that he had obtained from his father [*Crosses*, Chap. XIV.] At one period of his life Jonas Coaker, long known as the Dartmoor poet, kept the inn at Newhouse, and once had a very exciting experience with a party of miners who invaded his premises. Jonas was compelled to seek safety on the moor while the men helped themselves to his liquor. From the road near the inn the small newtakes said to resemble the four aces on the cards are plainly seen eastward (Ex. 22, S. Ex. 87). King's Oven, which is quite near to the inn, is described in Ex. 21, and other objects in the vicinity are noticed in S. Ex. 58.

½ m. distant, and R. of the Moreton road, is Bennet's Cross, described in Ex. 22, and from this the route to Grim's Pound, also described in that excursion is given. A more direct way from the inn is to strike E. across the common towards the gap in the ridge (Ex. 22), beyond which the pound can be seen. The distance is less than 2 m., or about 4 m. from Post Bridge. The way to Hameldon Cross from the pound is described in S. Ex. 60, and the hill itself in the section devoted to it in the *Bovey Tracey* District. L. of the Moreton road is Bush Down and the Lakeland Valley, with Castle Hill, above Hurston Castle, Ex. 21.]

Behind the Warren House Inn is Water Hill, or Waters Down, as it is more often called, and to this we shall now make our way. We pass upward by the E. side of the house, and striking N.W. shall reach the cairn mentioned in Ex. 21 in about ⅓ m., not far from which is the stone row also noticed in that excursion. From this point we shall strike westward for 1 m. to the corner of Stannon Newtake, ¾ m. N. by W. of the summit of Meripit Hill. A short distance from this, and near the Vitifer Mine leat is a single row of stones running northward from the wall.

[Assacombe is due N. from the corner of Stannon Newtake. This is described in Ex. 21, and is also noticed in the *Tracks* Section, T. 77. Should this be included in the ramble it will increase the distance by about 1 m. Then on leaving the Assacombe row the visitor will strike up the hill W. by S., and passing over the northern side of White Ridge (R. 10b) will reach the upper end of Lade Hill Bottom near Beach Holt. The distance from one combe to the other is about 1½ m.]

Leaving the wall of Stannon Newtake we strike W. by N., and in about 1 m. shall reach the same point as will the rambler in coming from Assacombe.

[If the excursion be extended to Sandy Hole, which will increase the distance by about 2 m., a S.W. course from the head of Lade Hill Bottom must be followed for 1 m., when the point where the Vitifer Mine leat is taken in will be reached (R. 10b). Sandy Hole Pass is just above this. Here the Dart is confined within walls built of large granite blocks, apparently for the purpose of storing the water, a dam, or hatch, having probably been placed at the lower end. Northward of the pass is Winney's Down ; above the pass is Broad Marsh, where is an extensive stream-work, at the lower end of which is an old tinners' building. For Cut Hill the river should be crossed at the head of the pass, and followed up, R. bank, to where the Cut Hill stream comes into it, as described in Ex. 46. In the angle formed by the Dart and the stream named is a small tinners' hut. (The route by Drift Lane and Broad Down is the best for Cut Hill from P. B., Ex. 46). In returning from Sandy Hole the rambler should keep near the river. A short distance below the Hole is a fine waterfall, and in the gorge through which the river runs when it bends N. there is a cache on the R. bank. When it abruptly turns S. the rambler will find himself at the lower end of Lade Hill Bottom.]

Turning southward from the head of Lade Hill Bottom we follow the little stream nearly to the Dart. Our course is then S.E. to the deserted building known as The Sheepfold, ½ m. distant. This consists of a spacious courtyard, said to cover three quarters of an acre. It is oblong in shape, and the wall is of considerable height and thickness. Every 9 or 10 feet a large granite post is let into it. The entrance is at the N. end, and at the S. are the ruins of a dwelling-house, one gable still standing. In the yard are a number of small courts, or pens, which I learnt many years ago had once been roofed in, and were used as cattle shelters. The place was built by a Scotchman for the purpose of folding Scotch sheep, and was burned down between 1820 and 1830, when, it is said, a child perished in the fire. (I have never been able to ascertain the exact date). [*Hundred Years*, Chap. III.]

Stannon Tor, 1,517 feet, rises close by the Sheepfold, and about ¾ m. S. is Hartland Tor, 1,368 feet, and either may be conveniently included in this excursion. Should the visitor decide upon ascending the latter he will afterwards make his way to Hartland Farm, one of the ancient forest tenements. In this locality are the vestiges of several pounds and hut circles. Near Hartland is Ringhill. In the former, in February, 1801, Jonas Coaker was born ; in the latter, in February, 1890, he died, and was buried at Widecombe. Not far from the farm, at Muck's Hole Gate, is a blowing-house with a mould-stone. The gate is between Ring Hill Newtake and Hartland Moor, and not a great way from the Stannon Brook. A path leads from the farms to Post Bridge.

Stannon Tor is not much more than ¼ m. from the cottage to which it gives name. Making our way to the latter we shall there cross the Stannon Brook, and follow the road over Stannon Hill to the lodges in the village. The reverse of this is the best route to the Sheepfold from Post Bridge.

Ex. 46.—*Drift Lane, Roundy Park, Broad Down* [*Sandy Hole,* add 1 m.], *Hollow Combe, The Cherry Brook,* 6 m.

In the section dealing with the old tracks on the moor we have spoken of Drift Lane (T. 78), a path which branches from the high road not far from the western end of the bridge, and runs up by the side of the Dart. This we shall now follow, having the Archerton enclosures L., and shall be led past Still Pool, and Hartland Farm on the opposite bank. The path then turns away from the river, and about ¼ m. beyond this point is an enclosure to the R. of it, the wall of which is built on the line of a much older one. This is known as Roundy Park. It contains a few hut circles, and close to the wall is a fine kistvaen. Some of the stones composing it have been replaced. Two fragments of flint were found in it, and some bone charcoal, as well as a cooking-stone which had been used to trig one of the end stones. Still following the path, which passes up the hill towards Rowtor Gate, we cross a little stream, to which the name of Broad Down Brook has been given, and then the Powder Mills leat. Here on the slope of the hill R. is a large enclosure built, like the smaller one just noticed, on the site of an ancient pound. It contains a number of hut circles. These were noticed by the Rev. Samuel Rowe, in 1827-8, and were spoken of by him later as being in Hamlyn's Newtake. Not far from this group is a small pound, which bears the name of Broad Down Ring, locally Broad'n Ring, the down being not infrequently spoken of as Broad'n Down. This arises from the moorman's habit of duplication. Mr. Rowe noticed this enclosure also, which, he says, was situated in Templer's Newtake. Below it, and close to the Dart, is another pound with hut circles.

[Sandy Hole (T. 79, R. 10b) is 1 m. N.W. by W. of Broad Down Ring, the way lying over the side of Broad Down. In going from Post Bridge direct to Sandy Hole the large enclosure with the hut circles must be kept R., and the track followed up the hill to Rowtor Gate, when a course about N.W. by N is struck. The route to Cut Hill from Sandy Hole will take the rambler along the bank of the Dart through the pass above it, and thence by the great stream work at Broad Marsh to Kit Steps, near which crossing place the river bends, and flows from the N. Here it receives two small tributaries, one from the W., the other from N.W. Between these is good hard ground, forming the approach to Cut Lane (T. 79). The summit of the hill must be kept L. in ascending, so as to reach the ridge to the N. of it. Hollow Combe, to which we shall make our way from Broad Down Ring, is 1 m. S. of Sandy Hole. If the excursion be extended to the latter it will increase the distance by about 1 m.]

From Broad Down Ring we shall strike W.S.W. for 1 m. towards towards Lower White Tor with Rowtor Wall R., to the Cherry Brook, which here runs down through the deep and narrow gully bearing the name of Hollow Combe, and which seems also to have been known as Gawlers Hole. Not far below the head of this the brook is crossed by the great reave which is by some regarded as a road, and to which we have elsewhere alluded (see *Reave* in *Terms* Section). It runs up the steep western side of the combe to Lower White Tor, where it terminates. In the other direction it can be plainly traced over part of Chittaford Down running towards the Dart, which it crosses at Still Pool, and thence goes through Webbs' Marsh towards the

Wesleyan Chapel, to be seen again on the moor beyond the village. Mr. Robert Burnard has given some interesting particulars concerning it in a paper read before the members of the Devonshire Association.

Nearly ½ m. S. of Lower White Tor is Higher White Tor, called in the neighbourhood Whitten Tor (Ex. 5), and not far from this, and running S. from it, is a double stone row. It is over a hundred yards in length, but has been much despoiled, no doubt by the builders of the newtake walls near by. Still further S. is Longaford Tor, conspicuously placed on the ridge that forms the eastern side of the valley in which the oaks of Wistman hide themselves (Ex. 5). Westward of the Powder Mills are a couple of ruined kistvaens.

At the lower end of the combe we shall take leave of the Cherry Brook, which we have met on so many of our excursions, and strike S.E. over Chittaford Down towards Arch Tor, near which we cross the Powder Mills leat. Below this is Gawler Bottom, where the roots of trees and bushes of various kinds have been found by peat cutters. In 1892 an object of antiquarian interest came to light here. This was a bronze ferrule, which was buried some four feet beneath the surface. (Cf. Ex. 5). Crossing this shallow valley, down which Gaw Lake, or Gawler Brook, runs to fall into the Dart, we reach the Princetown and

Littaford Tor.	Longaford Tor.	Higher White Tor.

Powder Mills.

FROM ROAD AT LAKEHEAD HILL. LOOKING W. TO N.W.

Moreton road, and turn L., having Lakehead Hill R. Soon we arrive at the enclosures of Archerton, in the midst of which is an ancient pound, now planted with trees, and also a ruined kistvaen. When these are passed we find ourselves once more at the spot whence we started, and close to the ancient clapper that gives name to the village around which we have been rambling.

ROUTES TO CRANMERE.

Cranmere pool is situated on the northern slope of a ridge which rises between the springs of the Dart and the West Ockment. It has sometimes been spoken of as the source of the last-named stream, and in the days when it was truly a tarn its overflow of water certainly contributed to swell the volume of the infant brook. But for more than a hundred years Cranmere has been a pool only in name, and the Ockment receives no water from it now. The true source of this is a boggy hollow several yards from the northern bank.

Cranmere is first mentioned in the Itinerary of William of Worcester, which was written about the close of the fifteenth century. On

Sittaford Tor.   Hartland Tor.   White Ridge.   Stannon Tor.

FROM NEAR ARCHERTON. LOOKING N.N.E.

Donn's map of Devon, 1765, it is marked as " Craw-mere-pool, vulgo Cran-mere-pool." Polwhele, in his *Historical Views of Devon*, 1793, also mentions it ; and an account has been handed down to us of a visit to it in 1802 by Mr. E. A. Bray, afterwards Vicar of Tavistock, when he found the pool dry. The name has been supposed by some to mean the lake of cranes, or herons. This may be so, but it is more probable that in the first syllable we have the Celtic *an*, or *aun*, *water*, and that it has no reference to the bird in question. (Cf. Crane Hill, Ex. 30). According to tradition the pool is haunted by the spirit of a former Mayor of Okehampton, who, the stories say, has sometimes appeared as an ugly dwarf—usually referred to as Binjie Gear (Benjamin Gayer)—and at others as a black colt. [*Gems*, Chap. III.]

In 1854 a little cairn was built in the pool by the late Mr. James

Black Ridge.   Ockment Hill.   Cranmere X   Steeperton.   Hangingstone Hill.   White Horse Hill

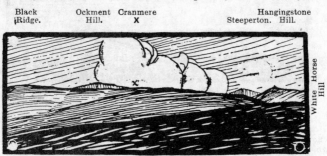

FROM CUT HILL. LOOKING N.

Perrott, of Chagford, so long known as the Dartmoor guide. In it he placed a bottle for the reception of visitors' cards. Fifty-one years later, that is, in April, 1905, Mr. H. P. Hearder and Mr. H. Scott Tucker, of Plymouth, both enthusiastic moorland ramblers, placed a visitors' book there. The number of signatures to the end of 1908 is as follows :—

	1905	1906	1907	1908
January	—	5	12	17
February	—	—	6	3
March	—	1	136	16
April	34 (from 9th)	170	92	128
May	76	61	62	154
June	54	113	102	264
July	71	104	88	190
August	179	247	294	538
September	128	153 (to 16th)	502	159
October	50		39	252
November	4	108	16	18
December	13		3	2
	609	962	1352	1741

C. R. 1 and 2.—*From PRINCETOWN AND TWO BRIDGES*, 7½ m. from T. B. (A) *via* East Dart. Higher White Tor, as in Ex. 5, 2¼ m. from T. B. Leave it R. Thence N. by Lower White Tor to Cherry Brook above Hollow Combe, and across Broad Down to the stream-work at Broad Marsh on the East Dart, 2 m. (Or the course may be N.N.E. from the Cherry Brook as in R. 10b, in which case the

Yes W. Mill Ockment
Tor. Tor. Hill.

N.E. X
Cranmere.

FROM ¼ MILE WEST OF E. DART HEAD.

Dart will be reached at Sandy Hole, and must be followed up through the pass to the stream-work. This will add another ½ m.) About ¼ m. above the point where the Dart should be struck the river bends R., flowing from the N. Follow it to its source—sheep paths on L. bank

—2 m. From this point Cranmere is ½ m. distant N.W., or N.W. by W. from the highest spring, which comes from a heathery hollow in which there is a small rock. This hollow is in the higher corner of the swampy source. R. in ascending. Between the river head and the pool the ground, which is spongy, but not difficult to pass over, rises gently to the top of the Cranmere ridge, so that the goal is not in sight. When the summit of the ridge is reached High Willes with the deep cleft marking the valley of the West Ockment, comes into view. Make for this and the pool will be struck.

(B) 7¼ m. from T.B. Valley of the West Dart to the bend ¾ m. above the wall that crosses under Row Tor (Ex. 5). Leave the river L. and strike N.N.E. for nearly ¾ m. to the East Dart, which should be reached at Kit Steps, at the head of the stream-work near Broad Marsh. Thence as in A. (A or B form the first part of the route from T. B. to Belstone ; see R. 3. *Reverse*, R. 29).

(C) *via* Cut Hill, 8¾ m. from P.T. ; 7¼ from T.B. The route to Cut Hill from P.T. and T. B. is given in Ex. 11. Thence to East Dart Head, see R. 3, also R. 63. From Dart Head to the pool, see A.

(D) *via* Cowsic Head. 7½ m. from T. B. ; 9 m. from P. T. From T.B. to head of Cowsic, see Ex. 5. From P.T. the first point is Rundle Stone ; thence to New Forest Corner ; thence N.E. over the S. side of Black Dunghill to the Cowsic, near the Bear Down wall. Follow the stream to its head. Thence due N. over the ridge to the Tavy, which is struck a little below its source. (Cut Hill is R.) The next point is Fur Tor, N.N.W., which must be kept L. Thence as in E.

(E). From P. T. *via* Walkham Head, 9 m. (This is an easy route). Rundle Stone and New Forest Corner, as in Ex. 6. Turn R. to the Prison leat. Thence as in R. 3 to Walkham Head and Tavy

Great   Black   Cranmere
Kneeset.   Ridge.   X

FROM LITTLE KNEESET. LOOKING N.E.

Hole. E.N.E. to Fur Tor, which keep L. ; and descend Cut Combe to Fur Tor Wood* ; R. bank of Cut Combe Water ; when it bends L. leave it ; strike N. across Rush Bottom and over eastern side of Little Kneeset to Black Ridge Water, rather over ½ m. from Cut Combe

---

* The name still attaches to this spot, though no wood now exists here. Oak has been found buried in the peat near by. (Ex. 11).

Water ; this should be struck where two branches meet. Follow up
L. branch to source. (Should the R. in ascending be followed it will
not throw the rambler out much). Rising ground. Cranmere is ½ m.
N.N.E. If ground is bad ascend Little Kneeset, and cross it N.W. by
N. to Black Hole. Follow up the branch of the Black Ridge Water
that comes down L. or N. This branch joins the other less than ½ m.
due N. of the summit of Little Kneeset, 1,665 feet. Great Kneeset is
about ¾ m. northward. Follow this branch nearly to its source, ¼ m.,
under Great Kneeset, and then strike E. by N. along the edge of Kneeset
Pan—Black Ridge, fen, R. ; the pan, good ground, L. This will lead
directly to the pool).

Return routes to P. T. and T. B. are shown in R. 27 to Hollow
Combe ; also by way of Tavy Head and Cut Hill, in R. 29 ; and from
Cut Hill in Ex. 11.

C. R. 3.—*From TAVISTOCK via* Pork Hill, 11½ m. To the com-
mons as in Ex. 8, ¾ m. beyond Moor Shop. Strike L. with Cocks' Tor
Hill close L. ; thence to Roose Tor, N.E., from which the course is the
same along the ridge, keeping above the valley of the Walkham R.
When the stream bends R. above Mis Tor continue N.E. ¾ m. beyond
this the Lich Path (T. 18) will be struck where it descends to Sandy
Ford. (This point may also be reached by way of Peter Tavy, as in
R. 10). Take the L. branch, *i.e.*, T. 16, and follow it to Walkham
Head. Thence as in C. R. 1e.

C. R. 4.—*From TAVISTOCK via* Wapsworthy, 12 m. (This
also forms a route from Mary Tavy and from Brent Tor, Wapsworthy
being reached by way of Hill Bridge, or, in the case of the former, also
by way of Horndon Clam). By road through Peter Tavy as in Exs. 8, 9.
From Wapsworthy the old peat track (T. 19) is followed to Brook's
Head, whence Outer Red Lake runs down through The Meads to the
Tavy. Thence N.E. to that river, which should be struck near where
the Fur Tor Brook falls into it ; below this, on the L. bank, is Tavy
Hole Stone. Keep on N.E. under Fur Tor, which is R., for over ½ m.
to where Cut Combe Water comes from R. into the Amicombe. Leave
the Cut Combe stream R. and follow the Amicombe L. for a very short
distance, when turn R. into Black Hole, and follow the stream running
through it to the first fork. This is ½ m. due N. of the summit of Little
Kneeset. Turn L. and follow the instructions given in R. 1e.

C. R. 5.—*From LYDFORD*, 5½ m. from the Dartmoor Inn, *and*
BRENT TOR, 8½ m. (Mary Tavy visitors will join by striking R.
into the Dartmoor Path, T. 21, beyond the fifth milestone from
Tavistock, and following it to the Rattle Brook, or by reaching that
stream *via* Lane End and Tavy Cleave, Ex. 11. But this cannot be
done during rifle practice at the camp. The Dartmoor Path is also
followed to the Rattle Brook by Brent Tor visitors). From the Dartmoor Inn to the High Down stepping stones, reached by keeping L.
by the wall on gaining the down ; thence between Bra Tor, with the
cross R. and Arms Tor L., to the top of the ridge, and down to the
Rattle Brook with Chat Tor R., the course from the steps being E.
(This stream may also be reached by way of Wheal Mary Emma Steps,
when Bra Tor is kept L.) This course is continued over Amicombe

Hill (referred to in 1346 as the Preda de Aunnacombe) to Great Kneeset, nearly 2 m. from the brook. Keep L. of Kneeset when approaching it ; it rises like a peak (Ex. 14). From that point, which is reached soon after crossing the head waters of the Amicombe, Cranmere is 1 m. E., Newtake being seen against the sky beyond it. But a direct course must not be followed, as such would lead the rambler over broken ground. Keep R. of an E. line and cross Kneeset Pan. When the ground rises a little the line described in C. R. 1e will be reached. Turn a little L., keeping the fen close on the R.

Another plan is to leave Great Kneeset on the R., and bear N.E. from the head of the Amicombe towards the West Ockment, which must be kept L. Continue N.E. and the stream will be struck at the foot of Jackman's Bottom, which is on the L. bank. Follow the stream upward. At the confluence above the stream coming from the L. in ascending is a tributary from Vergyland Combe. At the next confluence the tiny stream from the R. is a tributary. The source of the Ockment is just above this, and close to the pool. A little mining building will be passed on the way.

The return is by R. 37.

C. R. 6.—*From BRIDESTOWE,* 5½ m. from the Fox and Hounds. The road by the side of the Fox and Hounds is followed to Noddon Gate (Ex. 13), and the Lyd crossed at Noddon Steps. The way then lies up the hill with Arms Tor L., and from the crest of the ridge the route is the same as C. R. 5, as also is the return.

C. R. 7.—*From SOURTON,* 6 m. The pool may be reached from this place by way of Kitty Tor, T. 30, 31, 32, from which Great Kneeset is about 1½ m. S.E. by E. Thence as in C. R. 5. Another way is by the West Ockment valley, passing under Branscombe's Loaf, and striking the river opposite to Black Tor Copse. This is then followed to Sandy Ford, where it must be crossed. From this point C. R. 8a gives the way. If the stream cannot be crossed at the ford it should be followed up to where Brim Brook (Ex. 14) comes into it from the N., above which no difficulty in gaining the R. bank will be experienced. Thence C. R. 8a.

C. R. 8.—*From OKEHAMPTON* (A) *via* West Ockment Valley, 7½ m. Fishcombe Head and Black Tor as in S. Ex. 36. Keep the tor R. Then strike S.E. by S. above Black Tor Copse, drawing near Sandy Ford on the Ockment, 1 m. from the tor, but not descending to it. Thence over Lints Tor, keeping the rocks R., to Kneeset Nose, where Brim Brook falls into the river. Cranmere is 1¼ m. S.E. by S. of this, but that course must not be followed, as it would lead the rambler through boggy ground. Strike due E. for ½ m., taking care not to bear too much L., when the Ockment will again be met. The little lateral valley L. at this point, in which there are streaming remains, is Vergyland Combe. This runs up northward, and must be crossed near its foot, and the Ockment followed to its source. One little feeder falls into it above the combe. Here the Ockment is the L. branch. As already stated Cranmere is close to the head of the **stream**

(B) *via* Dinger, 7 m. Moor Gate ; Creaber's Hole as in Ex. 15.

Thence by the L. track over Dinger Plain southward (T. 34). Leave Dinger Tor R. (¾ m. S.E. by S. of High Willes), and descend to Brim Brook, which will be struck near its source. Thence the way is S.E. across the side of Ockment Hill to the head of Vergyland Combe, about ½ m. (see A). On leaving Brim Brook keep a little L., the lower ground R. being bad around its source. If the S.E. line is followed there will be no difficulty in reaching the combe. On crossing the latter bear a little R., and the Ockment will soon be struck (see end of A).

C. R. 9.—*From OKEHAMPTON via* New Bridge, 6½ m. Summit of Ockment Hill, as in Ex. 16 and T. 35. From this point, which is about ¾ m. S. of the old wall (Ex. 16) the head of Vergyland Combe is ½ m. S.W. (C. R. 8, a, b). Cranmere is 1¼ m. due S. There is some broken ground between, and it is not advisable to pursue a direct course. The rambler should bear a little R. in order to strike the Ockment about ½ m. below the pool (see end of C. R. 8a).

Another way from the summit of Ockment Hill is to bear S.E. to the Taw, but it is further. C.R. 10.

Cut Hill.   Black Ridge.

X
Cranmere.

FROM SOUTHERN SLOPE OF OCKMENT HILL, ABOUT ¼ M. S.E. OF SUMMIT.

The return route to Okehampton by way of New Bridge forms the latter part of R. 63. The rambler will follow the Ockment downward for about ½ m., and then strike N. to the New Bridge track, 1 m. (T. 35). This he will follow to the bridge, and thence to the town as in Ex. 14, 15. If he desires to go by way of Dinger he will strike N.W. by N. when ½ m. down the Ockment, and so onward across Vergyland Combe to Brim Brook, taking Willes for his guide. When the weather is clear the track he is making for near Dinger Tor can be seen from the pool. On reaching this (T. 34) he will turn into it R. and follow it to Moor Gate and the town.

C. R. 10.—*From BELSTONE via* the Taw, 5½ m. The way lies by Watchet Hill to Oke Tor, 2½ m., and thence to Knock Mine, 1 m., as in Ex. 17. From that point the river is followed to its source, from which Cranmere is less than ½ m. distant W. by S. The ground between the head of the stream and the pool is rather spongy, but will present no difficulties. Care must be taken not to keep too much to the L. or the pool may be missed. It is better to steer W., which course, if it does not bring the rambler to his goal, will at all events bring him to the Ockment—here a tiny rivulet—which he will follow up to the pool.

The return to Belstone forms the latter part of R. 63. Strike E.N.E. or N.E. from the pool, and in ½ m. the Taw will be seen R. Trace it down to Knock Mine Bridge, then mount the L. bank. and follow the track by Oke Tor along the ridge to Watchet Hill (Ex. 17).

A camp road runs up W. of the Taw, and crosses it near its head.

From ST-ICKLEPATH the route is first to Belstone ; thence C. R. 10. Or C. R. 11 may be followed, the Peat Road being reached by way of Cosdon. A path runs up through the wood from near Sticklepath Bridge to the common. From the summit of Cosdon keep S. till the track is struck.

C. R. 11.—*From SOUTH ZEAL*, 6 m., *and THROWLEIGH*, 6 m. The Peat Road (T. 41) is followed past Raybarrow Pool to the stone circle, where visitors from Throwleigh join it, making their way thither by the track from Clannaborough Down to the E. side of Raybarrow Pool (T. 42), or by Shilstone, when ½ m. will be saved. From the circle the track goes on below Wild Tor Ridge L. to Bow Combe, at the head of which is Bow Combe Hill, L. Cross Steeperton Brook to Ockside Hill, on which are some cairns and a small pool. Strike over this ridge S.W. to the Taw, and follow it to its head. Thence as in C. R. 10.

The return to the Taw is also as in C. R. 10. Follow it down a little way, and then strike N.E. into the track.

C. R. 12.—*From CHAGFORD*, 7½ m., *and GIDLEIGH*, 5½ m., *via* Walla Brook Bridge. The way lies first to Batworthy Corner, as in Ex. 20, and thence down by the wall to Teign Clapper. Cross the Teign, and then cross the Walla Brook by the single stone clapper. Gidleigh visitors will reach this point by way of the Berry Down Stroll. From the confluence of these two streams Cranmere is 3½ m. distant W. by S., Watern Tor, which is seen rising on the ridge, being about

| Great Kneeset. | Great Links Tor. | Amicombe Hill. |

x
Cranmere.

FROM NEAR SUMMIT OF NEWTAKE.

midway between the two. This is a little N. of a direct line to the pool, but as it will probably be desired to include it in the ramble we make it the next point. Should the ground be swampy, as it sometimes is on this level, it will be well to keep rather near to the Walla Brook. From Watern Tor (Ex. 19) the way lies across Walla Brook Combe to Newtake, not quite 1 m. W.S.W. This is a rounded eminence, and is sometime known as Hangingstone Hill, as mentioned in Ex. 19, where the view from it is described. Four miles away, a little N. of W., is Great Links Tor (Ex. 13), and by taking this for a guide the visitor

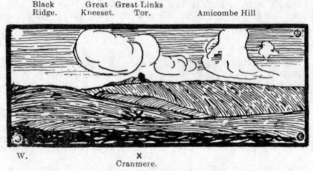

Black   Great Great Links
Ridge.   Kneeset. Tor.   Amicombe Hill

W.　　　　　　　　　　**x**
　　　　　　　　　Cranmere.

FROM NEWTAKE, ⅓ M. S. OF SUMMIT.

will be led to the pool, which is 1 m. distant. To do this he passes over a stretch of fen, and if this should be in a bad state it will be well to keep a little to the R. of the distant tor. By so doing Taw Head will be struck, from which point the way is shown in C. R. 10. But at all events he must not keep L. or he will miss Cranmere. Taw Head is W. of Newtake, and about midway between it and the pool. East Dart Head is ¾ m. S.W., or ½ m. S. of Taw Head.

A more direct route from Chagford is by way of Hew Down (Ex. 19). From Batworthy Corner a little S. of W. to the Teign ; cross the river and climb the ridge, passing about ½ m. S. of Watern Tor ; thence, still S. of W., by Walla Brook Head to the S. side of Newtake, and straight to the pool. The former route, is however, the most convenient one.

In returning strike E. by N. to Newtake, and then follow a N.E. course for a short distance gradually turning more nearly E. towards Watern Tor, as in Ex. 19. A track will be seen leading up to it. On reaching this cross the stream and follow it downward for a short distance, and then strike E. to Teign Clapper. To Chagford see S. Ex. 51 ; to Gidleigh Ex. 19.

C. R. 13.—*From CHAGFORD via* Fernworthy, 8½ m.. Tawton Gate, as in Ex. 21 ; thence by the road to Fernworthy, and up the lane by the farmhouse as in Ex. 20 ; from the gate at the head of the lane follow the green track (T. 45) to Teign Head Farm. A carriage can be driven to this solitary dwelling, from which Cranmere is 2¼ m. distant W.N.W. The hill facing the bridge may be ascended by the pedestrian leaving the farm L. The course given must be followed to White Horse Gate, ¾ m., from Teign Head Bridge. Here the farm enclosures are left behind, and the way lies W.N.W. over White Horse Hill. On the L. is the source of the Varracombe Brook. ½ m. on is Moute's Inn, the scanty remains of a peat-cutter's hut. From this W. by N. for ½ m. to East Dart Head. Thence as in C. R. 1a.

East Dart Head will be the first point in returning, ½ m. S.E. of the pool. Keep it R. and strike E. by S. past Moute's Inn to the wall of the Teign Head enclosures. This will bring the rambler to White Horse Gate ; it is better to bear a little L. of the line on leaving Dart Head, and on reaching the wall follow it S., so that the gate may not be missed. E.S.E. across the enclosure to Teign Head Farm. Thence by the track to Fernworthy and on by the road to Tawton Gate, near Yardworthy. To Chagford as in S. Ex. 56.

C. R. 14.—*From MORETON and NORTH BOVEY*, 11½ m. By road to Tawton Gate and Fernworthy. Thence as in C. R. 13. From Moreton the road runs by way of Thorn and Stiniel.

C. R. 15.—*From the WARREN HOUSE INN*, 6 m. N.W. over the side of Waters Down to the head of Assacombe, 1¼ m. Thence over White Ridge to the Grey Wethers, 1½ m., the course being the same. Follow the wall of the Teign Head enclosures northward for 1½ m. to White Horse Gate. It is well to enter the enclosures at the Grey Wethers, keeping the wall L., the ground being better there than outside. From White Horse Gate as in C. R. 13.

The return to White Horse Gate is shown in C. R. 13. Thence by the wall to the Grey Wethers ; S.E. over White Ridge to the head of Assacombe, and onward to Waters Down.

C. R. 16.—*From POST BRIDGE via* Stannon, 6 m. By this route it is possible to drive to White Horse Gate, 1½ m. from the pool. By the road leading from the lodges, over Stannon Hill with Stannon Bottom L., 1 m. Thence by the newtake wall to White Ridge and on to the Grey Wethers, 1¾ m., the direction being N.W. by N. Turn L. inside the gate as in C. R. 15 (see T. 77).

The return route to the Grey Wethers is shown in C. R. 13, 15, Although Stats Brook rises over 2 m. from the Grey Wethers the name is found in this locality in the ruin known as Stats House. From the circles strike S.E. by S. over the shoulder of White Ridge to Stannon. To the village by the road.

C. R. 17.—*From POST BRIDGE via* the East Dart valley, 6 m. In Ex. 46 the route to Sandy Hole, and the stream-work above it, has been described. At the head of the working the Dart bends, coming from the N. From this point the route to the pool is shown in C. R. 1a. On the way up stream the remains of two little mining buildings will be observed on the L. bank, one close to a tiny feeder.

The return from the pool is shown in C. R. 13, which will bring the rambler to the head of the river. This he will trace downward to Sandy Hole, and thence strike S.E. to Drift Lane.

From the southern part of the moor the starting-points of the Cranmere routes are Princetown and Two Bridges, C. R. 1, 2 ; Post Bridge, C. R. 16, 17 ; and the Warren House Inn, C. R. 15.

Great Links Tor. Amicombe Hill. Foresland Ledge.

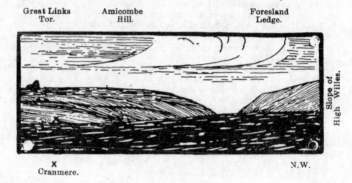

Slope of High Willes.

X
Cranmere. N.W.

FROM NEAR E. DART HEAD.

LYDFORD GORGE.

Perhaps no beauty spot on the borders of Dartmoor is better known than the romantic Lydford Gorge. [*Gems*, Chap. XXIII.] At one point it is spanned by a bridge thrown across a deep and narrow chasm. This is not far from the castle, and visitors are admitted here on the Monday in each week on payment of a small charge. At the lower end of the gorge is the celebrated Lydford Waterfall, formed by a small stream, which rises on Black Down, leaping from a considerable height into the Lyd. To this part of the beautifully wooded ravine visitors are admitted at all times ; tickets are to be had at the Manor Hotel, near Lydford Station, where it is entered. For railway service see *Lydford District.*

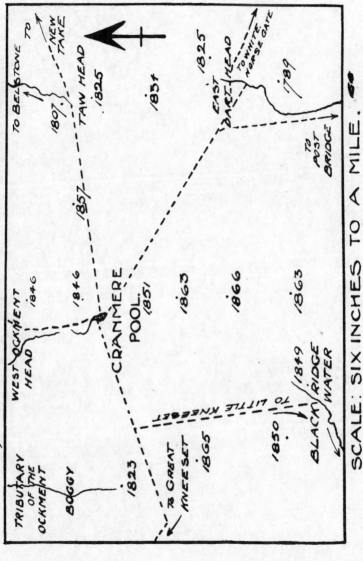

19. SURROUNDINGS OF CRANMERE

SCALE: SIX INCHES TO A MILE.

NOTES.

A valuable addition to the literature of Dartmoor has lately been made by the appearance of *The Story of Dartmoor Prison*, by Mr. Basil Thomson, late Governor of the convict depot. The book is particularly interesting, and contains much information.

The grave of the " Three Valiant Soldiers," in Princetown Church-yard (Ex. 1), has been recently restored.

At a meeting of the U. S. Daughters of 1812, held in New York, in January, 1909, it was voted that the Society place a memorial window in the church at Princetown.

INDEX.

Many of the places are named in the Guide several times ; the references are to those pages on which a place is mentioned in its more important connections. Figures in brackets indicate the pages where the fullest notice of the place or object will be found.

SUBJECTS.

DAVID & CHARLES BOOKS ON DARTMOOR

All illustrated — full details in our current catalogue available from Brunel House, Forde Road, Newton Abbot, Devon.

CROSSING'S HUNDRED YEARS ON DARTMOOR
Introduced by Brian Le Messurier

An account of the life, work and environment of the ordinary Moor people in the 19th century. First published in 1901.

CROSSING'S AMID DEVONIA'S ALPS
Or Wandering and Adventures on Dartmoor

Edited and introduced by Brian Le Messurier

This most personal of Crossing's books describes his own rambles across Dartmoor, companions, routes, favourite stopping places and incidents on the way.

THE INDUSTRIAL ARCHAEOLOGY OF DARTMOOR
Helen Harris

A study of the various industries which for centuries were based on the Moor's natural resources, including tin mining, granite working, peat, milling, agriculture and various forms of communication.

GEOLOGY EXPLAINED: DARTMOOR AND THE TAMAR VALLEY
John W. Perkins

How scenery, geology and the lives of man interrelate in one of Britain's most beautiful areas, with separate sections on the better known beauty-spots, the most geologically interesting features in each area, map references and suggested excursions.

WORTH'S DARTMOOR
R. Hansford Worth

Introduced by G. M. Spooner

A collection of the author's work on the physical geography, vegetation and archaeology of Dartmoor and an account of the activities of the stannaries, first published in 1953 in the *Transactions of the Devonshire Associations*.

DARTMOOR (Leisure Series)
Crispin Gill

DAVID & CHARLES BOOKS ON DEVON